Over The Edge:
Death In Grand Canyon

Books by Michael P. Ghiglieri

The Chimpanzees of Kibale Forest

East of the Mountains of the Moon: Chimpanzee Society in the African Rainforest

Canyon

The Dark Side of Man: Tracing the Origin of Male Violence

First Through Grand Canyon: The Secret Journals and Letters of the 1869 Crew Who Explored the Green and Colorado Rivers

Off the Wall: Death in Yosemite (co-author Charles R. "Butch" Farabee, Jr.)

In the Back of Beyond: The Education of an International Wilderness River Guide (forthcoming)

Through the Great Unknown (fiction, forthcoming)

Books by Thomas M. Myers

Fateful Journey: Injury and Death on Colorado River Trips in Grand Canyon (with Chris Becker and Larry Stevens)

Grand Obsession: Harvey Butchart and the Exploration of Grand Canyon (co-author Elias Butler)

The Desert Doc: Canyon and River Medicine—A Field Guide for the Southwest (forthcoming)

Books by Thomas M. Myers and Michael P. Ghiglieri

Flipped Out on the Colorado: Boating Mayhem in Grand Canyon, Cataract Canyon and Colorado Tributaries (forthcoming)

Over The Edge:
Death In Grand Canyon

Michael P. Ghiglieri

and

Thomas M. Myers

Over The Edge:
Death In Grand Canyon

Gripping accounts of all known fatal mishaps in
the most famous of the World's Seven Natural Wonders

Michael P. Ghiglieri

and

Thomas M. Myers

PUMA PRESS

Flagstaff

FIRST EDITION

eighteenth printing

thirteenth revision

ISBN: 0-9700973-0-1 (Hardcover)
ISBN: 0-9700973-1-X (Paperback)
LCCN: 00-108448

Maps by Bronze Black
Book Jacket design by Bronze Black
Geology schematic by Michael P. Ghiglieri
Cover concept by Michael P. Ghiglieri, Thomas M. Myers, and Becky Myers
Front cover photographs by Connie S. Ghiglieri and the Emery Kolb Collection,
Cline Library, Northern Arizona University.
Author photographs by Conan Michael Ghiglieri and Mark Middleton
Rear cover photograph by Ken Klementis and (again) Emery Kolb
Interior Puebloan rock art designs by Kim Besom
Book production by Mary Williams

DEDICATION

For the millions who come to Grand Canyon in the future, that they each may walk away enriched—and in one piece.

And also in recognition of each member of every search and rescue team from Arizona and Utah and Nevada and of every guide, companion, and Good Samaritan who has risked his or her life to save those of us who otherwise never would have walked away at all.

For want of a nail, the shoe was lost.
For want of a shoe, the horse was lost.
For want of a horse, the general was lost.
For want of a general, the battle was lost.
For loss of the battle, the war was lost.

TABLE OF CONTENTS

FOREWORD

"How many people die here each year?" This refrain from visitors to Grand Canyon is asked repeatedly. Who can blame them? Each of us has an underlying morbid curiosity that draws us to ask such a question, but admittedly not always openly. It may be the very reason that the title of this book caught your eye.

Although deaths and near-misses occur regularly in national parks, it is difficult for any other national park to match the range and scope found in this book. The range of drama at Grand Canyon includes the harrowing technical rescue of injured photographer Franklin Nims from Robert Brewster Stanton's 1889-1890 Expedition under conditions that today seem unsurvivable. And it expands to June 30 of 1956, when the calm of the park was shattered by the mid-air collision of TWA and United Airlines aircraft that resulted in the worst civilian aviation disaster up to that time, one so bad that it led to the creation of the Federal Aviation Administration (FAA). The scope of this book even includes the saga of the largest criminal manhunt in the history of Arizona, one which focused the spotlight of the nation on this park during the summer of 1992, when that manhunt intensified here as fugitive Danny Ray Horning eluded law enforcement for weeks with incredible cunning.

Despite the obvious dangers of Grand Canyon, a frequent observation I have made of many visitors is their tendency to have a "911 mentality." They often make the assumption that help will always be immediately forthcoming when they place themselves in harm's way. Such visitors suffer from the misguided belief that a national park is a close cousin to an amusement park. The realities are that Walt Disney did not have a hand in constructing Grand Canyon, and the inherent risks associated with this park are unbelievably real. And all too often, tragically so.

As a National Park Ranger at Grand Canyon for over a decade and a half, I have been involved in over a thousand search and rescue operations. Many of the mishaps that Michael Ghiglieri and Tom Myers recount here are very vivid personal memories for myself and several other rangers who have participated in these operations. Many of us have experienced our own close calls in the Canyon and have learned personally that the margin between life and death here is narrow.

Tragically, beyond the hundreds of victims of fatal Grand Canyon accidents mentioned in varying detail here, there also exist many more unreported victims. These are the relatives and friends of those who lost their lives at Grand Canyon. In my own efforts to provide solace for the parents, friends, and companions of the victims of these tragedies I have experienced the senseless waste that such a loss of life may bring to a family. It is astonishing how suddenly a high-spirited act or a bit of high jinks can take a life.

For example, consider the tragic aftermath caused by a father pulling a practical joke on his daughter as he pretended to fall backwards off the Canyon rim down to a ledge hidden from her view. His momentum carried him beyond that ledge to a death plunge into the Canyon. That short moment in their lives cannot be reversed; it irrevocably leaves a young girl fatherless and baffled by the forces that rule our fates. Likewise is the needless loss as two companions attempt a hiking shortcut from Phantom Ranch by swimming downstream in the Colorado River, a shortcut in which one of them drowns and the other barely escapes death. The grief and suffering of the families of such victims continues permanently with an emptiness which that loved one used to fill. These families will always see Grand Canyon not as an incredible natural wonder, but as a place that stole away life. This book not only chronicles such unwarranted tragedies, it opens our eyes to preventing them in the future.

Also punctuating this book are incredible tales of survival, near misses, and rescues that fate has allowed to end on a happier note. Just one of many is the epic of David Whittlesey, who survived alone, battered and freezing, for six days in Lower Granite Gorge after losing his raft and gear and all of his food. During his rescue, I offered David my lunch. He devoured it in barely more than a heartbeat.

Traditional Canyon "lore" comes to life in these pages—in fact, some established historical legends are strongly challenged. Tom and Michael present new information which questions, for example, the originally published outcomes to the three members of John Wesley Powell's first 1869 expedition down the Colorado—William Dunn, Seneca Howland, and Oramel G. Howland—after they hiked away from the expedition at Separation Canyon. Also re-examined provocatively here is the infamous demise of the honeymooning couple—Glen and Bessie Hyde—who vanished in Lower Granite Gorge in 1928.

The many accounts of death and near-misses contained here make exceptional reading, but there exists a much greater value in compiling this research under one cover. This book analyzes recurring patterns of fatalities for commonalities in their contributing factors. And it examines ways to prevent such tragedies in the future. Hopefully, as you and other readers study the many fatal errors made by previous Canyon travelers, you will carry a valuable education with you long after you put this book down. What you learn here could truly prevent a life from being lost.

We all should keep in mind that *"there are no new accidents—only new people having the same old accidents."*

Ken Phillips
Search & Rescue Coordinator
Grand Canyon National Park, Arizona

ACKNOWLEDGMENTS

In executing a project of this magnitude and complexity we found ourselves repeatedly relying on the good will of people who lacked the sense to just say no. Our first hurdle in writing this book was in locating reliable data and information regarding fatalities. No one source existed from which these data might be drawn. Even NPS records turned out to be incomplete for our needs, occasionally erroneous, and often impossible to locate. Hence, we owe a vast debt to those who helped locate (or recall) missing details. Some of these people were researchers who went prospecting for us to mine lost information from old newspaper records. Others, working for Grand Canyon National Park, searched NPS incident reports—and their memories. Yet others, who had the bad luck to be in the wrong place at the right time, simply told us what happened, from their perspectives, during fatal episodes. All of these people shared a trait at which we were surprised and for which we are extremely grateful: they each wanted the record to be set straight in this book, and they wanted that record to be accurate.

At the risk of inadvertently omitting the names of those who made personal contributions of time and energy in seeking out and/or providing records or details regarding several of the episodes in this book, we wish to acknowledge and thank the following people who helped (whether they knew they were helping or not) it become accurate: Joe Alston, Ann Anderson, Martin J. Anderson, Bruce and Susan Armstrong, Jeffe Aronson, John S. Azar, Bruce Babbitt, Chris Becker, Paul Berkowitz, Kim Besom, Camille Bibles, George H. Billingsley, Garth Bundy, Harvey Butchart, Carolyn Castleman, Jeff & Laurel Casey, Frankie Chamberlain, Chris Coder, Pat Coffey, Jay Cole, Michael Collier, Kim Crumbo, O'Connor Dale, Peter Dale, Regan Dale, John Davenport, David Desrosiers, Brad Dimock, Becky Douglas, Jeff Drayton, Dan Driskill, Colleen Dunleavy, Michael Ebersole, Darla Ekbom, Tim Ellis, Jack Fields, Dave Foster, Laura Fulgineti, Tiffany George, Daniel Graber, Karen Greig, Bill Grundy, Cathy and Rich Hahn, Curtis ("Whale") Hanson, Michael Harrison, Tony Hillerman, Bruce Hooper, Colleen Hyde, Terry Jacobson, Daniel D. James, Teresa Janecek, Kevin "KJ" Johns, Bert Jones, Steve Knisely, Peggy Kolar, Karen Kovalik, Martha Krueger, Arlan Lazere, Sylvia Leimkuehler, Bruce Lenon, Robert R. Marley, Scott Mascher, George Marsik, Tom Martin, Chris McIntosh, Nancy Mecham, Dove Menkes, Greg Moore, Shane Murphy, Jim Ohlman, James Peshlakai, Ken Phillips, Richard D. Quartaroli, Mike Quinn, Christopher Reynolds, Sheriff Joe Richards, Gary E. Robbins, William C. Roberson, Michael Schulte, Jean-Marc Sellier, Tim Simonds, Drifter Smith, Joan Staveley, Sara T. Stebbins, George Steck, Larry Stevens, John N. Stryker, David Swickard, Barbara Theilen, Muir Thompson, Scott Thybony, Paul Toberg, Jim Traub, Bil Vandergraff, Vic Vieira, Michael S. Walchle, Mike Walker, Susan Warner, Steven Wells, Tim Whitney, Mary Williams, Bryan

Wisher, Tom Workman, and Mike Wynn. Without the various contributions of these people, *Over the Edge: Death in Grand Canyon* would not be as complete a book as it is.

An even more onerous task once a book like this begins to assume draft form is reviewing it for accuracy, for readability, and for tone. We had helpers here too. Richard D. Quartaroli not only read an early draft for accuracy, he went well beyond the call of friendship to make it a personal quest to cross-check the numbers of fatalities in various categories and even to cross-check a few river flow levels attending whitewater incidents. As an accomplished historian of the Colorado River in Grand Canyon in his own right, Quartaroli made suggestions and corrections too numerous for us to list here, but vital to improving the quality of this book. We owe him a large debt.

Likewise Canyon historian Michael F. Anderson perused and combed a later draft of this book and found a few more gaffes and some prose offering gray instead of black and white—or technicolor—exposition.

Several other people read working drafts of this book for readability and tone, vital services from our point of view. Hazel Clark, Connie Ghiglieri, Daniel D. James, Tom Martin, Becky L. Myers, Sharon L. Myers, Ken Phillips, and Bil Vandergraff all made very important observations and suggestions, which again improved *Over the Edge: Death in Grand Canyon* beyond our original work. The latter two, NPS Rangers in Grand Canyon, also offered additional details on incidents during which they had responded as rescuers. Sharon L. Myers, Tom's mother, deserves special thanks for reviewing yards and yards of microfilm records in search of illusive incidents, until bleary-eyed.

Kim Besom of the Grand Canyon NPS Study Collection not only went beyond the call of duty in helping us locate missing data from hard-to-find incident reports, as a student of ancient Puebloan rock art she also discovered and designed the petroglyph elements heading each of our chapters. We owe extra thanks to Kim for improving the book's accuracy and also for enhancing its look and feel.

Grand Canyon National Park Superintendent Robert Arnberger remained interested in this project throughout; one of his most important suggestions was to incorporate several more "near-misses" than we had intended (due to space considerations). Doing this turned out not only to vastly increase the number of upbeat stories in this book—and thus improve the book's feel—it also revealed several lessons in survival, techniques of rescue, and amazing tales of both foolish adventure and heroic rescues.

We also want to acknowledge help from a source that is all too easy for a parent to forget: our children—Conan, Cliff, Crystal, Brittany, Alexandra and Weston—have provided us with daily reminders of how precious the gift of life is and that it is our duty to preserve it.

Introduction

Why A Book On Death?

At first glance, this book's title may seem only lurid, exploitative, and even macabre. Nothing could be farther from the truth regarding its contents. We are now convinced that very few people have died in Grand Canyon due to causes that can honestly be assigned merely to bad luck or an unforeseeable act of God. Instead, nearly all of the violent and/or traumatic fatalities known within the Canyon have resulted from a series of decisions by the victims and/or by those responsible for those victims' safety. In short, as trite as it may sound, traumatic death in Grand Canyon is rarely an "accident" as defined by Webster's Dictionary as an "unforeseeable incident."

Hence, if most "accidental" fatalities are not unforeseeable events in the true sense, but instead are what statisticians would term the "rare outcome" *that one would expect to happen* given a set of specific conditions or decisions (such as not wearing a life jacket while boating the Colorado River), then many of us would benefit from learning what these given conditions and decisions are which increase the odds of being killed while visiting, boating through, hiking in, or flying over Grand Canyon.

We realize too that when we look here at decisions which contributed to some people's deaths we may also be treading on someone else's toes. Our intent in this book is not to assign blame. It is instead to identify the kinds of mistakes and decision making which commonly kill people in Grand Canyon. By identifying these and sharing them, we may all be in a far better position to avoid or prevent such lethal errors in the future. Again, instead of blame we seek *understanding*. It is, after all, only this sort of knowledge—combined with common sense—that saves lives.

Indeed, both of us have spent years within the Canyon, boating, hiking, bouldering, and orienteering cross-country. And we both admit that we have made decisions that we survived partly because of luck. Because luck is an undependable commodity, we admit here to a certain humility in our judgement of others' lack of it. There, but for the grace of God, might have gone either of us.

Beyond the life-saving lessons that the episodes in this book may teach us, most of its stories of Grand Canyon death and disaster are amazing, a few are truly unbelievable, some are absurd, and yet others heroic. We hope you find them fascinating as well as illuminating. But be warned: the amount of astonishing history in this book may keep you up past your bedtime.

How important are these life and death issues in America's national parks? The U.S. National Park system, if combined into one geographical entity, would be bigger than its fifth largest state (New Mexico). In 1999, for example, 287 million people visited U.S. national parks. Not all of them had a pleasant time: 4,603 of these people needed to be rescued, and about 211 of them died from falls, drownings, and other accidents. Nor has Grand Canyon been immune to this. As veteran Ranger Charles R. "Butch" Farabee, Jr. notes, in Grand Canyon in 1996 alone, National Park Service (NPS) rangers performed 482 searches and rescues (SARs) involving 377 injured or ill people, 18 of whom died. The one-day record for Grand Canyon is reputedly 12 SARs in one meltdown July day in the mid-1980s. Within America's National Park system, Grand Canyon seems a top ranking trauma zone offering a wide array of unfamiliar opportunities to make fatal errors.

And hundreds of victims have made at least one of them. Overall, the known number of traumatic fatalities in Grand Canyon National Park itself (including the plateaus) exceeds 700 people. The record year (not counting 1956 when 128 people died in a mid-air collision) was 50 fatalities in 1986, when twenty-five of these died in yet another midair collision. Many deaths in the park itself over the years—carbon monoxide poisoning accidents in tents and campers, heart attacks, and motor vehicle accidents (32 deaths from these alone)—occur on the plateaus. The causes of most of the 600 or so traumatic fatalities below the rims are different. They occurred among a far smaller number of visitors than those crowding the plateaus above.

This 600-person tally who fell victim to the "larger-than-life" dangers below the rims, however, remains tentative due to incomplete Park Service records and difficult-to-access Coconino County Sheriff's Department records. Indeed, until 1974, the NPS at Grand Canyon did not keep a list of traumatic fatalities in the park. Worse, some reports of fatalities before 1974 have been misplaced, lost, or even discarded to make more space. Unfortunately, NPS employees prior to 1974 are no longer available for queries on the numbers and types of fatalities during their watches. This confusion is further complicated in that, if a visitor sustained a fatal injury in the Canyon but was evacuated from Grand Canyon National Park only to die in a medical facility elsewhere, he or she is not listed on NPS fatality lists or records. The same thing happens with Arizona Department of Public Safety medical evacuations but is further complicated by the lack in their log books (*if* DPS were keeping a log book during the era of the incident) of the victim's name, age, circumstances, mechanism of injury, and, again, whether or not the victim survived. Compounding all of these problems, this book is not strictly a list of fatal accidents occurring within the administrative boundaries of Grand Canyon National Park. With the exception of homicides and aircraft fatalities, it is predominantly about deaths *in* Grand Canyon, below the rims. Why the hair-splitting? Because much of the park is above the rims and outside of the Canyon, and because much of the Canyon itself is outside the park and is instead on Navajo land, Havasupai land, Hualapai land, Lake Mead National Recreation Area, Bureau of Land Management land, National Forest, mining claims, and on private land. We have tried to track down fatalities beyond these many complications, but we may have missed a few.

Enough of political zones. Yet another complication is multiple reports of an incident are often inconsistent or even contradictory regarding how or why or even where someone died. Witnesses often fail to agree on what happened, while NPS rangers or Coconino County or Arizona Department of Public Safety SAR personnel focused on rescue or body recovery sometimes miss details in how these incidents happened to begin with. Moreover, some witnesses giving official reports following a fatal incident are reluctant to accurately describe their own role in the ontogeny of death. Years later these same witnesses sometimes report a far different story about what happened, and how. On top of these problems in seeking accuracy, published newspaper reports are commonly skimpy and vague. And sometimes wrong. Hence, in some of the incidents we discuss we've had to make judgement calls to interpolate between all accounts. We have sifted the reports for what appears to be the closest fit to reality.

Again, that reality can teach us something.

We want to say that we know that there exists another danger here in our writing this book. That danger is the possible hubris accompanying our approach. We attempt here to identify the reasons why hundreds of people died as they did. Inherent in our doing this is the assumption that we know what we are talking about. We think we do. But we do not think we possess God-like omniscience. We are simply trying to do our best based on the data available and our experience.

What *is* our experience? One of us, Ghiglieri, has, during the last quarter century, rowed more than 125 commercial whitewater trips down the Colorado in Grand Canyon and also worked as a Grand Canyon National Park Service river ranger. The other, Myers, an accomplished backcountry hiker, worked as a physician in Grand Canyon Clinic for nearly a decade, during which he saw, responded to, treated, and tried to understand the ontogeny of thousands of injuries and of all too many traumatic Canyon fatalities.

To us, this book is far more about life than about death. It is as much about preventing the great canyons that erode in the hearts and lives of families from the loss of loved ones as it is about this awe-inspiring physical canyon where these losses might occur. We empathize with the surviving family members who feel deep chasms ripped into their lives. But to save future lives, these lost lives must not be forgotten. Instead they must be remembered—and understood. Understanding, however, requires critical analysis. Such analysis can be painful for surviving family members. Unlike exploratory surgery, the only anesthesia we have to offer through our analysis here is a sense of compassion such that each death is discussed with some respect and sensitivity. It is not our intent to add humiliation to the pain of loss. But in that we are committed to exposing the *true* reasons for why these fatal errors occurred, we all too frequently have had to call a spade a spade. We apologize for any perceived failure on our parts to retain an attitude of respect to survivors. After all, the goal of *Over the Edge: Death in Grand Canyon* is to increase the survival of Canyon visitors—whether casual viewers from the rims or serious route-finders in the inner Canyon.

Finally, we believe accurate documentation of fatal accidents is vital to preventing future ones. Without such documentation significant details might well be lost forever or simply fade into incomprehensibility due to time, rumor, myth, and failing memories.

The bottom line here is we are convinced that the lack of prevention of preventable deaths in Grand Canyon is a serious issue. Thus we believe our analysis in *Over the Edge: Death in Grand Canyon* is not just a leap forward in the quest to prevent future fatalities; more than this, it would be lethal *not* to have written this book. If, in our quest to identify exactly where that preventability might reside, we step on some emotional toes, we ask that the owners of those toes also embrace this goal and sincerely examine their own values and concerns before taking umbrage.

Having now explained our goals to give you the best we could, it's time to drop over the edge.

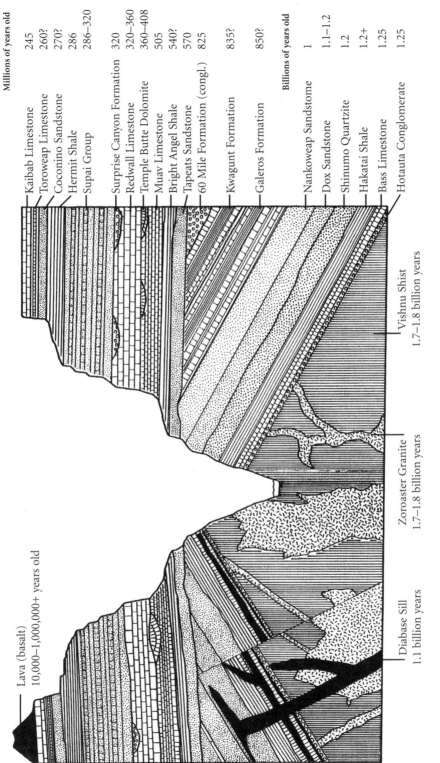

Grand Canyon Geology

Millions of years old

Kaibab Limestone — 245
Toroweap Limestone — 260?
Coconino Sandstone — 270?
Hermit Shale — 286
Supai Group — 286–320
Surprise Canyon Formation — 320
Redwall Limestone — 320–360
Temple Butte Dolomite — 360–408
Muav Limestone — 505
Bright Angel Shale — 540?
Tapeats Sandstone — 570
60 Mile Formation (congl.) — 825
Kwagunt Formation — 835?
Galeros Formation — 850?

Billions of years old

Nankoweap Sandstome — 1
Dox Sandstone — 1.1–1.2
Shinumo Quartzite — 1.2
Hakatai Shale — 1.2+
Bass Limestone — 1.25
Hotauta Conglomerate — 1.25

Lava (basalt)
10,000–1,000,000+ years old

Diabase Sill
1.1 billion years

Zoroaster Granite
1.7–1.8 billion years

Vishnu Shist
1.7–1.8 billion years

Map of Grand Canyon

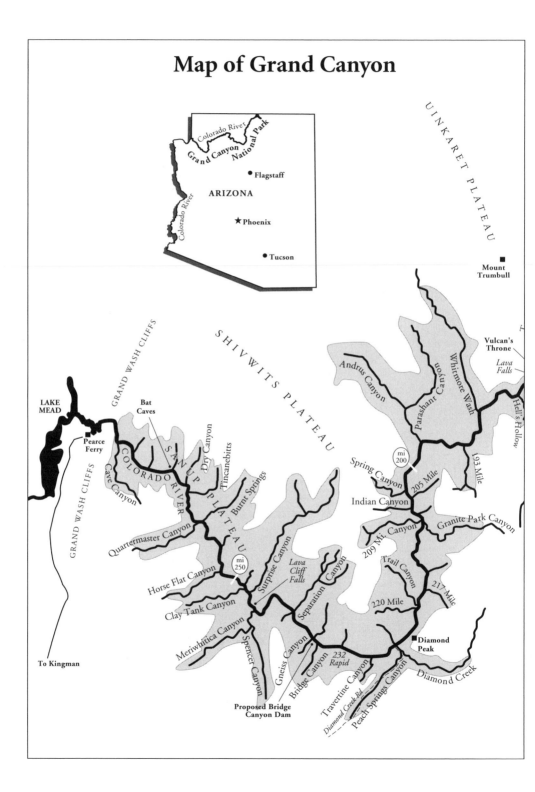

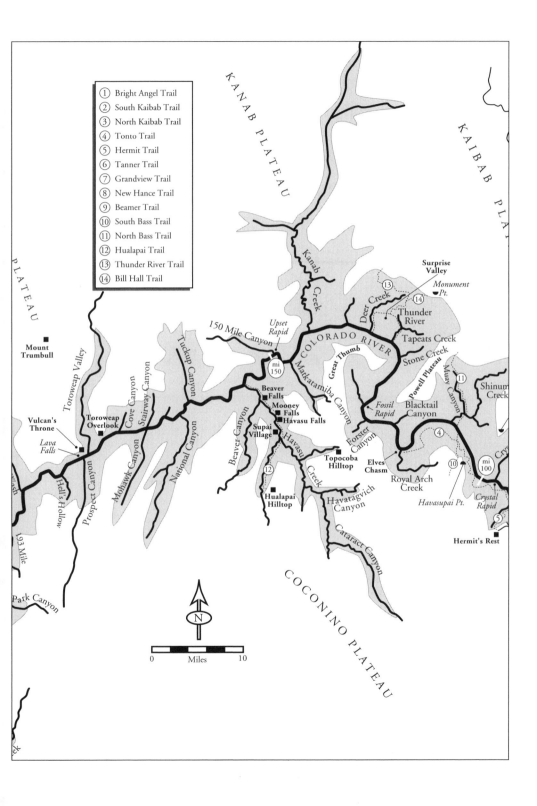

1. Bright Angel Trail
2. South Kaibab Trail
3. North Kaibab Trail
4. Tonto Trail
5. Hermit Trail
6. Tanner Trail
7. Grandview Trail
8. New Hance Trail
9. Beamer Trail
10. South Bass Trail
11. North Bass Trail
12. Hualapai Trail
13. Thunder River Trail
14. Bill Hall Trail

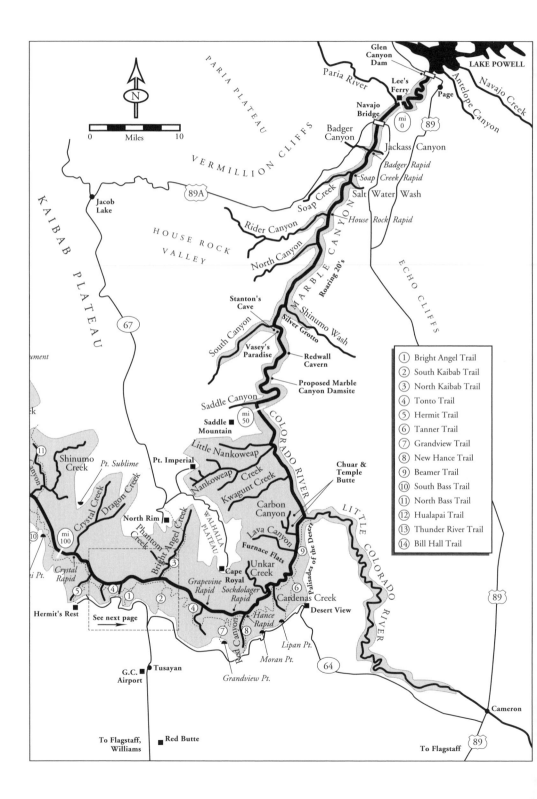

South Rim Village Area and Phantom Ranch

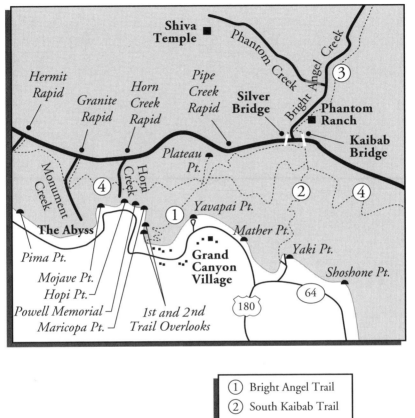

<u>Chapter One</u>

"Say, how many people fall here?"

Falls From The Rims

"Get her off that wall before she falls off!" Chief Ranger Perry Brown grumbled to Ranger William Bowen as they neared the rim.

Bowen and Brown both stared in disbelief. They had each seen some stupid stunts in their careers, but this one took the cake.

It was the morning of September 15, 1946, the day when stunning Hollywood fashion designer Dee Dee Johnson, age 33, and her entourage were planning a major public relations shoot on the South Rim. They would model several new styles that they were about to market. One of these fashion blasts into the Atomic Age was "pedal pushers," skin tight pants.

Ranger Bowen and his boss, Chief Ranger Perry Brown, had just arrived out of curiosity to watch the fashion show. Hollywood was not a common visitor here. Besides, Dee Dee herself would be modeling these "pedal-pusher" things.

And there she was, the two rangers saw horrified, glamorous Dee Dee clad in a halter top and pedal pushers and posing provocatively on the parapet wall on the brink of the abyss in a death defying pose.

Brown's alarmed "Get her off that wall before she falls off" echoed in Bowen's ears as he hurried toward Dee Dee on the wall. Flash bulbs flashed blindingly. Bowen made it maybe three steps, he would later report, before Dee Dee Johnson fell off the wall and vanished into Grand Canyon....

"How many people fall here each year?" Ironically, *this* is the question that nearly every National Park Service ranger hears most often from South Rim visitors once they first view the shocking abyss called Grand Canyon.

Questions about geology and so on emerge only after this first visual shock begins to wear off. Sometimes this prime question is phrased: "How many people *die* here each year?" But "die" in this context almost always means "fall." Either way, the two questions seem nearly identical.

Most NPS rangers don't know the accurate answer to either question. But most of them do know a true answer: "It varies from year to year; in some years only one person falls from the rim, in other years the number can be far higher...."

Again, a fall almost always equals death. Surviving a fall from either rim is about as likely as being struck twice by lightning. Even so, a few people have survived falls. Their stories tend to verge on unbelievable. Ranger William Bowen, for example, explains what happened next with Dee Dee Johnson in her "death plunge" off the wall in front of a small platoon of photographers:

> *If you know Grand Canyon you know there isn't much of anything "over" that parapet wall but a lot of scenery and open space. I quickened my pace considerably upon her disappearance, looked over and noted that she was in a sitting position, facing the Canyon, on a very steep slope and about 5' from a 300' drop. I wouldn't have regarded her as a good risk for life insurance, as the only thing holding her was some debris that had accumulated in her crotch as she slid. Perry hollered at her to sit still. I went on up the wall about 30', went over and worked my way back above her. When I got there I saw a little stunted pinyon about 3" in diameter which was so situated that if I could get a hold of it with my left hand I ought to be able to get a hold of her with my right. She was sitting very still indeed but the debris in her crotch was gradually trickling off into the void, and there didn't seem to be time for a full scale planning meeting so, much against my better judgement, I slid down the route she had just taken and grabbed the Pinyon Tree [sic]. Thank God it was well rooted or Dee Dee and I might shortly have been airborne. I reached out and got a firm grip on the seat of her pedal pushers and there we were. I wouldn't say we were comfortable, but at least we were immobile and we did have an excellent, unobstructed view of the Canyon.*
>
> *In a very short time Dean Dazey came over the wall on a rope and tied another rope under Dee Dee's arms and up she went. Having no further business in the vicinity I hung onto Dean and we too joined the crowd on top.*
>
> *There was one feature of the rescue that did cause some comment. In 1946 the "topless era" was well in the future. Pedal pushers featured a halter top. Dean had tied the rope around Dee Dee and, when the rope was pulled from above, Dee Dee arrived on the rim topless.*

With a half dozen photographers on hand this was well recorded
to Dee Dee's intense distaste. She seemed to blame Dean.

Dee Dee Johnson, topless in her soon-to-be-wildly-successful pedal push-ers (but now also with a sprained ankle and a new phobia for heights) was not unique in failing to grasp the magnitude of her error of tempting fate while standing on the rim. Since Day One, it seems, the magnitude of the dangers posed by the sheer immensity of the Canyon's cliffs has consistently failed to compute in the minds of many human visitors. Even worse, for some visitors, the immense vista holds a fatal attraction that exerts an almost magnetic pull. Right up to the edge. Then, as with Dee Dee Johnson, over it.

Half a century later, at the same wall, Fate played out a similar tableau. At half past midnight on May 11, 1997, NPS Dispatch received a frantic call from the lobby of the Bright Angel Lodge. The caller, Clifton Reeder, reported that there was an intoxicated woman outside. She was walking atop the wall behind the lodge, he said, and she was insisting that she wanted to go "climbing."

Alarmed, the dispatcher broadcasted this same message over the park radio. Ranger Keith McAuliffe responded first, hurrying into the lobby barely a minute after the dispatcher's alert. The lobby was empty. McAuliffe contin-ued outside to the rear wall overlooking Grand Canyon. He found Reeder there standing in the dark and peering downward. Reeder turned and franti-cally gestured into the dark abyss to McAuliffe. "She is over the edge," he said. "You have to help her!"

McAuliffe peered down to where Reeder pointed. All he could see were the branches of a tree vibrating jerkily. Then from the depths came a very scared and clearly feminine call, "Help me!"

Still seeing no one, McAuliffe shifted his position and shined his MagLite downward, sweeping toward the chasm. The beam revealed a woman in a light blue shirt sitting precariously on a steep ledge twenty feet below him. McAuliffe recognized her as Lana Virginia Smith, age 28. McAuliffe had met Smith at a neighbor's house. She was a local Grand Canyon Village resident and an employee of the Fred Harvey Company.

"Don't move," McAuliffe cautioned her, "I'll find a way to help you."

Smith, McAuliffe now saw to his alarm, was not just sobbing; she was so upset and unstable that she was an extreme danger to herself. Smith's perch lay only a few very dangerous feet above a sheer cliff.

McAuliffe crossed the wall for a better look. Yes, Smith's position appeared sketchy in the extreme. McAuliffe wracked his brain for a safe plan to get a rope or a hand to her. The option of him descending the steep, unstable slope to her in the dark was far too dangerous without the protection of a rope. As he feverishly scanned the treacherous terrain again for a safe route to Smith, she sobbed louder and cried out again for help. Smith was so distraught, McAuliffe now realized, that whatever he was going to do, he had to do it fast.

As if to underscore this urgency, Smith tried to shift her location. She slipped downward a few feet. Rocks and debris dislodged and tumbled into a long silent free fall.

His heart racing, McAuliffe studied the terrain again and tried to calm Smith down with assurances as he meanwhile struggled to devise a plan to rescue her. "Don't move," he advised her again. "Let me find a way to help you where you are."

"I'm really scared," Smith gasped to McAuliffe; "I want to get out of here."

Now, less than five minutes after McAuliffe had rushed into the empty lobby of the Bright Angel Lodge, Ranger Donny Miller joined him. Miller too knew Smith. The two rangers quickly agreed that Miller should assume the full-time role of talking to and calming Smith while McAuliffe formulated a plan to get to her with a rope before she tried to move again.

Miller climbed over the wall and onto the steep eroding slope. He talked soothingly to Smith as he too scanned for a safe way to get a hold of her. McAuliffe meanwhile radioed Dispatch to immediately send technical rescue expert, Ranger Michael Nash. He next radioed for Ranger Matt Vandzura to assist. Meanwhile Reeder had become so distraught and unsafe near the edge that McAuliffe had to order him away from the wall.

Minutes of waiting now ticked by as he tried to review what he would need to do to reach Smith and bring her up without casualties. Meanwhile Reeder explained to McAuliffe why Smith was such an emotional mess. At 12:30 a.m., Reeder said, the bartender at the Bright Angel Lodge had refused to sell her another drink. Smith was despondent over child custody, her ex having been switched from every other weekend to every other week, and had been drinking heavily. The bartender had already served her three shots of Yukon Jack and two beers. But when he had said, "No more," Smith had become agitated and headed for the wall. Now her teetering above the cliff while not being in her right mind was a disaster about to happen.

Maybe, McAuliffe hoped, Miller will calm her down enough that she will stay put until they could harness her into a rope.

McAuliffe heard a scream from beyond the wall. He rushed to peer down beyond Miller, himself now inching precariously downslope. Smith had again tried to move and again she had slipped and slid further downslope toward the edge of the cliff. Both rangers' hearts skipped a beat. They were running out of time. Running out fast. They knew it. And they still had no rope.

Smith's situation now looked even worse. She lay on her back in the dark on the steep slope now fifty feet below the wall, spreading her friction thin, and clutching loose, rattling gravel between her fingers.

"Hold on, don't move!" both men yelled to—and at—Smith.

McAuliffe thumbed his transmit button and radioed to Nash to expedite.

At 12:52 a.m., less than fifteen minutes after McAuliffe had awakened him from a dead sleep, Nash arrived with his technical gear. McAuliffe told Nash emphatically that they were running out of time and had to move fast.

As Nash secured a high strength anchor for a belay, the distraught woman lay half on her back and her side and gripped a small tree very close to the cliff. Her screams for help now merged into wailing.

Ranger Vandzura had arrived a few minutes after Nash. He now buckled himself into his rappelling harness and top roped himself from Nash's anchor.

At 1:04 a.m., McAuliffe saw their sands of time running to zero. He yelled at Nash to throw him a rope. McAuliffe caught Nash's rope then tossed it to Miller, yelling at him to catch it and pass it down to Smith.

"Catch this rope!" Miller encouraged the now hysterical Smith as he yanked and gathered slack and then tossed it further.

Instead of catching the rope, Smith screamed as she slid the last few feet to the edge. Rocky debris rattled off into thin air. And this time, instead of stopping, Smith kept on sliding to, and then over, the edge. At the brink of disaster Smith grabbed a stunted bush anchored in the thin soil.

Miller dared risking a scramble downslope to her a few feet further, as had done Ranger William Bowen for Dee Dee Johnson half a century earlier. But this time, the slippery and steep terrain, far more treacherous in the darkness, stopped Miller several feet short of being able to grab Smith. Indeed, Smith had now slid over the edge and was almost invisible. Her wailing for help was unnerving.

All that McAuliffe could see of Smith now were her hands and head. This was as far as she could go, he realized, and still survive. Her body now seemed to be dangling off the edge in a hideous cliff-hanger.

Screaming and frantically gripping that stunted bush with both hands for dear life, Smith could neither focus on the rope Miller had tossed to her, nor was she willing to risk letting go of that bush to grab anything else.

"Hang on, hang on!" the rangers yelled again.

Smith again screamed for help.

Ranger Vandzura was still not yet fully harnessed, but he hurried over the wall toward Smith anyway.

Abruptly the other rangers' stomachs sank as they saw Smith's last visible hand release the bush, then vanish.

Smith called out then screamed in terror in a sickening Doppler effect. A few more rocks clattered downward and dropped off. Then silence.

Hoping for a one-in-a-million last reprieve, McAuliffe shined the beam of his MagLite along the edge of the drop-off. Still nothing. Smith was gone.

Hoping now for a true miracle, McAuliffe ordered Nash and Vandzura to execute an immediate hasty rappel over the edge. Vandzura, still not fully harnessed, immediately rappelled downward over the cliff and to the end of his 150-foot rope. He then dangled in the dark and searched the cliff face. Smith, he soon realized, had fallen a lot further than where he now dangled. Sickened by the realization that he and his three comrades had run out of time by mere seconds and run out of space by mere inches, he slowly ascended back to the wall.

An hour and a half later Vandzura and Nash had descended further and finally spotted Smith's lifeless body crumpled 230 feet below the edge.

Alcohol and the world's most frightening drop-off is a lethal combination whose tragic outcome few of us find surprising. Far more shocking, however, is this sort of outcome stemming from a practical joke. On November 28, 1992, Greg Austin Gingrich, age 38, visited the South Rim with his family and friends, including a college buddy who was a former basketball player for the Phoenix Suns. They strolled along the Rim Trail between the Visitor Center and El Tovar. The group separated here with plans to meet back at their cars in the parking lot. Gingrich and his young daughter ended up walking back last.

Playing around to tease his daughter, Gingrich jumped atop the rock wall separating terra firma from the abyss. He paused precariously and dramatically atop the wall. Then, facing his daughter on the path, he wind-milled his arms comically and said, "Help, I'm falling...."

Then he jumped off backwards, toward the Canyon.

His daughter said something like, "Oh, Dad," in impatience at her father's clowning. She continued walking along the Rim Trail reluctant to fuel her father's pranks by acting shocked. Expecting her father to pop up out of nowhere any second, she returned to the parking lot for their rendezvous. Once there, however, Gingrich was the only member of the party who failed to appear.

Concerned, the entire party retraced their steps along the Rim Trail, back and forth, searching for Greg Gingrich. After an hour or two, the sun was setting. The searchers became alarmed.

They contacted an NPS ranger. The Park Service then initiated a missing-person search. They went first to the section of wall where Gingrich had been goofing around, teasing his daughter. He was not there. Fearing the worst, the search team peered over the edge of the rim looking for a body. They saw no one down below.

At this point, some of the searchers were wondering just how far Gingrich would carry his prank. NPS searchers more or less expected to find Gingrich off the beaten path somewhere and embarrassed in being caught in a joke that went a little too far.

As nightfall became a reality, the search and rescue (SAR) team suspected something far worse than a prank. They launched a helicopter equipped with infrared (heat) sensors and a powerful searchlight. They searched closely with these along the South Rim. But, yet again, they found nothing.

Finally, searchers spotted Gingrich's jacket about 400 feet below where he had been clowning around on the wall. Dropping closer near the sheer cliff, they saw the jacket was still wrapped around a crumpled body.

The morning after Gingrich's disappearance, Rangers Ken Phillips and Chris Pergiel re-examined the section of wall where Gingrich had vanished. The Canyon side of the wall was not an immediate drop-off but instead a ledge and then a talus slope that one could walk on, if one were very careful. Scuff signs on the slope revealed that when Greg Gingrich had dropped off the wall backwards while facing his daughter, he had tried to land on that 3 to 4-foot-wide ledge below the base of the wall. The scuff marks suggested that he had immediately lost his footing on contact here and had somersaulted backwards and out of control down the talus before launching off the 400-foot cliff.

Rangers Dan Kirshner, Kent Keller, and Tim Reid rappelled down the cliff that morning to retrieve the body.

Gingrich, of course, was a rare exception. Most visitors don't experience this sort of outcome. Yet all too many have. How bad does it get? Near the end of 1993's grisly, record-setting toll of falls from the South Rim, journalist Susan Trausch summed it up.

> *Chilling statistics from the Grand Canyon this week. Seven people fell to their deaths in 1993, and park officials can't remember a worse year for fatalities.*
>
> *With the exception of a tourist* [in fact a local resident] *who had been drinking and a drifter trying to grab coins tossed on a ledge, the lives were lost by sober, solid citizens who simply had no sense of danger standing on the rim of the mile-deep gorge. They died posing for pictures, leaning over for a better look, or strolling along rocky paths as nonchalantly as they walk through a shopping mall.*
>
> *Warning signs, guard rails, stern words from rangers, and fear did not register. They were in a park, and that meant the authorities were responsible for their safety, didn't it?*

Are such seemingly foolish deaths truly due to our having grown up in a culture so paranoically obsessed with paving the natural world that we can no longer cope with any terrain that has not been laser-leveled?

"You have to look at each one of them [the falls]," notes NPS spokesperson Maureen Oltrogge, "as a separate incident. But, in general, the falls mostly result from carelessness or ignoring warnings....we issue warnings all the time [handed to each visitor entering the park]. We talk about the dangers of getting too close to the rim. Beyond that, I don't know what else it is you can do."

Speaking also of the bonanza of foolish fatalities in 1993, Chief Ranger Ken Miller noted, "The one common thread from these incidents has been the complete lack of regard for personal safety."

"A lot of tourists approach Grand Canyon like a ride at Disneyland or some other amusement park and think it's idiot-proof," notes Tom Jensen, Executive Director of the Grand Canyon Trust. "The Grand Canyon wasn't built by attorneys and engineers."

But even Grand Canyon *has* been modified (however slightly) by busy engineers. At a price. In 1908, for example, a team of men was trying to pry up a tree of eight inches diameter on the edge of the South Rim at Grandview. It was spoiling the grand view.

One of the men, D. Johnson, paused for a moment. At that same moment all hell broke loose. The "problem" tree not only jerked loose from the limestone bedrock, so did the bedrock itself in which the tree had been anchored for the past couple of centuries.

As the uprooted tree and the loose rock around it all obeyed the law of gravity by toppling into the Canyon, the tree's heavy roots caught Johnson in the back. These literally catapulted Johnson off the rim and into space.

Johnson sky-dived head first into the atmosphere below. He plummeted between two narrow, projecting ledges of jagged Kaibab Limestone. Either of these might have crushed his skull like an eggshell. Then, one hundred feet below the rim, and after glancing blows from sloping projections, Johnson slammed into a large clump of thick brush clinging above a ledge only three feet wide. Still conscious and aware that the man-made avalanche of stones still raining down might kill him despite his miraculous survival thus far, Johnson dragged himself under a shallow ledge.

After the final stone rattled past him and whistled into infinity, Johnson risked a glimpse off his tiny ledge to the world below. This world dropped away vertically for almost one thousand feet. That patch of brush had saved his life.

A physician examined Johnson but found no broken bones. But Johnson was now sporting a colorful collection of bruises. Johnson's survival was so infinitesimally improbable that he should have limped off to buy a few lottery tickets before the clock struck midnight and ended what had to be the luckiest day in anyone's life.

At further risk of making light of the normally tragic denouement of a fall from either rim of the Canyon, consider Tommy Manis' sky dive. In late May 1966, Tommy, the ten-year-old son of the assistant manager of Babbitt's General Store at Grand Canyon Village, decided to give his new bicycle a work-out. Manis pedaled furiously as he blazed along the Rim Trail a half mile west of the Bright Angel Lodge. He was pedaling so hard that it seemed he could get that bike to fly.

And then he did. Manis came to a curve, rolling fast. He knew he had to brake. His old bike had a foot brake; but this new one had handle bar brakes, which now escaped his memory—and his feet. He launched off the rim into thin air. With no E.T. to keep him aloft, Manis and his bicycle plunged 120 vertical feet into the Canyon.

This length of fall in the Canyon has killed everyone else who has tried it. When rescuers got to Manis, however, they found him with a broken arm, scalp lacerations, multiple bruises, and several not so obvious, but potentially serious, internal injuries. His bicycle was not in such hot shape either. Manis ended up in critical condition but did okay during his long stay in the hospital. "Rescuers," the newspaper reports said, "termed the boy's survival a miracle." Just like D. Johnson's survival back in 1908. (Despite the obviously slim odds of surviving a fall into the Canyon, on May 21, 1999, motorized daredevil Robbie Kneivel deliberately launched his standard 500-cc motorcycle off a jump set on the edge of the deep upper drainage of Quartermaster Canyon on Hualapai Tribal land near the Tribal Casino. He gained 55 feet in altitude and shot horizontally a record 228 feet to the ramp on the far side—at the cost of only one broken leg.)

Sadly, however, unlike the miracles of Tommy Manis's bicycle descent or Robbie Kneivel's Canyon daredevil stunt, and completely unlike Dee Dee Johnson's topless fashion fall, during most accidental long falls from the rims, the bag of Canyon miracles has come up empty.

To understand what leads to these fatal falls, one must peruse Table 1–A at the end of this chapter. This table—as does every table ending each chapter in this book—offers rewarding reading. Tables 1–A and 1–B reveal that the conditions under which people have managed to fall into Grand Canyon are amazing, but at the same time not consistently predictable. A look at the dates, for example, in Table 1–A reveals that, while common, accidental falls from the rims are not regular events. During a two-year span in 1983 and 1984, apparently no one fell off either rim accidentally. Yet millions of people visited the Canyon during those years. Earlier yet, before 1971, a decade passed when, reportedly, no one fell off either rim. In contrast (and as mentioned earlier), in 1993, seven people accidentally and independently fell to their deaths.

Why did all these 50 people listed in Table 1–A fall? Each of them was doing something that influenced their fatal outcome. The most cliche activities that many of us assume are the most common causes of "stupid" falls are posing for a photo on the edge and taking one step back too many, or else taking a photo of the Canyon from the edge of either rim and falling off while gazing absent-mindedly through the view finder. Sadly, these cliches match reality.

This failure to exercise common sense has often been fatally coupled in Grand Canyon with the desire to "win" the most dramatic photographic footage. Veteran pioneers of Canyon photography, the indefatigable Ellsworth and Emery Kolb, for example, epitomized this gambler mentality. For a stunning photo, they would leap over chasms as mid-air subjects or dangle themselves above precipices by a rope to get that perfect perspective—or even to get a photo documenting their incredible daring to get that perfect perspective. But while the Kolb brothers were experienced and calculatingly competent—and frequently lucky—others seeking the most dramatic images have been neither. Indeed their misfortunes arrived along with the first cameras to enter the Canyon.

This sort of mishap is now so cliche that it has its own punch line: "Take just one more step back...." An early example occurred on March 22, 1925, barely six years after Grand Canyon had become a national park. Lewis W. Thompson stood on the edge of the South Rim to pose—as millions of people by now have done—for a scenic photo proving that he had actually been to Grand Canyon. Thompson's position, however, proved less than ideal for a perfectly composed photo. So he took one more step. Into a crack.

Thompson tripped, lost his balance, tottered, then fell off the rim. He plunged hundreds of feet to his death.

Another tragic camera "killing" involved Yuri Nagata, age 21. While visiting with friends on March 12, 1989, at the West Rim, Second Trailview Overlook, Nagata stepped around the guard rail to climb down to the lower ledge. Then she sat on the very edge of the picturesque precipice. A friend asked her to turn around for a photo. As Nagata stood to pose for that photo, she lost her balance and fell off the rim.

Another senseless fall occurred on September 8, 1993, at Mather Point. James Merriman, age 51, was a daredevil transient who haunted this overlook to gather "good luck" coins tossed onto small jutting ledges by tourists. Merriman, a Flagstaff resident, used to periodically ride his bike 80 miles to Grand Canyon to collect these coins. Afterward he would ride back to Flagstaff and treat his buddies to a feast at Sizzlers restaurant. A week earlier Merriman had gotten himself so trapped on an exposed ledge that he had to be rescued from the "zone of coins" by NPS rangers. Apparently this episode created little lasting value as a deterrent. On September 8, Merriman again climbed beyond and below the safety rail to collect "good luck" coins on ledges.

When Merriman saw tourists above watching him in horror, he hammed it up by jumping from rock to rock, inviting them to take his "action" photo (allegedly in exchange for a fee). "Watch me!" he bragged. Then he jumped. Merriman missed his footing and fell to his death.

Only two months later, on November 9, 1993, Timothy J. Rowe, age 24, botched his action photo, too. While visiting the Second Trailview Overlook on the West Rim, Rowe jumped from rock to rock to create dramatic action for the ideal photo. He missed his footing and plunged to his death.

A recent "posing" tragedy occurred on August 19, 1999, at Moran Point on the South Rim. Gabriel Comerford, age 25, asked nearby tourists if they would use his camera to take his photo. These bystanders agreed. Comerford explained that he wanted to pose out on a precipice where the shot would be dramatic. The bystanders nodded in understanding. Comerford then crossed the guard rail, climbed over a retaining wall, and walked out to his chosen, highly exposed position.

Just before arriving at his chosen spot a rock crumbled under his foot. Comerford slipped off the level Kaibab Limestone and tumbled down a rubble-strewn, bush-clumped talus chute for more than a hundred feet.

Meanwhile the bystander with Comerford's camera continued to photograph him during his battering tumble. The bystander snapped the final photo as Comerford slid off the edge at the end of the chute and into vertical air. Comerford next fell 875 feet.

Yet other people have plunged off the rim to their deaths while *using* the camera. On July 7, 1978, Bobbey Kay Kendrick, age 45, shuffled along the edge of a truly dizzying precipice in search of a perfect vantage point for a photo from Yaki Point. She lost her footing and fell over the edge 600 feet. Less than a year later, on April 8, 1979, Roger Sydnor, age 30, walked out on the Rim Trail near the Visitor Center for a dramatic dawn photo. Sydnor lost his footing on the rim and fell 250 feet. The next such fatality occurred not long after this, on April 27, 1981, and in nearly the same place. But in an amazingly different way.

Essentially walking backwards while looking back toward the Bright Angel Lodge in an attempt to get an ideal photo of *it*, John Eric Hastrick, age 20, climbed over the rock guard wall. He continued the few feet to the rim itself. Again, Hastrick wanted a shot of the lodge, not of the Canyon itself. Astoundingly, *while holding his camera to his face, Hastrick continued backing up toward the Canyon.* He soon lost his footing, lost terra firma, and fell 330 feet.

Yet another tragic attempt to get the perfect photo was caused by a crumbling ledge of Kaibab Limestone at Cape Royal. On September 7, 1993, Lori Newcomb, age 31, walked far out on the edge of a ledge to take a photo. The ledge itself crumbled under Newcomb's weight. She slipped and fell 20 feet, rolled and slid down a terrace, then plunged 60 more feet to her death.

These two activities—posing for or taking photographs—account for 6 and 4 victims (20 percent) of the 50 total victims of accidental lethal falls from the rims.

What killed the many other victims of falls from the rims?

Only five—all males—of the 50 victims were rock climbing or scrambling without technical protection (ropes, pitons, chocks, nuts, friends, etc.). On June 7, 1958, for example, Donald L. Mark, age 43, took a break from his job as a Grand Canyon motel clerk and climbed over the guard wall behind El Tovar. He descended partway down the cliff as a solo, recreational climber. An audience gathered above him to watch his climbing technique and to marvel at his incredible nerve above such a dizzying exposure. Mark next appeared to be "putting on an act" by "playfully jumping from rock to rock." He "continually looked up at the crowd" still gathering to watch. He had fair footing, one witness later reported, but poor handholds. On Mark's next climbing move, he lost his grip. And his balance. He fell over backwards into the abyss, plunging 300 feet.

Three other victims—again all male and most fairly young—were not even climbing but simply "goofing-off" in the most ridiculous of locations. As mentioned earlier, on November 28, 1992, Greg Austin Gingrich, age 38, jumped atop, then over, the rock wall along the Rim Trail near El Tovar. Again, he missed his landing and fell 400 feet. On September 5, 1993, Andreas Zimmerman, age 24, jumped from one ledge to another on the edge at Cape Royal just for the hell of it. He slipped and fell to his death. Two months later, on November 16, 1993, James Hyland, age 21, decided to walk atop the frosty guard wall built to separate people from the abyss below El Tovar Hotel. He too slipped and fell.

Since the first recorded falls from the rims, such reckless ones have been standard—like the following one reported in the July 30, 1920 edition of the *Coconino Sun*:

> *Tourists at El Tovar hotel, Grand Canyon, came very near being treated to a thrill on Saturday that is not down on the regular schedule. A lot of them were standing near the wall in front of the hotel watching a chap about a hundred feet below the surface of the rim, who had managed to get a couple of hundred feet down the side of the cliff and was working his way back up to the top. Everyone was holding their breath and suddenly everyone lost it, for the young man lost his hold and fell. Twenty feet lower he struck on his back on a narrow ledge, by a miracle sticking there. But for the ledge he would have dropped several hundred feet. He got up lighted a cigarette, and finished his climb to the top.*

Many of the accidental falls off the rims discussed so far seem so bizarre as to beg reality. How so many people could manage to mismanage their footing on such relatively easy terrain offering a dizzyingly nearby vista that screams "WATCH OUT, DON'T FALL!" almost defies belief. Consider the case of Richard Peña.

Late on a cold January day in 1985, Richard Peña and his family visited the West Rim to take in the view. Snow had fallen days earlier and the exact position—or edge—of the rim itself lay somewhat hidden under a few inches of frozen white fluff. For reasons known only to Peña himself, he climbed over the National Park Service safety railing at the First Trailview Overlook to get a couple of feet closer to the view.

His young son warned him, "Hey, the sign says you're not supposed to go past the rail."

Peña turned to him and allegedly said, "You gotta take some chances in life."

Then, stepping on snow which had nothing underneath it but a few hundred feet of air, Peña vanished from view and plummeted into the frozen abyss.

By a strange coincidence, NPS Ranger Rod Losson was hiking up the

Bright Angel Trail at this instant. He heard Peña scream. Losson looked up and watched Peña plunge more than three hundred feet.

Meanwhile, his shocked family tried to see where he had hit. Failing in this, they hurried to find an NPS ranger. They explained to the ranger what had happened. He activated an NPS search and rescue (SAR) chopper that launched almost immediately. The SAR personnel searched the cliffs and terraces in the fading light of dusk. Minutes after launching, they spotted Peña's body 350 feet below the rim sprawled on a terrace. The body lay contorted, broken-looking, and apparently lifeless. In that the sun had set and darkness was falling and recovery of the body would be extremely risky for the rangers, the SAR team decided that it would be much safer to recover the body in the morning during daylight.

The family was appalled. What if Peña were still alive down there? They were so upset at this perceived self-serving attitude of park personnel that they threatened to sue the NPS. Meanwhile rumors circulated at the South Rim that a routine background check on Peña allegedly revealed that he was wanted for two counts of murder in Los Angeles County. (Law enforcement officials at the South Rim recall these rumors but, in 2000, were unable to substantiate their source.)

Park SAR personnel recovered Peña's body the next day. A post-mortem exam determined the time of death to have been upon impact.

Peña's nonchalance in the face of such a strong possibility of violent death was not unique. At least six other victims, five of them women, revealed much the same attitude of nonchalance and seemingly were felled by their neurophysiology. All six had either sat right on the edge, at the brink of infinity, or had approached it on foot. Yet each one, through dizziness or loss of balance or suffering vertigo—caused perhaps by each victim having lost her or his habitual visual cues of the "normal," i.e. level, world—slipped into that infinity. Some of these victims may have slipped or tripped simply because they were only accustomed to walking on artificially leveled and surfaced terrain. This is a very likely extenuating factor. For every fatal fall from the South Rim, for example, possibly twenty other victims on the rims have simply tripped on imperfections of the Kaibab Limestone and suffered injuries (some of these victims threatened to sue the National Park Service for not leveling the paths perfectly).

These six fatal falls mentioned above include the July 17, 1947, episode of Herbert E. Kolb, age 17, again due to some sort of dizziness. Kolb crawled through the guard rail with his girlfriend to sit on the edge of the cliff at Hopi Point. When they got up to leave, Kolb lost his balance and fell 950 feet. Two years later, on September 14, 1949, Minnie Edith Kindig, age 63, walked to the rim. The view was apparently so shocking that she fainted and collapsed to her knees. She toppled off the rim, falling 500 feet from Yaki Point. On April 12, 1971, Elizabeth Hazelhurst, age 21, was sitting on the edge of the rim with her sisters at Mojave Point. When she tried to get to her feet, she slipped and fell about 350 feet. Informal information from one sister instead suggests hallucinogenic drug use and a possible desire to "fly off the rim." On October 8, 1981, Maria C. Alfaro, age 23, walked to the edge, off the Rim Trail near the Visitor Center, to sit on the rim and watch the sunset. She slipped and fell 400 feet. On March 9, 1989, Gesela Elixmann, age 34, walked to the edge at Mojave Point. She became dizzy and fell off, plunging 500 feet. Yuri Nagata, age 21 (mentioned earlier as a photo-posing fatality on March 12, 1989) also became disoriented and lost her balance as she tried to turn around and stand. She fell to her death.

A common factor in these deaths is each victim seemingly became disoriented due to the visual shock of looking down into such an immense hole and, in seeing nothing for an instinctive reference point, lost her or his balance. Notably, all of these victims had ignored warning signs and also bypassed or climbed past guard rails or walls to get to the edge from whence they fell.

Another fatal factor is nightfall. Six other victims—five of them males— fell at night while camping or walking alone. A possible culprit in many of these fatalities may be the male urge to urinate off high places combined with dizziness (and possibly alcohol consumption). Other male victims likely have fallen to their deaths from heights *within* the Canyon or into the river to drown, while urinating (see next section).

Surprisingly, another category for unplanned plunges involves motor vehicle accidents, usually at very slow speed—or even parked. Five people have died accidentally this way. The most tragic of these is the case of James Lloyd Qualls, age 5, and Harold Frank Qualls, 15 months old, visiting with their family from Brownsville, Texas. On June 8, 1958, the two boys' father had parked the family sedan (with both boys in it) at a lookout point on the rim above the Little Colorado River eight miles west of Cameron. The father, Frank Qualls, age 28, had left the transmission in gear, but in the highest gear of "overdrive" (which offered the least resistance to the vehicle rolling). Qualls also had not set the parking brake.

While the adults were 200 feet away admiring the view, they sent another relative, Kenneth Dull, age 10, back to the car to fetch a camera in the glove compartment. Dull said the car started rolling as he opened the door. Dull jumped aside. After rolling only 25 feet, the car plunged over the rim 100 feet into the gorge, ricocheting off rocks, then exploding into flames.

The earliest victim of a vehicle plunge into the Canyon was Waddy Thompson Ligon, age 73. On October 29, 1925, Ligon drove his converted Ford Model A down the old, very narrow "Dugway" about 2 miles south of Lees Ferry. The wheels on the right side of the Model A slid off the narrow dugway as he backed up. The vehicle slid off the steep road and jammed into a crevasse, pinning and killing Ligon.

The only high-speed motor vehicle fatality not suspected to be a suicide, was that of Elroy Ponyah, age 17. On May 1, 1971, Ponyah missed a turn and drove his Ford sedan off Highway 64 at Tappan Springs Canyon. The vehicle leaped the gorge and hit the opposite wall 40 feet lower.

Bennett Hanna experienced an almost unbelievable accident on Hualapai Hilltop on August 19, 1972. Hanna had just dropped off some friends at the trailhead into Havasu. As he backed up to turn his car around, he reversed too far and plummeted backwards off the vertical edge for 500 feet.

Two victims of work-related falls include accidents while working near the edge. Philo Anderson became entangled in a rope while lowering a section of pipe on November 24, 1927. He fell 300 feet off the North Rim. Months later, on June 12, 1928, Lane McDaniels, age 42, was working on the partially constructed Navajo Bridge at River Mile 4. Despite this being the tallest steel bridge in the world at this time, the supervisors vetoed rigging safety netting under the bridge because they were sure that hot rivets dropping by accident might ignite it. McDaniels, unfortunately, missed his footing on a scaffold. He fell. And there being no net, he plummeted about 470 feet into the Colorado River. His fellow workers stared down in horror. They said that, upon impact, McDaniels' body seemed to "burst and flatten out" on the surface of the water. Four steelworkers quit after McDaniels death, not from fear of falling, but from the dismal prospect of being swallowed up by the turbulent waters of the Colorado if they did fall, with no hope that their bodies would ever be recovered.

Some rim-falls are not merely suspected but known to have been alcohol related. Lawrence Jackson, age 24, who fell off the rim above Badger Overlook on August 14, 1993, had been drinking "heavily." As mentioned earlier, so had Lana Virginia Smith, age 28, who fell off the wall (and the South Rim) behind the Bright Angel Lodge on May 11, 1997. It is unknown, however, to what degree, if any, alcohol may have contributed to the actions that led to the falls of other victims in Table 1–A.

That these 50 rim-fall victims seem almost evenly divided as to their activities during the time of their demise obfuscates a couple of major risk factors. What are *the* truly big culprits leading to such a hideous death? At least ten of the victims—and possibly as many as 25 or more of them—had deliberately crossed the guard rails or walls to frolic, walk, stand on, or sit on the very edge. In short, before they fell over the edge, 20 to 50 percent of these victims were intentionally reckless.

Add to this snow and ice. At least five, and as many as seven, victims died due to slipping on ice and snow on the rim—often after passing the guard rail or wall.

A further risk factor, a glaring one, is being male. In contrast, while youth does seem to play a role, the average age of fall victims (excluding the two Quall children innocently trapped in the parents' car) was 34 years old. While many of these victims were young adults, when considered as a group they were all of a mature age. Yet Table 1–A does reveal a slap-in-the-face pattern of males being the predominant victims. Of 50 falls, only thirteen were women. Even though only a quarter of accidental fatal rim falls have been of women, this is the highest proportion of women victims in any group of people dying traumatically in any one way in Grand Canyon. In other words, for women at Grand Canyon, this is a very high level of representation. Women, it appears, are less careful of falls from the rims than they are, as we will see in later chapters, of all other Canyon dangers except flying with male pilots.

Looked at another way, however, Table 1–A also reveals that men take far more risks, even at the relatively "tame" lookout points on the rims, than women do. Again, glaringly, all eight victims who were rock-hopping and trying to appear fearless for an audience of friends, family, or even strangers—and often doing so for someone's camera—when they slipped off bedrock to their long death plunges were men. All five victims who dropped off the South Rim in motor vehicles were male, and all died due to the actions of men. All five victims who died while rock-climbing or scrambling on the rims were also men.

How do we know that these 50 falls were accidents and not suicides? Each fatal incident has a report. And most falls were witnessed by observers who reported them as obviously unintended mishaps. And, as we'll see in a later chapter on suicide, most suicidal jumps differ from accidental falls in a couple of interesting respects. Most accidental falls, for example, happen during summer season and its shoulder seasons. In contrast, suicides (see Chapter 7) are clustered in the colder seasons. Even so, one or two of the falls described in Table 1–A might have been intentional; we may never know.

Another glaring reality is clear among those 50 rim falls. Excluding the two Qualls children trapped in the family car, none of the 48 other fatalities were of children. In short, as immature and reckless as children can be (as with Tommy Manis' miraculous 100-foot plunge), none of them has killed himself or herself by falling into Grand Canyon. This may be due to the reality that children possess a more recent familiarity about the dangers, risks, and consequences of falling in the natural world (while many adults have been too long out of touch with vertical drops). Or, instead, the lack of children falling may be due to many parents exerting a double standard on their kids ("It's okay for Daddy to stand this close because he's taking a picture, but this is too dangerous for you"). Either way, this would be an interesting focus for further research. We predict the outcome of such research to be that children possess—and exercise—a far more realistic and careful appreciation of the dangers of the natural world than do more jaded adults.

Either way, this holds some interesting ramifications. The first—one hard for many parents to swallow—is that children seem significantly smarter, when it comes to common sense, than many adults. Perhaps the NPS caution signs posted to warn visitors against the danger of falls would be far more efficacious if they specifically admonished children:

"IF YOU ARE A CHILD, PLEASE KEEP A CLOSE EYE ON
ANY ADULTS NEAR THE EDGE. ADULTS HAVE A TRAGIC
TENDENCY TO BE CARELESS OR RECKLESS. DOZENS OF
THEM HAVE DIED HERE DUE TO LACK OF ADEQUATE
SUPERVISION BY CHILDREN."

Falls Within The Canyon

Once one descends even ten feet below either rim of Grand Canyon, one has
entered a new and different world. This world is the most convoluted, massive,
and jaggedly vertical landscape on Earth, a vast complicated labyrinth carved
by the vagaries of erosion as it removed 1,000 cubic miles of rock in a den-
dritic drainage pattern that gnaws into bedrock cliffs thousands of feet high
and fractures the landscape into 600 tributary canyons. The vast majority of
rock surface here is so nearly impossible to access that it may never be visited
by humans. The few practical routes penetrating this landscape—most of
which were pioneered millennia ago by Native Americans—are themselves
fraught with precipices and pitfalls and decaying sedimentary rock that weed
out the unwary. Accidental falls within this Canyon, however, bear only slight
resemblance in their conditions and victims to the falls *from* the rims discussed above.

This might be because trekking into the Canyon—and then getting back
out alive to tell of it—can demand a high degree of skill. But such skill can be
gained only in places like the canyons of the Colorado Plateau. Canyoneering
is not mountaineering. Canyoneering demands negotiating huge and lethal
exposures on crumbling cliffs soaring to vast heights or plunging to even
worse depths. It also requires managing this on bone-dry, 120-degree-hot
traverses leading to routes that ultimately prove not to be routes at all, but
instead heart-breaking, dead-end cul de sacs. In short, the Canyon's dangers
and pitfalls tend to be larger and worse than those of normal, dangerous life.

From the beginning of recorded history, these dangers have fooled newcomers. The Canyon's very first European, would-be hikers, for example, tried
for three days to climb down to the Colorado River but failed. This happened
in 1540, less than twenty years after Cortez and his small army had toppled the
Aztecs' huge Mexican empire to double the territory of Spain. This 1540 expedition, led by 26-year-old Francisco Vasquez de Coronado, consisted of yet
another army of conquistadors assembled in Mexico. Coronado's quest was to
discover—and then empty—the fabled Seven Golden Cities of Cibola located
somewhere far to the north beyond a vast arid desert of shifting sands.

Several weeks north of Mexico, Coronado led his 336 Spanish soldiers and
700 Indian allies against the Zuñis of Hawikuh (in future New Mexico). After
ransacking Hawikuh, Coronado's troops moved farther north along the upper

Rio Grande. They looted, extorted, raped, pillaged, and murdered along their way. Despite these local conquests, those elusive Seven Cities of Gold continued to evade discovery. Coronado knew that if he returned to Mexico without having discovered the legendary gold, he could kiss his career—and maybe his life—goodbye.

Finally Coronado heard of another seven cites, those of Tusayan. These were the Hopi pueblos. Coronado sent Pedro de Tovar west to reconnoiter them. Tovar returned and reported that these pueblos too held no gold, no silver, no precious gems; they were not even surrounded by fertile lands. But, Tovar said, the Hopis had spoken of a great river to the west.

Coronado ordered Lieutenant Garcia Lopez de Cardenas and a dozen conquistadors to find that mysterious river. At Tusayan, Cardenas enlisted Hopi guides. Twenty days march to the west of the Hopi Pueblos, his reconnaissance force reached a region of low twisted pines, where, looking north, they beheld a huge canyon with a river running south and then west. North beyond and above this river was a high, barren plateau. The river down at the bottom, the conquistadors reckoned, looked about six feet wide.

The Hopis insisted that the river instead stretched half a league (1.5 miles) across.

Cardenas sent his three lightest and most agile men—Captain Melgosa, Juan Galeras, and one other man—to climb down the least difficult route to ascertain the river's true dimensions. The trio spent three days trying to find a feasible route down to the river. They failed. But they did manage to find a route one third of the way down. But at that point the Redwall Limestone stopped them cold. Even from atop the Redwall, however, they realized that the Hopis were probably right about things here being bigger than they had looked from above. Boulders that had appeared no higher than a man from the rim, they now saw were taller than the 300-foot high Tower of Seville. Continuing downward from the Redwall now looked like suicide.

The conquistadors' inability to comprehend the scale of Grand Canyon topography had nothing to do with the century these men lived in. Of course, Cardenas' Hopi guides knew well their own nearby "Salt Trail" route to the river; they likely smiled inwardly even as they impassively watched Cardenas' three "agile" conquistadors struggling in vain for three days in growing thirst atop the Redwall cliffs. Hopi mirth aside, our point here is that even these tough little men in armor who toted Toledo steel and conquered empires embodied the same two failings that nearly every non-Indian visitor to Grand Canyon since 1540 has exemplified: an inability to comprehend the scale of Grand Canyon and a marked—and often fatal—tendency to underestimate it.

The earliest known deaths due to falls in the Canyon happened to men lured into its depths by hidden mineral riches they imagined must be waiting in its inaccessible nether regions. After all, God would never have built such an immense treasure room—one He guarded with a million pitfalls—unless He had hidden some very valuable treasure in it. These riches, they believed, would be claimed by the man with the greatest faith and the most grit. The Canyon attracted scores of such miners. As George H. Billingsley, Earle E. Spamer, and Dove Menkes note in their *Quest for the Pillar of Gold: The Mine & Miners of the Grand Canyon*:

> *When silver was not found in abundance, copper became the number one commodity sought in the Canyon, although visions of gold veins were probably always in the minds and dreams of early prospectors. Asbestos was discovered and mined from the canyon, too, but it was not widely developed, probably because the markets were too distant. In most cases minerals were mined because they were there. It was better than nothing.*

The Canyon felt the onslaught of a slow motion, "almost" mineral rush, much of which pre-dated the more organized—and more limited—official explorations of the Canyon funded by the U.S. Government. Indeed, as Billingsley, Spamer, and Menkes report, in search of riches: "By 1890, prospectors had explored virtually every side canyon in Grand Canyon."

But these 600 or so tributary canyons within Grand Canyon were not explored without casualties. Billingsley, Spamer, and Menkes note how "Old Man Snyder," for example, failed one time to make his regular pass through Paiute territory from his mine to St. George, Utah. A few of the local Paiutes checked on him. They found him dead at his mine. Before this mine was rediscovered east and north of Diamond Creek in Western Grand Canyon, it had become one of the "lost mines" that fueled dreamers' quests for lost gold. The mine itself was relocated by George and Sue Billingsley in a breccia pipe above the Redwall in the Watahomigie member of the Supai Group. Its ore contains a fairly rich concentration of copper minerals as well as arsenic, cobalt, nickel, molybdenum, and zinc. But, as usual, no gold.

Perhaps the earliest witnessed fatal fall of a prospector was that of Daniel W. Mooney. Formerly a sailor, and then a rancher in the Williamson Valley near Prescott, Arizona, Mooney too had been bitten by the lure of mineral riches. Bitten hard. Mooney and four other miners filed one of the earliest claims in Havasu (a.k.a. Cataract) Canyon. They found lead and silver, fairly common in Havasu but economically challenging to extract. Mooney and a few others among the dozen associated miners who prospected Havasu's canyon system felt teased by the mystery of what might lay below the biggest falls along the last seven miles or so to the Colorado. This mystery tortured Mooney.

The Havasupai people apparently never traveled downstream of this point, and for good reason: the falls dropped 196 feet and offered only the most hellishly exposed, expert-only climbing route.

Finally, in 1880, Mooney decided he could pull off a descent. As Billingsley, Spamer, and Menkes tell it:

> *On a fateful last trip, Mooney took a rope down into the canyon and, trusting his sailor's experience with ropes and rope climbing, let himself down over the falls. Once he was over the falls, the others in the party lost sight of him and the roar of water precluded any verbal communication. Soon they felt the rope slacken and, running around to the side of the falls, they saw the rope dangling nearly half way down. Mooney lay on the rocks below. Unable to reach him, all they could do was leave.*

A prospecting associate, Edward I. Doheny, described Mooney as red-headed, red-bearded, and possessing a violent temper. Mooney was also the spokesman with the Havasupai Indians for the dozen prospectors allied in combing their canyons for paydirt. "Mooney," Doheny said, "was very reckless and did not exercise the caution that 100 percent sanity would dictate. His fall from the place where he had started to go down over a bluff on a very small rope, was not altogether unexpected by those of us who constituted the party."

A few years later, in 1883, Matthew Humphreys would blast out a descending tunnel along the creek's left side. Mooney's friends then buried him almost exactly where he fell. In less than four years, however, the thin sands atop Mooney washed away, as prospector William Wallace Bass noted, to reveal his "grinning teeth and eye sockets."

The next known fall victim also sought gold, but the kind to be made by selling real estate. Shortly before Christmas in 1889, Robert Brewster Stanton arrived at the Lees Ferry entry to Grand Canyon with a well-equipped river expedition to survey the Canyon for construction of a railroad within the Inner Canyon. This expedition had launched in Glen Canyon at Crescent Creek, four miles downstream of the Dirty Devil River in Utah on December 10, 1889. Shortly after Christmas, the expedition floated the Colorado into Grand Canyon.

On New Year's Day of 1890, photographer Franklin A. Nims climbed a bit higher than he should have to artfully compose—a thing Stanton had warned him not to do—a photo with the men, the boats, and the river canyon all in it.

Nims lost his footing and slipped. He fell 22 feet onto the rocks and sand below. The other men rushed over and found Nims unconscious and with blood oozing from his mouth and right ear. Nims' right lower leg had been badly broken, as had the bones of both feet.

Nims remained partly conscious but vomited repeatedly through that first freezing night and into the next morning. That day Stanton and the crew decided to carry Nims out of the Canyon. As they were only about 1,000 feet below the rims of what would soon become a mile-deep gorge downstream, such a carry did not seem ridiculous.

But it soon became insane.

The expedition splinted Nims' leg. Next they improvised a stretcher from oars and canvas. Then they pondered possible evacuation routes. Seeing no tributary canyon that looked inviting, the men decided to row Nims a few miles downstream. Near River Mile 17 they recognized what should have been an exit to the northwest via Ryder Canyon.

Stanton climbed out the 1,500-foot ascent first and fastest. Once atop the Kaibab Limestone he hiked 20 miles across the Marble Platform in the moonlight. His goal was Lees Ferry. There he hoped to fetch the ferryman and his wagon. Meanwhile the other men began a 6.5-hour, harrowing carry of Nims up nearly the same route to the Canyon's North Rim. They hauled him, still unconscious, over boulders, and they hoisted him, suspended by ropes, up cliffs. Had Nims seen and understood what his companions were doing to help him, he might have died of fright.

The evacuation team—with Nims still alive—reached the rim that afternoon, only to be forced to spend the night without blankets in a snowstorm while they waited for Stanton.

He arrived the next day by wagon with the ferryman, W. M. Johnson. Johnson hauled Nims back to Lees Ferry. There Nims lay unconscious on the cook house floor for a week. He awakened as a group of Mormons from the north passed through on their way into northern Arizona. Responding to Nims' pleas to take him to see a doctor, they agreed to take him on the 9-day, 185 mile wagon ride to Winslow, Arizona, for $85.

After this ride—a hellish one for anyone in Nims' condition—the doctor in Winslow discovered several other broken and dislocated bones in addition to the obvious damage in Nims' leg. He also diagnosed Nims' skull fracture. After administering minor treatment, the doctor sent Nims to Denver for further care.

Strangely, although Stanton's crew had gone through tremendous effort and risk to get Nims out of the Canyon, as soon as Johnson arrived they abandoned Nims on the rim to return to the river. Nims was embittered by this experience. During his month and a half of convalescence, Nims wrote that Stanton's company paid none of his expenses, and "cut off his salary as of January 1, 1890, the day of the accident." Indeed, Stanton never did pay Nims another dollar.

But Nims survived. In this alone he was very lucky. Most episodes of falling off cliffs in the Canyon end fatally. Of course Nims fell "only" 22 feet. By Canyon standards, 22 feet would be considered lucky.

The identities of a few other victims of fatal falls in the Inner Canyon have been illusive. For example, commercial rafting guides commonly used to take their clients up to the Redwall caves immediately upstream of South Canyon near River Mile 31.5 to see, among other things, the "Mystery Skeleton." This was a human skeleton. And it was indeed a mystery as to whom it belonged. Courtesy of river historian P. T. Reilly, however, we have a tidbit as to how it came to lie in its niche at the foot of a Redwall cliff near the ancient Puebloan ruins. Reilly quotes the 1934 river diary of Alton Hatch:

> *July 22. Left camp at 7:30 and passed two or three bad rapids and at last we came to some that were navigable. We stopped at Vasey's Paradise and went exploring. Found pottery, rock houses, and dug up the skeleton of a man. He had dark hair, wore buckskin clothes. Had both legs broken and still had a bad odor to him. I dug back in a cave about 15 feet and found a piece of canvas and an old gun scabbard, a flour sack, and some nails. There were two caves together and this was the top cave. I had to crawl on my stomach to reach it. Bus found several little horses made out of willows and sticks. I think that they were toys for the children to play with. We camped here and enjoyed the good fresh water.*

Who the mystery man in buckskins was will likely remain a mystery (all these bones vanished by the late 1980s), although, with both legs broken, it seems fairly certain this man died in a fall somewhere in or near the sheer drops of South Canyon. He may, of course, have been an Indian visiting a sacred area including the Puebloan ruins themselves. Reilly determined that Alton Hatch found the rifle scabbard and canvas inside Stanton's Cave several hundred yards downstream of the skeleton. Indeed, they may have belonged to Stanton's ill-fated crew of 1889 (see Chapter 4).

Although several other early pioneers, most likely lone prospectors, may also have met their end via accidental falls inside the Canyon, their stories are lost to us. The miners themselves were replaced in the late 1930s by a new wave of seekers. These were seekers of adventure and diversion.

A trio of these included a 30-year-old Catholic priest, Eugene A. Gavigan, and two teenage boys, John Manson Owens III, age 15, and Walter J. (Pete) Mahany, Jr., age 16. They arrived at the South Rim from Savannah, Georgia, in the summer of 1959, seeking precisely these two goals: adventure and diversion. From there they headed down the Tanner Trail. Their quest—which the two boys had begged for—was to visit an abandoned "silver" mine that Father Gavigan had said he had visited as a teenager. This mine was likely the McCormick/Tanner copper mine along the river about 13 miles from the South Rim trailhead.

The three started their descent from the South Rim on a Friday in late July, the hottest month of the year, a time when temperatures in the shade below can hit 120 degrees Fahrenheit. In full sun, of course, it gets hotter yet. The distance by trail to the river by Father Gavigan's route was about nine miles. The mine lay another four miles upstream from the trail's foot. The round trip would be about 26 miles.

What followed was a massive National Park Service and U.S. Army search and rescue effort all begun by the thinnest of threads. Father Gavigan had told no one of his plans, hence there existed no way any NPS personnel would have known anything was amiss when the trio failed to return. Almost incredibly (when one remembers just how big Grand Canyon is), however, visitors to the South Rim near the park's East Entrance on Saturday reported hearing yells for help drift up from its super-heated, shimmering depths.

Could these visitors have heard the real thing, a ranger wondered? He checked to see whether any cars were parked near the Tanner trailhead. There was one south of Lipan point, not parked where he would have expected. Inside it he found a group-kept journal. The latest entry written in it stated: "Tomorrow, we are going to the silver mine."

So there *was* someone down there. And in this heat it was likely to be someone in trouble. The NPS and U.S. Army began their search and rescue.

The day before this search began, Father Gavigan and his two charges had gotten a shockingly late start down from the rim. They had left the parking lot on Friday at noon—almost inconceivably bad timing given their goal to hike 26 screaming hot miles, including a vertical mile down and back up, and yet return to their vehicle on this same day. Compounding this bad planning, the three carried only one bottle of water each and a can of beans. They had left their camping gear, food, and additional water in the car. They did, however, carry first aid and snake bite kits.

Again, Father Gavigan's intent was to reach the mine and return to the rim that same day. This simple plan would fail for a number of reasons, most of which are spelled H-E-A-T. And, making a badly planned hike far worse, beginning atop the Redwall, Father Gavigan somehow missed the standard, NPS-maintained trail. Instead he descended at least partway on the Old Tanner Trail (possibly the route he had taken as a teenager). Had Father Gavigan looked a bit farther west, he would have seen the marked and maintained New Tanner Trail.

The trio consumed all of their water that afternoon as they followed trails, some false, some real. They managed to descend below the cliffs to the long slope of Dox Sandstone flanking the river. By now the trio was painfully dehydrated. When Walter Mahany finally saw the river only a half mile away, he panicked. Mahany ran down the slope willy nilly to the river. Neither Father Gavigan nor Owens could restrain him.

All three made it to the muddy Colorado and finally drank, but it is unclear how much. The late hour, the intense heat, Mahany's panic, and their general unpreparedness now made it clear that hiking more miles upstream to the "silver mine" was not in the cards. So the three hiked back toward the rim, to their car and their food and equipment.

Dusk darkened the cliffs as they trudged upward, now less than halfway up. Already their water bottles were empty and hot to touch and they themselves were parched with thirst and, again, dehydrated. Nightfall caught them still below the Redwall cliff. In the dark they missed the all-important switchback trail at its base which allowed an ascent. This trio found themselves in the same predicament as Coronado's three would-be Canyoneers centuries earlier, but they were stuck at the foot of the Redwall instead of at its top. At this point, as Ranger Dan Davis of the search and rescue team would later explain, things went from very bad to worse.

Having lost their route in the dark thousands of feet above the river yet thousands of feet below the rim—and having made the mistake of having followed parts of the Old Tanner Trail, officially "abandoned" and unmaintained and unmarked for the previous half century—the three gave up and sat down. Unable to sleep due to thirst, they spent a night of torture.

At dawn they started walking along the base of the 600-foot Redwall cliff again where they were stranded in hopes of finding their lost route upward. Survival was now their only priority. But after miles of wandering in the superheated oven of exposed Paleozoic sedimentary strata, they again ended up worse off than before. They still had found no trail, and now all three hikers were gripped in the throes of advanced dehydration.

They gnawed cactus pulp and wracked their fevered brains for a means of escape.

Ranger Davis explains:

> *They made so many fatal errors and did so much meandering around that it was almost impossible to figure out what they did and where they went by the[ir] tracks. After they missed the Redwall switchbacks when they were hiking back out at night they followed the base of the Redwall on up the west fork of Tanner Canyon almost to the head where they spent the night, then dropped into the streambed several miles up from the switchbacks in the Redwall.*

Well off both the Old and New Tanner trails and hopelessly lost, Father Gavigan continued to be baffled by the location of either trail. So the boys yelled for help. Someone in the distance answered by hooting like an ape. The hikers ignored the ape calls and continued yelling for help. Finally someone who sounded like they were up on the rim responded by hollering: "Do you really need help?"

Owens yelled, "Yes." (The willingness of this Good Samaritan on the rim to tell a ranger that he had heard faint yells for help emerging from the shimmering heat waves deep in the Canyon was what set NPS search and rescue efforts into action.)

Despite having made this tenuous contact, the trio's need for water became so acute that the location of any trail upward became academic. Father Gavigan and both boys decided that, instead of searching more for a route upward, they now had to short cut their way back down to the river for water as soon as possible.

They descended about five hundred feet then hit the same problem that they had just faced at the Redwall, but now in reverse. They could not find a route downward through the 250-foot cliff of Tapeats Sandstone. Desperate from thirst and heat atop the Tapeats, the Trappist Priest found a flash-flood-polished, dry "ravine" that seemed to him to provide a route. He would, he explained, lead the way.

The heat was so intense that Father Gavigan, now possessed of diminished mental capacity due to dehydration, instructed the boys to strip off their clothes except for their pants. He also said they should discard their shoes too, and thus have cooler feet (and maybe better traction?). The three hikers tossed their shoes and clothes down the cut in the Tapeats for later retrieval.

Father Gavigan led the route down. He carried a short rope. With about one-third of the immediate cliff descent behind him, the bare-footed priest lost his footing in the Tapeats chute and fell off a high ledge about 150 feet to his death. He rotated in the air about eight times then hit his head, slammed onto yet more rock, bounced a couple of times, then rolled to a halt on his back.

Mahany stared open-mouthed then went into hysterics. He wanted to hurry down and help "the Padre," as the two boys called him. Owens too was appalled. But he knew they could never make it down that crevasse in the cliff to Father Gavigan. Besides, there was no question of helping the Padre; he was dead. This hike had disintegrated into a waking nightmare. One that might end their lives at well. Owens insisted that they search for some other route down to the river.

The two desperate teenagers wobbled bare-footed and woozily dehydrated across the torturously sharp, hot rock. Fortunately they discovered a nearby route around Father Gavigan's cliff toward the river. They managed this descent on increasingly abused feet. Dehydration had taken such a toll on them that, even though they passed within a few hundred feet of their shoes and clothes, they did not detour to retrieve them. As they struggled toward the river, Mahany grew more and more exhausted in the blistering heat. Suffering from foot injuries and severe thirst and now staggering, both boys made it to within a fairly close descent of the river. Only a fairly easy (with shoes) mile and a half slope of eroded Dox Sandstone lay between them and the river, now life itself.

Mahany, exhausted by dehydration and heat, sat down on a rock. Owens stared at him and asked, "Pete, are you coming with me or not?"

Mahany just sat in silence. The temperature in full sun now likely shimmered at close to 120 degrees.

Desperate with thirst, Owens pushed on. "That's the last time," Owens would later report, "that I saw him."

Owens reached the river. He drank his fill, went swimming, then drank some more—spending an unknown number of hours here between River Miles 68 and 69. Likely because of his seriously wounded feet and his state of dehydration, Owens never retraced his tracks upslope to assist Mahany. Owens instead decided to build a raft of driftwood by strapping logs together with his elastic belt.

Before he launched this to float downstream, Owens scrawled three desperate notes in the sandy soil. One said, "Manson Owens going on raft downriver to bridge."

The second note said, "Pete Mahany okay the last time I saw him in ravine."

Owens' third note said: "Help. One may be dead. Fall of 150 feet. Upper ravine."

Meanwhile, Mahany, shoeless and nearly naked, died of heat stroke and dehydration upslope and close to where Owens last saw him, roughly a 45-minute walk from the river.

Owens launched his raft and drifted down the Colorado. From here onward he prayed "every minute of every day. I never prayed so much in my life." He explained why:

> I hit those rapids. I like to drown. I kept praying. The water was like a washing machine. The raft turned over and I went under. I made it to the bank.

Inconveniently, after this truly terrifying swim through the long, huge wave-train of Unkar Rapid (River Mile 72.7), Owens swam to the side of the river where no vegetation existed. He decided that, if he were to survive, he had to be on the other side, where plants grew. To get there he had to swim across the Colorado. But the river now terrified him. Indeed, despite seeing Father Gavigan die horribly in that 150-foot fall and despite having walked away from a zombie-exhausted Mahany, the *only* time that Owens thought of his own death was when his little raft had tipped over in Unkar. Owens now told himself: "Owens, you ain't a man unless you do it." Then, he reported, "I jumped in and swam to that sandbar."

For these next few days Owens became an unsolved mystery. Two and three days after the three hikers had descended from the Tanner Trailhead, SAR personnel had found the bodies of Walter J. Mahany and Father Gavigan, respectively, well off the Tanner Trail and in divergent locations on Sunday and Monday. Why they had died where they had and what decisions had led to their deaths, the searchers had no idea. Nor could searchers explain the macabre trail they had found littered with Mahany's and Owen's clothes. Days passed before they found Owens' notes scratched in the silty sand. And even then, they seemed to have missed note number one about his rafting down the river. Hence the most perplexing question for the searchers remained: Where was the body of John Manson Owens III?

After a week of unsuccessful searching in the melt-down heat, most of the searchers had given up Owens too for dead. "We're just looking for a body now," searchers admitted.

During the end of this unsolved mystery phase of the search and rescue, doyen Canyon hiker Harvey Butchart suggested to SAR personnel that Owens might have built a raft or tried in some other way to descend the river to help. Butchart even volunteered to leap onto an air mattress and go search for Owens.

While the NPS rejected the air mattress concept, the U.S. Army chopper search crew from Fort Huachuca and a few NPS rangers, Dan Davis among them, took the possibility to heart of Owens having gone rafting. They decided to take their huge, H-21 "flying banana" for one last run over the Canyon, again following the river but now more closely. They were pretty sure that Owens was not along the river upstream of Mile 74 because the Canyon was so wide here that they had been able to fly close to the beaches and search them for Owens and for his footprints and had found none. The Canyon downstream of Mile 74, however, was too narrow for the large H-21 to fly low enough to search thoroughly.

Riding on very hot, diffuse air that gave the machine a sickeningly weak amount of lift, the crew was elated to spot a crude "*H*" on the beach on the left side of River Mile 75 (Nevills Rapid). The house-high letter had been built of stones on a steep, castaway beach about seven miles downstream from where Owens had scrawled his sad notes in the sand. Immediately downstream of the "H" lay 75-Mile Rapid. Below that Hance Rapid.

The air was so hot and of such low density that the chopper felt ticklish to lower. The pilot could not land it and hope to lift off again. So he set it in a semi-landing on one wheel on the narrow "H" beach and ran his motor at full power in order to hover.

Blinking against the solar glare from behind the windbreak he had constructed, John Manson Owens, III stared at the huge machine and the sandstorm it was creating. He finally knew his ordeal was about to end...in his favor. Owens would later recount to the *Deseret News* his strange odyssey toward the head of Upper Granite Gorge:

> *After leaving my companion and arriving on the river I built a raft from three logs, strapping them together with my belt.*
> *I laid on the raft and paddled down the river* [west] *from Saturday until Tuesday. Because of the sun, I decided to stop on a sand bar. The raft was still together when I saw it float on down the river.*

I built a large letter X from sticks and a large letter H from mud along the river bank. Helicopters flew over but couldn't see my distress signals. The mud dried out and blended into the sand bar.

Each time a `copter came over I would take off my pants and wave them, but I couldn't attract anyone's attention. That's when I decided to make a large letter H out of stones. This was on Thursday [Day # 7].

It took a long time to make and was about thirty feet long.

I had a knife with me and tried to flash it in the sun in the hopes a pilot would see it.

I cut cactus plants and chewed the pulp and also found some beans on what I later learned was a mesquite tree. The beans were very hard and had to be soaked in water before they could be eaten. ["I had to search for food on my hands and knees. My feet were so sore."]

If it hadn't been for the heat I would have stayed with the raft—and I guess I wouldn't have made it. I thought I could reach Santa Fe [hundreds of miles east and nowhere near the Colorado River] *on down the canyon. I guess I drifted about eight miles.*

After nearly a week of long conversations with God and of making practical efforts at survival, Owens hobbled on his own badly bruised, blistered, swollen, and cut feet—now clad in makeshift moccasins that Owens had made from the lower legs of his blue jeans—to the semi-landed chopper. Ranger Dan Davis appeared spectral and surreal as he dropped out of the huge machine into the wild sandstorm. ("The pilots," Davis reported, "were flying on instruments as the rotors under full power were causing a regular tornado in the loose sand, and the pilots couldn't see 5 feet.") Davis hoisted Owens, now thirty pounds lighter, up into the machine. The first thing Owens asked of his rescuers was: how was his companion?

Unfortunately, Davis had to tell him that Mahany had died on Owens' same route, roughly a mile from the river.

Despite this seemingly Hollywood ending to this horrific search and rescue, neither the SAR team nor Owens were out of the woods yet. In fact things looked dicey for everyone who got close to Owens' "H."

"All this hovering caused some damage to the engine," Davis noted, "because it was held wide open too long...we had a heck of a time climbing out....[When the pilots finally coaxed the dying helicopter above the rim, they] landed in the local ball park because they didn't think the machine would make it to the G.C. Airport 15 miles away."

Of this incident the *Deseret News* concluded that Owens' companions, Gavigan and Mahany, were "victims of the treacherous canyon and heat."

More accurately, Owens was the lucky recipient of the actions of park visitors who reported faint yelling from the middle of nowhere, of a ranger who had the imagination and initiative to search a vehicle and read a journal, of a hiking expert who imagined a boy desperate to survive building a raft and trying to run the Colorado, and of U.S. Army and NPS personnel who felt it was still worth one more try after nearly a week of unsuccessful searching even in superheated air that might crash their helicopter. True, young Owens had used his head to make the best of a very bad situation. As Dan Davis summarizes:

> *Owens at times really used his head and at other times did exactly the wrong thing—of course a 15-year-old boy that's never been west can't expect to do everything the way it ought to be and I think he did better than most would in like circumstances etc. Had he only waited on the beach at Tanner a little longer our crew would have gotten there before he took off on his log—but at the time all he wanted to do was get away from there. We were there early in the PM.*

But, after all is said and done, Owens' survival ultimately had pivoted on luck and several people having gone beyond the call of duty against the odds to try to rescue him.

Also lucky was twenty-year-old Paul Benson of Gaylord, Michigan. He hiked down the Bright Angel Trail in early October, 1963, solo—except for his faithful dog, Scotty. For reasons unknown, once deep in the Canyon, Benson impulsively decided to try his hand at rock climbing. He ascended a decaying wall and terrace system. About 75 feet up, he lost his handholds and footholds.

Benson tumbled down fifty feet of 60-degree slope then launched off twenty-five feet of cliff to crumple onto the Bright Angel Trail. Another hiking tourist saw Benson's precipitous descent. He alerted rangers, who wheeled Benson out on a stretcher. In Flagstaff Community Hospital Benson was diagnosed with a skull fracture, broken wrists, a likely broken spine and ankle, internal injuries, plus multiple cuts, abrasions, and bruises. Scotty, who had not been enticed by rock-climbing at all, was fine.

As hiking within the Canyon became more well publicized, casualties began increasing. In late August of 1968, for example, Rita Julie Burkhalter, age 25, left her river-running group, including two cousins, on a Western River Expeditions trip at River Mile 65.5 to hike alone up Palisades Canyon. No one had noticed that Burkhalter had hiked off on her own (she had not told anyone of her intent) but when she failed to appear in camp that evening, members of the trip began searching for her.

They found her in good spirits atop a 150-foot cliff on the south side of the creek bed. Burkhalter assured them that all was well and that she would find her way down from her high ledge. So the searchers turned back to camp.

But, yet again, Burkhalter failed to show up in camp. At daybreak the next morning searchers found her body 150 feet below the ledge where she last had been seen. How she fell remains a mystery, although suicide cannot be ruled out.

The four above-mentioned victims died in fairly well-known and easy territory. Once one enters terra incognita in Grand Canyon, survival becomes far more iffy. At the end of August in 1974, for example, two students of Arizona State University (ASU), Frank Costa, age 21, and Edwin Heisel, Jr., age 23, decided to make one of the most beautiful hikes on Earth. They parked their car near the Big Saddle Hunting Camp on the North Rim. Then the two young men descended into the Canyon. Their goal was Thunder River flowing out of a sheer cliff face about 400 feet below a wide slump zone named Surprise Valley, itself about 3,000 feet below their parked car.

The note the hikers left on one of their vehicles indicated that they planned to be back out of the Canyon and be finished with their 4,000-foot descent and ascent the next day, or the day after at the latest. By the way, they added, they planned to do some rock climbing. They were carrying ropes.

Even to educated neophytes in the Canyon, this plan sounds naive. And it was. Instead of following one of the two standard NPS trails off the North Rim down onto the Esplanade and then down again to Surprise Valley and then down yet one more pitch to Thunder River, the two young hikers followed a faint game trail descending somewhat easterly off Bridger's Knoll, a route neither man had ever seen before.

No one ever heard from Costa and Heisel again. Fellow students at ASU alerted the pair's parents that neither had shown up for classes.

Thirty personnel from the NPS, National Forest Service, and Coconino County and Fredonia Sheriff's Departments' formed SAR teams and went to work. Because no one had a clue which route the two hikers had taken—or even whether the pair might have made it to the river and then hitched a ride out with a river trip—the search was difficult. Jeeps drove the rims. Searchers rode horses along the upper trails. Two helicopters scanned the cliffs and terraces.

Well below Monument Point and "some distance off" the standard route to Surprise Valley but on a "little-used trail near" to that standard NPS route, searchers found the two men's abandoned backpacking gear. With it were two notes. Both were dated September 2, day #3 of the pair's hike. The first note, written at 11:00 a.m. that morning, explained:

> We have run out of food and water. God help us. We're trying
> to get water.

A second note, written 2.5 hours later, explained that the two were trying to head back down into the Canyon again (the two had stranded themselves on the then waterless Esplanade roughly 2,000 feet below the rim yet 1,500 feet above Thunder River). They intended, this second note explained:

—to reach a small stream. We have ropes, too. Please look for us. It looks bad, but we're tough. Don't give up looking for us. God bless whoever finds us.

Searchers followed what remained of the pair's week-old tracks after thunderstorms had pounded their route. SAR personnel found bits of gnawed cactus, but otherwise the searchers rarely felt certain that they were following the right route. *If* this were the route taken by Costa and Heisel, however, the two hikers had continued to miss the nearby feasible route and had instead headed toward a thousand-foot cliff overhanging Thunder River and Tapeats Creek.

The SAR team finally found Edwin Heisel's body about 125–150 feet down this cliff, where he had obviously fallen.

Later searchers also found Frank Costa dead on a rock ledge halfway up the north side of the Canyon above the Esplanade but below Monument Point, miles away from Heisel. Apparently, after Heisel had died in the fall, Costa had changed his survival/self-rescue plan yet again to abandon the strategy of trying to reach Thunder River down the huge cliff and instead decided to hike back up to Monument Point and to their vehicle. But, without water at temperatures exceeding 100 degrees in the shade—and on a "route" where no shade existed—Costa had died of dehydration and heat stroke.

Again, even on ground known to be dangerous, the Inner Canyon precipices seem to tempt people fatally. On May 31, 1979, for example, a recurring nightmare of most professional river guides on the Colorado came true on the second day of a Cross Tours trip. Trip leader Dick Clark and boatman's assistant Peter Weiss made an unplanned stop at River Mile 31.5 to take their passengers from a Whitworth College geology charter on a hike up to see that "Mystery Skeleton" discussed earlier. Weiss led two passengers, Gordon Stanley Grace and David Olson, to a high cave penetrating the Redwall Limestone above the skeleton. This cave opens into empty air at least one hundred vertical feet above the floor of South Canyon and above a sheer cliff. Weiss led the way out to the narrow ledge above this cliff, then he returned into the cave proper.

Olson next exited the small hole onto the slim ledge for a look, then returned to Weiss in the larger part of the cave facing the river corridor. Gordon Stanley Grace, age 20, was the third and last person to exit the small cave opening out to the narrow ledge perched above South Canyon.

A moment earlier, Weiss had complimented Grace on his ability to move on rock. Grace had responded by saying that he had some rock-climbing experience. Weiss had also told Grace and Olson that they should return into the cave via the same route that they had taken out, noting that any other route would be "sketchy."

Weiss and Olson waited for a couple of minutes for Grace, who was out of sight and alone on the narrow ledge. Once he rejoined them they could return together to Clark's motor rig.

Weiss and Olson heard rocks sliding from the South Canyon opening of the cave and then a long scream. And then a thump. Feeling a stomach-tightening jolt, Weiss returned through the narrow opening to check on Grace. Grace was gone.

Weiss saw a wet section of the hundred-foot-high Redwall cliff face where Grace had apparently urinated. Weiss exited the cave via its river-facing mouth and yelled to trip leader Clark below that Grace had fallen into South Canyon. Clark rushed into the Canyon. He found Grace unconscious with angulated limbs, a severe crushing injury to the back of the head, and cranial bleeding from the ears, nose, and mouth. Both of Grace's shoes had flown off, the sole of one was almost completely peeled off the shoe. Apparently Grace had contacted the Redwall with his feet at high speed.

Amazingly, Grace also still had a weak carotid pulse. Five minutes later Grace's pulse stopped.

As these examples suggest, and as Table 1–B reveals in spades, accidental fatal falls in the Inner Canyon are the province of young males. The patterns are consistent with one another, yet a bit different from many of the falls from the rims discussed earlier in this chapter. First, only five of the 40 inner Canyon fall victims were women (12.5 percent). Moreover, the ages of these victims, both male and female, were a bit younger than rim-fall victims. Although the average age of Inner Canyon fall victims was 32 years old, 24 of the 40 (60 percent) were between 17 and 28 years old. What these victims were doing in the Canyon before they died also reveals a significant trend or risk factor.

At least 28 of the 40 victims—70 percent—were solo hikers or alone at the time of their demise. The significance of this is clear when one remembers that the vast majority of hiking and river-running trips contain several people. What this means is, for every solo hiker, there are many groups containing hundreds of people. Statistically, for every solo hiking fatality due to falls within the Canyon, there also should be dozens of social hiker deaths. But there are not. Being solitary is not just the number one risk factor for these Inner Canyon falls—even greater than being male—as Table 1–B reveals, being alone is apparently an overwhelmingly powerful risk factor. For many young male hikers, as we will see, it is the kiss of death.

Why are young male solo hikers at vastly greater risk of self-destruction? At least 16 of the 40 (40 percent) who died were "shortcutting" from an established trail or route across country in a personal cheat-route to eliminate apparently "unnecessary" distance. All but two of these fatal decisions were made by solo young male hikers. In several cases, these decisions were influenced by dehydration, impatience, and diminished mental capacity. Take a look at Table 1–B again; the patterns are an eye-opener.

Young *solo* males are also significantly the most prone to making fatal mistakes in all other endeavors in life. Insurance companies figured this out decades ago. Indeed, the mere condition of being male and alone on a hike, with no other person to offer an opinion on the issue of whether or not a "shortcut" looks safe, is what probably killed nearly half of these forty fall victims. As we will see in the next chapter, it has killed yet more solo male hikers in other ways.

A further contributing factor leading to hikers' decisions—solo males or otherwise—that ultimately result in falls in the Canyon is environmental. The physiological impacts on hikers of heat and cold—especially on unprepared hikers—has played a role in dozens of deaths.

Although heat has caused far more poor decisions than cold has, hypothermia seems to have been the primary factor in Dennis E. Daboll's loss of decision-making ability on January 2, 1974. Daboll, age 27, had been solo hiking up the Tanner Trail during an increasing snowstorm. The thickening snow apparently prompted Daboll to decide that speed was of the essence. Roughly four miles below the rim he abandoned his backpack and supplies. His decision may have been made in panic or under the diminished mental capacity that accompanies hypothermia—or both.

Either way, Daboll ascended the trail two miles higher through ever heavier snow. Approximately 2.5 miles below the rim, he slipped off the trail and fell 50 vertical feet. Then he slid or possibly crawled another 400 feet off the trail. There the storm buried him. Searchers found his body days later.

Heat has contributed to far more tragic incidents than cold for two reasons. First, more people hike the Canyon during the hot months than during midwinter. And, second, the heat in Grand Canyon is far more intense than what many hikers anticipate (see the next chapter for more on this). Hikers are sometimes taken by surprise to find themselves out of water, distant from any source of water, and seriously dehydrated—as if ambushed by some assassin. But it is a self-ambush. And, in that one's need for water is as remorseless as one's need for oxygen, dehydrated hikers frequently make bad decisions in deciding upon the shortest feasible route to a water source. We suspect that many of these decisions were not simply "bad decisions;" they were instead acts of flat-out panic spurred by desperation. This is the same sort of desperation that one feels if one's head is being held under water—only in slow motion. The sad demises of Father Gavigan and Walter J. Mahany and of Edwin Heisel, Jr. and Frank Costa (described earlier) are just a few of the many examples of this.

Another such heat-driven tragedy unfolded on June 24, 1974, one of the driest and hottest days of the year. That day four men—including Gregory DeYoung, age 17, Lee Meister, age 18, and David Smith, age 31—had tackled the Grandview Trail (a trail that at no point nears the river). The four ran out of water roughly halfway through their hike. DeYoung separated from his companions and hiked a couple of hours ahead of them "to cut cross-country down a steep drainage to the Colorado to renew their water supply." Desperately committing themselves to a perceived shortcut, the entire group stranded themselves on a ledge with severe vertical exposure.

Even so, DeYoung continued his attempt to descend to the river. He slipped and fell off a 125-foot cliff. His fatal fall would likely never have happened had the men supplied themselves with enough water for their hike.

It was at the end of August in this same year when Frank Costa and Edwin Heisel, Jr. made the identical error on the north side of the Canyon.

A few years later, on a very hot July 26, 1977, Charles Walter Rienecke, age 27, had hiked alone into the Canyon with inadequate food and only an 8-oz instant coffee jar of water. Rienecke, a former Fred Harvey Company busboy, had received some food and water from other sympathetic hikers. But, alone again and having run out of water on the Tonto Trail, Rienecke made a terrible decision.

Although he was only about two level miles by trail from Indian Garden, he tried to hike down a steep drainage between Plateau Point and Horn Creek to reach the river. Arriving at a pitch that seemed too steep, Rienecke stopped and tried to dig in the stony soil for water. This yielded nothing but dust. Rienecke tried again to descend to the river. He fell—or jumped—down a 40-foot cliff in the Tapeats Sandstone (barely missing a cushioning ponderosa pine tree that he may have been aiming for to break his fall). From there he left a 150-yard trail of blood before he collapsed at the top of large drop off. Rienecke died there from his injuries and dehydration.

Again, being young and male is a greater risk factor in falls than merely being unprepared for environmental circumstances. A typical episode of young solo male's faulty route-planning comes from Abdulla Balsharaf, age 27, from South Yemen. A college student in California, Balsharaf was hiking in the Canyon for two mid-October days in 1982 with a young German male he had just met. The two had arrived at Cottonwood Campground on the North Kaibab Trail. Balsharaf decided that he wanted to hike the Canyon more and longer than his original plan. Gale Burak, a ranger at Cottonwood, helped Balsharaf arrange for two extra nights of camping in the Canyon at Indian Garden and offered him a list of alternate—and longer but not unreasonable—hikes to Indian Garden, including a detour over to the Clear Creek Trail as far as Sumner Wash and then back again to the North Kaibab Trail and then down to the river—and then up to Indian Garden in late afternoon.

Both young men then set off down the North Kaibab Trail.

Two days later the rangers at Phantom Ranch were perplexed because a tent containing the belongings of Abdulla Balsharaf had been sitting unused for two days. His German companion, it was soon found, had hiked out of the Canyon at least a day or two earlier and had then traveled south to Phoenix. When contacted, this German said he had no idea what Balsharaf had planned to do when he had decided not to hike out with him as originally planned. Furthermore he was indignant that the U.S. government had tracked him to Phoenix. Wasn't America supposed to be a free country?

Search and rescue teams combed all the hiking routes that Burak had suggested to Balsharaf. Tracking dogs hit the trails. Two helicopters searched visually.

Finally three men hiking out of Clear Creek near Sumner Wash said they had seen Balsharaf "tearing past" them alone on a "day-hike to Clear Creek," with just his daypack. Close to the mouth of Clear Creek (River Mile 84—a ten mile hike from Balsharaf's tent at Phantom Ranch) Ranger Sam West found the footprints of Balsharaf's size 8 Nikes in the sand (Ranger Gale Burak had informed SAR personnel that she and Balsharaf wore the same size and style of Nikes). But after this footprint, West found nothing.

West and his fellow SAR personnel suspected that Balsharaf, upon arriving at this point, was, as were so many young male hikers, unprepared with food, equipment or the mental state for bivouacking. He had, they surmised, therefore been tempted to try to shortcut, or "cheat," the energy-demanding, ten-mile return hike to his tent. Again, short-cutting established trails by traversing across virgin terrain because the standard trail seems to demand unnecessary effort is virtually a "signature" lethal decision of young solo male hikers.

Balsharaf could have attempted his shortcut in one of two possible ways: by jumping into the river and swimming it for four miles or instead—and far more likely—by climbing along the 60-degree slope of the Vishnu Schist and then the Tapeats cliff up to the Tonto Plateau more than 1,000 feet above the river and, from there, trying to work his way downstream toward Phantom.

West figured that Balsharaf would have tried the dry route up the schist. West climbed, belayed, to the first small shelf above. He found a size-8 footprint crushing a patch of grass. Above this point the rock turned steep and slick. And no amount of searching above, below, or adjacent to this ledge added any more clues as to where Balsharaf had vanished.

The SAR coordinator, Butch Farrabee, called in an infrared-detecting Huey helicopter to skim the Clear Creek tributary at dawn. They found nothing. During the entire ten-day SAR effort, that last footprint remained the last clue. Balsharaf most likely had either fallen onto dry rock or into the river itself in an attempt to shortcut the Clear Creek Trail. Either way, the precise mechanics of his fate remain a mystery. His body was never found.

Less mysterious was the fate of Julie Chaibineou, age 25. At least after rescuers found her. As Ranger Ken Phillips' NPS incident report begins:

On October 4th Grand Canyon Dispatch received a call for assistance from the Tipoff Emergency Phone on the South Kaibab Trail. Hikers reported hearing yells for help coming from the Old Miner's Route west of the South Kaibab Trail. A second report received from the Fred Harvey wranglers on their radio frequency indicated a hiker was severely injured after suffering a fall in the area. Rangers responded from Phantom Ranch and a short haul rescue team was immediately dispatched from the South Rim to the scene. VIP [volunteer in park] Sjors Hortsman and Ranger Brian Furbush found Julie Chaibineou, 25, an employee of Phantom Ranch Lodge, who had suffered a 90 foot fall down a talus chute while solo hiking off route.

October 4, 1994, had been a good day to hike in the Inner Gorge. It lacked the blazing heat of summer. But Chaibineou, as the above dispatch report indicated, had chosen a very sketchy route. Why?

Among some of the Phantom Ranchers years ago it became somewhat of a tradition to have climbed the Old Miner's Route which ascends steeply from the river trail between the Kaibab and Bright Angel trails up to the South Kaibab Trail. The unmaintained Old Miner's Route short-cuts a mile or more of the South Kaibab's switchbacks in a relatively short but, again, very steep ascent. The problems with this route, however, include angle-of-repose talus, a repeated need for fairly expert three-point-contact for ascent or descent, crumbling or exfoliating Precambrian rock that can fail as handholds or footholds, and a lack of marking of the route itself. In short, this is an advanced, not an amateur, scramble route—and then only if the climber is cautious—and on the correct route.

Chaibineou, however, had lost the route, straying east of it, and was attempting to climb through the Tapeats Sandstone on a shortcut route she had decided might reconnect her.

During her hideous 90-foot tumble, Chaibineou suffered bilateral pneumothoraxes (collapsed lungs), a fractured pelvis, fractures of the wrist and jaw, a myocardial contusion (heart bruise), a suspected concussion, and bleeding in her airway. What saved her life was the sheer luck to have retained consciousness and the additional luck that her yells alerted a Fred Harvey mule packer, John Berry, who was a few hundred yards away on the South Kaibab Trail. Berry radioed to his dispatch, who passed on the message to the NPS Dispatch. NPS personnel evacuated Chaibineou to Flagstaff Medical Center for emergency surgeries.

Extremely notable yet again is the statistical sample for fatal falls from the rims include no children. This same lack (an encouraging one) of fatal falls for children held true for episodes within the Canyon. But then Jared King, age 14, of Bakersfield, California, decided that he had to urinate at 11:00 p.m. on the night of March 13, 1996.

That day he and his companions had made a long hike from the rim to the Clear Creek Trail. Rain had started falling. And King was tired. Still, he needed to urinate. Half asleep and in his underwear, he followed a typical male impulse to walk to the edge of a seventy-foot cliff to relieve himself. He lost his footing and fell.

Waking from unconsciousness after an unknown span of time, young King screamed for help. He was alive but very seriously injured. His companions, panicky, could not climb down to him. Eventually they tossed him a tarp so he could cover himself from the rain. One of them then ran to Phantom Ranger Station for help and alerted Ranger Mary Litell.

Because a helicopter was impossible to fly in the Inner Canyon during darkness and foul weather, Ranger Bryan Wisher at Indian Garden ran with a 50-pound pack of gear down to Phantom Ranch (5+ miles) in 45 minutes. Then he jogged partway up the Clear Creek Trail to King in 20 more minutes (another 1.5 miles). Wisher had brought oxygen, an Advanced Life Support (ALS) pack, and IV fluids. He had also instructed NPS maintenance operator Frank Corey to heat water on every available stove burner in the ranger station, to fill up every available bottle with that hot water, and then to get the trail crew to help bring the hot water up to the accident site along with a backboard and yet more gear.

Using technical climbing gear, Litell rappelled down the cliff to King while Wisher climbed up to him from below. They found King perched, silent and only half under the tarp. He was naked except for his underwear. He was wet and cold—but he was not shivering. Indeed, young King was nearly dead. Wisher inserterd a rectal thermometer. The mercury failed to move up the column at all. King's body core temperature was a frighteningly low 84 degrees. Worse, the rangers felt no pulse and detected no blood pressure. They did auscultate a faint heart beat. And King did respond, albeit minimally, to painful stimuli. King's faint heartbeat and response to pain did give the rangers hope—not much hope, merely a splinter.

Wisher examined King's spine. He felt a deformity indicating a serious spinal injury. Still encumbered by working while dangling against the face of the cliff, Litell and Wisher placed King on oxygen, stabilized his spine, and started an IV line using a solution warmed by wrapping the line in the warm water bottles brought up by NPS trail crew workers. Wisher positioned more warm water bottles around King's body to try to re-warm him. Then the entire crew stayed on vigil with King for the rest of the night. The warm water bottles slowly raised King's level of consciousness. Eventually King warmed up enough to start him shivering. His core temperature inched up to 89 degrees. By dawn he was stable enough for a short haul evacuation by NPS Paramedic Tammy Keller via an Arizona Department of Public Safety (DPS) helicopter out of the Canyon.

King was flown to Flagstaff Medical Center and diagnosed with multiple spinal and extremity fractures. Ultimately, the 14-year-old made a full recovery.

King was a very lucky young man.

One of the more memorable experiences of a river trip is the brief hike at Elves' Chasm (a.k.a. lower Royal Arch Creek at River Mile 116.5). Elves' Chasm, with its tiers of waterfalls and pools carved in the thick, ledgy Tapeats Sandstone, its beds of crimson monkey flowers, and its walls of maidenhair ferns and columbines, is a "must" stop for river trips. But seeing all of Elves' natural wonders requires serious scramble climbing on highly exposed, narrow ledges.

One of the most beautiful sets of falls and pools exists only about three hundred yards from the river and requires only a few minutes to visit. Above this pool, however, lie eight more waterfalls, often with shallow pools below them. The problems posed by visiting these upper pools are the various necessary climbing or bouldering moves, again on exposed faces of the Tapeats.

Thousands of river trips over the decades have taken at least some of their passengers on this scary and demanding scramble to see the first seven pools (the next higher falls are far more ridiculous). And probably without exception every professional guide or trip leader who has taken people on this scramble has worried: 1. "What am I *doing* here with these people?" and 2. "I wonder when someone will finally peel off of one of these exposures and eat it."

Around midday on August 21, 1986, Connie Wernette, age 28, stopped with the other members of a private rowing trip down the Canyon to "hike" Elves' Chasm. In large part due to the stunning and mysterious reputation of Elves', Wernette's party decided to make the scramble up the Tapeats Sandstone from the first idyllic pool to see the more hidden wonders above. At least some of the members of this group, however, had ill-prepared themselves. Some apparently did not know the correct route, and those who did know failed to ensure that those behind them followed on that same route.

Wernette apparently lagged behind other members of her group after she and they reached the first high waterfall. Her companions had made the next dangerous ascent traverse past the first large waterfall to the second waterfall. By the time Wernette decided to climb after them beyond the first falls to the second, her companions had passed beyond the critical part of the difficult ascent and disappeared from her view.

Wernette tried to solo rock scramble after them. At first she followed a correct route to where continuing upcanyon demands that the climber crawl/creep along horizontally on all fours under a low overhang of Tapeats above a narrow ledge. Apparently deciding that this could not be the correct route—and possibly thinking the rough sandstone would abrade her knees as she crawled—Wernette decided to continue up higher. She soon climbed another thirty feet upward, alone and now on a much higher, non-route.

She next followed a small horizontal ledge yet thirty feet higher than the one she had bypassed. This too led deeper into Elves' Chasm, but it was situated sixty-five feet or so above the narrow floor of Tapeats at the first pool and thirty or more feet above the floor of the second pool area where her friends had just vanished. Wernette, wearing wet, canvas deck-type shoes, soon found herself "ledged out." She could no longer proceed upcanyon because her route had fizzled out into sheer cliff.

Wernette tried to turn around to reverse her direction and thus descend by retracing her steps. But she lost her balance, or lost her friction on the Tapeats. She slipped and screamed. Two of her companions—Craig Byrne and Richard Learned—heard her scream.

They spun around and witnessed Wernette fall—although they did not see exactly what action of Wernette's had led to it. She fell head first to below the floor of Tapeats and into a "hole" between the huge boulders wedged and cemented on the creek left atop the first falls. The crushing impact instantly knocked her unconscious.

Wernette's companions looked at her in shock. One of them hurried back to the boats for first aid. Upon his arrival, he saw a Grand Canyon Dories trip pull to shore for a hike.

Peter Dale, a guide on this trip, said the man asked in a shocked way: "Do you have a first aid kit?"

Dale said, "Yeah, we do, why?"

The man did not answer. He simply stared at Dale.

Peter Dale and his fellow guides knew that something must have gone very wrong up in Elves' Chasm. They grabbed their first aid kits and hustled up to the scene of Wernette's fall.

The Dories guides attempted first aid, but one look at Wernette revealed that she was beyond their abilities. Blood and cerebrospinal fluid now drained onto the rock from a basilar skull fracture via her nose, ears, and mouth. Wernette's neck had also broken, apparently at the third, fourth, and possibly fifth cervical vertebrae. These guides' one ace in the hole was a brain surgeon who was a passenger on their trip.

This neurosurgeon examined Wernette. His prognosis was anything but favorable. Wernette's cranial and cervical injuries were beyond what even the most skilled team of surgeons in the best facility on Earth could repair. Still he and the Dories guides tried to keep Wernette alive.

A half hour later Wernette's heart stopped.

The Dories CPR team worked to keep Wernette biologically alive—despite her neurological death—for the sake of her organ donor potential. Meanwhile, the guides also radioed an overflying aircraft to pass a fatality message on to NPS Headquarters at the South Rim. Wernette became the first Elves' Chasm fatality.

Such tragic climbing mishaps as Wernette's are not the exclusive province of amateurs. Even veteran guides fall. And the geological Siren calling them most often to climb where they should not be climbing is again Tapeats Sandstone. Many guides who work in the Canyon decide that the Tapeats

Sandstone is their favorite of the Canyon's thirty or so named geological formations, or rock types. Tapeats is a ledgy, coarse-grained sandstone that typically erodes into smoothly sculpted slot canyons, such as the one at Elves' Chasm. It also erodes into cliff shelters offering shade from a remorseless sun and into wide patios of smooth stone that make wonderful picnic spots. Cracks in the Tapeats frequently erode into chimneys that can be climbed for fun via bouldering moves. The problem with this sandstone is, despite its 570-million-year age, it decays and crumbles unpredictably. In short, Tapeats is very unreliable stuff.

During the evening of September 21, 1990, on a Moki Mac River Expeditions' trip, trip leader Michael Jacobs free-climbed (without rope protection) alone in the Tapeats. He chose an ascent downstream of the trip's camp on the south side of the river at River Mile 120.25 at the head of Conquistador Aisle. Jacobs had free-climbed along several sections of bedrock during this trip. A witness said that this time Jacobs was ascending very quickly up a tall chimney next to a sandstone column.

Near the top of the Tapeats, one of Jacobs' handholds broke away from the bedrock.

Jacobs immediately lost contact with both hands and with his right foot. He fell. His left foot, however, remained wedged in a crack. As Jacobs tried to recover from this nasty slip, his left foot yanked loose. Jacobs free-fell fifty feet onto scattered blocks of Tapeats.

Jacobs sustained multiple internal injuries, including massive cranial ones. Under a tarp set up to protect him from monsoon rains, his companions, including six physicians, struggled to save him. They were desperate enough that a neurosurgeon among them attempted to relieve pressure on Jacobs' brain due to intracranial bleeding by drilling a hole in his skull. Despite every measure, however, within three hours, the 43-year-old Jacobs had succumbed to his injuries. "Michael made a courageous fight," noted Vaughn Short, "but it was not to be." Jacobs died that evening in camp.

So what can we learn from all these tragic falls detailed in Tables 1–A and 1–B? At the risk of being insensitive in this analysis, of the 90 accidental fatal falls from the rims and from various dangerous precipices within the Canyon, nearly all were due strictly to the serious lack of judgement of the victim himself or herself. "Acts of God" rank low on the list as a cause of fatal falls. Bad judgement ranks at the top. The significant preponderance of solo victims (solo at the time and location of the incident) drives home how very important the role of a "second voice" of reason or caution is for anyone hiking or climbing anywhere in the Canyon—or even standing on its rims. The available statistics do reveal that young solo male (and female) climbers—or solo male hikers who become climbers—are at vastly higher risk of injury or death from inner Canyon falls than hikers with companions. Although the data are "invisible" or irretrievable to prove that this is how the mechanism of "social safety" works, it seems that when a hiker has a companion, that hiker normally makes a verbal proposition of intent to try some uncertain route before tackling it. And it seems that the hiker's companion has frequently been the voice of reason, which by merely saying something to the effect of, "It looks sort of sketchy to me," has prevented many fatal falls.

As Canyon hiking expert and author George Steck puts it, "A solo hiker often has a fool for a companion."

The lesson? If you don't possess your own Jiminy Cricket, hike with a companion.

TABLE 1–A.   ACCIDENTAL LETHAL FALLS from RIMS of GRAND CANYON.

Name, age	Date	Location on Rim	Circumstances
Lewis W. Thompson, age ?	March 22, 1925	South Rim	

Thompson took a side step while posing for his own photograph on the edge of the rim. He stepped into a crack, lost his balance, and fell off. (see text)

| Waddy Thompson Ligon, 73 | October 29, 1925 | On "Dugway" 2 miles from Lees Ferry | |

The wheels on the right side of Ligon's converted Ford Model T slid off the narrow dugway as he backed up. The vehicle slid off the steep road and jammed into a crevasse, pinning and killing Ligon.

| Philo Anderson, adult male | November 24, 1927 | North Rim at Pipeline | |

While working on the construction of the water pipeline from Roaring Springs to the new North Rim hotel, Anderson helped lower a pipe to a ledge 50 feet below. He became entangled in the rope used to lower the pipe and fell 300 feet. (see text)

| Lane McDaniels, 42 | June 12, 1928 | River Mile 4, Navajo Bridge, Marble Canyon | |

McDaniels, a construction worker, missed his footing on a scaffold while constructing the highest steel bridge in the world and fell about 470 feet into river. Observers said McDaniels' body seemed to "burst and flatten out" on impact. No net had been placed below due to the worry that hot rivets might ignite it. Four steelworkers quit after McDaniels death, not from fear of falling, but of being swallowed up by the turbulent Colorado with no hope that their bodies would ever be recovered. (see text)

| L. C. Hunley, adult male | August 18, 1935 | Lookout Point | |

*Hunley, a C.C.C. enrollee at Camp No. 847, was last seen walking at 2:30 a.m. on the rim at night as a **solo hiker**. He fell 600 feet.*

Hepzibah Watkin,
adult woman

December 2, 1939   Hopi Point
Watkin was walking on the footpath to Hopi Point, fell off, and died of a broken neck.

Herbert E. Kolb, 17

July 17, 1947   Hopi Point
Kolb "crawled" under a guard rail with his girlfriend to sit on the edge. When he later got up to go, he lost his balance and fell. Rangers had trouble locating Kolb's body so they got a bale of hay and nudged it off the exact spot from where Kolb had fallen and watched its descent. They found Kolb and the hay scattered 950 feet below. (see text)

Minnie Edith Kindig, 63

September 14, 1949   Yaki Point
Kindig apparently fainted, collapsed to her knees, then toppled off the rim, falling 500 feet. (see text)

Donald L. Mark, 43

June 7, 1958   behind El Tovar Hotel
*Mark, a Fred Harvey desk clerk, had climbed over the guard wall behind El Tovar and a short way down the cliff as a **solo climber**. He smoked a cigarette then appeared to onlookers to be "putting on an act, playfully jumping from rock to rock" on edge of rim. He "continually looked up at the crowd" gathering to watch. He had fair footing but poor handholds. He lost his grip and fell over backwards, plunging 300 feet.*

James Lloyd Qualls, 5
Harold Frank Qualls, 1

June 8, 1958   Little Colorado Overlook,
June 8, 1958   8 miles west of Cameron
The two children's father, Frank Qualls, age 28, had parked the family sedan in gear, but still in overdrive, with both boys in it. The parking brake was not set. While the adults were 200 feet away, another relative, Kenneth Dull, age 10, returned to the car to fetch a camera in the glove compartment. He said the car started rolling, so he jumped aside. After 25 feet the car plunged over the rim 100 feet into the gorge, ricocheted off rocks and caught fire. (see text)

Elizabeth Hazelhurst, 21

April 12, 1971   Mojave Point
Hazelhurst had crossed guard rails to sit on the edge with her two sisters and a friend. The other three got up to return to the car to make sandwiches, but turned around when they heard a scream. They saw Hazelhurst "slip" and fall about 350 feet. (see text)

Elroy Ponyah, 17

May 1, 1971   Tappan Springs Canyon
Unwitnessed drive off Highway 64, Ponyah's Ford sedan leaped the gorge and hit the opposite wall 40 feet lower. (see text)

Bennett Hanna, age ?

August 19, 1972   Hualapai Hilltop
Hanna had driven, then dropped off, friends to the trailhead. While backing up to turn his car around, he drove off the edge 500 feet. (see text)

McCormick, (unknown first names), 50s

Summer, 1973   Scenic Overlook at Navajo Bridge
McCormick, an heiress to the McCormick farming machine company, was picknicking with her son and a friend. They crossed the guard rail, beyond which she lost her footing and fell about 200+ feet.

Joseph Fielding Smith, Jr., 61

August 22, 1974   Cape Royal Overlook, North Rim
Smith attempted to jump from a ledge on the rim to a dirt slope about five feet lower. He lost his balance and slipped into a free-fall of 35 feet.

Douglas Pritchard, 22

June 18, 1976   Lipan Point
*Pritchard was scramble-climbing **solo** on edge of rim, lost his footing, and fell 200 feet.*

Bobbey Kay Kendrick, 45

July 7, 1978   Yaki Point
Kendrick lost her footing while seeking a vantage point for photo, fell 600 feet.

Peter Leonard Robertson, 19

November 3, 1978   Pima Point
*Unwitnessed fall of 200–250 feet; **solo hiking** Robertson was wearing warm clothes and carrying back-packing gear, sleeping bag, etc. Body with several broken bones was not discovered for 2.5 years and then by chance by a hiker.*

Roger Sydnor, 30

April 8, 1979   Rim Trail near Visitor Center
*Sydnor attempted a dawn photo, **solo walker** from edge of rim, suffered unwitnessed fall of 250 feet.*

Richard Keith Jop, 26

December 27, 1979   Rim Trail near Visitor Center
Jop stood on snow-covered edge of rim, slipped, and fell 400 feet.

John Eric Hastrick, 20

April 27, 1981   behind Bright Angel Lodge
*Hastrick, an Englishman, had climbed over the rock guard wall to take an ideal photo from the edge of what was on the rim (not what was in the Canyon). While holding a camera to his face, **he backed up toward the Canyon**, lost his footing, and fell 330 feet. (see text)*

Mary Lee Ranahan, 52

August 26, 1981   the Abyss
*Unwitnessed fall of **solo hiker** 400 feet. Body recovery took NPS personnel 6 difficult hours.*

Maria C. Alfaro, 23

October 8, 1981   Rim Trail near Visitor Center
Alfaro climbed past guard rail, went to edge to sit and watch sunset, slipped and she fell 400 feet.

Frank Taylor Jolly, 20

August 31, 1982   Yavapai Point
Jolly was leaping from rock to rock while "climbing." He slipped and fell 300 feet. (see text)

Richard Peña, 46	January 9, 1985 First Trailview Overlook *Peña had climbed over the guard rail at dusk, slipped in 3 inches of snow, and fell 350 feet. (see text)*
Roy Bundens Jones, 38	January 22, 1987 Hopi Point *Fell 1,000 feet.*
Brian J. Vordahl, 32	April 15, 1987 Tuweep Campground Overlook *While camping, Vordahl became a **solo hiker** from camp and fell off 300 feet.*
Gesela Elixmann, 34	March 9, 1989 Mojave Point *While Elixmann stood on the edge, she became dizzy and fell 500 feet.*
Yuri Nagata, 21	March 12, 1989 Second Trailview Overlook *Nagata stepped around guard rail, sat on lower ledge. She stood to pose for photo, lost her balance, and fell. (see text)*
Jeremy Fahl, 19	July 1, 1989 ¼ mile east of El Tovar *Fell 310 feet.*
Scott Awodey, 29	June 25, 1992 Francois Matthes Point *Awodey was "rock-hopping" on the edge of rim, reportedly hamming it up for photos. Conflicting reports: One says a rock gave way beneath him; the other says high winds may have blown Awodey off the edge. Either way (or both), Awodey fell 140 feet.*
Greg Austin Gingrich, 38	November 28, 1992 Rim Trail near El Tovar *Gingrich jumped atop, then over, the rock wall to the sloping edge of the rim while goofing off to tease his daughter. slipped and fell 400 feet. (see text)*
Lawrence Jackson, 24	August 14, 1993 Marble Canyon/Badger Overlook *After drinking heavily, Jackson was sitting with a friend on the rim at Badger Overlook to watch boats below. The friend turned away to look at something else. When he turned back, Jackson had vanished over edge hundreds of feet below.*
Andreas Zimmerman, 24	September 5, 1993 Cape Royal *Zimmerman was jumping from one ledge to another on the edge. He lost his balance, slipped, and fell 400 feet.*
Lori Newcomb, 31	September 7, 1993 Cape Royal *Newcomb walked far out on the edge to take a photo. The rock crumbled under Newcomb's weight. She slipped and fell 20 feet, then 60 more feet, eventually falling a total of 150 feet.*
James Merriman, 51	September 8, 1993 Mather Point *Daredevil **solo climbing** transient Merriman was jumping from rock to rock beyond and below the safety rail to collect "good luck" coins on ledge. He was also "hamming" it up for cameras, said "Watch me!"; jumped, and fell 360 feet. A week earlier, Merriman had to be rescued from this same "zone of coins" by NPS rangers. (see text)*

Timothy J. Rowe, 24   November 9, 1993   Second Trailview Overlook
Rowe was jumping from rock to rock to pose for the ideal photo. He fell 200 to 300 feet.

James Hyland, 21   November 16, 1993   below El Tovar Hotel
*While **solo walking** atop frosty guard wall, Hyland slipped and fell 300 feet.*

Glenn Higgins, 25   May 8, 1995   Yaki Point
*While camping, as **solo hiker**, Higgins fell at night 500 feet off rim.*

Daniel Sloan, 44   May 30, 1995   River Mile 1, south of Lees Ferry
*While camping as **solo hiker**, Sloan fell at night 120 feet off rim.*

Hideya Yamamoto, 73   September 25, 1996   Rim Trail near Visitor Center
*Yamamoto was **solo walking** on edge, then turned to hurry away to catch a tour bus. He slipped on the edge, fell, screamed, and hit less than 70 feet below.*

Lana Virginia Smith, 28   May 11, 1997   behind Bright Angel Lodge.
*During late evening, after drinking at Bright Angel Bar, Smith walked outside with a friend and sat on a retaining wall. Her friend walked away to phone for help. Smith **solo walked** atop the guard wall, slipped off, and slid 25 feet. From there she yelled for help to people on rim. As rescuers positioned themselves, Smith became impatient, moved, but slid 30 feet farther down. She grabbed a tree branch above the precipice. As rescuers fixed a rope for a rescue, Smith could not retain her hold; she fell 234 feet. (see text)*

Maria Sophia Edovist, 24   August 23, 1997   Tuweep Overlook
Fell 600 feet, details unknown.

Michael L. Hankins, 26   October 30, 1997   Yaki Point
During a witnessed event, Hankins slipped and fell.

unidentified man, 40s   April 13, 1998   Near Hopi House
Unwitnessed fall of 400–500 feet.

Nash Jamarillo, 36   July 4, 1998   Worship Site, Rim Trail
*Jamarillo had been listening to his radio and watching the view, became **solo walker** and apparently slipped and fell 150 feet.*

Gyula Tamas Szakallas, 32   September 9, 1998   Bright Angel Point on North Rim
(male)   *Szakallas slipped on gravel-covered ledge and fell 250 feet.*

Murray Marshall, 51   November 19, 1998   Maricopa Point
Marshall fell an unknown distance due to unknown circumstances.

Gabriel Comerford, 25   August 19, 1999   Moran Point
Comerfold crossed guard rails, climbed over a retaining wall, asked bystanders to take his photo when he posed in a scenic spot. A rock crumbled under Comerford, and he slipped. Witnessed (and photographed) fall of 875 feet. (see text)

The following entries are not included in text, statistics, or the index

Hiroko Kawakami, 66   August 8, 2001   Mojave Point
The guide of a sunset tour made a head count of his tourists and missed Kawakami, having been left behind. She had fallen 350 feet.

Fern Beuchart Shelton, 72   November 23, 2001   Tuweep Overlook
Shelton of St. George, Utah asked her husband to take her photo; she positioned herself on the overlook, slipped, and fell 675 feet.

Paul Stockhfs, 16   August 24, 2005   Walhalla Overlook, North Rim
Paul ran downslope ahead of his father and out of view to the small peninslar, guardrailed overlook. His father failed to find him. A SAR team failed too but dad walked 100 feet laterally and spotted Paul's body 140 feet below the guardrail. Had Paul run into, and then flipped over, it?

TABLE 1–B. ACCIDENTAL LETHAL FALLS WHILE HIKING or ORIENTEERING within GRAND CANYON

Name, age	Date	Location	Circumstances
Daniel W. Mooney, 40s(?)	January 20, 1880	Mooney Falls/Havasu	

While descending 196-foot travertine falls, prospector Mooney lost his grip and/or ran out of rope and fell. (see text)

| "Mystery Skeleton," age ? | pre-1934 | South Canyon (a.k.a. Paradise Canyon) | |

Dead adult male found and disinterred by Alton Hatch in 1934, with two broken legs and buried in buckskins. (see text)

| Irene Johnson, 19 | August 4, 1940 | near tunnel on Bright Angel Trail | |

Johnson, with several friends., was jumping from one rock to another and apparently lost her balance and fell 180 feet.

| Lee Smith, 50 | June 17, 1951 | near top of Bright Angel Trail | |

Smith was a Fred Harvey Company guide/mule skinner riding double with Lee Roberts. Their mule was crowded off the trail by other mules. Lee Roberts survived; the mule and Smith fell. The mule landed atop Smith, who was killed. (see text, Chapter 6)

| Ronald T. Berg, 22 | July 30, 1954 | Tanner Trail | |

*Berg was a seasonal NPS ranger and a **solo hiker** who fell from a cliff. Body recovery was so difficult and hot that it nearly killed several rangers and a trail crewman. A fixed wing drop of "emergency" ice blocks crushed several items of gear and nearly brained the rangers, but the fragments, once gathered up, saved their lives. This incident prompted NPS Ranger Dan Davis to write his first giveaway booklet on inner canyon hiking and water needs.*

Eugene Gavigan, 30 | July 23, 1959 | Tanner Trail in the Tapeats Sandstone
Gavigan ran out of water, tried to shortcut trail to river by descending a cliff/crevasse bare-footed, fell 150 feet. (see text)

Rodolfo Marcello Ledesma-Vilmar, 28 | April 7, 1965 | near Bright Angel Trail in the Kaibab Limestone
A Cuban National hitch-hiker, Ledesma-Vilmar tried a solo hike to shortcut his way across cliff, by rock scrambling, from the rim Trail to the Bright Angel Trail, slipped and fell 200 feet.

Rita Julie Burkhalter, 25 | August 20, 1968 | River Mile 65.5/Palisades Canyon in the Tapeats Sandstone
On a motor trip run by Western River Expeditions, Burkhalter made solo hike up Palisades Canyon, fell from cliff 150 feet during attempted solo—and unwitnessed—descent. (see text)

Steven Dustin, 18 | September 28, 1971 | The Battleship in the Supai Sandstone or Redwall Limestone
Dustin, a novice solo hiker, detoured off the Bright Angel Trail and tried to shortcut by roping down the sheer west face of the Battleship. He fell 65 feet and was found later wedged in a crack.

Thomas J. Weiner, 28 | April, 1972 | Little Colorado Gorge tributary canyon in the Kaibab Limestone
Weiner was hitchhiking through the West and stopped to solo hike and gaze into the Gorge about 500 yards west of the junction of U.S. Highway 89 and Arizona 64. Weiner either slipped or the rimrock collapsed.

Paul Laurence Mysyk, 25 | April 25–29, 1973 | ½ mile below Bright Angel Trailhead
Mysyk, a solo hiker suffering from health and psychiatric difficulties, experienced an unwitnessed fall of 250 feet off the trail.

Kevin Cochran, 19 | July 18, 1973 | Hopi Point in the Kaibab Limestone
Cochran and a friend were scrambling up a scree slope 200 feet below Hopi Point. Cochran slipped and fell 1,200 feet.

Dennis E. Daboll, 27 | January 2, 1974 | Tanner Trail, 2 miles below rim
Solo hiking and ascending during an increasing snowstorm, Daboll may have become hypothermic. He had abandoned his backpack. Daboll walked off the trail 2 miles higher but 2.5 miles below the rim. He fell 50 vertical feet then slid or crawled another 400 off the trail and was buried in snow. (see text)

Gregory DeYoung, 17 | June 24, 1974 | below Grandview Trail
DeYoung and three companions (including Lee Meister, 18, and David Smith, 31) ran out of water on their hike. DeYoung separated from his companions and descended 2–3 hours distant ahead and out of view as a solo hiker "to cut cross-country down a steep drainage to the Colorado to renew their water supply." DeYoung's companions stranded themselves on a ledge. DeYoung fell off a 125-foot cliff while trying to descend to the river. (see text)

Edwin Heisel, Jr., 23

September 2, 1974   below Bridger Point, on North Rim
Heisel and partner Frank Costa, 21, were descending a deer trail "not far" from main NPS trail to Thunder River. They abandoned their camping gear and left notes explaining they had run out of food and water and would try to descend to a creek—Thunder River. Heisel apparently fell off a 200-foot cliff in the Redwall Limestone during this attempted rope descent. (see text)

Thomas Velzy, 18

September 28, 1975   1.5 miles down South Kaibab Trail
*Velzy, a **solo hiker**, suffered an unwitnessed fall of 100 feet off the cliff adjacent to the trail.*

Charles Walter Rienecke, 27

July 26, 1977   near upper Horn Creek Drainage in the Tapeats Sandstone
*Rienecke **solo hiked** into the Canyon during extreme heat. He carried only an 8-oz coffee jar of water and inadequate food. He bummed some food and water from other hikers. After running out of water, he tried to hike down a drainage between Plateau Point and Horn Creek to the river (instead of hiking 1–2 level miles to Indian Garden). Next he tried to dig for water. He next fell (or jumped) down a 40-foot cliff in the Tapeats and left a trail of blood before collapsing 150 yards away at the top of large drop off. Died from injuries. (see text)*

Jeffrey F. Ridenour, 63

May 28, 1978   Tanner Trail to New Hance Trail
*Ridenour, a **solo hiker** on his 2nd Canyon hike ever, vanished and was never found. He may have lost the trail and fallen to his death on land, or instead have fallen in the river and drowned.*

Ruben D. Rodriquez, 22

June 14, 1978   below Navajo Point
A backpacking hitchhiker, Rodriguez and 3 friends had been drinking alcohol. They hiked below the rim. When Rodriguez tried to scramble/descend lower, he slipped and fell 200 feet.

Leland J. Marsh, 39

September 29, 1978   North Kaibab Trail, 4 miles below rim
Hiking after dark via flashlights with one companion, Marsh sat too close to the edge. Top-weighted by his pack, he fell 175 feet.

Tsue Wang, 18

April 19, 1979   Havasu Canyon between Beaver and Mooney Falls
*Hiking with a Seventh Day Adventist group, Wang split from party, with the leader's permission, to try an alternate shortcut, an unscouted trail as a **solo hiker**. 24 hours later Wang's body was discovered. He had died above Beaver Falls due to a fall.*

Ronald T. Drabik, 22

August 7, 1979   ½ mile W of Bright Angel Campground
*Drabik, with no previous climbing experience, was apparently rock scrambling as a **solo hiker** to traverse a cliff of exposed and crumbling schist. He fell 250–500 feet. Drabik's two companions, from whom he had separated, had hiked out of the Canyon without reporting Drabik's separation/ disappearance. Drabik's backpack left at the campground was the only clue of his mishap.*

Gordon Stanley Grace, 20   May 31, 1979   South Canyon cave/window in the
Redwall Limestone
*On a commercial motor rafting trip run by Cross Tours, Grace, during or after urinating while being left as **solo hiker** on an exposed cliff face, fell off the sheer cliff about 100 feet. (see text)*

Joseph Anthony Dean, 43   November 1, 1980   Horseshoe Mesa
*Dean, an NPS Albright Training Center instructor, got up during the night (possibly due to stomach problems or the need to urinate) and walked away from group camp as a **solo hiker** 200 yards, leaving his boots behind but wearing his socks. He sat down, pulled a sock off, then dropped it about 60 feet. He then walked 700 more feet down Miner's Spring Trail nearer to the lost sock. From there, Dean mysteriously fell more than a hundred feet. Was found with his fly zipper unzipped, belt unbuckled, and his feet badly lacerated.*

Abdulla Balsharaf, 27   November 14, 1982   Clear Creek (River Mile 84) in the
Vishnu Schist (?)
*Balsharaf split off from a German hiking companion to **solo hike** into Clear Creek drainage from Phantom. His Nike, size 8 footprints were found by SAR personnel at mouth of Clear Creek where he arrived after 10 miles, carrying only a day pack. No other positive evidence was found; no body found. Suspected death by a climbing fall (possibly into river) while trying to shortcut the 10-mile hike back to his gear at Phantom. (see text)*

Allen Kelling, 47   November 28, 1982   off old Supai Trail /Topocoba Hilltop
*Kelling became a **solo hiker** after rolling his truck while driving the road above Topocoba. He apparently decided to hike into Supai for help but slipped off the Topocoba Trail (possibly while shortcutting?) at one of the switchbacks. Kelling fell 80–100 feet.*

Theodore Levin, 38   May 6, 1984   Near confluence of Salt Canyon and
Little Colorado river in the Tapeats
While hiking with two friends in Salt Canyon, Levin fell 150 feet.

Charles M. Mays, 42   June 9, 1984   Bright Angel Trail
*Mays walked **solo** off the trail onto a narrow ledge to take a photo at sunset. He lost his footing while preparing to take the photo, and fell 300 feet.*

Jonathan Paul Bladel, 21   March 5, 1985   Pipeline route off Bright Angel
Trail in the Vishnu Schist
*Bladel detoured as a **solo hiker** off the Bright Angel Trail, shortcutting between switchbacks up along the pipeline during icy conditions. He slipped and fell 75 feet. Possibly died of combination of fall and exposure. He was found the next morning.*

Randy V. Fischer, 22   August 17, 1985   Plateau Point/Tapeats Sandstone
***Solo hiking** on the Tonto Trail along Tapeats Rim, Fischer slipped and fell (shortcutting?) 200–600 feet.*

Connie Marie Wernette, 28	September 21, 1986	Elves' Chasm (River Mile 116.5) in the Tapeats Sandstone

*Wernette lost and strayed from the climbing route while lagging behind, and out of view of her friends. She continued her own **solo hike** ascent on a non-route which dead-ended. Wernette fell 30+ feet head first onto bedrock. (see text)*

Ronald Dwayne Hight, 47	August 16, 1989	off Tonto Trail near Boulder Creek

***Solo hiking** cross-country route during high temperatures, Hight's shortcut route was a few hundred yards above Tonto Trail. Hight fell 50 feet. When last seen (by a companion who had exited earlier) Hight was seeming ill and spitting up blood. Hikers found Hight's body 7 months later, on March 10, 1990.*

Timothy A. Burris, 39	March 17, 1990	Sheep's Head Trail, (River Mile 4)

Burris, during hiking/fishing trip to river, slipped and fell 60 feet.

Ronald Shortt, 21	June 6, 1990	below El Tovar Hotel in the Kaibab Limestone

*Shortt was free-climbing **solo** in sandals in a highly exposed position not far below the South Rim. He fell 750 feet.*

Michael Jacobs, 43	September 21, 1990	River Mile 120.25 in the Tapeats Sandstone

*Jacobs was trip leader on commercial trip and free-climbing an exposed chimney in the Tapeats as a **solo climber**. He lost both hand-holds plus friction on one foot and fell 50 feet. (see text)*

Beverly Ann Collins, 26	May 5, 1994	Pipeline route west of Bright Angel Trail below Plateau Point in the Vishnu Schist

*Collins, a Phantom Ranch employee, **solo hiked** the pipeline route. She slipped and fell 100 feet to the foot of the Tapeats Sandstone.*

Richard Flowers, 35	July 2, 1994	Lake Mead National Recreation Area near Grand Wash and Shivwits Plateau

*Flowers was camping with girlfriend near Twin Points off Shivwits Plateau. During the day of July 2, he had been drinking vodka and grapefruit juice and beer. At 7:00 p.m., he started on a **solo hike** without food or water and failed to return. On July 3, Flowers' hat was found in nearby tributary canyon. On July 4, helicopter SAR personnel located Flowers 600 vertical feet below plateau; he had fallen into a pine tree. Death had occurred upon impact.*

Gabriel Parker, 21	October 29, 1995	near North Kaibab Trailhead, within Canyon atop the Coconino Sandstone

*Unwitnessed fall of 380 feet to foot of Coconino. Parker's body, equipped as a **hiker (solo?)**, was found six months later. His death was ruled accidental.*

Sheryl Flack, 48	May 8, 1998	Plateau Point near Bright Angel Trail in the Tapeats Sandstone

*On a mule trip, Flack was alone (**solo**) for a few minutes on the edge of the Tapeats. She suffered an unwitnessed fall of 400+ feet.*

The following entries are not included in text, statistics, or the index

Andy Drugg, 13

June 12, 2001   North Canyon, ¼ mile from river
Drugg was hiking as a client on a Moki Mac River Expeditions trip when, on the route adjacent to the waterfall amphitheater, the 6 foot, 3 inch, 240-pound boy missed his footing and fell 35 feet.

Aaron Tyree, 18

September 6, 2001   Mooney Falls, Havasu Canyon
Tyree, from Mesa, Arizona, was visiting with friends and family. Possibly under the influence of amphetamines, Tyree scooted on his butt 20 feet over the lip of Mooney Falls with the intent to dive off. Bystanders talked him out of diving. Next Tyree tried to downclimb off-trail next to the upper chain along the descent path. He fell about 100 feet onto bedrock.

Hannah Stehlin, 13

October 3, 2001   Windy Ridge, South Kaibab Trail
Stehlin had been petting a mule in a tied off mule train and was standing on the edge of the trail exposed to a major vertical drop. She lost her footing for unknown reason(s) and fell 150 feet.

Sabra Jones, 44

August 12, 2002   Havasu/Dry Beaver confluence
Jones, a river guide for Tour West, was descending an exposed route down a travertine cliff after visiting a ceramic "protector" idol known as the "Fox Man" or "Beaver Man" tucked into the cliff face. She lost her balance and fell about 40 feet.

Lucas Fara, 28

November 29, 2002   First Tunnel on Bright Angel Trail
Fara, a Czech citizen, made his way past an NPS sign warning "Dangerous footing. Do not enter" and entered, descending to an exposed ledge to pose for a dramatic photo. Fara fell 150 feet.

Clayt Cuppy, 35

November 28, 2002   Plateau Point
Cuppy was an overdue hiker on the Bright Angel Trail. Searchers found Cuppy's body 600 feet below Plateau Point. Cause unknown.

Maris Serafimovs, 28

June 8 or later, 2004   Grandview Trail area (?)
Serafimovs, an athletic Nevadan, embarked on a solo hike with a day pack but no backcountry permit from Grandview Point. Six days later a family friend reported him missing. A 5-person SAR team found his parked car and searched until June 17 without success. Possible fatal fall (?)

Gordon Robert Wagner, 57

September 5, 2004   North Canyon, ¼ mile from river
During a private river trip, Wagner was hiking past the narrow section of the route between a cuboid boulder and the dry waterfall where Andy Drugg (above) fell. As he stepped up one foot onto a ledge he lost his balance and toppled about 35 feet.

Marlin Lindquist, 70

September 18, 2004   N Kaibab Trail, Eye of the Needle
Lindquist hiked behind his wife and fell unwitnessed. She heard him and returned to find him spread-eagled on the talus 25 feet down and on the brink of the cliff. He said he was OK and did not need help. As he tried to climb he lost his footing and fell 500 feet.

Randy Rogers, 45

September 10, 2005 tributary off Bright Angel Trail
Rogers of Phoenix vanished on a solo hike during the last of his
many annual Canyon visits. A large scale ground and air search
failed (the dogs used led rangers to another body—a Texas suicider).
On August 20, 2006 a routine helicopter patrol saw remains (35%
of a skeleton) scattered in an unnamed drainage. Forensics indicated
Rogers had a fractured tibia suggesting a hiking fall off trail.

Reinhard Kirchner, 61

April 1(?), 2007 Hellhole Bend area, Little Colorado Plateau
Kirchner made annual solo visits from Germany to the Little
Colorado Plateau, methodically making notes on his map of each
area he explored. After he failed to rejoin his girlfriend in Las Vegas
on April 9, a multi-agency search found his car and map but not
him. Searching narrowed the possibilities to abduction—or a fall.

Chapter Two

The Desert Crucible: Environmental Death within the "Inverted Mountain"

"Polliwogs!" Paul Stryker mumbled in disgust to his wife Karen as they stared down into the bedrock pool of water in the otherwise dry bed of upper Cottonwood Creek. The inferno of late June had sucked almost every molecule of moisture from this part of the heart of Grand Canyon—except for this little bedrock pool. The tiny polliwogs in the life-giving pool now scurried for cover to escape the two huge bipeds standing over it.

"We can't *drink* this——"

It was late June in 1990. The weather was as hot and as dry as it gets in the Canyon. The mercury soared well above 100 degrees. Karen and Paul Stryker, both age 26, from Pennsylvania, were making a two-day hike from Grandview to the South Kaibab Trail and then down it to the river.

Knowing that it would be hot, the couple had carried six liters of water each, three liters of water per day per person, for their two-day trip. Having never hiked before in Grand Canyon, the Strykers reckoned this amount would be adequate. Tragically, this would not be even half enough. They had also done their arithmetic on the trail. Their downhill route to the river had looked to them to be about 18 miles. Here they had underestimated yet again. In reality, the route they had tackled was at least 25 miles.

On their first day they each drank three liters, leaving the remaining three for the next day. Having brought only about one-third of the water they should have carried for their location, season, exposure, and activity level, they were extremely fortunate to find water in the potholes in the dry bed of Cottonwood Creek.

The couple stared in disappointment at the water in the stone basin as those tiny polliwogs wiggled for cover. No amount of wishful thinking could transform this natural pool into the office water cooler back home in Pennsylvania. "I can't drink that...."

Neither Paul nor Karen overcame their sqeamishness enough to drink this water. Nor did they even refill their empty bottles with this life-giving fluid "just in case" the heat became too much. This decision to favor fastidiousness over survival would become a fatal error.

The Strykers camped the first night in the dry drainage of Grapevine Creek. Paul and Karen had back-packed before—Paul starting with Boy Scouts and both of them later across Europe and in the Rockies. But backpacking in the desert, notes Paul's brother John, was a new thing. That night, due to the heat, Paul did not eat dinner, but he did plan to eat breakfast in the morning.

The next morning Paul did not feel like eating breakfast. The couple started hiking at 4:30 a.m., with the first faint light of dawn. By noon they had been hiking for several hours under full sun and now realized that they had to find shade. Paul had finally eaten: an apple, an orange, and some trail mix. The two hikers found a tiny patch of shade, but soon the movement of the sun erased it.

Karen and Paul walked on in the screaming heat of day under full sun. It was too hot. Finding no shade on the Tonto Trail, they stopped and set up a shade tarp. They huddled under it to try to "wait out" the heat.

Paul quickly became frustrated with the heat, far hotter than 100 degrees even in the shade of the tarp. "Let's go," he said. So they began hiking again.

As had been the case all that day, Paul encouraged Karen to drink more water. In so doing, he himself drank far less. Their three liters each were not enough to last either of them until noon—if they had known what to do to survive in the desert on a hike such as theirs, they each would have had nine liters for this one day alone. Instead, here it was afternoon and they were eking sips and swallows from their bottles as if to save the last water for when they might "really" need it. Meanwhile both of them were losing pounds and gallons of body moisture as their bodies battled desperately to survive the heat.

By the time they reached the upper drainages of Cremation Canyon, heat and dehydration were making it hard for either of them to make an intelligent decision. The trail that was supposed to connect with the South Kaibab Trail veered uphill. Could this uphill trail really connect with the Kaibab? Could it be right to go uphill like this when they wanted to go downhill to the river?

Of course it did connect, and it was correct, and it was only a little over a mile away to the Kaibab. But neither hiker at this point thought that they could walk uphill at all. They were down to one liter of water between them. Karen had swallowed the lion's share of the woefully inadequate water the two had consumed that day.

So instead of hiking the easy, though initially upward, main Tonto Trail, they decided to drop down into the Cremation drainage and make a cross-country, unknown, downhill, short-cut traverse to the river.

Scramble climbing in Grand Canyon inevitably proves far more difficult—both technically and in effort expended—than following a NPS maintained trail, especially if descending. This descent of Cremation again proved this rule.

After a couple of hours of struggling, Karen and Paul started shouting out loud in hopes that someone might hear them. They next tried mirror flashes at overflying aircraft. But neither tactic seemed to alert rescue. At only 2:00 p.m., the sun vanished beyond a cliff. Now flashing a mirror from inside the drainage became impossible.

Paul and Karen started walking downhill again. Paul stumbled and fell. Then he stumbled again. He could not seem to keep his balance anymore. Paul's loss of balance was a glaring signal of advanced dehydration.

Karen helped him up. But now Paul admitted that he could not manage to descend Cremation—nor, of course, could he now ascend back up to the Tonto Trail. Paul told Karen to "go on and save yourself."

Karen told Paul that she would rather stay with him and die with him—if he died.

They were out of water. It was barely 2:30 p.m. The afternoon would continue to grow even hotter.

Karen stayed with Paul. He became semicomatose and delirious, mumbling unintelligibly. Then Karen suspected that he was dead. Soon she knew he was dead. Eventually she realized that she might still have a chance to make it to the river during the final few hours of daylight remaining. So she started down Cremation again. But after only a short distance she decided to sleep and then try the descent in the morning.

At dawn of day three, Karen awoke, grabbed one empty water bottle, and continued her hike. This time she ascended. She soon found the Kaibab Trail and hiked it, passing the Tipoff emergency phone maybe 20 minutes after starting her hike down to the river. By 5:30 a.m., she reached the Phantom Ranger Station. In short, while Paul lay dying in a delirium of dehydration and heat stroke, he had been only an hour-plus from the river by trail. Sadly, Paul Stryker died of self-induced dehydration spurring his death due to heat stroke.

During her investigative interview, Karen repeated one statement: that she and Paul had no idea that the temperatures in Grand Canyon could be so hot.

In the winter of 1939, two young friends, Casimar Pultorak, age 22, and Paul E. Des Jardins, age 17, drove out from Detroit to Grand Canyon in Pultorak's 1937 Ford. On February 9, the young men signed the register at the Bright Angel Trailhead and descended the 9-mile trail to the river with the intent of hiking back up to the South Rim on the same day.

The soon-to-be-written Superintendent's Report and *Coconino Sun* article both reported that an NPS ranger warned at least one of these hikers that their planned 18-mile hike was over-ambitious and overly-optimistic for the trail and for the season of the year (the dead of winter). Fifty-eight years later, however, Des Jardins still insisted that no one warned him that they were biting off more than they could chew.

Either way, the two hikers descended the trail dressed only in jeans, light shirts, and light jackets. They reached the Colorado River in good shape. After a lunch of crackers and pork and beans, the two began their return ascent. Now they noticed a storm coming in. The rain quickly turned to snow. In the fading, or absent, light the two shivering hikers walked up past Indian Garden without even seeing it.

The two stopped at a rest house, likely at Three-Mile (measured downward from the South Rim). What happened next is as muddled as the minds of the two hypothermic young adventurers. (The original reports of this episode disagree somewhat with a letter written by Des Jardins nearly 60 years later in 1997.) According to a report in a fatalities file kept by Fred Harvey Co., amidst heavy snowfall, the two built a fire 3.5 miles from the Rim. Later, they tried to continue on up through the storm, but eventually they stopped again and built a second fire. Pultorak was so cold that he could hardly stand. He fell over into the fire, putting it out.

Des Jardins reportedly stood him against a rock ledge and tried to continue up the trail. When Des Jardins reached the next "shelter" (Mile-and-a-Half House), a small, roofed dwelling with no walls, he was so chilled that he was too confused to figure out how to use its emergency phone. He was also too exhausted to hike any farther, up or down. He climbed into the rafters to escape the driving wind and snow blowing into the hut from its open sides.

Pultorak, however, exited the ledge where he had been left. Or else (in the other version of the story) he exited the lower, Three-Mile Rest House— or he did both—and continued up the trail. Roughly two or three miles separated him from the Rim.

The next morning Wilbur Wright and his wife descended the trail on mules through heavy fallen snow. About two miles down, the mules spooked. Wright investigated. He found a hand sticking out of snowbank beside the trail. It was attached to Pultorak's frozen body.

Wright went to the nearest rest house (a half mile back up the trail) to report his grisly find. Here Wright heard a noise from above him in the rafters. It was Des Jardins, nearly frozen, but still propped up in the rafters in the chill air.

Rangers evacuated Des Jardins first to Indian Garden then up to the Rim via mule litter through two to three feet of new snow. For the next five weeks in the hospital in Williams, Dr. Ewell carefully removed blackened tissue from the 17-year-old's severely frost-bitten feet. The doctor knew what he was doing. Des Jardins lost only his left big toe—instead of both feet as first anticipated.

Des Jardins' thoughts during his night of misery while cramped into the rafters of the Mile-and-a-Half House—as well as his thoughts during the following five weeks in the hospital—and Pultorak's thoughts during his last few hours of life on the Bright Angel Trail were likely both haunted by the same surprising revelation: "I had no idea that Grand Canyon could be so cold."

Karen and Paul Stryker's revelation about the extreme heat of summer in the Canyon and Des Jardins' and Pultorak's revelation about how unbelievably cold the Canyon can be in winter epitomizes the *single most common misconception that visitors to the Canyon share*: "Lots of people hike in Grand Canyon; it can't be that dangerous."

Of course some people die in Grand Canyon merely because the sands of their physiological hourglass have run out due to nature's normal slow course, and they happen to be in the Canyon at that moment. Yet even in many apparent cases of this sort it remains uncertain whether or not the Canyon environment also played a role in their deaths. In nearly every death, the Canyon remains a suspicious accomplice. In other cases, as with the Strykers above, it is all too clear that the Canyon—and ignorance of the Canyon environment—was the only cause of death. A couple of examples in the more equivocal category include those of Wilson "Willie" Taylor and Ed L. Agnew. Wilson Taylor, age 59, took a turn for the worse on June 6, 1956, almost immediately below Lees Ferry. He died on shore of a heart attack near River Mile 44.5. Willie had a known serious heart condition. Whether or not his "routine" heart attack was triggered by the extreme heat of June is anyone's guess. At 9:45 a.m. on July 30, 1981, Ed L. Agnew, age 50, sat near the moored Grand Canyon Dories at River Mile 230.5 to rest in the shade, a shade which bordered on hot. Forty-five minutes later boatman Michael Jordan returned with other hikers to find Agnew still sitting in the shade, but now deceased, apparently from cardiac arrest. Again, whether the heat of July had anything to do with Agnew's heart attack remains anyone's guess.

Yet in other cases the sands in some people's physiological hourglasses have spilled to zero due directly to the intense and waterless heat—or cold—of the Canyon. And the ways in which some victims have shattered their own hourglasses in the Canyon defies belief.

For example, James Higgins, age 19, decided on a fairly reasonable itinerary for hiking the Inner Canyon. On July 7, 1977, he would park his Honda 350 cc motorcycle on the South Rim and hike down to Hermit Campground. On July 8, he would continue down Hermit Creek to the Colorado then back up onto the Tonto Trail. On the 9th, he would hike east to Monument Creek. On the next day (day #4), he would hike farther east on the Tonto to Horn Creek (which is a seasonal creek only, except during flashfloods). On July 11 (day #5), Higgins would hike to the Bright Angel Trail and Indian Garden, and then back up 2,600 feet to the South Rim. This was not a bad itinerary—except for Higgins' timing.

It was early July, the very hottest time of the year in a place that is almost unbelievably hot for five months of the year. So hot that the coolest hour of darkness may plunge only to a sizzling low of 100 degrees.

But as a long-time resident of Boulder City, Nevada, another very hot place that owes its existence only to the building of Hoover Dam, Higgins might have been expected to understand heat, what it can do, and what precautions to take so that it won't. So, even with young Higgins' admission on his permit application "Does not know the area," at least he did know heat.

On July 11, Higgins failed to appear at Indian Garden or at the South Rim.

The search began. Early on the morning of July 9, searchers learned that other hikers had seen Higgins leave Hermit Campground one day later than he had planned. From there Higgins' movements became hazy, but ended in a gruesome trail.

About midmorning of July 12, three hikers came across the first clues. As they hiked the Tonto Trail eastward toward Horn Creek Canyon and beyond, they found a set of motorcycle tools abandoned on the trail. Farther on, they found motorcycle boots. Three pairs of motorcycle boots. Next they found a receipt made out to Higgins. Next a pair of Levis. Then, far more ominous, the trio of hikers found a plastic soap dish. Inside it were Higgins' driver's license and his library cards.

When the three finally came upon Higgins himself, he was clad only in his underwear. He was unconscious, severely dehydrated, hyperthermic, and very close to death. In his backpack was only one water bottle, an empty glass jar.

One of the hikers stayed with Higgins. The other two ran two and a half level miles to Indian Garden to alert the ranger there. An NPS helicopter arrived on the Tonto and evacuated Higgins. During that less-than-five-minute flight to the Grand Canyon Clinic, Higgins died of extreme dehydration and heat stroke.

Chalk up Higgins to a case of Canyon ignorance? Maybe. But let's not jump the gun. It is not just "outsiders" or "noncanyoneers" who succumb in the Canyon. Even men of the Four-Corners' canyon country have been trapped by the Canyon's vast, complicated, waterless labyrinth. Consider, for example, this following note scrawled on the inside of a U-tah-na cherry chocolate bar wrapper and found sealed in a tobacco tin stashed below Point Imperial.

Ray Hoggan
Bert Hall
Dick Carlson
Rex   "
Sept. 29th 1929
Manti, Utah
Sanpete Co
4 days without food or water
Lost

What happened to these four men after this desperate note was sealed in the tin remained a mystery. But, thanks to Becky Douglas, who grew up in

Manti and who quizzed her grandfather, we learned that all four had survived.

Heat is a killer, especially of the naive or ignorant. A hard lesson here is: canyoneering is emphatically not mountaineering. In any group of mountaineers, the number of potential summiteers shrinks as the mountain lets people know just how hard it really is to gain altitude solely via one's own power. In other words, mountains often weed out the unfit so early in the game that, once they realize they have bitten off more than they can chew, they can often return fairly easily downhill to their staging zone. In complete contrast, canyons do the opposite. While descending most Canyon trails, the ease and coolness of the descent are seductive. It's a breeze even for the unfit or the unprepared. Until the time comes to hike back up. Then, when it's all too often a hot, dry, hard, agonizing, and often torturous physiological contrast to the descent, the unfit get weeded out late in the game and get weeded out brutally. Sometimes fatally.

Almost routinely—despite the Canyon's infamous heat, its lack of water, and its lethal cliffs acting as ramparts to imprison the parched hiker away from the river of life flowing within view so far below—hikers underestimate levels of heat and thirst in Grand Canyon. That a hiker may need *more* than two gallons of water per day for summer day-hiking in the Canyon may seem unbelievable. But, under some conditions—pivoting on the weight of the hiker, the weight of his pack, the air temperature in the shade, the amount of wind, and the lack of shade—these two gallons-plus per day may not be enough.

Table 2 lists 65 known victims—only six of whom (less than 10 percent) were women—of "environmental" deaths while hiking (or simply being) in the Canyon. The predominant cause of death listed is heat stroke. With 30 victims known or suspected, heat strokes account for nearly half of all victims. The second most common cause of death listed is "cardiac arrest," which of course simply states that the victim's heart stopped beating. "Cardiac arrest" is often a catch-all category for trail deaths. The question of *why* the hearts of those particular hikers stopped beating in the intense heat of the Canyon while hiking uphill has a short list of answers. In most cases, the cause certainly includes the victim's past medical cardiac history. But the common threads connecting these cardiac fatalities were not simply that "their time was up." Instead, the hot, arid Canyon environment, the "inverted mountain" effect of an easy initial descent followed by a very demanding ascent—combined with the victims' behaviors—often severed their timelines. In fact, most of these "cardiac-arrest" victims *were* hiking uphill, often under direct solar heat (heat that can be unrelenting even in April and October), and in the dry Canyon air. On top of all these, they often were hiking without having drunk enough water.

The human body's methods of cooling itself demand an adequate perfusion of blood to the internal organs and to the head and extremities in a "radiator" effect. Accomplishing this requires an adequate circulating volume of blood—which is mostly made up of water. The body also requires enough water for sweat to cool the body via an evaporative heat-loss effect. Lack of adequate sweating and loss of adequate perfusion due to dehydration and/or cardiac clogging and/or cardiac muscle death creates an instant and automatic danger to the hiker's homeostatic mechanisms—similar to what happens to a car with a bad radiator or a failing water pump laboring uphill in heat. On top of these problems, a normal person requires about two weeks of acclimatization in a hot environment in order to fully adjust in a homeostatically and metabolically efficient way to the high heat of summer in Grand Canyon. Acclimatization, for one thing, reduces loss of the body's electrolytes. For another, it increases the body's ability to sweat to effect its most efficient cooling, which is the only way the body cools itself at temperatures exceeding 95 degrees.

In a Canyon Catch-22, however, almost no one has that two-week, active acclimatization period in extreme heat *prior* to engaging in his or her Inner Canyon hikes—unless he or she has been working as a summer construction laborer in Phoenix. Instead, many of us hiking in Grand Canyon seem more like bizarre medical experiments tossed into an alien landscape of hostile temperatures, desiccating winds, and fierce solar radiation to see how long we can walk before we collapse. An all too typical NPS "Morning Report" by Patrick Brasington on June 12, 2000, illustrates how mindless people become as the heat soaks in.

> *On May 25th, rangers received a report that 61-year-old John O'Donnell had failed to return from a day hike in the canyon. His cousin advised that he planned on hiking down the South Kaibab Trail, across the Tonto Trail, and back up the Bright Angel Trail. O'Donnell had only two small water bottles, no food, no flashlight, no map, and no extra clothing. Temperatures in the canyon that day ranged from 111 degrees during the day to 102 degrees at night. Rangers established containment points at the South Kaibab and Bright Angel trailheads and swept the three trails. No sign of O'Donnell was found. An aerial search ensued on the following morning, but initial efforts were fruitless. Rangers familiar with the history of lost people in this area made a second flight of the area and this time spotted O'Donnell. He was found to be suffering from severe dehydration and was hallucinating. He had also been hiding from searchers, who he thought were "bad guys." O'Donnell had water in one of his bottles, but told rangers he hadn't drunk it because a man sitting next to him said it was bad water (O'Donnell was found alone). He was flown out and treated at a medical facility. Doctors said he would not have survived another day if he hadn't been found.*

While the heat alone is bad enough, hikers with cardiac inadequacies are at far greater risk of dying on the trail in Grand Canyon from environmental challenges than are healthy hikers. And as Table 2 suggests, laboring in the Canyon environment may have precipitated these cardiac deaths on the trail. In short, "cardiac arrest" listed as cause of death emphatically does not mean a fatality independent of environmental causes. We suspect several of these "cardiac" deaths were due to combinations of dehydration, hyperthermia, and exertion on steep trails, which turn people, inch by inch, into heat zombies.

These complications are further compounded by age. The most well-camouflaged victims of dehydration/heat stroke are fairly young and athletic. Kids and young adults seem to run at full function in the heat, sweating appropriately and seemingly going strong, but abruptly, when dehydration kicks in, they crash quickly and often unexpectedly. And die.

A classic example of this sort of run-until-you-crash mentality was embodied by Arthur Clarence "Jack" Anderson, age 19. On July 1, 1925, Anderson decided to hike down the Bright Angel Trail to the Colorado and then hike back up to the South Rim—all in one day. That day was one of the hottest days of the year. On top of his already overambitious goal, Anderson added a somewhat typical young male's macho twist: He boasted that he was "going to make a new record" on his Rim-to-river-to-Rim hike of 18 miles. Did he? Anderson made it to the river quickly but was slammed into the dust by heat stroke before returning more than a few hundred feet back up. He was evacuated to the Rim by a "drag out." Anderson died hours later while being evacuated homeward to Phoenix by train.

The common problem exemplified by Anderson is twofold. First, young hikers, especially athletes, often possess such a well conditioned cardiac system that they—especially males—are able and accustomed to blasting along where other people move more slowly. Second, all too many of them do not understand heat or what it does. In extremely hot climates these young men are a lot like muscle cars with big engines but undersized (unacclimated) radiators. They drive at their usual high speed, spurred additionally by testosterone-driven thinking that denies the consequences of breaking the speed limit, until they overheat. And this potentially lethal overheating takes them almost completely by surprise. Meanwhile nonathletic or older people are neither capable of, nor inclined to, push themselves nearly as hard.

In complete contrast, only six of the 65 victims in Table 2 are known or suspected to have died due to hypothermia, or exposure to cold. This reflects two realities: first, and as mentioned in the previous chapter, far fewer people enter the Canyon during the cold season than the hot one. Second, people in North America understand cold better than they understand the Canyon's extreme heat, wind, and dryness; and such people are better prepared to combat cold via clothing.

Even so, as we saw earlier with Casimar Pultorak and his friend Paul Des

Jardins, people hiking in the Canyon since the first trail was marked have underestimated how such a supposedly hot canyon can get so cold. In his excellent book, *Through the Grand Canyon from Wyoming to Mexico*, for example, Ellsworth Kolb notes finding in 1911 an unidentified hiker wearing the hob-nailed shoes of a prospector and double layers of denim plus an overcoat and mittens. The body had been originally discovered in 1906 lying "halfway up the granite" in Upper Granite Gorge on river left about two miles downstream of Pipe Creek (see book cover).

> *He was lying in a natural position, with his head resting on a rock. An overcoat was buttoned tightly around him. No large bones were broken, but he might have had a fall and been injured internally. More likely he became sick and died. The small bones of the hands and feet had been taken away by field-mice, and no doubt the turkey-buzzards had stripped the flesh. His pockets contained Los Angeles newspapers of 1900. His pockets also contained a pipe and pocket knife, but nothing by which he could be identified....Such finds are not unusual in this rugged country. These prospectors seldom say where they are going, no track is kept of their movements, and unless something about their clothes tells who they are, their identity is seldom established. The proximity of this grave made us wonder how many more such unburied bodies there were along this river.*

The "unburied" part bothered the Kolb brothers. So, after photographing the peacefully reposed victim, there being no soil, they buried him under rocks.

A final factor, one clearly implicated in Inner-Canyon falls in the previous chapter, also plays a role in environmental injuries. This factor is hiking *solo*. There exists no question that, when it comes to appreciating and avoiding lethal dangers in the Grand Canyon, two heads are better than one. Thirteen of the 65 environmental victims in Table 2 are known to have been solo hikers; several other victims may also have been, but records are incomplete.

It is also clear from Table 2 that having passed the age of forty among men seems clearly to increase their odds of dying due to heat-related cardiac arrest in Grand Canyon. Ironically, however, *being* below the age of 25 vastly impacts the odds of young men in the Canyon living long enough to reach forty. Hence, neither youth nor maturity offers immunity. Fourteen heat stroke victims (about half the total) were young males between the ages of 10 and 28 years old. How do these sorts of unusual deaths happen to such young men? Consider the following examples.

In early 1975, Charles Myers, age 20, had to get out of New York. Myers was a student in history, philosophy, and religion at Columbia University. He felt "bothered by people in New York City." To escape the crowd there, Myers hitchhiked west. He briefly visited Yuma, Arizona, then spent a month living alone, fasting and walking in the woods, near Taos and Jemez, New Mexico. Myers planned to return to New York by July 4, but when someone suggested a detour to Grand Canyon, a place he had never seen, Myers veered west.

On June 28, Myers hiked alone down the Hermit Trail into the Canyon. He rested at Hermit Creek and ate all of the food he had. Realizing that, indeed, this had been *all* of his food, Myers decided to hike out that same day—despite the heat. He also decided to take a shortcut off the trail during his return. "I had a topographical map of the canyon," Myers explained, "and it looked like I could take a shortcut out. It's my nature to want to do things two different ways."

Myers' decision to shortcut an established Canyon route was virtually a cookie-cut fatal error, a *signature* error made by the majority of young, solo male hikers in the Canyon who have ended up dying from Inner Canyon falls and/or dehydration and heat stroke. Shortcutting is the mother of all hiking errors.

You guessed it: Myers' alternate route proved not to be a shortcut. By night-fall he found himself distant from the NPS trail yet less than halfway to the rim. He slept fitfully on rock. He retackled his personal route the next morning. He walled out against a cliff that did not look overly difficult. He started climbing it. He soon lost his footing and fell about 30 feet.

The impact not only fractured a vertebra in his back, but maybe even more seriously, it also cracked one of his two canteens. The water leaked out onto the superheated rock. In pain and sweating profusely, Myers quickly gulped nearly all the little water he had remaining. Realizing that his predicament was now desperate, he decided to send up an SOS via a signal fire. One problem with this idea—other than the slim odds that anyone would see a fire—was the lack of tinder where he had fallen. In his wishful thinking about the efficacy of a fire, Myers torched his backpack.

When this short-lived blaze failed to attract a rescue helicopter, he then stripped naked and burned his clothes.

Still no one came.

Now naked, with no backpack and very little water, and suffering a cracked vertebra, Myers continued trying to light small brush fires. Again to no avail. As the day wore on and the sun baked him dry, Myers not only ran out of faith in a signal fire, he was also down to his last few gulps of water.

Desperate, Myers discarded his knife and wallet near where he had fallen. Next he stumbled and crawled to a grassy area where he tried to sleep for the night. His night was miserable, to put it mildly. For some strange reason, Myers still believed that someone would find him. But he also knew that, before they did, the extreme heat here might kill him. So the next day, day #3, he found a small rock overhang offering a patch of shade.

Myers stayed in his postage stamp of shade for two days. He tried to flash-signal over-flying aircraft by reflecting sunlight off a medallion he wore around his neck. He also tried to eat a little cactus. But he found the taste bitter. In pain, hot, exhausted, starving, dehydrated, and with his mouth now bleeding, he was ready to give up and die.

Instead of dropping dead, on this, his fourth day, Myers railed at his Maker by shouting a prayer-tirade. This bout with a God who had failed to equip him with common sense finally gave him the strength he needed to go on. That night and the next day, as he chewed on more cactus, he struggled back down into the Canyon. He realized finally that by being off any established route, as he was now, he might never be found.

On day #5 he found a small seep spring. He spent the night here. Eventually, he hobbled all the way back to Hermit Creek. Now, on day #6, he had plenty of water. But he was still short on decision-making ability. He decided to head down the creek. By now, almost a week after hiking down from the South Rim, Myers was so weak and injured that he could walk only fifty yards at a stretch before needing to lie down and rest. Myers' rate of travel shrank to less than five percent of a normal person's. As he staggered through the brush and heat and boulders and cacti along the creek, he screamed like a child and he moaned and groaned.

It took Myers, still railing against the powers-that-be, five *more* days of stumbling down Hermit to locate his original campsite. A normal hiker might have done this in two hours.

A couple of hours after Myers found his original campsite—and more than ten days after running out of food—two hikers found Myers.

Myers spent the next ten days recuperating in Flagstaff Community Hospital. He contemplated his ordeal, Native American life, religion, and his future hitchhike back to New York. To Myers, having people around him somehow had become more attractive.

The numerous baffling episodes of foolish death in the Canyon have prompted many an NPS ranger to ask herself: Are these people who kill themselves in the Canyon by hiking without enough water merely ignorant or....Or what? Journalist Elliot Almond writes in his *Los Angeles Times* article "Summer danger in the Grand Canyon: Hikers risk heatstroke and death:"

> *Hikers have died of heatstroke after having their pictures taken next to a sign at Indian Gardens warning them not to go farther. Rangers have found people dead of dehydration who were carrying water in their packs. Rangers lament that many simply expect to be saved when in danger.*

What this "of-course-someone-will-rescue-me" mentality among some hikers can produce is tragedy. In October of 1975, for example, NPS rangers were faced with another mysterious disappearance. Arizonan Brad Riner, age 22, had planned an ambitious and challenging, solo, experts-only hike for eleven days in the heart of Grand Canyon on both sides of the river. His previous Canyon hiking experience included the Bright Angel, Kaibab, Tonto, Hermit, Boucher, Clear Creek, Hance, and Tanner trails. This is a respectable list, although it comprises only the easiest small fraction of the 500 miles of trails in the Canyon recognized officially by the Park Service and includes, significantly, all of the mere 33 miles of those trails that the NPS routinely maintains aggressively. Thus, Riner did have Canyon experience, but most of it had been on visible, well-traveled trails relatively easy for hikers of medium ability.

On September 20, Riner's father had dropped him off at the trailhead. Eleven days later, on October 1, Mr. Riner called the NPS Backcountry Reservations Office and told them that his son had failed to show up for work. Brad Riner was an "overdue hiker."

The NPS launched a helicopter search of Riner's proposed route—down Hermit Trail to Hermit Campground, then west along the Tonto Trail to Boucher Rapid (River Mile 96.7), across the Colorado in his small inflatable raft, then down to Crystal Rapid (River Mile 98.2), up Crystal Creek, up Dragon Creek toward Shiva Saddle, over Shiva Saddle, down Trinity Creek, around Cheops Pyramid, then up again to Shiva Saddle, then to the headwaters of Phantom Creek, and then down Phantom Creek to Phantom Ranch.

Although Vibram-soled foot prints thought to be Riner's were found heading up Crystal, then Dragon, creeks, the air search found no other sign of him.

On October 2, three two-person NPS search crews plus five more SAR crews from the Coconino County Sheriff's Department choppered into the Inner Canyon to search Riner's route. Meanwhile helicopter air searches continued. The day ended with one team having found tracks appearing to be Riner's around the Shiva Saddle area.

On October 3, nine crews of two to five persons each scoured the tortuous, convoluted maze north of the river in more detail. A four-person NPS crew on Shiva Saddle at the 5,250-foot contour (roughly 3,000 feet above the river) found not only footprints but also a two-inch square of blue ensolite pad snagged on a tree branch just above the Redwall Limestone cliff. They tracked this trail to the 5,600-foot level but, as night fell, they were recalled.

On October 4, a three-person NPS crew followed the previously discovered tracks. Soon they arrived at a half-acre area that had been burned by a recent fire. In it they found two expended flare tubes, then, 75 feet below the edge of a short cliff, they also found a stuff sack containing freeze-dried foods, foot powder, trash, empty water bottles, an itinerary, blue tennis shoes, a pair of old green fatigue cut-offs, two hiking books, et cetera, plus a light raft paddle. The searchers admitted that these might have rolled off the ledge accidentally rather than have been discarded. Above these, in the main burned area, searchers reported: "It appeared that RINER had spent a good deal of time in this area as evidenced by sleeping areas where he had done a great deal of rolling around."

This burned area seemed to have been undisturbed for four days. Riner's stride from here, they noted, was now shorter than it had been (Riner was 6' 2" tall) but it was still normal and strong.

All search crews now focused on this trail. Meanwhile a private boater phoned in the information that he had taken Riner from the south to the north shore across the river from Hermit Rapid (River Mile 95) to Crystal on September 21. Riner therefore had not had to use the small raft he was carrying. The NPS tracking team followed Riner's tracks for 2.5 hours, until "the tracks headed down a wash at almost the head of the Phantom Creek Drainage."

The helicopter now scrutinized this Outlet Canyon/Phantom Creek headwater area. At 10:38 a.m., chopper personnel located a body at the base of a cliff near a shallow pool in upper Phantom Creek.

Climbing crews and trackers converged here. Rangers Chase and Stan Stockton made a series of technical rappels and were first to reach the body. It was Riner's body. The NPS incident report stated that Riner:

> had apparently lowered his pack with string, then attempted to
> jump 30 [vertical] feet to a sandy area adjacent to a water pool.
> He struck his head on a large nearby boulder. Signs allude he made
> his way to his pack, and removed his...raft and ensolite pad. The
> body was found on this pad and raft lying on the left side, curled
> slightly with feet extending into the pool.

Chase and Stockton noticed that Riner's right leg appeared to be fractured and, worse, that blood had seeped from his nose and ears, and his eyes were blackened. Riner's glasses were found near the original landing imprint. This imprint location appeared to have been deliberately chosen and hit by a person who jumped (not one surprised by an accidental fall). It also looked like the best possible landing spot below the cliff—though, again, it was the termination point for a vertical fall of thirty feet.

An autopsy revealed that Riner had suffered a dislocated hip, a broken back and ribs, a punctured lung, and a skull fracture. Death had occurred on about September 29.

Inside Riner's pack were two, half-filled quart water bottles. Riner had carried no rope, nor hat, nor knife, but among other things (including his small raft and an inflatable life jacket) he still had plenty of food, a topo map with no route marks, plus pages torn from the *Inner Canyon Trail Guide* and Harvey Butchart's *Grand Canyon Treks*. Both these books were in the stuff sack discovered earlier above the 5,600-foot contour, which suggests that Riner had discarded everything in that sack to lighten his load. But, if he had done this, why then keep a raft when his planned route out and across the river was over a bridge at Phantom?

What went wrong here?

Riner died at the foot of a 100-foot dry waterfall the bottom thirty feet of which were unclimbable because the waterfall was fully blocked by a wall-to-wall chockstone boulder which was undercut. Riner had tossed his sleeping bag, walking stick, and life vest down separately. He had carefully lowered his pack by a string. Then, because he carried no rope to lower himself down short pitches on which a ropeless descent might risk injury, he jumped into space.

This *is* hard to understand. Riner made the decision to jump off a cliff that guaranteed *certain* injury regardless of how well he (or anyone else) could have landed, even if everything went perfectly. In short, he made an impossible jump that no sane person could have expected to walk away from. Why?

For a ghost of a chance of understanding why, let's back up to his long, possibly multi-day camp above the 5,600-foot contour. Why had he stayed there so long? Why had he shot off his only two flares there? Why was the area all burned—as if ignited intentionally as a signal? And why had he abandoned roughly ten pounds of non-critical supplies and equipment only 75 feet below his sleeping spot (remember, he tore the critical pages out of the two books he had placed in that dropped stuff sack before abandoning it.)

It is only conjecture, but the two most likely explanations for Riner's behavior are: a. he might have injured himself somewhat and felt that going on would be too difficult, or b. he may have, for psychological reasons, felt that he had gotten in over his head in backcountry orienteering and was worried about achieving his orienteering goals. Riner's experience in the Canyon consisted only of hikes on established, visible trails. He was not experienced with Canyon orienteering, route-finding, terrain evaluation, and free-style Canyon scrambling or "bouldering" over serious exposures that inspire deep fear even in experienced Canyoneers. Worse, Riner had not just entered new, trackless territory whose challenges were a quantum leap above his experience level, he had done it solo, and with no back-up. Yes, he was carrying a lot of stuff, some of it useless. But he had not even brought a hat. Back to the bigger issue, was Riner, just before his fatal leap, worried about having pushed solo too far beyond his confidence level or, instead, was he injured—or were both true? Either way, by this point above the 5,600-foot contour he clearly had wanted to be rescued. But no rescuers had responded to his flares or fire.

Does any of this explain why, after carefully lowering his backpack so that *it* would not be damaged, *he* jumped into thirty feet of air? Was he dehydrated and thus afflicted by the typical irritable snap-thinking that accompanies it? He had a half liter of water in each of his two bottles (or had he filled these *after* jumping?), and he was staring down at several gallons of water in a pool. It remains unclear whether or not Riner had been drinking enough water.

Did Riner decide to commit suicide? If so, why lower his pack carefully and why choose a "soft" landing spot for himself that would guarantee a lingering, horrible death?

Our conclusion is that, days before he jumped, Brad Riner had found himself way over his head and very alone. And he had come to realize it so intensely that he may have begun obsessing about it. Hour by hour in the trackless and often terrifying route he had chosen, his fear grew, and his rational thinking declined. With the specters of failure and absolute helpless solitude lurking in every decision, Riner hurried—too panicked perhaps to believe he could re-ascend his feeder route—when instead he should have exercised infinite patience and contemplative judgement by climbing back up and reassessing his route.

Riner, in fact, had apparently lost his route after crossing Shiva Saddle shortly before his leap into space. He descended down the far left (the northern) option into his fatal "no-go" feeder wash into Phantom Creek instead of descending well to the right into Trinity Canyon as he had originally planned—and also instead of taking the more center route down the "scramble" cliff into Phantom Creek. Riner's entering a "no-go" feeder was a natural enough mistake. But when he hit that unclimbable drop he *knew* he was on the wrong route; the NPS ranger at the Backcountry Office had warned Riner when approving his proposed route not to do any exposed climbing because only scramble climbing was required. Riner knew that Trinity and Phantom creeks *were both possible via scramble climbing*. But he apparently did not add up two and two when he was faced with an unclimbable 30-foot fall to come up with "four," that he was in the wrong drainage and on the wrong route.

The perplexing question remains: Why did Riner not turn back and spend 30 minutes re-evaluating his route (and his location) when faced with an undescendable cliff? Only someone who had lost his ability to reason or who was inordinately worried about water (and perhaps was dehydrated due to having hoarded his water) would have refused to spend an extra 30 to 60 minutes to find a safe route that he *knew* must exist. Indeed, to Riner's right, to the south, lay the climbable route he had missed but had been told existed. Again, why did he refuse to re-evaluate his lethal predicament?

Riner apparently lost his head. But which environmental factors (dehydration, fatigue) versus which psychological or physical factors (fear, insecurity, anxiety, loneliness, bullheadedness, injury, or being 22 years old and possibly naive) were responsible for this became moot points once he leaped off that 30-foot drop.

Again, as is all too clear from a look at Tables 1-B and 2, solo hiking in the Canyon proves beyond the shadow of a doubt the old maxim that two heads are better than one.

Another example, a harrowing one, illustrates in technicolor this danger of solo hiking. But this time the victim was not a stubborn young male, but a young woman....

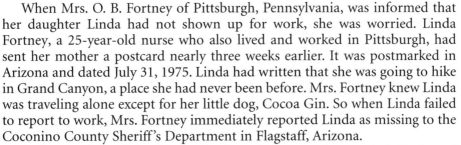

When Mrs. O. B. Fortney of Pittsburgh, Pennsylvania, was informed that her daughter Linda had not shown up for work, she was worried. Linda Fortney, a 25-year-old nurse who also lived and worked in Pittsburgh, had sent her mother a postcard nearly three weeks earlier. It was postmarked in Arizona and dated July 31, 1975. Linda had written that she was going to hike in Grand Canyon, a place she had never been before. Mrs. Fortney knew Linda was traveling alone except for her little dog, Cocoa Gin. So when Linda failed to report to work, Mrs. Fortney immediately reported Linda as missing to the Coconino County Sheriff's Department in Flagstaff, Arizona.

As it turned out, Mrs. Fortney had good reason to be worried. Linda and Cocoa Gin had hiked down the trail to Havasu Canyon on August 1. But other than that postcard, Linda had left no specifics of her plans. Her postcard did say, however, that she was hiking to Supai Village.

Having never been to Grand Canyon before, let alone hiked it, Linda Fortney was stunned almost immediately by the heat and the confusing terrain. Temperatures soared well over 100 degrees. Worse, she had gotten a late start. Even so, she was determined to make it to the village by dark.

She never even got close.

Near sundown, still on the seven-mile trail in Hualapai Canyon, Fortney took off her pack containing her food, water, and gear. She laid it in the trail. Then she wandered off trail carrying only her purse. Becoming disoriented, she could not find her way back to the trail or to her pack—even though she and the trail and her pack were all in the bottom of the same narrow canyon. Fortney continued downcanyon without her gear. She reached the junction (or confluence) of Hualapai Canyon and Cataract Canyon in fading light.

At this point Linda Fortney had a fifty-fifty chance of turning in the correct direction. Left would take her to Supai Village in a couple of miles. Right would take her upcanyon but deep into a lot of lengthy "nowhere."

Fortney veered right, up the huge side canyon called Cataract Canyon, and walked southeast.

She followed a cattle trail. This major tributary snaked miles upstream and south of Havasu Village. Again she was headed *up* it, to the south, in the opposite direction of Supai and the main trail and, eventually, water.

Night fell. Fortney realized that she was lost. The darkness scared her so much that she could not sleep. She had matches in her purse but she was too frightened even to light a fire. As the temperature dropped into the 50s, her halter-top and blue jeans also left her too cold to sleep. The next morning she found herself cold, foodless, and waterless—having already walked upstream past the source of Cataract (a.k.a. Havasu) Creek into the dry zone. She felt extremely anxious to reach Supai or, instead, to escape the Canyon altogether.

Again Linda Fortney had a fifty-fifty chance of going in the right direction. If she returned downcanyon, she would reach Supai Village in a few hours. If she continued upcanyon, she would be entering a desert prison and death row.

She looked both ways, then hiked farther upcanyon. En route, maybe ten or more miles upcanyon from her "bivouac," Fortney veered out of the main Cataract Canyon into Havatagvitch Canyon, a true middle-of-nowhere location.

By nightfall, once more having walked in the wrong direction, and this time, all day, she was 15 miles from Supai Village, and now 20 miles from her car.

By day three, she had become severely dehydrated—and even more desperate. Miraculously, she found a small spring up Havatagvitch. But it dripped so incredibly slowly from a cliff crack that it took 45 minutes to fill her eyeglass case. This would at least postpone death from dehydration. In fact, as pitifully tiny as this spring was, it would hold death at bay for at least 17 more days....

For the first four of those days, Fortney screamed for help. She gave up eventually when she decided that her voice was not carrying very far. The nights remained so cold and so frightening that each night seemed to last an eternity before sunrise. To fight the cold, she stood and walked around and, being Catholic she said the rosary, or sang. When the sun finally did come up, it heated the Canyon so hot that she feared she would not be able to bear it. She still refused to light a fire, even to try to attract attention. Before she lit anything, she decided, she first wanted to be sure that someone was up there and looking down. No one was looking (she was not due back at work for two more weeks). And even if there had been someone "nearby," Fortney would not have known it.

For her first 15 days of inadvertent but self-imposed exile, Fortney kept track of the days in her address book. She also wrote dinner recipes to keep busy. But when this became too depressing, she quit. She found an old whiskey bottle. By filling this at her dripping spring, she could venture away from it for a full day at a time before fear of dehydration urged her back. This bottle alone might have gotten her to Supai had she been willing to walk downcanyon, but not long after finding this precious bottle, she dropped and broke it.

Hunger drove her to eat cactus blossoms. Cocoa Gin, weak and starving, eventually wandered off.

When finally, on August 19, Linda Fortney's mother reported her missing to the NPS, the park and the Coconino County Sheriff's Department started a search. They found Fortney's car parked at the Rim at Hualapai Hilltop. Cocoa Gin had already been found wobbling down in the correct direction toward Supai Village by hikers a few days earlier. The search team concluded that Fortney was most likely still inside the Canyon. But where?

On day #20 of Linda Fortney's adventure in orienteering—and the second day of the search—Hardy Jones, a Supai Indian, spotted human footprints up Cataract "where nobody should be." He returned later with his son Darrell and his friends Stanley Manakaja and Roy Young, also Supai, to follow those tracks. At 6:30 a.m. on August 20, the four Native Americans found Linda

Fortney in Havatagvitch Canyon (12–15 miles upstream of the Hualapai Canyon/Cataract Canyon junction) branching to the east of Cataract.

She stared at them and cried.

After her helicopter evacuation to Flagstaff's Hospital, Linda Fortney was still 5 feet, 4 inches tall, but now, instead of weighing her normal 110 pounds, she weighed only 85. Otherwise she was in good condition—even better for having been reunited with Cocoa Gin, now nursed back to health.

Linda Fortney's near-death, wrong-way hike briefly earned her fame. Several articles capitalized on her ordeal. She was even invited to make a guest appearance on the national television game show "What's My Line?"

The lesson? Linda Fortney had lost her pack, lost her food and water, lost her bearings and sense of direction, lost her way, lost her dog, lost even her common-sensical ability to plan her own self-rescue, and lost 25 pounds. But she did make it on TV. In short, she became a modern American story.

On a more serious note, she did survive—and through her example she may have influenced other hikers not to enter the Canyon as ill-prepared as she had been. Perhaps her example has even saved a life or two.

Even so, others would continue to enter the Canyon ill-prepared mentally to match wits with its heat and dryness and its immense, sheer, and convoluted terrain. Another tragic but classic example of this occurred in June of 1996. A group of eight hikers from Bountiful, Utah, five Explorer Boy Scouts and three adults, hiked from near Saddle Mountain down to Little Nankoweap Canyon and the Colorado (Mile 52). The group was led by scout leader Guy C. Davis, age 44. The other two adults were Earl Pace, age 64, and his brother, Loren Pace, age 71. Loren Pace had been asked by Davis to be the group's guide. Loren Pace was in charge of all provisions and was the only person to have hiked this route before. The hike was intended to be what Davis described as "a super activity" for the varsity scouts. Neither Davis, who was on medication for a bronchial condition (medication which required water for him to swallow), nor Earl Pace had ever before hiked in Grand Canyon. Nor had any of the Scouts.

Davis said that Loren Pace had recommended that each hiker carry a minimum of 3, 2-liter bottles of water plus a 2-quart canteen—a total of about 2 gallons of water per boy for three days of trekking. All the boys carried only this minimum, except, Davis thought, David B. Phillips, who maybe carried only four liters plus a two-quart canteen for a total of about 1.5 gallons. Again, this amount of water was to last each hiker for three days; it was also intended to be used to prepare dehydrated food. Davis had asked Loren Pace whether these two gallons would be enough for all that. Pace had answered that they would run out of water before reaching the river, but he had done this before. No one, it seems, carried more water than this minimum.

On day one, Monday, June 3, the group hiked only about two hours along the hilly plateau, maybe five miles, then camped in a flat area. During nearly all of the next morning they hiked to the end of Trail 31. The Saddle Mountain Pass to Little Nankoweap route that they were following along the Boundary Ridge area is emphatically not the traditional, more clear cut trail route into Nankoweap near Point Imperial. It is a far more advanced route—with no trail at all—for experts only. NPS spokeswoman Maureen Oltrogge noted that the route was only for "highly experienced Grand Canyon hikers with proven route-finding ability."

That afternoon, under a scorching sun, the eight descended "The Chute." Partway down, one of the adults told the boys that they were off the correct route. The hikers spent more time in the hot sun re-locating it and then descending again. The Chute used up a lot of their remaining water. One of the boys said later that Loren Pace told them at this point that he had hiked this area before "but never once had he made it down to the river with water."

Here the adults, especially Loren Pace, had a hard time keeping up with the boys, and thus slowed them all down. The boys, one of them later said, wanted to go ahead and continue more quickly toward the river, but Loren Pace insisted that they stay together. Loren Pace "was not sure of the trail," Boy Scout Jordan Winegar later said, "and was one of the people who slowed the group down." Other survivors agreed with this.

By day's end the group was almost out of water. They now knew that none of them would make it to their destination, the Colorado River, with any water remaining. Indeed, at this point, possibly because of earlier "Canyon" stories told by Loren Pace about having run out of water during his previous Canyon hikes and about other people dying after they had lost their route, the five Scouts were already privately discussing the possibility of dying on *this* hike.

That night, Scout Leader Davis reckoned that each boy had 1.5 liters of water remaining. Phillips perhaps only 1 liter. In that the temperatures had exceeded 100 degrees during most of the day but they all had been rationing their water, everyone at this point was already dehydrated, likely dangerously so. Most of the hikers did not eat that night for fear of losing the last of their precious water by mixing it with dehydrated food.

On the morning of day #3, Wednesday, after skipping breakfast, the hikers descended another "chute." Because the adults were so slow, the boys descended ahead of them. Loren Pace yelled at them to come back up because they had again missed the route. Even the surviving boys later admitted that they did a lot of backtracking throughout the entire hike after they went ahead but missed the routes.

Eventually everyone made it down this chute except Davis, who refused to attempt it. He was now unable to take his medication due to a total lack of water and was having trouble breathing. Trying to coax Davis down ate up more hours and more water. And in vain; Davis refused to budge.

Now the boys openly discussed the possibility of dying on the hike. They were exhausted and had no energy. But they agreed that they did not want to die here where they were. David Phillips, the most active of all, shared his water with some of the other boys. Very soon after Davis had stopped cold, Loren Pace, their guide and the only one who knew the route, also dropped out. Now, by noon or even earlier on day #3, the scouts were not only guideless, they had also run out of water completely. The temperature now climbed well above 100 degrees in the shade. And almost no shade existed.

Finally Earl Pace, the last adult still on his feet, guided the boys across another difficult area, and then traversed around a cliff. Now they were only about 1.5 miles from the river, even so the heat next felled Earl Pace as well. Too exhausted and dehydrated to take another step, he dropped out to hide from the sun under a boulder. He advised the boys to stay where they were until evening and then to hike to the river in cooler air.

The five boys had been completely out of water for several hours and, worse, had been very inadequately hydrated for three days. They decided instead to continue through the blazing heat down Little Nankoweap to find water.

The river seemed very close. Other than assuring their own survival (the survivors would later say), once they reached the river they were also "supposed to" purify river water and carry it back up to the adults.

By now every boy was so exhausted and dehydrated that he could not walk straight. Phillips complained to his companions that he could not see the trail very well (deterioration of vision is a *well advanced* symptom of dehydration). He not only staggered, but fell several times. All five staggered down the bone-dry Little Nankoweap. But exhaustion and dehydration stopped all of them every few minutes. Several of them fell asleep as soon as they stopped.

Of the five boys, three fell back. David B. Phillips, age 15, and Mark Coons were in view of the Colorado, several hundred feet and only a few minutes away. The shade temperature at the river was 111 degrees. Both boys stumbled on.

David collapsed. Hard. He hit his head. His eyes rolled back and his breathing became very hard and extremely fast.

Coons stared at him then "ran" to the river. He desperately tried to fill bottles. Then he returned to Phillips. He tried to pour some water down Phillips' throat. This did not seem to work. Next Coons poured water all over Phillips' body to cool him off. At roughly 6:00 p.m., Coons hurried back to the river for more water and saw a rafting trip. He waved frantically and yelled at them that his friend was dying.

Tom Barry, a member of this private rafting trip, said that he heard Coons yelling. So he walked downstream. Several people on Barry's trip had been hearing a faint cry for help but had had trouble locating its source. When Barry got to the beach, he found Coons looking very scared and "almost delirious and attempting to fill one or two plastic jugs with water." Barry tried to talk with Coons for about a minute as he gulped two quarts of water, sorting through the confusion about eight people in trouble and one of them, David, only 400 feet up a dry creek bed.

Barry hurried to Phillips then yelled for his other two companions Mark Diedrick and Dave Scalia. The two grabbed water and first aid and also sought out David Phillips.

Scalia, a paramedic, found Phillips hatless and "all jumbled" under a mesquite tree, as if he had just fallen. While still breathing, the 5-foot, 10-inch and 130-pound boy's temperature was higher than the 106-degree cap of the thermometer. Phillips was in deep heat stroke. His pulse was 180, his respirations 72 per minute, and his blood pressure was extremely low. Phillips was dry to the touch and also unconscious and unresponsive to pain.

Realizing that Phillips' prognosis was extremely bad, they too poured water all over him. Then they organized a bucket brigade to keep him wet. They improvised a stretcher and carried him to camp. They also alerted an Outdoors Unlimited commercial river trip camped downstream of them of the emergency and asked them to radio for help. Its trip leader, Bert Jones, said he got on the radio and also sent up a medical doctor and two other people to help.

David Phillips died that evening, just under five hours after Coons reached the river. Phillips died of heat stroke and dehydration. Barry slept next to the body that night to make sure no animals got to it.

Melanie Miles, co-leader of the private river trip, spent most of her time with the four surviving boys. She described them:

> They were initially delirious, frantic, pale, filthy, and had assorted scrapes and scratches. Some were stumbling, most were afraid they were going to die, but within three to four hours they were all able to eat and drink and keep the food and water down without throwing it up and had definitely become more stable.

Miles added that the boys were confounded over why their leaders had let them down; they had, the boys told her, even asked the Scouts to carry their backpacks! Scout Leader Davis, they said, had wanted them all to wait in the shade, but "the Scouts were afraid that they were going to die and just wanted to get to the water and also wanted to do the right thing."

Around midnight, Earl Pace had been found up the wash "in very bad shape" on his hands and knees leaning over a boulder. Rescuers brought Pace to the river without his pack. He was shocked the next morning to find David Phillips dead. He said that their problems resulted from the boys having drunk their water too soon.

That night Bert Jones of Outdoors Unlimited finally managed to make radio contact with an overflying aircraft en route to Los Angeles International Airport; this aircraft relayed the distress call. The next morning an Arizona Department of Public Safety helicopter and an NPS SAR team found the two missing adults.

They found Loren Pace sitting in the shade up Little Nankoweap. He was disoriented and swayed unsteadily when he tried to walk on level ground. Pace did not seem to know that he was dehydrated. He never asked about the welfare of anyone else in his group but he did mention to rangers that he was fine and that he had done this hike several times and was not worried.

The searchers—Rangers David Trevino and David Desrosiers—found Guy Davis well above a cliff in little Nankoweap Canyon. Davis was "slightly confused mentally, somewhat disoriented, dehydrated, depressed, and crying." When told of Phillip's death, Davis said, "I can't believe it. Of all of us, he should have made it." Next he expressed the sentiment that he himself should have been left up on the cliff to die. He felt that, by being the weak link holding everyone back (at the lower chute) he had contributed to their prolonged and lethal exposure during the hike.

What went wrong here?

The obvious errors were:

1. No one on this hike carried enough water to make it safely (one, who died, had two liters less than the others but was allowed to do the hike undersupplied). The Scout Leader apparently had not brought to the trailhead the sixteen or so extra 2-liter bottles (old plastic soft drink bottles or whatever) of water that prudence would dictate and then "forced" each hiker to carry plenty. Given the season, conditions, and terrain, each hiker on this trek had far less than half of the water he needed (about 2+ gallons per day) for good health.

2. Those responsible not only chose one of the very hottest times of the year to hike, but also the very driest.

3. The hiking route itself was only a "route" for experts in route-finding; it was not an established trail, let alone a maintained or marked one.

4. Only one person on this hike—a 71 year old—had ever seen the route. No one else had ever hiked anywhere in Grand Canyon. Thus, this experienced-experts-only trip was made up of novice Grand Canyon hikers.

5. The guide on the hike could neither keep up with the pace of the other seven hikers with him, nor could he remember with facility each section of the unmarked route.

6. The group had no information backup: if the only person with information on the route were incapacitated, or if the group had to split up during a rescue or emergency, no one else knew the route.

7. The group did split up. And the person who knew the route dropped out.

8. The trip apparently had no emergency signaling devices, such as signal mirrors or radio.

9. Despite the full glare heat of June, these Scouts did not hike during dawn and dusk and then spend the in-between times resting and cooling off during a long mid-day siesta under whatever shade they could find or rig with tarps. Instead they simply hiked all day, hatless, under full sunlight during "banker's hours."

10. The scout leaders had obtained (by mail) from the NPS Backcountry Reservations Office the legally required overnight hiking permit for a hike in the Nankoweap use area, but they had not specified their route. On the permit the NPS had written of Little Nankoweap, "Trip not recommended for 1st time hikers in G.C.—know your limits." The reservation was also for a starting date of June 10, not June 3 when they actually began hiking. Hence, no one in the Park Service would have known to look for them specifically where they were at the time. *Except for young Mark Coons—the only one of the eight hikers to make it all the way to the river without collapsing—having flagged down a river trip, several more of the Scouts and perhaps all of the adults might have died.*

All of this may seem to clash with the motto, "Be prepared." David Phillips was at least the sixth Utahn to have died on Scouting trips in the past five years (two others drowned, one fell, and two were struck by lightning). Significantly, less than a week after Phillips died, a troop of ten more Boy Scouts and three adult leaders from Chireno, Texas, would have to be rescued after hiking beyond their abilities and their water during the hottest time of the year on yet another trail recommended only for experienced hikers, the New Hance Trail. River-runners on a hike found them and radioed out for help. The Scouts, all dehydrated in the extreme heat and spread along the trail for miles, had to be medically evacuated. All of this may sound bad, but it gets even worse.

Coconino County Detective Sergeant Kathy Palaski was assigned to this investigation. She found, from inside Guy Davis' pack, a manuscript written for, but never submitted to *Backpacker Magazine* (dated May 23, 1993) by Bradley W. Pace, son of Loren Pace. This 10-page article describes a September 1991 trail-less trek that Brad and Loren Pace and others made from Saddle Mountain Pass to Little Nankoweap. Pace described a "chute," the traverse of which took twice as long as expected. Two hikers along were injured, one with a broken ankle, the other with a dislocated shoulder. The group ran short of water due to the injuries and had to carve out hollows on the 45-degree slope and then line them with rocks to bivouac so they would not fall into the abyss during the night. They hiked for 17 hours and covered only 10 miles of the 25 they needed to when they ran out of water. They lowered their packs with ropes. They stumbled and they staggered. Loren Pace and others gave up, letting the others go ahead for water. Brad Pace and another hiker made it to the river. When they returned with water, Loren Pace and another man, Ron, were in delusional states. It took Loren Pace, Brad wrote, two more days of recuperation just to begin hiking down to the river. All of this mayhem, moreover, happened during the much cooler month of September.

Loren Pace explained that his son had used literary license in this unsubmitted article, combining events from more than one trip to embellish it. He also said that on this 1996 trip the boys were "like mice" running ahead and spreading out. He also insisted that he never expected or asked the boys to get water and bring it back to him.

One can conclude many lessons from this tragic hike—and we have. But one of the burning conclusions and questions which haunts us is: What might have happened had all eight hikers made it to the river without deaths or rescues and then recuperated? How many of them would have made it back *out*, *up* the much tougher uphill climb with only two gallons of water and under a blazing June sun, alive?

Tragedies from failing to heed, through ignorant denial, the Canyon's obvious forces of nature come in all nuances. The most tragic, however, are, as in the above incident, when children die needlessly in the charge of adults who ought to know better. While it is true that every year in Grand Canyon thousands of hikers experience symptoms of heat injuries, in 1996 alone, six or seven of them independently died from heat. Each of these deaths could have been prevented.

Only a month after the well-publicized tragic death of David B. Phillips to dehydration and heat stroke, the Grim family traveled from Ohio to Arizona for their semiannual hike into the Canyon. Among their eleven members was 10-year-old Phillip. His grandmother had organized and was leading this visit, which she had decided would be during July solely because this was the only open date she could reserve for a camping spot at Bright Angel Campground. Phillip's mother felt very apprehensive about it, however, because not only was this Phillip's first plane ride, it was also his very first hike in the Canyon. In reality, only a few members of the Grim family had ever hiked in the Canyon at all, and none during a month of peak heat.

Like most ten-year-old boys, Phillip Grim seemed oblivious to his mother's worries and instead felt very excited about hiking into the Canyon from the South Rim and out via the North Kaibab Trail to the North Rim, where his mother would be waiting to meet him the next day. Phillip and the several other hiking Grims started down South Kaibab Trail toward Phantom Ranch at about 10 a.m., an exceptionally late start by anyone's book, and a deadly time in July. Adding bad luck to bad planning, this day, July 23, would turn out to be the hottest day of the year.

Consumed with excitement, Phillip started down by skipping and half running down the trail. He paid little attention to the water he carried in his backpack. Less than an hour into the hike, at Cedar Ridge, the hikers encountered NPS Ranger Peggy Kolar, who cautioned them for thirty minutes about the dangers of heat and the need to drink lots of water. Assessing these hikers against the extreme heat of this day, Ranger Kolar suggested strongly that they cancel their hike and return to the South Rim. The Grims chose not to.

The group fissioned into faster and slower hikers. Phillip, the fastest, paired off with his 50-something great uncle. Phillip complained that his backpack was uncomfortable. His great uncle offered to carry it—and the water it contained—

for him. By the half way point down, Phillip looked slightly fatigued and complained of feeling tired. But his great uncle felt no concern because Phillip still was running ahead. Nor did Phillip ask for his water very often—possibly because the more-than-blood-warm fluid seemed unappetizing to an Eastern boy.

As the two hikers neared the bottom, mid-afternoon thermometers in the Inner Gorge hit 116 degrees in the shade. By now several Grims of various ages had scattered themselves over two miles. Shadeless miles. Phillip's grandmother and great aunt already were suffering severely from heat exhaustion on the trail well uphill from little Phillip.

Finally seeing the river so close, Phillip ran down to the Kaibab Bridge (a.k.a. the "Black" Bridge). Then he crossed it over the Colorado to the north side. Once there, he meandered along the gravel and sand trail against the cliff wall heading toward Bright Angel Creek. The heat was suffocating.

Abruptly, as the Kaibab Trail now failed for the first time to take him any closer to the river, Phillip likely felt psychologically defeated as well as exhausted. He sat down within a couple of hundred feet of Bright Angel Creek but unfortunately still out of view of it. His great uncle caught up with him. But he walked past Phillip saying something like, "Come on, we need to keep going." Leaving Phillip sitting alone and heat-exhausted in the hot sun, his great uncle walked a few hundred yards farther to Phantom Ranch.

Minutes later Phillip stood up and tried to walk. He collapsed face down on the trail. Some hikers found him. Alarmed, they quickly notified the closest NPS ranger. NPS Maintenance Technician Frank Corey and Ranger Marty Johnson arrived at Phillip minutes later.

Phillip, they found, was unresponsive to all stimuli. Phillip's eyes were open but glazed and covered with sand. His pulse was very weak. His breathing had ceased altogether.

The two started CPR and radioed for help. They also tried to cool Phillip with water—his rectal temperature now exceeded 106 degrees.

Meanwhile Phillip's great uncle had continued to Phantom Ranch, mixed up some Gatorade and had then returned to fetch Phillip. When he arrived, Phillip was in the throes of death to dehydration and heat stroke.

NPS rangers, Paramedic Nancy Mecham, I-EMT Ken Phillips, and EMT Bil Vandergraff arrived and performed advanced resuscitation efforts on Phillip for over an hour.

After a helicopter evacuation, the Grand Canyon Clinic staff, including myself (Myers) and my colleague, Dr. Jim Wurgler, continued resuscitative efforts on Phillip. Nothing worked. It was hopeless. Eventually we had to pronounce him dead. It was one of the most heart-rending and saddest moments of my medical career. And not just mine. There was not a dry eye in the clinic.

Still on the South Kaibab Trail, Phillip's grandmother and great aunt—experiencing severe heat problems themselves—saw the helicopter carrying Phillip to the South Rim Clinic. They had no idea, of course, that it was transporting Phillip. Minutes later and about a quarter mile above the Black Bridge, one of these two women also plunged into full-blown heat stroke.

At roughly this same moment another hiker reached Phantom Ranch and reported that he had passed two women who seemed to be in severe heat distress. Rangers Bil Vandergraff and Matt Vandzura found both women. Phillip's grandmother looked so far gone to Vandergraff that he felt compelled to tell her, "Ma'am, I need you to drop your pants to take your temperature."

Vandergraff rolled the older woman on her side and inserted his thermometer in her rectum. Her core temperature read 105 degrees. This was, he realized, the last remaining moment in which it was still possible to save her life. Vandergraff and Vandzura cooled her down with water. Then they evacuated her by litter, hauling her by hand down the sun-blasted trail. They carried her across the Black Bridge and then down to the small flat pad for a helicopter evacuation.

About three hours after young Phillip died, the helicopter returned to emergency evacuate both older Grim women. They eventually learned about Phillip's death, and, at Grand Canyon Clinic, each woman was in psychological shock. Each was also a dehydrated "mess" verging on the same lethal heat stroke catastrophe as young Phillip.

At Grand Canyon Clinic we put both women on intravenous fluids immediately. And just in time. Another hour of delay in their evacuation could have meant one or even two more fatalities. The medically evacuated and emotionally devastated Grims joined the ranks of the 280 other Canyon hikers who got lost or who injured or killed themselves in 1996 and had to be rescued by NPS rangers. Two hundred of these hikers had to be helicoptered out of the Canyon. Eight of them, including poor Phillip Grim and David Phillips, emerged too late for anything but their own funeral.

Tragically and almost unbelievably, young Phillip Grim died of dehydration and heat stroke within a couple of hundred feet of Bright Angel Creek and of the Colorado River. A few more seconds of easy walking to either water source could have saved his life. But, then, so could having drunk the water that he, and then his great uncle, had carried.

TABLE 2.   ENVIRONMENTAL DEATHS WITHIN GRAND CANYON.

Name, age	Date	Location in Canyon	*Circumstances*

W. E. or F. R. Mendenhall adult.   1894   near Soap Creek Rapid (River Mile 11)
A not-quite identified body was found by John Schubert of Pathe'-Bray/Clyde Eddy expedition in Dec. 1927/Jan. 1928, along with mining equipment and letters dating from 1893/1894. Personal checks on body were from a bank in Moab, Utah.

Mystery Man, adult   March, 1900   Upper Granite Gorge about 300 feet above the river near River Mile 91, south
*Skeleton of a likely **solo hiker** found by prospectors Clarence C. Spaulding (an employee of Ralph Cameron) and Howard Noble in 1906. Skeleton was dressed in double layers of denim and an overcoat with mittens. No traumatic injury evident. Copies of* Los Angeles Times *and* San Francisco Examiner *dated March, 1900, were found in the overcoat pocket. Apparent **hypothemia/ exhaustion** scenario of tourist or hob-nail-booted prospector 2+ miles off the beaten track. (see text and cover photo)*

C. R. Moore, adult male   August 7, 1903   Bright Angel Trail 1 mile below rim
*Moore was a **solo hiker**/tourist from Kansas who collapsed during a rim-to-river-to-rim hike during his ascent in August heat. Likely **heat stroke**. Body was found later.*

Pat Donovan, adult male   March 1905   middle Grand Canyon
*Donovan, a **solo hiker** from Williams, vanished permanently.*

Arthur Clarence "Jack" Anderson, 19   July 1, 1925   Bright Angel Trail
*Anderson, before hiking down the Bright Angel Trail to the Colorado, boasted that he was "going to make a new record" on the rim-to-river-to-rim hike of 18 miles. Anderson was stricken by heat near the river and overcome by **heat stroke**. He was carried up by "drag out," but developed a "pneumonia" type reaction and died while being evacuated by train. (see text)*

Casimar Pultorak, 22   February 9, 1939   Bright Angel Trail
*Pultorak and his friend Paul E. Des Jardins, 17, attempted a 1-day descent to river and ascent to rim. May or may not have been warned at outset that the 18 miles was over-ambitious. 2–3 feet of snow fell. Pultorak froze to death (**hypothermia**) in snow bank on trail. (see text)*

Wilson Taylor, 59 (a.k.a. "Necktie Willie")   June 6, 1956   near River Mile 44.5
*Willie had a known serious heart condition and suffered a **cardiac arrest** during the extreme heat of June. Willie's comrades wrapped him in a tarp and buried him on shore. (see text)*

Walter J. Mahany, 16   July 23, 1959   Tanner Trail, 1 mile from the river
*Mahany and his two companions left their hiking gear on the rim. He suffered **dehydration/heat stroke** at temperatures close to 120 degrees in shade. (see text, Chapter 1, part 2)*

Bennie Tohe, 72   June 23, 1960   Beamer Trail near River Mile 65, about two miles upstream of the Tanner Trail and only 25 yards from the Colorado River
*Tohe, a Navajo medicine man from the Chinle area, was **solo hiking** back from having visited the confluence of the Colorado and Little Colorado rivers on a private quest/pilgrimage (the confluence is a sacred area for Navajos, in part because it is a place to which Salt Lady sometimes returns). While well-hydrated and leaving firm footprints spaced at a healthy pace, Tohe died suddenly of **heat-related cardiac arrest** at a temperature of 114 degrees in the shade.*

Alfred Milton Hillyer, 33   January 27, 1964   Bright Angel Trail, 3 miles from Phantom Ranch
*Hillyer, during a **solo hiking** ascent in cold weather, died of **hypothermia**. His body was located in June 1966.*

Kirk Hanson, 16   June 10, 1966   South Kaibab Trail, 4.5 miles from Phantom Ranch
*Hanson suffered a massive **brain hemorrhage/heart failure** sustained while hiking with 84 other high school students from Sioux City, Iowa. Hanson's death was possibly spurred by **heat and dehydration**.*

Howard Mangas, 50   May 28, 1967   Bright Angel Trail
*Phoenix Boy Scout leader, Mangas, while hiking, suffered a **heat-related cardiac arrest.***

Harold Murray Keller, 38   June 5, 1967   Bright Angel Trail at Mile-and-a-Half House
*While hiking uphill in extreme heat, Keller suffered a **heat-related cardiac arrest.***

Elmer Watahomigie, 69   December 13, 1967   under ledge in tributary canyon of Cataract Canyon (Havasu)
*Watahomigie abandoned his pickup truck 7 miles away after it had run out of gas during an abnormally heavy snowstorm. Next, as a **solo hiker**, he took shelter in the Canyon, wrote a note, then died of **hypothermia**.*

Jon Herbert Freeler, 28   May 31, 1969   Tonto Trail, 7 miles from Grandview Point
*Freeler was hiking the Tonto with other people from the Los Angeles Sierra Club, three more of whom were affected by 110–112-degree heat and were air-evacuated out. Freeler complained of fatigue before collapsing. He died from **heat stroke**.*

Elmer Wallace Martin, 48   May 14, 1974   South Kaibab Trail
*Martin, a **solo hiker**, experienced a cardiac arrest upon his return toward the rim from below Cedar Ridge. Was found with one, 1-quart water bottle...**dehydration-related cardiac arrest.***

William Maxey, 60+   August 16, 1974   Phantom Ranch
*During hot weather, 110–112 degrees, Maxey, a 205-pound man, suffered a **cardiac arrest/heat stroke**.*

Frank Costa, 21   September 2, 1974   below Bridger Point, North Rim
*Costa and partner Edwin Heisel, 23, were descending a deer trail not far from main NPS trail to Thunder River/Tapeats Creek region. They abandoned their camping gear, and left notes explaining that they had run out of food and water and would try to descend to water. Heisel apparently fell off a 200-foot cliff during this attempted descent. Costa attempted re-ascent out of Canyon, died of **dehydration/heat stroke**. (see text, Chapter 1, part 2)*

Michael Irvin, 28   May 21, 1975   South Kaibab Trail below Cedar Ridge
*Hiking with companion during hot weather, Irvin complained of feeling ill. He died of **heat-related cardiac arrest**.*

Brad Riner, 22   October 1, 1975   head of Phantom Creek
*Riner was a **solo hiker** who, after a week on cross-country route, voluntarily jumped off a 30-vertical-foot drop. Died from impact, but was decision induced by **dehydration**? (see text)*

Raymond H. Daniel, 56   June 9, 1976   Bright Angel Trailhead below corral
*Daniel died of **cardiac arrest**, details unavailable.*

James H. Higgins, 19   July 12, 1977   Tonto Trail, 2 miles west of Plateau Point
*Higgins was a **solo hiker** who, during extreme heat, carried only 1 water bottle, a set of motorcycle tools, three pairs of motorcycle boots, canned food, etc. He died of **dehydration/heat stroke**. (see text)*

Enrico Cane, 65   April 4, 1978   Bright Angel Trail at rest house
*Cane suffered a **cardiac arrest**, details of activity unavailable.*

Reed Watahomigie, 60   December 26, 1978   below Yaki Point
*Watahomigie, a **solo hiker**, was last seen on Christmas Day, but not reported missing until January 22, 1979. He reportedly had been feeling sick and having respiratory trouble. On May 5, his remains were found on a ledge below point. Likely died of **exposure/hypothermia**.*

Renate Schroter, 22   August 8, 1980   North Kaibab Trail near Ribbon Falls
Schroter, a German woman, was hiking with a TrekAmerica guide from the North Rim to the Colorado River and back to the rim in one day during very hot weather. Carried only one water

bottle (1 liter?) and collapsed on ascent about two hours after noon. Her body temperature reached 105 degrees. She died of **heat stroke**.

Richard Carter Funai, 43   February 8, 1981   Kaibab Suspension Bridge
Funai suffered a **cardiac arrest** *after hiking the South Kaibab Trail with eight companions.*

Harold Forrest Gustavson, 31   April 12, 1981   Tanner Trail
Gustavson, who suffered from a thyroid condition and was on medication, was backpacking as a **solo hiker** *when he died of* **heat stroke**.

Ed L. Agnew, Jr., 50   July 24, 1981   River Mile 229/Travertine Canyon
Agnew was resting in the shade near the river after very little exertion, but in hot weather. At 10:30 a.m. Agnew was found dead of apparent **cardiac arrest**.

John L. Herr, 50   July 25, 1981   North Kaibab Trail
Herr hiked to Roaring Springs on an extremely hot day, died of **cardiac arrest/heat stroke**.

Forney M. Knox, 56   May 26, 1982   Bright Angel Trail
Knox hiked from rim to Plateau Point and back during the heat. He died of **heat-related hypertension/cardiac arrest**.

John E. Shakleford, 48   May 13, 1983   Bright Angel Trail at 2-mile corner
Shakleford started his hike from the rim to Plateau Point at 9:00 a.m. with little food or water. Was in apparent good health. Died of **cardiac arrest/heat stroke** *(?).*

Sheila Rowan, 26   June 4, 1984   Bright Angel Trail at Three-Mile House
Rowan attempted to hike from the rim to the river and back to the rim during summer heat. Rowan's body core temperature exceeded 106 degrees while climbing back uphill during late morning. Her three companions noted that she suddenly had leg cramps, acted disoriented, was breathing rapidly, and her lips turned blue. She suffered death from **heat stroke**.

Lee C. Stern, 62   September 4, 1984   Bright Angel Trail, 3 miles below rim
After a river trip, Stern was hiking up from the river and in the heat. He suffered a **cardiac arrest**.

Paul M. Christie, 58   May 26, 1985   Bright Angel Trail
Christie and his wife had hiked to the Inner Gorge and back. Victim consumed "extreme amounts of water" while hiking. Witnesses said Christie looked "ashen," and was complaining of leg cramps. He suffered a **cardiac arrest**.

Father David Andrew Casper Gensler, 45	August 12, 1986	south of Tonto Trail, east of Bright Angel Trail

*Gensler, a **solo hiker**, was reported as missing on August 8. Long after a major search, Gensler was found on October 4, 100 feet south of Tonto Trail with an empty water bottle. Died of apparent **dehydration/heat stroke**.*

Frank Crowe, 70s	April 29, 1987	Bright Angel Trail near Kolb Seep, ¾ mile from rim

*While hiking, Crowe suffered a **cardiac arrest**.*

Peter E. Pastor, 76	August 5, 1987	Bright Angel Trail

*While hiking, Pastor suffered a **cardiac arrest**.*

George L. Ortyer, 43	May 28, 1988	River Mile 234.5

*Ortyer collapsed on a beach in **presumed cardiac arrest**.*

Ian Hay, 39	August 23, 1988	South Kaibab Trail

*Hay hiked down the Bright Angel Trail from rim to river, then attempted ascent up South Kaibab Trail to rim. Collapsed 2.5 miles below rim of **cardiac arrest/heat stroke**.*

Ali Govindan, 27	July 2, 1989	South Kaibab Trail

*Govindan, in poor physical shape, hiked down the South Kaibab Trail at temperatures exceeding 100 degrees. Resting, he became irrational and violent, died of **heat stroke**.*

Carolyn Guerra, 61	October 10, 1989	Crystal Rapid (River Mile 98.3)

*Guerra suffered a **probable cardiac arrest/"natural causes"** on shore near Crystal Rapid during cool weather.*

Michelle Sutton, 15	May 9, 1990	North of Mt. Dellenbaugh

*Sutton was on a "program for troubled teens" trip run by Summit Quest, Inc. on its first wilderness trip. Sutton complained repeatedly of not feeling well. Group carried total of only two liters of water per person for multi-day trip. Sutton died of **dehydration/heat stroke**.*

Paul Stryker, 26	June 22, 1990	Tonto Trail/Cremation Canyon

*Stryker and his wife, Karen, from Pennsylvania, were making a 2-day hike during temperatures exceeding 100 degrees from Grandview to South Kaibab Trail and to the river. Planned 3 liters of water per day per person. Stopped at Cottonwood Creek to refill, but refused to drink pothole water due to polliwogs. Paul let Karen drink more water. Ran out of water at head of Cremation. Paul died of **dehydration/ heat stroke**. Karen hiked 1 hour to Phantom Ranch. (see text)*

Vernon Bollinger, 54	April 21, 1991	Bright Angel Trail

*While hiking, Bollinger suffered a **cardiac arrest**.*

George Fairchild, 42   September 3, 1991   Bright Angel Trail
*Attempting over-night rim-to-river-to-rim hike in 105-degree heat, Fairchild collapsed of **heat stroke** four miles into ascent.*

Jose Ordierez, 35   April 17, 1992   Bright Angel Trail
*Ordierez hiked from rim to Tonto Plateau. While returning back to rim, died of **cardiac arrest.***

Robert Kier, 62   September 11, 1993   North Kaibab Trail
*Kier hiked the North Kaibab during warm weather and died of **cardiac arrest.***

James Cumings, 47   February 14, 1994   Visitors Entrance, Highway 67
*Cumings had hiked the Canyon from South Rim to North Rim successfully, but, dressed inadequately, died of **hypothermia** at the top and was buried under three feet of snow.*

Gary Clausen, 47   March 24, 1994   Bright Angel Trail
*Clausen died of **cardiac arrest,** details unavailable.*

Roland F. Kruse, 54   May 27, 1994   River Mile 250
*Kruse complained of being hot while boating up Lake Mead. His left arm got numb, he got dizzy. He suffered a **cardiac arrest.***

Miloslav Hanacek, 66   June 10, 1995   Bright Angel Trail
*Hanacek, a Czeck citizen, hiked the Bright Angel 6 miles to Plateau Point. During re-ascent he collapsed during 110-degree heat. Died of **heat stroke/cardiac arrest.***

Larry Selander, 52   April 14, 1996   Beamer Trail
*Selander was hiking the Beamer Trail in the Furnace Flats area and died of **cardiac arrest.***

David Phillips, 15   June 6, 1996   Little Nankoweap Canyon
*Phillips was on a Boy Scout hike doing an "experts only" route, ill-prepared with less than half the water needed for safety in 111-degree heat, lacked NPS permit for route and date, died of **dehydration/heat stroke.** (see text)*

David Helmer Kruse, 57   June 14, 1996   North Kaibab Trail at Roaring Springs
*Kruse was attempting a 21-mile rim-to-rim hike during high heat; he died of **cardiac arrest/heat stroke** shortly after sunset.*

Janet Katson Comella, 57   July 1, 1996   Hermit Trail, 1 mile from the creek
*During severe hot weather, Comella, while hiking with her husband, died of **dehydration/heat stroke.***

Phillip Joseph Grim, 10   July 23, 1996   on trail near Bright Angel Creek/ Colorado River confluence
*Grim hiked down the S Kaibab Trail at temperatures of 116°F ahead of his uncle, who carried all the water. His uncle passed him, crossed the Kaibab Bridge without giving him water, but later returned with Gatorade. Grim, however, had already died of **heat stroke.** (see text)*

John Holforty, 43

September 8, 1996   Tonto Trail between Mineral & Red Canyon
*Holforty, who had "considerable Grand Canyon backcountry experience," died of possible **heat stroke** while hiking.*

Wesley S. Johnson, 63

October 16, 1996   Bright Angel Trail
*Johnson was hiking uphill from the river to rim after a river trip and died of **cardiac arrest** en route.*

James Ray Mansfield, 55

November 2, 1996   Tanner Trail
*Mansfield (a.k.a. "the ranger" for his love of the outdoors and who holds Pittsburg Steelers' record for the most consecutive games played [182 between 1964–76]) was troubled by a hurt ankle and lagged behind his son and a friend while descending the trail. He told them to go ahead and that he would catch up, or maybe even camp on the trail. When he failed to catch up, they returned in search of him the next morning. They found him collapsed on the trail still wearing his backpack. Mansfield, who had a family history of cardiac problems, had died of an unwitnessed **cardiac arrest.***

John Henry James, 55

October 11, 1997   North Kaibab Trail
*James was attempting a 21-mile rim-to-rim hike. He died two miles north of Phantom Ranch from a **cardiac arrest**.*

Mary Jane Beaver, 75

April 28, 1998   Havasu Canyon
*Beaver, a small but avid hiker from Phoenix on her fifth Havasu hike, collapsed in sudden death syndrome at the bridge over Havasu Creek about two miles upstream from Supai Village. Death was due to **cardiac arrest**.*

Thomas A. Pacewicz, 50

April 28, 1999   Bright Angel Trail
*Pacewicz, a client on an oar-rafting trip, was exiting a river trip from Phantom Ranch. He had hiked up then out to Plateau Point via Bright Angel Trail en route to the rim. He later collapsed above the 3-Mile Rest House of **cardiac arrest**.*

Nuria Serrat, 42

June 28, 1999   Tonto Trail, 0.8 mile west of Hermit Creek
*Serrat was a **solo female hiker** "experienced" in Grand Canyon. Carrying only 4, 1-liter water bottles (all of which were empty), she succumbed in 110-degree weather to **heat stroke**; her body was found the next day by another hiker less than one mile from the creek. (This was the third Inner Canyon heat stroke within one week; the other two victims—both males in their twenties hiking with companions—survived after medical evacuation.)*

Orda Seth Smedley, 48

February 6, 2000   Bright Angel Trail, 1.5 miles below Rim
*Smedley collapsed during return leg of 12.2-mile, rim-to-Plateau-Point-to-rim hike and died of apparent **cardiac arrest**.*

Paul Van Hoof, 47

June 2, 2000   Tonto Trail, 2 miles west of the South Bass, 1000 feet above River Mile 109.5
On Day #4 of a hot, exposed Inner Canyon hike planned for three days from the South Rim down the South Bass Trail (River Mile 108) to upper Royal Arch Creek (River Mile 116.5) and

*back to the South Bass Trail and up, Van Hoof's three other Belgian hiking partners said they had difficulty finding water. Van Hoof drank some water but rationed it during temperatures exceeding 108 degrees in the shade. Van Hoof, stumbling along in full sun, dropped dead in **sudden death syndrome, cardiac related, but triggered by heat exhaustion, dehydration, and likely electrolyte imbalance**. Van Hoof's companion had hiked ahead of him to the river at Mile 108 but refused to acknowledge waves and greetings from a river trip (Ghiglieri's) who passed him. Two hours later at 4:30 p.m., he reluctantly spoke to a Diamond River trip run by Leslie Diamond. They radioed for an NPS helicopter. It reached Van Hoff at 4:47 p.m, finding him dead. Errors made included: failing to plan for the heat, to carry enough water and to recognize natural water as drinkable.*

The following entries are not included in text, statistics, or the index.

Andrianus Grootenboer, 62   October 16, 2000   Bright Angel Trail, Devil's Corkscrew
*On a day hike from the South Rim to the river at Pipe Creek, Grootenboer began experiencing chest pain while ascending back up the trail. He died during an NPS helicopter evacuation from a **cardiac arrest** upon landing at Flagstaff Medical Center.*

Douglas Isaia, 63   June 7, 2001   Phantom Ranch wrangler bunkhouse
Isaia died in his sleep to unknown cause(s).

John Rudolph Young, 68   December 5, 2002   Bright Angel Trail, 3/4 mile below rim
*Ascending from river to rim, victim collapsed from **cardiac arrest**.*

John Fawcett, 65   May 23, 2003   Bright Angel Trail, below Jacob's Ladder
*On a hot rim-to-river-to-rim day hike, Fawcett collapsed and died due to **cardiac arrest**.*

Elma Hickman, 74   May 28, 2003   Phantom Ranch cabin
After a mule ride, Hickman felt poorly and went to her cabin to lay down. She died in her bed from apparent natural causes.

Margaret L. Bradley, 24   July 9, 2004   Cremation Creek
*On July 8, Bradley, a U of Chicago medical student and gifted all-America runner, with the help of a friend, "Ryan," attempted a marathon-length run via the Grandview, Tonto, and S Kaibab trails during weather that hit 105–110°F. They started late, at 9:00 a.m. with Bradley carrying a puny 1.5 liters of water and no map. By 3:00 p.m., 12 miles into their planned 27, Ryan drank his gallon and, overheated, he shaded-up under a bush for 14 hours. Bradley ran on alone for help. Dehydrated, she short-cutted as the Strykers had done, off the Tonto Trail 1 mile from the Kaibab Trail and descended 300 feet down Cremation Creek. She downclimbed a 20-foot dry waterfall and trapped herself above a 50-footer, 500 feet above the Colorado. 12 hours after Bradley's partner had reached a USGS worker with a sat phone, but had neither reported Bradley to the Park, nor inquired as to her situation, sadly she died of "**dehydration due to heat exposure**."*

Joseph Roitz, 45

June 30, 2005   North Kaibab Trail, 2 miles below Rim
*Roitz and Boy Scouts were day hiking up from Cottonwood Campground. Five miles up from there he collapsed of **cardiac arrest**.*

Avik Chakravarty, 28

July 13, 2005   Devil's Corkscrew, Bright Angel Trail
*Chakravarty from England and a partner descended the South Kaibab on a planned rim-to-river-to-rim hike. An NPS ranger advised the pair to wait until evening before hiking back up. Instead the two began in mid-afternoon at about 113 degrees in the shade. Chakravarty died of **heat stroke** after 3 miles in an area in which, 2 hours later (6 p.m.), the temperature read 120°F.*

Darlene Duffington, 66

February 1, 2006   Bright Angel Trail, Devil's Corkscrew
*While riding a mule down to Phantom Ranch, Duffington of South Dakota became dizzy. She soon died of a **miocardial infarction**.*

Richard Howard, 53

June 18, 2006   Escalante Trail (aka "River Trail") RM 75
*While trekking west from the Tanner Trail on day #2 of backpacking with his stepson, Howard of Yuma, Arizona collapsed and died of **heat stroke** 600 yards from the Colorado in Escalante Drainage.*

Thomas J. Nisson, 70

August 14, 2006   Coconino Switchbacks, Bright Angel Trail
*During late morning, while on a Geo Cache hunt using GPS coordinates, Nisson of Palm Bay, Florida died 1/4 mile from the rim of **cardiac arrest** while hiking up from 1 1/2 Mile House.*

April Goode, 56

May 17, 2007   junction of Tonto Trail with Ruby Canyon
*Backpacking with five others, Goode faltered. Three hikers stayed with her, two hiked to contact a river trip with a satellite phone. **Heat related** death.*

Donald Keyes, 67

May 19, 2007   Saddle Canyon Narrows
*With "a history of heart trouble," Keyes was hiking on a commercial river trip and suffered a sudden **cardial arrest**.*

Chapter Three

"Flash Flood!"

"It's great to be back...." Roger Clubb, Sr., thought as he gazed into the Canyon after such a lengthy absence. Eighteen years had passed since 1945, when, at age 18, Roger and his father had climbed Wotan's Throne and Vishnu Temple together. These had been serious ascents, not mere plods along the Bright Angel Trail. The Inner Canyon had not only been the scene of some of the earliest triumphs of Roger's life, it was also a place of fond memories of having made these triumphs with his father, Merrel D. Clubb, Sr., doyen Canyon explorer and mentor to the likes of the legendary Harvey Butchart. Small wonder then that Roger Clubb, Sr., now age 36, would return to the Canyon and bring his own son, Roger, Jr, age 8, for his introduction to the most astounding mosaic of landscapes on this planet.

Leaving his wife, Jean, and four-year-old son, Eddie, on the rim in El Tovar, Roger, Sr., took Roger, Jr. down the Bright Angel Trail to Indian Garden. This was more than 3,000 feet below the South Rim and about halfway to the river. It was August 3, 1963. Monsoon season.

The still young veteran of Wotan's Throne and Vishnu Temple and his impressed young son made it to Indian Garden okay. Then the rain fell. As it typically does during the monsoons, it pounded down hard and fast. Nearly an inch and a half fell on the elevations above them.

Upstream of Indian Garden, in the Garden Creek drainage, much of this water funneled and cascaded in a gathering flood racing and tumbling down toward the normally peaceful oasis once farmed here by the Havasupai (until Teddy Roosevelt arrived and personally told them that the U.S. had made it a national monument for all Americans and now they would have to leave). Meanwhile several hikers, the Clubbs among them, took refuge from the rain

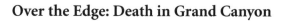
under the giant cottonwoods of Indian Garden. No one, it seems, was imagining that the canyon above them was funneling a new river of mud, boulders, and desert vegetation in a semi-liquid monster soon to explode upon them. If anyone did imagine it, apparently no one voiced his suspicions.

The rain stopped. So, after eating lunch, father and son headed back up the trail from the Garden. This trail is one of the safer looking places in the Canyon. Deceptively so. About 400 yards up the Bright Angel Trail, Roger, Sr., heard the roar.

The deep rumble presaged the arrival of the debris flow by several seconds. Clubb saw that they would have time to rush to a safe high point on the canyon slope. As he turned to hurry his son, he saw to his horror that the boy was missing. Where was young Roger?

As a ten-foot wall of water and mud exploded into view from the canyon immediately upstream, Clubb saw that his young son had lagged dozens of yards downstream—in the path of the tumbling flood.

Forsaking the close, easy route to safety, Roger, Sr., made a mad dash downstream to scoop up his son before the flash flood hit. Other hikers who witnessed his desperate race against disaster reported that, although he was running as wildly as any human being could, he never made it.

The tumbling wall of slurry engulfed Roger Clubb, Sr. and then his son with supreme indifference. The two vanished in a flash of mud before the horrified gazes of the hikers who had fled safely upslope.

Searchers later found the faithful father's body about 400 yards downstream, nearly buried by debris. Five days later, after a second, much smaller flood had eroded some of the debris deposited by the first flood, searchers found little Roger, Jr., too, only about 100 yards downstream of where his father had been found.

Roger, Sr.'s brother, Merrel Clubb, Jr., flew in from Montana to assist. Later, Merrel Clubb, Sr. considered the question of what sort of memorial might be fitting to commemorate the tragic deaths of the accomplished explorer and his young son. No manmade memorial would be appropriate, he said, "After all, the Canyon is their monument."

Among the most notorious of dangers of the American Southwest, second perhaps only to dying of thirst, is its opposite: being swept into oblivion by a flash flood. The alleged danger of flash floods here is not a product of media hype or a plot device of Zane Grey potboilers, it is instead a genuine meteorological phenomenon peculiar to the geography of this region and caused by a nearly unique constellation of geographical features.

First, the northern and eastern portions of Arizona sit at relatively high elevations. The North Rim of Grand Canyon, for example, lies at 8,000–9,000 feet elevation and is part of the huge Colorado Plateau, the world's second largest and highest plateau after that of Tibet. Plateaus such as these, it is now known, actually create their own weather.

Second, the American Southwest lies in the northward monsoon "migration route" of storms, especially hurricanes, in the Gulf of Mexico and sometimes the Gulf of California during the height of summer. Prevailing winds from the ocean begin around mid-July to blow north, carrying moisture-bearing fronts onto the Colorado Plateau. As these wet masses of air are forced ever higher above sea level by the rise of topography, they cool. When they cool sufficiently to hit their dew points, they drop their moisture as rain or hail, both often violent, abrupt, and copious.

Third—and the most difficult for newcomers to believe—many of these abrupt, violent, and copious storms form and persist in very localized regions. It may rain a quick inch, for example, in one drainage, or even rain several inches for hours of downpouring, yet eight to ten miles away a similar drainage may receive virtually no measurable precipitation.

The fourth and final element in the formula for flash floods is their being paradoxically exacerbated by lack of water. The high elevations which cause these violent storms experience two or three very dry months prior to the monsoons. Hence much of the Canyon region consists mostly of desert that receives an average of less than ten inches of precipitation per year and thus lacks the soil-retaining forests and grasslands that elsewhere suck up rain like a sponge. When rain falls in canyon country, only a little is absorbed by soil. Often no soil even exists over vast areas (again due to the violence and infrequency of the rains themselves), only bare rock. All the rest of that violent rain here hits, splashes, and obeys the dictates of gravity to flow downhill.

In canyon country these flows funnel down canyons. Indeed not only do the famous "slot" canyons of the Southwest act as charmingly narrow funnels for these violent storms, these canyons are themselves the stone children of these storms. Perhaps the easiest way to visualize the power of these watery sculptors of the Southwest's stunning canyons is to imagine just how much water, carrying how much silt, sand, rocks, and boulders up to and bigger than the family sport utility vehicle, would be necessary to whack out one of these canyons from solid bedrock. Contrary to popular belief, these canyons were not carved a micromillimeter at a time by the slow passage of small streams of water in a sort of geological Chinese water torture in accordance with Lyell's *"Principle of Uniformitarianism"* in his famous *Principles of Geology* of the 19th century. While many canyons are *polished* in this gentle, insistent way, they were more often *carved* brutally and catastrophically by the corrasive power of rare but massive debris flows/flash floods which often contained more rock than water. Canyon country is by its very existence a warning sign that violent processes have been at work. Add a few clouds to the scene and this warning sign changes tenses to become "violent canyon carving now at work."

Knowing this alone can save your life. Do not hike narrow canyons during monsoonal weather (July through September) or during any other times of potentially rainy weather. Grand Canyon and its tributaries are nothing more than giant conduits for storm run-off. That walking the floor of a storm drain during a storm is playing Russian roulette should be obvious. What makes it less than obvious to many people (and victims) is the storm itself may be miles away, and the sky above may be blue flecked with cute white cotton balls that look like dragons, Aunt Martha, or atom bomb tests.

All of this is pretty simple, and we apologize if we are being too elementary in spelling it out. But a surprising number of nature-lovers have failed to understand this aspect of nature in the Southwest and have ended up as nature's fertilizer because of it.

One of the more recent episodes made the front page coast-to-coast. It occurred in Antelope Canyon, 20+ miles upstream of Lees Ferry and east of Page and of Grand Canyon. This example does not enter into our analysis of Grand Canyon fatalities. We include it here, however, because it offers a perfect illustration of local flash flood dynamics—and life-saving lessons.

Antelope is a six-mile long slot canyon that "ends" in Lake Powell (were the reservoir not present, Antelope Canyon would be walkable for miles farther into Glen Canyon to the Colorado River). It is one of 96 named tributaries in Glen Canyon. Because this classic, sinuous "slot" canyon carved through the Navajo Sandstone and polished to a sensuous smoothness is the closest classic one to Page, it is a seductive local tourist attraction.

On August 12, 1997, an unusually violent El Niño year, during the height of the monsoons, Ken Young, concessionaire for the Antelope Canyon Tribal Park, rescued a man. He found 28-year-old Pancho Quintana clinging to a rock at the bottom of the canyon. Quintana was battered, bruised, scratched, and stark naked. He had lost his shoes and every stitch he was wearing in a flash flood.

Quintana had also lost his grip on two of the people he had been escorting down this beautiful canyon of death.

He had been leading a tour from a Los Angeles-based company named TrekAmerica. Quintana's tour group that day included four men and a woman, three from France and one each from Britain and Sweden. Along with this group, six other people had been hiking in Antelope Canyon. These included five from France and a man from New York.

That day rain fell about 15 miles southeast of Page on the Kaibito Plateau about 2,000 feet above the canyon. Yet while the town itself and the six-mile slot of Antelope Canyon received only trace rain, storms were visible from Page in the distance. The storm on the plateau was no freak event. Instead it was "not terribly unusual—your garden variety summer storm," noted Frank Richards, head of the Hydrologic Information Center at the National Weather Service Headquarters in Silver Spring, Maryland.

Pancho Quintana was a hired guide, but the Los Angeles welder had not been one for long. This was his third TrekAmerica trip; he was leading it after

21 days of company training. This training did not include specific operating procedures for monsoon storms: "We don't specifically define what a thunderstorm is," said TrekAmerica personnel manager Jack Aakhus. Quintana took his five clients into Antelope Canyon not only while the entire widespread region was under warning for extreme thunderstorms—but also on the very next day after a headlined mass evacuation of 100 tourists and residents of nearby Supai, in Grand Canyon, due to a massive flash flood there generated by a very quick 3 to 4 inches of rain on the Coconino Plateau (discussed later in this chapter).

After hiking for a while in Antelope Canyon, where a ten-foot-width is considered wide, Quintana told his five clients that it was time to climb out. He then climbed out of the 80-foot deep canyon and yelled back down at them.

No one, he told police, followed him.

Instead, a French couple still in the canyon bottom agreed to leave but said that first they wanted him to come back down and take their photograph in the narrow slot. Quintana (who refused to grant a press interview) actually did climb back down to take their photo. As he reached the bottom, a ten-foot high, chocolate-colored wall of water, mud, logs, cacti, cow manure, and other desert debris slammed down the canyon like a sewer from hell.

Quintana and his five clients heard the roar and looked up. They tried to outrun the rushing wall by scampering downstream. Seconds later the wall of semi-liquid debris slammed into them. They struggled to capture an eddy, but the flood kept increasing its intensity. One by one Quintana's clients vanished downstream and under the mud. Quintana got a grip on one or two of his clients, he said, but the flash flood ripped them both loose from his grip.

After Ken Young rescued Quintana, a helicopter flew over the canyon searching for more survivors or bodies. They found one body. A week of searching by dog teams and SCUBA divers finally unearthed eight other victims. Even after a year of deeper searches armed with ultrasound equipment, the final two victims of the eleven killed have not been found.

A major take-home lesson in all this was that these hideous deaths occurred despite the Navajo concessionaires (Antelope Canyon is in the Navajo Nation and received 20,000 visitors in 1996 alone) at the head of Lower Antelope Canyon having warned the victims emphatically that, due to monsoonal storms, it was a not a safe time to enter the slot canyon. The dozen people, nearly all of whom had traveled a long distance to see the Southwest, entered regardless.

"It's really hard," explains Effie Yazzie, office manager for the Navajo Nation agency responsible for canyon tours, "to get through, especially to people who are not from this area. They have no concept of what it's like to be in a flash flood."

The conditions under which Quintana's five clients died were questionable enough for Coconino County to review the episode for possible gross negligence or manslaughter charges. "In my mind, it's clear cut as to the criminal aspect of the case," County Attorney Terry Hance concluded, dismissing criminal culpability. "Whether there is a civil liability or not will rest in another venue."

Surviving members of five of the victims' families have filed suit against TrekAmerica in the U.S. District Court in Phoenix.

Was this tragedy simply bad luck? Fate? Or an act of God? That none of the eleven victims included residents of any of the Southwestern states may be only the result of chance, but likely not. In short, knowledge and understanding of how slot canyons were formed and are still being enlarged are far better to possess in advance of a flash flood than is having one's surviving relatives file a suit afterward. And while education and publicity do help save lives, common sense is the last and surest defense against flash flood fatalities.

Just a few weeks after this extremely well-publicized tragedy at Antelope Canyon, for example, on September 11, 1997, three people—John and Patty Moran, age 40, and John McCue, age 36, (Patty's younger brother)—from Metaire, Louisiana, repeated Pancho Quintana's error. The trio had hiked up Bright Angel Creek during a very light, almost unmeasurable scattering of rain. Less than two miles from the river they veered off trail into Phantom Creek. Phantom, 15 to 50 feet wide, is a narrower, steeper tributary canyon of Bright Angel.

Meanwhile, on the nearby North Rim at the head of Phantom Creek Canyon less than ten miles away, a spin-off of Hurricane Linda dropped about two inches of rain in thunder showers. Just two days earlier, similar monsoonal storms had sent an eight-foot wall of water down this same canyon—after ripping through Haunted Canyon higher up—from nearly two inches of rain that had fallen then on the North Rim.

Phantom Creek, the three hikers were finding, was an amazing canyon. As deep as something in a Tolkien fantasy, it seemed like a different world. A different planet even. The hikers walked upstream in awe. Roughly a half mile upstream of the Bright Angel/Phantom Creek confluence, McCue helped his older sister across the creek to see a pretty waterfall ahead. This idyll was shattered by Patty's sudden scream: "Water!"

Instead of water, McCue would later explain, it was a "thick, dark, red mud." And rather than claw their way up one or the other of the 70-degree walls to attain higher ground, the trio huddled for safety on the downstream side of a boulder in the middle of the canyon bottom. Within about fifteen seconds, the five-foot high wall of water and debris careened and cascaded along the canyon floor to the trio's sanctuary. It instantly filled with violent water and obliterated the imaginary safety zone in which the three had huddled. This flood then blew all three hikers into the mainstream of mud cascading and roaring downcanyon.

This flood peaked at only chin deep—but, again, it was fast and violent and dense. As McCue felt himself tumbling out of control in the nightmare flood, he remembered some of the life-saving lessons he'd had. He now fought for his life by swimming with all of his might. The flood swept McCue about half a mile downstream before he was able to haul himself out, abraded and covered in mud, on shore along Bright Angel Creek. He painfully crawled out of the slurry like some desperate primeval amphibian caught in a prehistoric cataclysm. On solid rock again, he coughed up mud.

As a traumatized McCue struggled down the edge of Bright Angel Creek, he cried rust-colored tears from mud-caked eyelids. Search as he might for his sister or brother-in-law, they were nowhere to be found. Eventually a frantic and crying McCue found NPS Ranger Bryan Wisher, who then duplicated McCue's unsuccessful search.

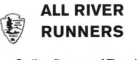

ALL RIVER RUNNERS

On the afternoon of Thursday, September 11, a flash flood occurred in Phantom and Bright Angel Creeks. This event swept two adults, one male and one female, down Bright Angel Creek. Neither of these victims could swim, and it is possible they were carried into the Colorado. Please be aware of this situation and be on the lookout for any evidence of the victims in eddies below Phantom Ranch.

The Morans had both drowned. The implacable flood carried their bodies down into Bright Angel Creek, then into the Colorado, and then miles downstream. Despite intensive searching by thirty searchers and dozens of river runners, the Morans' bodies were only discovered one and three weeks later, 30 and 46 miles downstream, by river trips.

Knowing when to and when not to hike in slot canyons is vital. I (Myers), with several years of inner Canyon off-route and remote hiking experience, had solo-hiked through the entire five-mile drainage of Phantom Creek on September 10, less than 24 hours before the Morans were killed—thereby "splitting" both flash floods. Coming off the North Rim at Tiyo Point, I had climbed Shiva Temple before dropping into the narrows of Phantom Creek. From these vantage points—as opposed to being within the blind confines of

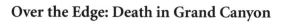

Phantom Creek—I saw no significant monsoon activity within fifty miles. Even so, flash floods weighed heavily on my mind. But what were the odds of two flash floods happening in the same drainage out of the hundreds in this neighborhood, I asked myself, on two days in a row? Low, very low, I kept telling myself. Had there been any active rain visible, though, I would have waited until it cleared or else I would have avoided the drainage altogether and detoured it by traversing along the slopes to the dry-land Banzai Route to Phantom Ranch. But from the extremely constrained view the Morans had had in the bottom of Phantom Creek, they had possessed no way to visually check against the possibility of distant rain. Instead they had gambled blindly, perhaps even unknowingly. And lost when an in-season flood had killed them.

When I reached the river after my hike, I joined a river trip run by OARS, Inc. and led by my co-author, Ghiglieri. Within two days our entire trip was put on alert by commercial motor rigs that had passed Phantom Ranch twenty-four hours after our rendezvous. The alert? Watch the river and the eddies for bodies: two people had drowned in Phantom Creek the day after I had hiked it. This sad news and this grim duty pounded home to us yet again how important it would be to do what we could to *prevent* these sorts of tragedies—rather than simply search eddies for corpses. For me personally, having hiked Phantom Creek only a day before the Morans, this tragedy was a sobering experience. Two flash floods in three days....

These two fatalities were so glaringly "in-season" (like those in Antelope Canyon a few weeks earlier), that the National Park felt obligated to conduct a criminal investigation of the Morans' demise. A post-disaster interview with John McCue conducted by NPS criminal investigator Franco Sidoti revealed: 1. McCue was acting as "trip leader" because he had been in Grand Canyon a few years earlier and thus "knew" it; 2. McCue also knew about the danger of flash floods in small canyons; 3. he had heard about the mass death episode in Antelope Canyon only a few weeks earlier; and 4. it was his idea to hike up the narrows of Phantom Creek on this occasion.

The investigator concluded that no criminal intent was involved.

As we have seen, being hit by a flash flood "coming out of the blue" is a hideous way to die. Its opposite, actually knowing that a flash flood is on the way, however, can produce some amazingly positive results.

Consider, for example, the outcome of Papillion Helicopters pilot Michael Moore's flight down Havasu Canyon on August 10, 1997 (two days before the Antelope Canyon disaster). While making a routine flight into Havasu, Moore had seen a flash flood ripping down Havasu Canyon from its upper reaches. Moore knew that dozens of unsuspecting tourists were frolicking in the blue-green waters downstream. Moore veered his machine down the canyon. Flying at an illegal altitude, Moore searched for people and warned them from the air to seek high ground.

Things were going well. Everyone whom Moore had tried to warn had understood his hand-signaling to run for high ground. But when, miles downstream, Moore hovered above 23-year-old Elizabeth Nemeth and her companion, both from Tennessee, the two young women could not figure out what the pilot wanted. Nemeth and her friend were part of a group of private river runners who had scattered themselves along lower Havasu Creek that day for a big taste of Paradise. And this pilot, as friendly as he seemed, was not really improving their experience. In fact, he was becoming irritating.

Waving frantically with his hand, Moore again signaled the two women to get out of the creek where they had been swimming and to go uphill. Initially thinking that this friendly pilot from nowhere was just waving hello, they waved back. Pleasantly—even if he was irritating.

But because Moore persisted in waving them out with ever more exaggerated gesticulations, the two young women reluctantly left the creek. Seeing this, and knowing that the wall of mud upstream was now that much closer to yet more people downstream, Moore sped downcanyon to try to save yet more lives.

Once Moore's noisy machine had whomp-whomp-whomped downstream, however, and everything looked as calm as before, Elizabeth Nemeth ventured back down into the creek and its pleasantly gurgling blue-green flow.

Her companion, perhaps more impressed with Moore's gesticulations, stayed on high ground. Seconds later she heard a thunderous roar. She looked upstream. To her horror, the red wall of a flash flood was bearing down from upstream like something from a computer-enhanced disaster movie.

She screamed at Nemeth to get out of the water. Nemeth, however, could not understand her screams over the noise of the creek. Nemeth turned her head to try to hear her companion's yells better. As she turned, a 6-foot-high wall of mud, water and debris slammed into her. It tumbled and somersaulted her as just one more piece of debris in the "desert batter" of logs, rocks, and liquid mud. Nemeth felt herself career helplessly into boulders and over them as she accelerated down Havasu Creek.

Finally, several hundred yards downstream, a log pinned her against a boulder. Luckily, and this fluke saved her life, the cresting current pushed her even higher up onto this sloping rock. She clung to it with a death grip. And she kept on clinging to it for several minutes until the flood receded a bit.

Nemeth was air-lifted to Grand Canyon Clinic. There, I (Myers), found her severely bruised and battered and with a broken nose. It seemed a near miracle that she was otherwise unharmed. Strangely, despite her near brush with death and despite not having heeded Moore in his risky race against the flood to warn potential victims in time to save them and despite Nemeth owing her life only to the shape of a lucky boulder upon which chance alone had thrust her, she seemed a lot less impressed with her survival than the Clinic staff was.

But Michael Moore's desperate warning flight down Havasu Canyon was not over yet....

Downstream, the mouth of Havasu looked like a typical summer traffic jam. For river guides, the apparently dry "holes" during the monsoons are tempting. After all, their emotional logic runs, we're here, and it doesn't look like rain, and some of my passengers may never be here again...let's hike it, at least a short way up. Again, this "lottery of death" mentality nudges people into decisions to hike slot canyons that later may seem a lot less smart.

As Moore had begun his race against death down Havasu from one group of hikers to the next, a commercial rowing trip run by Wilderness River Adventures had pulled into the mouth of Havasu Canyon. A few hundred yards downstream two other trips, motorized—Western River Expeditions and Wilderness River Adventures—had parked in the "motor" eddy in the main Colorado adjacent to low Muav Limestone ledges. A private river trip—Elizabeth Nemeth's—was also moored in the mouth of Havasu. All these boats had stacked up to be a garden variety traffic jam.

Those who scanned the sky upstream above Havasu that morning had seen only scattered clouds. "Okie," (a.k.a. Paul Jones) leading the Wilderness River Adventures trip, however, viewed those clouds with suspicion. He changed the trip's plan from a four-hour-plus hike to Beaver Falls and back to a more prudent one-hour hike to the nearer pools.

Later, a stay-behind Wilderness boatman, Tom Janecek, heard a strange sound as he lolled on his boat in the Mouth. It was a low frequency roar from up Havasu Canyon. Strangely, it sounded rhythmic. It grew louder.

As Janecek's personal alarm bells started ringing, he spotted a helicopter 100 feet above the floor of Havasu. He stared into the cockpit and saw:

> *a hand making a wave-like motion much like splashing water in a pool. I screamed over the chopper's roar along with four other boatmen, "FLASH FLOOD! EVERYBODY OUT!!! OUT, OUT, EVERYBODY OUT!! NOW!"*
>
> *It was mass confusion. Some people thought that we meant get on the boats to leave. Parents ran around looking for their children. One parent came up to me as I was screaming at her son, who was deep in the mouth of the pull-in spot, trying to get the vest that was blown into the water from the chopper. He finally heard the panic in our voices and left the life jacket in the water and ran across the boats.*

Once the Wilderness guides had evacuated the mouth safely, they tried to figure out whether they had time to rescue their boats. Was the chopper's warning a two-minute warning or instead maybe even a twenty-minute warning? "None of us," Janecek writes, "would commit to going into the mouth where there was no immediate escape route."

Even so, while wearing life jackets, they untied one boat and moved it 25 feet downstream into the Colorado, below the mouth.

While returning to move the second boat, "we heard the horrible sounds—absolutely terrifying...not of water, but of people way upstream screaming in terror and warning those downstream."

Okie and Janecek froze in the mouth of Havasu for about ten seconds listening to the screaming get even louder. Then it came, a beautiful, nearly six-foot-high wall of blue water with a 45-degree slope. It metamorphosed into a ten-foot high, nearly vertical wall of muddier water in the narrow mouth. Okie and Janecek had leaped to a high ledge. Below them the flash flood snapped all the remaining bowlines "like popcorn."

Eight boats in a vibrating mass of ropes, gyrating oars, and logs shot from the mouth into the river and under the still-hovering chopper.

Several guides hurried down to the Western rig at the lower pull-in to watch for victims shooting out of the mouth of Havasu. Every life jacket or piece of clothing popping to the surface caused at least one of their hearts to skip a beat.

As the guides at the mouth watched the river, people upstream enacted mini-scenes from a disaster movie. Not only had Elizabeth Nemeth been caught, then miraculously shoved atop her boulder, another woman as well had been caught in a pool when the flood hit. She was slammed in the ribs by a log and her halter top ripped off. A guide, Patrick, plucked her from the current. Another passenger, intent on "getting to high ground," climbed up and kept on climbing. He finally dead-ended on a narrow ledge on a sixty-foot cliff. There he froze in fear in a dangerously exposed position. Now, he found, he was unable to go up or down.

Matt Penrod, another guide, used climbing gear for protection to orchestrate a harrowing 90-minute rescue. He painfully helped this man descend thirty feet down the cliff to a place where a harness could then be used to get him down the other thirty feet to safe ground.

Many hours later and eight miles downstream, at Tuckup Canyon (River Mile 164.5), borderline chaos ruled during a monsoonal downpour. With assistance by the NPS, and with all the guides and passengers nearby working together, ninety people from the several trips visiting Havasu that day struggled, some in vain, to find their own gear, their own boats and guides, and to somehow get warm in the pounding storm. The "hole" had closed. The monsoon had become itself again. Multiple waterfalls plunged and roared off the Redwall rims surrounding the struggling knot of bedraggled humanity in awe-inspiring streamers and fountains into the inner gorge. Janecek noted that everyone was present and accounted for—and alive—due to the actions of one man:

> The chopper pilot, Michael Moore, had saved the day. His warning was all that was needed to get everyone to high ground. Apparently he saw the flood coming upstream, and broke some rules of radio

contact and flight zones, and went on the warning mission. You could easily argue that he saved a dozen lives that day.

All in all, the above incident was an almost picture-perfect example of how to "have" a flash flood at Havasu. Unfortunately, most episodes of flash floods are considerably less than perfect; they occur with no chopper pilot present to act as knight in shining armor.

On August 6, 1988, during the peak of yet another monsoon season and again at Havasu, the narrow, cliff-bordered mouth was again loaded with motor rigs. Tim Whitney and Richard Quartaroli were running a two-boat Arizona River Runners trip. Because it had rained lightly within a mile of Havasu as they had approached, and because the mouth was already some-what crowded with two Western River Expeditions motor rigs and two Wilderness River Adventures rigs, the two boatmen opted to moor their rigs in the lower "motor" eddy along the riverside. Quartaroli next decided to take a few people up to the very first crossing only. His plan was to allow them to see the aquamarine creek plunging picturesquely over the polished boulders and waterfalls between slick ledges and walls of Muav Limestone. Quartaroli had weighed the ominous signs in the sky and vetoed going farther upstream due to the risk of a flash flood.

"Okay, everybody, here it is," he informed everyone as they arrived at the first crossing of the Southwest's most famous blue-green waters, "This is as far as we go today."

After about ten minutes of oohing and aahing, Quartaroli announced that they all would now be heading back to the boats.

As Quartaroli walked back along the route bypassing the mouth—a three-minute walk—he detoured into the mouth to ask Carl McDonald and Mike Reyes, who were running the Wilderness trip tied up along side those two Western motor rigs, where they were planning to camp. As he stepped aboard and asked....

BOOM, the creek started to rise.

Pretty close timing, Quartaroli thought to himself, getting his folks out of the creek minutes before this thing hit....

Unbeknownst to Quartaroli, three of his and Whitney's passengers, a family from New York, were not as safely out of the creek as he thought. Katherine K. was a 110-pound marathon runner about fifty years old. She was traveling with her daughter and son-in-law. As the three had followed Quartaroli and their group up and out of the Havasu drainage moments ago, Katherine's son-in-law had decided that he had to have a photo of the three of them in the creek. So he called his wife and mother-in-law back. The trio had quietly turned around and re-entered Havasu. As with the tragic demise of Pancho Quintana's clients in Antelope Canyon, this flash flood hit the trio as they sought the perfect family photo.

The flood caught Katherine in mid-creek above the first crossing. The wall of water whipped her off her feet, flushed her downstream, swept her over both sets of falls, rolled her down the narrows, and spurted her out of the mouth.

The flood also took Katherine's daughter. But a fellow passenger grabbed her as she flushed past. Katherine' photo-bug son-in-law ended up trapped on a pair of trees in the middle of the flood. He was rescued later via a rope extraction.

Meanwhile Quartaroli spun around and leaped off the Western River Expeditions' boat to escape the flash flood. Behind him a two- or three-foot wall of red muddy water hit the mouth. Someone in the mouth saw a face in the muddy water. It shot out into the river.

McDonald tossed a life jacket into the water near the face. Both jacket and face vanished separately down the rapid.

Tim Whitney, downstream at the ledges in the motor eddy, was saying hello to small groups of his and Quartaroli's passengers as they reboarded the boats in twos and threes. He glanced upstream and saw the flash flood disgorge from the mouth. Both Western rigs shot out with it, still tied together bow to stern and spinning out of control. He saw Darrell (a.k.a. BamBam) scrambling to get his motor started to power the boats back to shore in Whitney's eddy.

As Whitney warned everyone on the boats to brace themselves and hold on against an impending collision, Whitney looked down into the roiling muddy water. A life jacket, floating loose, bobbed past. Then a face appeared. No body, not even hair—just eyes, nose, and a mouth open and desperately gasping for air.

This was decision time. But with no time to think. Whitney jumped off his large raft into the flood. He grabbed the body belonging to The Face. The woman (he only discovered her gender later) crawled all over him as if he were an island.

"Take it easy," he told her, "relax, breathe, I've got you...." In reality, Whitney's life jacket was not doing all that well holding both of their faces out of the water. Even so, he realized, they could float safely for miles if forced to.

Then, abruptly, his view was blocked. Ahead of him the two loose Western rigs slammed into the left wall and bent into a V. He heard Darrell's 30-horsepower motor screaming as he tried to power both rigs to shore via one motor.

Whitney grabbed with his free hand for a lifeline on the nearest Western boat. But he missed it. Instantly he and The Face vanished underneath the boat into the dark and the roar. From the front of boat number one to the stern of number two lay a potential underwater swim of seventy feet. This, Whitney knew, could be like being flushed down a seventy-foot storm drain with no air and toward a whirling propeller that could slice and dice him and The Face he was trying to rescue.

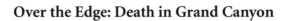

Meanwhile, as Whitney and The Face bumped along under the tubes of the boats, she throttled him by the neck in a death grip.

Worried now that The Face might kill him, Whitney pried her hands off his neck.

Poof, she was gone.

Oh, my God, Whitney thought as he reached out for her in the dark, turbulent flow and found nothing. Oh, my God. She's gone. Just hold your breath, he told himself. This can't last forever.

Finally, light brown water. Then air. "Well, that was the one chance you had, bucko," he rued to himself in despair. "You're never going to see *her* again."

The woman with the face popped up a few strokes away. She tried to catch a breath but sank too quickly. Following her under water, Whitney stroked hard then dived as best as his life jacket would allow. He grabbed her hair. Still underwater, he shifted her to a cross-body carry across the chest. When he surfaced again, he looked around.

Still grasping Katherine K. against himself, he now found himself caught between the two Western rigs and the cliff face. One of these boats—like the closing walls of the trash-compactor in the Death Star in *STAR WARS*—was about to crush him and his rescued woman against the Muav Limestone.

Whitney yelled up at Darrell, "Don't run me over!"

Darrell finally spotted Whitney. He pivoted the boat to place Whitney and the woman beside it. An adult male passenger tried to help the two up, but he fell off into the river. Now he too had to be rescued. At last a goggled-eyed thirteen-year-old boy hauled the woman with the face onto the boat.

Whitney now swam to the stern of the non-powered Western boat and hauled himself out. He struggled for a while before he managed to coax its Johnson into firing up.

What impressed Whitney most about this rescue was not that he had succeeded in saving Katherine's life against serious odds—to his mind, this is exactly what professional guides do. What really haunted him was that he had lost her under the boat. This reality recycled through his mind like a close-looped tape.

These two stories of successful rescues illustrate some important points about Canyon flash floods. First, Havasu—being the single most popular hike/stop for river trips in Grand Canyon—is fed by a huge drainage. While not as large as those of the Little Colorado River or Kanab or Diamond creeks, this drainage is huge. This means flash floods can, will, and do appear near the mouth with no warning at all from local rain. Indeed the source of the flood could be nearly forty miles south and be completely invisible to anyone in the Canyon. Second, the mouth is a dangerous place even when the creek is flowing as its charming, blue-green self. The mouth, circled by Muav cliffs and often with not even a shred of gravel beach exposed, feeds its swirling water directly into Havasu Rapid. So far no one without a life jacket has swum this alone and survived. Instead, at least three people have drowned here (see next chapter). More than in Lava Falls (again, next chapter).

The mouth is clearly an area where life jackets should be worn by anyone on the boats or in the water. Even the several other guides, AzRA's Dave Edwards for one, who have managed truly heroic rescues (episodes of which were not covered in this chapter due to space consideration) would have been useless or suicidal had they not been wearing life jackets. A further lesson here is flash floods appear with so little warning that, if the weather appears questionable, trip leaders are serving their fellow Canyoneers' best interests if they make the difficult and unpopular—but safe—decision to not hike Havasu Canyon at all but instead go find a safe replacement activity. Go play horseshoes or something. Or sit in a safe place and read Tony Hillerman.

It may only be the luck of the draw or instead a happy product of experience and skill, but none of the half million people who have run the river in boats (as of 2000 AD) has been killed by flash floods anywhere in the Canyon. A few have come very very close—some of their escapes being matters more of luck than intelligence—but, again, no fatalities of this sort have occurred to members of river trips. Sadly, and as we've seen, the same cannot be said of recreational hikers in the Canyon.

On August 24, 1992, U.S. Air Force Investigative personnel contacted Grand Canyon NPS rangers because two of their personnel were overdue in returning to Onizuka Air Force Base (the Consolidated Space Center in Sunnyvale, California) from a hike in the Canyon. Second Lieutenant Walter A. Jaskowiak, II, age 24, and 1st Lieutenant Miriam Leigh Epstein, age 26, he explained, were both "stellar performers" working on top secret projects with high security clearances. They had not returned. More ominous, they had failed to rendezvous with another hiking party as planned on August 17, day one of their hike.

Jaskowiak's and Epstein's backcountry hiking permit listed the following itinerary: On August 17 they were to hike from the rim to Hermit Creek (River Mile 95), on the 18th, Monument Creek (River Mile 93.5), and on the 19th, Indian Garden (roughly halfway up the Bright Angel Trail from the river at River Mile 89). Although these daily goals sound close to one another and therefore easy, the standard hiking route "paralleling" the river demands that hikers traverse inward and back upward, then downward and outward, within a sidewinder's posture of side canyons such as Monument or Hermit, for miles to gain about 1,000 vertical feet and the top of the Tapeats Sandstone, also known as the Tonto Plateau. The Tonto provides a safe, spacious, and relatively level hiking surface in the inner Canyon between tributary canyons. Its downside is it meanders sinuously from river-ward, immediately above the Upper Granite Gorge, to rim-ward as it follows the contours of the tributary canyons, thus multiplying the horizontal straight line distance that the raven flies from one tributary to the next. Moreover, the Tonto normally offers neither water nor shade. During cool weather, this is not serious. During summer, it is. Either way, the Tonto does offer a remarkably safe passage in a topography riddled by a myriad of extremely dangerous alternate routes.

So what happened to Walter Jaskowiak and Miriam Epstein?

For some reason, rangers found, their permit had been edited so that only the first night of the itinerary was used. Did this mean the pair had hiked down the Hermit Trail, camped, and then hiked back early but then vanished?

No. Their "plan A" was to have met two friends, Stephen and Virginia De Martini, at the Backcountry Reservations Office. From there the foursome were to have hiked together to Hermit. Jaskowiak and Epstein did not show up at this office. The De Martinis did. And, even though their friends never showed, the De Martinis went ahead and did hike to Hermit. They next camped in the Hermit area on the 17th, as had been decided as the foursome's plan B (in the event that the two couples missed one another at the Backcountry Office). But Plan B also failed. The De Martinis never saw Jaskowiak or Epstein here either. Disappointed but only mildly concerned, the De Martinis hiked back out of the Canyon and went home.

Here the plot thickens. NPS rangers found Jaskowiak's Dodge parked at the Bypass Lot on the Village Loop Drive. It was covered in dust. A background check of both hikers—seeking a motive for vanishing deliberately—revealed that Jaskowiak and Epstein were romantically involved. But it also revealed that the two normally traveled (including climbing Pike's Peak) with other people, as with the De Martinis.

NPS personnel contemplated the clues. Jaskowiak and Epstein jogged and were in good condition. Neither owed unpaid debts or had a criminal background. Nor had either seemed suicidal. Instead, both had recently appeared to their families, their roommates, and their co-workers to be in normally sound mind and body.

On top of all these positive signs, Jaskowiak and Epstein had also completed the Air Force Academy's one-week survival class.

Yet they had vanished. So completely that not even interviews with river runners camping in the general vicinity of Hermit Creek and Monument Creek turned up anyone who had seen the missing hikers.

Soon NPS rangers began uncovering small but tantalizing clues. Late on the morning of August 26, NPS Rangers Sue Cherry and Dave Chapman hiked the Tonto Trail about two miles west of Horn Creek (River Mile 90.25). The two found a cache of clothing abandoned on the Tonto Trail. Based on the rain-spattered dust on it, it appeared to have been there for roughly a week. Inside it the rangers found two or three MREs (military "meals, ready to eat"), jeans, sweatshirt, towels, a U.S. Army shovel, shorts, a book (*Catch 22,* checked out from San Jose State University, where Jaskowiak was a student), a receipt from San Jose University, toothpaste, socks, and a t-shirt.

At about this time, U.S. Air Force Special Agent Lieutenant Colonel Ron Parker phoned Ranger Keith Lober to inform him that the missing persons had possessed extremely high security clearances. Parker also told Lober that the information that Walter Jaskowiak and Meriam Epstein possessed could be sold.

An hour after Cherry and Chapman found the abandoned pack, on August 25, at 2:45 p.m., two hikers from New York City, Daniel and Linda, told rangers over the phone that on their second day out, August 18, they had met and briefly hiked with two other hikers named Walt and Miriam on the Monument Creek Trail. Walt and Miriam, they said, had been planning to camp by the river at Monument (River Mile 93.5). But they had changed their minds around noon when Daniel and Linda told them that they themselves needed a rescue.

Daniel was vomiting at this time. Linda was even worse; she had, she explained, "lost all body functions."

One day before this, during Daniel's and Linda's first night's camp, they both had already felt ill. The NPS ranger at Indian Garden, Bil Vandergraff, had tried to convince them to switch their itinerary from Monument Canyon to the much easier, closer, and phone-friendly Phantom Ranch. But despite their feeling ill already from the extreme heat, Daniel and Linda had rejected Vandergraff's sound advice and instead followed their original plan.

Hence, a day later, on August 18, Walt Jaskowiak and Miriam Epstein met an even more desperately uncomfortable Daniel and Linda. Here Jaskowiak and Epstein decided against their own original plan to continue down the Monument Trail. Instead, Walt and Miriam decided to be Good Samaritans and hike out in the blazing heat to request a rescue for Daniel and Linda.

So Jaskowiak and Epstein veered from their descent and instead headed east onto the Tonto Trail. This route led past Horn Creek and continued on to Indian Garden and the ranger station, roughly seven miles from where Jaskowiak and Epstein had met Daniel and Linda. There the two Good Samaritans could alert Ranger Bil Vandergraff, who had originally warned Daniel and Linda not to hike the Tonto, that his advice had been correct: Daniel's and Linda's physiological situations had deteriorated to life-threatening.

Walt, the two heat-stricken hikers said over the phone, was wearing a grey Australian cowboy hat. Both Walt and Miriam also wore shorts and tank tops and seemed to be in good shape. Miriam also wore a bandanna and had an ace bandage on her knee. Dangling off their packs were several water bottles, one of them a "Dromedary" type. Before veering onto the Tonto, Walt and Miriam had also told Daniel and Linda that they had missed meeting their friends at Hermit.

The weather that day, August 18, was clear and very hot. The Phantom Ranch Ranger Station recorded a high of 111 degrees in the shade. The next day soared to 113 and was hit by a severe windstorm. The next day, August 20, climbed to a stupefying 115 degrees in the shade. No measurable rain fell at Phantom Ranch (River Mile 88) until August 21, when the high temperature dropped to 110 degrees, and it rained 0.59 inches. On August 22, it rained another 0.37 inches. Aside from these specifics, the region in general had been hit all that week with scattered, severe, but unmeasured local monsoonal thunderstorms.

An hour after this phone chat with Daniel and Linda, Rangers Sandy Hand and Jesse Farias found a pack at the bottom of Horn Creek drainage well above the river's edge. Inside it they found Miriam Epstein's credit card.

That same day, August 25, at 2:45 p.m., 70 minutes after finding Epstein's pack, searchers aboard one of the three contract helicopters combing Upper Granite Gorge spotted two bodies sprawled in a dry creek bed near the foot of the extremely narrow, steep, tortuous Horn Creek drainage. The bodies lay only about 300 feet upcanyon from the Colorado River at River Mile 90.25. The topography of Horn Creek Canyon above the bodies was punctuated by several high, sheer drops. In short, it was unclimbable and undescendable without climbing gear.

One hundred horizontal feet separated the two bodies, as also did a 20-foot, sheer, vertical fall. The upper body, a woman's, was sprawled at the foot of a 50-foot, dry waterfall. It was dressed in shorts, shoes, and a t-shirt, and partially enwrapped in a piece of plastic. Decomposition had begun. Strewn around it in the vicinity lay two military canteens on a web-belt, a large, broken flashlight, two bandannas, a "Trails Illustrated" map of the Canyon, sunglasses with a neoprene band, parachute cord, and a "Dromedary" water container still holding a quart of water. Twenty-five feet from this body, at the lip of the 20-foot falls that separated the two bodies, was a man's watch partially buried in sand.

The lower body, a man's, was also dressed in shorts, shirt, and shoes filled with red sand. The rangers found no equipment nearby, but they did find in the man's pocket a wallet containing Walter Jaskowiak's ID cards.

Upstream, roughly 350 yards up the Horn Creek drainage from the bodies and above a few more high waterfalls, sleeping bags and other camping equipment lay damaged and scattered as if they had tumbled down the drainage from the Tonto Trail.

Dental charts confirmed both identities. The Coconino County Medical Examiner, Dr. Thomas Vorphal, concluded that both victims had drowned.

How?

Dr. Vorphal noted that Epstein had an abraded right knee (still wrapped in gauze) and a fractured left wrist and a skull fracture to the left side of her head which occurred *well before* her death. Jaskowiak himself had suffered an abdominal injury prior to death. Both autopsies concluded that no foul play was involved.

Rangers Richard Perch, David Trevino, and Keith Lober examined Horn

Creek Canyon itself and concluded: "The rock on the side of the canyon was clean, with no mud, and the drainage did not appear to have flash flooded significantly in recent times."

If this conclusion were true, *how* then did Epstein and Jaskowiak end up where they had?

The clues were worthy of an A. Conan Dolye mystery. Investigators from the park, from Coconino County Sheriff's Office, and from the U.S. Air Force figured out that Miriam somehow must have been seriously injured in a fall while hiking—this accounted for her broken left wrist and the fracture in the left side of skull—on or near the Tonto Trail. Jaskowiak, who weighed 155 pounds, apparently carried her, possibly unconscious (she weighed 138 pounds), in a sort of fireman's carry dangling down his back. The toes of Epstein's otherwise brand new tennis/running shoes were very badly worn through, consistent with their having dragged along the abrasive surface of the Tapeats Sandstone for quite a distance. This task also would explain Jaskowiak's having jettisoned 15 pounds or so of clothes, etc. on the Tonto to lighten his overall load. It might also explain his abdominal injury as being due to the strain of carrying her.

It appears that Jaskowiak's first big mistake, a potentially fatal one, was not to sequester the injured Epstein in whatever protected area he could find or create near her place of injury. He could have erected a quick shade shelter and left Epstein with water. He also could have written her a note, if she was unconscious but woke up after his departure—or to inform anyone else who happened by—to tell her to stay put and to explain what had happened and where and when and how he had gone for help. Lightly loaded with nothing but a water bottle, he then could easily have reached the Indian Garden Ranger Station in a couple of hours and arranged for a helicopter evacuation in less than an hour more. If worried about Epstein's rolling while unconscious or asleep, Jaskowiak also could have tied her ankle to a large stone with parachute cord, or have built a rock retaining wall to keep her from rolling into danger.

The team of investigators concluded that Jaskowiak's second mistake—without doubt *the* fatal one—came next. After dragging Epstein for quite a distance along the sun scorched Tapeats of the Tonto Plateau, he apparently sought shelter from the blistering sun, from the sand-blasting, super-desiccating wind, or from both. The flash flood-carved head of Horn Creek offered shade and a windbreak on an inviting ledge under an overhang of Tapeats Sandstone. With plenty of food, water, and now this shade, Jaskowiak, who now was hurt himself, may have decided that the shelter of the Tapeats was a heaven-sent haven in which to wait for Epstein to regain consciousness—and hopefully even her ability to walk to Indian Garden.

There, after being sequestered safely perhaps for three days and nights, lying on a plastic tarp, a flash flood caught and killed Jaskowiak and Epstein. The flood slammed them, then scattered their bodies and equipment down

Horn Creek Canyon almost to the Colorado River.

Forensic entomological assessment (based on larval development in tissue) placed their times of death on the evening of August 21, the date of the heaviest rain at Phantom Ranch, and four days after starting their hike.

What about the NPS rangers' initial conclusion that little mud was present in the Horn Creek drainage therefore it must not have flashed? It seems that this conclusion was wrong. Some mid-sized flash floods in the Canyon, especially in steep drainages, are fairly clear; sandy, yes, but more or less silt free. This flood had been one of these—as the piles of red sand in Jaskowiak's shoes hinted.

A brief Associated Press article summarized this incident: "Two Air Force officers whose bodies were found in a drainage area were seeking help for another couple when floodwaters apparently swept them down a creek, authorities said Thursday."

Ironically, before Jaskowiak and Epstein were hit by the flash flood, while trying to rescue distressed New Yorkers Daniel and Linda from consequences of their poor decision making, the latter two had hiked down Monument Canyon to the river. There, on August 20, a Hatch River Expeditions trip radioed an emergency call for them, and an NPS chopper arrived to air-lift them to the South Rim.

Again, huge flash floods are so rare that most short-term visitors to the Inner Canyon, either hiking or boating, are unlikely to witness one. Often it is only the people who work in the Canyon for many months (or years) as rangers, guides, mule skinners, and other concession employees, and so on who gain the experience to expect, fear, and predict them. Thus many short-term visitors tend to doubt the danger that flash floods pose.

But the power of flash floods can be far more gargantuan than even what this chapter has so far spelled out. On July 26, 1984, I (Ghiglieri) was rowing on an OARS, Inc. trip with fellow guides Michael Boyle (who was trip leader), Craig Alexander, and Richard Haratani, and with trainees Geoff Gourley, Renee Goddard, and my older son, Conan Michael. We stopped at Diamond Creek. We couldn't help ourselves. Nearly five days before arriving here, an NPS helicopter piloted by Dana Morris had materialized over us in the narrow and fantastically sculpted depths of Matkatamiba Canyon (River Mile 148). A uniformed arm had appeared and dropped us a little baggie of sand with a streamer attached. The airship then rose between the close, thousand-foot cliffs and vanished.

Like a message in a bottle, this baggie held a warning: "Diamond Creek flash flooded. Take out at Pearce Ferry."

Again, even though we could not take out our 23-person trip as planned at River Mile 225.7, we had stopped here anyway to ogle the newly scoured Diamond Creek Canyon. As we and our passengers stepped off our boats, I noticed the newly-exposed and only five-day-old Diamond Creek delta extending fifty yards farther than usual into the Colorado. Only twelve hours earlier the Colorado River had dropped for the first time in months, by about 4,000 cubic feet per second (cfs), thus exposing for the first time this new, flash-flood-created delta. Curious, I walked out onto this new landscape. Everyone else wandered up Diamond Creek.

Right away I spotted a swatch of green nylon emerging from the mud. I yanked on it, pulling up bowling-ball-sized boulders with the fabric. Cool, I thought to myself, a fly for a Eureka tent, and still in good shape. OARS used this exact same model. Having an extra fly can never hurt....But what is it doing *here*?

I walked farther onto the delta. No foot prints existed out here. I was the first human being to tread this tiny addition to the Inner Canyon. I saw a military rocket box lid half buried. I wiggled it hard to yank it out. A strange sensation fluttered in my stomach. The lid had been hand painted to say "COAL 1." Almost instantly I saw yet another lid. It had been painted to say "EGG 2." I knew who had painted these. Connie Walker, the OARS foodpacker, had hand-lettered both of them.

Now feeling very uneasy, I continued farther out onto the delta. A cast iron cooking griddle lay wedged between two boulders. It was polished squeaky clean. It was the same type we used.

Did our new stakebed truck carrying the trip nearly a week ahead of us drop all this stuff? Maybe the stakebed gate fell off and let this gear fall out. Or maybe....No, that was unthinkable.

Farther out on the delta I spotted a twisted length of red-painted steel. It looked exactly like one of the steel stakes from our new stakebed. 1 tried to pull it out. It would not budge.

I stood there and gazed around me. More red-painted lengths of steel oozed twisted from the mud and boulders like giant worms caught in the act and frozen into fossils.

The answer to this puzzle seem pretty obvious now. It also seemed horrible. What the hell had happened to our truck? And, more importantly, to the crew who had been riding in it?

With a feeling of dread, I turned away from this graveyard of mud and walked up Diamond Creek to join everyone else. I saw two Hualapais with Boyle.

"You'll never guess what happened!" Boyle said to me astonished.

"Our truck got caught in the flash flood and went down the drink," I said, trying not to think about what this meant in terms of lost crew members.

He eyed me strangely, "How'd you know?"

"The delta," I explained. "Pieces of the truck are scattered all over it."

Eventually we heard the story from most of the survivors. A week earlier, when our other trip had beached here to take out, it had been drizzling slightly. Our trip had been slower than usual in getting ready to leave. So too, had been the Outdoors Unlimited trip taking out here. Even slower was the AzRA trip doing the same thing. Up on the plateau to the south, near Route 66, however, it was not drizzling. It was cloudbursting from an ink-black sky.

The road that day (July 20) was already a mess because during the previous 24 hours minor monsoon storms had already gullied and slurried it, especially in the final mile or so closest to the river.

Early that afternoon, the OARS passengers and part of the crew from that trip had walked out less than a mile then rode the Hualapai school bus the other 22 miles to Peach Springs. The remaining crew—Sam West, Greg Schill, Bill Brisbin, and Charles Rau—plus the OARS manager, Mike Walker, finally got all six boats and the gear loaded into OARS' new two-ton GMC stakebed truck (OARS' previous GMC stakebed had burned to the ground not long before). Walker drove the new stakebed with the four crew up Diamond Creek.

He followed Outdoors Unlimited's Dodge Power Wagon, also hauling crew and gear. A half mile up the creek from the Colorado, the Power Wagon bogged down in the slurry of the "road" in a creekbed section of canyon between steep walls of schist called "the Narrows." Debbie Jordan, driving the Dodge, and another woman, Amy, could not get the Power Wagon moving again.

So Walker, West, Brisbin, Rau, and Schill jumped out of the GMC to help Outdoors Unlimited's guides Doug Carson and Dennis Silva to push it.

As the six men were about to push the Power Wagon, they heard a roar. Walker said the roar brought to mind a passing jet, thunder, and the Caterpillar the Hualapais used to grade the road. But the sound was not right for any of those. Simultaneously Walker looked up at the bend of the canyon two hundred yards ahead. Fingers of red-brown water five to ten feet high tumbled around the bend, rebounded off the schist wall, then rumbled toward them. These fingers swelled quickly to a wall of slurry that doubled its height to about fifteen feet and filled the entire canyon from wall to wall.

"RUN!" several people yelled. As everyone scattered, Walker ran back to the new GMC. He opened the door and pulled out the ignition key, then rolled up the driver's window. Then he sprinted at top speed after the men heading for the high ground to the east.

When Debbie Jordan saw Walker rolling up the stake bed's window in her rearview mirror, she told Amy, "Don't get out, just roll up the windows."

Amy glanced through the windshield at the approaching wall of slurry, now taller than either truck, and said, "No way!" Then she yanked the door handle open.

This spurred Debbie to change her mind. Both women leapt from the Power Wagon. Now the wall of flash flood was a lot closer. Clad only in panties and t-shirts due to the heat, they sprinted for the nearest cliff. This happened to be to the west. They climbed the weathered schist like squirrels until they reached an overhanging section of slick rock beyond which they could not climb. They had trapped themselves, but turning back now would have been suicidal.

Diamond Creek, now a river of mud flowing at about 5,000 cfs (instead of its usual 1 or 2 cfs) walloped both trucks and engulfed them. Walker told me that he knew the flash flood would hit both vehicles hard, but he was hoping that the GMC would stay where it was as the flood washed around it. But the wall of the red-brown debris flow picked up the Power Wagon like a leaf and tumbled it on top of the GMC two-ton. In seconds both vehicles were engulfed and rushing downstream. Due to their relative lightness and their flat-surfaced shapes, however, they continued to flow and surf half submerged on the surface, like two sinking ships dancing a slow motion fandango. Both trucks vanished downstream.

When they next heard the roar, the AzRA guides were upstream of the confluence and hauling their boats from the Colorado. They stared at the sudden flood a hundred yards downstream. For an instant the dual wheels of the GMC surfaced in the flood as the truck rolled end over end in a twenty-five-foot wave into the Colorado. The AzRA guides were horrified. The OARS crew *had* to still be inside that cab.

Meanwhile, upcanyon, Walker and the other five men watched the flood of red-brown debris slam and thunder from wall to wall below them. The terrain here allowed them to walk up or downstream. In complete contrast, Debbie and Amy, on the west side, could not have trapped themselves in a more terrifying predicament. The overhanging slick rock stopped them from ascending higher. Nor could they traverse laterally. The deafening flood with its thousands of boulders rolling suspended in it cascaded beneath them. Almost malevolently, the flood yawned directly below them several feet in a gaping hole that seemed a duplicate of the famous killer hole in Crystal Rapid (next chapter). Not only were these two women trapped, they were trapped on an awkward cliff face that they had to cling to or die. This flood would last for hours. If either woman lost her balance for even an instant during those hours, she would die.

Unable to help Debbie and Amy, Walker and the other men hiked upstream to view the flow where it entered the Narrows. Schill had a hard time now. In his haste to escape the flood he had outrun his flip flops. Now he limped tenderly on bare feet on the sharp schist. Soon the others ahead of Schill sent back one of their number with another one's sandals on loan.

Upstream, the men now saw, the flood filled the much wider section of canyon from wall to wall. This was one hell of a lot of water.

And boulders, rocks, sand, silt, trees, dead animals...and now two perfectly good trucks, six river boats, two dozen oars, six rowing frames, everyone's personal gear, et cetera, et cetera. Now and then a cactus emerged from the flood, rolling to the surface as if desperate for a gulp of air. Several species of cacti swirled past the six watchers as if in some hallucinogenic vision of desert hell.

Walker stared at this flood for several seconds before the reality sank in. He reached into the pocket of his Patagonia Baggies, found the GMC's keys, pulled them out, and studied them. Then he admitted, "I guess we won't be needing these any more." He tossed the keys into the racing slurry.

About an hour later, the AzRA guides hiked upstream with ropes, wondering if they would find anyone to rescue. The six men had settled into ringside seats across from the two trapped women and were still trying to guess the volume of the flow of the now monster creek. Debbie and Amy might as well have been clinging to a crater wall on the moon.

As dusk approached, the flood ebbed. An hour or so later, Sam West strapped two life jackets on himself and swam across it. On the west side, West caught a rope tossed from the east. He set up a Tyrolean traverse to get both women back to the east side. After several hours of clinging to two-billion-year-old rock, West was Mister Right. He rigged each of them into the traverse. Guides on the opposite side hauled them over.

OARS' GMC 2-ton stake bed truck ended up on the opposite side of the Colorado River and partway down Diamond Creek Rapid. At low water, even by the year 2000, it was still visible. The nearby camp on the far side of the river over there is called "Truck Stop."

Despite the ultrasaurus power of such flash floods, however, many naive hikers fail to believe that flash floods can truly wreak the unrelenting havoc that they are reputed to. One of these campers, Bill Grundy, for example, on the night of September 15, 1992, at Cottonwood Campground on the North Kaibab Trail sat in his tent and, even after noting that its floor was surging "just like my waterbed," laid down on his Thermarest.

A flashlight seemed to be bobbing in the rising flood racing past and under him. "It's flashing out," warned NPS Ranger Bryan Wisher from the dark. "You need to gather up your gear and get out of this spot."

"Since Bryan had seemed unconcerned," Grundy would later write, "I was in no hurry… [I sat] on my mattress figuring out how to pack up my gear."

Mud and water next engulfed Grundy's tent, ripped its stakes out of the ground, and started floating it away.

Grundy said, "I forced the tent down with my hands and knees…."

Earlier that evening, Ranger Bryan Wisher also had been listening to the rain. He knew that what little soil existed in this drainage was already saturated from several rains over the last week. Indeed, this very evening, he had warned campers here at Cottonwood about a potential flood. And now, as the rain fell harder and harder—the hardest rain he had ever heard in his life, he admitted to himself—he knew a flood had to be on its way.

Wisher radioed Phantom Ranch of an imminent flood. Then he yanked his boots on and grabbed a MagLite. Racing outside, Wisher stared in amazement: the eastern wall of Bright Angel Canyon appeared to be an endless sheet of cascading waterfalls. Realizing anew the extreme danger this posed to campers, he ran fifty yards downhill to the lower campground.

Wisher yelled at two campers still inside their tent. The pair was struggling to hold it down as a six-inch-deep flow of water pushed against it. "Leave your tent behind," Wisher yelled, "and head immediately to the Ranger Station at higher ground."

As the floodwater inched deeper across the campground, Wisher frantically ran to another campsite. He shouted the same instructions to its occupants.

During Wisher's scrambling, the flood rose. He found two more campers sitting on a picnic table amidst the flow. They were watching it rise and swirl around them as if somehow the implications of the flood's final peak level were incomprehensible to them. Wisher instructed them on the run. "Get off that table and head to higher ground near the Ranger Station."

Running south, Wisher saw yet another flash flood hurtling down through the blackness of the normally dry drainage south of the ranger station. Across the flood, barely visible through the thundering rain, Wisher spotted a tent wrapped around a rock, pinned by the current. Was someone trapped inside that tent?

Trying to time his crossing so as to avoid getting hit by boulders or logs, Wisher listened for crashing rocks. What the hell? Wisher ran out into the flood, struggling to stay on his feet and angling his way downstream to the other side. The collapsed tent, he found, was empty, except for mud. Good. Now there existed only one more campsite in the upper campground that might lay in the floodplain.

Wisher recrossed the swollen new creek. Again he played a dangerous game of Russian roulette in trying mostly by luck alone to avoid being hit by rolling rocks and careening debris. He made it across. He ran to the north end of the campground. Visibility had diminished, it seemed, to about 10 feet.

Wisher strained his eyes to peer back across the wash. Penetrating the downpour, his Maglite beam caught a distorted yellow object in mid-flood.

It was Grundy's tent, still in its original location but now perched on a little island submerged and surrounded by racing flood waters. Inside the trapped tent a light burned. Wisher's stomach sank as he realized the implications of that light: Grundy was still inside that tent....

Again listening to the rocks crashing in the stream—as if to detect some sort of pattern—Wisher tried to time his crossing. Again he managed not to be hit by boulders or debris crashing through the waist deep water. The flood level rose even higher as he reached the tent. Wisher screamed over the roar of the water to whomever was inside the tent, "Get out of this tent, now!"

As if in a very bad nightmare, the rising water chose this moment to engulf the yellow dome tent and float it downstream with Grundy still inside. The nylon death trap now wrapped around Wisher and pushed him downstream into deeper water and toward a six-foot waterfall that drained into Bright Angel Creek, now a river.

Grundy finally agreed to exit his tent. Desperate, Wisher and Grundy, now outside but still in his underwear, started to drag it back across the rising stream. Wisher dragged them both across the flood. Amazingly, the "trio" arrived on the shore unharmed.

Wisher sagged onto the bank exhausted.

Grundy wrote, "I credit him with saving my life."

Grundy, by the way, is still using that same tent.

Later the following year, Secretary of the Interior Bruce Babbitt awarded Bryan Wisher the National Park Service's Valor Award for his heroic performance at Cottonwood. Wisher was credited with saving 28 lives.

Nearly three years later, on March 5, 1995, nonstop rains again pounded the Inner Canyon in the vicinity of Upper Granite Gorge. It poured all day and into the night. Enough rain fell on the Canyon's huge north side to build the biggest flash flood since the 1966 supermonster in the upper drainages of Bright Angel and Crystal creeks. At about 11:00 p.m., the roar of this flood woke up Phantom Ranch employees as it ripped down the creek less than a hundred yards from their bunkhouse.

To everyone, this flood was a novelty. Some went outside and took pictures. Five employees—Leslie Aldrich, Julie Chaibineou, Stephanie Hettinger, Laura Tibbetts, and Wanda Woodbury (all in their mid-20s to early 30s)—walked the trail down to the bridge 200 yards upstream of the confluence with the Colorado River. They were keen to witness even more of Mother Nature's power where the great flood slammed into the river.

The creek, they saw, had already climbed to eight feet deeper than normal. What a sight it must be, they agreed, where the flood pounds into the Colorado itself. The five walked to the confluence, first crossing the dry wash east of the creek. This was separated from the creek itself by a large delta-debris fan built in part by remnants of that mammoth 1966 flood. Indeed, this dry wash had been dry ever since then, almost thirty years....

The five women reached the confluence. It seemed anti-climactic. The two flows mixed with only a little turbulence and a lot of boring foam.

Several minutes later, the women tried to retrace their route back. Now, however, the view was anything but anti-climactic. Floodwaters raged along the formerly dry (for the previous 29 years) east side of the delta. Operating under the hopeful disbelief that perhaps they were only disoriented and had walked west instead of east, the five women walked to the other side of the delta. Here the flood roared past far deeper and faster.

Suddenly all five women realized that they had trapped themselves on a shrinking island. If the flood rose much higher, the odds were that they would all die.

The rising flood had risen above and jumped the main drainage. It now cut around the delta, shrinking it. With the Colorado River to their south, the five were completely cut off from terra firma. But dredging up some optimism after finding that they had walked into an unescapable trap, they speculated that merely being stranded here for awhile might be the worst outcome of their error.

A desperate Phantom Rancher who had seen the trapped women now pounded on Phantom Ranch Ranger Patrick Suddath's door.

Suddath ran to survey their plight. Impressed, he radioed a request for assistance. Next he grabbed a throw bag and ropes from the ranger station and tried to get a rope out to the stranded women.

Several rangers were dispatched to hike down the South Kaibab Trail to help. Bryan Wisher, now the ranger at Indian Garden on the south side of the Canyon, received Suddath's distress call at 1:00 a.m. For Wisher this was deja vu, although this time the people at risk were not naive campers who refused to listen to him, but instead people he knew personally, some as friends. Maybe this flash flood would go more easily.

Wincing from the pain of a recently broken rib, Wisher gathered his gear. Next he recruited Jerry Chavez (NPS pumphouse operator and pipeline maintenance specialist), also a strong hiker, climber, and an assistant during Canyon medical emergencies and rescues. The two men ran out into the rain.

Garden Creek flowed a foot deep. The two men ran a couple of miles in the dark down the Bright Angel Trail. Wisher's rib hurt with each step. In the lead, he stopped at Pipe Creek. It now roared past them as a sluice of rocks and debris. In the worst places it flowed more than four feet deep. This, Wisher thought to himself, was not good. Not good at all.

As Wisher stood in the rain and radioed a ranger on the North Rim to check what was happening with the weather there, Chavez ran past Wisher and into Pipe Creek. The rain, this North Rim ranger told him, had begun to turn to snow. This meant that the floods in Bright Angel Creek might stabilize in the next two to four hours.

As Wisher listened he also watched in disbelief as the flood instantly swept Chavez off his feet. He disappeared into the flood. Wisher ran downstream along side it. Chavez surfaced. Wisher helped his friend struggle out of the current. Chavez had lost his radio. Both men were badly shaken.

But their friends' lives were still at stake, so they braced up against each other and entered the flood. For every foot they struggled across, the current shoved them several feet downstream. They finally made it across. Heading down the Bright Angel Trail again, they had to cross their own personal flood four more harrowing times.

A half hour later they crossed the big steel bridge to the north side of the Canyon. The two men found the situation at Phantom Ranch anything but improved. Rain continued to pound down. Bright Angel Creek now looked like the Colorado River. The flood slapped the bottom of the campground bridge walkway. The roar was incredibly loud as boulders crashed in the current. Logs, trees and other debris flushed down in a freight train of lethal weapons. From even one hundred feet away the two men felt the entire ground vibrating due to nonstop concussions of rolling boulders in the flood.

The highest point of the five women's delta, normally 12–14 feet above the creek bed, now stood only three feet short of being covered by the flood. Bright Angel Creek itself now flowed at 3,000 to 4,000 cfs, much higher than many historic low flows of the Colorado River itself. The five trapped women now huddled together in the dark on an area shrunken from more than an acre to only 30 by 50 feet.

Seeing Wisher and Chavez across the flood, several of the trapped women now jumped up and down and yelled for joy. Wisher looked back at them on their shrinking postage stamp of real estate and his stomach sank.

Meanwhile Suddath had been trying to heave and float a throwrope out to the island, but with no luck. Wisher studied the horrendous, 100-foot-wide flood and decided that any attempt to have the trapped women cross this "creek" via a rope was out of the question anyway; being *in* that flood and fixed to a rope would spell certain death. Wisher again considered the report of snow, instead of rain, falling on the rim. According to logic and experience, this flood should be peaking, maybe even now ready to subside.

Wisher took over the operations role. Instead of extricating the women, getting life jackets and supplies to them to prevent hypothermia and maybe prevent drowning would now be the rescue team's top priority. Thus equipped, the women could maybe ride out this storm. Any attempt to extricate them—given that a helicopter would be impossible to use in the dark *and* in this storm—should be viewed as an absolute last resort to be tried only if the floodwaters threatened unequivocally to carry them off. For now, the five were safe on their tiny island of delta. Messing up that safety unnecessarily would not be smart. Still, Wisher instructed the trailcrew to don life jackets, hike downstream of the delta, and set themselves up on shore to be ready with throw ropes in case the flood flushed anyone into the river.

Next Wisher tied a rock to parachute cord. He yelled to the women over the roar that a cord was on its way, Wisher threw the rock out to the island.

Wisher's rock clattered onto the delta. A woman grabbed it and reeled it in. Attached to it was an 11 mm rope. Wisher screamed instructions to the trapped women on how to tie the rope around the mesquite tree on their island. Next, using a carabiner attached to this rope, he sent life jackets, a radio, and a pack with food and supplies out to the island.

The women radioed that they were freezing. Wisher's crew—strengthened now by the arrivals of Rangers Nick Herring, David Trevino, Craig Patterson, and Todd Van Alstyne, who had just descended the scary South Kaibab Trail on this dark and stormy night—next sent over clothing, rain gear, a tent, sleeping bags, and a lantern. Again, Wisher was betting that keeping the five trapped people warm was far safer than risking anyone's life in trying to get them off at night. After dawn, he said, a helicopter evacuation could be safely attempted. But, again, if the flood rose much higher, the rescue team would be forced to try an emergency evacuation off the island across that horrendous, raging, 100-foot-wide flood.

Wisher bet right. At 6:30 a.m., a helicopter lifted all five women off their island safely. None had been injured. And, yes, after all, the women agreed, the flood, where it hit the Colorado, *had* been impressive.

Neither Grand Canyon nor the American Southwest in general are the only places on Earth where flash floods wreak havoc. The lesson in this is that such havoc is not merely a product of cloudbursts and canyons. It is more a product of people naive to the ways of Mother Nature voluntarily placing themselves *in* these canyons when Mother Nature floods them. In the Swiss Alps, for example, a relatively new sport called "canyoning" has caught on in a big way. Rather than hiking or boating down a canyon though, "canyoning" includes rappelling, jumping, sliding, clambering, and swimming down steep narrow canyons. In Switzerland alone, 50,000 people do this per year. In early August of 1999, almost two dozen international thrill-seekers on a commercial canyoning descent run by Adventure World had dropped into central Switzerland's Saxeten River Gorge and were clambering down it. From upstream a black wall of water from heavy rains cascaded into the group killing at least 21 people and injuring several others. Grand Canyon's flash flood fatalities pale in comparison. Perhaps this is due to sheer luck. Then again, maybe just enough smart people have been in the right place at the right time to prevent such mass drownings.

So, even though the low number of Grand Canyon fatalities from flash floods may at times seem nothing short of miraculous, in reality only the rarest flash floods appear out of the blue as unpredictably as a meteor crashing to Earth. Instead, most are "telegraphed" by severe storms in the general vicinity of the drainage. Even the canyons themselves provide an audible warning system shortly before the floods arrive. For each of the many flash floods we have personally witnessed and for those witnessed by others, a deep roar often has preceded the wall of debris flow by as much as a minute. Sometimes even longer. Such a roar—during weather that could give birth to cloudbursts—is about as close to receiving God's personal warning on a silver platter as one can get. And, although some flash floods arrive as a massive wall flowing and tumbling down an absolutely dust-dry creek bed, when a creek is already flowing there may be other clues. These may include a sudden muddying of the creek, the muddy smell of clay and other minerals in the air, and a sudden shift of wind or sound in the air.

Despite the presence of some clues and the absence of others on a case-by-case basis, the bottom line on hiking slot canyons during potentially rainy weather is: it is exactly like playing Russian roulette.

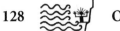

Table 3. VICTIMS OF FATAL FLASH FLOODS IN GRAND CANYON

Name, age	Date	Location	*Circumstances*
Unnamed older woman	January 2, 1910	Havasupai Village	

During the most severe and destructive Havasu flash flood known, a warm rain storm (2.3 inches) fell during December 31–January 1 and melted a heavy snowpack. The flood breached four earthen dams to create a 20-foot-high wall of water in Havasu/Cataract Canyon, filling it wall to wall. Only one victim, a blind and feeble Supai woman, drowned. The flood destroyed Supai Village and downcut Havasu Falls by 30 feet and Beaver Falls by 33–50 feet. (not in text or text statistics or index)

Claud Hallmark, 20	Summer, 1921	Big Wash, 6 miles N of Bundyville	
Claud's horse			

During a storm, Hallmark rode his horse into a flash flooding wash to retrieve coats from a wagon on the opposite side for his sister and mother. The bodies of Hallmark and his horse were found the next day. (not in text or text statistics or index)

Rogers Clubb, Sr., 36	August 3, 1963	Bright Angel Trail, 400 yards uphill from	
Rogers Clubb, Jr., 8		Indian Garden	

A ten-foot wall of water and mud exploded from the canyon immediately upstream engulfing the Clubbs, killing both father and son. (see text)

Walter A. Jaskowiak, II, 24	August 21, 1992	Horn Creek Canyon (River Mile 90.25)	
Miriam Leigh Epstein, 26			

Jaskowiak's and Epstein's bodies were found in the bottom of lower Horn Creek Canyon separated by 100 feet horizontally and by a 20-foot vertical fall. They and their gear had been deposited by one or two flash flood(s), most likely on August 21 and/or 22, when significant rain fell on days whose temperatures reached 110 degrees in the shade. Reconstruction of this incident suggests that Jaskowiak had dragged Epstein, possibly unconscious from a fall on the Tonto Trail, into the shade under the ledges of Tapeats Sandstone in upper Horn Creek Canyon, where the flash flood hit them. (see text)

Patty Moran, 40	September 11, 1997	Phantom Creek	
John Moran, 40			

The Morans, plus Patty Moran's brother, John McCue, age 36, were hit by a chest-high wall of "thick, dark, red mud." The Morans drowned. (see text)

George Lamont Mancuso, 46	August 7, 2001	Little Colorado/Big Canyon/Emerald Pool	
Linda Brehmer, 51			

On August 18, NPS SAR personnel found that Mancuso and Brehmer had left their gear in camp at the confluence of Salt Trail Canyon and the Little Colorado. Brehmer last wrote (on August 7) in her journal, left in camp, that she and Mancuso intended that day to visit "Emerald Pool." This is one half mile from camp, in Big Canyon, a steep boulder-choked drainage offering limited "high ground." Major flash floods scoured the Little Colorado and several tributaries that day during the pair's unpermitted camping trip for Mancuso's "La Femme de Grand Canyon" photo shoot. Mancuso, an accomplished canyon photographer, was an "expert" remote Canyon hiker with a passion for the Little Colorado gorge. Mancuso's vehicle was found parked at the head of Salt Trail. Brehmer's body was found wrapped around a tamarisk just below Emerald Pool on August 22 by searcher Scott Thybony. Alerted by ravens days later, NPS boatman Greg Woodall found Mancuso's body lodged in driftwood and boulders on the island at the confluence of the Colorado and Little Colorado rivers. (not in text or text statistics or index)

Melvin Presta, 39
Denice Cooper, 40
Aaron Presta, 2

August 10, 2001   Hualapai Canyon/Havasu
En route to the Havasupai Peach Festival, Presta and Cooper and their four children, Aaron, Christa, Drey, and Yvonne, became separated; the latter three going ahead. The three behind were hit in Hualapai Canyon, as flood witness Jim Furgo said, by a 20-foot high wall of water that "sounded like a 747 jetliner." The three victims' bodies were recovered 3.5 miles upstream of Supai village. (not in text or text statistics or index)

Chapter Four

The Killer Colorado

*I never want to see it again anywhere. Near the Grand Cañon it proba-
bly will remain unvisited for many years again, as it has nothing to recommend it but its general desolation as a study for the geologist....What
I have seen of Arizona I do not consider worth settling. As a disgusted
woodchopper put it: "The whole damned Territory is a Bilk."*

John Colton Sumner confided this appraisal of the Colorado River to his
journal on August 31, 1869. Sumner had only one day earlier fulfilled his
contract as head boatman for John Wesley Powell on the first-ever river trip
down the Canyons of the Colorado in 1869 (see Chapter 8 for more on this).
Upon exiting Grand Canyon after 98 days of river exploration beginning in
Green River, Wyoming—and also having survived one of the most harrowing journeys in the annals of North American exploration—Sumner had
earned the right to express an opinion. Nor was this opinion formed in
haste. He had just spent 26 days thoroughly convincing himself that nothing
of material worth could possibly exist in this 1,000-cubic-mile hole in the
ground that some fool had named Grand Cañon.

Nor was Sumner merely a grumbling boatman disgusted with having been
welshed out of what he expected as his due financial reward (one he never did
receive, see Chapter 8). Instead Sumner was simply measuring the arid Southwest
with the eye of a man born in the green East. Indeed, Sumner's assessment
echoed that made by U.S. Lieutenant Joseph Christmas Ives eleven years earlier
on April 18, 1858. After struggling *upstream* by boat from Mexico to the head of
Black Canyon, well downstream of Grand Canyon, and then riding and hiking
overland into western Grand Canyon, Ives too concluded:

Ours has been the first, and will doubtless be the last, party of whites to visit this profitless locality. It seems intended by nature that the Colorado River, along the greater part of its lonely and majestic way, shall forever be unvisited and undisturbed.

Yes, both Ives and Sumner were wrong. And for reasons they both would have denounced as demented. Grand Canyon's desolation and immensity—the very same hideous qualities that Sumner and Ives condemned as being so inhospitable and worthless—would soon sound as the song of a Siren to those seeking their fortunes from railroad projects, from publicizing their adventurous exploits, or from wresting precious metals from the hidden rocks themselves. Yet not even these fortune-hunters ever suspected that eventually millions of people would seek the Canyon's unfriendly depths in search of spiritual solace—or to experience the euphoria of adventure. After all, a century ago, nearly anything anyone did in Arizona was an adventure. Furthermore, "adventure" was best avoided if you didn't want to cash in your chips before you were ready to play your last hand.

At any rate, long before the first tourist would hazard the taxing journey across the Coconino Plateau to the South Rim, the Colorado River in Grand Canyon had seduced its first known victims. The river's reputation quickly became that of a killer. And for years this reputation was well-deserved. But exactly how well-deserved—and why—has long been shrouded in myth and hyperbole.

Strangely for such a reputedly deadly river, during most of the Colorado's length between its headwater regions in Wyoming's Wind River Range and in Colorado's Western Rockies, the river appears deceptively calm. Even most of its 277 miles in Grand Canyon appear harmless. Between Lees Ferry at elevation 3,117 feet and Lake Mead (River Mile 238 or so) at 1221 feet, the river descends less than a mere eight feet per mile. Those who run technical whitewater rivers elsewhere tend to smirk when they hear this eight-feet-per-mile gradient. For example, rowers and paddlers on California's Tuolumne River routinely navigate whitewater plunging almost sixty feet per mile. One of us (Ghiglieri) has run an exploratory first descent of the Alas River in Sumatra, a river that drops for three of its miles at 165 feet per mile. How dangerous could a mere eight feet be?

When it comes to the power of a river to grab a human being and exert total control over him or her, descent is only one part of the equation for danger. The Amazon River during its final couple of thousand miles to the sea drops only one foot per *each thirty miles*. Yet the Amazon's tremendous volume, more than the next three largest rivers in the world combined, exerts immense power.

Overall, the Colorado River flowing within Grand Canyon gobbles people because of a constellation of hydrodynamic features. First, while it ranks only 26th in size in the U.S., it is still a respectable-sized river. Before Glen Canyon

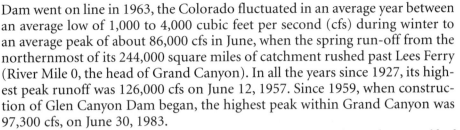

Dam went on line in 1963, the Colorado fluctuated in an average year between an average low of 1,000 to 4,000 cubic feet per second (cfs) during winter to an average peak of about 86,000 cfs in June, when the spring run-off from the northernmost of its 244,000 square miles of catchment rushed past Lees Ferry (River Mile 0, the head of Grand Canyon). In all the years since 1927, its highest peak runoff was 126,000 cfs on June 12, 1957. Since 1959, when construction of Glen Canyon Dam began, the highest peak within Grand Canyon was 97,300 cfs, on June 30, 1983.

The next factor in the equation of danger is the river's gradient. Half of those eight feet of drop per mile happens in about 160 rapids of varying size. These constitute only 9 percent of the river's 240 miles downstream of Lees Ferry. This means that for 21.6 of its miles, the Colorado drops an average of 45 feet per mile. And, since passage of the Grand Canyon Protection Act by Congress in 1992, it descends with an average flow of roughly 8,000 to 25,000 cfs. Beyond its flow and gradient, the Colorado used to possess yet one more deceptive feature that spelled doom for those trapped in it.

This third factor was most obvious prior to the 1963 completion of Glen Canyon Dam, which created a huge sediment settling "pond" (also known as Lake Powell) upstream of Grand Canyon. Before the building of Navajo Bridge in 1928 at River Mile 4 of the Colorado, livestock were driven across the calm stretch of river at Lees Ferry. Oral history has it that many animals never reached the other side. It was not the cold that drowned these animals. True, the Colorado did once run cold as ice in winter then up to 80 degrees in summer instead of today's constant 46–47 degrees at Lees Ferry. Instead, the problem lay in what the river carried.

"Too thick to drink but too thin to plow" used to be the wry description for the water quality of the Colorado. During high flows or periods of monsoonal runoff from the Painted Desert and the spectacular regions adjacent to it, the Colorado River seethed and hissed with silt and sand. At flows of 100,000 cfs, nearly half of what flowed down the Canyon was sediment, the other half water.

So what? Stories have been told for years that when sheep tried to swim across the river under these conditions, their wool captured so much silt that the animals sank. Stockmen watched their animals plunge in the muddy flow and bravely swim across with heads held high and noses aimed at the rimrock of the cliffs. Slowly those heads sank deeper and deeper until only the animals' nostrils protruded from the silty river. Then nothing. Likewise, it would turn out, for men.

Lethal Errors Made While Running the River

The first recorded mishap attributed to the Grand Canyon Colorado may have instead occurred downstream of its mouth. We may never know for sure. It happened during a classic Western adventure, the stuff of Zane Grey thrillers. On September 8, 1867, at Callville, Nevada, (now submerged under Lake Mead) a couple of men saw what looked like a person lying on a crude log raft on the Colorado River. They waded out and snagged it as it drifted near shore. Aboard it was an emaciated, bruised, half-naked, severely sunburned wreck of a 30-year-old human being who gave his name as James White. White's story of how he came to be where he was—and in the state he was—has been disputed and debated almost since the moment he told it.

In a letter White wrote to his brother on September 26, 1867, he explained what had happened to him. He had been prospecting since April with Captain Baker and George Strole in the San Juan Mountains in southwestern Colorado. In search of better prospects, the three headed down the San Juan River about 200 miles. They crossed over to the Colorado River. But the argonauts saw that they could not travel down it with horses. So they decided to turn back. On August 24, while ascending the tributary out of the canyon, identified by anthropologist Bob Euler as Moki Canyon, 15 to 20 Indians—Utes, White guessed—attacked them.

Baker was shot to death almost instantly. White and Strole gathered their guns, four ropes off their horses (losing seven head to the Utes), and a ten-pound sack of flour. They fled on foot fifteen miles downcanyon back to the Colorado River. They reached it at night and built a driftwood raft in the dark.

Then they escaped downriver. They had smooth floating for three days. On the fourth, however, they ran a small rapid and capsized. Here Strole saved White's life by grabbing him by the hair. The two men next built a new, bigger raft. Bad luck, though, in the next rapid Strole fell off it and drowned in a whirlpool.

Fearing that he would be next to die, White pulled off his boots and pants (so he could swim) and tied himself by his waist to the raft by a fifty-foot rope. Given his situation, this was a good decision. His raft floated over 10- or 15-foot falls and flipped upside down three or four times per day. Seeing no sign of civilization, not even a road, White stayed on the river.

This float was no picnic. The remains of that sack of flour had been lost even before Strole drowned, leaving White alone. For seven days he ate nothing. Gaunt with hunger, he finally ate his rawhide knife scabbard. After eight days, he found some honey mesquite beans and ate them. On day nine his raft disintegrated, and he had to rebuild it. Two days later he had to build his fourth new raft of the trip. Then, on the 12th day, he saw about 75 friendly looking Hualapais.

A few of them waded out and pulled him to shore. A squaw gave him a bit of honey mesquite loaf. Meanwhile other Indians stole one of his revolvers and a hand axe. When they would give him nothing more, he set sail again. The next day he traded his last revolver to another group of Indians for the hind quarters of a dog they had butchered. He lost one hind quarter acciden-tally in the river. The following day the men at Callville grabbed his raft. Ever since, White's claim of having been first to traverse the entire Grand Canyon by river has been doubted, disputed, or, by a few, half believed.

After interviewing White in 1907, Robert Brewster Stanton, in his role as historian, takes a highly skeptical, superior, even supercilious view of the sug-gestion that White had floated through Grand Canyon: "It is my conviction that at the time White wrote his letter he knew neither where he had been, how far he had come, or how long he had been on the river—only that he had been on a raft, somewhere on the Colorado."

Instead of floating for 500 miles of the Colorado, Stanton concluded from White's own testimony of passing 300-foot walls of sandstone on his float, and seeing only one tributary (from the north), and running only one big rapid, and never seeing extremely high canyon walls at all, that White instead had floated only 60 miles from Grapevine Wash near the Grand Wash Cliffs (River Mile 277 and 330 miles from the San Juan River) to Callville. On the other hand, White's mention in his letter to his brother of having seen a very high tributary waterfall suspiciously resembling Deer Creek Falls (at River Mile 136 in Grand Canyon), would seem to suggest that he indeed did float through the Canyon.

So George Strole's whitewater death, as tragic as it was, may or may not have happened in Grand Canyon.

Ironically, the firm honor of the first certified whitewater boating deaths in Grand Canyon go to the trip on which Stanton himself became its leader.

This chapter of the Great American Dream to trick the West into laying eggs like those of the proverbial golden goose began in late 1870. In that year, a prospector, S. S. Harper, alone and down on his luck, became desperate as his store of flour and bacon dwindled to zero. Harper came across a small band of men driving a herd of cattle north from east of the San Francisco Peaks. The men offered Harper a piece of the action if he would help them with the herd. Harper agreed.

Harper noticed, however, not only that the herd did not shrink due to loss-es, daily it *grew*. And the cows' brands were mixed. Harper added up two and two and came to the conclusion that he had fallen in with a band of rustlers intending to sell their stolen stock to Mormons in southern Utah. Harper knew that, were a posse to catch them, if he was not shot immediately, he would be hanged with these rustlers.

The men and cattle reached the south side of the Colorado across from what soon would be Lees Ferry. That night some of the stock strayed back south. Harper volunteered to round them up so that no posse would find them and thus back track the cows to find the rest of the herd. Harper's "part-ners" agreed to this. Harper immediately rode south and kept on riding as fast as his bronco would carry him—stray and stolen stock be damned.

Harper's day and night on the Colorado, however, had planted in him the seed of a grand idea to build a railroad from the Colorado Rockies to San Diego via a route that followed the river itself—within its canyons.

Many years later, after Harper had finally struck serious paydirt in Colorado, he confided his plan to another member of Denver's new rich upper crust. The man was lawyer Frank Mason Brown, a real estate and mining magnate. Brown was captivated by the grandeur of Harper's scheme—and also by its potential profits. He immediately formed the Denver, Colorado Cañon and Pacific Railroad and launched a survey expedition from Green River, Utah, down the Green and Colorado rivers. Brown hired as his chief surveyor, Robert Brewster Stanton. Stanton notes that Brown was optimistic to a fault. For example, though Brown met for an hour with John Wesley Powell, who had commanded the original explorations of the Colorado in 1869 and 1871–72, Brown had somehow walked away from that meeting with little sense of what would be necessary as equipment to survive the river. Stanton listed three main faults in Brown's planning.

First was the boats themselves. While Powell had used three, 21-foot-long Whitehall haulers constructed of oak and double-ribbed, Brown chose five cheaper, 15-foot-long canoe type boats only 40 inches wide, a mere 18 inches deep, and built of thin planks of brittle red cedar. On top of being far too small to carry sixteen men plus the several months of provisions and equipment they needed, Brown's tiny, fragile boats were round bottomed and easy to capsize.

Next was Brown's choice of boatmen. Stanton asked Brown to hire four men who knew moving water. Brown said that boatmen would not be necessary; two of his own friends, fellow lawyers, would come along as his "guests" and they would row the easy stretches. And the men would line or portage the boats around the rapids themselves, just as Powell had done.

The third fault in Brown's planning was his decision not to buy or bring life jackets. (Powell himself had used one on his first trip down the river; and on his second trip he had also issued them to his crew.) Stanton says that he beseeched Brown:

> Then came up that much vexed question of life preservers. I urged
> President Brown to provide them for all of the men....I could make
> no impression upon Brown, and called my friend S. S. Harper, the
> real father of the enterprise, to help me. We both urged more cau-
> tion and better preparation for the journey. It was no use, even
> though the air grew blue as Harper tried to convince Brown that
> he was going into dangers that he knew nothing about. Harper and
> my other friends urged me to take a life preserver myself,
> because...in my early childhood, I had had a battle with my Irish
> nurse, and, I suppose, getting the better of her while in her arms,

she dropped me on the pavement and so smashed up my left arm that it has been of little use to me since; hence...I could not swim a stroke, especially in the whirlpools of the Colorado. No life pre-servers were gotten for anyone....

Brown's survey expedition left Green River, Utah, on May 25, 1889. Three days earlier, Stanton had been aghast when he had stared into the railroad car hauling Brown's five boats. Two of them had already split almost end to end. Brown's crew had repaired the injured boats and then added a sixth boat, a flat bottomed dory they purchased locally, as the cook's boat.

The necessary provisions failed to fit into the bow and stern compartments of Brown's fleet of six. So the men built a raft of zinc-lined boxes to tow the food down the sluggish waters of Labyrinth and Stillwater canyons (the gradient here is only about 1.5 feet per mile). A week later Brown's crew rowed their boats onto the Colorado River flowing into Cataract Canyon. Cataract immediately introduced itself as a 40-mile nightmare that would last more than two weeks.

For starters, the men lost that towed raft of food. Next they pinned a boat underwater and lost almost everything in it. A day later, another boat flipped upside down. Then, soon afterward, the cook's boat was pinned against some boulders. Although the men were finally able to rescue some of the cook's equipment, most of the messware and the food were lost. On top of this, the river utterly destroyed the cook's boat.

After these first few days of poor boating decisions, Stanton's surveying crew began openly criticizing the "management" by Brown and his lawyer buddies.

Only a day after this open criticism began, yet another boat was badly smashed. Luckily, it was salvageable. Four days after criticism began, with all five boats now leaking and as most of the men openly muttered their disgust of the situation, the cook's "new" boat flipped upside-down—losing all the rest of the expedition's plates, et cetera. Yet another boat was sucked into the vortex of a whirlpool to half sink in a nose-stand. Three days after this, the men lost a boat altogether (recovered intact four days later). As more days passed, each day had its crashes, and each lost yet more food and gear.

Finally, on day #14 in Cataract, Stanton suggested to Brown that, since the expedition now had less than a week's rations, Stanton and five of his surveyors should *hike* the rest of the canyon on half rations, while Brown tried to get the boats and nine other men several miles down to Hite where a re-supply was possible. Brown agreed. The expedition prepared to split in half.

Unfortunately, Brown's crew promptly demolished yet another boat—permanently—before the division could even take place.

Discontent now boiled over into mutiny. Stanton ordered the cook to cook every last bit of food remaining and divide it into sixteen shares, one per man.

Discouragingly, each small pile now added up to only one day's ration.

At this point, on day #17 in Cataract, everyone but Stanton and four of the men loyal to him headed downstream in three of the four surviving boats to float ten miles to Hite. In their first rapid—the last one in Cataract—one of Brown's three boats immediately lost most of their remaining food and clothes.

Meanwhile Stanton and his tiny crew toiled on, hiking and surveying the walls of Cataract and Narrow canyons. Lunch on these hikes was three lumps of sugar plus as much Colorado River as one cared to drink. Three days later, Peter Hansbrough, having rowed a few miles *up* the Colorado from Hite into Narrow Canyon, met Stanton with a load of fresh supplies.

What, you might ask in all fairness, do all of the trials and tribulations of this amateurish expedition, with its almost slapstick river-running mistakes, have to do with death in the Grand Canyon? Plenty. The "can-do" and "brave-but-ill-advised" actions of the principal men during this first month of the Brown Expedition explain their otherwise nearly unbelievable decisions next in Grand Canyon. These decisions set the record, still unbroken, for boating deaths on one trip in Grand Canyon.

Brown decided that he and Stanton and a half dozen of the crew who had proved their loyalty—oarsmen Peter M. Hansbrough and Henry C. Richards, engineer and surveyor John Hislop, photographer F. A. Nims, carpenter Harry McDonald, and cook George W. Gibson—should continue their survey down Grand Canyon in three of their original boats. Brown planned to eyeball and photograph the inner canyon, rather than run time-consuming transits.

Many people still wonder today why Brown made this decision "merely" for a railroad bed. The answer is, Brown and Company had far more in mind than just two lengths of steel rail connected by ties. As written in its Articles of Incorporation, Coconino County, Territory of Arizona (Recorder's office, Flagstaff), the Denver Colorado Cañon and Pacific Railroad's stated purposes were: "the operations of mines along the Canyon, located by the Stanton expedition, the location of new claims, the establishment of toll roads and a ferry across the river, the operation of hotels on the rim, and the acquisition and sale of real estate."

Stanton agreed to Brown's plans, he says, because "I considered it my duty to remain with my superior officer."

On July 9, 1889, Brown's party of eight headed downstream in their three repaired and heavily resupplied boats. They portaged Badger Creek Rapid (River Mile 8), then Soap Creek Rapid (River Mile 11+), and camped at its foot. For the first time during the entire survey, Brown, that night, dreamed of rapids. The next morning, at 6:20 a.m., Brown's boat, with McDonald steering and Brown at the oars, pulled away from shore. The next two boats took a few minutes longer to get off shore and to break into the current. They lagged behind.

Several hundred yards downstream, Brown and McDonald passed through a narrow "gateway" of Esplanade Sandstone bracketing the Colorado. Next they entered a series of haystack waves bisecting a sudden widening of the river where the Supai-Esplanade bedrock has been carved into a deep cove by debris flows from Saltwater Wash and by the river itself. The river here widens into a massive, powerful eddy system walled on the left by low cliffs. The standing waves of the downstream current raced past the eddy's very powerful upstream current on the left side of the river with a few feet of "eddy fence" whirlpools between them.

Brown yelled to McDonald, "Mac, we want to make this eddy and look at the rapid below—this is where Stanton wanted to stop and look at the rapid which he could not see."

"Alright," McDonald said, as he steered the boat left. Instantly a heavy wave erupted from the eddy fence. As the upstream eddy current grabbed the bow, the round-bottomed hull rolled over in an instant upstream flip.

This flip tossed McDonald from the stern into the main current. He emerged to see Brown to his left, already on the surface. As the rush of warm, silty water carried McDonald and the boat downstream, he "hallooed" to Brown to "Come on!" Brown cheerfully answered "Alright!"

The river swept McDonald through a series of small haystack waves for two hundred yards and toward the left shoreline. McDonald gasped for air. Then he swam like a madman for that left shore. He grabbed solid rock and hauled himself out. Next he looked for Brown.

Brown had hit the water farther left, toward the bow of the boat. This was not a good location. Brown had plunked into a whirlpool in the eddy fence swirling between the rushing downstream flow and the powerful upstream eddy current. Brown probably saw the left shoreline of smoothly sculpted Esplanade Sandstone only a hundred feet away and decided to swim for it— instead of trying to follow McDonald's route down the river. To a whitewater novice, McDonald's downriver swim would have looked anything but desirable.

As Harry McDonald raced back upstream along the boulder-cluttered sandstone ledges, he saw Brown. The would-be railroad magnate was still struggling in the eddy, now less than fifty feet from the shoreline cliffs. Brown, McDonald saw, was slowly being swept back upstream. At this same instant, McDonald also saw Stanton's boat, with Henry Richards and Peter Hansbrough rowing, only 200 feet upstream of Brown.

Stanton and his crew, however, could not yet see Brown. But Stanton did see McDonald frantically waving. He also heard him yell, "Mister Brown is in there!"

Stanton's crew steered into the eddy and searched the muddy surface. But they saw no one. Brown's notebook suddenly shot to the surface in the eddy. Stanton saw it and yelled. Hansbrough grabbed it. Brown himself, however, had vanished. Stanton's boat had arrived a few seconds too late.

The seven survivors spent the day rowing around the eddy and walking miles of the shoreline below in hopes of rescuing Brown's body. But Brown had vanished. The men did find their missing boat a mile downstream. That afternoon, Nims would later report, Hansbrough carved an epitaph in inch-high letters in the black desert varnish of the Esplanade a few feet above the racing eddy:

F. M. Brown Pres. D.C.C. & P.R.R. Co
was drowned July 10 1889
opposite this point

"Thus it was," Stanton writes, "that President Brown sacrificed his life, which could so easily have been saved if he had had a life preserver to keep him afloat one-half minute longer. A noblehearted man and a true friend, he had won the love of everyone associated with him."

It was at this point that this strange and tragic trip became irrational—and soon far more tragic. The seven survivors camped here at the mouth of Saltwater Wash. In a bit more than an hour they could have hiked the easy one-thousand feet up the wash to the plateau above. Another three hours of walking could have returned them to Lees Ferry, where friends, food, and transportation to the outside world could have been had.

Instead, as Stanton would write:

> *It was a day of terrible experience....*[But] *In this world we are left but little time to mourn. We had work to do, and I determined, if possible, to complete the whole of that work. That such a determination at that time was unwise, I can freely admit, as I look back upon it today, but neither Hislop nor I ever thought of leaving the river then. That we did not sufficiently appreciate the difficulties, even after such a warning, knowing the outfit we had, is also clear as I see it now, but who is there that can say our decision was culpably wrong?*

Remember, however, that Stanton himself had beseeched Brown on the issue of life preservers:

> *I urged President Brown to provide them for all of the men....It was no use, even though the air grew blue as Harper tried to convince Brown that he was going into dangers that he knew nothing about.*

Indeed Stanton's actions from this time after Brown drowned make little sense except in light of his own vision of what marvels—and economic remunerations—the Denver Colorado Cañon and Pacific Railroad Company might

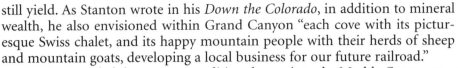

still yield. As Stanton wrote in his *Down the Colorado*, in addition to mineral wealth, he also envisioned within Grand Canyon "each cove with its picturesque Swiss chalet, and its happy mountain people with their herds of sheep and mountain goats, developing a local business for our future railroad."

Stanton now led the survey expedition deeper into the Marble Canyon section of Grand Canyon. They were now so careful about whitewater that they portaged everything with a wave in it, thus making only three miles per day. Four days downstream, as the crew rested on Sunday, both Hansbrough and Richards, Stanton reports, independently expressed deep worries over drowning in the Colorado. Each man also discussed the possibilities of life after death.

The next day, July 15, at 25-Mile Rapid, the crew lined their three boats halfway downstream on the left. Then, stopped by a cliff face in the Redwall Limestone, they had to run the rapid's large tailwaves.

The first boat, rowed by McDonald and Gibson, after one false start, tried again and made it. They beached on a strip of sand a few hundred yards downstream.

The second boat, Stanton's, rowed by Henry Richards and Peter Hansbrough, followed. The two (Stanton had decided to walk around this rapid, atop the low Redwall cliff) failed to row far enough to the right. The river swept their boat back to the left, into the cliff face, which was slightly undercut. The current here was mild enough that Hansbrough and Richards could use their oars and hands to push back away from the wall. But, in so doing, their round-bottomed boat abruptly flipped upside down.

The river sucked both men under. Both were good swimmers. Even so, no one ever saw Hansbrough break the surface. Richards, however, did appear in midstream where he swam to save himself.

McDonald and Gibson pushed out from shore to row upstream to intercept Richards. But the man sank forever in the thick Colorado before their horrified eyes.

What killed these two men was a series of bad decisions to continue running the river at all, inadequately equipped and untrained as they were. These and the river itself, which might have been flowing at about 25,000 cfs or less. On top of these, however, the Colorado was living up to its name. Two days earlier the monsoon rains had started with a vengeance. Countless tributary canyons had dumped millions of tons of mud, silt, and sand into the river. Both Richards and Hansbrough were fully dressed, as had been Brown. Their clothes, like the wool of those sheep at Lees Ferry, may have loaded ever heavier with sediment with each passing second in the river to the point where neither man could remain on the surface regardless of his swimming ability. If so, they might as well have been wearing weight belts loaded with lead.

A bit late in the game, one concludes, Stanton finally believes his own and Harper's admonitions about life jackets:

Then I realized fully what it meant to be without life preservers....

At last fully realizing that he and his four survivors were on a suicide mission, Stanton resolved at this point to abandon the survey. But now the convenient exit of Saltwater Wash was—Stanton thought—at 14 miles upstream, too far behind them to use. So, paradoxically, the five survivors continued downstream, with eyes peeled for a tributary canyon to the north that might offer them deliverance from this river that "seldom gives up its dead."

Two days later—having passed five other potential routes by which they might have exited the Canyon downstream of where Brown had drowned—they found a route labeled almost in neon. Tipped off by ancient Puebloan Indian ruins at South Canyon (River Mile 31.5), they decided that, if Indians could get in and out here, so could they.

The next day, after the most awful monsoonal symphony of lightning and thunder that Stanton had ever witnessed, the survivors cached their gear in a cave in the Redwall Limestone and readied themselves to hike out. At the last moment, however, Stanton spied Brown, identifiable by the coat he was still wearing, floating down the river.

McDonald and Hislop scrambled to get a boat back into the water in time to snag Brown. Not only was this the Christian thing to do, Brown had had all of the expedition's money in his pockets when he had drowned. But Brown drifted past his few surviving crew members too quickly to be intercepted.

On July 18, the five survivors hiked up South Canyon through "solid sheets of water" dumped by the monsoons. Four of the five vowed to return and complete the survey.

And those four (Gibson, the cook, had had enough) did return just before January of 1890. One of the four, Nims—as recounted in Chapter 1—was badly injured in a fall only five days into this second expedition. This time, however, Stanton had brought good life jackets and suffered no fatalities during his 86-day survey of Grand Canyon.

Many more people would seek their fortunes in the Canyon. In the winter of 1895–1896, Al Marsh took his string of burros with supplies into the upper end of Grand Canyon in search of paydirt. He reckoned that he prospected nearly one hundred miles of the Canyon without finding good prospects before he ran out of food. Deep in the Inner Canyon, Marsh found it impossible to climb out. After some disappointing non-routes on snow-covered cliffs, Marsh abandoned his burros and his outfit and headed downstream on a raft he built from driftwood.

Marsh reckoned he had drifted down about fifty miles of river before being stopped by his fear of a huge rapid. He abandoned his raft and started hiking to the South Rim again. This was likely a smart move even though days passed as he wandered and struggled along the high cliffs searching for breaks that might allow him to escape the Canyon walls. Finally, during early January,

1896, Marsh, half-starved and footsore, found a break in the wall. A few days later he reached Aubrey Valley and the railroad.

"He will not attempt to regain his burros or camp outfit," noted the staff writer for the *Mohave Miner*, "as he has seen enough Grand Canyon to last him a lifetime."

Almost forty years passed after Brown, Hansbrough, and Richards drowned during their attempted railroad survey before the river claimed new known victims trying to navigate (rather than cross, see next section) the Colorado. The most famous of these victims died during a romantic bid for stardom.

The pivotal event of this epic took place one day during early summer in 1927, when a shy, twenty-one-year-old woman named Bessie Haley embarked with a girlfriend on an overnight trip by ship from San Francisco to Los Angeles. Bessie had come west a year earlier from Parkersburg, West Virginia, to attend the California School of Fine Arts. Weeks earlier, in Kentucky, she had secretly married her high school sweetheart Earl Helmick. But after living with him for less than two months, their marriage had failed. After Bessie vanished to the West, however, Helmick had allegedly wired her money for an "operation." Some historians conclude that Bessie was pregnant. The money, they say, was either for an illegal abortion or for the medical costs of childbirth coupled with adoption. On the other hand, this "operation" story may be a false rumor.

Once in San Francisco, Bessie attended classes, worked in a large local bookstore, and she also wrote poetry. She shared a room with a nineteen-year-old nude art model, Eraine Granstedt (a.k.a. Irene Granstedt, a.k.a. Greta Granstedt). Bessie's roommate was not only a young and beautiful blonde, but also an ambitious one. And perhaps a very persuasive one as well. After less than a year of studying art, Bessie and Eraine purchased one-way tickets south to the City of Angels on that overnight ship. Eraine's goal was to make it big in Tinsletown. Bessie's goal was, well, a mystery.

Fate, however, placed on this same southbound ship a tall young adventurer named Glen Rollin Hyde. Glen was the son of a boom-and-bust-cycle rancher and builder, Rollin C. Hyde, from Twin Falls, Idaho. Glen had run a few Idaho and British Columbian rivers—the Salmon, the Fraser, and the Peace—and had learned "drift," or "sweep" boating techniques from veteran boater Harry Guleke. (Idaho drift boats were built like gigantic horse troughs thirty or more feet long. Riding on the steeper gradient of Idaho rivers, the boatmen rarely found the need to power their boats downstream. They simply drifted. They positioned their long sweep oars off the bow and stern strictly to be able to move their boats out of the way laterally of obstacles in the river.)

Electricity must have flowed between Bessie and Glen. On that short voyage down the California coast to the City of Angels, their destiny became the stuff of a Hollywood fantasy—a tragic one. When Bessie disembarked in Los

Angeles she and Glen had already become inseparable. Eraine stepped off the gangway with Bessie and Glen—and legally vanished. As pods of grey whales near their ship had spouted geysers onto Pacific waves, she had assumed a new identity; Eraine was now Greta Grenstedt. Greta, as river historian Brad Dimock notes, "went straight to Hollywood for thirty-some years of bit part roles."

Bessie, in contrast, left Los Angeles with Glen for Idaho. She married him several months later, in April of 1928, one day after her uncontested Nevada divorce from Earl Helmick. Glen had a dream that had captivated Bessie. His dream was to be the first man and woman team to run the Colorado River through the Grand Canyon. Glen also wanted to maximize their publicity, fame, and money for having done so.

Bessie could draw and write poetry. Glen too could write. Glen's grand plan incorporated her talents as well as her gender. They would run the river, the two of them. And they would run it in a boat that Glen built. They also would set a speed record for traversing the canyons. On top of all this, like trapeze artists defying death without a safety net, Glen and Bessie would run the treacherous Grand Canyon Colorado without life jackets—just as Idaho boatmen had been doing for decades.

Not only would all of this make them famous, it would open the door to the lucrative vaudeville lecture circuit and also land them a book contract. Bessie and Glen could write the book and illustrate it with her drawings.

It seemed like a perfect plan.

In October, 1928, Glen and Bessie arrived at Green River, Utah. Here Glen spent $50 on materials to build an Idaho drift boat, a flat bottomed scow of the type that the legendary Harry Guleke had taught him to build on the Salmon. Two days later, Glen's scow measured twenty feet long by five wide by three deep. He equipped it with a pair of long sweep oars off the bow and stern. He also installed conveniences such as bedsprings and a stove consisting of a metal box of sand into which kerosene could be poured, then burned. These would free the honeymooners from any need to camp on shore. Speed was the thing.

Harry Howland, a Green River local who helped the two with facilities for building, stared at Glen's boat. Howland appraised the poorly angled cuts of the boards and the imperfect vertical rows of nail heads holding Glen's big box together and said, "It looks like a floating coffin."

On October 20, Glen and Bessie set off down the Green in their scow. After 100 miles of flat water they struggled through the 28 rapids of Cataract Canyon. One of these ejected Bessie from the scow. Glen somehow retrieved her. The two arrived unscathed at Lees Ferry in mid-November on 14,000 cfs. By this time they had named Glen's scow "Rain-in-the-Face" because of how the squared-off bow snowplowed into waves with huge splashes instead of slicing through them.

Here boatman Owen Clark, veteran of the 1927 Pathé-Bray Expedition down Grand Canyon, warned the Hydes that they needed a second boat and also should be wearing life jackets for safety. Clark, having run the river himself only to River Mile 95, also told them that the worst rapid they would encounter would be Soap Creek (River Mile 11). Glen ignored Clark's safety warnings, then he and Bessie continued downstream.

Days later, Earl Boyer and some companions would hike down Soap Creek Canyon to retrieve the body of Royce E. Dean, who had drowned on June 7 in a tragic accident during the last cross-river run of Lees Ferry (discussed later in this chapter). Boyer and company were surprised to find a man's and a woman's foot prints heading up Soap Creek Canyon for *three miles* and then reversing to return to the river. Apparently, after Glen and Bessie Hyde had scouted Soap Creek Rapid, which never had been run at low water, they had decided to abandon the trip and hike out of Marble Canyon. But, after walking miles up Soap, the Canyon walls either frightened them or their own sore feet convinced them that continuing downriver remained their best option after all. Either way, the honeymooners returned to the Colorado and managed to get their scow past this rapid.

Later, in Sockdolager Rapid (River Mile 79) or Grapevine Rapid (River Mile 81.5), a big wave beguiled Glen. His sweep oar thumped him in the chin and knocked him out of the scow. Bessie grabbed the sweeps and kept the scow straight. Next, once Glen grabbed a gunnel, she hauled him back into the scow.

Twenty-six days—a record time—and 424 miles downstream of Green River, Glen and Bessie tied up their scow near Phantom Ranch (River Mile 88). From there they hiked up to the South Rim Village. This stop had multiple purposes. First, it was a perfect way for the world to learn that Glen and Bessie Hyde were alive and well in their conquest of the Colorado. Second, the honeymooners had run out of food. The rim offered them a chance to resupply—if only Glen had brought enough money to buy enough food.

On the rim, the couple was treated as royalty. But quickly, Emery Kolb, an inspired photographer and an experienced Grand Canyon boatman who had rowed the entire Canyon twice, swept Bessie and Glen out of the limelight and into his studio. There, perched on the South Rim overlooking the Bright Angel Trail, Kolb tried to convince Glen to take Kolb's own life jackets. Glen refused, saying, "We don't need any artificial aids."

Emery, who had done his share of unplanned swimming in the Colorado, beseeched Glen to at least buy an inner tube or two to keep on the scow as throwable life preservers. Glen refused, this time, more angrily, announcing in a letter from the rim, "I am going to do it without life jackets, or else."

Ranger Bert Lauzon met the Hydes on the rim and reported, "The little woman was sick of it when she reached this far. He wanted to make a record—taking the first woman thru—she would have quit long before if she had her way—she just had no enthusiasm—she was dejected…Mrs. Hyde had enough of the Canyon and went on only because Mr. Hyde insisted."

Before hiking down the trail to their scow, Bessie gave some of her good clothes to Edith Kolb, Emery's 20-year-old daughter. Then she gazed longingly at Edith's new pair of shoes. "I wonder," Bessie mused, now sobered by Emery's warnings of the dangers awaiting the honeymooners downstream, "if I shall ever wear pretty shoes again."

A San Francisco businessman, Adolph Sutro, solved Glen's other problem of not enough money to resupply on food by offering Glen a trade. If Sutro could ride along in the scow for seven miles from Phantom Ranch to Hermit Rapid, Sutro would provide a couple of weeks of food—to be delivered at Hermit Creek by mule. Glen agreed.

Sutro rode with the Hydes for seven miles, including through Horn Creek Rapid (River Mile 90.25). They camped one night en route, likely at River Mile 91. Sutro would years later report to river historian Dock Marston, however, that he had never seen a boatman as indifferent and irresponsible to boating techniques as Glen Hyde—nor one as consumed with his own feat and the money it might get him. Glen seemed slipshod. He had, Sutro said, the habit of jamming an oar into the sand and then securing the scow only with one rope tied to that oar. Indeed, Sutro's impression at this point was that Bessie was both tired of the trip, terrified of the rough water, and fearful of continuing, even while Glen mostly discussed the possibilities for making money by cashing in on their fame. "It was," Sutro wrote, "the most inadequately equipped outfit I have ever seen. I couldn't understand how they got to Bright Angel. [But] it was obvious that [the] whole object of the trip was to make money in show business."

On November 18, at a Hermit Rapid now flowing well under 10,000 cfs, they found Sutro's mules with food. After loading the scow, however, the Hydes' bid for stardom took an ominous twist.

One account told to mule packer Bob Francy, who wasn't looking, by other men present has it that Bessie refused to get back into the scow to continue the trip. Glen, the men said, physically picked her up and placed her in the scow. Although the story of Glen carrying Bessie may be apocryphal, Sutro himself did note that, once Bessie was back in the scow, "Her face registered stark terror."

The last and final photo taken of Bessie and Glen (at Hermit Camp) prior to their launch onto the River at Hermit Rapid reveals body language shouting despair and lack of confidence—or worse.

Either way, Glen and Bessie ran Hermit Rapid at low water—then vanished.

Glen's 69-year-old father, Rollin C. Hyde, waited at Needles to pick up Glen and Bessie on December 6. When the honeymooners still had not appeared by December 16, R. C. Hyde reckoned that the scow had somehow escaped his son and daughter-in-law and marooned them. He called the governor of Idaho and requested an aerial search by the U.S. Army of the river corridor. On December 19, L. G. Plummer and H. G. Adams, piloting a Douglas O-2 airplane out of March Field, California, spotted what appeared to be the scow floating in an eddy at River Mile 237.

On December 21, Emery Kolb, his brother Ellsworth, and Chief Ranger Jim Brooks, along with R. C. Hyde and Deputy Sheriff John Nelson of Yavapai County, borrowed a Hualapai wagon and saddle horses to get down Peach Springs Wash to Diamond Creek and the Colorado (River Mile 225.7). The Kolbs and Brooks re-hammered together a skiff abandoned by the James Girand Dam Site Survey party several years earlier. On Christmas Eve, the three put in at Diamond Creek.

The three Christmas boaters found the Hydes' scow in the same eddy as where the search plane had located it. Its bowline seemed to have caught underwater between boulders. But searches up and down the river—initially, by the Kolbs and Brooks below Diamond, and by R. C. Hyde and Deputy Sheriff Nelson upstream of Diamond, and then later by the Hualapais, by cowboys, and by the NPS and Fred Harvey personnel enlisted by R. C. Hyde (who had lost his other two sons as infants and was now 100-percent dedicated to rescuing his only surviving one)—discovered no other definite signs of the missing honeymooners beyond an abandoned camp several miles upstream of Diamond Creek near Mile 212 containing empty tins and a jar from Idaho, and Glen's foot prints scouting Mile 217 Rapid.

Aboard the scow sat virtually all of the Hydes' possessions: their coats, Glen's rifle, Bessie's camera, diary, and even her purse. But, oddly, no sketchbook. Glen had carved forty-two notches, including crosses for Sundays, in the gunwale of the scow, one per day. The last would have been incised on November 30. Bessie's diary, a skimpy document in simple code of dashes for quiet stretches and circles for rapids and with few words, placed them three days downstream of Lava Falls (River Mile 179.5) on this date, floating on about 8,000+ cfs. This translates to the area of Diamond Creek (River Mile 225.7) or beyond. Whatever had happened to the Hydes had occurred on the November 30 or on December 1. But what *had* happened?

Five miles upstream of the self-moored scow, 232-Mile Rapid was pouring its entire narrow sluice of Colorado into a carnivore's dentition of jagged fangs of Precambrian bedrock. The Kolb brothers and Brooks had had the devil's own time figuring a way around it in the rickety old boat they had re-hammered together. They finally had to line the boat along the shore. What, they had wondered, had Glen done here?

The three found no foot prints, which suggests the Hydes ran 232-Mile unscouted. This rapid, all three men figured, was the likely culprit—that and Glen's obdurate refusal to bring life jackets.

If Glen had simply run the scow in the main current, flowing at 8,700 cfs on December 1, it would have collided with those surprising fangs sieving the mainstream. It easily could have jarred Glen and/or Bessie into the cold river. Without life jackets in the rapid.

Indeed the scow did show minor collision damage to its hull and also had a foot of water in the bilge, though it otherwise remained ship-shape. After searching both shorelines at River Mile 237 and finding no sign of humanity, the Kolbs and Brooks off-loaded the Hyde's possessions into their small boat, severed the scow's bowline, then rowed downstream.

About three miles downstream, the searchers capsized their own little rig in Separation Rapid. Jim Brooks was trapped under the upside-down boat with one of the upright standards caught in his overalls. He finally got loose. But at least he had a life jacket. With only two jackets for the three men, Ellsworth had strapped an empty five-gallon can to his back for safety.

Ellsworth now struggled in the icy flow to keep his face above water. All three men escaped alive, but now were freezing. Ice formed on and in the boat itself. The three shivering, would-be rescuers continued to Spencer Canyon (River Mile 246). From there they rode out on horses with the Deputy Sheriff Nelson of Yavapai County, R. C. Hyde, and some Hualapais. This ride avoided their otherwise being forced to run Lava Cliff Rapid, then considered by those who had run the entire Grand Canyon to be the worst rapid on the entire Colorado (Owen Clark and the Pathé-Bray Expedition had quit the river at River Mile 95; hence his warning to Glen Hyde at Lees Ferry that Soap Creek would offer the worst challenge).

Glen and Bessie Hyde were chalked up as victims of drowning (or maybe even murder, see Chapter 8). But no matter how she died, Bessie Hyde had become the first woman to run the rapids of the Colorado from Cataract Canyon through Grand Canyon to somewhere near River Mile 232, for a total of 565 miles. Bessie is rarely credited with this "first-woman-to-do-it" because she did not make it past River Mile 237 to the foot of the Canyon at River Mile 277—at least alive and in a boat. The women normally credited as having been the first, Elzada Clover and Lois Jotter, were designated thus by the self-appointed "bean counter" of who had "really" boated Grand Canyon—"Dock" Otis R. Marston (who perhaps eliminated 150 names of those who did not run all 277 miles in order to include himself among the first 100). Clover and Jotter, however, descended the river a decade later, in 1938, as paying passengers on one of Norm Nevills' early commercial trips. This was during a time when, ironically, the rapids below River Mile 237 had been drowned by Lake Mead. Moreover, Nevills portaged or lined many of the rapids that Bessie and Glen ran. In short, Bessie Hyde was the true "first," a woman who also, for many miles, manned one of the sweeps, thus "rowing" the Hydes' boat downriver. The next two women to follow her ran only a couple of minor rapids beyond what she had but ran far fewer big ones before River Mile 237 than Bessie and, of course, did no real rowing whatsoever.

The Grand Canyon Colorado took its next river-running victim less than three years later, during the depth of the Great Depression, a time when a steady job, no matter how back-breaking, was life itself.

This next amazing story became known—in part, anyway—at about 8:00 a.m. on June 23, 1931, when James R. Ervin walked up to a Hualapai ranch house about five miles from Peach Springs, in Peach Springs Canyon. Ervin was pin-cushioned with cactus thorns, exhausted, and had lost twenty pounds off his normal 130. He had eaten no food for four days. And he had just traversed a landscape offering little water.

Ervin fell under the Hualapai's artesian water hydrant and gulped like a dying man. Then he vomited. Charles McGee, the young Hualapai owner of the ranch, dragged Ervin away from the hydrant and forced him instead to take small sips. Ervin explained to McGee that he had a partner, Bill Payne, somewhere in the Canyon behind him, to the west, in Lower Granite Gorge. But his partner, Ervin added, was exhausted and probably had been unable to follow him out.

How Ervin and Payne had gotten themselves into the mess they had comprises an odyssey of non-planning and poor decision-making that would make Custer's Last Stand look clever.

Bill Payne of Hollywood, California, and James R. Ervin had been working for Anderson Brothers Boarding and Supply Company which housed and fed construction crews on site at the Boulder Dam project. Payne (whose true name was reportedly William Talmadge but who said that he used the alias "Payne" to avoid possible bad publicity for his famous sister, Hollywood actress Constance Talmadge) held the job of checking the men's names as they entered the mess hall at the foot of the thousand-foot canyon wall. Ervin was a waiter. Both men—and hundreds of others—considered the 120-degree-hot dam project a boiling "Hellhole" (nor were they wrong; 110 men would die building Hoover Dam).

In late May, Payne suggested to Ervin that they drive Ervin's stripped down Model T to Denver, Colorado, and work instead on a dude ranch run by some friends or relatives of Payne's. Ervin agreed. Not even waiting for payday, the two arranged for their final checks to be mailed to them in Denver. Then they drove east. Ervin was thirty years old, Payne twenty-seven. The two were an odd couple. Ervin had worked physical jobs all of his life, had served a stint with the Coast Guard, and was an excellent swimmer. He described himself as in "perfect condition physically" and probably was. In contrast, Payne had never resorted to physical labor in his life and was, in Ervin's opinion, what today would be called a wimp.

In Denver, Payne could not find the people who were supposed to offer them employment. Nor could the duo find other work. Worse yet, the two men's final paychecks also failed to arrive. The pay steward in Boulder City, Nevada, had "forgotten all about it."

So the pair drove south. Ervin's Model T broke down in Cobero, New Mexico. With no money to pay for repairs, the pair abandoned it and their luggage in a Navajo garage in hopes of retrieving it all later. They hopped a freight train on the Santa Fe line with the goal of picking up their old jobs—and their paychecks—in Boulder City, Nevada.

Railroad guards tossed the two off. Multiple times. Finally Ervin and Payne gave up on the rails. They hitchhiked west. By the time they reached Peach Springs on Route 66, roughly 150 round-about miles short of Boulder City, they had gone two days without food. Desperate in an era when bumming food was a tough go, they perused their road map again for inspiration. The map showed the Colorado River flowing past them only 23 miles north.

To Ervin, the river distance from the mouth of Diamond Creek to Boulder City seemed to be far fewer miles than overland by road. Besides, Ervin reasoned, because this western half—133 miles—of the Grand Canyon Colorado was not within the national park boundaries (it was not included in the park until 1975), it must not include any of the rough rapids that made the river so famous. "I assumed," Ervin admitted, "the river to be rather calm from there on down." So, thinking that it was smooth sailing—and, perhaps more importantly, that it would not require them to hitchhike or to hop trains— the two men narrowed their dire straights by walking 23 miles down Peach Springs Canyon.

Neither man carried food or water. Payne, exhausted, sat down to rest. Ervin continued downcanyon. He scooped the mud out of a wet burro track and drank what seeped into it, missing the clear spring nearby. From there he made it to Diamond Creek. After drinking his fill of clear water, Ervin headed back upcanyon with an old coffee pot he had found and filled with water for Payne. Ervin soon found Payne stumbling along in tears—Payne had thought that Ervin had abandoned him.

The two walked the last mile to the Colorado River. The Colorado had peaked that year on June 17 (measured at Phantom Ranch) at a mere 32,000 cfs. Now, on June 21, it had dropped by 8,000 cfs. Ervin walked along the new clean beach, then he poked his nose into the bushes and buildings higher up from the river. "Imagine my elation," Ervin later would write, "at finding an old boat pulled up with boards and pipe rollers."

At Diamond Creek in Lower Granite Gorge, Ervin and Payne found their short-cut to the Boulder Dam site assured in the form of this serviceable river boat, the *Bright Angel*. It was one of six wooden boats built in California with water-tight compartments of galvanized steel, and painted white. The 1927 Pathé-Bray expedition had used these six boats during the dead of winter to film a movie in Grand Canyon. Due in part to an undecided screenplay and a hideously bad lead actress, Rose Blossom (who never entered the Canyon), this movie flip-flopped in both its title and concept from being the *Bride of the Colorado* to the *Pride of the Colorado*. It had no woman on the expedition;

instead, one of the boatmen dressed in drag. The film was never released. Pathé-Bray had abandoned their filming and the expedition itself, including the *Bright Angel*, 130 miles upstream of Diamond Creek at Hermit Rapid (River Mile 95). Soon afterward, Bob Francy, a handyman at Phantom Ranch, had enlisted some friends to help him row, line, winch, drag, and portage the *Bright Angel* back upstream to Bright Angel Creek (River Mile 88) and Phantom Ranch. Months later, Rollin C. Hyde had implored Francy with the lure of a $1,000 reward to use his hard-won *Bright Angel* to search for Glen and Bessie—or at least to find firm information on what might have happened to them. Francy had enlisted Jack Harbin to help him. Assistant NPS Superintendent P. P. Patraw had ridden with the two for the first twenty miles—until social friction drove Patraw to hike out alone up the South Bass Trail to the Coconino Plateau (where he got lost in the snow for two days). Francy's search and rescue expedition in the dead of a very nasty winter had been a truly horrible experience for all three men, the *Bright Angel* having flipped once, wrapped once, and frozen the men constantly. Worse, it had uncovered nothing that R. C. Hyde defined as "firm." Hyde, who had mortgaged virtually everything he could to raise search money, refused to pay the two men any of the $1,000 reward he had promised. Francy, now had had no choice but to abandon his dearly-won *Bright Angel* in the early winter of 1929 at Diamond Creek. He felt disgusted with R. C. Hyde. Finally, Francy threatened to sue. Hyde settled for $700. At any rate, this serviceable, though anything but lucky, boat sitting on shore at Diamond Creek with a good pair of oars and one cork life jacket eliminated Ervin's and Payne's need to build the raft that they had planned to build (without tools or supplies).

Before they shoved off the next morning, Ervin quipped to Payne that the boat might be called the *Dark Angel* before they got out of the Gorge. Payne answered, "Yes, it will be a great story to tell your grandchildren if you live to tell it."

Shortly after dawn on June 22, the duo set off downriver. For the past couple of days the river had been flowing an almost steady 23,600 cfs. While this was a low flow for a normal June, relatively speaking, it was a very serious high flow in the Lower Gorge, especially for a novice boater. In fact, it would prove to be nuts.

In the first six rapids, by Ervin's count, they capsized the *Bright Angel* an amazing five times. But, in that sixth rapid, Ervin lost one of the oars. (A packrat had nibbled through its tether, and, despite having extra rope aboard, Ervin had not bothered to replace this tether.) Even before this loss, however, Ervin admitted that he could not control the boat at all in the rapids. But now, upside down yet again, he leapt off the boat's hull toward the wall on the south side, swam, and made it. This fifth swim without a life jacket—Payne was wearing their only one—had taxed even his "excellent physical condition."

The duo tied up the *Bright Angel*, still upside-down, above a large boulder somewhere near River Mile 234. Evidentially trusting the seals of the hatches of its watertight compartments to allow no water to leak in that might sink it—or, more likely, not even thinking that the boat might leak—Ervin decided to leave the *Bright Angel* upside down and to hike out of the Gorge.

By now, mid-morning of June 22, both men were weak and starving after more than three days without food. Ervin, believing it would be impossible for Payne to climb out, told him to wait there with the boat. He would come back, he promised Payne, when he found help.

Roughly a thousand feet up, Ervin found a spring. He drank his fill, wetted his face and shirt, then climbed higher. He hit a wall in the Redwall. It looked sheer and unclimbable. Ervin searched along it but could not find a breach. Finally he gave up and walked back down to his spring. From there he walked over to the edge of the Tonto to see what Payne was doing. Payne, he saw, had started up the first sloping wall of Vishnu Schist. Payne looked up and saw Ervin. He yelled to him, "Hey, wait for me!"

Ervin explains how things continued to go wrong:

> *This is where I made another mistake. I yelled back, "Go back and stay there." If I had told him to come on up and also about the spring, he might have, just might have, stayed there, as he might have been too exhausted to go back down to the boat from up there. However, I knew that if I saw him fall it would unnerve me to the point that I would be unable to climb out, granting I had a chance at all.*

Now late morning, Ervin searched again for a breach in the Redwall looming so high above him. He finally found a chimney crack extending hundreds of feet up. He ascended this but was stopped at 80 feet by a chock boulder blocking him. He chimneyed around this, scaring the hell out of himself. He then continued to ascend the last 150 feet, the top of which seemed to be vertical. And impossible. "This is where I almost collapsed from sheer fright."

But, continuing up, he found a small bench to the right with a barrel cactus growing on it, the only one he had seen. He hacked it open for the pulp. He reached the rim about a half hour before sundown on what was one day short of the longest day—and one of the hottest—of the year. That night, under a half moon, he walked southeast, pin-cushioning himself with cactus thorns. Ervin got so woozy before dawn that, as he descended a wash littered with round boulders, he was afraid he would fall and bash his brains out.

So he laid down and fell into a tortured sleep while awaiting the dawn. When it finally came, Ervin awoke to see only trackless desert. The absence of any evidence of human presence, even in the far distance, almost sent him "into a tail spin again."

A half-hour of walking, however, brought him to a barbed-wire fence. At about 8:00 a.m. on June 23, Ervin walked up to Charles McGee's ranch house and guzzled madly from his faucet. Then retched.

Ervin had hiked out of Lower Granite Gorge, from roughly eight miles downstream of Diamond Creek, possibly twenty or more miles and thousands of feet of elevation, including scaling the dreaded Redwall Limestone. The soles of his new shoes were worn completely off.

John Nelson, deputy sheriff at Peach Springs, led a six-man search party, including Ervin, back to the head of Bridge Canyon (River Mile 235.3).

Descending into it, they picked up Ervin's tracks coming out of the canyon and the Inner Gorge itself on the Tapeats Sandstone, the Tonto Plateau. On June 24, they reached the spring Ervin had first found on the 22nd and saw more of Ervin's tracks. The party then descended into Lower Granite Gorge. There, however, they could find no sign at all of Bill Payne or the *Bright Angel*.

A hard rain set in and likely obliterated the possibility of finding at least some of the tracks. Ervin showed Nelson the exact spot where he and Payne had tied up the boat at River Mile 233.6. Nelson, however, saw no sign of anything and remained unconvinced that a boat had ever parked there (Nelson, incidentally, had been the person who had originally dragged the *Bright Angel* above high water back at Diamond Creek after Bob Francy had abandoned it in disgust. Hence, Nelson now may have been annoyed with Ervin not just for all the hassle he was causing, but also for having hijacked the *Bright Angel* to begin with and then losing it).

Ervin also explained to Nelson how Payne had started to follow him. But the search party found no signs of that having happened either. At this lack of material evidence—no boat, no Payne, no foot prints, no boat drag marks, nothing at all—Nelson, again possibly already irked at Ervin for "stealing" his *Bright Angel*, began to doubt Ervin's story. Nelson reports in June 1931:

> *Camping at a spring on a bench that night that* [over-] *looked the Country after looking a while Ervin seemed to be satisfied and started back toward bridge* [sic] *Canyon by him Self. After looking around a while longer we all decided from Ervin's actions, that they had an accident at this point Ervin getting to shore and he was not sure whether his partner had reached shore or not but after making this search around 2 miles in vicinity of where he came out he was satisfied in his own mind he was drowned, which he would not admit. After we reached the head of Bridge Canyon Ervin was in camp. I accused him of being doubtfull* [sic] *of his friend getting out of the river. He still maintained that he started to follow him out of the Gorge after they tied up boat being up side down at the time. After making the search from Point of Accident to bridge* [sic] *Canyon I still believe his partner never reached the bank of the river and was drowned.*

But Ervin's explanation is different. "I think he [Payne] must have taken the boat and gone on the day I left him or not later than the next morning."

Maybe so. But muddying this mystery even more, the river had spike-flowed another 500 cfs during Ervin's hegira through the desert, possibly raising the river enough to float the *Bright Angel* loose and to erase any marks made by its bow on shore.

Ironically, only three miles downstream of the place where Ervin had left Payne a cabin stood in a camp left by the Bridge Canyon Dam surveying team. Its shelves lay stocked with $75 worth of canned food, a large larder in 1931. "You know," Ervin wrote later, "it took me three months to get over my hunger."

So what happened to Bill Payne and the *Bright Angel*? A week of searching found no trace of either man or boat or even the life jacket. Nor was the boat or body ever seen by anyone downstream beyond the Grand Wash Cliffs. Likely Bill Payne drowned in the Colorado and the *Bright Angel* sank, but, even more likely—and as with the unsolved mystery of Glen and Bessie Hyde (more on this one later)—we will never know exactly what happened. But when, back in 1931, Ervin had tried to retrace William Payne's Hollywood connections to inform his relatives of his loss, he allegedly found no firm record that William Payne was related to Hollywood's famous Talmadge sisters. He did find instead that William Talmadge had quit his restaurant job in Hollywood prior to arriving at Hoover Dam. And when Talmadge had left, the restaurant proprietor informed Ervin, he had absconded with the entire day's till, a whopping $700. So, after all, William Talmadge may have become William Payne for reasons other than what he had disclosed to Ervin.

Even so, Payne's mysterious disappearance would haunt Ervin for the rest of his life. So much so that, in 1965, Ervin returned to Lower Granite Gorge with Harvey Butchart to retrace Ervin's harrowing, 1931 escape route out of the Canyon. Ervin considered his tragic adventure so gripping that he tried to sell it as a Hollywood screenplay. While the route was every bit as difficult and frightening as Ervin remembered, Hollywood passed on Ervin's saga of survival.

Far more river runners in Grand Canyon would die. Some of them would be unsuspecting passengers who trusted in the expertise of their guides; a few would be fortune hunters; some would be partiers who mixed too much alcohol with their river, or vice versa; some would be quixotic wayfarers, unrealistically prepared and living, then dying, a fantasy. Yet others would apparently be suicidal.

In October, 1938, members of the Amos Burg-Buzz Holmstrom-Willis Johnson trip down the Grand Canyon Colorado spotted a boat half-sunk and half filled with the sand on the north shore immediately downstream of Lava Canyon Rapid (River Mile 65.5). The boat was a 16-foot punt, square at both ends, built of new pine lumber. It was 4-feet wide and had 3-foot-high ends.

Holmstrom reckoned that it was Jack Aldridge's boat. Aldridge had put in at Green River about two months ahead of them. Aldridge, Holmstrom thought, had planned to manage the punt with a sweep oar off the stern. The boat was a very rough copy of the earliest boats that Norm Nevills had used on the San Juan River, the prototype of which was constructed from an old horse trough and a privy, whose knot holes and cracks were patched with tin and caulked with old undershirts. At any rate, nothing remained in this derelict boat now wrecked below the Little Colorado but sand.

Upon investigation by the NPS they learned that in Glen Canyon just downstream of California Bar at Hansen (roughly Mile 100 upstream from Lees Ferry and one of the few Glen Canyon tributaries passable by wagons or Model Ts off Highway 276), two Japanese visitors reported seeing Jack Aldridge. Aldridge had explained to these two tourists that he was planning to row through Grand Canyon all the way to the newly completed Boulder Dam (roughly 430 miles downstream). As bad as Holmstrom thought Aldridge's boat to be ("impossible to control in heavy rapids"), Aldridge *had* somehow navigated it in one piece through the forty difficult miles of Cataract Canyon.

But no one had seen the boat float past Lees Ferry. This could have been because Aldridge had passed at night, or during the day but was not seen (and in neither case had Aldridge stopped, which would be surprising), or because the boat passed without Aldridge aboard, either afloat, or half afloat. In any case, Aldridge's fate was a mystery. Did he drown in Glen Canyon, drown in Grand Canyon, or had he hiked out somewhere?

River sleuth Dock Marston pursued the mystery further in December of 1948. He tracked down an acquaintance of Aldridge (who was normally a painter in San Diego) named Waldo Watkins. Watkins wrote back, "Regarding Mr. Jack H. Aldridge. Met him last as I remember in late Spring 1940 at Palm Springs, Calif., have not seen or heard of him since that time, have inquired of others who also knew him to no avail. It seems he quietly disappeared." [punctuation added.] If Watkins' memory was accurate, then somehow, somewhere, Aldridge escaped the Colorado and abandoned his boat only to vanish yet again from civilization. We include Aldridge's incomplete saga here only because, if Waldo Watkins' memory had instead failed him over the years as to the last date he had seen Aldridge, and if all of Aldridge's other friends' memories were correct in recollecting their not having seen him, then Aldridge may indeed have drowned in the Colorado River or died while trying to hike out.

Aldridge may seem eccentric, but a far more bizarre example of an eccentric lone boatman exists in the *Superintendent's Monthly Reports* for October, 1946:

> *On Oct. 24 one man in a rubber raft was sighted passing the
> mouth of Bright Angel Creek. Subsequent investigation revealed the
> man, who refused to give his name, had been put into the river*

near Lees Ferry on Oct. 19 by employees of Marble Canyon Lodge. The man, who may be Charles Roemer, of 353 E. 19th St., New York City, started without adequate food or equipment, and the success of his mission seems doubtful, although his knowledge of the river, obtained by extensive reading, was complete and accurate. On Oct. 26 Chief Ranger Perry E. Brown chartered a plane, and with Ranger Lauzon and Deputy sheriff John Bradley, flew over the river from Havasu Creek to the Bright Angel without sighting either man or raft. Subsequent investigation discloses that if the man is Chas. Roemer; he is a retired engineer from Hungary but recently arrived in the United States. The New York Chief of Police states that the man has no known friends or relatives in this country. [punctuation added]

Roemer's one-person attempt to traverse the full Grand Canyon Colorado in his small inflatable—allegedly without oars or paddles—was the first such attempt to run the entire river in five years and also the only try of the first 198 miles below Lees Ferry in 1946. A solo run had been done before Roemer, by Haldane "Buzz" Holmstrom in 1937. Holmstrom, however, had worn a life jacket.

At any rate, Roemer was not a recent immigrant as the report above stated. He had immigrated from Hungary shortly after World War I, abandoning his wife and three children in Budapest. He then had lived in New York City for more than twenty years. Months before arriving at Lees Ferry he had quit his job and planned to move to California. En route, he also planned a solo run of the Grand Canyon Colorado. To get ready for this, he memorized the rapids from a book. He named off to Art Greene, owner of Marble Canyon Lodge, which rapids he could run and which he would have to line.

While preparing for his descent, Art Greene tried to dissuade the fifty-something-year-old Roemer. But to no avail. Even if things went wrong, Roemer insisted, he was a good swimmer and could simply swim to shore. On top of this level of confidence, Roemer impressed people as a stingy man. He bargained hard with Greene for two loaves of bread, two Bermuda onions, and five small packages of raisins, *apparently as his only provisions for the entire 277-mile* (ten-day) *journey*. Roemer's crash diet alarmed Greene even more. "Even if you just rub the onions on your belly," Greene warned Roemer "and don't even eat them, they still will be gone by the end of the trip."

We likely will never know whether Roemer failed to provide himself with a life jacket because he was miserly or because he was so self-confident in his swimming ability. Maybe it was both.

Roemer floated past Bright Angel Trail (River Mile 89) on 7,100 cfs at 3:20 p.m. on October 24, in his little "five-man" inflatable. He waved and called out to a surprised tour guide on shore. At this point, the guide said, Roemer seemed to be in fine spirits. Horn Creek Rapid, very nasty at this medium low water level, awaited Roemer less than two miles downstream. Indeed, Roemer was never seen nor heard from again.

The following June, despite searches by air and by water on Lake Mead by Harry Aleson, still no sign had been found of Roemer. A "memo to [Park] director" concluded, "The fate of this adventurer is still unknown, but he is presumed to have perished in the treacherous rapids below Bright Angel Creek. This incident emphasizes the need for better control of river parties, although the mechanics of such control are uncertain."

Only three years later, the Grand Old Man of the Colorado, Bert Loper, ended his rowing career in 24.5-Mile Rapid. Albert Loper was an enigma of sorts. No doubt he loved the Colorado River system. Since the late nineteenth century, he had worked as a boatman on the river's upper tributaries: the San Juan River, the Green River, and the Colorado in Glen Canyon. And he had worked in as many capacities as it was possible to do: as a mining employee, a free-lance prospector, and as head boatman on the 1922 U.S. Geological Survey expedition on the Green River. He had also worked as a Boy Scout leader in Glen Canyon. He built his stone cabin in Glen Canyon. For Loper, the Colorado River system seemed to be life itself. And then his exit from life.

Despite being known as "The Grand Old Man of the Colorado," Bert Loper had only rowed his first Grand Canyon trip in 1939, at the age of nearly seventy. That trip had worked out so well that Loper had built a new boat, the *Grand Canyon,* for his second Grand trip: a July, 1949, reunion trip with Don Harris and a few other friends with whom he had run in 1939. Loper made this trip, notes Dock Marston, "against the advice of four doctors who warned him that his proposed traverse of the canyon at the oars would be an excessive strain on his weak heart."

On July 8, three weeks short of his eightieth birthday, Bert unwisely rowed well ahead of Harris and company and entered 24.5-Mile Rapid with DeWayne Nichol riding on his deck. Both men wore life jackets. 24.5-Mile is a respectable rapid at all flow levels. At super-high flows, it is hideous. Bert Loper had entered this rapid in a solo boat at 51,500 cfs, an unforgiving flow.

As waves now filled their view, Nichol turned around. He was startled to see that Loper was not rowing. Nichol turned to Bert and allegedly uttered an admonition which today is cliche for Canyon boatmen: "Look to your oars, Bert!"

Instead Loper stared glassy-eyed at 24.5-Mile Rapid and let his oars lay idle. Speculation has it that, at this moment, he was either in the grip of yet another heart attack or instead was experiencing his first stroke. Either way, the *Grand Canyon* flipped upsidedown. Bert floated out of sight into 25-Mile Rapid—itself a killer since Hansbrough and Richards had drowned there in 1889. Meanwhile Nichol clawed his way to the bottom of the upset boat. The current shoved it toward shore. Nichol leaped from it onto shore. But without the bowline. Now, as the boat drifted after Loper, Nichol wondered what to do next.

Reunited with Harris, Nichol explained how Bert Loper had vanished downriver. And "vanished" unfortunately turned out to be an accurate description of Loper's demise. Until a quarter of a century later. In 1975, a hiker found what was decided to be Bert's skeleton on the south bank in the driftwood near the mouth of Cardenas Creek at River Mile 71 (this location has also been reported as instead being 75 yards below Lava Canyon Rapid near River Mile 65.7). Despite Bert's expressed last wishes that if he died on the river, he wanted to be buried on shore, Loper ended up buried in Sandy, Utah. Even so, Bert Loper's own words still ring down to us from his diary written while he was leading the 1922 U.S. Geological Survey trip down the Green River. Indeed, Loper's words comprise the most succinct explanation for most boatmen's decisions today to keep running the river. Right after portaging Hell's Half Mile in Lodore Canyon, Loper wrote, "Who in the hell wants to be a white collar sissy when one can enjoy such grandeur and beauty such as this?"

Months later, by 1950, only about 345 people had traversed all or part of the Grand Canyon by boat since John Wesley Powell's first expedition in 1869. From 1950 to 1954, the number of new river runners per year averaged only 31 (the average was 62 per year for the entire 1950s decade) for completing first-time, full traverses. Commercial river running remained in its infancy. Such operations were polarized at one end with exclusive and expensive trips on small, plywood cataract boats modeled after the ones used by their commercial innovator, Norman Nevills (Nevills had run the first commercial Grand Canyon river trips in 1938 and had invented the profession of river-running in the Canyon). In the 1950s, these small hard-hulled boats were often run by Frank Wright, by Jim and Bob Rigg and their associates, and by Gaylord Staveley. At the other end of the spectrum were large inflatable boats, often rigged together and pushed by outboard motors. These operations were epitomized during the middle to late 1950s by Georgie White's Royal River Rats' "cost-sharing" trips. Such commercial trips regularly carried life jackets for everyone, even if many boatmen failed to wear them.

Ironically, it may have been none of these types of boats that kicked Grand Canyon river-running into third gear. Instead it was running with no boats at all. The biggest single boost to the numbers of clients demanding river trips came directly from Bill Beer's and John Daggett's painful 26-day swim of the Grand Canyon Colorado begun in April 1955. Although poorly equipped due to lack of funds, they were smart enough to wear swim fins, long johns, neoprene jackets, and most importantly, Mae West life jackets. They also took movie footage. Good enough footage to support their future lecture circuit.

Beer and Daggett swam and shivered in the cold river. They ate and breathed flying sand (occasionally they wore swim goggles to see what they were eating). They bled though cracked hands and feet. Meanwhile, newspapers in the outside world printed headlines of their deaths in the Canyon. This odd odyssey is recounted beautifully in Bill Beer's engaging book *We Swam the Grand Canyon: The True Story of a Cheap Vacation That Got a Little Out of Hand*.

Soon after surviving this cheap vacation, Beer's and Daggett's movie aired on television. The two also ran their lecture circuit. Public awareness of the magnificence of the river corridor in Grand Canyon grew in leaps.

In 1955, the year Beer and Daggett swam the river, only 70 people ran it in boats. The next year, however, 135 people ran it. In the five years following Beer and Daggett's big swim, the number of people running the entire Grand Canyon portion of the river per year averaged 92. Also in 1955, Georgie White began running triple "G-rigs" of surplus U.S. Army ten-man rafts. These—plus her huge triple inflatable bridge pontoon rig—played a large role too in increasing numbers of tourists carried. In 1962, 372 people ran the river. The demand for river trips grew exponentially for years after that. In the 1990s, for example, *every* year saw more than 25,000 people run all or part of the Grand Canyon Colorado—in boats, and with life jackets. Since 1972, more than half a million people have run this river.

The pioneer era of running the Grand Canyon Colorado began with John Wesley Powell's expedition in 1869 and lasted nearly 70 years, until 1938, when it was ended by Norm Nevills taking women clients who paid him for a Canyon river trip. But even by the end of 1955, when Beer and Daggett swam the Canyon, a grand total of only 570 people had run all or part of the river (101 of them by 1914).

In July of 1955—only two months after Beer's and Daggett's epic swim—yet another "river runner" drowned. George D. Jensen, age 28, embarked on a copy-cat swim down the Colorado. Instead of starting at Lees Ferry (River Mile 0), however, Jensen started near Furnace Flats (somewhere between River Miles 68 and 72, near the Tanner Trail) on a flow between 20,000 and 36,000 cfs. Jensen had no life jacket and is thought to have embarked on the river on a driftwood raft. His body was discovered near Hermit Rapid (River Mile 95) on July 13.

Despite ever heavier traffic, the Colorado claimed no new victims from among river runners for a decade. When it did, its next victim was an NPS ranger.

It happened on a chilly February 21, 1965, when two NPS rangers paddled their canoe out from Lees Ferry for fun. Phillip D. Martin, age 27, had been stationed at Lees Ferry for about five months. His paddling partner, Don Pledger, was a ranger in Great Smokies National Park. The two drifted downstream of Lees Ferry into Paria Riffle flowing at 9,000 cfs. They capsized. Fortunately, both men wore life jackets.

But it was February, a cold month, and the river itself was only 47 degrees. Pledger and Martin tried to right their boat, but failed. Next they discussed swimming for shore. Pledger stroked for shore and made it. Martin, however, stayed with the canoe, clinging to its limited buoyancy.

Phil Gentless, an NPS maintenance man, hauled Martin out of the river an hour later about 1.5 miles downstream of the Paria. He was still floating but had died, perhaps from drowning, though Page physician Dr. Ivan Kazan suspected that hypothermia had taken Martin's life.

As Grand Canyon grew bigger on the tourist map, more people got in trouble. On a relatively warm November 5 or 6, 1966, three young teenage hikers from Flagstaff camped near Phantom Ranch. They decided that riding a driftwood log on the Colorado sounded like a good idea. David Rider, age 14, Harold Lindstrom, age 15, and Peter Scott Le Brun, age 14, launched their log from the Boat Beach at River Mile 88. Very soon the 9,000 cfs current grabbed the log and hurried it downstream. As their log romped into Bright Angel Rapid, all three boys got nervous and swam toward shore. Peter Scott Le Brun never made it.

The next tragic whitewater death was a boatman. Moreover, he was a good, thoughtful boatman. And he was wearing his life jacket.

Shorty Burton's tragic death was enigmatic in many ways. First, he was not even short. He was nearly six feet tall. Second, he was a very careful, organized boatman who developed techniques in the early 1960s to cover nearly every aspect of a Grand Canyon trip from cooking great food over a driftwood fire, to repairing and rigging a boat to make it tight and safe, to caring for passengers as if they were his own family, and, of course, to running rapids. Shorty Burton was mentor to a small legion of green boatmen for Hatch River Expeditions, all trying to learn the profession.

So what went wrong in Shorty's thirteenth year as a guide?

On June 14, 1967, one day after Shorty's 44th birthday, he powered into the top of Upset Rapid (River Mile 150) on 12,750 cfs. Shorty hated Upset. He had talked of it on this trip even 150 miles upstream at Lees Ferry. Moreover, in his previous dozen runs, he had run it left, not right. As the flow here lowered, however, the left run became far more rocky. Yet the more difficult right run also remained very tight and rocky, and required more finesse and more power at exactly the right moment. Any minor mistake could send a boat through the big hole at the foot of the rapid. Shorty tried to convince his twenty-horsepower, long-shaft Mercury (Shorty preferred oars) to push his boat all the way right to the narrow slot along shore that by-passes that big hole.

He did not make it.

Shorty's boat was sucked into the steep hole, very likely at some angle other than straight-on. It flipped upside down in a flash. His passengers, more than half of the thirteen on the trip, scattered like jetsam and raced downstream willy nilly.

Shorty's fellow boatman, Clarke Lium, also ran the hole behind him, but punched through it. He gave chase, picking up swimmers en route. He hurried because, not seeing Shorty, he suspected that he was trapped under his boat. When, close to ten minutes later, he finally pushed Shorty's upside boat to shore and reflipped it right-side-up, Shorty was indeed underneath, but already dead.

The new style life jacket that Ted Hatch had talked Shorty into wearing on this trip had caught on one of the open eye-bolts suspending a floor board. Lium reckoned that, as cool under stress as Shorty was, had he been conscious he would have tried to use his knife to extricate himself. Hence, Lium suspected that Shorty had been knocked out during the flip.

But the causes of 44-year-old Shorty's last run may have been more complicated. Shorty was a diabetic and he smoked, both of which put him at risk for early heart disease. And, as will become clear in this chapter, traumatic immersion in cold water can trigger a quick cardiac arrest in such people at risk. Be that as it may, three hours of CPR failed to resuscitate Shorty.

After Shorty's death, new victims of Grand Canyon Colorado River running belong to what we think of as the "True Modern Era." In this era professional boatmen would no longer be the Colorado's predominant victims.

Some of them would continue to be Tom Sawyer-type amateurs. On April 23, 1971, for example, two young men at the boat beach at Phantom Ranch (River Mile 88) would be inspired like Rider, Lindstrom, and Le Brun had been five years earlier, to raft downriver. Bruce Allen and John Zombro, both in their early 20s, found an abandoned "raft" of driftwood combined with an air mattress. The two young men tightened up their salvaged rig and launched it onto 15,000 cfs. Two other companions—Joseph Tomaselli and Steven Anderson—watched them from shore.

The two Huckleberry Finn rafters made it almost a mile before hitting the area above or in Pipe Creek Rapid (River Mile 89). This moderate whitewater disintegrated their raft. Zombro and Allen swam successfully to the north bank. But the hiking "route" back upstream along shore on this side cliffs out. So both men tried to swim across the Colorado to the south bank of the river to join their companions waiting on the river portion of the Bright Angel Trail. Allen dived in and made it across. Zombro dived in too but was never seen to surface at all.

But the modern era of surviving boatmen and drowning passengers finally had begun. On July 10, 1972, one of Georgie White's (a.k.a. Georgie Clark) G-rigs piloted by one of her guides flipped on day one in House Rock Rapid (River Mile 16.8). These rigs, used seriously in Grand Canyon for decades only by Georgie's company and, less so, by Dick McCallum's Grand Canyon Youth Expeditions, consisted of three inflatable U.S. Army, ten-man rafts roped side by side in a triple rig powered by a small, 10-horsepower outboard motor astern the middle boat. The outer two boats were rigged with one oar each. Georgie invented these rigs in a flash of insight in 1954, as a means of avoiding so many flips when running the ten-man rafts as individual boats through big rapids. She considered them safer than the more flip-prone single boats. But she never managed to upgrade them to be adequately powered. She called them her "thrill boats" because, in part, they were so under-powered that they could not be finessed around the worst dangers in certain rapids. Instead, they just slammed into or through the worst hydraulics the rapid offered, creating unavoidable thrills. Adding to the thrill, Georgie often "hired" fairly inexperienced boatmen, whom she sometimes paid, sometimes not (depending on her end-of-the-season profit margin) to run these G-rigs. Georgie herself ran a much larger boat (discussed later).

Mae Hansen, age 64, rode one of these G-rigs during this July 1972 trip. Hansen was an annual passenger with Georgie—she had run the river 14 times in 14 years—though she had ridden only once before on one of these small triple rigs. The other times she had ridden with Georgie herself on her huge boat.

Hansen's G-rig flipped upside down in House Rock Rapid in 14,000 cfs. Hansen and two other passengers became trapped beneath it. Although many boatmen today shudder at the thought, Georgie used to instruct her passengers to *stay* under the boat when the boat flipped—Georgie admitted, "Having a boat flip in a rapid was just a way of life for me, and an enjoyable one at that." By staying under, or at least with, the boat, her passengers would not be scattered from hell to breakfast up and down the river. It is unclear whether Mae Hansen and her cohorts were thus instructed on this trip. But Georgie's "cardinal rule" for all passengers throughout her Canyon career *did* remain that everyone should stay with the boat if it flipped, instead of swimming the rapid independently or swimming to shore.

The other two people in Mae Hansen's predicament in the 47-degree water under the G-rig found air pockets. Mae Hansen apparently never was able to find enough air under the vast floating carpet of heavy rubber boats. She cardiac arrested in a laryngeal-spasm, "dry" drowning. Mae Hansen became the first commercial passenger to die as a river-running casualty in the history of river-running in the Canyon.

Curiously, Georgie excluded Mae Hansen from this category of dying due to a river-running mishap. Only a few years after Mae Hansen's death, Georgie, who believed that our lives and deaths are ruled by Fate, would write in her 1977 autobiography of river running, *Georgie Clark: Thirty years of River Running*:

> Fortunately my trips have few major problems and I have the best safety record on the Colorado River. I have never had a fatal accident on any of my boats or even a minor one. Over more than thirty years of rapid running however, two people with me have suffered fatal heart attacks, including my very good friend, May [sic], who went with me for years.

Interestingly, the other passenger who died of a heart attack on one of Georgie's trips was a 70-year-old man who collapsed—apparently due to natural causes—while taking photos from the back of her rig while running the Salmon in Idaho. Despite his natural and thus innocent demise, Georgie quickly hid his corpse under a tarp. After a prompt evacuation, she told her remaining passengers that the man had become ill and had to leave.

Georgie, who was unique in a number of her stylistic decisions on how a Grand Canyon trip should be run, was also known for her tendency to respond to tragedies with denial. Mae Hansen's and the unnamed 70-year-old's deaths are examples. But this was standard for Georgie, whose mother had insisted to Georgie as a girl that she never cry nor feel sorry no matter what went wrong. As the years passed, Georgie, who, again, believed that Fate (and luck) ruled all, took her mother's injunction to heart. As one biographer, Richard E. Westwood, wrote of Georgie's response to one of her passengers having sustained serious skull and spinal fractures in a fall while trying to assist others of her passengers who had gotten stuck on a high rock at Elves' Chasm, "Georgie's reaction to all of this was to pretend it hadn't happened."

Ironically, this seriously injured victim, Vernon Read, of Milwaukee, Wisconsin, became—once he was evacuated from Elves' Chasm after his fall—another first. Read's evacuation was the first ever by helicopter of an injured river-runner in Grand Canyon history. The year was 1959.

While Mae Hansen was the first commercial river passenger to drown or suffer hypothermia-induced cardiac arrest in the Colorado in Grand Canyon, by no means would she be the last. On April 27, 1973, for example, on a research trip run by the Museum of Northern Arizona, Charles Lyon, age 25, drowned or died due to hypothermia while running Sockdolager Rapid (River Mile 78.7) at 34,000 cfs in an inflatable kayak. Other members of the research trip did not catch Lyon, who apparently was unable to recover his boat or swim to shore in the 47-degree water. Despite his life jacket, Lyons was spotted hypothermic and singing to himself as the river carried him to, then past, the Silver Bridge near Phantom, below which, he drowned.

Three weeks later, on May 19, 1973, Michael Koenig, age 29, and his friend, Tony Burdick, of San Diego, put in a motor boat at Diamond Creek (River Mile 225.6). They intended to make a powered uprun of the river against 17,200 cfs. This trip not only lacked the necessary private permit to boat the Colorado upstream of Diamond Creek at all, it was also an up-run of the river, a type of trip banned entirely. On top of being illegal on these two counts, Koenig and Burdick also committed the so-commonly-fatal error of not wearing a life jacket. This last omission was illegal in yet a third way, as all river runners are required by NPS regulations to wear a life jacket while on the water. Far worse, it again proved fatal. After their boat capsized, apparently in 217-Mile Rapid, Burdick managed to swim to shore. Koenig drowned.

Four years would pass before another boater would drown in the Canyon.

And it ultimately happened for the first time in Lava Falls, the most infamous, hyped, and dreaded Grand Canyon rapid of this century.

At 8:45 a.m. on August 22, 1977, George "Butch" Hutton, ran his Sanderson 33-foot motor rig down the notorious Right Side of Lava on 23,000 cfs. Almost immediately, in the V-wave, water swamped Hutton's motor. Out of control like this, a 33-foot rig still might float through okay. Then again, it might turn sideways and flip. This had already happened to another big, motor rig here a few years earlier, earning a prize-winning photo in *LIFE Magazine* (and our rear cover).

Hutton turned around and pulled the start cord of the motor. The T-handle at the end of the cord broke off. Hutton tried pulling the rope. His pulls refused to coax the drowned motor back to life. Meanwhile, the mere four or five seconds that a boatman is allotted to accomplish anything in the Right Side of Lava elapsed.

The big boat slammed up onto the big Black Rock near the right shore and near the foot of the rapid. Still powerless, the boat rode up on the left side of the rock like Godzilla emerging from the ocean. The left side tube sucked under and submerged. The boat slid into the main waves immediately to the left of the rock. As the left tube of the rig had submerged the powerful waves had stripped a half dozen passengers and the boatman's assistant off the boat.

Hutton and his still-on-the-boat passengers, including a "hitchhiking" future AzRA boatman, Drifter Smith, scrambled along both sides of the boat hauling passengers back in. In less than a minute everyone was aboard. They thought.

Then the real nightmare began: someone spotted an empty life jacket floating near the boat.

Hutton had been running boat number two. Downstream, just below "Son of Lava Rapid," Sanderson's first boat had already pulled to the beach. Many of its passengers had walked back upstream to photograph Hutton's boat. In short, the boat ahead was not a safety boat, it was a "helpless" witness boat tied to shore.

Two of the passengers swept off the left tube when the rig slid off the Black Rock were 118-pound Andalea Buzzard, age 49, and her husband, Forrest. (Ironically, Forrest Buzzard was the liability insurance agent for Sanderson River Expeditions and had been invited on this trip many times by Jerry Sanderson before he finally agreed to go.) Forrest said he had gotten a hold of Andalea's ankle in the rushing water with one hand, then he had also grabbed a front D-ring of the boat with the other. In the immediate vicinity of the Buzzards at this moment, the force of the current rushing away from the stalled rig was so powerful that the D-ring in Forrest's hand ripped off the boat. Then Forrest lost his grip on his wife's ankle.

Speculation has it that it was during this moment of being held by Forrest as he held the D-ring that Andalea's life jacket, a Holcomb Industries type 5, though apparently securely fastened before the rapid, failed to remain strapped to her body. Being held by the ankle against the current would have whipped her headfirst downstream and also have caused her life jacket to act as a "parachute." This situation was worsened by her also wearing a rain jacket beneath the life jacket. It too acted like a parachute. The force of current on the lower hem of the jacket and life vest likely yanked both garments over her head and off her arms and then down the river.

People on the now drifting motor boat heard a faint scream. At least 100 feet upstream of them and slightly left of the main current, Andalea's head emerged briefly from the waves. She screamed for help.

Because the boat was still unpilotable due to lack of motor power, the boatman, Hutton, did the next best thing he could: he leaped into the river and swam upstream toward Andalea, who was a nonswimmer. But she sank life-jacketless in the eddy fence whirlpools on the river left before he could reach her. Hutton continued swimming. Andalea surfaced briefly a half dozen times. Yet, each time, she emerged too far away for Hutton to grab her. At last, she sank and was not seen again.

Drifter Smith witnessed all of this in amazed horror. He said that the entire rig had now drifted into Son of Lava. As the rig exited this and floated past the right beach, and as the swamper tried to get the motor started, Drifter dived off the rig into the river. He swam to shore and to the other Sanderson rig. There he informed the other Sanderson boatman, trip leader Armand-Didier "Frenchy" Cadol, what had happened. One of Andalea's and Forrest's two children had witnessed this mayhem from Hutton's boat, the other from Cadol's on shore.

As Drifter jogged back upstream along broken columns of black lava to rejoin his own party, he saw Hutton on the opposite side of the river. By now he had escaped the river via the tiny beach by the warm springs. He was, Drifter saw, retching his guts out behind a bush.

Andalea's life jacket was found floating six miles downstream. When recovered, the straps needed to secure the back portion of her jacket were missing. Without them it could not have remained cinched onto her or anyone else in the water. Ironically, Andalea had worn this jacket, assiduously fastened in front, even on shore, because she was a non-swimmer. Andalea's body was discovered by boatman Perry White eight days later, on August 30, ten miles downstream, floating in an eddy at Whitmore Wash.

Years would pass before yet another river-running tragedy happened. And this time it would happen in technicolor in a huge rapid on a phenomenally high flow. On the morning of June 25, 1983, Lane Jackson Parmenter piloted a 33-foot Tour West motor rig into Crystal Rapid (River Mile 98.5) on a horrendous flow of 69,000 cfs. Parmenter's job on the rig was boatman's assistant. Parmenter had run the Idaho Salmon 38 times, but he had been on only two Grand Canyon trips before.

Tour West's assigned boatman was Darryl Roberson. Roberson and Parmenter had scouted Crystal for at least 30 minutes. They had then decided that the latter should make a hard right run. This meant starting his cut to the right very early to avoid plowing into a now monstrous Crystal Hole at center left. It also meant, Roberson explained, continuing to motor their rig so far toward the right shore that they should "try to ram the trees."

Parmenter, however, missed his cut. He later complained, "the boat didn't have enough power."

Other guides who watched this run in stunned disbelief (personal, private communications from witnesses), however, alleged that, as Parmenter was running the boat in his entry to Crystal, Roberson was sitting in front of Parmenter and gesticulating to him via emphatic gestures of his right arm pointing to the right side of the river, signaling, "GO TO THE RIGHT NOW." Roberson continued gesturing like this throughout the entry and into the wave train of rapid, signaling Parmenter to steer to the right side of the rapid, away from Crystal Hole.

Parmenter, however, seemed unable to—or was unconvinced that he should— steer his boat into an aggressive angle to the right early during his run. He committed a double-error: he entered Crystal far too near the middle of the tongue instead of well to the right to begin with, and then he began his break-out move late instead of early. A haunting series of 14 photographs taken by Dick Kocim from shore of Parmenter's run (and later published in *Fateful Journey: Injury and Death on Colorado River Trips in Grand Canyon*) shows his too-far-left entry in the main flow of the tongue—and next shows that his boat stayed in the tongue. Worse, they reveal a very weak downstream right ferry angle, one that vanished two or three seconds into Parmenter's entry to become a nearly straight downstream angle and mainstream run.

By the time the Tour West rig dropped into the sixty-foot-wide Crystal Hole, Parmenter had angled the rig directly downstream into it. Then he yelled, "Oh God, we're going to hit the hole!"

Kocim's photos at this point show the 33-foot Tour West rig buried almost three-quarters and nose first in Crystal Hole and vanishing into and under the 25-foot-high standing wave. This 3- or 4-ton boat quickly pivoted to the left. Next it surged up, vibrated, then slid back down into the hole fully sideways. The next frames show the boat standing vertical on its left tube, then flipping. The rig stayed in the hole a few more seconds as its metal frame bent, nylon straps snapped like cotton thread, and the boat itself partially de-rigged while contorting pretzel-like. Meanwhile everyone who had been aboard flushed into Lower Crystal at blurring speed.

William R. Wert, age 62, was one of those passengers. He drowned in 69,000 cfs despite wearing his life jacket and despite having been in "reasonably good" physical condition. Two other passengers injured their legs during this mishap but were rescued in time. Both had to be evacuated.

On November 10 of this same year, a bizarre and mysterious boating tragedy occurred. It began when a pair of fishermen, next-door neighbors from La Mesa, California, drove most of the day from San Diego to Lees Ferry. Dick Benjamin Roach, age 71, and Richard Bruce Sheperski, age 50, then launched their Monarch 16-foot aluminum motor boat at the Ferry. For November, the river was flowing an unusually high 23,000 cfs. The two men intended to power upstream into Glen Canyon to "Camp 9" via their 10-horsepower motor, an ambitious goal considering the high flow and their low horsepower.

Four days later, after this pair of fishermen was overdue to return, the NPS initiated a search and rescue. A fixed-wing overflight spotted a small aluminum boat and a blue tarp on the north side of the river in an eddy below Soap Creek Rapid (River Mile 11.25). Rangers Tom Workman and Joe Evans landed in a helicopter to investigate. The boat, the two rangers found, was badly damaged. It also appeared to have been pulled up onto shore by hand. Had Sheperski and Roach survived and then abandoned this stuff?

While Evans overflew the river at 50 feet, Workman hiked up the nearby, four-mile Soap Creek Trail toward the rim. He found footprints, but as this is a prime hiking route for fishermen, they could have been anyone's. Meanwhile Evans landed at River Mile 52 to talk with a four-person private river trip led by Ron Stark, which also had put in at Lees Ferry on the 10th, the same day that Sheperski and Roach had intended to motor upstream.

Stark's group had camped that night below Badger Rapid (River Mile 8) on the left shore. After dark, at 7:30 p.m., one of the group, Fred Stasek, noticed a light coming downstream. The four campers had a campfire blazing and—to celebrate their first night of finally making it onto the river—had been drinking wine. Now the four stared at the approaching light. Why anyone would be boating through Badger Rapid at night and on 23,000 cfs puzzled all of them.

The mystery light drifted into Badger Rapid but remained pointed at the campers and their fire. Stark's group aimed their flashlights into the rapid to try to see what was happening in the peek-a-boo wave train. They saw what looked like a boat. They yelled questions over the roar of the waves. Fred Stasek said that, through the "pitch dark" they saw "a long narrow object riding the center of the current; it cleared the water by less than a foot, and a dark irregular shape appeared near the leading edge of it—apparently a person, holding on. I yelled, and I believe I heard a response—'Hello!' or 'Help!' barely audible over the roar of the river."

Ron Stark reported, "I yelled 'Hello' and I heard someone on the boat yell back something like 'Help!' I was not willing to go downriver at night to try to catch them."

The light grew brighter and still aimed at them. Then it passed them and continued downstream beyond the rapid's tailwaves. None of this made any sense to the four on shore unless: a. someone who really knew the river well was running it in the dark to make up lost time (this has been done by several deadhead [passenger-less] trips running into Phantom Ranch); or b. someone was in real trouble and could not start his motor, could not use his oars or paddles to go to shore, and could not even lean over the gunwale of the boat and use his hands or another paddle-like object to paddle to shore; or c. someone was in even worse trouble: their boat was already upside down.

Stark's party knew that if some variation of "b" or "c" was the true answer, then whatever was happening was unsafe. So the group set off three or four aerial flares toward small planes they saw. Meanwhile two of the four campers, Stasek and Nigel, walked downstream over the boulders in the dark about a mile "in hope that the person(s) had eddied out or swum to shore." But the two men saw nothing, not even the drifting light.

The next morning Stark's group found a Monarch 16-foot boat upside down in the eddy below Soap Creek Rapid. The hull had holes punched through it. A large blue tarp and some other items floated nearby. But they found no footprints on shore. The four dragged the boat onto shore and spread the tarp as a signal. When they turned the boat right-side-up they found two life jackets and another flotation device bundled and *tied* to its bow. Stark's group left a note of explanation of their discovery wrapped in a brown rain poncho weighted down with a rock. Then they rowed downriver to puzzle over this tragedy for days.

What had happened to Roach and Sheperski? The NPS launched an intensive, multi-team search on land and water. No team had any luck.

What went wrong here? This is not an easy mystery to solve. Roach and Sheperski's boat had a ten-horsepower outboard, a three-horsepower backup engine, and a pair of oars. The ten-horsepower engine was still mounted on the boat when Stark and friends found it. But when the boat drifted into Badger Rapid, they had heard no motor noise. Again, a ten-horsepower motor provides a very limited thrust when traveling upstream against 23,000 cfs unless the boat is piloted by a very savvy river boatman.

On March 23, 1984, more than four months later, Walter M. Gregg found most of Dick Roach's badly decomposing body (an arm and lower leg were missing) in an eddy near Vasey's Paradise (River Mile 32).

On August 28 of that same year, nine months after Roach's and Sheperski's mishap, Skip Bell, a boatman for Grand Canyon Expeditions, reported that one of his passengers, Wayne, had discovered a human skull with soft tissue still attached. The skull was under a honey mesquite tree and next to mule deer bones and an antler. The mesquite was 75 yards from the river, well above the historical fluctuation zone, and 150 yards downstream of Nankoweap Creek (River Mile 52). Obviously some person or animal had placed the skull in this location. Despite diligent searching, no other human body parts were found nearby. Mountain lions do frequent the Nankoweap drainage. And these predators sometimes cache kills or scavenged carcasses. Dental charts identified this skull as Richard Sheperski's.

Yet how these two fishermen drowned remains an unsolved mystery. Capsizing a 16-footer on the quiet water of Glen Canyon is uncommon, but it would have been easy had they allowed their underpowered boat to lodge against a projection of shoreline that was being hit by downstream current. Capsizing also would have been easy in Paria Riffle (River Mile 1) at 23,000 cfs, had the two accidentally drifted downstream past Lees Ferry in the dark. That neither man had donned his life jacket may suggest they had experienced an abrupt and unexpected capsizing, wherever it took place. Once they began drifting, with their boat upside-down and out of control, hypothermia would have set in quickly in the 47-degree water, well before reaching Badger Creek Rapid and then floating past the river-runners camped there. Rapid hypothermia and psychological shock might also explain why neither man retrieved and donned his life jacket from under the bow. These scenarios seem to be the only ones that make sense.

Except that all four people in Stark's party camped at Badger that night apparently thought they had witnessed (albeit in the dark) a boat *floating right side up and with a light aboard it being aimed at them by a person inside that boat, not* in *the water.*

Indeed these four witnesses were nonplussed in trying to imagine a realistic scenario to explain what they saw. They spent days afterward trying to make sense of it. Only several months later did they learn that one of the two fishermen had had a serious heart condition which may have lead to cardiac problems during that first afternoon on the swollen Colorado. Had he experienced a cardiac arrest, and if the other man was unfamiliar with the river, or with the boat's motors, or with the location of unlit Lees Ferry in darkness, or all of the above, this second man could have allowed the boat to drift downstream for hours in the expectation that Lees Ferry would be well illuminated—and thus noticeable—and that it would offer them help in the form of an NPS ranger.

The alternate possibility also exists that the pair may have, after driving several hundred miles from San Diego that morning, arrived at Lees Ferry so late that they launched their boat at twilight or after dark. Next, in the darkness and against the surprisingly powerful current, they may have ended up going downstream instead of upstream without noticing it. Why no motor was heard running at Badger, however, remains a mystery—unless it was drowned out by the roar of whitewater. In any case, perhaps only upon pounding through the huge waves of Badger did either fisherman realize their serious error. Stark and his three companions had neither the confidence nor state of mind to abandon their camp in the dark at a moment's notice and then risk their lives giving chase on the ink-black river downstream of Badger to rescue someone from what may or may not have been an emergency.

Only seven months later, yet another boater drowned. On June 7, 1984, a private boatman, Tom Pillsbury, age 66, and an heir to the famous Pillsbury flour and baking mixes company, rowed his inflatable boat on a private trip into Crystal Rapid (River Mile 98.5). Pillsbury had erred, as so many boaters have done here, by entering too far left to make the cut to the right. Not only was Pillsbury rowing against a very difficult flow level, according to trip member Carolyn Marley (now Carolyn Castleman), he was trying to identify his critical "landmarks" in the rapid with one bad eye and very poor vision otherwise. Perhaps this helps explain why trip members on shore—Bob Finkbine and Jeff Jackel—were surprised to see Pillsbury entering the rapid out of sequence, unprotected by a companion boat, and also making no solid attempt to execute a break-out-of-the-tongue cut toward the right shore. In spite of his previous trips down the Canyon (on lower flows), on this very challenging flow of 43,500 cfs, Pillsbury allowed his raft to be sucked down the center of the wave train toward Crystal Hole.

Pillsbury had been told to run last of six boats. But he had ignored this and entered, carrying two passengers, Pauletta Davis and Monica Corella, as a surprise third boat late in the first, planned "pulse" of two boats. This trip had split its boats during this run so that some of the boatmen could take photos instead of running all the boats in one tight pulse for mutual support. This 43,500 cfs level was so difficult and so dangerous at Crystal that many commercial rowing trips during this period and flow level routinely walked their passengers around Crystal Rapid on shore as they ran their boats through empty in one pulse on a conservative "cheat-" run hugging the right shoreline. Then those who walked would reunite in the boats below the first half of Crystal. After having watched NPS rangers successfully run the right side of Crystal in oarboats, however, members of Pillsbury's trip had decided not to use these tactics.

When Pillsbury failed to cut to the right, a large wave near the top of Crystal swept him off his rowing seat and flipped his fifteen-foot inflatable upside-down. Next he, Pauletta, and Monica swam the rapid. To complicate matters, the number-two boat, ahead of Pillsbury's, had also capsized. Luckily, the three people aboard it—boatman Scott Berry, trip permit holder Susan Groth, and passenger Linda—swam to the right shore.

As the NPS incident reports and letters from Bob Marley and from Carolyn explain: Bob Marley had rowed the lead boat with his son Scott, wife Carolyn, and Don Johnson aboard and had kept it right side up, but swamped. By the time Pillsbury, his passengers, and his upside-down boat washed downstream unexpectedly, Marley was already "engaged in securing boat number two and its crew" by tying multiple ropes from the boats—one swamped, the other upside down—to shore. One of Pillsbury's two passengers, Monica, swam to the right shore well upstream of Marley's position and unseen. Meanwhile, as Carolyn reports, Pauletta did not try to swim to shore but instead held onto the bowline of Pillsbury's upset raft such that Marley and the others did not see her. She would not grab terra firma until a mile later, after abandoning Pillsbury's boat, below Tuna Rapid. (She was so hypothermic and traumatized by this swim, Carolyn noted, that she almost could not continue with the trip).

Pillsbury, separated from his boat, floated past the Marleys on the opposite (left) side of the river and close to the far shore. Members of this trip had already seen Pillsbury, with his low body mass, become hypothermic quickly. Now, as Bob and Carolyn and other witnesses interviewed in the NPS report indicate, Pillsbury waved his arm to attract attention and yelled out to Marley as he passed, "Help, Bob!"

Carolyn said that she and the others yelled back to Pillsbury, "SWIM OUT! SWIM OUT!"

Pillsbury yelled back, "Help! Help, I can't!" Indeed, although Pillsbury drifted close to the left shore, no witness saw him try to swim toward it. On the contrary, as Pillsbury drifted downriver from here, Don Johnson saw him instead simply hold both of his arms across his chest in a "gripping-your-life-jacket" position suggesting hypothermia and/or to hold his life jacket snugly prepatory to entering Tuna Rapid.

With two of the first three boats upside down, and two of the people who had been riding in them scattered in the river downstream, Marley says he made a "triage decision" to continue his "commitment to the previously over-turned raft [boat number two] and its crew."

The next boats to arrive were part of the group's second planned pulse through Crystal, delayed after Pillsbury's episode, and were rowed by Jeff Jackel and Bob Finkbine. Both boats had emerged from Crystal right side up. When Jackel caught up with Marley, as Carolyn notes, Marley told him there were two people who had swum into Tuna Rapid and to try to catch them.

Jackel picked up Pauletta below Tuna Rapid (River Mile 99.3 to 99.8) where she had self-rescued. Jackel tried to combat her hypothermia, then continued to row downriver in hopes of catching Pillsbury, now downstream with a lead of unknown distance.

Meanwhile, four miles downstream, an NPS river patrol had already run Crystal ahead of Pillsbury's party and parked for lunch near River Mile 103 (Shady Grove). At noon they saw Pillsbury's upside-down boat drifting toward them. Ranger Dennis Haskew rowed out to capture it. Ranger Becca Lawton paddled her kayak out to help. To her alarm, she spotted a person floating in midriver face down. At Becca's call, Haskew abandoned the drifting boat in an effort to rescue the victim.

It was Pillsbury. His pupils were fixed and dilated. He was not breathing. He showed no pulse.

The rangers initiated CPR immediately.

The time was 12:57 p.m., 57 minutes after Pillsbury had flipped his little boat. The river rangers radioed for assistance. Ranger Paramedic Sherrie

Collins arrived with Ranger Larry Fredricks at about 3:00 p.m. Pillsbury had been on shore in 105 degree heat for two hours as the river rangers performed CPR. Yet now Ranger Collins found his core temperature to be only 78 degrees. Even so, he still had heart activity, albeit ventricular fibrillation. Unfortunately, despite a prompt (at this point) evacuation to Flagstaff Medical Center with advanced life support en route, Pillsbury was finally pronounced dead at 5:39 p.m.

Pillsbury had been wearing a kayaking-type life jacket which does not orient a swimmer face upwards. Ironically, he also had a farmer-john wetsuit offering both warmth and more flotation, but instead of wearing it, he had packed it while rowing into Crystal. He had drowned as he careened downstream below Crystal, despite his U.S. Coast Guard-approved life jacket.

Only a couple of months later—on August 25, 1984—the legendary Georgie White had her own out-of-control ride. On Georgie's personally-guided Royal River Rats' raft trips, she used a boat that some guides had nicknamed the *Queen Mary*. Georgie simply called it her "big boat." Some of her boatmen called it "Mama's boat." The *Queen Mary* title came naturally because the boat was so huge. Georgie invented it in 1955 with the twin goals of increased safety and high passenger capacity in mind. She simply rigged together three "donut" military bridge pontoons, each about 33 feet long but with the center donut staggered sternward about four feet. This giant triple rig, filled internally with yet more "sausage" tubes, was about 37 feet long by 27 feet wide. Georgie considered this mammoth rig unflippable. And she probably was right. Yet staying on this big rig in some of the routes she chose through big rapids was problematic for some of her passengers.

Georgie's technique at Lava Falls (River Mile 179.4), for example, was to raise her passengers' expectations to a frenzy of anticipation of impending whitewater mayhem. While we other boaters stood and scouted Lava from above, we could hear Georgie's boat approaching (Georgie herself rarely scouted Lava). Even over the roar of Lava Falls, we could hear her passengers screaming like maniacs as the *Queen Mary* drifted into the rapid. Sometimes nearly twenty passengers would be seated, facing outward and wildly kicking their legs in the air. Georgie normally instructed her passengers to keep their feet up and off the boat so that they would not become entrapped between the strapped-together tubes of her hybrid rig during its convolutions in the radical whitewater that Georgie ran. At Lava Falls, Royal River Rats' tradition had evolved this feet-in-the-air, safety position among some passengers into a two-footed kicking frenzy.

Then, immediately upstream of the center of the rapid, Georgie would yank her 20-horsepower motor out of the river, cut it, and don her construction hard hat (if she were not already wearing it). Next she would slip down into her "hidey hole," a semi-private compartment forward of the motor well where she had rigged two high wrist straps. She would slip her wrists through these. Then, in a crucifixion position, she would ride out whatever the Ledge Hole of Lava Falls dished Mama's Boat.

Back in 1955, Georgie had christened her Big Boat by running the center Ledge Hole (a run no other commercial company makes on purpose). Everyone aboard had survived that experiment. So the Ledge Hole too had become tradition. Tradition or not, however, running the Ledge Hole normally entailed gut-wrenching gyrations of Georgie's entire boat. Once the *Queen Mary* hit the tail waves, Georgie would drop her motor back into the river and frantically yank its start cord. Again, this was her standard run. And by August 25, 1984, she had run Lava Falls at least 150 times.

Passengers on this wild ride knew they had to hold on tight. Norine Abrams, however, was 58 years old and weighed 240 pounds. And at 11:00 a.m., when Georgie arrived at Lava, she had let the *Queen Mary* drift off center. As she motored into view above Lava, a Moki Mac commercial river trip already stood on the left shore scouting. They wanted to be dead sure they had their entry to the left route figured out to safely run left of the dangerous Ledge Hole. One of these witnesses, river guide John Davenport, reported Georgie's—to him—astonishing approach to Lava Falls:

> She [Georgie] *was pretty far left in her entry. It looked like she was going to run left. But then I saw her stand up and look toward the Ledge Hole. As soon as she saw she was going to miss it, she fired up her motor and powered over to the center of the river. She was too late to reach the Ledge Hole and also straighten out. So she entered the Ledge Hole at a 45-degree angle. It was the worst example of gross incompetence I have ever seen.*

As Georgie dropped her *Queen Mary* powerless over the center Ledge Hole, it stalled in the reversal water. The 33-foot donut in the upriver section of the Ledge Hole submerged and folded under the center donut. Norine and a few other passengers were sucked overboard into the rapid flowing at 24,500 cfs.

As she slid off the *Queen Mary*, Norine's husband Ray Abrams grabbed her. By lower Lava, however, the force of the current was injuring his arm and he had to let go. The river swept Norine ahead of the boat. Georgie's efforts to catch her before Son of Lava failed. After a chase of a mile or so, Georgie eventually caught Norine, now apparently lifeless. She transported her to shore.

CPR for 30 to 45 minutes failed to resuscitate Norine Abrams. The entire trip spent the night at the old helicopter pad near River Mile 183. As the pilot arrived the next morning to evacuate all of the passengers and to bring in new ones, as per Georgie's pre-arranged routine, Georgie told him that Abrams was a casualty who had to be evacuated. He radioed the NPS, who sent in Rangers Kim Crumbo and Culhane for Norine Abrams' evacuation.

Crumbo explained in frustration that 73-year-old Georgie had been exhorting him in irritation to hurry up before anyone else arrived and saw Abrams' body bag. Crumbo, who injured his back moving the heavy victim, responded, also in irritation, "Georgie, you just killed this woman, now you want me to hurry up and hide the body?" Georgie stared Crumbo in the eye and said, "You're damned right I do. Now get her out of sight before you scare these new people."

Two years later, yet another whitewater misadventure occurred at the notorious, "post-1983" version of Crystal Rapid. On the morning of September 21, 1986, Wilderness World ran one of its last trips (the company had already been sold and was pending Park approval; it would soon be reorganized and renamed). This trip ran their paddleboat through River Mile 98.5 on a flow far higher than normal for fall. At about 10:30 a.m., this boat entered Crystal under the command of paddle captain Bob Lippman, following two oar boats. The boat hit the right diagonal wave where intended, "high on the right." The boat stalled, failed to cross the diagonal, surfed left, then ran the "guts" of the main wave train at 27,800 cfs. The boat seemed to run the "New Wave" okay but stalled on the crest of the diagonal wave off Slate Creek, where it capsized.

All seven of the crew—six paddling clients plus Lippman—from the 16-foot inflatable paddle raft were tossed into a long wild swim through the severe hydraulics and rocky second half of Crystal Rapid.

Ray L. Interpreter, Jr., was rowing the oarboat closest to the capsized paddleboat. He started pulling people out of the river within two minutes. Interpreter grabbed passenger David Sandrock. Sandrock was reportedly "blue and non-breathing [but] began to breathe spontaneously upon being lifted into the boat." Then Interpreter saw passenger William B. Blair, age 65, floating face-down in the river. Interpreter jumped into the river to rescue Blair. When hauled out of the water, however, the mildly obese Blair was pulseless, not breathing, and had a mouthful of water. Ominously, his eyes were fixed open and staring.

Interpreter started CPR on Blair within a few minutes, just below the foot of the rapid. Assisted by four fellow boatmen plus two physicians (who intubated Blair and injected him with epinephrine), the CPR team worked for an hour and a half. But without success.

William Blair had drowned and/or suffered medical cardiac arrest due to hypothermia in Crystal's long, brutal whitewater—despite his life jacket and farmer-John wetsuit—in only about two minutes. (Sadly, a half dozen years later, Blair's almost rescuer, Ray Interpreter himself, also drowned, in Arizona's Salt River.)

For several years after the June 1983, 97,300 cfs flood of the Colorado remodeled Crystal Rapid, this rapid would prove to be not only The Scary One in Grand Canyon—eclipsing the terror of Lava Falls hands down—but, far more sinister, The Lethal One. At 1:30 p.m., on June 14, 1989, for example, Martin M. Hunsaker, the 54-year-old pilot of a 33-foot motor rig, entered

Crystal as trip leader for a Georgie's Royal River Rats trip. He lost motor power in the second tail wave after entering the rapid on 13,250 cfs. Hunsaker had aimed for the wild left run, standard for many motor companies.

Every effort Hunsaker made to restart his motor in those five seconds above the Hole and the left wall failed. Tellingly, as that brief time ran out, passenger Kjeld Harris heard Hunsaker exclaim, "Oh, shit!"

Hunsaker's 33-foot "baloney" rig slammed directly into the left cliff wall of schist downstream of the mouth of Slate Creek and to the left of Crystal Hole. The rig inched up the wall, stood on edge, sucked a lower side tube, then flipped upside down.

More than a dozen people aboard flew, dropped, or were slam-dunked into the Colorado. In the ensuing several hundred yards of whitewater, nearly all of them but Hunsaker swam to the upside-down boat. They held onto it, or climbed up it, or were dragged aboard by Hunsaker's two other crew members who had already clambered aboard.

Other swimmers agree that Hunsaker did not try to return to the upside down boat. Assistant boatman Paul Semerjian reported seeing Hunsaker not far upstream of it. Hunsaker gave Semerjian a "thumbs-up" signal "indicating that he was alright." As Semerjian pulled more passengers aboard, he lost sight of Hunsaker, who he thought was swimming after yet another passenger downstream of them.

Even after Semerjian managed to tie the rig to shore immediately above Tuna Rapid (River Mile 99.3), he said he was not worried at Hunsaker's absence. Only after Semerjian motored the rig downstream (the rig was still upside down; the crew simply reversed the motor mount, et cetera, and *ran the boat upside down*) to join Georgie at her camp at River Mile 107.8 did he learn that Hunsaker was missing in action.

At 6:30 p.m. that evening, a Hatch River Expeditions trip led by Curtis "Whale" Hanson found Hunsaker. Steve E. Hatch spotted Hunsaker floating "mostly submerged" in the main current below Tuna Rapid (River Mile 100.1). When Hatch pulled Hunsaker aboard, he was pulseless, without respirations, and his pupils were fixed and dilated. Whale told me (Ghiglieri) that a physician aboard checked Hunsaker's core temperature then pronounced him dead. An autopsy concluded that Martin Hunsaker had drowned in Crystal Rapid despite his life jacket, an Extrasport, "shorty" type III with 22 pounds of floatation displacement. *Hunsaker was the fourth victim to drown/or cardiac arrest due to hypothermia in Crystal Rapid while wearing a life jacket.*

Whale, in tears, and Steve Hatch stopped in Georgie's camp to deliver Hunsaker's body and to inform her that her number-one guide and trip leader had just drowned. Georgie, Whale said, just stared at him. Eight of Hunsaker's passengers decided to leave the river due to this Crystal flip. An NPS helicopter evacuated them to the South Rim.

Crystal Rapid would remain a terror. Just before noon on April 27, 1990,

Gene Elliot Stott, age 54, ran Crystal as a member of a private trip. Stott rowed his little 13.5-foot inflatable *Miwok* to the right, but he failed to make the cut out of the rapid's tongue on a flow of 10,250 cfs. Stott's little boat flipped in Crystal Hole.

Fellow trip members plucked Stott and his passenger, John Prior, out of the river "5 to 10 minutes later," downstream of Crystal Rapid but upstream of Tuna Rapid. Almost immediately after re-flipping Stott's *Miwok*, Stott complained of feeling exhausted and fatigued. His complaints escalated to feeling his jaw stiffen, then to pain radiating in his left arm, and to substernal chest pain. While Stott's alarmed companions tried to attract the attention of over-flying aircraft with signal mirrors, Stott collapsed, suffering a massive heart attack and died. Three hours of CPR failed to resuscitate him. *Stott was the fifth victim to die "in" Crystal Rapid—due most likely to cardiac arrest spurred by hypothermia—despite his having worn a life jacket.*

Indeed, Stott emphasizes the clear lesson provided in common by all four of the other victims of heart failure in Crystal. Crystal is emphatically the most dangerous rapid for a person in middle age or later to be dumped into due to its violence, boulder field, and great length of cold water swimming. Of the five victims who died in Crystal, William R. Wert was 62 years old, Tom Pillsbury was 66, William B. Blair was 65, Martin M. Hunsaker was 54, and Gene Elliot Stott was also 54. Hence Crystal is also the most dangerous rapid to run when carrying older people aboard (whether as guide or passenger) in any manner beyond the most conservative possible.

Running the Colorado River conservatively is a good idea in general. Even so, many boatmen tend to be seduced into complacency by their success or by the ever-increasing state of the art of the equipment they use—or by both. On top of this complacency, some professional guides succumb to pressure from clients to go for the biggest possible rides. Complicating all of this, many people entering Grand Canyon at the end of the twentieth century also assume that recent triumphs of human technology—especially in improved communication devices—render the consequences of human error in the river corridor far less dire.

Maybe they are right. Then again, maybe not. Dead is, after all, still dead. A good example of the maybe not, during which a Canyon voyager was reduced to the most helpless mammal on Earth, comes from a fascinating 1991 incident. As with most tragic episodes in the wilderness, this one started off looking like good clean fun.

Perhaps the most effective way to tell this story is to begin when Grand Canyon Dories' guide Chris McIntosh and the rest of the crew tied up their boats above 232-Mile Rapid to scout it on November 2, 2000. "I hadn't run 232-Mile left, and it was flowing at low water [about 10,000 cfs]," McIntosh explained to us, "and I was nervous because I knew it could destroy our boats if we hit the fangs at the bottom right." McIntosh and company scouted for several minutes, then "We all ran it down the left side."

Several minutes downstream of the Dories' uneventful run of 232-Mile they encountered a tiny private trip. One of its two boatmen, David Whittlesey, age 54, had just suffered a far less pleasant outcome at 232-Mile. He and passenger Darla Ekbom, age 44, had spent ten minutes sitting in Whittlesey's 14-foot raft above and out of view of 232-Mile Rapid while they waited for the second boat in their two-boat, four-person trip to catch up with them. As Ekbom tells it, Whittlesey elected not to scout the rapid. Next, with the goal in mind of getting splashed as little as possible, Whittelsey rowed down the right side of the rapid. His boat slammed into those fangs of sculpted schist near the right shore that had likely killed Glen and Bessie Hyde in late 1928. Whittlesey's boat pivoted sideways and began climbing to vertical. Whittlesey and Ekbom "high-sided" frantically. The boat flipped, however, almost in slow motion. So slow that Ekbom was in the river already when it slammed down, she said, and hit her on the head. She inhaled water as she fought her way to shore. Whittlesey ended up making a fifteen minute swim with his boat, one which ended only when boat number two finally caught up.

When boatman McIntosh next caught up to Whittlesey and his three companions, he was flabbergasted to learn what had happened. On an earlier commercial trip on which McIntosh had been a guide and Whittlesey a trainee the latter had shown McIntosh several critical sites between River Miles 232 and 234 where a heart-rending struggle for survival had unfolded on and after November 17, 1991, a struggle against pain and endurance and disappointment that would scar most of us....

David Whittlesey, age 45, from Prescott, Arizona, had made two previous Colorado River trips down the Canyon, both with other people. On October 28, 1991, he next launched his 14-foot inflatable boat from Lees Ferry on a three-and-a-half-week solo voyage.

As insurance against loss, Whittlesey had supplied himself with provisions for six weeks. Whittlesey was concerned about food. Being hungry in the middle of nowhere in cold weather is not what he considered a good time.

For 232 miles he enjoyed "a wonderful trip," having safely navigated all rapids. Then, as it likely had with Bessie and Glen Hyde, 232-Mile Rapid, in its low-water, demonic form, took control.

Shortly before noon on November 17, with only five rapids (of 160 plus) and a half-dozen miles left to run before hitting Lake Mead, Whittlesey entered 232-Mile on about 10,500 cfs. The guide book rated this rapid lower than many of the upstream rapids that had turned out to be not so difficult to run. Besides, floating down toward 232-Mile, it appeared harmless.

Whittlesey's boat rollicked over the standing waves just fine. Then it slammed up onto a large cluster of sculpted knobs and fangs of bedrock semi-hidden in the main current. The boat pivoted, stern into the current. Whittlesey tried to maneuver his raft off the rock. It flipped upside down.

The good news was Whittlesey was uninjured. He clung to the overturned raft as the river swept it into an eddy flanked by a wall of schist. For an hour Whittlesey tried to right his overturned 14-foot raft. Unsuccessfully.

Desperate to get the thing right side up and then unload his gear, especially some warm clothes and shoes, Whittlesey got careless about the current. His raft floated into the riffle below 232-Mile. He tried to stay on its slick floor. But waves in this riffle washed him off.

Whittlesey clung to the side of his raft. He narrowly avoided being crushed against or dragged over rocks in the riffle. By now severely hypothermic, he tried again to drag his raft to shore as quickly as possible, even while in the riffle. As Whittlesey scrambled onto shore, he lost his grip on his boat. The raft followed the downstream current. As Whittlesey stared at it in disappointment, it floated away serenely. Then it disappeared around a bend.

Although being safely on shore was a definite improvement over freezing to death in the river, the shore quickly metamorphosed from salvation to prison. The rock here inclined steeply, with numerous cliffs. And having lost his shoes, along with everything else, Whittlesey realized that he needed to either find his boat or at least get to a safer place to wait for help to happen along. With these two options in mind, he started walking downstream.

While traversing a cliff ledge twenty-five feet above the water, his handhold crumbled off. Whittlesey fell backwards. He slid head first down an incline. His jaw struck a rock. The blow knocked him unconscious. He somersaulted into the river. The cold water revived him. He scrambled out. His chin, he now found, had been punctured by that impact during his fall. Four of his teeth were now broken. The pain became intense.

Still, he *had* to get farther downstream. Whittlesey started walking again. While perched precariously on another cliff, a loose boulder rolled onto his bare foot. It broke two of his toes.

Desperate, cold, and in insistent pain from multiple sources, he finally hobbled to a beach on the right bank above 234-Mile Rapid. (This is about where James R. Ervin had left Bill Payne back in 1931, never to see him again.) En route to this patch of beach Whittlesey had also found a can of beer wedged in a crevice by the high water of 1983.

That eight-year-old beer—along with one lizard and one grasshopper— would constitute Whittlesey's provisions for the next six days.

As each day passed, the seriousness of his plight impressed Whittlesey ever more deeply. This being November, and river trips being vanishingly rare in November, he might not see anyone on the river in time to be rescued. Without a rescue, he now knew he would die. He was stranded, crippled, and his food consisted of one can of skunked beer. He was dressed only in a life jacket, t-shirt, and shorts. On the positive side of the list, however, he was carrying a Bic™ lighter and a knife.

Whittlesey dug a pit in the sand and bivouacked under sand and grass. To

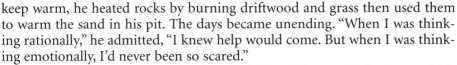

keep warm, he heated rocks by burning driftwood and grass then used them to warm the sand in his pit. The days became unending. "When I was thinking rationally," he admitted, "I knew help would come. But when I was thinking emotionally, I'd never been so scared."

During one bout of despair, when he believed he would die, he used his knife to carve his farewell letter into a piece of driftwood.

Five days after losing his boat, a friend of Whittlesey informed the NPS that he had failed to arrive at Pearce Ferry (46 miles downstream) on November 21, as planned. The NPS launched a search and rescue effort. On November 22, the sixth day after Whittlesey had watched his boat float away without him, NPS Rangers Susan Cherry and Ken Phillips spotted Whittlesey from a helicopter. He was still alive. And hungry.

Phillips offered Whittlesey his lunch. Whittlesey almost inhaled it.

Other private boaters would be less lucky. In late afternoon of November 15, 1994, a private rowing trip stopped at Hance Rapid (River Mile 77) to scout their "low" water run on 9,000 cfs. John Littels rowed first down the right tongue. Mark Miner followed, rowing a new "Protar" raft with two passengers aboard, Emilio X. Solares, age 26, and Lisa Abell.

Miner miscalculated the flow and entered too far right. Abell, an experienced kayaker, warned him during his entry that he was heading for "the hole." Miner, she added, had acted very nervous as he had scouted Hance. A raft had already capsized during this trip and another had been badly ripped. And Hance had looked worse than anything they had encountered thus far.

Solares, meanwhile, was holding onto Miner's boat with one hand, having jammed his leg between the frame and the boat for stability, so he could operate a video camera with his other hand.

Two oar strokes after Abell's warning, Miner's boat dropped into a large hole near the top of the rapid and flipped upside down. Littels, well below, rescued both Miner and Abell at the foot of the lengthy, 30-foot drop.

Solares, meanwhile, stayed with the boat, even grabbing one of its oars. The upside-down boat had snagged on a boulder in the rapid itself. Witnesses on shore said they could see Emilio Solares still with the raft. Through binoculars it was apparent to them that at least one of Solares' legs or feet was somehow trapped in the boat's rigging.

Solares struggled violently for several minutes to get out from under the raft. Failing to extricate himself, he continued to lay on his back under the water with his head aimed downstream. At least one of his feet, it still seemed, remained trapped under the overturned raft.

Those on shore watched in dread as Solares struggled frantically to keep his face above water and gasp for air.

Abell later said that, as they had pulled away from shore, she had noticed a loose rope trailing. But it was then too late, she thought, to have secured it.

Mark Miner, who had kayaked for three years but had purchased his

"Protar" raft only four months earlier, reported that he had told Abell and Solares that Hance "was powerful—and, if they went over [capsized]," he advised them not to try to highside but to "just go with it."

Amazingly, two more video cameras were operating from shore. Tapes from these two, however, failed to show Solares in his struggle. Solares' own video tape recovered later shows Mark Miner rowing as Lisa Abell warns him in the background that he is heading for the hole. Miner shouts "Oh Shit! Hang on!" as his raft flips in this hole. Solares' camera continued to film for several ghastly seconds under water before it shut off.

Those on shore groped for a way to get out to Solares before it was too late. They made several attempts to paddle kayaks from the right shore—with a rope—to Solares' position in the rapid. But they failed in this even as they watched Solares still clawing at the water and the boat to escape. Apparently Solares was not carrying a knife with which to cut whatever line had snagged his legs. Or else his leg or foot was trapped in some other way, perhaps still wedged between the frame and the boat.

In the end, the boat's lodged position in the river proved too challenging for his would-be rescuers. Finally, after Solares' face vanished under water a last time, his companions gave up. Two of the kayakers paddled eleven miles downstream to Phantom Ranch to seek NPS ranger assistance.

The weather had turned so foul that a helicopter landing was deemed too dangerous. Rangers Jim Traub and Bil Vandergraff hiked down the New Hance Trail after dark through a blizzard to reach the river. Of course they were not able to do much at this point except collect statements and try to avoid hypothermia themselves. When the NPS finally recovered Miner's boat, which drifted off the rock that night, they saw the boat had been rigged with a frightening "spiderweb of loose netting" that can trap a person's arm or leg instead of with safer, tight straps. They also found several stashes of marijuana aboard in Miner's personal gear.

On January 8, 1995, 45 days after Solares' drowning, NPS Ranger Marty Johnson spotted Solares' body floating past River Mile 88 at Phantom Ranch. A Glen Canyon Environmental Studies trip recovered it at River Mile 100.5.

The bodies of other river fatalities have proven nearly as elusive to recover. One of Georgie White's favorite stopping spots in Grand Canyon was at the cliffs soaring upward with almost unearthly grandeur near River Mile 53. Nankoweap Camp was one of Georgie's very favorites. The place offers one of the most spectacular sights in Grand Canyon. But in the summer of 1957, Nankoweap surprised Georgie in a different way.

It began when one of Georgie's Royal River Rats ran anxiously to her yelling, "Hey, there's a grave!"

The grave, six feet long and lined with rocks, had been built not long before by Gaylord Staveley's Mexican Hat Expeditions trip. The trip had found a

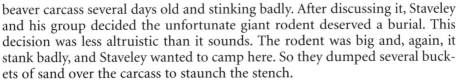

beaver carcass several days old and stinking badly. After discussing it, Staveley and his group decided the unfortunate giant rodent deserved a burial. This decision was less altruistic than it sounds. The rodent was big and, again, it stank badly, and Staveley wanted to camp here. So they dumped several buckets of sand over the carcass to staunch the stench.

Georgie's problem arose when Staveley's group had decided that the deceased beaver also needed a small wooden grave marker. They fashioned one and inscribed it: "Here lies D. Beaver, died June 15, 1957." (The "D." was short for "dead.")

In disbelief, Georgie and several other clients went to investigate the grave. Sure enough, a mound of fresh sand lay carefully pounded down. And at its head stood a marker lamenting the passing of D. Beaver.

It damned well looked like a grave. But maybe, Georgie suspected, it was just a joke. She knew Staveley had passed through here only a few days ahead of her. But if not a joke, Georgie realized, she would be smart to find out now. So she started digging. Soon the stench and sight of rotting flesh was unmistakable. No question now that a corpse had been buried here! Disgusted, she stopped digging and covered up what she had exposed.

Georgie later called the NPS from Phantom Ranch and asked to be transferred to John McLaughlin, Superintendent of Grand Canyon National Park. "Staveley lost a passenger," Georgie told him. She next explained that she had found buried a Mr. D. Beaver at Nankoweap.

As bureaucrats are wont to do when they have been left out of the loop, this NPS official became irate. Absolutely, McLaughlin said, Staveley should have reported this fatality. Unable to contact Staveley to verify who D. Beaver was and what sort of tragic accident had taken him, however, NPS officials instead checked the trip itinerary from Staveley's launch at Lees Ferry. Unhelpfully, the itinerary listed no "D. Beaver."

This was worse yet. Staveley had been carrying a passenger whom he had failed to list. Here was yet another violation!

National Park headquarters put out the word to the rangers at Lake Mead National Recreation Area, to the Arizona Department of Public Safety, and to the Coconino County Sheriff's Department to apprehend Staveley as his trip exited across upper Lake Mead into Pearce Ferry.

This army of law enforcement officials somehow missed Staveley's trip.

Because this was too early in Grand Canyon Park history for a helicopter reconnaissance of the grave, too early for beach sanitation rules, and too early even for good interagency communication, Mr. D. Beaver detonated an explosion of rumors and bizarre ideas as to who the dead person really was and what dastardly fate had placed him in his hideously isolated grave. Had a murder been committed? The Coconino County Sheriff's Department wondered. This explosion of weird hypotheses was a nagging thorn in the side of NPS headquarters for weeks. Park authorities were worried that "D. Beaver" was actually Gilbert H.

Hansen, a wealthy easterner who suspiciously vanished under water at Music Temple in Glen Canyon on May 17, 1957, while on a river trip.

Meanwhile the Arizona Game and Fish Department was worried that Mr. D. Beaver was not a human at all. Instead, they feared, it was one of their recently transplanted desert bighorn sheep. They were dismayed at the prospect of having lost one of their vital transplants because the new population they hoped to restore to Paria and Marble canyons was so precarious.

Later, Gaylord Staveley drove to Grand Canyon National Park Headquarters for his routine check-out for the season. To his surprise, he found himself in very hot water. McLaughlin read him the riot act over the seriousness of not reporting dead bodies.

Staveley told him that it was a dead beaver stinking to high heaven and he had simply wanted to camp there.

River Crossers Who Didn't

The early days of Canyon-Anglo relations resembled a geological cat and mouse game. The Anglos were the cat. The mouse was gold—or at least silver—hidden somewhere in the unfathomable vastness of Grand Canyon. That this gold *must* exist *somewhere* in the Canyon many men were dead certain.

Hence, it is no surprise that the strange saga of the first known historical death in the Colorado in Grand Canyon was that of a prospector positive that gold lay hidden here, in God's own secret treasure room. His story begins with this passage from the reminiscences of prospector Edward Schieffelin:

> *About the hardest trip I ever took was in the spring of '72 when I, with four others, went up the Grandest of all canyons, the Grand Canyon of the Colorado River. Although it was short, less than a month, it was a hard one.*

That spring, not just Schieffelin and his four argonauts but two hundred miners in Saint Thomas, twelve miles up the Muddy River from the Colorado River in southeast Nevada, had set their eyes on "the Grandest of all Canyons" where rumors of a gold rush had sparked an epidemic of gold fever. Many planned to travel upriver into it from its western end. Several of them hauled their boat lumber on wagons down Grand Wash to the foot of Grand Canyon near the Grand Wash Cliffs. There three cliques constructed, caulked, and loaded three separate craft. One young man, Bush Dulin, had done the lion's share of the work for his group, only to see all of them change their minds once the time came to row upstream. Ultimately Dulin convinced four others—Edward Schieffelin, George Magin, George Goodnow, and Oliver—to abandon their own smaller boat and instead use his own large pride and joy, the *Lady Jennings*.

In late March 1872, these five men headed upstream in company with another group, all Irishmen, using a similar boat, the *Shamrock*.

Attrition among these argonauts continued at a high rate. The *Lady* had just entered the Grand Wash Cliffs when downstream of them, not quite inside Grand Canyon, the *Shamrock* wrapped, sank, then emptied itself of all of its cargo in a minor rapid. Its crew salvaged the boat itself. But now destitute, they decided to give up and float forty miles downstream and then head up the Virgin and then the Muddy River back to St. Thomas.

Now only five prospectors of that potential two hundred rowed and hauled their boat upstream. They struggled, prospecting along the way, for ten days. Their only other companions were two ravens who dived on their camp each morning once they abandoned it. By April 10, they were possibly thirty miles upstream in Grand Canyon when they encountered a rapid that required them to haul their boat around a twenty-foot-long granite boulder projecting into the current.

As they tried to tow their unloaded boat around this rock, the current grabbed it. The sudden jerk yanked everyone off his feet and into a pile. The rope hissed through their hands and flew into the air. The *Lady*, finally freed, zipped downstream.

Thoughts of being marooned here "in hostile Indian country" flashed through each man's mind.

Abruptly, however, the large knot at the end of the *Lady's* bowline caught between two boulders. The rub was that the *Lady* had "moored" herself close to the opposite side of the river.

Dulin had hurt his knee in the dogpile when the *Lady* had leaped loose. As the other men grabbed the oars with the intention of building a hasty raft to row out and recover the *Lady*, Dulin said, "It might tear loose at any time and as soon as my knee gets well, I will go up the river somewhere and swim over."

Dulin and two others walked a mile and a half upstream to find a safe crossing. The first man in, George Magil, swam across successfully. Dulin and Oliver tried to follow him while carrying the oars. But they soon realized they could not make it. They turned back. Ashore again Dulin felt such urgency that, instead of retracing the shoreline upstream to follow Magil's route exactly, and instead of waiting until he had warmed up, he walked only part way upstream and dived into the river while still cold from his previous swim.

Dulin made it three-quarters of the way across before the Colorado became a rapid racing against a cliff face on the side of the river he had been swimming toward. At that point Dulin vanished under water.

His four horrified companions never found his body. Magil, however, did recover their boat by severing the bowline from shore. He used a knife lashed to a long driftwood pole. The four survivors now possessed their boat again. But without its rope they could no longer tow it upstream. So the four prospectors instead used the *Lady* to escape the Canyon.

Even as they floated safely downstream, the specter of Bush Dulin's death haunted Schieffelin, who wrote:

> *And to lose a comrade in that out of the way, wild, terrible, dismal place was too horrible to think about. And I imagined I could hear him calling not to leave him. Friends may die surrounded with comfort of Brothers or Sisters where they can see the flowers and trees or at least fields of level country and cause us a great deal of grief. But to die in that dark and life forsaken place and be left there was more appalling I believe than it is possible for it to occur in any other way or place.*

A far more mysterious pair of drownings occurred nearly twenty years later. During the summer of 1890 (uncertain date), John Fuller and Harry MacDonald were working as herdsmen on the Kaibab Plateau. Harry MacDonald was very likely the same "Harry McDonald" who, as mentioned earlier, had been steering F. M. Brown's boat when it overturned fatally for Brown at Salt Water Wash in 1889. Six months later, McDonald had returned to the Colorado River with Robert Brewster Stanton on his 1889–1890 Grand Canyon surveying expedition and worked as head boatman. But in February of 1890 he had quit in disgust at the men having destroyed in Horn Creek Rapid one of Stanton's three boats, the *Sweet Marie*, that he, McDonald, had just spent five days rebuilding. Fed up, he had hiked out to the North Rim. Now, in summer, Fuller and MacDonald rode and led their horses down Bright Angel Fault before the North Kaibab Trail existed along it. They were on a mission in search of the remains of a man whose identity was not mentioned, but who likely was Frank Mason Brown himself or, less likely, Henry Richards (the body of the third casualty of Brown's trip, Peter M. Hansbrough, already had been discovered in January of 1890 at River Mile 44 by McDonald and the rest of Stanton's crew).

Fuller's and MacDonald's descent down the treacherous deer trail following the Bright Angel Fault from the North Rim was hideous. Both men lost their horses to fatal falls. They ended up carrying their salvaged gear to the river. McDonald and Fuller trudged into a macabre mystery, a fully equipped but unoccupied camp set up along Bright Angel Creek near the confluence. The tent stood well set up and in ship shape. In it were two cots with the blankets pulled back as if just vacated. Two rifles and two revolvers lay next to them. An expensive gold watch (run down and no longer ticking) hung from the tent pole. A Dutch oven sat outside on cold coals and held half a loaf of bread baked about three days earlier. Tracks on the ground indicated that two adults had saddled horses and rode them to the Colorado—and then entered it as if to swim across.

Also standing in camp, waiting dutifully, was a gelding donkey, "Brighty" (named after Bright Angel Creek) of the Grand Canyon, made famous 60 years later in a book by Marguerite Henry, who read about Brighty in a 1922 *Sunset Magazine* article by Thomas Heron McKee.

The two missing men, Fuller learned later, were never seen again, but they originally had been seen passing through Flagstaff with their donkey—"Brighty"—en route to Grand Canyon. People on the South Rim also told Fuller that the pair with the donkey and horses had descended the early version of the Bright Angel Trail to the region of this mysteriously abandoned camp. Again, the two missing men were never seen to exit the Canyon—and, of course, had they been planning to do so, they never would have abandoned their valuables, even if they might have abandoned their set up camp. The identities of these original owners of Brighty of the Grand Canyon remain a mystery, though their fate seems very likely to have been one of drowning during an attempted crossing of the Colorado. Like Brown and Richards, McDonald's lost companions, these two men too were never found.

In the early years of human presence historically in Grand Canyon, the river took those most available to her. Hence, the most common drownings were at Lees Ferry because it was by far the most accessible crossing point of the river for more than four hundred miles. Every one of the eleven victims of drowning here while the ferry was in operation started out in some sort of boat. But every one of them shared two elements in common: mishandling of the boat and not wearing a life jacket.

The first such victim was Lorenzo W. Roundy, who drowned trying to cross the river on May 24, 1876. Not long after this, around 1880 or 1881, two unnamed Navajos drowned here. And soon after them, in June or July of 1884, Henry Rosely and his twelve-year-old son, Al, drowned while trying to cross. Two more Navajos, brothers, tragically drowned here while operating the ferry incorrectly in 1889. Next, Preston Apperson, a crewman with Charles Spencer's huge, but failed, mining promotion drowned here on March 9, 1911, along with a team of horses when the entire ferry sank in midriver. The most gruesome of incidents at Lees Ferry took place on its last attempted crossing.

All three people aboard the ferry's last journey across the Colorado on June 7, 1928—passengers Royce Elliot Dean, age 25, and Lewis Nez Tsinnie, age 26 (and their wire-cage Ford truck), plus substitute ferryman Adolpha Johnson, age 26—became victims of an apparent freak gust of wind on very high water. The ferry successfully crossed the river to the east with all three men and the Ford. But as Johnson tried to tie it up, a gust of wind hit. The ferry began drifting hard, back out toward midriver. Johnson dug in his heels to try to stop it, but found himself dragged to the river anyway.

At the river Johnson climbed hand over hand back to the ferry as the powerful current relentlessly shoved it back out toward midriver. Johnson needed to crank the forward windlass to change the ferry's angle so that the current would shove the boat back to the east shore again. Either of the two passengers still on the ferry might have done this quicker than Johnson. But neither

Dean nor Tsinnie did so—either from lack of understanding or from fear.

When Johnson reached the ferryboat, the upstream beam was dipping into the relentless 86,500 cfs current. The entire deck listed upstream at a precarious angle.

As Johnson's wife, Marva, and their small son, Milo, watched from the west shore, the cable broke loose. The entire ferry tipped over and hydroplaned under. Horrified, Marva watched as "everything went out of sight." She never saw her husband nor Dean (nor the Ford truck) again. After several minutes of searching, Marva Johnson did see Lewis Nez Tsinnie floating downstream apparently motionless.

Dean's body was discovered two months later embedded in a sand bank twenty feet above the water near Soap Creek. These final three fatalities hold the record for the highest known number of deaths for drowning victims not attempting to travel downstream. They also heralded the last gasp of the ferry service. After more than fifty-five years of service—and the "deaths" of 14 different ferry boats and 11 people—Lees Ferry became simply a place along the Colorado at the head of Grand Canyon, River Mile 0, as designated by the Colorado River Compact of 1922. The completion of Navajo Bridge about four months later replaced the ferry function at Lees Ferry altogether.

Aside from tragic mishaps at Lees Ferry, crossing the Colorado River in Grand Canyon has all too often been like playing tag with the Devil.

The next known victim of an attempted crossing well downstream of Lees Ferry was yet another prospector. On June 9, 1899, a party of prospectors from Williams—George H. Gibson, George D. Roberts, Henry B. Clifford, William F. Russell, Henry Sellers, and T. A. and George Fleming—descended from the South Rim along an early version of the Bright Angel Trail. Their intent was to explore some mining properties on the north side of the river. To cross the river they had brought along a folding canvas boat. The stumbling block was, by the men's own estimate, that snow melt and recent rains had raised the river a whopping 70 feet.

It being already 5:00 p.m., the seven hastily set up their canvas boat. T. A. Fleming and William F. Russell paddled the frail craft onto the racing spate. The river sped them downstream. The men's efforts to power their boat across the flood to the north side failed. As Russell shifted position in the boat, it capsized. True to form for those days, neither man wore a life jacket—even though they had been invented decades earlier. Fleming, a good swimmer, stroked back to the south bank. Russell, instead, clung to the capsized boat. The two raced hundreds of yards into the rapid below and vanished.

Half of Russell's companions hurried along the shore in the twilight, hoping to assist him. They never saw him again.

They camped that night, then hiked back up to the South Rim the next morning, counting Russell as dead.

On June 16, William Wallace Bass, pioneer asbestos miner and tour operator, along with John Waltenberg and R. M. Bleak, launched a search for Russell's body near River Mile 108. All they found during their four days of strenuous efforts was an inordinate number of rattlesnakes. On day four the two lowered Bleak off a short cliff to ascertain whether something in the river below was Russell's hat. The rope broke. Bleak fell and was knocked unconscious. They trio gave up their search. Bleak recovered days later. Russell, however, was never found.

Again trying to wring money out of the Grand Canyon Colorado, in 1903 the Grand Canyon Electric Company conducted surveys within Grand Canyon deep within Upper Granite Gorge for good locations to harness the river. Surveyor P. T. McConigle, age 37, who was quitting the company, was aiming to show his successor, surveyor Charles McLean, age 44, the company's camp on Bright Angel Creek. McConigle then planned to exit the Canyon with his personal effects.

The two men hiked down from Indian Garden on the morning of July 27. Two days later, launch marks in the sand from the company's aging pine scow showed that the two men had launched to make their crossing. The mystery arose in the lack of landing marks on the opposite side of the river.

Several days of laborious searching by Niles J. Cameron, Louis D. Boucher, and others found not only no boat marks on the opposite side of the river, but no footprints nor any other sign that either McLean or McConigle had ever crossed the river, safely or otherwise, or ever reached the company's camp.

Yes, the river was running high, but McConigle had crossed the river only ten days earlier in the same boat. All parties agreed, however, that this boat was weak from exposure to the elements and could have disintegrated if the men in her had inadvertently run a rapid. Exactly what went wrong to drown McLean and McConigle—a lost or crabbed oar, a man overboard, a shipping of too much water, disintegration of the boat itself—remains a mystery. It is only certain that the two men were not wearing life jackets and that they had vanished.

It also has been rumored for years that the skiff the two had used dangled a chain for a painter. The rumor continues that the dangling chain was found later by searchers, perhaps Godfrey Sykes and Harry Hussey, caught between two boulders, it having ripped the stern of their scow clean off when it caught.

Despite such notorious deaths during attempted crossings, not even NPS personnel were immune to repeating the fatal errors that caused them. On February 20, 1929, less than two months after the large-scale search for the vanished "Honeymooning" Hydes, three NPS personnel attempted a crossing below Phantom Ranch near Horn Creek Rapid. The three were Naturalist Glen E. Sturdevant, age 33, Ranger Fred Johnson, age 30, and Chief Ranger James P. Brooks (who, with the Kolb brothers two months earlier, had searched for Glen and Bessie Hyde). For nine days, they had been exploring the Tonto Plateau atop the Tapeats Sandstone for an inventory of natural history and archeological sites on the north side of the river, more than 1,000 feet above the Colorado. Meanwhile Rangers Michael Harrison and Carl Lehnert had explored the corresponding South Tonto across the river.

Once the trio on the north had finished their recon work, they wanted to cross to the south side to return to the South Rim. The trio portaged their 12-foot-10-inch folding boat about 100 yards upstream of Horn Creek Rapid. Then, at about 8:00 a.m., they started across the river. Sturdevant, who was wearing a kapok-filled life belt, Brooks later would explain, had insisted on rowing. But as the boat crossed an eddy fence, Sturdevant lost an oar. And Johnson, who was standing up and wearing no life belt, lost his balance and fell into the river.

At this point the trio and their little boat were about 75 yards upstream of Horn Creek Rapid, only seconds away, and flowing at 5,700 cfs, a horrible level for this rapid.

Brooks saw that Johnson, with no life belt, was in peril. He grabbed a kapok life belt and jumped into the river to rescue him. But he never did catch him. Meanwhile the river swept the two swimmers and also Sturdevant, still rowing with one oar in the folding boat, into Horn Creek Rapid. At low water like this, Horn Creek Rapid was a mass of crushing hydraulics and boulders.

All three separate entities—Johnson, Brooks, and Sturdevant in the boat—accelerated and funneled into Horn Creek Rapid. The racing current sucked Brooks under almost instantly. He thought he had caught one of his companions by the hair for a moment, but did not know whose hair he might have held. Brooks later found himself cast to the shoreline on the north. He looked around for his companions but saw neither them nor the boat.

Hypothermia had already taken a toll on Brooks. It took him several minutes to marshal the strength simply to drag himself out of the river onto dry land. Once out, Brooks climbed low cliffs to search the shorelines and river for two hours for his companions. But he saw nothing. He shouted, but also heard nothing.

At last giving up, he scrambled upstream along the broken schist and granite in his soggy, freezing clothes and reached Phantom Ranch at nightfall. Brooks next hiked across the Kaibab Bridge, then up the South Kaibab Trail to the South Rim, and finally to Park Headquarters to make his report.

Park Superintendent M. R. Tillotson ordered several search parties into action. Brooks, in an early version on the Iron Man Competition, returned to the river with one of them. Tillotson ordered Harrison and Lehnert to hurry to the mouth of Monument Canyon (River Mile 93.5) to join a party of Fred Harvey personnel searching the river by coming upstream (alternatingly rowing, towing, and portaging) from Hermit Rapid (River Mile 95) with a sawed-in-half-then-reassembled boat abandoned by the Pathé-Bray expedition.

These searchers soon found a body wearing a life belt floating in the large eddy below Granite Falls at the foot of Monument Canyon. Near it floated several other items belonging to the three swimmers, including Brooks' leather coat, which "now weighed 75 pounds." Harrison immediately identified the body as Sturdevant by a once-broken but still stiff finger on the corpse's hand. Despite his life belt, Sturdevant had either drowned or succumbed to hypothermia.

Four more days of searching, including the use of hard-core tactics, failed to find Johnson. As Michael Harrison recalled: "We dynamited the head and foot of Horn Creek Rapid....We threw in...a full case of dynamite." But the searchers never did find Johnson, who had not been wearing a life belt.

As might be guessed, crossing the river has likely always been a problem. Evidence from archaeology reveals at least casual visits from as early as 4,000 years ago by people of the Desert Culture. It also hints at visits as far back as 10,500 years ago by Folsom people, who likely were here to hunt giant ground sloths, Harrington's mountain goats, or other huge creatures of the now-vanished Pleistocene megafauna still lumbering within a Grand Canyon that was far more lush than today. Since 850 AD or earlier, Puebloan Indians lived in various sections of the Canyon at least seasonally, if not semi-permanently. They grew corn, squash, beans, and cotton. They also hunted and gathered. Their stone pueblos and metates, elegant pot shards, and flaked stone tools still litter the Canyon's deltas and creek courses. All of these people up to our highly technological "now," however, have faced the same problem when they hit the Colorado: How do you get over to the other side?

No one today knows how prehistoric Native Americans or PaleoIndians did it. They left no paddles, boats, rafts, or inflated bighorn sheep bellies behind for us to puzzle over. Nor did they leave pictographs painted on, or petroglyphs etched in, the cliff faces depicting river crossers that might give us a clue. Your guess as to how they did it, other than by fording shallow places, may be as good as anyone's. In some parts of the world in which primitive cultures face crossing good-sized rivers without a boat, they do use floats. Natives of Ethiopia's upper Omo River, for example, use inflated bladders or skins of animals such as goats or sheep. By contrast, some natives of the 1950s Southwest use inflated air mattresses.

Unquestionably the doyen of Grand Canyon hiking is Harvey Butchart. This former professor of mathematics at Northern Arizona University (NAU), logged 12,000 miles of hiking during 1,000 days in the Canyon. And Butchart's routes were anything but routine. He found 116 different approaches to the Colorado River from the rims, climbed 83 of the Canyon's named peaks, and logged 35 first ascents. Butchart's avocation to know the Canyon's maze consisted of brilliance flirting with obsession.

On May 26, 1955, only a month after Bill Beer and John Daggett swam the entire Grand Canyon Colorado, 48-year-old Harvey Butchart tried to talk his best hiking partner from the NAU hiking club, 22-year-old Carlton Boyd Moore, into following in Beer and Daggett's wake on air mattresses. Moore said, "no way."

So, instead, they hiked down the Nankoweap Trail from Point Imperial, reaching the Colorado near River Mile 53 and walked downstream.

Butchart wanted to cross the river somewhere upstream of the Little Colorado River (River Mile 61.5), but first he picked a quiet stretch of river about a mile upstream of Kwagunt Rapid (River Mile 56) to practice their mode of transport—paddling across on an inflated air mattress—with no other sort of personal flotation device. Moore, who was almost a nonswimmer, had been leery of the Colorado, so Butchart tried to aid him by lightening his pack and even towing him with a short rope. While towing proved futile, Moore seemed to catch on and was ready to continue, warily remarking, however, that he could see that once they were on the river, they were strictly on their own.

After safely landing and portaging around the huge Kwagunt Rapid, the two launched back into the cold, swiftly flowing river, heading downstream along the right bank before attempting a crossing near 60 Mile Rapids.

Butchart started paddling across on his air mattress first, while Moore elected to watch. To Butchart's surprise, once beyond the eddy the 26,000 cfs flow of the river swept him through a small rapid and back to the right shore, downstream and out of view of his starting point and of Moore. Butchart climbed out of the river onto a ledge to signal Moore not to try it. It was too late. Moore was already racing past him down the middle of the river on his own mattress.

Butchart quickly jumped back into the river and paddled furiously to catch up with him. He chased Moore for over two miles, and might never have caught him were it not for Moore getting stuck in a large eddy a mile *after* the Little Colorado River, nearly three miles downstream of their crossing point. Moore at this point was hanging upside down with his arms and legs wrapped around his air mattress from underneath. He was gripping the inflated rubber for dear life while he swirled around in circles in an eddy whirlpool.

The current then whipped Moore into another eddy on the opposite side of the river where Butchart finally reached him. Moore's face was pale and white. Butchart saw that Moore was "not thinking clearly." Butchart tried to get him to shore by first telling Moore to shrug off his waterlogged backpack and climb atop the mattress, which Moore did. Butchart then tried towing the panic-stricken Moore by having him hold onto Butchart's feet, but found himself unable to tow Moore against the current. Then, as Moore seemed to try paddling himself to shore, he was swept back into the main current and rushed downstream again.

Butchart paddled after him in the darkening twilight. The two were swept toward Lava Canyon Rapid (River Mile 65.6). Butchart thought Moore had too great a lead on him for Butchart to be able to catch him before the rapid, so he paddled to shore and climbed out among the willows on the left bank. Then he jogged downstream.

Butchart never saw Boyd Moore again. No one ever did. His body was never found, although P. T. Reilly later did find Moore's backpack, split open and empty, above River Mile 72.

Only afterward did Butchart learn that when Moore was 3 or 4 years old he had experienced a near drowning from which he had never recovered psychologically and which had left him too fearful of water to learn to swim.

Swimmers Who Drowned Between Phantom And Pipe Creek

The combination of brutally hot weather and a steep dustbowl of a trail winding for mile after mile under an unblinking desert sun has beguiled thousands of hikers who have descended to the foot of the Bright Angel Trail. The surprisingly intense heat and amazingly fast process of dehydration have sapped the mental acuity of many otherwise intelligent hikers like a brain vampire. This combination of heat and dehydration has made fools out of thousands of summer hikers, some of whom have literally walked off the trail and into the river fully dressed like zombies from a bad B-movie. Even NPS rangers have done this in uniform, radio and all.

The heat is that unnerving. Even veteran Canyon hikers can attest to this, without embarrassment.

This sort of "cool off" swim, however, has often turned fatal. On July 21, 1935, for example, on a day about as hot as it gets in Grand Canyon, three teenage trail workers for the Civilian Conservation Corps (C.C.C.) hiked to the foot of the Bright Angel Trail and decided to cool off. This location, only a few yards upstream of the head of the lethal whitewater of Pipe Creek Rapid (at River Mile 89), has tempted thousands of hikers. And even though it was only 9:30 a.m., a cool hour in many parts of the world, here, now, it was already torrid.

The three young men stripped down to their skivvies and jumped into the small eddy. They splashed and dunked, savoring the nearly 80-degree water. Abruptly two of the teenagers saw their companion, 18-year-old Kenneth E. Curtis of Kingman, vanish as he was sucked under the waves of the rapid flowing at 21,000 cfs. The two quickly tried to get near Curtis to help him, but they realized that they would likely drown if they followed him. They climbed out of the small eddy and headed downstream over the talus. They spent the rest of the morning searching the shorelines. But they found no sign of Curtis.

A large search party the next day scoured both shorelines for miles. But neither they nor anyone else thereafter ever found a sign of Curtis.

Two years later, on August 7, 1937, Wallace Peshlakai, a Navajo interpreter of the Christian Reformed Church Mission, of Rehoboth, New Mexico, also hiked down with several others to the foot of Bright Angel Trail. And, as the C.C.C. boys had done, he decided to ease himself into the Colorado to cool off.

As his hysterical eight-year-old step-son, Tommy Atchinson, reported, Peshlakai disrobed at the foot of the trail, just above Pipe Creek, and entered the warm river flowing at 9,500 cfs. A few moments later he saw Peshlakai, a horrified expression on his face, sucked into the swirling current and carried downstream. Peshlakai too was never seen again.

On June 20, 1955, Harold William Nelson, (age unknown), tried to swim across the river to cool off at a flow of 29,000 cfs near Phantom at today's "boat beach" area upstream of Bright Angel Creek. Nelson's body too was never found. Nelson was the third drowning victim in 1955, a possible "copycat" of Beer and Daggett's well publicized swim of two months earlier.

While it was once commonly said that the Colorado never gives up its dead, this is not exactly true. More true perhaps, is the Colorado frequently packaged its dead in mysterious circumstances. During their mid-April Easter vacation in 1968, for example, two Northern Arizona University students—Bruce Mitchell and Jan Jensen—hiked from the western North Rim area into Parashant Wash (River Mile 198.5). While admiring the grandeur of the western Canyon they were shocked to find a human skull protruding from the sand bar above the river. Upon returning to civilization, they alerted the National Park Service.

NPS personnel then hiked into Parashant and searched the area. They too found the skeleton, still clad in a woman's one-piece blue bathing suit, buried in the river sediments of the bank. The skeleton, forensic investigators concluded, was that of a young woman, 5-feet, 7-inches tall. The young woman's skeleton showed no indications of trauma. Nor did it possess any identification.

The investigators, however, suspected murder. Nearby in a recently-abandoned mine were a woman's clothes and also expensive mining equipment. It seemed fishy. As in a mystery novel, something sinister seemed to have happened here.

Ultimately someone remembered that nearly three years earlier, Carol Goldman, age 18, of Albuquerque, had stepped from the hot beach into the 17,400 cfs river near Phantom Ranch for a quick dip—on August 24, 1965. She had been careful, her 17-year-old companion Jeanne Putnam had explained, because Goldman could not swim. Yet despite her care, Goldman had slipped into an unexpectedly deep hole and had been swept away. Searchers had never recovered her body. Forensics in 1968 now indicated that the skeleton found 107.5 miles downstream of Phantom was that of Carol Goldman. The women's clothes with the mining equipment at Parashant was apparently an unexplained coincidence.

The combination of sweltering heat and a deceptively friendly river would continue to lure victims. On June 3, 1970, Dwight L. Miller, age 26, decided that it was so hot that he had to leap into the river. He plunked in just above Pipe Creek flowing at 16,000 cfs at the foot of the Bright Angel Trail. The powerful current swept him into eternity. His body was found 13 days later several miles downstream. On a hot August 4, 1973, Londoner Julian Griffiths, age 21, did the same thing in 11,500 cfs. He ignored the nearby sign warning against entering the river and decided instead that his own swimming ability would propel him across the Colorado to the north side. Twenty-five days later a commercial river-running trip found Griffith's body at River Mile 102. On April 8, 1977, a year of extreme drought, yet another hiker repeated Griffith's fatal error. Aparicio Gil, age 26, found himself gripped by the surprisingly tenacious current—even in an almost record low flow of 2,000 cfs. Sixteen days later, on April 24, an air search found Gil's body 4 miles downstream.

Thankfully, nearly eighteen years passed before someone else committed this same fatal error. On June 25, 1995, a pair of hikers, Tom Snashall and Gerald Deyo, arrived at the foot of the Bright Angel Trail at Pipe Creek and met Louis John Stano, III, age 21, from Tennessee. The three men talked for a few minutes. The pair noted that Stano, with a dirty blond ponytail, scruffy beard, and torn clothes, was a rough looking specimen. He had been badly sunburned, they said, and had old broken blisters on his face and shoulders. He looked worn out.

Stano told them he was traveling across the U.S. to California to see the San Diego Zoo and that he had just been hiking in Colorado. This morning he had lost track of his traveling partner on the Bright Angel Trail. Unknown to Stano, his partner, who had not been carrying any of their water, had drawn an unnoticed message to him in the dust of the trail several yards above the trio's heads, and was now awaiting Stano at Phantom Ranch.

Snashall and Deyo mentioned they were about to do some work in Tennessee, but Stano, they said, seemed distant and uninterested. He asked them for a match. They did not have one. Stano bummed a match from one of the six other hikers nearby and lit up a cigar. He then stood knee-deep in the river and smoked it.

During their conversation, Snashall and Deyo reported, Stano had asked the pair several times their opinion of the river, how deep it might be, and so on. The two said there was a sign that said swimming was illegal. They also said they thought the current was dangerous. They recommended against trying to swim in it.

After Stano smoked his cigar, the pair was surprised to see him walk behind a bush, strip naked in the 106-degree heat, then run to the shore and make a shallow dive into the river. Stano swam out into the Colorado, flowing at 17,800 cfs, as if to cross it immediately upstream of Pipe Creek Rapids.

The current funneled Stano into the 48-degree rapid. Witnesses say Stano kept swimming the whole time while in view, never disappearing more than briefly. Even so, as Stano vanished out of sight, the eight others on the beach were in shock. A woman from Denmark asked, "Why would anyone do something like that?" An Hispanic man said, "They'll find him in Yuma."

But Stano never got close to Yuma. Three weeks later a Western River Expeditions' trip led by Bill Skinner spotted Stano's body twenty miles downstream of Pipe Creek Rapid and floating near Shinumo Creek Beach.

Later that year, on November 25, eight day-hikers from Los Angeles descended the South Kaibab Trail with the intent of returning to the South

Rim via the Bright Angel Trail. At 1:00 p.m., two of the eight, Frederick Zernik, age 29, and Troy M. Fortney, age 26, decided to eliminate the nearly two-mile walk along the River Trail that connects the South Kaibab with the Bright Angel Trail. These two accomplished body surfers would swim instead of walk.

Ignoring the sign they had just passed saying "**Dangerous Currents Swimming Prohibited**," both men waded into the river, found it shockingly cold, then exited back to shore in a hurry. The only way to get into the river they decided, was to leap in from a high rock with full commitment. Zernik and Fortney jumped into the cold Colorado immediately below the Mile 88 Boat Beach. Mere seconds in the cold water convinced Zernik that he had made a serious mistake. It did even worse to Fortney.

As the two entered Bright Angel Rapid, flowing at 14,000 cfs, Fortney was already hyperventilating and panicking in the cold water. He climbed on top of Zernik. Zernick pushed Fortney off. Fortney crawled atop Zernick again.

The other six hikers ran downstream to the Silver Bridge in hopes of helping, but they arrived too late to do anything but witness the tableau unfold.

Zernick knew that both of them were about to drown. And probably he first. He fought his way free of Fortney again and stroked for the south shore. He swam into a tight eddy. Fortney followed him. After cycling around and around in the eddy with Fortney close behind him for a minute or two, and getting colder by the second, Zernick managed to self-extricate onto dry, but nearly vertical rock. At his precarious haul-out on a cliff face, Zernick perched, self-trapped, just upstream of the Silver Bridge. From here he would require a technical rescue via ropes.

Meanwhile Fortney was swept out of the eddy and back into the downstream current.

Zernik became irrationally combative due to hypothermia. He was no plum for his rescuers. Indeed Zernick was so cold and scared by the time that Rangers Mary Litell and Patrick Suddath dropped a rope to him that when he harnessed himself into it, he also looped it around his own neck.

Fortney never again escaped the current. It swept him under the bridge into Bright Angel Rapid. His body was found two weeks later at River Mile 95.25.

Swimmers Who Drowned Elsewhere In The Colorado

As we have seen, swimming in the Colorado to foil the heat waves shimmering from every square yard of exposed surface in Grand Canyon is all too tempting, even to those who should know better. On April 19, 1931, for example, 22-year old Iven Bundy and his cousin, Floyd Iverson, were grazing the family's sheep along the Colorado River near Whitmore Wash (River Mile 187.5). Floyd decided to swim across the river for fun, a thing both young men had been forbidden to do by their families.

Floyd swam alone across the 9,700 cfs current and made it to the other side. He called back to Iven that the swim was not all that hard.

Iven followed Floyd into the Colorado but was sucked under by a whirlpool. He vanished. Floyd searched for him desperately, but never saw a trace of him again. Floyd then faced the swim back across the Colorado and, after that, the long hike up to the family ranch at Mount Trumbull to explain how Iven had died—or had he merely been swept downstream?

Iven's father, Roy Bundy, had been crippled by arthritis. He asked his brother, Chester Bundy, to help search for Iven—or his body. Chester and Floyd plus Pat and Ensign Griffiths returned to the river. They searched in the rain, but found nothing. They plodded back up to Mount Trumbull to get a better outfit for searching properly. They next dragged a 180-pound, galvanized iron boat with watertight chambers fore and aft down to the river and loaded it with supplies, including a box of dynamite "for fishing." Chester, Floyd, and Pat now began their search for Iven in earnest.

During the first twenty miles or so of river they found no sign of Iven. But they did manage to flip their metal boat in a rapid "south of Parashant" (River Mile 198.5). This may have been 205-Mile Rapid. They also managed to lose most of their supplies, including their dynamite. Fortunately, no one else drowned.

The searchers continued downriver for five days in total to Diamond Creek (River Mile 225.7). Dissolute and hungry, Chester Bundy sat down in the old blacksmith's shop which had been built at Diamond by a government survey camp nearly a decade earlier. Chester sat on a bed spring under a two-foot wide plank that had been a tool shelf. As he looked up he read pencilled on the wall, "Glen and Bessie Hyde, November 31st [sic], 1928." This inscription, assuming that it was genuine, helped pinpoint where Bessie and Glen had vanished, i.e., downstream of Diamond but upstream of 237-mile. But it did nothing to help the searchers recover Iven, dead or alive. Nor did it help fill the three searchers' empty bellies.

They continued searching downstream and portaged their small boat around rapids. On day eight, they reached Separation Canyon and Rapid (River Mile 239.5). Although none of the three knew where they were, they did know they could not run this rapid and emerge from it alive. Nor could they portage it.

So they resorted to "ghost-boating" it with a log tied onto the tow rope as a float in the hopes that two of them could swim out below the rapid and rescue the empty boat. The searchers shoved the empty boat into the slick, silky vee feeding the already notorious rapid and watched from shore.

The rapid gulped the boat. The craft ruptured an air chamber, filled, and half sank. The searchers waded into the river downstream and rescued it, but the boat was a mess. On top of this, the three men were out of food. So out of food that the whole enterprise of boating down the Colorado now seemed insane.

The trio gave up. They hiked up Separation Canyon, taking the east fork. They shared a one-quart canteen. They ate tiny birds' eggs right out of the nest. Chester shot a jackrabbit with his six-shooter. This was like Thanksgiving. Up on the plateau, many hours later, they found an old mining road. From there they hiked from ranch house to ranch house, finding most of them unoccupied. Eventually they made it home.

Much later, the Bundys learned that Iven's body had been discovered by two prospectors while fishing at Gregg's Ferry, west of Grand Canyon, and was buried there.

In August of 1973, during a time of low releases of water from Glen Canyon Dam, four hikers made the trek from the Havasu Campground to the Colorado River. They arrived during morning when the flow was about 5,000 cfs or lower. This flow was low enough that the sand bar across the mouth of Havasu Creek (River Mile 156.8), often submerged, was exposed to sunlight. The creek still bisected this bar, but otherwise it offered a walkable route upstream to the Inner Gorge of the Colorado above the outflow of Havasu.

The four hikers stared at it and wondered what was upstream. Two of them decided to wade across Havasu and walk up the Colorado shoreline to find out what lay beyond the bar and the ledges of Muav Limestone so tantalizingly near. After all, this was the Grand Canyon. It seemed crazy to have hiked this far—nearly twenty miles—and then not even take a look.

Both men walked up the bar to the Muav and, walking its ledges, vanished from the view of their two companions remaining at the mouth.

At about 2:00 p.m., the two adventuresome hikers returned. In the meantime, the release from Glen Canyon Dam had risen another 3,000 to 4,000 cfs. The exposed bar of sand and cobbles that had allowed the pair a fairly safe route upstream was now deeply submerged by swift eddy currents. The two could not walk back as they had come.

They decided instead to swim downstream in the Colorado from their ledge. And to swim together. As their two companions waiting at the downstream side of Havasu watched them, both men jumped into the main river with the intent of swimming into the creek/eddy as soon as they came opposite it. Both men started swimming, one a few feet ahead of the other.

The lead man missed the eddy. Havasu Creek and the eddy flow of the river itself, a far more powerful entity, had shoved him out into the river. Now, try as the lead swimmer might, nothing he did countered the outflow of Havasu *and* the current of the Colorado. Even getting to shore before Havasu Rapid swallowed him looked questionable.

As the current shoved the lead man away from dry rock, the second man decided to help him. He too tried to stay near shore. But the current gripped him as tenaciously as it had his companion. Not only was he unable to help his

companion, he found that he could not even help himself.

As their horrified companions watched helplessly from shore, both swimmers, without life jackets, struggled unsuccessfully to swim to shore. Fighting them, however, the relentless funnel of current feeding Havasu Rapid swept the two men into the rapid itself. And though their two companions ran along shore in hopes of helping somehow, the two swimmers vanished under the Colorado.

An hour or so later an ARTA trip hiked back down from upper Havasu to their boats in its mouth to head downstream. One of the two remaining hikers explained what had happened. Mike Wynn, one of the boatmen on this trip, with others, searched the immediate shorelines on foot. Finding no one, they next had floated downriver. They searched for the swimmers for the next two days, but both young men had vanished.

Almost immediately after this incident NPS rangers at Lees Ferry issued to some commercial trips body bags to be used in the event that either young man was found. Other details on this episode, however, have proven illusive. No one whom we interviewed can remember the victims' names or the precise date of this mishap, and the NPS incident report on it likewise has been misplaced.

An even stranger, almost eerie misadventure occurred on August 5, 1976. A male passenger on a Hualapai river trip named Minoru Oda, age 31, decided to swim, also without a life jacket, 200 yards from the Hualapai River Runners boat on which he was riding to the shore at Pearce Ferry ("River" Mile 280). Despite this location being 40 miles onto Lake Mead—and therefore on quiet water, it was deep. NPS regulations, however, do not require a life jacket on Lake Mead.

Despite the deceptively inviting water, those on the boat warned Oda not to try to swim in the cove to shore. But they had warned him in English, and he spoke only Japanese. At any rate, Oda dived off and swam several yards.

Abruptly he began thrashing and flailing his arms. He quickly drowned and sank only four feet from a buoy not far from shore. The ensuing searchers never found his body. It was as if Oda had discorporated his molecules into the reservoir.

Bizarrely, eight days later, Oda's body surfaced four feet from this same buoy.

Several years later, on August 7, 1983, at River Mile 2.5, a somewhat similar mishap occurred. Less than an hour into an OARS, Inc. rowing trip, the group stopped for lunch. After the trip leader's safety talk, and as the guides cleaned up lunch, three young passengers on the trip, Jeffrey Kaplan, age 16, Jeff's younger brother Rick, and Kenneth Richard Kleeburg played a sort of "follow-the-leader" game sliding down the sand dune bank toward the eddy. Abruptly, Jeff, without a life jacket, jumped into the water about twenty yards downriver of the boats.

He swam with the eddy current up past the sterns of the boats. Rick, also wearing no life jacket, followed. Rick reported that the cold water took his breath away. Kenneth, still on shore behind the two brothers, decided not to enter the river.

Jeffrey, Rick saw, was doing a slow-motion breast stroke ahead of him. Then Jeffrey submerged out of sight. When Rick reached the upriver end of the boats, he still could not find Jeffrey. Rick looked around for a few seconds. He poked his head in likely hiding places. He suspected that his brother was trying to trick him. But as his searches continued to come up zero, he finally asked, "Where is Jeff?"

The last person to see Jeff was a fellow passenger and Kenneth's father, Richard Kleeburg, on this father-son trip. Jeff, Kleeburg said, had been twenty feet from the boats. He was floating "in the eddy face down, moving his arms, then his face came up and went down. These were gentle motions and Jeff appeared to be OK." Kleeburg did not watch Jeff after seeing this.

But at Rick's worried question, the boatmen now scoured the eddy. They looked in, stepped in, then checked under the boats. That done and nothing being found, they rowed around the eddy and probed its depths with oars. But still they found nothing. Later, neither did NPS divers, land searchers, nor helicopter searchers.

What happened to Jeffrey Kaplan? He had experienced an epileptic (petit mal) seizure a year and a half earlier. He was on the medications Dilantin and Tegretol to control a recurrence. Despite these, he had apparently suffered yet another seizure anyway. And none of the guides, three of whom were on their boats stowing food away at the time, had seen him. The chilly Colorado, it was surmised, had triggered a seizure in Jeffrey despite his medications, and he had silently sunk out of sight into a powerful flow of 36,000 cfs at a moment when no one was looking.

On August 30, 23 days later, a motorist stopped atop Navajo Bridge (illegally) to treat himself to the inspiring view into Marble Canyon from 470 feet above River Mile 4.3. This tourist, however, saw more than he had hoped to. Below him floated something that looked all too much like a human body. It was, it turned out, Jeffrey Kaplan's body, floating barely two miles downstream from where he had vanished.

On March 22, 1990, Boy Scout Matthew Cranny, age 13, hiked with his Utah LDS Troop 189—14 boys and 8 adults—down Saltwater Wash. The troop camped at River Mile 11.5. The next morning, Cranny and another scout, Scott Dillon, and his father, Steve Dillon, walked a mile or so upstream to a few hundred yards upstream of Soap Creek Rapid.

Steve Dillon saw Cranny sitting despondently on a rock. Steve asked him how he was doing. Cranny answered that he was not doing too well and that he probably would not catch a fish during the whole trip. Steve asked Cranny to come upstream and join him and Scott where they were fishing and to use their bait instead of salmon eggs.

Cranny walked upstream and baited his line with the Dillons' worms (illegal bait in Grand Canyon at this time). After baiting it, Cranny set his pole down and walked to the water. Steve Dillon thought Cranny was just going to wash his hands. But Cranny waded into the cold Colorado. Dillon yelled at him, "It's no wonder you don't catch anything, you just screwed up a good fishing hole." Cranny, only two merit badges short of Eagle Scout rank, looked at Dillon but said nothing, then he continued walking into the river. When he was chin deep, Steve Dillon yelled, "Matt, come on out."

As Jeffrey Kaplan (above) had done, Cranny dunked over his head and swam, sort of, upstream. Cranny surfaced, and looked directly at Steve Dillon. Dillon said, "Matt, get out!"

Cranny looked away. Frustrated at Cranny's lack of response, Dillon watched him tread water for "a short time" while drifting upstream. Then, speaking loudly of Cranny's lack of etiquette, Dillon turned away from Cranny to pick up his own tackle, preparatory to moving to yet another fishing spot. (Every member of this hike had been briefed that there would be no swimming.)

Steve Dillon's son, Scott, then told his father, "He's gone."

Concerned, Dillon ran up the beach 25 feet. Both father and son saw Cranny surface. Young Scott said Cranny was struggling and could not stay above the surface. But Steve Dillon later said, "not knowing exactly how long he had been under, I was undecided as to whether to attempt a rescue."

Steve Dillon turned away for a moment to remove his vest and hat and toss them to higher ground. When he turned around, Cranny had vanished yet again into the 11,500 cfs current. Now finally alarmed, Dillon dived into the water but each time found a boulder instead of Cranny. Meanwhile Scott yelled for help. After 45 minutes of searching by Troop 189, two adults hiked out to notify NPS rangers at Lees Ferry.

Troop leader John R. Whitmer reported to NPS Ranger Lenore Grover that Cranny had a history of epileptic seizures—and that indeed he had just had one only 3 or 4 months earlier on a troop bicycling trip. Scott Dillon then described how Cranny's petit mal seizures manifested themselves: he "would walk around as if he were in a trance, he would just stare off and not say anything. After a while he would fall down."

Much like Jeffrey Kaplan, Matthew Cranny had drowned apparently as a victim of a seizure. This would happen again to another fisherman (see below). Indeed, the susceptibility of some epileptics to experiencing seizures when they watch flickering lights—such as the bright reflections of sunlight dancing on the rippling surface of the water—may put epileptics at higher risk of drowning than other people.

NPS divers from Glen Canyon National Recreational Area scoured the nearby eddies but failed to located Cranny. Dog teams on shore also failed.

The next day Glen Canyon Dam operators lowered its outflow to 1,000 cfs, dropping the river level by about ten vertical feet. Divers still could not find Cranny. A few months later a leg wearing his style of hiking boot washed ashore at House Rock Rapid almost six miles downstream.

In mid-June, 1990, Elmer Meredith Akers, age 40, drove down Peach Springs Road in his VW squareback sedan to Diamond Creek (River Mile 225.7) to camp. Akers stayed there for several days. A Cherokee, he was well-tanned and had recently come from Florida. He bragged to river runners that he had swum across the Colorado and back earlier on the day of June 21. He was a strong swimmer, he told them, grinning.

Possibly misjudging the power of the river based on his experience with the Atlantic Ocean, that same day he decided to swim Diamond Creek Rapid at 17,500 cfs, for fun. But, river runners saw, Akers wore no life jacket. A week later a Hatch River Expeditions' crew found Akers' body in the eddy at River Mile 269.

Only a month later, on July 26, 1990, a Navajo woman from Wingate, New Mexico, Bert Francisco, age 28, also rode down Peach Springs Road with three friends to the Colorado River. They spent the day at Diamond Creek, from 8:00 a.m. onward, drinking beers. Then, after 4:00 p.m. and after eating chicken, Francisco impulsively decided to jump into the river to cool off, also without a life jacket. Almost instantly the 16,000 cfs current swept her into Diamond Creek Rapid. Like Akers, above, she drowned. A Mark Sleight River Expeditions' trip found Francisco's body the next day in the eddy below 234-Mile Rapid.

On August 28, 1992, Boy Scout Troop 17 from Mankato, Minnesota, started their backcountry hike into the Inner Canyon. George Fischer led the troop. Accompanying him was his grown son, Paul. Four 15-year-old Scouts from Troop 17 were on this hike. The six descended the South Kaibab Trail and made their way west on the Tonto, descending into Hermit Creek Canyon on September 2. They camped at Hermit Creek (River Mile 95).

That same afternoon, one of the Scouts, Christopher Guetschow, dived into the Colorado without a life jacket about 100 yards upstream of Hermit Rapid. The investigation by NPS rangers into this incident revealed that Guetschow had been socially "outcast" by his peers in the troop. Being odd man out in a tiny group of three other peers could become nightmarish after a few days in a place as isolated—and isolating—as Grand Canyon. Guetschow may have been trying to redeem or prove himself by showing that he had the guts and the ability to swim across the Colorado.

Indeed, Guetschow's intent did seem to be to swim across the river. But only halfway across, the slick tongue of water funneling into Hermit Rapid gripped Guetschow and accelerated him into the rapid. His companions last saw him above the surface in the upper swells of the rapid. Two weeks later Guetschow's body was found in the eddy at River Mile 104.

The common thread in these nineteen drownings of deliberate swimmers is that the victims—most of them young men—all vastly underestimated the power of the current in the Grand Canyon Colorado, and, after 1963, its coldness as well. Driven by heat and the promise of cool relief in the river, all of them had willingly entered the flow. Their outcomes, however, would have been much the same had they stepped off the South Rim into a thousand feet of vertical air. Hopefully, if future visitors understand this, they will approach the Colorado River as if it were a hungry man-eating crocodile.

Accidental Swimmers Who Fell In From Shore

Although falling into the Colorado accidently, unseen and unheard, while being surrounded by people, and then never leaving it alive may seem like a pretty unlikely chain of events, several people have done exactly that. A few of these victims were witnessed as they slipped into the river, or else heard as they cried for help. But more victims have vanished unseen and unheard.

On May 17, 1919, two young male hikers from the Eastern United States, of surnames Van de Bunt and Betts, arrived at the South Rim by train. Next they hiked down the Bright Angel Trail. They camped halfway down but then lost the trail. Confused by the weave of trails left by feral burros, the two hikers followed a wrong route, the old Wash Henry Trail (unused at this time for about twenty years, but likely following the unusually steep "Miner's Route" leading to today's river trail between the South Kaibab Trail and Pipe Creek). Then, near the river, they deviated from this trail too.

The two found no trail along the river at all. The trail was supposed to be here somewhere, they reasoned. But not only was the trail not where it was supposed to be, neither was the cable (put in place a dozen years earlier by David Rust) visible that was supposed to cross the river to Roosevelt's Camp (which would become Phantom Ranch three years later, in 1922).

The two young men decided to walk along the river and find the missing trail and cable. They felt certain that they would eventually reach both in a short distance. Soon, however, the banks of the river became almost vertical walls of Vishnu Schist. And still no trail or cable were in sight. Betts started climbing this wall. Behind Betts and unseen by him, Van de Bunt tried walking in the water against the cliff face.

Betts turned around and saw Van de Bunt in the water. Alarmed, Betts yelled at him to either wait where he was or else back up onto dry land.

As Betts turned around to backtrack himself off the cliff to rejoin Van de Bunt, he slipped and fell at least twenty feet. Battered, Betts pulled himself together and checked on Van de Bunt. To Betts' added consternation, Van de Bunt had vanished. Searching failed to locate any trace of him.

When Betts later showed Emery Kolb the place where he had fallen, Kolb wondered aloud how Betts could even have survived. Betts next showed Kolb where he had last seen Van de Bunt. Kolb nodded. Van de Bunt, Kolb noted, had been walking on a ledge about two feet underwater. Kolb knew this area at lower water. Van de Bunt's ledge dropped off a vertical twenty feet almost directly in front of where he was last seen by Betts. The missing man, Kolb concluded, almost certainly had taken one step too many, a fatal one. Then the hugely swollen current of late May in the steep gradient of Upper Granite Gorge had swept Van de Bunt downstream and underwater as if he were no more than a mouse.

How quickly the unwary can be swept into oblivion by the Colorado can be nothing short of appalling. On April 29, 1983, for example, the San Diego Nomads, a Sierra Club hiking group of 44 people, hiked from Hualapai Hilltop down to the Havasupai Campground and camped. The following day some of the Nomads, including a woman, Jody Mack, M.D., age 31, hiked up Carbonate Canyon. The next day, May 1, again several of the Nomads, including Mack, whom everyone agreed was in a very positive mood and in excellent physical condition, reached the mouth of Havasu Creek at the Colorado River (River Mile 156.8). There the group ate lunch.

The air temperature was below 70 degrees. Mack had goosebumps as she talked briefly with boatman Bruce Simbala of Grand Canyon Dories, whose boat was tied in the mouth of Havasu.

One of the Nomads, Jerry Herrman, later saw Jody Mack 30 to 40 feet away and crouching on a low ledge of polished Muav Limestone jutting into the river about 150 feet downstream of the mouth of Havasu Creek and along the edge of Havasu Rapid. Mack, Herrman said, was leaning out and seemed to be trying to put her hand in the river. Abruptly, Mack's feet slipped (she was wearing Sierra Sneakers). Mack kerplunked feet-first into the swift current. Herrman immediately yelled, "Jody's in!"

The 19,000 cfs current instantly swept Mack into the mainstream. She seemed, however, to remain in control. Even without a life jacket, she kept her head up and faced downstream. But she continued to funnel down the mainstream instead of swimming back toward the left shoreline. Horrified onlookers watched her until she floated out of sight a few hundred yards downstream between cliffs of Muav.

Upon hearing Herrman's yell, Bruce Simbala grabbed several life jackets and one of the hikers. He sliced his bowline and rowed into the river to give chase. Despite his relatively quick response time of under five minutes and his rowing hard for more than half an hour, Simbala never saw Mack again. Her hundreds of yards of lead plus her submersion into invisibility cut her odds of rescue drastically. Sixteen days later, a river trip found Jody Mack's body floating in the river forty miles downstream near River Mile 196.

During a very similar episode in 1997, a woman passenger from New York on her second trip down the Colorado slipped and fell off a commercial boat in the Havasu eddy. She quickly swirled upstream into Havasu Creek's flow and then zipped into the rapid itself—without a life jacket. (While many commercial guides since the 1980s caution their clients to wear their life jackets until they have climbed well up onto shore at Havasu, for whatever reason, this woman had doffed hers prematurely.)

Hearing cries of alarm, boatmen Billy Ellwanger and Kirk Burnett, running an unconnected research trip, fired up their small motor boat and blasted out into the rapid. The victim surfaced rarely and briefly as she submarined down Havasu Rapid. When the woman's head surfaced close by in the waves, Ellwanger yelled at Burnett, "Jump!"

Burnett jumped into the rapid, grabbed the woman, and towed her to the boat. She lived only because of these guides' prompt actions.

The episode illustrates at least two lessons. First, if boatmen are very quick, they sometimes can save the lives of accidental swimmers. But this sort of quickness pivots on having devised or imagined or rehearsed rescue procedures in advance of any incident to enable timely and appropriate action. Second—and all too obvious—life jackets are vital while on the water. This life jacket part *is* easy to ensure. In our opinion, these are a good idea even while fishing in the Grand Canyon Colorado from shore, even if it may not look stylish. Two separate fishermen at Lees Ferry—Robert G. Arceire, age 48, on January 18, 1987, and Robert Wiel on July 24, 1988—fell into flows of 23,500 cfs and 11,000 cfs, respectively, without life jackets. Both drowned in their waders, the wide rubber legs of which acted like two huge buckets of water. On January 29, 2000, Jamie Padilla, age 22, suffered a petit mal seizure while fishing without wearing a life jacket above River Mile 8 near the mouth of Jackass Canyon. Despite his companions witnessing the seizure (caused perhaps by sunlight flickering on the water), they could not reach Padilla in time. He drowned in the rapid. So too did fisherman Todd Strickland, age 49, on May 30, 1999, when he fell in below Nevills' beach at River Mile 75 in search of a good fishing spot, again without wearing his life jacket.

At times the Colorado River seems almost treacherous. On June 14, 1989, the same day that boatman Martin Hunsaker flipped his 33-foot rig in Crystal Rapid and drowned, only an hour downstream the river took yet another victim.

Things had started off well enough for Karl Sebastian Jacobi. The 21-year-old from Germany had been touring the U.S. on a motorcycle. He had motored down between the soaring Triassic cliffs framing Lees Ferry for a look at the Colorado River. There, on the launch beach, was a private party with gear scattered across the beach preparatory to loading for a three-week trip. Jacobi chatted with them.

Having been required to wait for several years after their application to the NPS for the actual issuance of a permit to launch a private float trip, this trip's members—like many others—had lost many of its originally-intended fellow boaters. To finally use their long-awaited permit, the surviving original members of this intended trip had patched it back together to a dozen members by adding several people who neither knew one another nor understood one another's abilities in whitewater. Several of these new people, the group was now finding out, had little to no experience on big rivers. And now, as Karl Sabastian Jacobi walked up, several members of the trip's paddle crew were already very worried about being able to paddle their boat safely. Consensus at this moment was that they needed at least one more strong, aggressive paddler to complete a safe crew.

The group of worried boaters stared at the youthful, athletic Jacobi and could not believe their ears when he asked if he could go along with them.

Almost instantly, Jacobi, a total stranger, became a last minute, thirteenth member of this trip and was assigned to its paddle crew. He did not remain a stranger for long. Other members of the trip found him a very positive addition: he was young, quiet, self-confident, undemanding, optimistic, and enthusiastic. On the flip side, he was over-confident, did not seem to appreciate the danger of the Colorado, and frequently had to be reminded to put on his life jacket while boating. Indeed, Jacobi's "I-can-do-anything" attitude may have set the stage for tragedy on day nine.

That morning, the trip was camped near River Mile 103.8. At 11:00 a.m., Jacobi had asked the trip leader if he could hike alone from camp upstream along the shore. The trip leader said yes, but for no more than 40 minutes.

Jacobi failed to return by 60 minutes. One of the women in camp said she thought she heard someone call for help. Several of them listened and searched the slope with binoculars. Three of the trip members began searching for Jacobi. One, Frank Leuthold, hiked upstream and uphill hundreds of feet above the river. He looked down and, to his shock, saw Jacobi shouting and breast-stroking toward shore in an eddy bordered by vertical cliffs about 40 yards upstream of camp.

Leuthold went briefly out of sight of Jacobi to yell downslope to get rescuers into motion. Leuthold never saw Jacobi again.

Meanwhile a second searcher, Esther Graw, had also climbed high upslope, thinking too that the original calls for help were coming from up there. Graw too now heard frantic shouting from the river. She saw "a white person in the middle of the river with arms outstretched, head out, and shouting." As Graw ran back down to the shore, she too lost sight of Jacobi, who likely entered 104-Mile Rapid flowing at 13,250 cfs. Neither Graw, nor anyone else, ever saw him again.

Although several people involved assumed that Jacobi had somehow fallen into the river from a short cliff while hiking, at least one member of the trip, Arlan Lazere, thinks it may have been otherwise. "He may have jumped into the river, planning to swim back down to camp," she reflected. "He was that kind of guy, really confident, but he did not understand the power of the river."

Helicopter searches that afternoon failed to locate Jacobi. Twelve days later, a commercial river trip found his body at River Mile 105.5. An autopsy revealed death by drowning.

Luckily, members of river trips becoming casualties of drowning from shore during daylight, like Jacobi had, are very rare. But, unfortunately, they are not unheard of. As mentioned briefly above, for example, Todd Strickland, age 49, was walking along shore below Nevills' Beach at River Mile 75 in search of a good fishing spot when things went wrong. Roughly 300 yards downstream of the camp chosen by the commercial motor rafting company, Wilderness River Adventures, with whom Strickland was a client, he somehow fell into the river. Again, he was not wearing a life jacket.

As Jacobi had, Strickland too yelled for help repeatedly as the current swept him downstream. Members of another commercial company, AzRA, camped on the opposite side of the Colorado, heard his cries. Then they saw him careening along in the powerful riffle. The AzRA guides gave chase in their motorized raft. A few minutes later they caught Strickland.

But by the time they had pulled him from the water, his breathing had already stopped. The AzRA guides performed CPR on Strickland for almost two hours. They meanwhile used a satellite phone to call for a medical evacuation by the National Park Service. An hour after Strickland's med-evac, he was pronounced dead due to drowning.

Mysterious Disappearances Who Drowned From Camp

As is all too clear by now, the Colorado River is far more deceptively lethal than many people guess. Yet no single type of fatality seems quite as bizarre and puzzling as when a person vanishes unseen and unheard into the Colorado—even while "surrounded" by other people—at night.

On June 8, 1973, Desi Baca led a party of eleven children backpacking down from the South Rim to Indian Garden. The party dropped off their camping gear there, then Baca took his eleven charges a few miles further down the Bright Angel Trail to the Colorado River at Pipe Creek. This hike took longer than he expected. Now the hike back to Indian Garden would require traversing the trail at night. Baca next found that his flashlight was not working right. So he told the boys to bivouac at the mouth of Pipe Creek for the night.

Baca made a head count at midnight. Two boys, Kenneth Baca, age 9, and Marcos Ortega, age 11, had disappeared. Worried, Baca yelled for the boys. Kenneth, Baca's son, answered from the other side of the creek where he was stranded for unexplained reasons on a rock ledge above "camp." But no amount of yelling or searching located Marcos (Mark) Ortega, whose shoes were still in his sleeping spot. Nor did a six-hour ground search or seven hours of searching by air by NPS rangers on the next day (June 9) turn up further clues. Additional searches continued for a week. They too found nothing.

None of the boys seemed to know what events had led up to Ortega's disappearance. But young Mark, it turned out, had a history of sleep walking—hence his bare-footed disappearance into a flow of 11,000 cfs that night. On June 26, 18 days later and six miles downstream, river runners found Ortega's body in the river just below Hermit Rapid.

A year later, on July 18, 1974, a woman passenger, Teresa Rainey, age 25, was camped with Fort Lee Company at Trail Canyon (River Mile 219.2). While Fort Lee was credited in those years with running one of the best trips in the Canyon, one of the amenities they offered was an open bar. Wearing no life jacket and also after drinking heavily, Rainey fell off Fort Lee's 33-foot motor rig unseen and unheard at night into the river. Immediately downstream of this camp the river swirls into a very dynamic eddy system of "keeper" water in Trail Rapid. Rainey drowned in 23,000 cfs.

Several years later, on August 4, 1980, a 19-year-old male passenger, David Bret Lasater, on a Canyoneers motor trip, vanished at their first camp at River Mile 22.5. This is a stretch of Marble Canyon with sheer cliffs and hiking routes possible only for the most expert climbers. "He was seen as being heavily intoxicated [that] evening," reported Coconino County Sheriff Joe Richards. Lasater had retired to his sleeping bag after dark. At 4:30 a.m. that morning, "it was discovered he was missing."

What happened? One possibility arises from a simple and innocent NPS policy: all passengers are advised that when they urinate, they must do so in the river or in the wet sand of the fluctuation zone to avoid polluting the rare campsites with urine. Lasater may have gone to the river, flowing at 22,500 cfs, to urinate while intoxicated. Once there, he may have lost his balance, fallen in, and drowned. No other credible scenario was offered to explain Lasater's disappearance besides sheer alcohol intoxication. On August 21, 17 days later, another river party found Lasater's body near River Mile 37.

The same thing may have happened a year later on July 8, 1981, to a 58-year-old male passenger, Charles Robert Hunter. Hunter was a client on a Diamond River Adventures motor trip camped at River Mile 19. Like Lasater, above, Hunter had been drinking alcohol heavily that evening—having started with four beers at lunch—before going to sleep on the motor rig with the crew at about 10:30 p.m.

Amazingly for only an 8-day trip, Hunter had brought along a full case of twelve one-fifth bottles of Seagrams 7 and yet another case of twelve one-fifth bottles of vodka. He had broken out several bottles that first evening for general consumption.

Hunter, whom all of the guides reported as having a positive attitude, drank bourbon by mixing it in a Sprite can and also straight from the bottle. Trip leader Daryl Diamond told Hunter, who was a local teacher at Page High School and had taught some of the Diamond guides as teenagers in his classes, that he could sleep on the boat if he wanted to. Hunter laid out his sleeping bag on the bow of the downstream boat, removed his shoes, and reclined atop his bag in the July heat. That was that last thing anyone saw him do.

An hour before dawn, Diamond boatman Max Hamblin (a.k.a. Garn) came down to the boat from shore. Still drunk (by his own admission), Hamblin saw an empty sleeping bag. Cold, he crawled into it. After he awakened later, he realized it was Hunter's bag. That morning, Daryl Diamond found Hunter's cigarette case in the wet sand of the fluctuation zone (the river had dropped after midnight) under the front pontoon of his rig.

Hunter too may have been urinating into the river off the edge of the boat, lost his balance, and fallen into the Colorado flowing at about 15,000 cfs and drowned.

Yet another mysterious disappearance from a river-running camp occurred during the night of September 13, 1997. Passenger John Anthony Frye, age 43, also on a Diamond River Adventures motor trip, was seen at the condiments table after dark at the middle camp at River Mile 220. This was the trip's last night. After saying good night to the others, Frye, his girlfriend Carol Burkhart reported, did not make it back to his sleeping bag. He had accompanied Burkhart to their camp around 9:00 p.m., she said, then he had returned to camp for the "party." Burkhart also said that she could hear Frye's voice among those of the very last people to be making any noise. Then nothing.

A subsequent search of lower 220-Mile Canyon, of the camp area, and of the beach found only a set of bare footprints leading from the far, downstream corner of the lower, downriver camp several hundred yards downstream and into the river, which had been flowing at 24,000 cfs.

Although this does not seem nearly as complicated a plot as Agatha Christie would concoct, the simple solution of suicide did not add up. Frye had been on the trip for four days since Phantom Ranch. He had seemed during that time to be in good spirits. He was on the trip with his girlfriend, and they seemed to be getting along. Indeed Frye seemed, if anything, more adventurous than most on the trip. He wanted to ride the "horn" of the motor rig's side tubes in rapids, for example. He even had to be reprimanded for climbing the cliff at Elves Chasm (River Mile 116.5) and jumping from it into the creek. Indeed, as Diamond guide Jeff Pyle explained, Frye was a prankster. He tied his hat, for example, to the float bag (containing beers, etc.) in the river to fool people into thinking it was a human being. More suggestive yet, Frye "was very eager to swim from one boat to another...with an open beer in his hand." Pyle also stated, however, that on this last day Frye "had been drinking beer since lunch time."

Another Diamond guide, Dave Panu, reported that Frye had said to him, "I belong here." Panu interpreted this in a spiritual context.

Even so, hours before Frye's disappearance he had been taking video recordings of his fellow passengers and writing down their addresses to later send them copies.

An NPS and Department of Public Safety combined search and rescue mission launched on September 15. They used a team of tracking dogs, helicopters, and so on. The searchers found no sign of Frye.

By coincidence, one of us (Ghiglieri) was running a rowing trip down the river from Lees Ferry to Lake Mead. We arrived on the lake on the morning of September 21. That morning, eight days after Frye's disappearance, our jet boat driver, Sam, spotted John Frye's body floating (no life jacket) in the eddy at Quartermaster Canyon (River Mile 260). One may imagine many scenarios regarding Frye's demise. But the two most probable are that Frye either fell drunk—and relatively fearless—into the Colorado on the night of the 13th, possibly while urinating into it; or else he decided, also while drunk, that he really did "belong here."

Lessons Of Safety & Survival From The Grand Canyon Colorado

The lessons from the 82 drownings discussed above are many. Perhaps it would be trite to simply say that the Grand Canyon Colorado is a dangerous river. Even after hearing this, however, many people would mentally answer, "Yes, of course it is, but *I* am a good swimmer." It well may be this thought alone that killed half of the victims discussed above.

Several patterns exist in these victims' drownings which teach us specific lessons of survival:

1. Testosterone is an accomplice. As with fatalities to falls, the primary and most numerous hiking-swimming-drowning victims are/were young men or adolescent boys. Of 69 victims of known age, at least 38–40 were at or under the age of 28 years old. Aside from age, of all 82 known or suspected victims, 74 (90 percent) were males. In short, again the main factor in these drownings—besides lacking a life jacket—is being male. Worse yet, a young male. The signature error such victims most often make is failing to respect the magnitude of the power of the river. And the number one manifestation of this lack of respect is denying their need to wear a life jacket.

2. Life jackets are aptly named. Being on the river or *in* the river beyond chest level without a life jacket is the primary situation in which nearly all drowning victims have drowned. Indeed 16–18 people (George Strole and Jack Aldridge remain questionable drownings) who were originally in boats or rafts on the Grand Canyon Colorado drowned after mishaps because they wore no personal flotation devices. Eleven more victims drowned from Lees Ferry without flotation devices. Eight to eleven more victims without life jackets drowned while trying to cross the river via a boat or raft or air mat-

tress—or just by swimming. These bring the total number of "boating" mishap deaths associated with a lack of life jackets to 35–39.

Added to these are 19 victims, nearly all hikers, who deliberately decided to enter the river without jackets, usually for a swim, and drowned. Yet fourteen other involuntary swimmers—including six disappearances from a river-running camp or hike plus hiker Jody Mack and four fishermen who fell from shore—also drowned without life jackets.

The total number of known drowning victims not wearing life jackets in all situations on the Grand Canyon Colorado is somewhere between 67 and 71 of a total of 82. In contrast, thousands of other people wearing personal flotation devices have been tossed into the river—and serious whitewater—via mishaps or have entered it voluntarily and survived.

Two other victims drowned despite having been dumped into the Colorado even with jackets because their jackets were torn off by the current. A possibility exists in both cases that a life jacket crotch strap might have saved their lives.

If only one thing is to be gained from this chapter, it should be: **Never enter the Colorado more than waist deep—or never allow yourself to be in the position to accidentally enter the Colorado—without wearing the best personal flotation device available, Coast Guard approved, fastened securely on your body.**

3. River guide: passenger ratios (as determined by boat type) and company culture both appear to influence survivorship. Contrary to "intuition"—and to river myth—during all of the many tens of thousands of commercial rowing trips by at least a dozen companies since the onset of commercial recreational river running in 1938, no commercial passenger riding on an oarboat has died in any whitewater situation. Indeed, except for the possible petit mal seizure-related drowning of Jeffrey Kaplan from shore, and the almost instant drowning/cardiac arrest of William Blair tossed into Crystal Rapid from a capsized paddleboat run by Wilderness World, no other commercial passenger on a human-powered (oar or paddle) trip run by professional Grand Canyon river guides has died in any sort of accidental or traumatic manner on land or in the water while on that trip during the entire history of river running in Grand Canyon.

In contrast, on motor-powered commercial trips since the 1950s, fifteen people have died traumatically. Four were passengers who drowned in whitewater accidents, six more drowned from camp or during hikes (these include all four recorded drownings of intoxicated clients at night), one more drowned while trying to swim to shore recreationally, and yet two more have died traumatically due to falls (see Chapter 1). Also two motor guides have drowned. When taking into account the greater number of people who ride on commercial motor trips compared to commercial human-powered (oar or paddle) trips, these mortality statistics reveal that the on-river fatality rate on motor trips is 2.7 times higher than on commercial oar-powered trips.

In the same vein, and again corrected for different proportions of motor versus oar passengers on commercial trips, off-river deaths are significantly higher for clients on motor trips compared to oar-powered trips.

Beyond the commercial fatalities, two dozen people have drowned on various noncommercial attempts to descend or ascend the river since 1889: 14 of them while rowing or paddling or while being rowed, 5 of them on motor boats, 4 while trying to raft it on driftwood rafts and one from shore.

What is really going on here? The two main differences between rowing versus motor trips are in types of craft—including their size, speed, navigability, and proximity to other boats on the same trip for mutual rescues—and also in the guide-to-passenger ratio for each trip on the water and on land (camping, hiking, etc.) Motor rigs tend to be 33 feet to 38 feet long. Most of these may legally carry up to sixteen people with two or three crew, often only one of whom is a qualified—and paid—Grand Canyon river guide. These boats travel solo or with one companion boat.

In contrast, most commercial rowing rigs are about 18-feet long and carry one fully qualified, experienced guide plus 3 to 6 passengers, usually 4. Boats on rowing trips travel in company with three to six or more other similar boats. In rapids recognized as more serious, the tendency for these latter trips is to run the first few boats tightly together to facilitate rescues. At least one of these first boats next acts as a safety net for subsequent boats.

This quick analysis is emphatically not intended to pinpoint the large motor rigs themselves as reasons for the higher death rates of their passengers on the river. Instead it is merely to highlight two obvious points: 1) Commercial *rowing* (as opposed to paddling) trips with a high guide-to-passenger ratio have had no fatalities of commercial passengers in whitewater, none "lost at night in the river," only one killed due to a fall while hiking, and, with the exception of the possible seizure-related drowning of Jeffrey Kaplan, no other traumatic deaths on-shore or off-shore. 2) Rowing boats, by their size and nature, allow such a small number of passengers that one well-qualified river guide apparently can advise and assist all of them in time to make a difference. Were this very same guide on his or her own on a large motor rig, he or she would be hard-pressed to rescue ten or fifteen people in distress, let alone keep an eye on them all to practice good preventative measures (advising and correcting individuals on their seating, life jacket fit, hand-holds, activities on shore, etc.).

Note, however, that it is neither the size of the boats nor merely the boatman-to-passenger ratio alone that makes this difference. The number of whitewater and on-shore fatalities on private rowing trips is also higher than on the same sorts of commercial trips yet the number of people on private trips have been far fewer overall than on commercial rowing trips. Most private trips use slightly smaller boats. Based on both the lower number of trips and smaller size of boats and higher boatman-to-passenger ratio, one might reasonably predict a lower relative fatality rate. However, the data—from all types of noncommercial river trips and evenly split between motor and human-powered craft—reveal that non-professional, non-Grand Canyon qualified river guides instead experience higher fatalities among their passengers and themselves than do commercial motor or rowing trips. Lest all this be misinterpreted, this discussion is, again, emphatically not intended to be anti-motor or anti-private boater. Neither of us has an "anti-motor" agenda, and both of us believe that private trips should become more fully represented on the river. The data do not pinpoint motor rigs themselves as more dangerous craft. On the contrary, the types of craft used, motor versus oar, and the size of craft used, 18 feet versus 33–38 feet long, seem to bear less on passenger and guide survival than does the boat's guide-to-passenger ratio and guide experience. Indeed, the clear factor here which correlates statistically with fewer fatalities—and which also can be seen in action on all types of trips—is the presence of a high ratio of qualified and experienced Grand Canyon river guides to the number of passengers carried or guided. The bottom line? Having two (or more?) qualified and paid guides on motor rigs carrying 10–16 passengers might be good insurance for the safety of everyone aboard. In fact, some motor companies often do this already. Hatch River Expeditions, to offer one example of a large motor company that likely has taken more passengers down Grand Canyon than any other, frequently runs their trips with such crews. Hatch, by the way, has experienced no passenger fatalities in the Canyon during their many decades of operation.

In addition to the above-mentioned considerations of why fatalities occur, or don't, on river trips, several guides and rafting company owners have confided to us that they firmly believe that accident rates are tied most firmly to "company cultures." Many companies, they say, strongly emphasize safety and live up to their words via their actions on the river. Other companies, they add, do not.

4. Age plays a role in who lives and who dies. Older victims of whitewater mishaps are at greater risk of dying. This is due to the greater metabolic susceptibility of older people to quick hypothermia from the river's 46- to 55-degree water, due to their greater propensity for cardiac arrest when plunged into such cold and turbulent whitewater, and due to their lower ability to self rescue. Worse yet, that first sudden gasp due to cold may include aspirated water. Aspiration causes instant panic. And, again, if all that were not bad enough, hyperventilation is a common automatic response in cold rapids. All of these involuntary responses bode worse for older people. Also evident from the examples above, a dozen or more accidental or deliberate swimmers from shore may have become fatalities due in large part to the very cold temperatures of the river produced artificially by the operation of Glen Canyon Dam.

5. Especially applicable to hikers, ignorance is bliss only if "bliss" is the Hereafter. Most hikers and river trip passengers who drowned from shore were

naive or ignorant of the river's danger (some not through any fault of their own). Most such victims have died within their first 24 hours on, or next to, the Colorado. In contrast, no Grand Canyon river guide has drowned from shore even though nearly all of them bathe in the river and sleep on their boats on the river on most nights. In short, people well educated about the river's dangers seem to survive at a higher rate. The preponderence of victims drowning within their first few hours of reaching the river shows that means of advising caution cannot be overdone. In other words, there may be no such thing as too many warnings. For example, the very high death toll of hikers drowning between the mouth of Pipe Creek and Phantom Beach is despite several warning signs posted on trails. Perhaps additional signs should be posted right on the beaches themselves.

6. Having drunk alcohol in significant quantity is the most common single precipitating factor in camp disappearances due to drowning. Although it is no secret that alcohol consumption reduces alertness and common sense, drinking alcohol has caused *millions* of fatalities while driving cars, hunting with firearms, arguing in bars, and, yes, boating. Consider the summary findings of the BOAT/US Foundation:

> *Most boaters think of collisions as the greatest threat when drinking on the water. Yet, according to BOAT/US Foundation for Boating Safety research, an estimated 75% of alcohol-related boating accidents and injuries do not involve collisions. In fact, falls on board or overboard, or missteps at the dock or getting into the dinghy, are a much greater threat when drinking afloat.*

This research concludes that drinking afloat is even more dangerous—due to its additional effects of life-threatening dehydration, of increasing risk of cardiac arrest in cold water, and of "boater's hypnosis"—than is drinking while driving! Having drunk alcohol was a factor in 46 percent of 586 U.S. boating fatalities in 1997 and in 37 percent of such fatalities in 1998. The U.S. Coast Guard also reported that a boat operator with a blood alcohol concentration above 0.10 percent (the legal threshold in 38 states) is ten times more likely to be killed in a boating accident than one with zero blood alcohol concentration. "No matter what the activity," the BOAT/US Foundation for Boating Safety added, "alcohol affects balance, vision, coordination and judgement. But in boating, stressors like wind, sun, noise, motion, and vibration can magnify the effects of alcohol and even accelerate impairment."

Eerily, one of the most common—and striking—errors that people make after even imbibing only one drink (when tested in a field situation) was failing to fasten their life jackets correctly. Little surprise then that all of the five adult disappearances from camp at night involved alcohol consumption.

7. A cardinal rule in river-running is: the welfare of people always comes before that of equipment. During runs of the Colorado between April through October, for example, even if boaters—as a result of chasing people in the river as a first priority—lose one or more boats or other critical gear, they are still safe in their decision that people get rescued first. This is because it is nearly impossible to be stranded along the river in Grand Canyon for more than 24 hours without another trip happening along and rendering assistance. This "people-first-gear-second" rule is "easy" to follow nearly all the time, and should be followed regardless of season.

8. Crystal Rapid holds the record as the most lethal rapid in Grand Canyon. All five fatalities there were of people who drowned/cardiac arrested *despite* wearing life jackets. Hence, prudence would suggest that this rapid be run in the most conservative manner available to boatmen, giving consideration to their types of equipment, the water level, the weather, the ages and health of passengers on the boats, and each individual boatman's overall experience.

9. High flows of the Grand Canyon Colorado have been presumed, and then claimed, to be more dangerous than "normal" (dam-controlled) flows. In 1983, for example, the river peaked at more than 96,000 cfs and otherwise ran at "high" flows for the entire commercial, "high-use-summer" boating season. Despite a nearly full summer boating season and despite many boating mishaps on this spate, however, only one river-runner drowned, a commercial passenger on a boat whose boatman had not yet run the, then, minimum NPS-required three trips down the river required of Grand Canyon river guides (the NPS changed the minimum to six trips after this incident). There exists no evidence in the patterns of fatalities observed in the past century of boating in Grand Canyon to demonstrate that high flows are more dangerous than other flow levels. If anything, high flow incidents analyzed by Tom Myers, Chris Becker, and Larry Stevens in their book *Fateful Journey: Injury and Death on Colorado River Trips in Grand Canyon* reveal that medium water levels correlate with more drownings. This again suggests that boatman competence and flow temperature (see next paragraph) are more important than flow level.

Interestingly—and as mentioned above—the temperature of the Colorado River may play a far more serious role in fatalities than its level of flow. During the extremely high water summer season of 1983, for example, hundreds of people were tossed involuntarily into the river. Indeed, hundreds were dumped involuntarily just into Crystal Rapid alone, the record-holding "killer" rapid, and were forced to swim for their lives often for long distances in treacherous flows. Yet only that one river fatality occurred during 1983's summer season. The river that year, however, flowed significantly warmer than usual for post-dam times because all water above 48,000 cfs was coming over the spillways from the warm *surface* of Lake Powell, not from 250 feet under it, as penstock water does.

Body heat loss during immersion hypothermia is up to 100 times faster in calm water than in air of the same temperature. In a rapid this lethal process proceeds far more quickly yet. Worse, the sudden immersion in cold water spurs an abrupt involuntary physiological response known as "cold shock." This syndrome sets a cascade of potentially lethal, maladaptive reflexes into motion: several huge involuntary gasps, lethal heart stoppage, heart attack, or rhythm irregularities. A person's breath-holding capacity is reduced to one third of normal. Hyperventilation and panic may occur, followed by muscular loss of coordination and increasing weakness. Those who die within minutes of falling into such cold and turbulent water *drown* due to a combination of all these cold water immersion-caused events.

The implications for safety here are twofold: First, instead of making whitewater boating "possible" or "safe" as claimed by a number of pro-dam publications, *Glen Canyon Dam may instead be killing far more people— including boaters, swimmers, and accidental fall-ins from shore—than the predam river would because of the river's extreme and unnatural cold even during summer.* Second, the proposed future release of warmer water from Lake Powell via the installation of redesigned penstocks may be a matter of life and death for human visitors to Grand Canyon, not solely a mechanism for the survival of endangered native fish species.

10. The act of urinating into the river while intoxicated may be (this is an untested and unproven hypothesis) a concomitant cause of drunk-drowning. In this regard, the use of a "pee"-bucket in each camp's porta-potty set-up might save a life or two in the next decade or so.

11. Boatman decision-making on how to enforce (or instead not to enforce) safety rules/behaviors based on all the above factors also may have played a role in some of the observed patterns of fatalities. This of course harkens back to "company culture" as it applies to safety concerns and protocols.

12. Although it has not been proven by otherwise avoidable fatalities, wearing a life jacket even on dry ground but adjacent to fast water while scouting rapids is probably a good practice.

13. Although this too has not been "proven" by otherwise avoidable fatalities, wearing a rain jacket—or worse yet a rain poncho—while riding a boat through dangerous rapids almost certainly raises the risk of injury if the wearer is dumped into the rapid and cannot manage good swimming strokes. If such rain gear is worn in such serious rapids as in the Upper Granite Gorge or in Lava Falls, etc., it is best worn *under* life jackets and should allow for tight wrist/cuff closures. Ponchos should be avoided altogether while on the water.

Table 4–A. RIVER TRAVELERS (upstream or downstream) WHO DROWNED IN THE GRAND CANYON COLORADO (most incidents are discussed in text). River flows in cubic feet per second (cfs) for dates of incidents are from the U.S.G.S. Historical Streamflows Daily Values Data Base, from Stations #09380000 (Lees Ferry) and #09402500 (Phantom) at wwwdaztecn.wr.usgs.gov/index.html.

Name, age	Date	River Location and Flow	*Circumstances*
? George Strole, adult	August 29, 1867	Maybe in Lower Granite Gorge in Grand Canyon or, instead, downstream of the Grand Wash Cliffs	

*Strole and James White built a log raft and headed down the Colorado from a now unknown put-in point fleeing from hostile Indians. Although White made a 14-day journey, Strole, **wearing no life jacket**, drowned on day four.*

Frank Mason Brown, 43	July 10, 1889	Saltwater Wash (River Mile 11.8)	

*As Harry McDonald steered it into the left eddy, Brown's small round-bottomed boat rolled and flipped. McDonald and Brown wore **no life jackets**. McDonald swam to shore a few hundred yards downstream. Brown drowned trying to swim directly to shore across the eddy.*

Peter M. Hansbrough, adult Henry C. Richards, adult	July 15, 1889	25-Mile Rapid	

*After lining, then running most of 25-Mile Rapid, Richards' and Hansbrough's boat was pinned against the left cliff. As the two men stood to try to free it, it flipped. Hansbrough, wearing **no life jacket**, never surfaced. Richards, also wearing **no life jacket**, surfaced, swam toward a downstream rescue boat, but sank in the silty water.*

Bessie Hyde, 22 Glen R. Hyde, 29	December 1, 1928	232-Mile Rapid (?), flow: 8,700 cfs	

*Precise circumstances of the Hydes' demise remain an unsolved mystery, but the most likely scenario is that the couple had trouble in or at 232-Mile Rapid and both—wearing **no life jackets**—drowned. Neither body was ever recovered.*

Bill Payne, 27 (a.k.a. William Talmadge)	June 22–24, 1931	234-Mile Rapid (?), flow: 23,600 cfs	

Payne and James R. Ervin, 30, tried running the Colorado from Mile 225.7 to Hoover Dam in the Bright Angel, one of six wooden boats abandoned by the 1927 Pathé-Bray Expedition. They launched on the ebb of the peak flow of the Colorado. They capsized several times, losing their oars in rapid "number six." Both men swam to the south side. Ervin hiked out. Upon returning on June 24, Ervin and the Deputy Sheriff found that Payne and the boat had vanished forever.

? Jack H. Aldridge, adult	October, 1938	Marble Canyon ?	

*Last seen by two Japanese visitors just downstream of California Bar at Hansen (roughly 100 miles upstream of Lees Ferry), Aldridge told them he was planning to row **solo** through Grand*

*Canyon all the way to Boulder Dam. Aldridge's boat was found at Mile 65.5 by members of the Amos Burg-Buzz Holmstrom-Willis Johnson trip. Aldridge wore **no life jacket**. One friend claimed to have seen Aldridge after 1938 (in 1940), but no other acquaintances did.*

| Charles Roemer, 50+ | October 24–26, 1946 | Inner Gorge beyond River Mile 88, flow: 7,100 cfs |

*Roemer made a **solo** attempt to fully traverse Grand Canyon in a small, "five-man" inflatable while wearing **no life jacket**. After passing Mile 88, Roemer was never seen nor heard from again. An air search on October 26 and an upriver search by Harry Aleson both failed to locate him.*

| Albert Loper, 79+ | July 8, 1949 | 24.5-Mile Rapid, flow: 51,500 cfs |

Loper rowed well ahead of his companions into 24.5-Mile Rapid at flood level and may have suffered a heart attack or stroke which led to flipping his boat and not surviving his swim.

| George D. Jensen, 28 | June–July 1955 | between River Miles 68 and 72, flow: 20,000–36,000 cfs |

*Jensen launched a driftwood raft in the Furnace Flats area and wore **no life jacket**. His body was discovered near Mile 96 on July 13 and identified by the shoes he was wearing.*

| Phillip D. Martin, 27 | February 21, 1965 | Paria Riffle (River Mile 1), flow: 9,000 cfs |

Martin and a fellow NPS ranger capsized their canoe in Paria Riffle. Both men wore life jackets. Martin stayed with boat and died of apparent hypothermia.

| Peter Scott Le Brun, 14 | November 5, 1966 | Phantom Beach (River Mile 87.8), flow: 9,000 cfs |

*Le Brun and two other teenage hikers rode a driftwood log down the Colorado. Upon entering Bright Angel Rapid, all three boys got nervous and tried to swim to shore. Le Brun, **wearing no life jacket,** drowned.*

| Jesse "Shorty" Burton, 44 | June 14, 1967 | Upset Rapid (River Mile 150), flow: 12,750 cfs |

While motoring toward the right cut in Upset, Shorty ran the steep hole and flipped. His new life jacket caught on one of the open eye-bolts suspending the floor and by trapping him under-water, drowned him.

| Mae Hansen, 64 | July 10, 1972 | House Rock Rapid (River Mile 16.8), flow: 14,000 cfs |

Hansen and two other commercial clients were trapped beneath one of Georgie White's triple, ten-man rigs after it flipped in House Rock. The two others found air pockets, Hansen apparently did not and drowned and/or cardiac arrested.

Charles Lyon, 25	April 27, 1973	Sockdolager Rapid (River Mile 78.7), flow: 34,000 cfs

*Lyon drowned or died of hypothermia **despite wearing a life jacket** after flipping an inflatable kayak in Sockdolager during a research trip run by the Museum of Northern Arizona.*

Michael Koenig, 29	May 21, 1973	217-Mile Rapid, flow: 17,200 cfs

*Koenig and a friend, Tony Burdick, put in a motor boat at Diamond Creek (Mile 225.6) to power upriver in an illegal run. Both men wore **no life jacket**. They capsized. Koenig drowned.*

Steve Brunette, 16	August 17, 1974	Gneiss Rapid (River Mile 236), flow: 21,000 cfs

*While riding in a motor boat from Lake Mead up the Colorado during an illegal upriver run, Brunette fell out dressed in heavy clothing and hiking boots but while wearing **no life jacket**. He sank instantly and drowned. Ten days later, a river rafting party found Brunette's body more than 30 miles downstream in Lake Mead.* (Not in text)

Andalea Buzzard, 49	August 22, 1977	Lava Falls (River Mile 179.4), flow: 23,000 cfs

*Buzzard was a client on a Sanderson 33-foot rig motoring down the right ride of Lava. The boat lost motor power, rode up the big Black Rock, slid back in, and the left tube submerged stripping off six passengers including Buzzard, a non-swimmer. She reappeared later **having lost her life jacket**, a Holcomb Industries type 5. Buzzard resurfaced but no one could reach her in time to rescue her. She drowned. When recovered, her life jacket was missing its vital rear straps.*

Terry D. Evans, 26	December 2, 1981	Bridge Canyon Rapid (River Mile 235.3), flow: 10,500 cfs

*Evans, a chief water quality researcher, was riding in an open, 25-foot, Duckworth aluminum boat in an attempted uprun during a Bureau of Reclamation research trip. The boat pilot nosed it into a hole. The boat swamped instantly and sank. Evans, wearing **no life jacket** (though eight life jackets were on board, none of the three persons aboard was wearing one), grabbed a Coleman cooler for flotation as he floated toward Mile 237 Rapid. Evans drowned. His body was found 27 days later near Spencer Canyon (River Mile 246). (Not in text)*

William R. Wert, 62	June 26, 1983	Crystal Rapid (River Mile 98.5), flow: 69,000 cfs

*Wert was a client on a 33-foot, Tour West motor rig piloted by a trainee running on flood flow. The rig flipped upside down. Wert drowned in Crystal Rapid **despite his life jacket**.*

Dick Benjamin Roach, 71
Richard Bruce Sheperski, 50

November 10, 1983   Soap Creek Rapid (RM 11+) at 23,000 cfs
*Fishermen Roach and Sheperski launched their Monarch 16-foot aluminum motor boat at Lees Ferry and headed upstream but that night floated possibly upside-down but possibly alive through Badger Rapid. Both wore **no life jacket** (but had them aboard); neither survived Soap Creek Rapid.*

Tom Pillsbury, 66

June 7, 1984   Crystal Rapid (RM 98.5) at 43,500 cfs
*Pillsbury, rowing a 15-foot inflatable on a private trip and carrying two passengers, entered too far left in Crystal Rapid at flood flow, flipped, and drowned **despite wearing a life jacket** after floating past other members of his trip.*

Norine Abrams, 58

August 25, 1984   Lava Falls (RM 179.4) at 24,500 cfs
*Abrams, a client on a Georgie's Royal River Rats motor trip, was, with other passengers, stripped off Georgie's triple rig as Georgie ran the Ledge Hole. The huge boat stalled and pivoted. The 33-foot donut on Abrams' side submerged and folded under the boat in the Ledge Hole. Abrams drowned **despite wearing a life jacket**.*

William B. Blair, 65

September 21, 1986   Crystal Rapid (RM 98.5) at 27,800 cfs
*Blair, a client on a Friends-of-the-River-chartered paddleboat on one of the last trips run by Wilderness World, drowned or died of a heart attack **despite wearing a life jacket** seconds after the paddleboat attempted but failed to make the safety cut to the right and flipped upside-down in the main wave train.*

Martin M. Hunsaker, 54

June 14, 1989   Crystal Rapid (RM 98.5) at 13,250 cfs
*Hunsaker, pilot and trip leader for a Georgie's Royal River Rats trip, lost power in his 33-foot motor rig in the second "tail wave" after entering Crystal while aiming for the left run. The boat flipped upside down against the schist wall. Hunsaker was dead at the foot of Tuna Rapid (Mile 100.1). He drowned in, or because of, Crystal **despite wearing a life jacket**.*

Gene Elliot Stott, 54

April 27, 1990   Crystal Rapid (RM 98.5) at 10,250 cfs
*Stott rowed his 13.5-foot inflatable raft, a Miwok, on a private trip and missed the cut to the right in Crystal and flipped in Crystal Hole. After rescuing Stott and re-flipping his boat, Stott suffered a massive heart attack and died. He was the fifth victim to die "in," Crystal Rapid **despite wearing a life jacket**.*

Emilio X. Solares, 29

November 15, 1994   Hance Rapid (RM 77) at 9,000 cfs
*Solares, on a private trip, wedged himself against the rowing frame of a new "Protar" raft to video tape the oarsman's run of Hance Rapid at "low" water. The Protar flipped immediately in the top hole on the right. Solares became trapped in the frame or the cargo netting used to secure his dunnage. Rescue efforts by the trip's kayakers failed. Solares drowned **despite his life jacket**.*

James Mehegan, 52

July 29, 2004   205-Mile Rapid
Mehegan, on a private trip, had just paddled his kayak through the rapid and to his buddy on a raft and told him he thought he

*was having a heart attack. He died of a **massive heart attack**.*

Leonard Gentry, 62

November 23, 2004   Hance Rapid (RM 77) at 41,000+ cfs
*An elderly, possibly "homeless," man had been "cajoled" onto a private rowing trip of mostly Phoenix firemen by two well-meaning brothers. The trip got lost on the huge muddy flow and entered Hance unscouted. 3 boats made the far left run. The 4th ran instead over the "hamburger rock," recycled, then flipped. Two rafters made it to shore in about "7 minutes," hypothermic. The elderly swimmer **drowned in his life jacket**, his lungs coated with silt. The terrified survivors spent a rainy night aboard their 3 boats, attached to the cliff by jamming an oar into it. They all quit the trip via helicopter at Phantom 3 days later.*

Marc Allred, 62

March 30, 2007   Crystal Rapid (RM 98.5) at low water
Wearing a type III pfd, wetsuit, and spray jacket, Allred rowed his Cataraft last attempting to nail the right run. He missed, hit the first hole, washed off his boat, swam Crystal, and, below, was rescued alive. He quickly succumbed to drowning despite CPR.

Table 4–B. RIVER-CROSSING TRAVELERS WHO DROWNED IN GRAND CANYON.

Name, age	Date	River Location and Flow	*Circumstances*
Bush Dulin, adult male	April 10, 1872	approximately River Mile 246–250	
	While trying to travel upriver into Grand Canyon 30 miles from its western end, Dulin and his four prospecting comrades lost their boat. Dulin drowned trying to swim across the Colorado to retrieve it.		
Lorenzo W. Roundy, adult	May 24, 1876	Lees Ferry (River Mile 0)	
	Roundy drowned while trying to cross the river by ferry.		
Navajo (unnamed adult male) Navajo (second unnamed adult male)	1880 or 1881	Lees Ferry	
	Both of two unnamed Navajos drowned during an attempted river crossing when the skiff overturned.		
Henry Rosely, adult Al Rosely, 12	June or July 1884	Lees Ferry	
	During an attempted crossing the Roselys' skiff overturned.		
Navajo (unamed adult male) Navajo (brother of unamed adult above)	1889	Lees Ferry	
	Both of two unnamed brothers, Navajos, "mismanaged" a ferry crossing and drowned.		
unidentified man unidentified man	1891 ?	Roosevelt Camp area at RM 88	
	John Fuller and Harry MacDonald (or, more likely, McDonald), herdsmen on the Kaibab Plateau, descended Bright Angel Creek in the summer of 1890 or 1891 to search for the remains of a man who had drowned the previous year (possibly Frank Mason Brown or Henry Richards). They arrived to find a fully equipped but unoccupied camp with a tent set up with two cots, two revolvers and rifles next to them, an expensive gold watch (run down) on the tent pole, bread baked three days earlier in a Dutch oven, and evidence that two adults had saddled horses and rode to the Colorado—and apparently entered it to swim across.		

Standing in camp, waiting, was a gelding donkey, "Brighty" of the Grand Canyon. The two missing men, Fuller learned, were never seen again, but had originally passed through Flagstaff en route to Grand Canyon and were known to have descended Bright Angel Trail to the region of this mysteriously abandoned camp.

William F. Russell, adult

June 9, 1899   above Pipe Creek Rapid (River Mile 89)
Russell and George Fleming, among five prospectors from Williams, Arizona, attempted a two-man crossing, with no life jackets, of the Colorado during flood stage via a folding canvas boat. It capsized. Fleming swam to the south bank. Russell clung to the capsized boat and drowned.

P. T. McConigle, 37
Charles McLean, 44

July 27, 1903   probably above Pipe Creek Rapid
                      (River Mile 89)
While trying to cross the Colorado at high water, with no life jackets, to visit the Grand Canyon Electric Company's camp in Upper Granite Gorge in a boat weak from exposure to the elements, both McConigle and McLean and the boat vanished forever.

Preston Apperson, adult

March 9, 1911   Lees Ferry
Apperson, a crewman with Charles Spencer's mining promotion, while wearing no life jacket, drowned with a team of horses when the entire ferry sank in midriver.

Royce Elliot Dean, 25
Lewis Nez Tsinnie, 26
Adolpha Johnson, 26

June 7, 1928   Lees Ferry, flow: 86,500 cfs
As the ferry made a successful crossing to the south, a strong wind blew all three men (with no life jackets) and the ferry back into the mainstream of a very silty flood flow of the river. A cable broke. The ferry overturned. All three men drowned.

Glen E. Sturdevant, 33
Fred Johnson, 30

February 20, 1929   Horn Creek Rapid (River Mile 90.2),
                          flow: 5,700 cfs
Sturdevant, Johnson, and Chief Ranger James P. Brooks (all NPS personnel) attempted to cross the Colorado to the south in a 12-foot-10-inch folding boat about 100 yards upstream of Horn Creek Rapid. Sturdevant, rowing, wore a kapok-filled life belt. He lost an oar. Brooks also had a life belt, but Johnson did not. Johnson fell out. All three swam Horn Creek Rapid. Only Brooks survived.

Carlton Boyd Moore, 22

May 26, 1955   near Lava/Chuar (River Mile 65),
                      flow: 27,000 cfs
Moore and Harvey Butchart hiked from Point Imperial down to the Colorado near Mile 53 and walked downstream. The two tried to cross the high flow without life jackets but with air mattresses. Moore had a phobia of drowning and lost control for seven miles of floating, mostly upside down. He drowned below Mile 65.6.

Table 4–C. SWIMMERS, VOLUNTARY OR OTHERWISE, WHO DROWNED IN THE GRAND CANYON COLORADO (all discussed in text). River flows in cubic feet per second (cfs) for dates of incidents are from the U.S.G.S. Historical Streamflows Daily Values Data Base, from Stations #0938000 (Lees Ferry) and #09402500 (Phantom).

Swimmers Who Vanished Between Phantom Beach (River Mile 87.8)) And The Foot of Bright Angel Trail at Head of Pipe Creek Rapid (River Mile 89)

Name, age	Date	River Location and Flow	*Circumstances*
Kenneth E. Curtis, 18	July 21, 1935	foot of Bright Angel Trail/head of Pipe Creek Rapid, flow: 21,000 cfs	

Curtis and two other young men working on a C.C.C. trail project jumped into the small eddy to cool off. Robert Demaree and Curtis swam in deep water and were carried into the current. Demaree made it back to shore, Curtis was sucked under the waves of the rapid and drowned.

| Wallace Peshlakai, adult | August 7, 1937 | foot of Bright Angel Trail/head of Pipe Creek Rapid, flow: 9,500 cfs | |

Peshlakai and friends hiked to the foot of the trail. Peshlakai jumped into eddy. With "a horrified expression on his face," he was sucked into the swirling current and carried downstream and drowned.

| Harold William Nelson, adult | June 20, 1955 | Phantom Beach, flow: 29,000 cfs | |

Nelson drowned in a high flow. As the Park Superintendent's Report 1955 stated, "Assistant Chief Ranger Lehnert and Ranger Davis made a trip into the Canyon to drag the Devil's Spittoon with a grapnel hook in an effort to locate the body of Harold William Nelson who drowned in an attempt to swim across the Colorado at the suspension bridge. Their efforts proved to be fruitless and they returned to the top on June 21."

| Carol Goldman, 18 | August 24, 1965 | Phantom Beach, flow: 17,400 cfs | |

Goldman, who could not swim, entered the Colorado to cool off. She slipped into an unexpected hole, was swept away, and drowned.

| Dwight L. Miller, 26 | June 3, 1970 | foot of Bright Angel Trail/head of Pipe Creek Rapid, flow: 16,000 cfs | |

Miller leaped into the river, was swept away, and drowned. His body was discovered downstream 13 days later.

| Anthony Krueger, 20 | March 24/25, 1971 | Phantom Beach, flow: 9,000 cfs | |

While camped with two friends under a rock shelter near Phantom Ranch, Krueger, from Bell Lake, Minnesota, drank a brew of Datura blossoms. Several hours later, after several inappropriate behaviors such as trying to lift impossible boulders, talking to nonexistent people for hours, and eating dirt, he stripped off his clothes and tried to cross the river but drowned. Death was mitigated by Datura poisoning. His body was found by hikers weeks later and six miles downstream, at Hermit Rapid, washed ashore. (see text, Chapter 6)

John Zombro, early 20s   April 23, 1971   Pipe Creek Rapid (River Mile 89), flow: 15,000 cfs
Zombro and his companion, Bruce Allen of Lynnfield, Massachusetts, found a driftwood and air mattresses raft combo. They tightened it then launched it from River Mile 88 while wearing **no life jackets.** *Two other companions—Joseph Tomaselli (Rochester, NY) and Steven Anderson (Milbury, Mass)— watched from shore. The raft disintegrated above River Mile 89. Both men swam to the right shore near Pipe Creek Rapid. To return to Phantom Ranch, both had to swim across the Colorado to the river-left trail. Allen dived in and made it. Zombro dived in but never surfaced.*

Julian Griffiths, 21   August 4, 1973   foot of Bright Angel Trail/head of Pipe Creek Rapid, flow: 11,500 cfs
Griffiths ignored the nearby sign warning against entering the river and tried to swim across the Colorado to the north side, but drowned.

Aparicio Gil, 26   April 8, 1977   foot of Bright Angel Trail/head of Pipe Creek Rapid, flow: 2,000 cfs
Gil also ignored warning signs and tried to swim across the river on a near record low flow and was swept downstream and drowned.

Louis John Stano, III, 21   June 25, 1995   foot of Bright Angel Trail/head of Pipe Creek Rapid, flow: 17,800 cfs
Stano also ignored warning signs and swam out as if to cross the Colorado against a high flow. He swam through Pipe Creek Rapid and drowned.

Troy M. Fortney, 26   November 25, 1995   Phantom Beach, flow: 14,000 cfs
Frederick Zernik, age 29, and Fortney descended the South Kaibab Trail intending on returning that day to the South Rim via the Bright Angel Trail. They ignored warning signs and decided to swim nearly two miles between the two trails. Zernik aborted and self-extricated, panicked, from the river but trapped himself on a ledge. Fortney was swept into Bright Angel Rapid and drowned.

Deliberate Swimmers Who Drowned Elsewhere Along The Grand Canyon Colorado

Iven Bundy, 22   April 19, 1931   near Whitmore Wash (River Mile 187.4), flow: 9,700 cfs
Iven's cousin, Floyd Iverson, swam across the Colorado from the north then called to Iven that the swim was not hard. Iven tried to follow but was sucked under by a whirlpool and drowned.

UNKNOWN,
   young adult male
2nd UNKNOWN,
   young adult male

August, 1973 ?   Mouth of Havasu (River Mile 156.8)
Two of four young male hikers waded upstream across the mouth of Havasu during a flow of about 5,000 cfs to see what lay upstream. When they returned the river had risen. The two tried to swim downstream across the mouth and into the eddy. The first swimmer missed the mouth and was pulled toward Havasu Rapid. The second tried to help him but failed. Both swimmers vanished into the Colorado.

Minoru Oda, 31

August 5, 1976   Pearce Ferry (River Mile 280), on reservoir
Oda, a male passenger on a motorized Hualapai River Runners' trip, tried to swim, without a life jacket, 200 yards from the boat to shore. Oda drowned four feet from a buoy near shore.

Jeffrey Kaplan, 16

August 7, 1983   River Mile 2.5, flow: 36,000 cfs
About one hour into an OARS, Inc. rowing trip, Kaplan, without a life jacket, jumped into the eddy at high water 20 yards down-river of the boats and swam with its current up past their sterns. Kaplan submerged out of sight. Possibly the cold or flickering water had triggered a petit mal seizure.

Matthew Cranny, 13

March 22, 1990   upstream of Salt Water Wash (River Mile 11), flow: 11,500 cfs
During a Utah LDS Boy Scout Troop 189 hike, Cranny waded into the 46-degree Colorado and ignored instructions to come back out. ("No swimming" was this troop's rule.) Cranny struggled, unable to stay above the surface, and drowned. Cranny had a very recent history of petit mal seizures and seemed to suffer one here.

Elmer Meredith Akers, 40

June 21, 1990   Diamond Creek Rapid (River Mile 225.7), flow: 17,500 cfs
Akers had been drinking alcohol and had bragged to river runners that, earlier that day, he had swum across the Colorado and back. Next he swam into Diamond Creek Rapid and drowned.

Bert Francisco, 28

July 26, 1990   Diamond Creek Rapid (River Mile 225.7), flow: 16,000 cfs
After eating chicken and drinking several beers, Francisco jumped in the river to cool off. The current swept her into Diamond Creek Rapid. She drowned.

Christopher Guetschow, 15

August 28, 1992   Hermit Rapid (River Mile 95), flow: 14,900 cfs
Guetshow, on a Boy Scout Troop 17 (from Mankato, Minnesota) hike that had forbidden swimming, dived into the Colorado with the apparent intent of swimming across the river. Halfway across, he was in the slick tongue carrying him into Hermit Rapid where he drowned.

Accidental Swimmers Who Fell In From Shore

Van de Bunt, (first names unknown), young adult male	May 17, 1919	Upper Granite Gorge on south side across from Phantom (RM88)

Van de Bunt, hiking with a friend, lost the trail but made it to the river. While trying to locate Roosevelt's Camp, he tried wading in the river at high flow against a cliff face. Van de Bunt vanished, drowning.

Jody Mack, 31	April 29, 1983	Havasu Rapid (RM 156.8) at 19,000 cfs

Mack, on a San Diego Nomads, Sierra Club hiking trip, crouched on a low ledge jutting into the river 150 feet downstream of the mouth of Havasu Creek. As she leaned out, trying to put her hand in the river, her feet slipped. She dropped into the swift current and drowned.

Robert G. Arceire, 48	January 18, 1987	Lees Ferry at 23,500 cfs

300-pound Arciere and his nephew were on the boat dock alone after dark. Arciere, wearing waders, allegedly grasped his chest and fell into the river and drowned—unable to swim, possibly due to his waders having collected water. The nephew apparently was unable to render assistance. This case was suspicious due to Arciere's multiple, million-dollar life insurance policies and also due to several alleged huge debts he owed. This drowning became an FBI investigation and also an "Unsolved Mysteries" TV episode.

Robert Wiel, about 40	July 24, 1988	Lees Ferry, 200 feet downstream of launch ramp, at 10,500–11,000 cfs

While fishing with a buddy, Weil stepped into the river, slipped on a rock, and fell in at low water. He grabbed another rock and screamed for help. This rock was too slippery to hang onto. Weil yelled for help again, slipped off his rock into the current. His waders swamped. He sank and drowned in the current. Weil's buddy seemed unable to render assistance. NPS Ranger Tom Workman injured his back during a retrieval of Weil's body.

Karl Sebastian Jacobi, 21	June 14, 1989	River Mile 103.8, at 13,250 cfs

Jacobi, while solo hiking upstream from a private river trip, either fell into the Colorado or jumped in to swim back down to camp. He was swept into midstream and drowned.

Todd Strickland, 49	May 30, 1999	Nevills' Beach (RM 75)

Strickland, fishing solo, fell into the Colorado 300 yards downstream of the camp chosen by the commercial motor rafting company, Wilderness River Adventures, and drowned. Rescue and CPR by AzRA river company crew were unsuccessful.

Jamie Padilla, 22	January 29, 2000	Jackass Canyon (RM 8)

Padilla, a Flagstaff resident, stood next to swift water upstream of Badger Rapid and baited a hook as he suffered an epileptic seizure (perhaps caused by flickering sunlight on the water). Padilla's two friends, upstream, witnessed this and saw him slip into the river. His two companions tried to, but could not reach

Padilla in time to prevent his drowning. Searchers found his body the next day 3/8 of a mile downstream, below Badger Rapid.

Iryna Shylo, 19   July 16, 2006   shoreline of lower Hermit Rapid, RM 95
A hiking partner reported Canyon concession employee Shylo of the Ukraine failed to return from a toilet break hike at 6 pm aside Hermit Rapid. On July 30, a private river trip found her in an eddy near Ruby Rapid, RM 105.

Mysterious Disappearances From Camp Who Drowned

Marcos Ortega, 11   June 8, 1973   foot of Bright Angel Trail/head of Pipe Creek Rapid (RM 89) at 11,000 cfs
Ortega, a sleep walker, vanished from a bivouac at Pipe Creek and drowned. His body turned up 18 days later, 6 miles downstream.

Teresa Rainey, 25   July 18, 1974   Trail Canyon (RM 219.2) at 23,000 cfs
While camped with Fort Lee Co., Rainey, intoxicated, fell off one of their 33-foot motor rigs into the river at night and drowned.

David Bret Lasater, 19   August 4, 1980   River Mile 22.5 at 22,500 cfs
While camped at night with a motor trip run by Canyoneers, Lasater, heavily intoxicated, vanished and drowned.

Charles Robert Hunter, 58   July 8, 1981   River Mile 19 at 15,250 cfs
While camped at night with Diamond River Expeditions, Hunter, heavily intoxicated, vanished off their 33-foot rig and drowned.

Robert Walker, 21   August 6, 1997   Diamond Creek Rapid (RM 225.7) at 24,000 cfs
Walker, a Hualapai, had been with friends hanging out on Hualapai River trip boats drinking alcohol at night. He disappeared that night. His body was found the next day on the gravel bar about a mile downstream. (not discussed in text)

John Anthony Frye, 43   September 13, 1997   River Mile 220 at 24,000 cfs
While camped at night with a Diamond River Expeditions motor trip, Frye, heavily intoxicated, vanished from camp and drowned.

Paul Smith, 48   September 8, 2004   River Mile 118 at 7,500 cfs
Smith, on a Tour West rowing trip and his 14th wedding anniversary, had complained to his wife of radiating pain in his left arm but attributed it to paddling. The two camped 75 feet from a broad, shallow eddy. At 10 p.m., a passenger heard faint calls of "Help!" from the eddy. He alerted the sleeping crew. In 3 minutes everyone had begun a 2-hour search of the eddy by wading it plus eddies downriver. Smith had admitted he was a non-swimmer and had promised to never get near the river without a life jacket. His family and personal history included early cardiac problems: he entered the eddy without his lifejacket maybe during a cardiac episode Six days later Dr. Michael Collier saw that a trip had jettisoned a load of french toast in the eddy at RM 122.5. Collier then saw Smith's body amid the debris. Collier, who had experienced the tragic death of Gordon Robert Wagner earlier that trip, now stabilized Smith's body for 4 hours awaiting Park rangers.

Chapter Five

If Looks Could Kill:
Death From The Air

Bombardier Lieutenant Charles Goldblum had just made an emergency parachute drop into an ink-black Grand Canyon. His long and terrifying night descent had jerked to a sudden halt on a three-foot-wide shelf of bedrock. What lay below this ledge was invisible. Goldblum now had a choice: he could dangle where he was and hope that his chute did not slip loose, or, instead, he could unclip from his chute and take his chances. Again, everything around and below him was imperceptible in the darkness. Directly below Goldblum, it turned out, yawned a 1,200-foot vertical drop.

In both Europe and the South Pacific, World War II was a raging storm claiming millions of lives. Mid-1944 was a pivotal time in this worst struggle known in human history. The United States would ultimately emerge victorious from this war by putting 17 million Americans in uniform and by training them as well as possible—though often in a hurry—for their military missions. But in June of 1944, this victory was less clear than it is now via hindsight.

In the European Theater, massive daylight bombing of Germany had exacted a horrible toll on Allied bombing crews. Thousands of U.S. airmen were dying. More yet were dying as the U.S. Army turned its bomb sights on Japan and its now crumbling, short-lived "Empire of the Rising Sun." "Replacing" these U.S. airmen with trained flyers was a struggle of titanic proportions.

On June 20, 1944, the five-man crew of a B-24 had just completed a routine celestial navigation exercise at 28,000 feet somewhere over a Grand Canyon shrouded by nightfall. Now the pilot banked the bomber around to fly back to the Tonopah Army Airfield several hundred miles to the west in Nevada.

The B-24's engines sputtered, then went dead. Knowing that no one could survive a crash landing into the tortured terrain below where they now were, its pilot ordered the crew to bail out. At 12,000 feet, three men made it out of the B-24's bomb bay door. Within seconds each man deployed his chute.

The three jumpers never saw each other in the midnight air, but they did see distant lights nearly one hundred miles away. Abruptly these lights were eclipsed as the three jumpers glided below an unseen Canyon wall.

This fairytale descent eventually had to come down to Earth. And it did. The navigator, Flight Officer Maurice J. Cruickshank, Jr., smashed into a steeply sloping cliff. He broke a bone or two in his foot, but amazingly, he otherwise "landed" in one piece. After skidding to a halt in the darkness, Cruickshank stayed right where he lay and waited for the light of dawn.

Instructor Aerial Engineer Corporal Roy W. Embanks waited four seconds to pull his rip cord. By his estimate, he then descended for fourteen *minutes* before landing uninjured.

Again, Bombardier Lieutenant Charles Goldblum found himself ricocheting from rock to rock in the darkness. Goldblum reported, "I came down within the arms of death when my chute was caught by a jagged cliff." Goldblum's landing on an invisible three-foot-wide shelf against a 1,200-foot cliff where he dangled all night in his harness was a cliff-hanger of the first order. Very fortunately, his decision not to unclip until dawn revealed his options. They turned out to be survivable. But only by climbing upward.

Meanwhile, up in the air at 8,000 feet, a mere thousand feet above the South Rim, after the "malfunctioning mechanism controlling the propeller's pitch" corrected itself, the B-24's engines re-started. The pilot and copilot, sweating bullets, nursed their bomber to those distant lights of Kingman only one hundred miles away.

At dawn Embanks awoke to see himself alone and surrounded by soaring cliffs and terraces in the heart of Grand Canyon. Being of sound body and sound mind, he decided to pack his chute and start climbing. No one, he knew, could ever rescue him this deep inside the Canyon. He climbed 1,200 feet up to a plateau. There he deployed his 24-foot canopy as a distress signal.

Cruickshank and Goldblum had both landed somewhere on the Tonto Plateau, also on the north side of the Colorado but about 1,000 feet above it. They both headed down instead of up, into Tuna Creek (River Mile 99.3). They spotted each other almost immediately and linked up. Cruickshank fashioned a makeshift crutch from a tree limb and hobbled with Goldblum on down toward water a vertical mile below the North Rim.

The first squadron of twenty search planes roared over Embanks. Standing beside his deployed chute, he waved at them like a maniac. The planes passed over Embanks as if he did not exist. "That," he admitted, "was probably the most disheartening sight I ever saw."

Cruickshank and Goldblum eventually made it to the tiny creek. There they expropriated (this was wartime) a bobcat's den for shelter. Goldblum scanned the walls for a break where it might be possible to hike out. Still climbing about and searching for a way out on day three, Cruickshank and Goldblum spotted Embanks' chute. They painfully hobbled and climbed to his plateau to join him.

A day or two later, another plane finally roared by and dropped smoke bombs signaling that they had spotted the trio on their mile-long, half-mile wide plateau. On day six, another plane came by and dropped K-rations, water, blankets, a walkie-talkie, cigarettes, and a note that read: "Greetings, you are in the Grand Canyon."

Once the three castaways had drained the canteens that had been dropped, however, they were forced to resume their previous, inconvenient climbs off the plateau for water. Each day, sometimes a few times, one of them would descend for four hours to a small spring that Embanks had found early on during his first ascent and refill the canteens. It being June, the two able-bodied survivors were forced to engage in a lot of very hot exercise.

Meanwhile, two rescue parties descended from the South Rim. To cross the river, one man shot a cable across. There being no one on the other side to catch it, this failed. They next brought from the South Rim to the river a dismantled, hard-hulled boat. But after staring at the ten-foot waves in the rapid at the foot of the trail, the team gave up the idea of boating across the river. It was, they decided, too close to suicide.

Colonel Donald B. Phillips, commander of the Kingman Air Field, flew around the stranded trio's location for two hours photographing the region. Upon studying these aerial photos, Phillips thought he had identified a breach in the cliffs that would allow a descent from the North Rim. The Army set up a base on the North Rim at Point Sublime and enlisted the aid of the veteran Toroweap Ranger Ed Laws, and the veteran Inner Canyon hiker, Professor Alan A. McRae (future mentor to Harvey Butchart), in strategizing a rescue descent.

Laws and MacRae—who had just been hiking in the Canyon with his bride on their honeymoon—teamed up and pioneered a descent. It turned out, however, not to be the one that Phillips thought existed. Balked by a 150-foot cliff in the Redwall Limestone on Phillips' route that had not been visible in Phillips' aerial photos, MacRae and Laws backtracked to search the Redwall the hard way, from afoot atop the Redwall. Zeroing in on some greenery on the far side of this tributary canyon, they circled around it. On the far side they found a spring and a rare break in the Redwall. They followed a deer trail down this break. It led, after a total of ten miles and 20 hours of hiking, almost directly to Embanks', Cruickshank's, and Goldblum's position on the plateau.

Had all of this happened in the 1950s or later, the story would have ended differently—with a helicopter ride. But this was 1944. Men had to be men and they had to use their feet, broken or not. Hence, all five men climbed out in a quasi-"self-rescue." Even Cruikshank with his crutch. All that the three downed fliers had really needed to rescue themselves was simply reliable knowledge of the location of a climbable route out.

After successfully exiting the Canyon, the three fliers proposed naming their ten-day camp spot EMOGO Point (for **Em**banks, for Cruickshank's nickname, "**Mo**," and for **Go**ldblum). Sadly, after surviving their unplanned night drop into Grand Canyon, then surviving their ten-day "camp-out" in the heat, and finally surviving their demanding, trail-less hike and climb a mile up and out of the Canyon during the blazing heat of late June, one of these three airmen, Goldblum, would die in the Pacific War with Japan.

Painful though it was for both the rescued and their rescuers, the story of this B-24 crew's "rescue" recounts one of the happiest air mishaps ever to occur over Grand Canyon. Indeed, these mishaps are so common and so commonly lethal that unsuccessfully attempting to fly over the Canyon has killed more people than have died by drowning in the river, by falling off cliffs within the Canyon or from its rims, by being killed by flash floods, and by dying from the heat *combined*. The airspace over the Grand Canyon region may be one of the most dangerous peacetime airspaces in the world.

The worst episode happened in 1956. At 10:01 a.m., Mountain Standard Time, on a reasonably clear morning of the last day of June, Trans World Airlines Flight 2, a four-engine Super Constellation, took off with 70 people aboard, six of them crew, from Los Angeles International Airport. It was en route to Kansas City. Flight controllers told Captain Jack Gandy to fly at 19,000 feet. Three minutes later, a faster United Airlines DC-7, Flight 718, took off with 58 people, five of them crew, aboard from the same air strip en route to Chicago. Air Traffic Control told its captain, Robert Shirley, to fly at 21,000 feet. Both pilots filed flight plans that deviated from standard, monitored "airways" (TWA 2's would have been via Albuquerque; UA 718's via Salt Lake City) in favor of more direct flight routes that would *intersect* near Grand Canyon but with 2,000 feet of vertical distance between them. An important issue to clarify at this point is that the flight environment immediately over the only 15-mile-wide Grand Canyon provides a rougher, not smoother flight. Both pilots, we submit, chose this narrow and lengthy bit of rough airspace instead of a nearby parallel but likely smoother route strictly for the view into Grand Canyon. Hence these flights became, in their way, scenic flights.

Well into his flight, Captain Gandy asked for permission to move his Super Constellation up to 21,000 feet to avoid turbulence. Los Angeles Air Traffic Control denied his request. There was, they noted, already another large aircraft overtaking him at that elevation.

Captain Gandy later asked again for permission to fly higher—perhaps because half of his passengers [30 plus] were TWA employees or dependents—this time for "one thousand on top." This was a request to rise one thousand feet above cloud cover, which apparently TWA 2 was in. Had he been granted this request, he could have moved TWA 2 to well above 20,000 feet, based on wherever the tops of clouds extended. Surprisingly, the Los Angeles controller this time said yes, but he did warn Gandy again about United Airlines Flight 718 at 21,000 feet in the same region, overtaking him, and flying in the same direction. Once Gandy gained his thousand-plus, he would be much closer to this United flight than before. And now flying on visual flight rules, it would be his responsibility to avoid it.

A half hour later, TWA 2 made its second routine call-in: "TWA 2, over Lake Mojave at 10:55, one thousand on top at twenty-one thousand, estimating Painted Desert eleven-thirty-one."

An air traffic controller in Salt Lake City heard this and noted to himself that TWA 2 and United 718 were now at the same altitude and in the same neighborhood of roughly a hundred-mile-wide airspace. But because this sort of situation was not unusual, he turned his attention to other tasks.

In reality, both aircraft now were near Grand Canyon. In the 1950s it was not only common for a pilot to modify his flight plan away from established airways, but to also alter his course to offer his passengers (and himself) this spectacular overview. On this day Grand Canyon weather offered "a reasonably clear sky" dotted with billowing thunderheads up to 35,000 feet.

Air Traffic Control next heard from United 718 at 11:28 a.m. as they "neared" Tuba City (roughly fifty miles east of Grand Canyon). Four minutes later, a westbound United flight heard a broken transmission from United Airlines Flight 718: "We are going...." Then brief static. Then nothing.

Three separate tourists, Eugene J. Sieffer, Blanche England, and Frederick Riley, saw something happen in the sky. Sieffer was driving near Flagstaff. He told Civil Aeronautics Board (CAB) investigators that he saw the two planes converge and then "fly as if stuck together." Seconds later they disappeared "behind some mountains."

Blanche England, driving many miles away near Winslow, reported:

All at once I saw a great puff of smoke, something came out of the sky like a parachute, then something came down with smoke following after it. The smoke spread out just like a parachute opening up. The object that came down didn't come straight down. It came down at sort of an angle.

Frederick Riley, driving along Highway 64 on the South Rim, saw the collision through his windshield much closer, only about ten miles ahead.

This plane here peeled right off and went over like this...it looked to me as if it had bent—broken....It didn't glide at all. It tipped over and went right straight down. The other took off at a gliding angle....It looked like it possibly kept on the same general flight, and then it tipped over and went down....

Riley feared the scene he had just witnessed was a hallucination, a visual trick played by the shimmering light. At first he did not even report it for fear of being laughed at.

Before 1:00 p.m., both United and TWA authorities were worried. Neither east-bound flight had checked in. And both failed to respond to radio hailing. Search planes took off and unsuccessfully scoured the regions farther east toward Tuba City. Meanwhile a tourist at Desert View at the national park's east entrance noticed a column of smoke near the confluence of the Little Colorado and Colorado rivers.

Hearing about this smoke (and the missing aircraft), Bill Deaver, a 20 year-old reporter for the *Arizona Daily Sun*, hired a Cessna 180 owned and piloted by Beth Wright to search for the smoke's origin in Grand Canyon. To get aerial photos, Wright explained to a terrified Deaver, just get rid of the airplane's door. At the last minute, a *Los Angeles Times* reporter, Jerry Hulse, jumped aboard with Deaver. As Deaver tried to shoot pictures, he worried that his ill-functioning seatbelt would disintegrate and dump him into a free-fall into the Canyon. So Hulse held Deaver inside the plane with a death grip.

The trio spotted the huge Super Constellation, down and burning in pieces on the shoulder of Temple Butte. A mile north of it, they also saw the United DC-7 exploded into fragments against the south face of 6,400-foot-high Chuar Butte, about a mile from the confluence of the Little Colorado River with the Colorado (River Mile 61.5).

Early the next morning, Clarke Cole, the 46 year-old undersheriff of Coconino County, flew his own small Ercoupe single engine plane to confirm for the Coconino Sheriff's Department where the collisions were. "I started down into the Canyon from the lower end," Cole explained, "and it was a rough day."

Cole too spotted the DC-7 disintegrated against Chuar Butte. Next he slowed to 80 mph to view the Super Constellation wreckage. Strong turbulence bucked his small plane. No way could anyone have survived either crash, Cole saw as he dropped as close as he could to survey the damage. Then, as Cole pulled up to escape the Canyon, he hit worse turbulence. Cole explains:

> *When I hit that turbulence, after I saw those two planes, my own plane flipped over and I was flying upside down. Gas spilled out on me. God, I thought I was a goner. But the next batch of turbulence flipped me right back over again.*

These overflights confirmed everyone's worst fears: 128 people had just died in a mid-air collision that sent both aircraft hurtling into Grand Canyon. The odds of anyone surviving either of the high impact collisions with the unyielding faces of Paleozoic rock were infinitesimal. Even recovering the bodies would be a very dangerous proposition. This collision was the worst peacetime civilian airline disaster in all of commercial aviation history (until it was exceeded in 1960). Indeed the carnage of this accident was so hideous that it alone spurred the formation of the Federal Aviation Administration (FAA).

The result of these errors—the United pilot had deviated 25 miles south of his route; the TWA pilot had climbed 2,000 feet higher than was prudent and also had deviated five miles off his own route—more than doubled the total number of people killed in Grand Canyon up to 1956 from all other causes combined since its recorded history began.

So how, exactly, did this disaster happen? Analysis of that final United 718 transmission received by Salt Lake and San Francisco revealed two voices over the radio. One, in the background, was saying, "Pull up! Pull up!" The other voice was that of United 718's First Officer Robert W. Harms: "Salt Lake City from United Seven One Eight...uh...we're going *in*!"

Reconstructing what went wrong would have to wait until investigators could examine the surviving fragments of the downed aircraft.

Almost instantly, coordination and control in recovering bodies and debris became a shambles. Every agency remotely connected with the incident—TWA and United Airlines, the Civil Aviation Administration, the Civil Aeronautics Board, the National Park Service, the Federal Bureau of Investigation, the U.S. Air Force, five separate bases of Army Rescue teams, and the Coconino County Sheriff, Coroner, and Attorney—all tried to make something useful happen. As Ranger Butch Farabee notes, "Finally, on the afternoon of the third day, Park Superintendent McGlaughlin and Chief Ranger Coffin got a top official from each agency together in one room and somehow orchestrated the chaos to calm."

The position of the Super Constellation wrecked on Temple Butte at 3,400 feet allowed fairly easy access. It had hit at a steep angle and upside down. Mixed with its debris was the left wing tip of the United Airlines DC-7. Fabric covering this wing tip matched the interior ceiling fabric of the Super Constellation. Later examination of the TWA wreckage, notes a collision report, "indicated that the left wing of the United DC-7 had slashed sideways and downward across the rear of the TWA plane, ripping off the latter's tail [and rear fuselage]." The TWA plane, tail-less, probably dropped like a lead Frisbee spewing coats and pillows and other cabin appointments over miles of desert landscape. No passenger had ever been killed on board a Super Constellation before.

The most likely collision scenario—a speculative one—was reconstructed to place the DC-7, at 345 miles per hour, overtaking the TWA "Super Connie," at 308 mph, from above and behind as each plane veered around a large anvil-shaped thunderhead and as the Super Constellation was possibly gaining altitude. In such positions, each plane would have been in the other's considerable blind spot. Indeed the pilot's field of vision from the Super Connie's cockpit was only 17.2 percent of an unencumbered person's; that from the DC-7 was an extremely narrow 13.8 percent. As veteran pilot, TWA Captain John Carroll, noted with respect to this collision, "The fact is a pilot often finds it almost impossible to see another airplane even when it is right beside him—particularly when its paint job camouflages it against the sun or sky, or when the sun glare is bad, as it often is at high altitude." Making a bad long-shot worse over Grand Canyon, Captain Robert Shirley of the DC-7 had no idea that anyone else was up there near 21,000 feet in his airspace. Air Traffic Control had not advised him of TWA 2's new 21,000-foot altitude.

Three days after the crash, Larry Wren, Deputy Coconino County Attorney, flew by helicopter to within 50 yards of the wreckage of the TWA Super Constellation. He was horrified.

> *There could be no one left alive. Blackened charred bodies dotted the ground among the debris....The stench was sickening. A part of the fuselage...contained the body of what we thought was a woman...we filled 28 bags with remains and one with personal effects and air mail letters.*
>
> *During the afternoon, two paramedics* [sic] *left for the treacherous peak where the United plane was down. They reported they had found only one body—the only body—that was not burned.*
>
> *Some of the bodies crumbled to ash as we lifted them. Aluminum parts of the plane had melted and run in rivulets between the rocks....We found a baby's body across the arms of a woman....We found a toy boat that wasn't even scratched.*

If the TWA Super Constellation was horrible, the wreck of Shirley's DC-7 was a nightmare. It was painted across the southern face of Chuar Butte on nearly inaccessible cliffs.

"Leave them where they fell," advised Flagstaff editor-publisher Platt Cline, who explained that the risk to rescuers of trying to salvage bodies from the pulverized DC-7—the first ever to crash—veneered against the cliffs of Chuar Butte was unconscionably high. "Grand Canyon is not an inappropriate resting place for these tragic crash victims."

Instead, officials dropped off climbers at the river at 2,700 feet elevation with orders to ascend Chuar Butte. They trekked up newly named "Crash Canyon" and began the final, challenging 800-foot ascent of Chuar Butte to the DC-7at 4,050 feet. But after two days of sweltering technical climbing during early July and of hammering hundreds of bolts into the weathered, decaying wall, the climbers still had not reached the impact site. They had, however, thoroughly terrified themselves.

Determined, TWA flew in a crack mountain climbing team of Swiss air rescue personnel and their 2,000 pounds of equipment from their training program in Colorado. U.S. Army Captain Walter Spriggs landed them, one by one, with his helicopter in a very hairy location on a narrow ledge—deemed impossible by the experts—about 30 feet above the wreckage of the United

DC-7. The Swiss rescue team set up their base camp on this ten-foot-wide ledge. For the next several days they pried from the crevasses and vertical cracks corpses and fragments of corpses that had been pressure injected into fissures and then subjected to six days of scorching heat.

In one of the most hazardous operations the U.S. Army had ever undertaken, their pilots brought their H-21 "Flying Banana" helicopters down through the superheated and treacherous air to evacuate these bodies. Only 30 of the 128 killed were ever identified, most of them from TWA Flight 2. The majority of the twenty-nine bodies recovered from the DC-7 were buried unidentified in the Grand Canyon Cemetery. Sixty-seven of the TWA victims were buried in Flagstaff.

Both the Hopi and Navajo tribes recognized that all these people had died on sacred grounds. They both held 24-hour prayer vigils for the victims. The entire city of Flagstaff and all of its businesses closed down in respect to the deceased.

How odd was this collision? This disaster was the 131st mid-air collision of civil aircraft to occur between 1947 and 1956. But it was far worse in casualties than all previous collisions. As mentioned above, it was the worst commercial air crash in U.S. history prior to 1960. And it was bad enough to spur U.S. Congress into action. Congressional actions included new flight rules to: 1. fly on Instrument Flight Rules (IFR) above 18,000 feet, 2. to achieve better and wider air traffic control of airspace, and 3. to form a new regulatory, investigatory, and advisory entity, the Federal Aviation Administration, today's FAA.

Despite all improvements in flight control, when it comes to Grand Canyon, the cliche "lethal beauty" unfortunately has been all too accurate all too often. Even if one has no interest in geology, planetary history, or even scenery in general, the quest to see the sheer dazzling phenomenon of Grand Canyon from the air can be a killer.

By the 1990s, Grand Canyon Airport was Arizona's third busiest, reportedly handling up to more than 1,000 take-offs and landings daily. By 2000, it had become Arizona's second busiest airport, handling yet more take-offs and landings. Yet some of those landings were made nowhere near the airport. On July 7, 1980, for example, Willis L. Woods, age 35, piloted his Piper Comanche from Page to the Grand Canyon Airport. With him were three passengers. Woods did not top off his fuel tanks in Page because "fuel was unavailable." Neither did Woods re-establish touch with reality by waiting at the airport for more fuel to arrive—or even by leaving by vehicle to go get some fuel himself.

Instead, undaunted by the inconvenience of not enough fuel in his tanks, Woods flew on toward Grand Canyon Airport. During this flight, he was fueled by determination. Dozens of miles short of this destination, near Grandview Point below the South Rim, Woods ran out of aviation gas. This was the moment of enlightenment: Woods found that determination does not at all affect the thrust vector in heavier-than-air flight.

Woods crashed onto an Inner Canyon plateau. His Piper rattled and banged along a rare stretch of semi-level terrain, denting and abusing the fuselage, but otherwise leaving the aircraft in one piece. With no fuel at all aboard, at least the possibility of a dangerous explosion was low. Miraculously, Woods and his three passengers survived and were rescued.

Others would not be so lucky. Less than twenty years after Glen Canyon Dam went on line 15 miles upstream of Lees Ferry in 1963, for example, the Bureau of Reclamation decided to rewind and upgrade their generator turbines to produce more kilowatt-hours of electricity per hour during daily peak, or "spike," releases. Since this upgrade would widen the difference between daily high spike flows of 31,500 cfs and nightly low flows as low as 3,000 cfs from the dam even more disparately by raising the highs to 33,200 cfs during the day and lowering the lows to even less than 3,000 cfs at night, it would change yet again the flow regime of the Colorado River in Grand Canyon National Park. The existing drastic daily fluctuations, many ecologists suspected, were already wreaking havoc with several native species in the park itself. Some species—river otters and the giant Colorado squawfish—had become extinct in the park due to the dam's operations—and these were barely the tip of the iceberg. Greater daily fluctuations yet, ecologists and conservationists worried, would cause even worse damage.

This being 1981, well after passage of the Federal National Environmental Policy Act (NEPA), the Bureau of Reclamation was now required to perform an Environmental Assessment before upgrading and then increasing daily flows of the Colorado (and also reducing nightly flows). The Bureau did this, but only in the most perfunctory way. They wrote it up in an office as bureaucratic paperwork without even looking into the river corridor in Grand Canyon to see what their fluctuating flows were actually doing to the park. Not surprisingly, the Bureau decided that their upgrade would produce no significant effect in Grand Canyon and issued a "finding of no significant impact."

Environmentalists sued the Bureau in 1982 for "bypassing" the NEPA process. In response, on December 6, 1982, the Bureau launched what would become one of the most expensive and protracted environmental studies on Earth, the Glen Canyon Environmental Studies (GCES) aimed at determining the effects of dam operations on the resources—both living and nonliving—within the river corridor in Grand Canyon. One of the most obvious resources being damaged at this time were beaches. They were shrinking drastically. Many had vanished altogether since 1963. To investigate this situation, the Bureau set up three stations in the Canyon to measure sediment transport by different flows of the Colorado, high versus low, and so on. This was necessary because, due to the damming of the Colorado, the natural sediment loads entering the Canyon—a million tons every two or three days—had decreased to a very small fraction. Most of what did exist in Grand Canyon was being deposited downstream in Lake Mead and was not being replaced.

One of these stations was installed upstream of National Canyon (River Mile 166.3). It consisted, as the other four did, of a steel cable stretched across the river about 35 feet above the water. This allowed researchers to cross above specific sections of the river in a cable car to collect water samples at various flows and depths. These samples provided sediment load data. GCES researchers were often poorly paid, or even unpaid volunteers. They were dropped off in the Canyon by boat and then, because the NPS had forbidden non-emergency helicopter traffic in the Canyon, the researchers were resupplied and/or relieved at multi-week intervals by other boats.

During summer months, these researchers experienced an idyllic life in the Canyon frequently punctuated by social visits from river-runners. During winter when river-running dropped to almost zero, however, those "trapped" at now sunless National Canyon were cold and monotonously lonely, experiencing an Inner Gorge version of cabin fever.

On the evening of December 8, 1983, two researchers, Heidi Herendeen and John Pittman, were readying their little cart at the National Canyon site. They were about to dangle above the river and collect the last sediment load samples of the day. Abruptly they both heard the echoes of a helicopter approaching low within the limestone walls of the Inner Gorge. This, to them, here, was a unique sound.

As they looked upstream, a Bell-206 swiftly rounded the bend and raced downriver thirty feet above the water. Again, helicopters—and all aircraft at this time—were requested to remain above 2,000 feet of this elevation except for search and rescue (SAR) missions. Even SAR missions rarely screamed down the corridor buzzing the river. This racing chopper was a novelty. Moreover, this BLM flight broke Federal regulations by deviating off its official route.

It was also in the wrong place at the wrong time.

Its pilot, William J. "Doc" Holliday, had two passengers: Bill Lamb, the District Manager for the Bureau of Land Management in Utah, and Charlie Houser, age 50, a BLM congressional liaison from Washington, D.C. These two federal bureaucrats had been comparing two regions of the plateau thousands of feet above and miles away to the north as candidates for wilderness designation. Once done up there, at least one of the two bureaucrats had convinced Holliday to buzz the river in a joy-ride (again, against federal regulations and at taxpayers' expense).

As Herendeen and Pittman stared in disbelief, the Bell-206's engine-cowling, then rotor mast, slammed into their one-inch cable. The 2,500-pound airship stopped on a dime. It flipped upside down as it dropped into the river. As it drifted downstream it started sinking slowly in the 15-foot-deep water near shore.

Herendeen dived out of the way as the cable snapped. The cart that she had been about to step into launched up in the air then crashed back down one foot away from her. All of this had been very lucky. Had Holliday's helicopter hit this cable a minute or two later, *all* five people involved likely would have been killed.

Pittman jumped into the cold river and assisted Holliday in his struggle to shore. Herendeen jumped in too. She grabbed the chopper's skid in one hand and a shoreline bush in the other, trying to stop it from drifting into National Rapid with people trapped underwater inside it.

Meanwhile, half underwater, Bill Lamb extricated himself from his harness. Next to him, Charlie Houser was unconscious, still strapped upside down, with his head underwater. Lamb pulled Houser's head out of the water by his helmet but then fumbled unsuccessfully with Houser's seat belt release buckle.

Pitmann entered the sinking chopper and made several dives to release Houser's buckle. Finally Lamb pulled Houser out and onto the belly of the Bell-206 and gave him cardiopulmonary resuscitation (CPR). Everyone made it—or was towed—to shore.

Secretary of the Interior Donald P. Hodel awarded Department of the Interior Valor Awards to Heidi Herendeen and John Pitmann—and, strangely, in view of the flight's regulation-breaking, joyride nature, also to Bill Lamb. Despite CPR, Charlie Houser died due to "delayed" drowning/lung complications several days later.

As we have already seen, the Canyon's stunning beauty combined with pilot error led to a major disaster in 1956, one so horrific that it became midwife to the FAA. Almost exactly 30 years later, the beauty of the Inner Canyon would yet again combine with pilot error to produce such tragic results that U.S. Congress would feel compelled yet again to re-attack the lethal problem of regulating commercial flights over the Canyon.

It was mid-morning, about 9:30, on June 18, 1986. The boatmen of a commercial river trip were scouting Crystal Rapid (River Mile 98.5). A few of their passengers heard a strange sound. As they looked downstream and north, a fixed-wing Twin-Otter and a Bell Jet Ranger helicopter had just collided above the drainage of Tuna Canyon (River Mile 99.3). Now both plummeted down to Earth.

Meanwhile an emergency call came over the radio. NPS Pilot Dana Morris heard it. Morris detoured away from his route to a noncritical river med-evac injury. Within five minutes he flew Rangers Ernie Kuncl and Charles Peterson to the smoking wreckage. The twenty-seat plane, a DeHavilland Twin-Otter operated by Grand Canyon Airlines, Inc. had indeed crashed. The three rescue personnel saw people still strapped in their seats in this aircraft, dead and burning. All twenty of the passengers and crew of the sight-seeing plane had died.

Twenty minutes later the NPS searchers also spotted the debris of a crashed Bell-206 helicopter owned by Helitech, Inc. strewn over a mile across the Tonto Plateau. All five persons aboard it too had been killed.

Why?

"Three good men died," a groundcrew member said of the pilots, "for no fault of their own. They died in an accident that couldn't be avoided. It was an act of God."

Whether or not God had been in on this disaster remains questionable; humans were piloting the aircraft. What had these humans been doing?

By informal agreement between air tour operators, helicopter tours were to stay below a ceiling of 6,500 feet while fixed wing flights were to stay above 7,000 feet, the intent being to create 500 vertical feet of airspace as a margin of safety between the two types of aircraft. Hence a crux question is: Where had these two aircraft been flying?

A tourist on that rafting trip at Crystal had taken three photos from the river of both aircraft in the air. Using photogrammetric reconstruction analysis, federal investigators bracketed the collision at between 6,401 and 6,613 feet. More than two months after the collision, the National Transportation Safety Board (NTSB) ballparked the collision as having occurred at about 6,500 feet. Years earlier, the FAA had issued an advisory urging pilots not to fly lower than 2,000 feet *above* the rim (9,000 feet elevation). Hence, the fixed-wing Twin-Otter and the helicopter had been flying well below their advised airspace (as many scenic pilots habitually were doing during the 1980s) and the fixed wing was apparently also flying 400–500 feet below its informal, conventional airspace. The helicopter had been flying at the ceiling of, but most likely within, its informal, conventional airspace.

Weeks later, however, the cause of this midair collision still had remained unexplained. Even after combing through and removing most of the wreckage, and after evacuating the 25 bodies, the FAA and the National Transportation Safety Board still could not figure it out.

Two months after the midair collision, the helicopter pilot's brother, Scott Thybony, hiked to the crash site on the shadeless Tonto Plateau. In the emotion of his quest, Thybony outwalked his water. He soon experienced classic symptoms of *advanced* dehydration: narrowed visual field, cramping stomach, tingling scalp, loss of judgement. Having made hundreds of Canyon hikes before, Thybony knew he was in trouble—enough trouble to now begin imagining the effect of his death upon his wife and son and the rest of his family so soon after his brother's death. How could he have been so stupid, he wondered now, as to not have filled up his canteen at that last pothole a few hours back? It had held at least two gallons of rainwater. Thybony looked toward the ridge above where, he reflected, he should have been walking, and thought ruefully about how distant that water was.

> Then I saw it. On the slope lay a piece of wreckage overlooked
> by the search parties. They hadn't expected to find anything this far
> north. It was the missing rotor blade from my brother's helicopter,

scarred from the impact of metal on metal. Later retrieved, it
turned out to be the critical piece of evidence used in reconstructing
the moment of collision. In the final instant, it's likely that neither
aircraft could have seen the other as the airplane overtook the heli-
copter from above and behind.

Scott Thybony had just found the key to understanding what had gone wrong. But he still had to survive to hand over that key to the ones who knew how to use it. In agony for that waterpocket a mile and half away, he finally found a ledge in the Tapeats Sandstone that offered a scrap of shade. He gave up his quest for water and hid under this from the sun.

Lying there on the rough sandstone he hallucinated an old Indian, maybe Apache, grim and unsmiling, sitting next to him. After what seemed like a long time, his new companion spoke: "Yes, we wait here, sun go down." Minutes later, the phantom Indian departed.

Five hours later, after Thybony had dredged up the energy and good sense to pull the cactus spines from his boots, the sun set. An hour later he reached that tiny waterpocket, life itself. Too burned by thirst to continue by foot in the twilight—or even to swallow any food—he bivouacked under a nearby ledge where, by eerie coincidence, he and his brother John had camped a dozen years earlier. The firewood they had gathered then was still stacked neatly nearby. Deja vu. Haunted now by his brother's stories then of the many terri-fying sorties he had piloted during the Vietnam War, Thybony kindled a small fire. Despite his deja vu—and everything else—Thybony felt relieved to be alive.

Later, Federal investigators would conclude from Scott Thybony's discov-ery that the rotor mast of the helicopter piloted by John Thybony at roughly 6,500 feet had been hit by the left landing gear of the fixed wing Twin-Otter piloted by Bruce Grubb and Jim Ingraham. Each aircraft had been in the blind spot of the other.

What is the overall tally of fatal air crashes in and around the Canyon? Unlike the media-blitzed airline crashes that populate our nightly news on television and win cover photos on U.S. news magazines, most of the 58 fatal crashes in and around Grand Canyon have received relatively little public attention. No aura of sensationalism surrounds the deaths of most of the 355 people who have died during these 58 fatal crashes (multiple additional nonfatal crashes have occurred which we have not tabulated) that we have determined to have occurred in and near to Grand Canyon. Nonetheless, as Tables 5–A and 5–B show, these 58 disasters caused 242 deaths from 29 air-craft crashing *in* the Canyon and another 113 deaths from yet another 29 aircraft in the environs *around* it. Together these Grand Canyon air deaths comprise a stunning total.

How could so many aircraft go down forever in one region?

Grand Canyon is not the Devil's Triangle, but somehow it has gobbled up more aircraft victims than that infamous Bermuda "hole" in so-called reality. One possible explanation may be that too many inexperienced private pilots fly over the Canyon's extreme turbulence and through its very changeable and dynamic weather from those same monsoonal systems that create flash floods and from those same winter storms that close the North Rim all winter. Some of these pilots, some critics say, are overcome by these challenges when matched against their own experience. This argument, as we will see, holds merit when matched against what is known about the causes of these crashes. These 58 aircraft that crashed fatally did include 33 under the control of private pilots. But of the other 25 aircraft down, 24 were piloted by men with commercial licenses (the April 1, 1999, helicopter crash is only one known to have been piloted by a woman, and she was in training). These 24 men possessed commercial pilot licenses and were trained in some way to anticipate the challenges posed by the airspace over and within Grand Canyon. Yet, within the Canyon itself, 16 commercial pilots have gone down in fatal crashes, while 13 private pilots have done so. In these within-Canyon crashes, 204 people have died inside the Canyon from commercial flights, 38 people have died from private flights.

The causes of these tragedies—involving both private and commercial pilots—do show some common threads. The discernable causes for these 58 fatal crashes are summarized in Table 5–C. Of these 58 crashes, causes were not determined (or not available to us) for ten. Of the remaining 48 crashes for which at least one cause is known or strongly suspected, mechanical failures and/or inadequate maintenance accounted for twelve or thirteen (25–27 percent).

On June 25, 1977, for example, George Lutteum was flying a private twin, piston-engined Piper Navajo on the Kaibab Plateau a half dozen miles south of Hermit's Rest on the South Rim. He lost one engine and crashed. Four of the nine people aboard (George Lutteum was not among them) fled the crash site before the plane exploded. Those four survived. The other five aboard died. On July 21, 1980 Richard T. Mierhouse, age 33, piloted a Scenic Airlines Cessna 404 twin, piston-engined aircraft on its takeoff for a scenic flight with seven passengers aboard. Almost immediately upon takeoff, metal fragments from incomplete repair work were sucked into the left engine, freezing it. The Cessna crashed shortly after takeoff and killed all eight people aboard. On May 13, 1991, all seven people aboard an Air Grand Canyon Cessna 207 died due to a cylinder-head explosion freezing up its one engine (piston-powered) a few minutes after take-off. On June 19, 1992, ten people died on an Adventure Airlines Cessna 402 twin immediately after take-off. It too had lost its right, piston engine due to a maintenance problem. On February 13, 1995, a Las Vegas Airline scenic flight crashed killing all eight aboard. The Piper PA-31 Navajo twin had also lost one piston engine. In summary, at least 60 people died in a dozen crashes due in part or in whole to mechanical failures, some associated with faulty maintenance of their piston engines, some not.

We looked for a pattern of fatal crashes that implicated certain models of aircraft. About 36 different models have crashed in these 58 known fatal incidents. We have not determined any specific "killer" model among them (although five Cessna 172s did go down fatally). On the other hand, two patterns do exist. First, among scenic commercial crashes single-engine aircraft seem less implicated in fatalities than twin-engined craft. Only four single-engine tour flights have gone down fatally, killing 21 among crew and passengers. Meanwhile eight twin-engine craft have crashed, killing 81 passengers and crew (more on this below). Second, there seems to be a difference between the numbers of scenic helicopters down fatally compared to scenic fixed-wing flights. This difference is masked somewhat by the fairly high number of ten fatal helicopter accidents. Of these ten, however, two crashed within the Canyon while filming commercial movies and flying too close to bridges or cables (described below). Three more crashed as "workhorses" while hauling equipment for pipeline or other construction. A sixth one, a joy-riding chopper on a BLM contract but on non-government business (described earlier) went down when it too hit a tram cable, at River Mile 166. A seventh machine became fatal when the pilot in training crashed in 1999 at the airport, possibly due to moisture in the intakes. Of the three scenic flights down, John Thybony's helicopter (also described earlier) was hit in mid-air by a fixed-wing scenic tour plane flying below the floor of its informal conventional airspace. Two other scenic flights have crashed—one due to engine failure, the other to unknown causes. These last three crashes killed a total of eight passengers and all three pilots. In summary, despite the statistic of ten machines—all gas turbine-powered—down fatally, only eight paying passengers of scenic helicopter flights have died—and none of them died due to a known error by the pilot of the helicopter they were in. In contrast, crashes of scenic fixed-wing flights have caused the fatalities of 91 paying passengers in or near the Canyon.

Even so, instead of aircraft type, and also instead of aircraft design or mechanical or maintenance failures (which we admit are important problems), a more lethal problem has caused a far greater number of the 48 fatal crashes due to known causes. As Table 5–A reveals, and as Table 5–C tabulates, pilot error has been implicated in 35 to 38 of these 48 crashes, or roughly 75 percent. Unsurprisingly, this approximate 75 percent figure matches the proportion of all crashes of jet transports in the United States determined to have been due to pilot error.

Pilot errors take many forms. The most common, it turns out, seem to occur in the actual flying ability or flying/maneuvering decisions of the pilot. These errors—analogous to the sorts of driving errors made by a driver of a car that mishandles the vehicle as road conditions change and crashes—

accounted for about 20 of the 48 crashes and comprised 42 percent of the total. Interestingly, these 20 flying errors are closely split between commercial and private pilots, with at least 9 and 11 each.

A clear example of pilot error occurred on April 19, 1982. Glenn Miller flew his Hughes 500 helicopter low along the river near Lees Ferry. He had three passengers aboard, the members of an EMI Productions crew who were filming an "American Eagle" adventure film. Miller failed to see the tram cable across the river. The rotor hit the cable. The aircraft skidded across the water for one thousand feet. Only one of the four people aboard, Laurie Gere, survived, rescued by river guide Dale Whitmore.

Doing a similar sort of job only about four miles downstream, on July 12, 1985, pilot Don Nasca, age 50, met a similar fate. Nasca was flying his helicopter as a motion picture "bad guy" airship during the filming of the Italian action film, "Hands of Stone." As the hero of this film dangled from Navajo Bridge, Nasca's aircraft rattled off blanks from a machine gun at him. For drama, Nasca maneuvered closer (for the camera) to the bridge. Too close. Nasca's rotor struck the bridge. The helicopter plunged 470 feet into the Colorado and sank twenty feet deep. Both Nasca and his actor-passenger died.

Slightly less dramatic, but even more lethal, Keith Crosson, age 42 and co-piloting a Grand Canyon Airlines DeHavilland DHC-6 Twin-Otter with 21 people aboard, mishandled his landing at Grand Canyon Airport on May 13, 1991. Only eleven people survived. Some of these were injured due to seat belt failures and were also trapped in the plane for an hour as rescuers worked feverishly—worried that the aircraft might explode—to free them.

Yet another incident of pilot error was made by private pilot John C. Walker, age 23. His piston-engined Cessna 172 had been having power problems periodically on September 4, 1988. But because he and his three passenger-friends could not find a room for the night at the South Rim and he was "anxious to get home," Walker decided to fly without fully correcting his engine problems. The heavily loaded Cessna 172 stalled after takeoff and crashed. All four aboard died.

Additional types of pilot errors in decision-making that led to fatal crashes included flying into dangerous weather systems. Eight pilots, four commercial and four private, did this fatally (accounting for 17.4 percent of all pilot errors).

After 600–700 flights over the Canyon, for example, pilot Wayne Leeth, age 47, flew a Scenic Airlines twin, piston-engined Cessna 402 with 9 passengers aboard on a tour flight on October 16, 1971, into an early winter snowstorm. Other pilots in the area said the storm was characterized by "clouds down to the ground." Fifteen miles south of Mount Trumbull, Leeth's Cessna hit the ground in Parashant Wash below the rim.

For many pilots used to flying VFR (visual flight rules), being inside a cloud can be instantly disorienting—despite the AI (altitude indicator), automatic direction finder (ADF), the horizontal situation indicator (HSI) gauge, altimeter, and other instruments intended to allow an instrument-rated pilot to fly "blind." Whatever went awry with pilot Wayne Leeth's situation, all ten aboard were killed. In total, three commercial pilots made the error of flying during cold, dangerous weather and iced up or otherwise crashed fatally. Four or five private pilots, however, made this same mistake.

Another fatal error made by three or four private pilots—but not by commercial ones—include attempting to take off and fly an overweight aircraft. Only one pilot, a private one, ran out of fuel fatally: on June 28, 1978, Arthur D. Meyers, age 28, committed the same error made by Willis L. Woods (described earlier), but without the happy ending. When Meyers ran out of fuel, he crashed his Cessna 170 into the Canyon near Cape Royal, killing all three aboard.

The upshot? While a known quarter of aircraft crashes and fatalities within and near Grand Canyon were due to mechanical problems and/or to faulty maintenance, the vast majority of crashes and fatalities were due to pilot error. This high proportion of fatal errors—as opposed to acts of God or unforeseeable malfunctions of aircraft—prompt a few questions.

The first might be: how are pilots trained before they fly over the Canyon? The answer for private pilots is: they were trained by whomever, wherever they got their ground school and in-flight training. In short, their in-the-air training was/is likely random and in no way uniform with regard to preparing them or honing their abilities to successfully meet the challenges posed by the dynamic air masses over the high canyon country of the Southwest. Not much will likely change in this situation. Hence it remains likely that future private pilots will crash in and around the Canyon in the same ways as their predecessors have done.

What about commercial pilots, especially the ones making multiple short, scenic flights each day, again and again, over the same itinerary? This is a tougher question. Just as we saw in the previous chapter analyzing Inner Canyon fatalities on commercial river trips—deaths to witnessed and unwitnessed drownings and disappearances and to fatal falls—the companies' safety records differ drastically. Several whitewater companies, for example, have been in business for three decades or more and have had no fatalities. Others of similar operational size have had as many as four separate fatal incidents. The same holds true for scenic air tour companies flying for hire over Grand Canyon but with far higher stakes. Some have had no fatalities. One has had three fatal crashes. Yet another air tour company has had five fatal crashes involving 44 fatalities. Of these five crashes, one occurred due to unknown causes, one to mechanical failure, and three flights went down (killing at least 36, but possibly as many as 43 of those 44 people) due to pilot error.

Several dangers and conditions specific to the Grand Canyon scenic environment conspire to make flying over it more iffy than flying over another

American wilderness of comparable size and elevation, say, Yellowstone National Park. First, flying over the uneven and unstable air masses created by the superheated hard rock maze of Grand Canyon necessitates repeatedly exiting updrafts and downdrafts. In addition to flying, pilots' take-off and landing environments often must be made at high density altitudes. "Density altitude" means the air density at an elevation and its prevailing local temperature and pressure compared to the density of air at sea level under the international standard atmosphere defined as being at a temperature of 59 degrees (15 degrees Centigrade) and a barometric pressure of 29.92 inches Hg (1013.2 millibars). Why is this important? Because conventional prop-driven aircraft fly "on" air much like ships sail on water. They gain their lift, thrust, and maneuverability based on how dense the air is. In general, the denser the better. Based on each aircraft's specific design, it possesses diminishing performance capabilities and ceilings in increasing density altitudes. Too high an actual altitude or too high a density altitude due to a combination of low air pressure and high air temperature can make aircraft unflyable. Commercial jetliners sitting on the tarmac at Sky Harbor in Phoenix, Arizona, for example, have been grounded en masse at low elevation simply because the air temperature exceeded 122 degrees in the shade and because this air was so "super-empty," or diffuse. At such high temperatures of dry air its density and pressure are so low that even a low elevation mimics the thin air found at high altitudes. Such air is so diffuse that the wings of the aircraft provide insufficient lift to get them safely off the runway and into the sky.

The problem over Grand Canyon is the take-off elevation is at nearly 7,000 feet, and everything in the air above higher yet. Air pressure drops by about one inch of mercury for each thousand feet of elevation gain. So at take-off the air pressure is already 23 percent less than at sea level. Add summer heat to this equation and the air pressure plummets even more. On top of this, over Grand Canyon the airmasses are often unstable, superheated, rising, and unequal even adjacent to one another. This also means that any aircraft flying a straight course from one air mass to another—as in off the edge of the Coconino Plateau to over Grand Canyon—may abruptly shift performance environments, sometimes drastically. To control an aircraft in such conditions, a pilot requires not only experience but thrust, or power.

Yet at 7,000 feet on a "standard" day a prop plane has only 75 percent of the engine power that it would at sea level. At 95 degrees at that same 7,000 feet, that power drops to the equivalent of flying at 11,000 feet, with only 63 percent of sea level power.

During the monsoons things get worse. The added humidity may further cut operational power during take-offs by another 1 to 10 percent. Far more hair-raising during monsoons, however, are microbursts of weather that consist of intense localized downdrafts. Often cues consist of streamers of vanishing rain called virga, or of expanding dust rings on the ground. But the vertical and horizontal wind shears within microbursts may instead be completely invisible, like mile-wide downdrafts (or "downbursts, see next paragraph) that can slam some aircraft onto the ground.

Monsoonal thunder storms—which occur during the prime tourist season—pose the worst wind shear hazards pilots face. These abrupt changes in wind speed and/or direction over very short distances can be horizontal or vertical (as in microbursts). The alchemy of thunderstorms spins off "first gusts" and "downbursts" (a.k.a. microbursts). The abrupt winds of first gusts can shift direction up to 180 degrees and blast at over 100 miles per hour as far as ten miles from the storm. Downbursts adjacent to the storm can not only reach speeds dropping at 720 feet per minute but, in so doing, may also exceed the climb capabilities of aircraft caught in them. Even high performance U.S. Air Force jets have augured into the ground due to such downbursts. The bottom line here is that such fierce winds can and do alter an aircraft's lift and indicated airspeed so drastically and also escalate the thrust requirements for escape so much that they can exceed the pilot's capability to recover. Such atmospheric phenomena may help explain fatal crashes during the monsoon season in or near Grand Canyon on July 26, 1967 (7 killed), August 3, 1975 (3 killed), August 21, 1981 (6 killed), August 5, 1983 (3 killed), August 17, 1983 (10 killed), August 1, 1984 (3 killed), August 2, 1996 (1 killed),

Clearly a vital performance element of all aircraft flying over Grand Canyon is thrust. Thrust allows for speed and lift. Lift makes airplanes go up. And engines provide this thrust. Increasing density altitudes, increasing humidity, and the possibility of microbursts and first gusts all demand reliable thrust for safety. Engine designs, of course, differ in thrust capacity and, significantly, in their price. Knowing that the Grand Canyon flight environment will predictably put aircraft abruptly into air masses demanding high thrust in order to retain a safe margin of lift and maneuverability, one might assume that all 11 companies of the air tour industry purchase aircraft powered by the most efficient and powerful motors, gas turbine engines, not piston engines, which provide poorer thrust and/or less reliable performance. Gas turbine engines, as used in helicopters and in the DeHavilland DHC-6 Twin-Otter fixed-wings which some companies use, provide far more thrust. To reduce the cost to the consumer/operator of the initial purchase, aircraft manufacturers install piston engines, but increase their thrust by also installing turbochargers. The problem here is turbochargers add to the aircraft's weight yet may not match the performance of the more expensive, reliable, and quiet gas turbine engines. Of course the faster a plane is traveling, the better its lift and gliding capabilities. But at what speed do most piston-powered air tour planes fly? Slowly. So that tourists can best see the sights below. Add to this piston-powered equation this low air speed and the plot thickens.

It thickens even more because many air tour companies have gone to twin, piston-engined planes. While this may sound promising, the reality is that most of these aircraft in most of the Canyon's summer flight environments cannot fly on only one engine. Instead, with only one working piston engine, they often can only descend in a controlled "glide." And the steepness of these "glides" may be exacerbated by increasing density altitudes. This "glide" capability has apparently seduced some pilots via a sense of added security which has prompted them to fly into air masses that pilots of single-engine craft have avoided through greater savvy and caution. Indeed, a look at Table 5–A reveals that some of the most serious fatal crashes of commercial flights here have been of twin, piston-engine planes "flying" on only one engine. Table 5–A also reveals that single-engine commercial planes seem to have a better record. As discussed earlier, among scenic commercial crashes only four single-engine tour flights have gone down fatally, killing 21 among crew and passengers. Meanwhile eight twin-engine craft have crashed, killing 81 passengers and crew.

With such variable and difficult flying conditions, one might conclude that the very best pilots for the job would be the very best pilots around. And one might further guess that the air tour industry would be preferentially hiring them. Instead, however, as local pilots have explained to us, many of the pilots who gain employment in the air tour industry around Grand Canyon are relative newcomers to the commercial scene; many are "flatland" pilots who are willing to accept the relatively low pay offered by scenic air companies and to endure the challenging flying conditions and back-to-back flights here in order to get their hours in to improve their resumes and flight experience record, and to thus make themselves more competitive in applying for more desirable commercial piloting elsewhere. In short, many air tour companies flying over Grand Canyon do not pay enough to attract and hold most top notch pilots possessed of solid mountain-flying experience. Nor do many potentially high-earning pilots want to live in the small, remote community near Grand Canyon. This is not to say that all air tour pilots are bad pilots; this is emphatically not true. Instead it is to point out that many of them stand on a low rung of the appropriate experience ladder.

Tellingly, the NTSB investigator and author of accident report NTSB/AAR-93-01 on the fatal crash of a Scenic Air Tour's Beech E18S on Maui on April 22, 1992 analyzed this crash against similar—and more numerous—crashes in and near Grand Canyon. He concluded (on his page 31) that some tour operators inadequately screen and train their pilots due to the lack of FAA requirements to do so—and that some of these pilots' flying errors prove lethal because of this weak screening. He further concluded:

> *I also agree with the majority that no single management action, no screening program, no training program can absolutely guarantee passengers freedom from risk. In the real world, one can realistically only alter probabilities; failure to take reasonable*

action to positively manage these risks also causes accidents. Since every pilot hired by an operator must ultimately pass through a sieve whose mesh size is set by management policy and practice, pilot screening and training programs effect real leverage on system safety. In my opinion, this Board ought to take every opportunity to bring its considerable moral authority to bear on the operators who are responsible for the conduct of such programs. I believe that we have missed such an opportunity.

Knowing these rudiments of safety requirements, one can see the wisdom of air tour companies that either pay for expert training to create "mountain pilots" out of "flatland pilots," or else pay well enough to attract extremely well-trained mountain pilots to begin with.

One example of how this pays off is revealed by the air record of the Arizona Department of Public Safety and Grand Canyon National Park Service. Their helicopter pilots—who fly search and rescue missions and maintenance runs—fly into the same scenic environment as the scenic flights above. But the NPS and DPS pilots also must drop into the Canyon, often in extremely challenging weather, and land their machines on frequently dangerous and unforgiving terrain. The NPS does this almost a thousand times each year. DPS pilots even do this at night. Tellingly, during the past 30 years from 1970 to the present, they have experienced no fatal accidents. Extensive pilot training prior to flying in/over the Canyon, NPS and DPS SAR personnel say, is what is responsible for their 30+ year, fatality-free flight record.

What has happened to improve the commercial scenic flight pilots' decision-making protocols and abilities and to improve the air tour industry's choice of aircraft type, maintenance protocols, pilot-hiring standards, and pilot training?

Closer federal examination of some of these issues was prompted in part by the June 18, 1986, incident (discussed earlier) in which that Grand Canyon Airlines De-Havilland Twin-Otter on a scenic flight collided with that Helitech, Inc. Bell 206 Jet Ranger helicopter over Tuna Canyon (River Mile 99.5), taking 25 lives. The NTSB and the FAA looked at this and several other crash histories recounted above and went to work to reduce their recurrences. That horrendous 1986 midair collision above Tuna Canyon led directly to Safety Recommendation A-87-91 and also to a congressional mandate sponsored by Arizona Senator John McCain. This passed as Public Law 100-91 on August 18, 1987, imposing flight restrictions at Grand Canyon and also at Yosemite and Haleakala (Hawaii) national parks.

Public Law 100-91 also spurred the FAA in 1987 to issue Special Federal Aviation Regulation (SFAR) 50-2. While prohibiting scenic flights below the South Rim—in most of eastern Grand Canyon—this complex regulation prescribed rules for operating aircraft specifically in the vicinity of Grand Canyon

National Park in a Special Flight Rules Area (SFRA) between Page, Arizona, and Lake Mead National Recreation Area, Nevada, and up to 14,499 feet elevation in flight free zones. Again, these new rules were spurred by the high numbers of crashes and fatalities mentioned above and were issued only for the Grand Canyon region, but the FAA intended SFAR 50-2 to examine and reduce the effects of aircraft noise on visitors and park resources, not to increase safety. To reduce noise, SFAR 50-2's Grand Canyon National Park Special Flight Rules Area restricts pilots to specific flight zones to allow other zones to remain quiet. Guidelines for these new rules were published in FAA Handbook 8400.10 Bulletin 92-10 to specify surveillance of the tour operators themselves. Despite all of this bureaucratic "control," however, an NTSB reviewer added, SFAR 50-2 "does not relieve the pilot-in-command from the responsibility to see and avoid other aircraft."

SFAR 50-2 also requires Grand Canyon operators to now hold 14CFR Part 135 certification, which, while restrictive, actually allows Part 135 commercial pilots to fly 2,000 feet *lower* than general aviation pilots may. Flight standards inspectors also mapped out and published new visual flight rules describing these companies' airspace, routes, and reporting points above the Canyon. The FAA next got to work to create automated weather reporting for the Canyon to help pilots avoid lethal environments.

One of the administrative problems in all of this is that scenic air tour flights—by definition—can only function in a VFR (visual flight rules) environment. With the exception of specifying even altitudes plus five hundred feet to fly west and odd altitudes plus five hundred to fly east, VFR flying is essentially open or "free-style" within the tour-flight routes allowed. Nor does the FAA directly monitor the interaction of VFR air traffic between the various operators and aircraft.

Sadly, as Tables 5–A, 5–B, and 5–C reveal, while the airspace in and around Grand Canyon seems to have proven to be as lethal as any peacetime airspace anywhere on Earth, the causes for its air fatalities remain all too mundane and all too human. And maybe too complicated to fully solve via FAA rules.

How serious is all this? Many of us have heard the oft-quoted "statistic" which says something like "you're far safer statistically to fly commercially than to ride in a car." Many of us instinctively respond to this assertion with, "It depends on who is driving that car." What is the reality here? True, aircraft have become far safer (partly because jet engines are safer than prop engines). Between 1964 and 1997, for example, the fatality rates on commercial air carriers in the U.S. fell dramatically from 28 dead to less than 3 dead per 100 million miles flown. How do cars stack up safety-wise? The U.S. Department of Transportation concluded in 1997 that cars have a fatality rate of 1.44 persons per 100 million vehicle miles driven. Airplanes, meanwhile, produce a fatality rate of 2.8 deaths per 100 million miles flown. Over Grand Canyon the aircraft fatality rate is higher yet, but the full statistics on total miles flown by all aircraft are not available and may never be.

As hinted before, aircraft noise is now considered by many people to be the auditory equivalent of DDT pollution in the natural sounds of Grand Canyon wilderness. As one traveler of literary bent wrote:

> From the river, another change is more wrenching. It floods the system with a kind of panic that in other animals induces nausea and sudden evacuation of the bowels; it is the descent of helicopters. Their sudden arrival in the Canyon evokes not jeers but staring. The violence is brutal, an intrusion as criminal and random as rape. When the helicopter departs, its rotor-wind walloping against the stone walls, I want to wash the sound off my skin.

Since the 1987 legislation, scenic flight helicopters no longer legally drop deep inside the Inner Canyon as they once did in the 1970s, so routinely and obnoxiously and by the dozens, as when the one above so disturbed Barry Lopez. But when they did do this, even most lovers of helicopters honestly would admit that they and their noise were heavily intrusive—even if not the equivalent of "rape." Indeed, the noise of low, overflying aircraft *within* the Canyon was not merely "intrusive," in some of the most scenic places it was virtually nonstop during daylight. These flights were so irritating that by 1981, Southwestern curmudgeon Ed Abbey joked:

> The prevalence of airplanes and helicopters in and above the Grand Canyon is a distracting, irritating nuisance which should no longer be tolerated by anybody. I look forward to the day when all river runners carry, as part of their basic equipment, a light-weight portable anti-aircraft weapon armed with heat-seeking missiles.

Ed Abbey's grumbling aside, restrictive changes in flight zones and altitudes in the Canyon, as intended by the FAA to increase passenger safety, were also intended to reduce levels of aircraft noise. Was such noise a genuine issue to more people than literary curmudgeons Abbey and Lopez? Prior to 1987, Grand Canyon NPS headquarters received one thousand visitor complaints about intrusive aircraft noise. So it does seem to have been genuine.

By 1999, U.S. Congress called specifically for a "substantial restoration" of natural quiet in Grand Canyon National Park to take place by the year 2008. This "quiet" is defined as 50 percent of the park being naturally quiet—no motor noise at all from aircraft or motor boats or vehicles—for at least 75 percent of the day (the "day" being defined as the 12 hour period from 7:00 a.m. to 7:00 p.m.). Based on these criteria, only 32 percent of the park in 1999 was "quiet." Even so, in 1999, NPS headquarters at the Canyon received only thirty complaints of intrusive aircraft noise. So, many visitors, at least, were less aware of non-quiet despite some aircraft noise carrying twenty miles. Yet even if the flight zone rules of 1987's *National Parks Overflights Act* were adhered to strictly, only 41 percent of the park on an average day would be "quiet." And on a day of peak use, only 19 percent. Aside from this degree of "quiet" or lack of it, however, the bigger question remains: By crowding more tour planes into smaller legal airspace, will safety improve? The answer to this is unclear.

This is because achieving "quiet" may be incompatible with safety *and* with current air tour businesses over Grand Canyon growing at 3 percent per year—up to 88,000 flights during the one year between 1997 and 1998. This computes to an average of 241 flights per day, or about 20 flights for every daylight hour of every day of the year over the Canyon. One new flight every three minutes! Predictably, several air tour companies, some of which are based in or near Las Vegas (and elsewhere), object to being limited to a quota of *only* 88,000 flights per year.

Should they? Are these flights a gold rush or instead are they a vital service for people who could not afford to see, or are physically unable to see, the Canyon in any other way? Thirty percent of the nearly 900,000 tourists these flights carry (for about $250 to $2000 each) are over fifty years old, and hence, by some standards anyway, maybe are less capable of seeing the Canyon on foot, from muleback, or by raft. Twelve percent of air tour clients, the air tour industry claims, are handicapped in some way.

Ironic in the face of this claimed 12 percent being "handicapped," Grand Canyon Airport is not yet compliant with the Americans with Disabilities Act (ADA). The airport, as busy as it is, has now become number two in Arizona, yet it still did not (as of December 31, 2000) have a wheelchair lift to embark wheelchair-restricted persons onto an aircraft. These lifts cost about $12,000 each. And while some of the scenic air carriers operating out of Grand Canyon Airport have allegedly grossed close to $100,000 in a *day* (a good day...), these same scenic air carriers refuse to buy these lifts. Instead, they repeatedly petition the State of Arizona to pay for ADA facilities on the basis that the airport itself belongs to the state. While this may seem reasonable, some state employees find this inconsistent with what they consider to be very low concession fees that these air tour companies pay in relation to the facilities and services that taxpayers now provide them for their operations. So, the issue of overall flight numbers, limitations on those numbers, and the rationale of what sectors of the public actually "need" versus simply "desire" such flights remains murky.

Finally, in spring of 2000, the FAA "slapped" Grand Canyon air tour companies hard enough to leave a red bureaucratic handprint. The FAA released new rules included in FAR 93 (Subpart U), to be enforced alongside the *National Parks Air Tour Management Act*. This additional FAR increased the "no-fly" zone from its existing 45 percent of the park to a far more restricting 75 "no-fly" percent. The FAA also raised the ceiling under which these rules apply to a new higher altitude of 17,999 feet (up from 14,499 feet). Again, these new rules were less aimed at safety than at restoring natural quiet to the region. Even so, perhaps the most significant specific restriction in FAR 93— beyond shrinking the available airspace from 55 to 25 percent of that above the park— is the unique, first-ever FAA rule to limit and freeze Canyon scenic flights to the 88,000 to 90,000 flights/year level that such companies flew between May 1998 and May 1999. (This rule applies only to scenic flights, not to the 30,000 Canyon overflights per year by civil air transportation, NPS maintenance, repositioning and training, and Grand Canyon West.) This rule limiting commercial tour flights went into effect in May, 2000. Although the rafting industry, the mule riding industry, and backcountry use in general has been limited by the NPS under a quota system for decades to prevent overuse of the park, the air tour industry has heretofore enjoyed limitless tourist loads in the sky. No surprise, several air tour companies discussed fighting FAR 93 in court with the claim that these new FAA regulations would drive them out of business.

In short, the $350-million-per-year Canyon air tour industry is a difficult enterprise to manage.

But for safety even more than quiet, managing it remains vital. In that more people have died flying in and around Grand Canyon during their quest (or their pilot's) to see it from the air than have died from all the other hundreds of mishaps in the Canyon *combined*—including falling from the rims or cliffs inside it, drowning in the Colorado, suffering fatal doses of heat or cold, being swept into oblivion by flash floods, hit by lightning or falling rocks or falling tree limbs—should remain a wake-up call.

But to be fair we should ask: Is the air fatality rate for the Grand Canyon region really all that high for an Arizona landscape? To try to answer this, we compared the air crash records for the Grand Canyon region with three other appropriate high use regions. We first compared the Grand Canyon region against that encompassing Phoenix, the seventh largest city in the United States. Phoenix not only has the busiest airport by far in Arizona, Sky Harbor International, it also holds several other private and commercial airports. Using all data on crashes posted on the Web by the National Transportation Safety Board, available only from 1983 to 2000, the Phoenix region experienced 16 fatal aircraft crashes resulting in 21 deaths. Meanwhile, during the same time span, the Grand Canyon region experienced 28 fatal crashes, 16 of these by private pilots and 12 by commercial, resulting in 43 private passengers and pilots killed and in 82 commercial passengers and pilots killed. This grand total of 125 people killed, which does *not* include the 1956, 128-fatality crash of TWA and United, over the Grand Canyon region is six times higher than the fatality rate during the same time period in the much busier Phoenix airspace.

Admittedly, the Grand Canyon region is larger than Phoenix. So, in fairness, we should also ask: Is the large Grand Canyon region's overall grand total of 355 air fatalities really all that high a tally for such a large chunk of *wilderness* landscape? Lee H. Whittlesey reports in his exhaustive 1995 book *Death in Yellowstone* that from the time of the first fatal air crash in May 23, 1943, when a U.S. Army Air Force B-17 crashed killing 10 crew members, until 52 years later in 1995, the *grand total* of all air crash victims in the huge, but similar-to-Grand-Canyon-region-sized Yellowstone National Park (2,222,000 acres, 3,272 square miles) is only 20 fatalities from a mere half-dozen crashes. During the same time span, through 1995, the Grand Canyon region experienced 53 fatal air crashes resulting in 345 fatalities, a rate more than 17 times higher than that in the Yellowstone region during this 52 year span.

A skeptic might object that comparing the Grand Canyon region's airspace with that over Phoenix is unfair due to its non-scenic nature and its being a radar-controlled environment—despite Phoenix's huge air traffic load. One might further object that comparing Grand Canyon with Yellowstone is unfair too, despite the two park regions' similar sizes and similar beauty, because Yellowstone experiences fewer scenic overflights. Hence we offer one more comparison. This one is with all flights, commercial-scenic or otherwise, over the Big Island of Hawaii (4,035 square miles) including Hawaii Volcanoes National Park. This region not only poses unstable and severe weather conditions and other flight hazards that challenge pilots, during times of impressive eruptions every aircraft of all of the ten or more companies offering scenic flights are swamped with clients. Indeed these island pilots have a reputation among some Grand Canyon pilots as "cowboys" who are "15 years behind the times" in terms of safety. How deserved is this? To compare crash histories we again perused NTSB records. As with NTSB records for Phoenix, those posted on the Web began on January 1, 1983. We looked at the records for flights from all scenic airports on the island—Hilo, Kailua-Kona, Waikoloa, Kanuela, and the Volcano golf course. For the nearly 18-year period between January, 1983 and August, 2000, the NTSB lists a grand total of 12 fatal crashes with 27 victims killed, including those on flights ditched into the Pacific. Comparing this to the grand total of 125 people killed over the Grand Canyon region during the same recent time period reveals that Canyon air crash fatalities are nearly five times higher than those over Hawaii.

So, yes: based on far less lethal air histories of these three other large, busy, challenging regions, the overall grand total of 355 people killed in 58 air crashes in and around Grand Canyon is high.

Perhaps this is an esoteric question, but some people wonder whether such a high fatality rate is worth that slightly different scenic vista. If an aerial perspective is so important to nearly a million foreign and American tourists each year, perhaps they might be better off if, instead of flying over the Canyon, they spent less money and simply bought the video and viewed its aerial footage. No one has been killed (so far) while watching a Grand Canyon video.

Significantly, few people who have been on the ground in Grand Canyon would agree that staring at the Canyon landscape from the window of a plane equals the experience of spending a few hours visiting it on foot. Indeed, many on-foot visitors to the Canyon have experienced profound revelations, even life-changing ones. This is not to say that flying a few thousand feet above the rims and over the Canyon does not offer one hell of a view. It does. That's why 25 percent of *all* scenic air tours in the United States fly over Grand Canyon. But in that it also is the one type of look that is most likely to kill, it also seems a far more risky view than any other. As one veteran Grand Canyon NPS/SAR pilot with 25 years in residence admitted, "I've often thought that the advertising phrase 'the trip/flight/view of a lifetime' was, sadly, too often true."

While these final words on air fatalities may be taken as cynical to the American dream of making a buck at every opportunity, they do address a very important issue. One of lives or deaths. No question exists that the greatest single cause of traumatic human deaths in Grand Canyon has been due—up until the present—to crashing while flying over or near it for the purpose of an "easy" viewing of it. But what about that important question of whether the new, more restrictive flight rules contained in Safety Recommendation A-87-91, Public Law 100-91, and in Special Federal Aviation Regulation (SFAR) 50-2 of 1987 actually improved air safety over and adjacent to Grand Canyon once they went into effect in 1988? A final look at Table 5–A reveals that, while new FAA regulations and decisions may have helped reduce noise, the "safer" decade from 1988 to 1997 still saw five more crashes of commercial scenic tour flights, most not within the Canyon but instead while trying to enter or exit the operating airspace connected with Grand Canyon overflights. These five crashes killed 40 more people. Meanwhile eight more private pilots crashed in or near the Canyon, killing 21 more people. This total of 61 fatalities for the post SFAR 50-2 decade is no lower than the average air casualty rates during the previous three decades before SFAR 50-2 went into effect though, admittedly, more scenic flights flew, and did so in less airspace, during this final decade. One hopeful trend is that, as of December 31, 2000, the last fatal scenic tour flight accident involving paying passengers was five years ago, in 1995. Still, the question of what safety repercussions will result next from the FAA's year 2000 FAR 93, which will crowd those same 90,000 scenic flights per year into only 25 percent of the airspace over Grand Canyon, remains open. At least for now.

When *all* types of flights—scenic tour, private pilot, NPS maintenance and SAR, Coconino County DPS or Sheriff, US military, and commercial passenger and freight transport—are considered, it turns out that the airspace above Grand Canyon on an average 24-hour daily basis for years on end is penetrated by some type of overflight at least every minute! Making the Canyon below this level of traffic "quiet" is one big challenge. Making the airspace itself safe is a bigger one.

Table 5–A. FATAL AIR TRAFFIC CRASHES IN GRAND CANYON AND ON ITS ADJA-
CENT PLATEAUS. Codes for each category of flight are as follows: "*C*" designates a commercial flight; "*P*" designates a private flight; "*Ca*" designates a crash within the Canyon;
"*Pl*" designates a crash on the plateaus or rims near the Canyon. Fatality totals for each
crash *within* the Canyon are underlined. Fatality totals for air crashes atop the plateaus are
not underlined. Probable cause(s) for crashes are discussed in "Accident Details;" symbols
(pe) indicate "pilot error" and *(ppe)* indicate "possible pilot error."

Name, age	**# Killed**	**Date**	**Location**	*Accident Details*

C/Ca
United Airlines #718 x 58   **128**   June 30, 1956   Chuar Butte & Temple Butte
TransWorld Airlines #2 x 70   *TWA Super Constellation Flight 2 entered vertical airspace of UA DC-7 Flight #718 at 21,000 feet. Both were bound east out of LAX on a reasonably clear day. Pilots of both aircraft were 5 miles and 25 miles off course, respectively (to purposely fly over Grand Canyon?). Mid-air collision—both aircraft were in blind spots of each other—was witnessed from ground when the DC-7 overtook and collided with the Super Constellation and its left wing sliced off the Super Connie's tail. Both aircraft crashed inside Canyon. All 128 aboard were killed. Worst commercial, civilian air line disaster in history (until 1960). (pe) x 2. (see text)*

United Airlines DC-7, Flight #718 Passengers & Crew:
Captain Robert Shirley, 48
First Officer Robert W. Harms, 36
Flight Engineer Girardo Fiore, 39
Flight Attendant Nancy Lou Kemnitz
Flight Attendant Margaret Ann Shoudt

John A. Barry, Lt. Col. C.E.A.U.S.	Christopher Balsat
Phyllis G. Berman, 45	Rosemary Bishop
Stephen Bishop, 3 mo.	Gertrude Coyne Book, 62
Frank C. Caple	M. Barry Carlton
Carol Jean Church, 6	Frank H. Clark, 46
L. David Cook, Jr.	Elizabeth Crider
Jeffrey Crider, 5	Elizabeth Francis Doering, 63
Thomas W. Doyle, First Lt.	Walter M. Fuchs, 75
Stella Blum Fuchs	Noel Gottesman, 30
Jack Groshans	James Hadfield
Lillian Ruth Hahn	Eugene B. Hoffman, 26
Russell Charles Huber	Frances Robert Johlie II, 31
Donald F. Kiel, 46	Dee D. Kovack
Ted M. Kubineck, 37	R.O. Lasby
Sally Lou Laughlin	Joseph M. Lewis, Jr., Lt. U.S.M.C.
Theodore Henry Lyman	Carl G. Matland, 39
Dwight B. Mims	John J. Muldoon
Gerald Murchison, 51	Floyd A. Nixon
Elsie W. Osterbock, 60	Hugo Pekrhun, 80

John George Reba, Lt. U.S.N.R.
Russell A. Shield, 31
Fred Staeckler, 11
J.P. Tobian, Jr. Captain, U.S.M.C.
Stanley Jerome Weiss
Albert C. Widdifield, 50
Donald L. Winings, 32
John E. Yeager

Alexander Eugene Rosenblatt
Carl J. Snyder, 59
Thomas J. Sulpizio, 30
Albert Vogt
Peter White, 15
Roberta E. Wilde
Weslau G. Wright

TWA Lockheed L-1049 Super Constellation, Flight #2 Passengers & Crew:
Captain Jack S. Gandy, 42 (pilot)
Co-Pilot James H. Kitner, 31
Flight Engineer Forrest Dean Breyfogle, 37
Flight Attendant Tracine Elizabeth Armbruster, 29
Flight Attendant Beth Ellis Davis, 24
Harry Harvey Allen
Thomas Edward Ashton, Jr.
Robert Vernon Beatty
Martha Ann Beck
Stephen Robert Bishop
Connie June Braughton, 6
Esther Ellen Braughton, 9
Linda Kay Braughton
Lois Klein Brock
Lillian Estelle Carrie
Lawrence Zay Chatten
Sally Ann Cressman
Chester Arnold Crewse
Helen Colleen Crewse
Selma Louise Davis
Robert Earl DeLonge
Donald Lloyd Elentie
Mrs. A. Evans
Jack Silvetus Gandy
Virginia Elizabeth Goppert
Janice Tracy Haas
Mildred Rogene Crick Hatcher
William Wallace Hatcher
Janice Mae Heiser, 24
Harry Robinson Holman
James Joseph Jang
Wayne Gardner Jeffrey
Sidney Roland Joslin
Joseph James Kite
Linda JoAnn Kite
Sharon Marie Kite
Peachie Marie Kite
Marie Jane Klemp
Lois Marie Laxton
Michael Anthony Laxton
Mary Lytle
Claire M. Maag

Howard John Maag, infant
John Otto Maag
Donald K. MacBain
William H. Markey, Jr.
Rosalie Maude McClenny
Alice Emma Meyer
Andrew Jackson Nasalroad
Marietta Thompson Noel
Richard Curtis Noel
Richard Darling Payne
John Walker Payne
Monica Jean Payne
Richard Michael Payne
Robert Farley Perisho
Dennis Joseph Phelan
Neal Alan Power
Edward Merrill Reaves
James Henry Ritner
Jeanette Karn Robinson
David Karn Robinson
Geoffry Brian Robinson
Robert Earnest Sanders
Esther Fair Sharp
Robert Frank Sontag
Gloria Kathleen Gipson Townsend
Bessie Whitmen
Carolyn Ruth Wiley
Elizabeth May Young

C/Ca

| Jack Pittman, (pilot) | <u>1</u> | April 12, 1966 | "The Box," 4 miles N of Phantom Ranch |

Bell G3B helicopter used for cross-canyon pipeline construction crashed due to unknown causes.

C/Ca

| Tom Rumore, 24 (pilot) | <u>7</u> | July 26, 1967 | 10 miles E of Village at |

Charles Wilhelm, 38
John Wilhelm, 12
Steven Wilhelm, 8
Carolyn Wilhelm, 34
Herbert Roscoe, 42
Scott Roscoe, 17

"Duck on the Rock", 200 feet below the rim

*Grand Canyon Airlines scenic flight in single piston-engine, Comanche Six crashed into cliff during "relatively clear" weather due to unknown causes (possible mechanical failure) and burned. Survivors of two victim-families sued for "negligent and careless management." (**ppe**)*

P/Pl

| Stephen Eugene Pritchard, 27 (pilot) | **5** | November 1, 1967 | ½ mile W of Grand Canyon Airport |

Carol L. Pritchard, 27
Patricia A. Burnes, 28
Jeffrey Pritchard, 4
Stephanie Pritchard, 19 months

*NTSB concluded the pilot misjudged his altitude while circling the piston-powered Cessna Skylane in a landing pattern, then crashed somehow. (**pe**)*

P/Ca
Paul McDonald, 24 (pilot) **4**
Mrs. Paul McDonald
David Wilson, 31
Mrs. David Wilson

May 6, 1969   Western Grand Canyon
Piston-powered Cessna 172 vanished in Canyon. Pilot McDonald had 80 hours of flight time; he had not filed a flight plan. (**pe**)

P/Pl
Wilfred Dugan, (pilot)   2
Mrs. Wilfred Dugan

July 5, 1969   North Rim 18 miles SW of
               Jacob Lake
Piston-powered Piper Cherokee Arrow crashed due to unknown causes.

C/Ca
Joe E. Savage, Jr., 31 (pilot) **2**
James D. Savage, 18

July 29, 1969   Yaki Point
As Bell 206 Helicopter took off, its sling load of fuel caught in a ground obstruction. The cable failed to disengage and the aircraft was yanked to the ground and caught fire, killing both men hired for cross-canyon pipeline construction. (**pe**)

C/Pl
John Harper, 29 (pilot)   3
Richard H. Hamblin, 24
Wayne W. Wright, 20

July 30, 1969   3 miles S of Grand Canyon
               Village
Scenic Bell 47G Jet helicopter crashed due to one engine failing during final approach to airport.

C/Ca
Arthur Ranger, 45 (pilot)   **1**

December 15, 1969   Along Bright Angel Creek
Pipeline construction helicopter crashed in Bright Angel Canyon when a cable used to haul pipe was left dangling and became entangled in the tail rotor.

C/Pl
Russ Marsh, 51 (pilot)   6
Frederich Meir
Klauss Spann
Helga Grueger
Karl Schwartz
unidentified Austrian stewardess

March 26, 1970   near Wolf Hole, Mojave County
Grand Canyon Airlines flight, piston-powered Piper Cherokee 6 crashed, NTSB concluded, due to pilot's decision: "continued VFR (visual flight rules) flight into adverse weather" combined with pilot "spatial disorientation." Flight, which took off during a "budding snowstorm," was missing for four months. It was found 50 miles north of pilot's planned route. (**pe**)

P/Pl
Merrill Shepro, (pilot)   5
Margaret C. Nejdl
William Vickers
Martin Rutsay
Robert Kostro

April 16, 1971   1 mile S of Grand Canyon Airport
Twin-engine, piston Beechcraft was 257 pounds over weight, crashed shortly after take-off. Cause of crash attributed to "inadequate preflight planning by the pilot." by NTSB. (**pe**)

C/Ca

Wayne Leeth, 47 (pilot)	<u>10</u>	October 16, 1971	5,500–6,000 feet in Parashant Wash,
James E. Allen, Jr., 60			15 miles S of Mt. Trumbull

Florence Allen
Dr. R. Lynch
Mrs R. Lynch
Walter Pilgram
Paul Haack
Mrs. Paul Haack
P. Dosmond
Mrs. P. Dosmond

Scenic Airlines' twin-engine, piston Cessna 402 tour flight flew into early winter snowstorm with "clouds down to the ground" and crashed. Pilot Leeth had flown 600 or 700 previous trips over Grand Canyon. NTSB concluded no structural problem with Cessna; crash instead due to pilot's error of having flown too far into the storm. (pe)

P/Pl

Priscilla Diane Ryan, 29	2	July 11, 1974	immediately at the end of Grand
Ibey Teresa Spurlock, 20			Canyon Airport Runway

Piston-powered Piper Cherokee 150's pilot (Thomas Ryan) encountered difficulty on take-off due to apparently over-loaded plane, tried to turn around, stalled, and crashed, augering in. Pilot plus two other passengers survived. (pe)

P/Ca

Curtis V. Gwynne, 42 (pilot)	<u>4</u>	Jan. 11, 1975	Dragon Creek, 1,600 feet below rim

Patrizia Feretti, 20
Renata Feretti, 41
Nicola Feretti, 17

Piston-powered Cessna 182 crashed during clear weather while pilot attempted to turn inside a narrow section of canyon and struck a wall. (pe)

P/Ca

Edward E. Sedwich, 33 (pilot)	<u>3</u>	August 3, 1975	South Canyon, a side canyon in Marble Canyon

Cecil C. Allen, 40
Janet Allen, 33

Piper Arrow (piston-powered) crashed due to unknown causes.

P/Pl

Phillip Creese, 59	2	April 23, 1976	Old Grand Canyon Airport
Patricia Creese, 52			

Cause of plane crash (augering in at 45 degrees and doing so upside down) was unknown, but is good candidate for mechanical failure.

P/Pl

Bonnie Watts, 28	1	September 21, 1976	Old Grand Canyon Airport

Four people in a single-engine (piston-powered) Cherokee Warrior were on approach to the airport when the pilot over-corrected for an off-approach position. The plane stalled, crashing. Three of the 4 aboard survived. (pe)

C/Pl

Saax Bradbury, 33	1	November 13, 1976	½ mile S of park south entry station

Four people were in a Beechcraft Muscateer (piston-powered) when its carburetor iced up on take-off. Three people survived, 1 woman (Bradbury) died. (ppe)

P/Pl

George Lutteum, 50 (pilot) **5**
Henry Lutteum, 20
Lois Jean Garcia, 46
Stephen Eisel, 16
Michael Eisel, 7

June 25, 1977   6 miles S of Hermit's Rest
Rented twin-engine Piper Navajo (piston-powered) lost one engine and crashed, flipped over, and exploded in flames. Four survivors fled before the plane exploded.

P/Ca

Arthur D. Meyers, 28   **3**
   (pilot)
Waldo C. Cross, 33
Debra R. Nelson, 26

June 28, 1978   near Cape Royal
Cessna 170 (piston-powered) ran dry of fuel while trying to fly from North to South Rim, apparently tried to emergency land on a nearby mesa but crashed into the side of a "mountain." (pe) (see text)

P/Pl

Nancy R. Day, 39   **2**
William C. Post, 48

July 4, 1978   North Rim
Overweight piston-powered Cessna 195 crashed due to failure of pilot to compensate for high altitude take-off. (pe)

P/Pl

Ernest P. Buntz, 42 (pilot)   **3**
June Buntz, spouse of pilot
Ferdinand E. Buntz, elderly

December 4, 1978   South Rim
Pilot radioed that his aircraft was "icing up," then crashed. (pe)

P/Ca

Lloyd Weir, 59 (pilot)   **4**
Mary Weir, 58
Leonard Grayson, 61
Lucy Grayson, 56

February 19, 1980   near Powell Plateau in Crazy Jug/
                     Tapeats Creek area at 5,800-foot
                     contour, 1,000 feet below the rim
Leonard Grayson's piston-powered Cessna crashed due to unknown causes (possibly icing). All four aboard were killed on impact. (pe)

C/Pl

Richard T. Mierhouse, 33   **8**
   (pilot)
William Calhoun, 31
M. Parab
D. Parab
L. M. Parab
B. M. Parab
Haroko Miazawa
Sawaka Minato

July 21, 1980   near Red Butte, 2.5 miles S of
                     Grand Canyon Airport
A Scenic Airlines Cessna 404 twin, piston-engine sight-seeing tour plane crashed shortly after takeoff and burned. Investigation revealed intake of metal fragments into left engine from earlier error in maintenance/repair. (see text)

P/Ca

Gregory A. Mathes, 26   **6**
   (pilot)
Daniel Bolware, 18 (co-pilot)
Michael Bailey, 39
John Bailey, 17
Mark Bailey, 15
Matthew Bailey, 11

January 12, 1981   5 miles SE of Fraziers Well
                    (south of Havasupai Canyon)
Pilot radioed that single-engine (piston) BE-36 Beechcraft Bonanza was icing up badly, then he crashed into a 200-foot-deep canyon, a tributary of Havasu, while seeking a lower elevation less prone to icing. (pe)

P/Ca
Herbert Redd, 51 (pilot) **2**
Anna Redd, 51

March 1, 1981   upper Nankoweap Canyon/
                       Brady Peak (?)
Piper Colt (piston-powered) reported trouble 15 miles south of Page while heading into bad weather, including snow. The Piper crashed about 50 miles farther south. This was the Redds' second crash in the Canyon Area. The couple had survived first one, crash landing a Piper Cherokee 140 into five feet of snow in the Buffalo range in House Rock Valley 2 years earlier. (pe)

C/Ca
Joseph Horace Baldwin, 68 **1**

May 24, 1981   below Horseshoe Mesa, 3,000
                       feet below South Rim, 12 miles E
                       of Village
Pilot of Grand Canyon Airlines scenic flight Cessna T207 with 7 passengers aboard lost only engine (piston-powered) and crash-landed. Six were injured, one killed from Romford, Essex, England.

P/Pl
Barton T. Watson, 47   **6**
(pilot)
Doris Watson, 43
Kelsey Ann Brady, 39
James R. Brady, 40
Deanne Hulett, 35
Larry E. Hulett, 38

August 21, 1981   1.5 miles W of Desert View
                       Ranger Station on East Rim Drive
Single-engine (piston-powered) Piper Lancer "shredded" during a crash landing into trees due to unknown causes.

C/Ca
Glenn Miller (pilot)   **3**
Diane Doherty, 27
Frank Novak, 49

April 17, 1982   Lees Ferry
A Hughs 500 helicopter flying 30 feet above the river at Lees Ferry with an EMI Productions TV crew impacted its rotor with a tram cable at high speed while filming an adventure film "American Eagle." The airship disintegrated as it skipped for nearly 1,000 feet across the water. A third passenger, Laurie Gere, was rescued by river guide Dale Whitmore. (pe) (see text)

P/Ca
Bob Wakeman, 60 (pilot) **3**
James Huffman, 41
Grant Huffman, 5

August 5, 1983   Western Grand Canyon
Wakeman's Mooney 231 turbo (piston-powered) aircraft vanished during flight plan to overfly the Colorado River over Western Grand Canyon.

C/Ca

Wallace S. Gustavson, Jr., 48 (pilot)	**10**	August 17, 1983 below South Rim near River Mile 209
Enrico Annibali, 49		
Maria-Vittoria Magnani, 48		
Giancarlo Annibali, 15		
Luciano Annibali, 45		
Guliana Ranieri, 44		
Francesca Annibali, 16		
Federica Annibali, 13		
Stafano Annibali, 22		
Daniele Vernava, 19		

*Las Vegas Airlines' scenic charter in twin-engine (piston-powered) Piper Navajo Chieftain crashed over the Hualapai Reservation during a "severe" thunderstorm, "disintegrated and burned" 70 feet below the top of a Canyon wall at the 5,800-foot contour. (**pe**) (see text)*

C/Ca

Charles Houser, 50   **1**   December 8, 1983   River Mile 166

*Two Bureau of Land Management officials were illegally (by breaking Federal regulations) joy riding down the Colorado River corridor at Mile 166, less than 30 feet above the water. The Bell-206 helicopter's rotor impacted a tram cable at a sedimentology research site and slowly sank. The pilot and other passenger were rescued by researchers. Houser died of delayed-drowning several days later. (**pe**) (see text)*

C/Ca

David Bauer, 23 (pilot)   **3**   August 1, 1984   Grand Wash Cliffs
Richard E. Reed, 50
Linda Sue Reed, 38

*Unknown mechanical problem or pilot error (?) caused impact of scenic tour Fairchild-Hiller FH1100 helicopter with treetop, then cliff. Of the Reeds' two sons, Bryan, age 12, suffered serious injuries and remained at the crash site, while Kevin, a 14-year-old Boy Scout with a broken wrist and facial injuries, walked six miles from site of Bauer Aviation crash, overnight, to Meadview to seek help. (**ppe**)*

P/Pl

Davis Baumann, 42 (pilot)   **4**   December 15, 1984   near Dog Lake on North Rim
Michael Corey, 23
Debra Jean Radez, 21
Peter Van Horn, 25

*Piston-powered Mooney single-engine plane developed problems during a heavy snowstorm; Pilot Baumann reported the plane "was icing up and going down". The plane disintegrated upon impact. (**pe**)*

C/Ca

Don Nasca, 50 (pilot)   **2**   July 12, 1985   Navajo Bridge, Marble Canyon
Claudio Cassinelli, 47

*Helicopter pilot during film shoot for Italian movie, "Hands of Stone," was simulating machine gun fire at "hero" hanging from Navajo Bridge. Pilot rose too high from under bridge and allowed rotor blades to hit it. Bell 206 (?) Helicopter plunged 470 feet into Colorado River and sank in 20 feet of water. (**pe**) (see text)*

P/Ca

Willard K. Martin, 55 (pilot) **2**
Eric Martin, 25

September 17, 1985   Crazy Jug Canyon near North Rim
*Vintage piston-powered 1940s Piper Cub crashed after clipping off a wing tip on cliff face. The aircraft's low altitude (flying within the Canyon) was due to unknown causes. Both persons aboard were killed. (**pe**)*

P/Pl

Ben Blecher, 34 (pilot)   **3**
Steven C. Tabbert, 41
Jim Elton Bobinson, 49

January 8, 1986   ¼ mile W of Grand Canyon
                        Airport
*Rented piston-powered Cessna 172 with three Michigan men aboard vanished after refueling at Grand Canyon Airport and taking off just after nightfall and after airport tower had closed. Arizona CAP searchers found the Cessna 5 days later almost hidden, having crashed nearby in heavy timber and rough terrain. Aircraft had crashed less than a minute after takeoff in the dark. (**ppe**)*

C/Ca

Bruce Grubb, 27 (pilot)   **20**
James Ingraham, 27 (pilot)
Mr. G. Tholenaars
Mrs. H. Bek
Mrs. K. Mulder
Mrs. K. Vandeelen
Mr. D. Feiters
Mrs. D. Feiters
Mr. Kleinjans
Mrs. Kempin
Mr. H. Schlegel
Mrs. H. Schlegel
Mr. Pigi
Mrs. Pigi
Mrs. Pakkert
Mrs. L. Meissner
Marcus Christian
Katrina Christian
Sherry Goss
Jay Whittenburg

June 18, 1986   Tuna Canyon, River Mile 99.5
*Grand Canyon Airlines' gas-turbine-powered DeHavilland Twin-Otter on scenic tour with 18 passengers apparently entered the ceiling of the informal conventional airspace (between 6,401–6,613 feet) of Helitech, Inc. Bell 206 Jet Ranger helicopter carrying 4 passengers—both aircraft were flying in the blind spots of each other. Midair collision killed all 25 people aboard. (**ppe**) (see text)*

C/Ca

John Thybony, 39 (pilot)   **5**
Rudolph Held
Wolfgang Banmann
Wern Geibold
Henietta Pearl

June 18, 1986   Tuna Canyon, River Mile 99.5
(see above)

P/Ca

Don D. Safely, 34 (pilot) **2**
Gentry D. Safely, 4

August 14, 1986   River Mile 19
Pilot Safely (a.k.a. "Smedley") "buzzed" a rafting party at low elevation in vintage 1948 piston-powered Luscomb monoplane to "wave his wings." As he tried to pull up into a turn, the plane stalled and fell into the Colorado upstream of the rafters. Father drowned inside the plane 30–85 feet deep, son drowned in river. He was found 3 months later, 32 miles downstream. (pe)

P/Pl

Edward Vernon Brown, Jr., **2**
  42
Aaron Brown, 14

August 24, 1986   Grand Canyon Airport
Pilot, Douglas Pound, of single-engine piston-powered Cessna 172 carrying four persons crashed on take-off; he and his son survived.

P/Pl

Renato Ricci, 47 (pilot) **4**
Glenda Jewel Ricci, 43
Paul William Lasley, 46
Goldie Ruth Lasley, 45

November 11, 1987   ½ mile S of Grand Canyon Airport
Trying to make emergency landing due to engine troubles during take-off, the single-engine, piston-powered Mooney aircraft struck a tree short of the runway and crashed.

P/Ca

Charles Frederick Arnold, **2**
  Jr., 62
Wesley Frensdorff, 61

May 17, 1988   Vista Encantadora 100 feet from rim
Cessna 182 was under full piston power, but at very low altitude 500 feet below FAA minimum altitude. It crashed through trees onto rim at full speed at 8,400 feet due to unknown causes.

P/Pl

John C. Walker, 23 (pilot) **4**
Christopher Watson, 23
Jeff D. Yardman, 25
Charles Sivils, 23

September 4, 1988   Grand Canyon Airport,
After not being able to find a motel room near the park, private pilot took off at night "anxious to get home." Hours earlier this plane had been plagued by engine power failures. On this later take-off, Walker stalled his still heavily-loaded, piston-powered Cessna 172, 200 feet above the runway. It crashed, killing all four aboard. (pe) (see text)

C/Pl

Keith Crosson, 42 (co-pilot) **10**
William Welch, 47 (pilot)
Lorraine Lou Murphy, 75
Joyce Anne Jones, 52
Barbara Ann Marchand, 61
Eugenia Sheehan, 78
John Sutton, 65
Donna Sutton, 63
Helen Zuckerman, 64
unnamed Scottish woman

September 27, 1989   Grand Canyon Airport
Grand Canyon Airlines gas-turbine-powered DeHavilland DHC-6 Twin-Otter scenic tour airplane crashed as "co-pilot" lost control during his landing attempt. FAA concluded "pilot error" by co-pilot had "botched the landing." Both pilots and 8 passengers were killed, eleven injured as several seatbelts failed. During its first impact with the runway, the aircraft sustained damage to the right wingtip, possibly making control of plane problematic. Rescuers required more than an hour to remove trapped victims. Survivors sued for damages in excess of $9.3 million. (pe) (see text)

P/Pl

Chris Jones, 22 (pilot)   **4**
Tim Jones, 21
Terry Dewayne Williams, 21
David Ross Bennett, 21

February 16, 1991   12 miles SW of Jacob Lake, on the Kaibab Plateau, north of Grand Canyon near Kaibab National Forest

During a flight from Bryce Canyon, Utah, to Grand Canyon, the single-engine, piston-powered Piper Archer II encountered large pockets of bad winter weather. Radar tracking reports indicate the aircraft made several abrupt and drastic course changes, including about-faces, and attained a surprisingly high altitude of 13,000 feet. An on-board video camera recorded full cloud-cover weather, leading to the suspicion that the heavily loaded plane iced up. The aircraft ultimately went into a flat spin, in a possible emergency landing or fuel-less descent, and "pancaked" into the ground relatively undamaged. The landing gear remained intact. All four aboard were killed by impact. **(pe)**

C/Pl

Robert R. Matthews, 26   **7**
  (pilot)
Gabriela Erikas Hoerler, 26
Max Johann Krucker, 28
Doris Maria Kaelin, 26
Franz Lueoend, 29
Paul Lipscombe, 26
Gitta Lipscombe, 27

May 13, 1991   National Forest near Grandview, 4 miles S of rim, 10 miles E of Grand Canyon Airport

Air Grand Canyon single-engine, piston-powered Cessna T207A scenic flight crashed minutes after takeoff due to engine cylinder head melt, cylinder explosion, and subsequent engine seizure. The plane burned, killing all seven aboard. (see text)

C/Pl

Perry Smallwood, 44 (pilot) **5**
Daisy Boukobza
Yardena Solal Cohen
Marie Sarfati
Ester Suid

December 10, 1991   25 miles W of Grand Canyon and ½ mile S of Indian Pass, Lake Mead National Recreation Area

Las Vegas Airlines scenic charter in twin-engine, piston-powered Piper PA31-350 Navajo Chieftain returning from scenic overflight tour of Grand Canyon crashed while flying through a thunderstorm. **(pe)**

C/Ca

Boris J. Orent, 61 (pilot)   <u>**10**</u>
Frederick Klenger, 23
Sylke Klenger, 21
Rico Thieleman, 23
Kevin Scully, 37
Janet Scully, 35
Rolando C. Valdez, 36
Dahlia Valdez, 29
Jerald Strnad, 54
Jane McNitt Strnad, 41

June 19, 1992   Hualapai Reservation 25 miles E of Meadview near Lake Mead

Heavily loaded Adventure Airlines Cessna 402 lost right piston-powered engine, then lost control, went into a right spin, and crashed. Cause concluded by the NTSB was scenic tour pilot's error in not maintaining minimal air speed, but also due to maintenance shortfall in tank plumbing. **(pe) (see text)**

P/Pl

Ralph Murray, 70+ (pilot) **2**
Clara Murray, 70+

November 29, 1992   about 10 miles SE of Grand Canyon
Piston-powered Cessna 182 crashed due to unknown causes
(it had possibly iced up).

C/Pl

Alivia W. Moore, II (pilot) **8**
Wei Chen Chang, 22
Mei Chi Tseng, 40
Hsiao Chi Tseng, 17
Chen Chuan Chang, 25
Hui Chuan Chen, 22
Chiang Yu Hsuan Tseng, 48
Hsiao Fen Chen, 24

February 13, 1995   2.5 miles NE of Tusayan
A Las Vegas Airline scenic charter in twin, piston-engine
Piper PA-31 Navajo crashed due to loss of one engine. Pilot
banked into higher, not lower topography, possibly
lessening odds of survival. Seven people killed were from
one family. Mechanical failure was possibly compounded
*by pilot decision-making. **(ppe)** (see text)*

P/Pl

Jason Evan Cook, 25 (pilot) **2**
Sondra Schuler, 23

November 22, 1995   ½ mile S of Grand Canyon Airport
Cook had earned his pilot's license 1 month prior to crash
and bought his piston-powered Cessna 210 one week before.
Cook, with no instrument rating, took off from a runway
at night south into total darkness with no horizon visible.
He may have overestimated his angle of attack and eased
off too much during "correction" while having lost his hori-
*zontal orientation. The aircraft nosed into the ground.**(ppe)***

P/Ca

Paul Capek, 39 (pilot)   **1**

August 2, 1996   below Pima Point
Capek crashed his piston-powered Mooney 20 doing loop-
de-loops (seen by witnesses) in a restricted airspace. He
*had apparently deviated around a thunder storm. **(pe)***

P/Pl

Dedier Brullemans, 29   **4**
  (pilot)
Olivier Brullemans, 25
Savine Lory, 25
Yves Krier, 30

October 6, 1996   On Highway 64, 1.5 miles inside
                       Grand Canyon National Park
Rented piston-powered Cessna 172 wingtip hit a tree
during pilot's attempt to make an emergency landing
on the highway as he veered away from vehicular traffic
which failed to yield. Plane crashed and burned.

P/Ca

James Eldredge, 56 (pilot) **2**
Darla Eldredge, 53

April 2, 1997   head of Fuller Canyon near
                       8,800 feet and Point Imperial
Pilot reported "having trouble" with piston-powered
Cessna 210 during increasingly bad weather and diminish-
ing visibility. Then he crashed. Darla Eldredge's body parts
not found for 18 days, 100 yards from crash. Government
search for this lost plane and body used 102 people, took
5,814 manhours, and cost $130,000.

C/Pl

Colleen Littlefield, 31 (Pilot) **1**

April 1, 1999   Grand Canyon Airport
Littlefield, a Papillion scenic helicopter pilot on a training

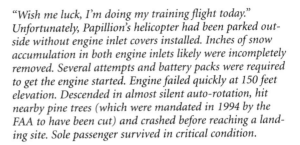

*"Wish me luck, I'm doing my training flight today."
Unfortunately, Papillion's helicopter had been parked outside without engine inlet covers installed. Inches of snow
accumulation in both engine inlets likely were incompletely
removed. Several attempts and battery packs were required
to get the engine started. Engine failed quickly at 150 feet
elevation. Descended in almost silent auto-rotation, hit
nearby pine trees (which were mandated in 1994 by the
FAA to have been cut) and crashed before reaching a landing site. Sole passenger survived in critical condition.*

P/Pl

Michael Regli, 39	2	August 3, 1999	100 yards from Highway 64 and
Christine Hostettler, 21			2 miles from rim

*Piston-powered Cessna 177B took off at Grand Canyon
Airport but failed to gain enough elevation to clear the
pines (engine problems?) and crashed. One survivor.*

The following entries are not included in text or the index.

C/Ca

Kevin Innocenti, 27 (pilot)	**6**	August 10, 2001	Grand Wash Cliffs at elevation
David Daskal			3,700 feet on 5,600-foot cliff on
Shiya Lichtenstein			BLM land 5 miles E of Meadview
Avi Wajsbaum			
Barbara Wajsbaum			
Aryeh Zvi Fastag			

*Papillon Grand Canyon Helicopters' American Eurocopter
AS350-B2 skimmed the Grand Wash Cliffs then crashed
(the fifth Papillon incident in 2 years). A local rancher,
Floyd Dwiggens, three miles from the crash site, noted how
tour helicopters has been "nose-diving" as a "thrill-seeking
type of thing." "There have been a load of them doing it,"
Dwiggins said. "They kick through here 100 feet off the
deck." Sole survivor, New Yorker Chana Daskal, age 25,
suffered a fractured spine and 80% burns. She told paramedics, "It got quiet and fell from the sky." NTSB prelimi-
nary mechanical evidence indicated the engine and rotor
were turning during a puzzling, almost vertical, straight
down descent to impact. An NTSB report concluded in June
2004 the probable cause of this crash was the pilot's decision
to descend too fast and too close to the cliff. A settlement
reached on behalf of Chana Daskal totaled $38 million.* **(pe)**

P/Ca

George Howard, 71 (Pilot)	**1**	September 8, 2002	Cataract Canyon

*Howard's Beechcraft Bonanza crashed within Cataract
Canyon due to unknown causes.*

C/Ca

Takashi Mezaki, 45 (pilot)	**7**	September 20, 2003	"Descent" Canyon near Quarter-
Joseph Hanna, 52			master Canyon, Grand Canyon West
Nouhad Hanna,			
Masami Kato, 24			
Makiko Hatano, 23			
Julia Hueyng, 33			
Wolf-Diter Mueller, 46			

*After an unusual 30–45-second hover during radio silence,
the French Aerospatiale AS-250 Helicopter run by Sundance
Helicopters made a routine descent from Hualapai Grand
Canyon West Airport toward an inner canyon landing pad
to deliver tourists for a boat ride but crashed into a cliff*

face. The aircraft had been serviced the previous day for problems with its main rotor—an apparently recurrent problem. No survivors. In October 2006, a jury awarded Makiko Hatano's mother $3.2 million in damages due to negligence by Sundance in not firing pilot Mezaki for his previously reported reckless flying as determined by NTSB interviews of previous passengers, some of whom had complained to Sundance. (pe)

P/Ca

Jerry Howie, 57 (pilot)   **4**   May 15, 2004   2 miles S of Tuweap on Hualapai
Albert Glenn Howie, 34   Land
Milena Stanoycheva, 26   *Jerry Howie, a Reno psychiatrist, flew his single-engine,*
Anna Dolinska Warszawa, 22   *"amateur-built" experimental plane, a "Lancer," out of Las Vegas to view Grand Canyon and climbed to 16,500 feet. 11 minutes later it disappeared off radar. Visitors at Tuweap, 2 miles distant, saw the Lancer spin to the ground and explode on the Hualapai side of the canyon. Howie's son, Glenn, and his fiance, Milena Stanoycheva, had experienced a fairy-tale courtship and were to be married in Las Vegas on the next day. Cause of crash is unknown.*

P/Pl

Thomas Redgate, 42 (pilot) **2**   September 2 or 3, 2004 1 mile SSW of Marble Canyon
Marianne Redgate, 40   airstrip
                                As discovered on September 4 by another pilot, Redgate, piloting his Redgate "Europa Classic" experimental aircraft N912EE, apparently ran out of fuel during an approach to the Marble Canyon airstrip then augered into the rolling desert terrain. The plane gouged a 75-foot swath and stopped at a 45-degree angle, destroyed. Being fuel-less, no fire started. Redgate had built and designed the plane, and Marianne was a Boeing safety officer, yet amazingly not only did the couple run out of fuel and crash, neither victim had fastened his/her seatbelt. (pe)

The following entries are not included in text, statistics, or the index.

P/Pl

Luis "Lucho" DeCastro, 44 (pilot) **4** October 25, 2006   25 miles NE of Meadview at 4,520
Laura DeCastro, 41   ft. msl "on rugged terrain" near
Nadia DeCastro, 7   Lake Mead
Trevor DeCastro, 4   *DeCastro flew IFR his single-engine, parachute-equipped Cirrus SR-22 (N121LD) from Lake Tahoe, violating military airspace, en route to Grand Canyon and tried to deviate around a cell of weather but into clouds during NTSB warnings of severe turbulence, icing, and low-level wind shear in his area. His final transmission to L.A. Center was a panicked "we got an ice…ice everywhere." (pe)*

Table 5–B. FATAL AIR TRAFFIC CRASHES IN GRAND CANYON (N=33) AND ON ITS ADJACENT PLATEAUS (N=30) LISTED BY COMMERCIAL OR PRIVATE FLIGHTS, AND BY HELICOPTER OR FIXED WING FLIGHTS. Average fatalities per flight of each category are denoted by ($\bar{X}$=).

Type of Flight	Crashes in Grand Canyon Aircraft crashed / Fatalities		Crashes on the Plateaus Aircraft crashed / Fatalities	
Commercial Fixed-wing: (after 1956)	6	58 ($\bar{X}$=9)	7	45 ($\bar{X}$=6.7)
Commercial Helicopter:	10	31 ($\bar{X}$=3.1)	2	4 ($\bar{X}$=2)
Subtotal:	__16__	__89__ ($\bar{X}$=5.6)	__9__	__49__ ($\bar{X}$=5.5)

[Subtotal of all Commercial Crashes after 1956, both in Canyon & on Plateaus: **25** aircraft & **138** fatalities (X=5.5)]

June 30, 1956 collision:	__2__	__128__ ($\bar{X}$=64)	
Subtotal of *all* Commercial Crashes in Canyon:	18	217 ($\bar{X}$=12.1)	

[Total of all Commercial Crashes in Canyon & on Plateaus: **27** aircraft, **266** fatalities ($\bar{X}$=5)]

Private Fixed-wing:	__15__	__43__ ($\bar{X}$=3.0)	__21__	__66__ ($\bar{X}$=3.2)

[Subtotal of Private Crashes in Canyon & on Plateaus: **36** aircraft, **111** fatalities ($\bar{X}$=3.1)]

Subtotal of all commercial & private crashes:	33	260 ($\bar{X}$=8.2)	30	115 ($\bar{X}$=3.9)

__GRAND TOTALS__: **63** aircraft in fatal crashes in and around Grand Canyon, **375** fatalities

Table 5–C. PROBABLE CAUSES OF FATAL AIR CRASHES BY COMMERCIAL AIRCRAFT (N=27) AND BY PRIVATE AIRCRAFT (N=36) IN GRAND CANYON AND ON ITS ADJACENT PLATEAUS.

Types of Pilot Errors

Type of flight	Unknown cause	Mechanical failure	Flying error	Ran out of fuel	Flew into bad weather	Icing of aircraft	Overweight aircraft
Commercial*	4	8	10–11	0	4	1–3	0
Private	8	4	12	2	4	4	3
Total:	12	12	22–23	2	8	5–7	3

* Total causes for 26 commercial flights exceeds 26 because two crashes were deemed by NTSB to have been due both to mechanical failure and to pilot error.

Chapter Six

Lightning Never Strikes Twice: Freak Errors and Accidents

"Last piece of nature's handiwork he should ever behold" reads the title of a century-old article that records the first known death in Grand Canyon caused by lightning. On July 25, 1895—monsoon season—Blachley H. Porter, age 18, from Connecticut, hiked several miles with his brother, Louis, and their friend Arthur Renton, from the Tolfree Camp (formerly Hance Ranch, three miles east of Grandview) to Bissell Point (now called Comanche Point). Although the day had been cloudless and unusually clear that morning, a sudden rainstorm set in.

The three hikers sought shelter in the Canyon under a projecting rock. Lightning flashed "all around them." Abruptly a blinding flash exploded in the three young men's faces. It hurled Louis Porter and Renton downslope and unconscious. Renton regained consciousness first. Still very disoriented, he dragged Louis upward and behind a log to prevent him from falling off a nearby cliff. Finally Louis, too, regained consciousness. It took both young men a while longer to regain their wits and to even realize where they were and why they were there. The two at last climbed back up to the rock where they had been "hiding" from the storm.

The two young men found Blachley Porter lying dead with his face turned toward an impressive view of the Canyon.

Almost a century later, on late Sunday evening of June 14, 1987, the NPS emergency rescue team was called to the Maswik Lodge. They found Robert Plsek, age 71, without pulse or respirations. This seemed a routine case of cardiac arrest. But the family soon explained that during that afternoon Plsek had been thirty feet from a man who was struck by lightning while photographing the Canyon. The man who had been struck directly survived. But Plsek himself did not.

As ideal as the north and south rims seem—if *being* struck by lightning is one's goal—lightning has taken fewer victims than one might guess. Overall, lightning strikes somewhere in the United States an estimated 40 *million* times per year. A bolt lasts less than one tenth of a second, strikes without warning, heats the air around it to 20,000 degrees Fahrenheit, and hits with up to 2 billion volts. These vital statistics imply that most people in America are doomed. But, in fact, while lightning does ignite about half of U.S. forest fires, it kills only a few people. And, again, the few people struck fatally at Grand Canyon by these huge electrical discharges from the sky have all been men. Possible reasons for such a non-random gender death from such a random source include more men than women placing themselves outside during storm seasons to begin with and fewer men than women taking cover when thunderstorms strike.

On May 13, 1993, for example, Daniel Mark Caesar, age 21, was struck by lightning and killed while hiking the Tanner Trail within the Canyon. CPR by his two companions was ineffective.

On September 11, 1997, a mere hour or so after a flash flood killed the Morans while hiking in Phantom Creek—and almost in view of the flood that killed them—lightning struck two people on the South Rim a few miles to the south. The two visitors, Heinrich Parvicini, age 26, and Jasmine Mischke, age 24, were from Germany. The two were sitting on a rock at Mojave Point, west of Grand Canyon Village. Weather throughout that day had been cloudy with scattered thunderstorms.

The German couple had chosen a perch at Mojave Point that was exposed. Too exposed. Lightning struck Parvicini directly, causing instant cardiac arrest. Mischke was hit indirectly, causing first- and second-degree burns over ten percent of her body. Bystanders performed CPR on Parvicini until NPS rangers arrived to provide life support. Happily, Parvicini regained cardiac function. Emergency medical personnel evacuated Parvicini to Flagstaff Medical Center where, the next morning, he was listed in fair condition.

Less than a year later lightning struck another visitor. On July 11, 1998, Stuart Wire, a 44-year-old tourist from London, stood and gazed over the Canyon as millions had done before him. It was 4:00 p.m. Wire stood at the guard rail at Lipan Point Overlook near Desert View. Wire peered at a tiny rectangle of Canyon within the tiny field of view offered by his video camera. Then he panned the Canyon to videotape his experience of "the Canyon during a thunderstorm."

Wire's wife stood beside him. Three other people also stood next to the same guardrail.

When the lightning bolt struck, the blast knocked everyone off their feet. Each person landed jarringly several feet away. The good news was that no one had been blasted over the rim into the abyss. The bad news was that the bolt of lightning had struck Wire directly on the top of his head.

It burned his hair and ruptured his eardrum, filling his ear canal with blood. The bolt traveled down the left side of Wire's face, causing first degree burns down to his neck. Crossing the left side of his chest, it next blew open his shirt to leave a long gash of burnt fabric and melted or missing buttons. It next singed the hair on his chest and burned the underlying skin. The bolt exited through the left front pocket of Wire's shorts, blowing a hole through the pocket, melting the zipper, and causing second degree burns to the skin beneath.

Wire collapsed onto the Kaibab Limestone as lifeless as the stone itself. His wife, trying to collect her senses, saw him lying motionless. She looked and listened for respirations. There were none. Panicked, she started CPR. Wire quickly woke up, as if in a CPR training film. But he seemed stunned.

Bystanders notified EMS officials. All the victims were taken to the Grand Canyon Clinic for examination. Amazingly, none of the victims was seriously injured.

How likely is it to be struck by lightning in Grand Canyon? In the past 41 years (since 1959), 62 people have been struck and killed by lightning in the entire state of Arizona. In the Inner Gorge of Grand Canyon near the river none have been struck and killed—although, granted, Daniel Mark Caesar *was* killed while hiking an open section of the Tanner Trail, miles from the river. By standing on open, exposed salients near or on the Canyon's rims, people inadvertently act as lightning rods. And the risk of being struck in such places during thunderstorm activity is predictably higher. Just as some people do win the lottery, some people are struck. Unlike players in the lottery, however, a person who chooses to stand as a potential lightning rod on open, projecting points in the higher elevations of Grand Canyon can definitely increase his/her odds of "winning."

Rock Falls

One of the most commonly asked questions by first timers floating the Colorado River at the base of miles and miles of cliffs and slopes littered with a trillion tons of loose rock lying at its angle of repose is, "Have you ever seen a rock fall?"

The honest answer given by most veteran guides is "yes, but not very often." This is usually followed by an explanation of why rocks fall, spalling, flash flooding, animals (humans included) setting a fall in motion, or, a favorite, frost-heaving. This is a process in which water in cracks or in spaces between rocks freezes, expands, thaws, and freezes and expands again in a cycle that ultimately wedges rock off a face or pushes boulders off their balancing points, making them fall. Sometimes they roll and fall for thousands of feet during which they convince other rocks to join them.

Of course, in the back of many peoples' minds is the second question:

"Aren't rock falls dangerous?"

Although it is possible to spend six months in the Canyon and see nothing solid larger than a grain of sand move, rocks frequently do fall somewhere in Grand Canyon, and more so during winter due to frost-heaving. Indeed, at least 1,000 cubic miles of rock over the past 20 to 30 million years have fallen here in one way or another—or no Grand Canyon would exist. But what are the odds of being in the wrong place at the wrong time so as to be hit by a rock fall? Incredibly low—but not nonexistent.

As Table 6 shows, the earliest known fatality due to a rock fall was of a miner. Prospectors William H. Ashurst, age 57, and J. Marshall both had worked in the 1890s in mining ventures with the colorful "Captain" John T. Hance, the first permanent white resident of the Canyon's South Rim (Hance was also a hosteler and a teller to tourists of the tallest Canyon tales ever told.) On January 18, 1901, after having discovered rich copper ore near Number Seven copper mine, Ashurst went prospecting yet again with the idea that he and Hance might still haul even richer paydirt out of the Canyon.

This time, alone near a mineral claim three miles downriver from Lone Tree Canyon (River Mile 84), Ashurst's keen eye roved the mineral deposits that he and Hance had thought promising in the general vicinity of River Mile 87 (near Cremation Canyon). Out of the blue, a rock fall, not mining related, caught him.

Hance did not find Ashurst until 49 days later, pinned to the ground by a slab of Vishnu Schist. Hance was appalled to see that his partner had apparently suffered a prolonged death.

Interestingly, Ashurst's son, Senator Henry Fountain Ashurst, played the key role, along with Senator Carl Hayden, in obtaining national park status for Grand Canyon. The two men introduced numerous bills—in the 63rd, 64th, and 65th congresses—to gazette the Canyon as a park. Not inclined to give up on this, Ashurst kept trying, eventually introducing S-390 on April 4, 1917. This legislation finally passed in 1919 (this success was ironic in that so many miners opposed national park status for Grand Canyon).

Hance buried William H. Ashurst's body near where he had found it. Ashurst's body remained there until 1908, when it was exhumed and buried at the top of Bright Angel Trail. Around 1934, it was moved again to the Grand Canyon Pioneer Cemetery.

Again, the odds of being killed in the Canyon by a rock fall appear far lower than of dying by other causes. This is because during a random rock fall a rock must hit an otherwise "well-behaved" victim. In most other fatal incidents in the Canyon the victim himself or herself normally contributes to his or her demise to some degree. Indeed, it is the very helplessness and randomness of lethal rock falls that make them a terror for some people. That one rare rock fall happening at the right time could smash a hapless victim in that tiny, unpredictable, billion-to-one place smacks of Fate and the vengeance of an angry God.

Yet, as minuscule as the odds are of such an event happening in the few hundred square miles of Grand Canyon actually visited by people, when people *are* visiting, rock falls do kill people.

On October 20, 1968, Masayuki Konno, age 24, was visiting the Canyon from Tokyo, Japan. He and his fiancee, Junko Morimoto, hiked down the Bright Angel Trail. Konno was to wed Morimoto in a few days. The two young lovers were walking about a mile below the South Rim. A recent rock slide had occurred just above this point on the trail. The two hikers had seen a mule deer moments before.

Acting all too much as an agent of cruel Fate, a boulder rolled abruptly from above the pair and hit Konno in the head. He died hours later. This one in a million type of accident, recalls Ranger Vic Vieira, was precipitated by kids on the rim, throwing rocks off, "trundling," to try to create a larger rock fall/avalanche. Apparently, this worked too well.

On August 6, 1982, 57-year-old Ralph R. Voss was acting as boatman's assistant on a Hatch River Expeditions' trip. Mr. Voss' son, Jeff Voss, was one of the two Hatch boatmen on this trip. While escorting a group of passengers up the trail to Deer Spring, one of the two source-springs of Deer Creek (River Mile 136.2), at noon, Ralph Voss became separated from them. Fifteen minutes later, when next he was seen, he was lying pulseless on the trail. Although at first Mr. Voss's demise was assigned to a cardiac arrest, a subsequent autopsy revealed multiple broken ribs, a punctured lung, and tension pneumothorax—all consistent with death to an impact from a large falling rock. No additional evidence clarified exactly how this incident happened.

Fatalities from rock falls, like those from lightning bolts, are random but eerily spooky. Certainly in the tragic case of Masayuki Konno, the boulder that took his life seemed like something out of fiction, or even from mythology. The same is true of the agent of Tom Gregory Standish's demise. Standish, age 32, of Boulder City, Nevada, had hiked down the trail into Havasu Canyon with his fiancee, Jody Pollins. The couple had set up their small tent by a ledge in the Havasu Campground downstream of Havasu Falls.

Heavy monsoonal rains during the afternoon of July 21, 1990, prompted the couple to seek refuge inside their tent. At about 3:00 p.m., a boulder peeled off the cliff above and plunged meteor-like into their tiny tent. It struck Standish in the head, killing him instantly. Pollins was unscathed by the rock itself but plummeted into deep psychological shock.

On May 19, 1992, Rosalee Heaney, age 33, from Australia was hiking with three friends along the upper Bright Angel Trail, below Mile-and-a-Half House. Shortly after 2:00 p.m., Rosalee and others heard the loud thunder cracks of a large rock loosened by recent heavy rains as it dislodged and fell from far above. Rocks tumbled and bounced into space for hundreds of feet above the hikers and sounded like cannon fire. One rock the size of a grand piano whistled through the air, witnesses said, then hit Rosalee. It crushed her chest and knocked her down hard. Her respirations stopped almost instantly. Ranger Paramedic Keith Lober and Ranger I-EMT Ken Phillips noted that had she been standing even ten inches to the side, she would have been unscathed.

On October 15, 1994, members of a private river trip camped about two miles upstream of Phantom Ranch on a small beach on the left, upstream of Zoroaster Canyon (River Mile 84.4). The weather had turned foul. A very early winter storm had dropped a foot of snow on the South Rim. Nearly half an inch of rain fell on the Inner Gorge. Everyone on this trip camped along the river and huddled in their tents hoping for the weather to clear.

Amid a heavy rain in the pre-dawn light, Rhesa Collins, age 25, of Buena Vista, Colorado, lay sleeping on her stomach in her tent. Well above her a loud crack echoed off the cliffs. Rocks began bouncing down the steep walls of schist. One small boulder ripped through Collin's tent, and smashed her pelvis. Three other people in this camp were hit as well. Their injuries included a broken arm, crushed feet, and a bruised thigh. While extremely painful, none of these injuries was life-threatening, except Collins'. With her pelvis crushed and large wounds over her buttocks, she now bled heavily both internally and externally.

In severe pain, she quickly passed into hypovolemic shock. Her companions recognized how serious her condition was. But they had launched from Lees Ferry with no radio. Attempting to flash a mirror to an overflying aircraft was impossible during the storm. Collins' companions sent a fast raft to the Phantom Ranger Station (River Mile 88) to ask for medical assistance when the slower one behind arrived with Collins.

Collins' companions had placed her on a table as a stretcher. They loaded it and her onto a raft. They rowed her downstream almost four miles, through two rapids and in a drizzling rain to Phantom Ranch. Every motion of the boat spurred excruciating pain.

NPS personnel Patti Thompson, Frank Corey, and Katie Gaines on the scene reported that, upon arrival, Collins was pale, lethargic, and had a low blood pressure and a rapid pulse. She was bleeding to death. Even so, Thompson would say of Collins, "She was a little fuzzy, but she was a great patient."

The paramedics started Collins on intravenous fluids and oxygen. NPS personnel also tried to arrange a helicopter evacuation for her. But a flight into the Canyon cloaked by near-zero visibility from snow mixed with rain was too unsafe. For nearly six hours at Phantom, Collins' condition deteriorated, despite additional help by Rangers Todd Van Alstyne and Bil Vandergraff. In a few more hours, all these rangers knew, Collins would die.

With the first good break in the weather, the NPS helicopter succeeded in evacuating Collins to the South Rim. But the weather again became so foul that direct air transport to the nearest hospital 80 miles away in Flagstaff was again unsafe. A quick re-assessment of Collins at Grand Canyon Clinic revealed anew that she was in critical condition. X-rays revealed her pelvis had been broken severely in nearly a dozen places. A blood count showed she had already lost nearly fifty percent of her blood volume. Unable to provide blood transfusions, Clinic staff gave Collins more intravenous fluid to keep her blood pressure up, morphine for pain, and intravenous antibiotics to prevent infection. Clinic facilities at the South Rim were far better than at Phantom, but did not include what Collins needed to save her life. EMS personnel transported Collins along those eighty miles of road to Flagstaff. Once there, she received multiple blood transfusions and surgical repairs of her vascular damage and pelvis fractures. Amazingly, after some touch and go post-operative complications, Collins did recover.

As hideous as Collins' odyssey was after that rock fall, she was lucky. She survived. Around 9:00 a.m. on February 26, 1996, 49-year-old Randy Thompson was working on the NPS trail crew in the Tapeats Creek Drainage (River Mile 134). The crew had scattered itself vertically in the first very steep ascent chute that hikers take when hiking upstream into Tapeats Valley from the Colorado River.

A trail volunteer levered a prybar to maneuver a 400-pound, rectangular slab of rock to be used as a stair in the trail near the top of a chute. Abruptly the volunteer lost control of it. As the slab dropped down the chute, he yelled "Rock! Rock! Rock!"

Two other members of the trail crew working with Thompson below the chute heard the warning. They immediately moved to a safe location. Several people echoed the "Rock!" warning. Witnesses said that Thompson hesitated, as if in indecision about which way to move (he was not wearing his prescription glasses). He first moved to the left, then he changed his mind and moved back to the right. Then he crouched down.

The falling block impacted another boulder and split into two equal-sized fragments, each weighing about 200 pounds. One of these continued down the chute, the other deflected onto a trajectory about 45 degrees to the right.

The deflected slab hit Thompson's back in the right scapula, inflicting a severe crushing blow.

At first, Thompson, still conscious, told his companions, "I'm hurt bad." Thereafter he lost consciousness. Later he regained consciousness and reported that he felt no sensation below the nipple line and could not move his legs. He complained too of having trouble breathing as he coughed up blood.

Fellow crew member and NPS Wilderness Ranger Nick Herring climbed a mile up and out of the Tapeats drainage to place himself in radio line-of-sight with NPS traffic. Even so, calls to NPS headquarters proved frustrating. A snow storm on the South Rim prevented the NPS and the Arizona Department of Public Safety (DPS) helicopter from completing a rescue run. The helicopter did lift off and began flying toward Tapeats, but the rotor iced up and nearly crashed the aircraft.

Herring looked around him for inspiration. If the South Rim was now out of the question as a source of rescue, did another option exist?

The North Rim was overcast, but no snow fell yet. Winds gusted around Herring in changing directions in a "squirrelly," undecided way. He continued his emergency calls, hoping that someone from somewhere might be able to penetrate the storm.

Meanwhile Thompson's fellow trail workers strapped him to a backboard for stability then hauled him down to the Tapeats Creek camp to get him into a tent and out of the snow. Though warmer, Thompson was still very seriously injured. His heart stopped beating. His companions began immediate CPR. Almost miraculously, Thompson responded with a renewed heartbeat but with very labored breathing as he still coughed up blood.

Eventually, after 11:00 a.m., a Blackhawk helicopter from Nellis Air Force Base in Las Vegas piloted by Captain Paul Youngblood (later unfortunately killed during another flight) dropped into the Tapeats Creek drainage. At 12:42 this aircraft evacuated Thompson to North Las Vegas Hospital one hour away. Despite this heroic extraction by Youngblood, which Grand Canyon Clinic nurse Karen Vandzura aboard described as a foul-weather nightmare flight, Thompson died from his multiple serious injuries within two days. Youngblood, Vandzura, and crew were awarded Sikorsky Aircraft Rescue Awards.

The Occupational Safety and Health Administration (OSHA) issued three willful safety violation citations against the National Park for Thompson's death. The trail crew, OSHA alleged, "allowed risky work practices, had an insufficient communications system, and had inadequate rescue and evacuation plans." "The situation," said Frank Strasheim, OSHA regional administrator, "could have been avoided with reasonable planning."

Grand Canyon National Park administrators made changes to improve safety. These included supervisor "hazards analysis," satellite phones, EMT-trained crew members, and restrictions on participation by VIPs ("Volunteers in the Park").

Venomous Creatures

After spending thousands of days in the Canyon guiding commercial rafting clients and after spending thousands more days on the South Rim treating injured clients and other park visitors, we are convinced that the greatest irony in the emotional "contest" between visitors and the Canyon is their extreme fear of its venomous creatures as death-slaves of the Grim Reaper. As is clear in this book, the Canyon is a dangerous place. Its sheer, dizzying heights, its implacably rushing river, its relentless and sometimes lethal heat, aridity, and penetrating cold, its exposure to lightning, and its labyrinthine maze of heart-breaking, "almost" routes and cul-de-sacs that sap the final molecule of vitality from a hiker, all offer the biggest and most deceptive larger-than-normal-life array of fatal dangers of any place we know of. Amazingly, however, many people stare directly at these truly lethal dangers and worry instead about the Canyon's tiny nocturnal crawlers as its real dangers.

In defense of this fear of desert venom, it is true that there are few among us, perhaps none, who have not witnessed a Hollywood rattlesnake kill a Hollywood actor, or a Hollywood scorpion kill a Hollywood actor, or a Hollywood spider kill a Hollywood actor. And as a monkey-see-monkey-do species, we humans learn from what we see. And we learn to fear, often paranoically, those little slithering or crawling predators furtively seeking a modest meal under the cover of darkness so that they themselves do not become food for the raven or the hawk during daylight.

So how bad is it?

Of the ninety or so species of scorpions in North America, all but four of them exist naturally west of the Mississippi. Arizona has six of the potentially lethal ones. At least one of these, the bark scorpion *Centruroides exilicauda* (formerly called *sculpturatus*) seems not only to be the most common scorpion in the Canyon, but, in a bit of weird luck during the ecological draw, it also seems to be the most common nocturnal arthropod. Inconveniently, the venom of the bark scorpion is the worst in North America. It's a complicated mixture containing at least fifteen protein toxins, all of which are neurotoxic, and some of which are 100,000 times as toxic as cyanide. The bark scorpion can control, via fine muscle command, the amount of venom it injects. No surprise, its sting in humans can produce a severe systemic reaction with respiratory distress, particularly in infants and toddlers. But these scorpions are not Hollywood plot devices; in reality they are tiny predators equipped with poison evolved to kill very tiny prey and to discourage predators.

Even the rattlesnakes here, of which the Canyon hosts several species, were designed by Mother Nature to kill small rodents not much bigger than a desert woodrat—not to slay pumas, bighorns, or human tourists.

How many of the Canyon's millions of human visitors have been killed by these toxic-nightmare scorpions? Although pediatric mortality records from the Anasazi and Desert Culture hunters and gatherers before them have not yet been discovered among the petroglyphs scattered in the Canyon, recent historical records reveal the answer to be: none.

But a rough estimate by Inner Canyon rangers is that about one in each 200 summer visitors who camp overnight is stung. Nearly all of these unlucky visitors who likely failed to follow the basic rule of shaking out all items of clothing or bedding before packing, wearing or sleeping in them, however, experienced only minor neurological symptoms radiating upward from the short-lived pain of the sting itself.

According to Arizona Poison Centers, several thousand Arizonans call in each year to report envenomations via scorpion stings. But the vast majority of victims never bother to call. Either way, none of these sting victims died.

The last reliably documented fatality in Arizona due to a *Centruroides* sting occurred in 1964 and was of a small child.

But, if not scorpions, then how many of the Canyon's millions of human visitors have been killed by the Canyon's black widow spiders, brown recluse spiders, hantavirus, killer bees, bumblebees, so-called "fire" ants, occasional Gila monsters, rabies, and all its other little venomous, noxious, and/or parasitic denizens?

None that we know of.

But how many of the Canyon's millions of human visitors have been killed by all those species of rattlesnakes or coral snakes?

Again, none. The last known fatality in Arizona (as of this writing) to rattlesnake bite was in 1994. The victim was a "biker dude" who kept a western diamondback as a "pet." The pet nailed his "owner" with venom due to inappropriate handling. The biker had survived previous bites. But this time he had been drinking a significant amount of alcohol. Instead of seeking antivenin, the biker shocked his own bite site with a stun gun then hit the sack. And woke up dying.

Rattlesnakes have also bitten people in the Canyon. For an agonizing example, consider Virginia Rice, age 32. On June 25, 1996, Rice and another member of a private river party had just swum to shore after the boat they were riding in had flipped in Lava Falls. Grateful to still be alive, Rice dragged herself out of the frigid current. She climbed a few feet above the racing river onto the rocks along the left bank. Again, preoccupied with her narrow escape from that swim in notorious Lava Falls—and now feeling emotionally that she was safe—Rice neither heard nor saw the snake that bit her. But she did feel a sudden sharp, searing pain in her left leg.

She looked down and saw a rattlesnake recoiling. Not only was Rice's action in spotting it too late, it was also too slow.

Before Rice moved away, the rattlesnake struck her again, biting her a second time on the same leg, just above the ankle.

The pain was immediate. Rice's leg swelled almost instantly as blood oozed from the fang marks. Rice was appalled, shocked, depressed, and alarmed that she might not live to see another day. Drowning in Lava Falls suddenly seemed a far better way to shuck this mortal coil.

Once Rice managed to tell the other members of her party what had happened, they flagged down a commercial trip. The guides on it radioed out to an overflying aircraft to relay a message to NPS Dispatch for Rice's evacuation.

Two hours later, an NPS helicopter with Ranger Medics Marty Johnson and Matt Vandzura retrieved Rice then dropped her off at Grand Canyon Clinic. Rice's left leg was swollen and had hemorrhaged under the skin up into her groin. Her pain was excruciating. At Grand Canyon Clinic Myers and staff intravenously infused Rice with antivenin and pain medication then evacuated her to Flagstaff Medical Center. Luckily, Rice eventually recovered.

Other people, though not many, have been bitten in the Canyon by differ-ent species of rattlesnakes (most of which have gone unidentified as to species). And while no one bitten has died, neither were any of them "improved" in any way by being injected with venom. Instead, many victims experience long-term problems. In short, rattlesnake bites remain serious business. And because most of us know this, most guides who work in the Canyon and most visitors in general have imagined snake scenarios and then tried to decide what to do about them to rescue themselves or their buddies.

I (Ghiglieri) had imagined several of these myself. But I had never imag-ined being a participant in one of the more challenging scenarios that I ulti-mately ended up being called upon to "fix." Working a Tour West rowing trip in 1987, we had camped at, of all places, "Rattlesnake Camp" (at River Mile 74 and named when a passenger on a much earlier river trip, who had been sit-ting on the porta potty, reached back for the toilet paper, and a rattlesnake bit him on the hand; amazingly, an identical incident would happen years later to another river runner reaching for the toilet paper at Tanner Camp). Anyway, a couple of hours after dark, I awoke when a lady on our trip appeared at the bow of my boat urgently calling my name. I asked her, "What's up?"

"A rattlesnake is coiled up on Barbara's chest. You've got to get it off before something happens."

Sure. A rattlesnake on Barbara's chest, I thought to myself. I've heard them all now. Rattlesnakes never coil up on someone's chest. That only happens in Gary Larson cartoons. But what if she was telling the truth? I suddenly real-ized that I would need something—a tool—to remove said snake. With no more time to think, I grabbed a short folding shovel, a G.I. "E-tool."

I followed the agitated lady to her and Barbara's nearby camp spot. Sure enough, there she lay on her back. She not quite all the way inside her sleep-ing bag. And despite the beam of my MagLite hitting her face, she was staring straight up into the starry heavens with the same permanent fixity of gaze as held by the inner golden coffin of young King Tutankhamen. On her chest a medium-sized rattlesnake had coiled.

Ever since having worked in rain forests and bush country of Central and East Africa populated with lightning quick mambas and absolutely lethal cobras, rattlesnakes have seemed to me far more like puppy dogs than true threats to life. Now, suddenly, this all changed. This rattlesnake's fangs were only a few inches from Barbara's carotid artery.

The handle on my E-tool now seemed to have shrunk. Even so, it would have to do.

As I approached the snake, it abruptly felt less satisfied with its warm snug-gling spot. It uncoiled. DO NOT, I tried to project mental commands to it (snakes being deaf), SLITHER TOWARD THIS WOMAN'S HEAD!

Instead it slithered toward her left shoulder, opposite from me and toward the river.

I circled around Barbara's feet to head it off. Gingerly, I slid the flat blade of the E-tool against Barbara's chest and under the snake's middle, but a bit forward. I knew that if I screwed this up, there would be hell to pay, and likely Barbara would be the one paying.

I lifted. The snake dangled off the E-tool but continued to slither forward. I carefully rotated the shovel to keep the snake balanced on it near midlength, This worked. But again, the handle of the E-tool was less than 18 inches long. And if this snake fell off, I'd have to recapture it—in a very agitated state—in the dark. Or else no one in this camp would sleep tonight.

Conveniently, the Colorado flowed past only a dozen or so feet away. What do you do with a hot-blooded, cold-blooded rattlesnake? Yes, it fell off my E-tool into the cold river.

Again, and contrary to popular misconception, even when considering the time before antivenin was available here, there have been no documented human deaths to rattlesnake or coral snake bites in the Canyon. In the United States as a whole, a whopping 40,000 to 50,000 bites are reported yearly involving nearly every one of the 115 species of snake in the country. Roughly 7,000 of these bites are from one of America's 19 poisonous species. How many of those 7,000 poisonous bites in the U.S. per year kill the victim? About fifteen victims (1 in 467) per year die. No surprise by now, 90 percent of bite victims are male. Moreover, 80 percent of bites known were inflicted on the victim's hand while he or she intentionally handled the snake. What this reveals is that most bites on humans are inflicted by the snake in perceived self-defense, and that men, not women, are the primary threats to such snakes. These statistics also reveal the one and only basic rule that a rational (non-snake-enamored) person needs to remember to avoid being bitten: Never put any part of your body—or your child's—*anyplace* where you have not *looked* in advance to check that it is not already a rattlesake's or scorpion's personal space.

Freak Errors and Accidents

Although this book so far has revealed that most fatal episodes in Grand Canyon result far less from Fate than from the decision-making of the victim and/or his or her guide, several spooky episodes have occurred. Consider the following one of August of 1912. Charles Bell and several other workers were blasting the face of the limestone cliff on the Bright Angel Trail to open a tunnel. Just before noon the crew set off five strategically located blasts. Only four exploded.

The crew waited about fifteen minutes. The fifth charge still failed to detonate. Finally, noon rolled around. Charles Bell volunteered to go get dinner ready. Inconveniently, the crew had to pass by the location of the hangfire charge to do so. They plodded up the trail with Bell in the lead.

Just as Bell reached the vicinity of the charge, it exploded.

The blast blew Bell into the air and off the edge of the cliff face to plummet about eighty feet. The impact broke both of Bell's legs and badly fractured his skull. Bell survived the errant blast for only an hour.

This kind of tragedy happened again in the line of duty a decade later. In 1922, trail foreman Rees B. Griffiths was working as part of a team building the South Kaibab Trail. On February 6, Griffiths decided to remove a large projection of rock blocking what he considered the perfect route near the suspension bridge. The crew detonated an enormous charge of dynamite here, blowing the offending bit of Canyon wall to smithereens. The placement of explosives had been perfect.

Minutes later, as Griffiths climbed to the top to inspect the blast excavation at close range, a "mammoth" boulder loosened by the blast rolled down on Griffiths, carrying him down to the rocks below half crushed. Griffiths died six hours later in Camp Roosevelt (now called Phantom Ranch). After careful consideration, NPS rangers and trail crew gave him a proper Mormon burial, interring him "about five hundred yards west of the bridge in an alcove in the Archaean rock which forms the Canyon wall."

A memorial plaque near Kaibab Suspension Bridge on the north side of the Colorado River states:

> Rees B. Griffiths
> Trail foreman, National Park Service.
> Born October 10, 1873. Died Feb. 6, 1922 in Grand Canyon he loved so well, as a result of injuries received near this spot while in the performance of his duty in building of Kaibab Trail.

In some tragic cases, common sense has been well exercised, but Mother Nature herself has been in a foul mood. During the night of August 27, 1970, for example, Raymond James Hock, age 52, was camped at the Supai Campground. While sitting at a picnic table that night, gusty winds tore off the top from a nearby tree. The tree top fell on Hock, killing him.

If treacherous trees seem a bit much, consider that stalwart friend of humankind for the past few thousand years, the horse. The January 28, 1921 issue of the *Coconino Sun* tells a grisly tale of horses losing it.

> The first serious accident in the history of the Bright Angel Trail at the Grand Canyon occurred Friday morning when three pack horses loaded with hay, grain, provisions, bedding, and 116 pounds of TNT for the construction camp at the foot of the trail, where the National Park Service is engaged in the erection of a bridge across the Colorado River, went over the wall of the canyon and perished on the rocks below.
> Among the horses was a black one recently acquired by

*Superintendent D. L. Raeburn. This horse was unaccustomed to the
trail and had acted badly on a previous trip. In rounding the first
curve immediately below the Kolb Brothers' studio it is supposed
either that the pack slipped upon the horse or that he was accidentally prodded from behind, whereupon he turned, reared and
plunged off of the trail.*

*The three horses were roped together and in its mad plunge the
black horse pulled the other two horses with it. The first horse to go
over landed at the second turn, 208 feet below; the second horse
landed at the fourth turn, 350 feet below; while the third horse did
not stop until it had reached the sixth turn in the trail, about 650
feet from where it took the fatal plunge or within a few feet of the
tunnel.*

The TNT did not explode....

Oddly, in view of the danger of nearly every other means of getting into or
out of or over the Canyon, the mules and the horses carrying people up and
down on the Kaibab and Bright Angel trails offer a near miracle of safety.
Among many hikers of the Bright Angel and Kaibab trails, mules are the Big
Uglies. They hog the trail; they block the trail; they pee copiously at every
switchback to create lakes of urine; and they poop prodigious piles of gooey
green globs of odoriferous, foot-clinging nastiness all over the trail. Worse yet,
the dudes who ride them don't have to grunt and huff and puff and suffer the
virtuous pains and sweat of the far more noble hikers who haul themselves
and their gear up and down these trails honestly on their own two Nikes.

On the other side of the coin, riding a mule into the Canyon is a symbolic
journey from the Old West. The rides possess an extraordinary allure. For city-
slicker "dudes" yearning to play cowboy in an Old West setting, riding a mule
down the Bright Angel Trail has no equal. For a century now, mules have been
hauling supplies for miners, hauling construction materials and food for the
Park Service and Fred Harvey concession, and so on. And for scores of years,
they have carried dudes as well—and have done so with a better record of success than any other mode of Canyon transport.

In terms of fatalities, some people would claim the mules have a perfect
record. The mules themselves, were they to be interviewed, might offer a
slightly different definition of "perfect."

Consider March 25, 1991. It had snowed hard during the night. Then it
snowed even more during the day. The wind howled, creating big drifts on the
Bright Angel Trail. To cap it all off, fog set in, swirling with the wind-driven
snow. Helicopter flights became unsafe. But for mule packer Stanley Sloan,
these demons of winter were unavoidable. "Since I had to get supplies down
to the inner canyon people, such as the rangers, trail crew workers and maintenance, I couldn't let the snow stop me."

Sloan prepared his mules with good winter shoes to prevent their sliding on the trail. Ominously, however, the trail itself had become not only hard to walk on, but hard even to see.

Sloan headed down the Bright Angel Trail. But he stopped after a few minutes to radio Dispatch to inform them of his intent and of the conditions on the trail. Sloan explains what happened from here:

> *What came next happened so fast that it was impossible to correct the chain of events. My #1 lead mule must have stumbled in a snowdrift. Next thing I knew we were being pulled toward the side of the trail. I guess the snow gave away and I felt the mule string falling. I bailed off the mule to save myself. I had a long lead rope to my first mule that went under my right leg to the saddle horn. After I bailed off, the rope came undone from the saddle horn. And Susan, my mule, didn't fall.*
>
> *By the time I got back on my feet and on the trail everything had already happened. All the mules were in a pile in a small wash below the trail. They had fallen 200 feet down the canyon.*

Sloan ran down the trail to find four of his mules amazingly alive, but all of them, having been tethered together and yanked off, were in bad shape. One of them, Gail, had a ten-inch laceration in her shoulder and was "in shock from the fall." Amazingly she—and she alone—survived, being well doctored by farrier Dan Cook.

No idle brag, the mule skinners running tourists down the Bright Angel Trail to Phantom Ranch hold an apparently perfect record: No client among the half million or so taken has been killed while riding a mule. Those riding mules have been well chosen.

But they still obey the law of gravity. On June 17, 1951, Lee Smith and Lee Roberts were riding double as they headed down the Bright Angel Trail. Smith was a professional Fred Harvey Company guide/mule skinner. As noted earlier in Table 1–B, the mule that Lee Smith and Lee Roberts were riding was crowded off the trail by other mules. As all three of them dropped off the edge, Roberts leaped for safety and survived. The mule and Lee Smith fell farther. The mule landed atop Smith. The mule survived. Smith was crushed to death.

The Canyon seems to pose a bewildering array of dangers. Yet some of them are camouflaged, appearing far more innocent and friendly than a mule ride along a narrow trail etched into the face of a soaring cliff. On March 24, 1971, for example, a few friends from Bell Lake, Minnesota, camped under a rock shelter near Phantom Ranch. This era was the "tune-in-turn-on-and-drop-out" age when the use of hallucinogenic drugs extracted from Southwestern plants—as inspired in part by Carlos Castaneda's *The Teachings of Don Juan*—had become a cliché in the Southwestern scene. True to form, at least one member of this small clique of back-to-the-desert seekers decided to make a brew of the poisonous but beautiful trumpet-shaped blossoms of sacred *Datura*.

One of these campers, Anthony Krueger, age 20, quaffed a cup or two (Table 4–C) of the essence of the ten-inch-long white flower.

His first reaction was insomnia. The anticholinergic effects of the atropine-like alkaloids of *Datura* have been characterized as making the person who ingested it as "hot as a hare, blind as a bat, dry as a bone, red as a beet, and as mad as a hatter." This brew of *Datura* induced all of this and more. By the next day Krueger's behavior had taken a serious turn for the inappropriate. He talked for hours to inanimate objects and to nonexistent people—and he was acting as if both were responding to him. He tried to lift huge, impossible boulders. He ate dirt. Finally, he stripped off his clothes and tried to swim—or walk—across the Colorado River.

Ranger Stan Stockton learned of this and tried to stop him from entering the river. But Stockton arrived too late. So he turned and raced downstream to the Silver Bridge with a rope to try to rope Krueger or snag him as he passed beneath it. While a valiant effort, it was the sort of challenge that might not be successfully met even once during twenty attempts.

Five weeks later a group of hikers found Krueger's body seven miles downstream along the shore of the Colorado.

The huge trumpet-shaped blossoms of *Datura*, however, would continue to entrap seekers of visions. During late summer a half dozen years later (August 28, 1977), deputies received a call reporting a dead body on the trail between Hualapai Hilltop and Havasu Village. The victim on the trail was Web Jones, age 26, a Havasupai resident of the Village. He was indeed dead, but no cause of death was obvious.

An autopsy found that Jones had died due to having ingested sacred *Datura* blossoms, also known as Jimsonweed and "locoweed," the same notorious plant of the nightshade group that led to Anthony Krueger's demise. When properly cured by an experienced Native American shaman, *Datura* reputedly induces hallucinations or "visions." Even when properly cured, however, users of the plant risk temporary blindness and other ill effects, such as Krueger's insane hallucinations. When eaten otherwise, every part of *Datura* can easily be fatally toxic.

If these beautiful, white, trumpet-shaped blossoms seem a devious package for Mother Nature to have chosen to hold a hideous deadly poison, even more deceptive is the most beautiful creek in the American Southwest. On June 27, 1965, for example, Otis Brown, age 40, went swimming in this idyllic creek. He swam behind its most famous waterfall. Somehow, his two swimming companions said, Brown was caught, then trapped, in a "whirlpool" under and behind Havasu Falls. Unable to swim out beyond the falls into the mammoth and nearly placid pool, Brown exhausted himself and drowned.

On a screaming hot July 10, 1972, Frenchwoman Christiane Haag, age 22, paused from her hike and eased herself into Havasu Creek. As her entry point she chose the foot of Navajo Falls, a beautiful location by anyone's standards. Haag, however, went swimming alone. Caught by current that was more powerful and rock-strewn than it may have appeared, Haag lost control and drowned.

Toward the end of her day at Havasu with a Western River Expeditions motor trip on July 26, 1998, Sylvia Ann Leimkuehler, age 18, from Ohio—and ironically a lifeguard—also made a fatal misstep. She had just hiked with an 18-year-old male friend, Derek, and a 50-year-old friend, Kim, on the very hot, eight-mile round trip from the Colorado River to Beaver Falls and back (or almost back). At 3:00 p.m., right on time, the trio finally arrived, after a hurried and likely dehydrating march, at the rendezvous point of their Western River Expeditions' motor trip where they reunited with the guides, families, and several other members of the trip.

This shallow ford so near the river is a rendezvous zone for members of many such trips. It offers shade, ledges, a small pool to dunk in, and a beautiful view. Downstream of the ford is a waterfall. Not a 196-footer such as can be found upstream at Mooney Falls (higher than Niagara Falls), but a mere less-than-ten-footer. This picturesque falls, however, funnels the creek between two boulders long cemented in place by travertine. The creek here narrows to five feet wide. From this gap it plunges straight down to pound into a recirculating eddy pool, then feeds into a millrace toward another, smaller falls.

Leimkuehler now followed Derek and Kim across the ford. Havasu was flowing murky due to recent rains. The bottom was hard to see. Both males plodded across the ford ahead. Behind the trio, Western River Expeditions' guide Tiffany George sat and chatted with another guide. When she glanced back at Leimkuehler, George could not believe her eyes. George saw Leimkuehler floating face down, her feet aimed downstream, toward the waterfall.

Leimkuehler herself explains what happened:

> *Derek and Kim crossed over and I followed. As I was walking the water was cloudy and I stepped on a large rock or something. My ankle turned and I fell down into the water. The current was pulling me and I could not stand up. I tried as hard as I could to stand but the water was too strong. I managed to grab hold of a rock at the top of the waterfall and held on for a few seconds. I was looking across at my family and the others on the trip yelling for help but I could not hear them. The rock I was holding on to was very sharp and the water was rushing over my body with my legs hanging over the waterfall. All at once I went over and I do not remember anything for about 5 seconds.*

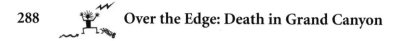

At first thinking that Leimkuehler was just drifting to cool off, George yelled at her to stand up. "When she didn't respond," George explains, "I jumped to my feet, screaming her name, and trying to get over to her when she caught the funnel that sucked her over the edge of the waterfall...she went over the top like limp spaghetti. I was horrified."

The recirculating "eddy" water at the foot of the falls—again opaque due to recent rains—held Leimkuehler in a Maytag effect, recycling her in a static location, tumbling, tumbling, tumbling under water.

George scampered to the base of the falls and scanned for Leimkuehler. Nothing. She shallow-dived in and tried to pull herself along the bottom against the current to reach the recirculating water where Leimkuehler must be. But, perversely it seemed, the creek swept George downstream. George tried again. Again no dice. She looked up at Kim and asked him if he had seen Leimkuehler.

Kim, in hysterics, sobbed, "No."

George, now as alarmed as it is possible for a human being to be, scanned the ledges for a less emotional helper. "Shut up!" she now hollered at Kim so that she could hear what other people were trying to yell down to her over the roar of the falls.

> *I must have been knocked slightly unconscious as I went over* [Leimkuehler sustained a fractured orbital bone and severe facial lacerations as she was knocked unconscious]. *The next thing I knew I was under water and my leg was trapped in something. I could not see the top of the water and realized that I was trapped. I have had lifeguarding and CPR training and knew that if I took even one breath of water in I would fill my lungs with water and drown immediately. I kept saying to myself, 'Don't breathe, don't breath in.' As I was doing this I was also trying to reach up because I knew they did not know where I was, and if only I could get my arms high enough, someone would see them and pull me out. At this time I was not aware of any pain or fear. I kept thinking, 'I am not going to die like this, not today.' I quickly realized that they were not going to be able to reach me and I needed to get my leg free from the rocks it was wedged in. I pushed and pulled and finally pushed one last time very hard with my right leg and felt my leg come free. Then I passed out from lack of oxygen.*

No one, George realized in dread, had seen Leimkuehler emerge from the Maytag pool of the falls. George asked another client to stand guard at the foot of the pool to play "catcher" in case Leimkuehler floated out while George was underwater trying to crawl again. She saw an arm break the surface then vanish, then wondered if she had really seen it.

Someone twenty feet above yelled, "She's out!"

The Good Samaritan catcher scooped up Leimkuehler. George and another guide, Kam, raced over and carried Leimkuehler to lay her on her back on a shelf of Muav Limestone.

"If I thought I was horrified earlier," George admitted, "I was truly horrified now!" Leimkuehler was severely battered and bleeding. One of her front teeth had been shoved back into her mouth. Her face below her lip had been punctured and torn. The travertine had lacerated her face and body in a random broad assault. Far worse, she was not breathing. Neither Kam nor George could detect a pulse. Sylvia Leimkuehler now stared sightlessly upward, pupils fixed. She had, to George's horror, "Doll's eyes."

George stared at her and thought, "Okay, cough and puke like they do in the movies." But nothing happened.

The next thing I felt was calmness and a sensation of floating but no awareness of my body. I saw faces above me in rows. They were faces of almost everyone I knew in my life including people on the trip. This seemed to go on forever until finally I could just see Kam and Tiffany's faces but nothing else, just black.

"You're not going to die on my trip, not today," George hissed to herself. George sealed her mouth against Leimkuehler's torn lips and exhaled hard. "I was amazed at how easily her lungs inflated. And when her lungs deflated there was a terrible moan, empty and hollow, yet she was still unresponsive."

George inflated her again. This time Leimkuehler's "eyes flew open wide as her lungs deflated but her pupils were still unresponsive. I was yelling at her, 'C'mon, Silvie, BREATHE!' It took about five seconds and she drew in breath, closed her eyes, opened them again, pupils dilated and constricted...."

Then I started to see more but I could not hear. They were yelling but I could not hear them or answer them. All of a sudden I felt like I was there again. I could hear them and see them and I felt tremendous pain all at once. For a couple of seconds I did not realize what had happened.

As Leimkuehler opened her eyes again, she said to George and Kam, "I had the strangest dream. I dreamt that you all were standing over me calling my name but I couldn't answer you."

As George listened to this, she admitted, "I could feel the hairs standing on end up and down my spine...."

It all came back quickly though. I remember my face hurting and not being able to move my leg at all. I felt so scared and upset I could not understand what had happened. Tiffany kept talking to me and telling me to calm down, that I was fine. She was holding me the entire time. She never left my side [even after having been carried to the Muav ledges above the river for the helicopter evacuation]. *Every once in a while I would feel as though my breathing was slowing and it might stop. I would start to panic but Tiffany would help me breathe by doing breathing exercises. I think that if she were not there to save me and breathe with me while we waited* [1.5 hours] *for the helicopter, I might not have made it.*

The NPS medical evacuation helicopter arrived and carried Leimkuehler to Flagstaff Medical Center. Sylvia Leimkuehler not only was lucky in her "choice" of rescuers, but also in her doctor; the physician on duty upon her arrival was a plastic surgeon.

No surprise, this traumatic "flat-line," as-close-to-death-as-one-can-get-yet-regain-life, experience left an impression on Sylvia Leimkuehler:

It changed my life in so many ways and it is not something I will ever forget or get away from. I still have nightmares and probably always will but I also have an experience that very few people in the world have. I have been given a glimpse into death and what it feels like just in the first stages. Death is not scary or painful or anything. I am no longer afraid to die and I feel that I was saved and given the rest of my life for a reason and until that has been fulfilled I will be here.

A bizarre—and still unsolved—disappearance in Havasu Canyon occurred less than two weeks later on August 8, 1998. A sixteen-year-old boy, Richard Tarr, III was a client on a Wilderness River Adventures motor trip with his family. Young Tarr apparently vanished from an unknown location along Havasu Creek. He was last seen less than a quarter mile upstream from the mouth of Havasu and near the same falls where Leimkuehler almost drowned. And, indeed this falls could also have trapped young Tarr, as it had done to Leimkuehler. Instead, his disappearance ultimately may have been into the Colorado River at Havasu Rapid. Mysteriously, no one on this trip at Havasu Creek saw what happened to Tarr. And, except for one of his shoes found floating in the creek, even after more than a year since his disappearance, no trace of him has been found.

Havasu is so unearthly in its beauty that it beguiles some visitors' sense of self preservation. On a hot July 10, 1983, for example, five-time Colorado State Heavyweight Boxing Champion James Gouge, age 27, decided to cool off. He and several friends had been hiking in Havasu Canyon and had stopped at Havasu Falls, a place of ethereal beauty. Gouge told his friends he wanted to jump into the 25-foot-deep pool—from the level of the lip of the falls, 115 feet up.

Several of his fifteen companions tried to talk Gouge out of this idea. It was way too high, they insisted.

But Gouge remained convinced that this jump was a desirable activity. He jumped the 115 feet. And landed on his back. The impact with the water killed him.

Fifteen years later, on July 16, 1998, David Matthew Kendig, age 41, had far better luck at Havasu Falls. Also known as Michael Lynn Jones, a.k.a "Coondog," the blond from Little Rock, Arkansas, had traveled to Havasu to visit a Rainbow Coalition event. Kendig, who reputedly had experience with cliff diving in Mexico, now found Havasu Falls to be irresistible. He swan-dived 115 feet into the blue-green waters successfully and emerged exhilarated. Next, about two miles downstream, Kendig stared in awe at Mooney Falls.

Kendig gazed off the travertine lip of the 196 foot plunge and studied his route. Yes, he was planning to dive off these falls too. Witnesses said Kendig walked to the lip and stared off then walked back away for his approach, then walked out to the edge again to recheck his planned dive repeatedly before satisfying himself that he had it figured out. Then he swan-dived off the dizzying lip of travertine in a seemingly slow motion, almost surrealistic descent of nearly two hundred feet. Kendig smashed to the bottom of the pool, 12 feet below the water's surface, where his luck ran dry. He died almost instantly due to the collision. A doctor at Havasupai Village pronounced him dead at the scene, and reported possible drug use by Kendig prior to his dive.

Many miles away from Havasu, in the sacred territory of their friends, the Hopi, two thrill-seeking buddies also pushed the envelope too hard. Jonathan Bolin, age 45, and Joe Walker, age 32, both from California, drove to the South Rim on a windy May 9, 1993. They parked near the edge of the cliff. The two donned their parachutes there, about 1,000 feet above the floor of the Little Colorado River Gorge. Their quest was to base jump into the Little Colorado Gorge all the way to that floor.

Like Butch Cassidy and the Sundance Kid, Bolin and Walker leaped together into space. A dazzling display of geology whirled past them as they plummeted toward bedrock. Each man deployed his chute successfully.

But the two men were so close to one another that their chutes entangled. Now whirling together and almost completely out of control, the lower talus slope 900 feet below the rim rushed up at them far too fast. Both men hit unyielding stone at high speed. The impact killed Bolin.

In closing this chapter, we are all too aware that it is unlike the others in this book. It contains acts of God back to back with acts of poor judgement. Hence its lessons are slightly more fatalistic. There is not much we can do about freak rock falls, for example, and only a little we can do about bolts of lightning. But we can easily decide not to jump 115 feet—or 196 feet—off the lip of a waterfall. Nor is it that hard to avoid entering Havasu Creek where it might kill us. Nor is keeping our bodies out of the small personal spaces of rattlesnakes and their venomous little fellow citizens of the desert that tough. Easier yet, we can claim to be the designated driver when someone offers us *Datura* tea. And we can just say no to base jumping with a buddy into the Little Colorado Gorge.

Table 6. FATAL ACTS OF NATURE AND FREAK ACCIDENTS AND ERRORS WITHIN GRAND CANYON (unless noted, all victims are discussed in text).

Name, age	Date	Location in Canyon	*Circumstances*

Blachley H. Porter, 18　July 25, 1895　Bissell Point (Comanche Point)
Porter was struck by lightning.

William H. Ashurst, 57　January 18, 1901　near Cremation Canyon
Ashurst was prospecting alone near a mineral claim. A rock fall (not mining related) pinned him, inflicting a lingering death.

Charles Bell, adult　August, 1912　Bright Angel Trail
Bell and other workers blasting the face of the cliff on the Bright Angel Trail to open a tunnel set off five blasts, but only four exploded. After waiting 15 minutes, Bell volunteered to get dinner ready. While passing the hangfire charge, it exploded. The blast blew Bell off the edge of the cliff face to fall eighty feet.

Rees B. Griffiths, 48　February 6, 1922　South Kaibab Trail
While building the South Kaibab Trail, foreman Griffiths removed a large projection of rock by detonating an enormous charge of dynamite. Minutes later Griffiths climbed to the top to inspect the excavation. A mammoth boulder loosened by the blast rolled down, crushing and carrying Griffiths down to the rocks below.

Francis Clem Cochrane, 43　September 13, 1933　Snake Gulch (?), Kanab Canyon, 12 miles from Hatch cabin
While prospecting, Cochrane was descending toward the Colorado River with fellow Los Angeles resident Gordon Smith when a rattlesnake struck at him but missed. The reptile frightened Cochrane so severely that he suffered a fatal heart attack, confirmed by autopsy. (not in text or text statistics or index)

Lee Smith, 50　June 17, 1951　Near top of Bright Angel Trail
Smith was a professional Fred Harvey Company guide/mule skinner. He was riding double with Lee Roberts. The mule they were riding was crowded off the trail by other mules. Lee Roberts survived; the mule and Lee Smith fell. The mule landed atop Smith, who was killed. (listed also in Table 1–A)

Otis Brown, 40   June 27, 1965   under Havasu Falls
While swimming under Havasu Falls, Brown was caught, then trapped in a "whirlpool," and drowned.

Masayuki Konno, 24   October 20, 1968   Bright Angel Trail, 1 mile from rim
Konno, visiting from Tokyo, and his fiancee—whom he was to wed in a few days—were walking beneath a recent rock slide. The young lovers had just seen a mule deer. Abruptly a boulder rolled from above and hit Konno in the head. He died with multiple fractures hours later.

Raymond James Hock, 52   August 27, 1970   Havasu Campground
While sitting at a picnic table, gusty winds tore off the top from a nearby tree which fell on Hock, killing him.

Christiane Haag, 22   July 10, 1972   Havasu Creek
Frenchwoman Haag eased herself into Havasu Creek at the foot of Navajo Falls **solo***. She was caught by current and drowned.*

Web Jones, 26   August 28, 1977   Hualapai Hilltop Trail
Jones, a Havasupai, had ingested blossoms of sacred Datura and died from its toxicity on the trail.

Ted Grounds, 29   May 4, 1980   Long Mesa west of Havasu
Victim was hit by tail rotor of Superior Aviation helicopter on the ground when it unexpectedly rotated on its axis. Grounds was about to ride on the chopper. (not discussed in text)

Name unknown,   July 14, 1981   Havasu Creek
Arizona Department of Public Safety Flagstaff logbook records a helicopter extraction of a drowning victim from Supai on this date but includes no details such as name, age, or situation in which drowning occurred.

Ralph R. Voss, 57   August 6, 1982   near Deer Creek Spring, (River Mile 136)
Voss, a swamper on a Hatch Expeditions' motor trip, became separated from group as **solo hiker***. Fifteen minutes later he was found on trail lying pulseless. An autopsy revealed multiple broken ribs, a punctured lung, and tension pneumothorax—consistent with death to an impact from a large falling rock.*

James Gouge, 27   July 10, 1983   Havasu Falls
Despite several of his 15 companions trying to dissuade him, Gouge, a 5-time Colorado State Heavyweight Boxing Champion, jumped 115 vertical feet into the 25-foot-deep pool from the lip of Havasu Falls for fun. Gouge landed on his back, fatally impacting against the water.

Robert Plsek, 71   June 14, 1987   South Rim
Earlier in the afternoon Plsek had been 30 feet from a man who was struck by lightning. The man struck survived. Plsek did not.

Tom Gregory Standish, 32   July 21, 1990   Havasu Campground
Standish was camping with his fiancee in a small tent by a ledge in the campground downstream of Havasu Falls to escape heavy monsoon rains. A boulder peeled off the cliff above and struck Standish in the head, killing him instantly. His fiancee was unscathed.

Rosalee Heaney, 33   May 19, 1992   Bright Angel Trail, below Mile 1.5
Heaney was hiking with three friends and heard loud reports of a rock loosened by recent heavy rains as it dislodged and fell from far above. A piano-sized rock hit Rosalee in passing, crushing her chest. Her respirations stopped almost instantly.

Jonathan Bolin, 45   May 9, 1993   Little Colorado River Gorge
Bolin and a friend base jumped into the Little Colorado Gorge wearing parachutes. The chutes entangled. The men lost control. Bolin died impacting the talus.

Daniel Mark Caesar, 21   May 13, 1993   Tanner Trail
Caesar was struck by lightning and killed while hiking. CPR by his two companions was unsuccessful.

Randal Thompson, 49   February 26, 1996   Tapeats Trail 1/3 mile from the Colorado
While working on the NPS Trail Crew in the first steep ascent chute of Tapeats Creek, a worker above Thompson lost control of a 400-pound rock. Upon hearing "rock!" Thompson, who was not wearing his glasses, hesitated, moved to the left, then back to the right, and crouched down. A 200 pound fragment of the block hit Thompson in the right scapula inflicting a fatal, crushing blow.

David Matthew Kendig, 41
(a.k.a. Michael Lynn Jones,
a.k.a. Coondog)   July 16, 1998   Mooney Falls, Havasu Canyon
Kendig was visiting a Rainbow Coalition event in Havasu and tried some recreational diving. Reputedly experienced with cliff diving in Mexico, Kendig dived off the 115-foot Havasu Falls and emerged from the blue-green waters unscathed. He next tried the 196-foot plunge off Mooney Falls. Witnesses said he studied the leap and seemed undecided, but then swan-dived off. Kendig smashed to the bottom of the pool, 12 feet deep, and died almost instantly due to the collision. A doctor at Havasupai Village pronounced him dead at the scene and reported possible drug use prior to Kendig's dive.

Richard Tarr, III, 16   August 8, 1998   Havasu Creek (or the Colorado River?)
*While hiking with his family on a motor trip run by Wilderness River Adventures, Tarr became a **solo** hiker and vanished. He is suspected to have drowned, either in Havasu Creek or the Colorado, but his body has never been recovered.*

Colin Hoagland, 57

July 22, 2000   Colorado River near River Mile 260
"Sandbar Alley"
Hoagland was riding in a empty, 45-foot commercial jet boat upstream from Pearce Ferry as the guest of the boat pilot to pick up river trip passengers. The boat hit a sandbar (the reservoir was at 1,199 feet, 23 feet below maximum) and abruptly stopped. The sudden deceleration threw Hoagland and his step-son forward. Hoagland hit an aluminum bench ahead of him. The impact caused internal injuries and internal bleeding to the older Hoagland. The boat carried no radio. Rescue was via the happenstance passing of a private trip, but the time delay, 3+ hours, was too great. Hoagland died 90 minutes after collision while still stranded on the sandbar despite more than one hour of CPR performed on him. (not in text)

Ben Bernal, 55

June 11, 2005   South Rim Trail, near outdoor worship site
*Bernal, from California, and a woman companion took refuge under a tree from a lightning storm. **Lightning** struck the tree and grounded through both people. Bernal suffered cardiac arrest. A good samaritan physician pronounced Bernal dead and discouraged CPR. He was resuscitated by rangers several minutes later, however, but died in the hospital.*

Chapter Seven

Suicide

"This is the best way out for you and for me. I'm going out peaceably and cleanly as possible. I love you all. Edward." After writing this, Edward jumped off....

No matter how you look at it, it is tough to find a silver lining on the cloud that a suicide leaves behind. In the U.S.A. alone, a land infamous for its rates of murder, far more people—at least 30,000 and possibly up to 100,000—take their own lives each year. This total vastly exceeds victims of murder (less than 17,000/year). In short, suicide is fairly common here—as it is in developed countries worldwide from Switzerland to Japan. And while America's rate of suicide may seem high, it is actually only a fraction of the rates in Japan and many European countries. Even so, America's suicide rate remains high enough that psychologists continue to argue over suicide's causes. They list depression, alcohol and/or drug addiction, unstable or dysfunctional families, antisocial tendencies, serotonin deficiencies, race (middle-aged black women, for example, almost never commit suicide), and also a family history of suicide. No one, however, has a reliable handle on what it is beyond sheer hopelessness that ultimately prompts a person to commit the final tragic act.

What makes suicide in Grand Canyon an important issue are two unique aspects. First, the Canyon, especially its rims, offers a spectacular, sure-fire, easy, and even a "Heaven-sent" opportunity to end it all. And, second, NPS rangers, Coconino County SAR personnel, professional guides, or even innocent bystanders in the Canyon who are called upon to try to rescue unsuccessful victims or to recover the bodies of ones who did succeed are often forced to expose themselves to significant dangers.

On June 15, 1980, for example, Edward Enzor Walters, age 36, wrote two elaborate suicide notes, one to his family and the other to the police. The first one explained that "the show received horrible reviews from the critics, myself included. All I've managed to do in my life is to bring distress and worse to others. The bad habits I've learned have simply become too ingrained to change at this late date." Were his body to be recovered, he asked further, do not send it back home to Troy, Alabama. Finally, after admitting that he could not interact successfully with people any longer, Walters concluded with the quote that opened this chapter: "This is the best way out for you and for me. I'm going out peaceably and cleanly as possible. I love you all. Edward."

Walters' letter to the police was twice as long. He explained who he was and how he had weighted himself down with heavy clothing and rocks and probably would never be found. But if he were, he added, check for dental records with his dentist (name and address provided). Once identified, he instructed the police whom to contact about his death and whom not to, providing more names and addresses. Then he explained what was good and not so good about his car and instructed the Coconino County Sheriff's Department to give it—and the food in the trunk—to someone deserving. Next he wanted the Sheriff's Department to find a worthy teenager for his camping gear, listing it and also a storage locker in New Mexico holding yet more stuff. The letter continued in the same last-will-and-testament vein—at great length and detail with numerous requests of the police to attend to this and that detail of his unfinished business. Then he apologized to the police, admitting that he would not want their job (especially, one might conclude, when they are being saddled with "clients" like Walters). He closed with his explanation: "If I could have found another way for me or another place, I would have done so. Time just ran out."

What all of this reveals are the common threads of complete self-absorption typical to suiciders. Apparently they often think they are solving other people's problems, not just escaping their own. How Walters "solved" everyone's problem was to weigh himself down with rocks, walk out to the center of Navajo Bridge (River Mile 4.3), and jump off. He plummeted 470 feet to the Colorado River.

In September, about eighty days later, Tour West boatman Michael Harris reported by radio that a private river trip had spotted a body floating seven miles downstream near Soap Creek Rapid (River Mile 11.25). A kayaker among the private boaters said he had found the corpse wedged under a snag along shore. It was decomposing and stank, but it was still wearing new hiking boots. He tethered the decomposing body to a tree with parachute cord.

But when NPS Rangers Sam West and Stephen Martin and Coconino County Deputy Steve Luckeson arrived by NPS chopper to evacuate the body, they could not find it. Finally the three SAR personnel helicoptered deeper into the Canyon to ask the original discoverer exactly where he had tethered the corpse. After being told the minute details, the rangers and deputy then located the body.

Because of fluctuating flows, the body had been exposed to air, ravens, flies, scorching sunlight, et cetera, repeatedly, then resubmerged. The decomposition was horrendous, and the recovery was anything but "peaceable and clean." The three SAR personnel managed to scoop and shovel Walters' maggot-ridden remains into two body bags for evacuation.

Yet not all suicide attempts in Grand Canyon have worked as well as Walters'. Consider the first known attempt, in 1922. John F. Finley, a thirty year-old elevator man from Cleveland, Ohio, was haunted by his father's attempt to commit suicide by cutting his own throat. This had failed, yet Finley's father did die later in an insane asylum.

Finley feared that his male heredity would ultimately overwhelm him. So to beat it, he joined it. But first he wanted to see Grand Canyon before he died. Just before he died.

Upon arriving at the Canyon, Finley walked in the bright sunshine to the Rim. The view was so spectacular and inspirational that he changed his mind. Life was too precious, he now felt, to simply throw away.

The problem with living, however, is that one needed to eat. And Finley was now dead broke. Realizing yet anew that living was hopeless, Finley decided that he might just as well go ahead with his original plan to commit suicide at Grand Canyon. Being fairly organized in his desire for privacy and anonymity, Finley removed all identification marks from his clothing. And even from his hat. He next tore the label off his cigarette box. These all attended to, Finley tested his .38 revolver by firing it twice at a tree. Strangely, the bullets failed to penetrate through the bark.

Resigned to nothing ever quite working right, Finley stood at Hopi Point for his final moment. But being fixed in his method of dying, he ignored the possibility of achieving a certain and easy death by simply stepping off the Rim. Instead he shot himself in his solar plexus with his not-so-powerful .38.

The bullet failed to kill him. Desperate and disappointed and in serious pain, Finley took out his pocketknife and tried to sever an artery in his wrist. The knife was too dull, or maybe his technique was faulty. Finally, Finley gave up on his attempt to move into the Great Beyond. Maybe he was afraid of heights.

Bleeding, Finley walked to El Tovar and sought medical help. A nurse bandaged his wounds. The next day, Dr. Felix Manning met him in Williams, from whence he was taken to the Coconino County Hospital in Flagstaff.

Like Finley above, Osan Kang also seemed like a figure from fiction. Indeed, Kang seemed a bit too strange even for fiction. He was born in 1913 in San Francisco of Korean parents. As an adult, Kang regaled listeners with tales of working with General MacArthur's intelligence staff during World War II in the South Pacific. In truth, Kang had passed a strict security clearance and had qualified as a language instructor—Korean, Japanese, Chinese, and English— for the U.S. Army. He worked for the Army off and on in California until 1961.

In the early 1960s, Kang registered as an older student at California's Reedley College. His fellow students found him dignified and charming. Student sponsors there, writes journalist Don Dedera, also found Kang "quick to borrow, free to spend, and slow to repay his loans."

As the 1960s became The Sixties, Kang's fortunes ebbed. He tried his hand at a number of trades—importing jewelry, investing in a radio and television station—but none produced profits. By 1965, Kang gained the sympathy of a Korean couple who ran a Washington, D.C. motel. The two respected and supported him. They even got him a job as a desk clerk at another motel.

But Kang's new employer soon fired him because he suspected that Kang was subletting his own quarters to patrons and pocketing the rent instead of renting to them the employer's normal rooms.

Kang appeared next in February, 1967, in Las Vegas, where he was detained by deputies on a bogus check warrant. The law released Kang when the Washington, D.C. bank informed them that they would not press charges. Kang stayed in Las Vegas for a month. He gambled heavily. And lost.

On March 24, Kang drove into Williams, 60 miles south of Grand Canyon, in a rental car from Las Vegas. There he tried to trade the car's jack for a tank of gas. When this failed, Kang tried to borrow money from a local motel operator. The operator turned out to be a Williams policeman. He called Las Vegas and learned that the rental agreement for Kang's car stipulated that it was not to be driven out of Nevada. Even so, the rental firm said, they would not prosecute Kang.

The policeman then countered Kang's attempt to borrow money by offering him a meal of plain food and a night in a clean, open-doored cell in the Williams jail.

Insulted, Kang refused.

Kang made a bee-line for the Williams Hertz rental car agency. On the strength of Kang's identification card issued by a high-security government agency, Hertz rented Kang a replacement car, one with gas in the tank. While waiting for the car, Kang talked of being a language professor and of being married to a woman who was a missionary teacher in Korea. They had two children, he explained. He was on vacation, he added, and temporarily out of funds. He was, Don Dedera reports, "witty, courteous and talkative."

Hours later Kang drove the Hertz car at 40 miles per hour toward the edge of Lipan Point. Kang must have done his homework. Lipan Point is well east of Grand Canyon Village. But of all the lookout points and scenic vista points, Lipan stands out in two ways. It offers a fairly good approach route during which one can accelerate on a level roadway without many trees in the way and with no guard wall. And it offers a thousand vertical feet of air immediately over the edge of the South Rim.

Kang and Hertz launched out over the Canyon for several scenic seconds before those thousand feet evaporated into solid rock. No one spotted the Hertz car for four days.

A half dozen years later, on February 2, 1974, Hertz lost yet another car. Stephen S. Steiner, age 24 and Peggy J. Horner, age 31, drove to the South Rim on their prized motorcycle. Once there, they rented a Hertz Car. They then drove it off the rim at high speed from Yaki Point. The car plunged an impressive 1,500 feet before being crushed with its two occupants. The motorcycle, parked in a safe place, escaped unscathed.

A dozen years later, Richard McMillan, age 50, and Lynn Allen, age 30, rattled toward the South Rim in McMillan's International Scout. Behind the pair, in Los Angeles, police had just issued arrest warrants for the two for seven counts of child molestation.

McMillan and Allen had lived together for the past two years and had a previous record of a few violent crimes. The present police charges were that the pair had sexually molested Allen's 9 year-old daughter and 8 year-old son. The two children, who normally lived with their father and stepmother, had spent the weekend with McMillan and Allen. After returning home they told their stepmother, "We don't want to go back!" Then, with coaxing, they explained why.

Not long afterward, Allen's mother, the children's maternal grandmother, told Allen that the children had reported being molested and that the police were issuing warrants. This had prompted Allen and McMillan to flee east.

A quarter mile east of the Desert View junction at the east boundary of Grand Canyon National Park, McMillan turned off the highway toward the nearby South Rim. On July 10, 1986, witnesses saw McMillan cut in front of an on-coming vehicle then steer across 147 feet of Coconino Plateau, dodging trees and leaving a trail of debris. Then McMillan's Scout launched off the edge. It hit bedrock nearly 500 feet down.

Twenty-four years after Osan Kang's last drive and 17 years after Stephen S. Steiner and Peggy J. Horner rented their Hertz car and 5 years after McMillan and Allen blasted off the rim to grab 500 feet of vertical air, Hollywood treated us to a similar denouement in the otherwise charming 1991 "chick flick," *Thelma and Louise.* This Academy Award winning screenplay ends—maybe because writer Callie Khouri could not figure out any other way to reconcile the plot—with Thelma and Louise being surrounded hopelessly by platoons of male police, some of whom have been chasing them for at least half of the movie.

Yawning before Thelma and Louise and their convertible is a Southwestern canyon a lot like Grand Canyon (Hollywood used Deadhorse Point State Park outside Moab, Utah). Thelma and Louise have had so much fun—some of it very illegal (although they were provoked by men)—that, now that they have been herded into this apparent cul de sac, they can only envision their future as a sad, anticlimactic trip to jail. But, no; one other option is still available....

Instead of going to jail, they could do what accused child molesters Richard McMillan and Lynn Allen had done. They could drive their car off the rim into space.

And so they do. In glorious slow motion. And somehow suicide seems a nice tidy end to coping with the problems that life throws daily into the faces of all of the rest of us who choose to go on with life's drudgery. In its defense, as is often the case in Hollywood, with *Thelma and Louise,* Hollywood was imitating life, specifically the drive-off-the-rim suicides mentioned earlier. But, as is even more often the case, life—and death—would soon imitate Hollywood.

The power of Hollywood has been known for years as an extremely effective model for shaping people's behavior—although the big studio lawyers are quick to point out that it is very hard to prove this in court. But consider an innocent example: when actor Clark Gable took off his white dress shirt in Frank Capra's 1934 Academy Award winner *It Happened One Night,* moviegoers were titillated to see that Gable was not wearing an undershirt. They were *so* titillated that for the next twelve months undershirt sales coast to coast plummeted to less than 50 percent of the numbers sold prior to that particular Gable movie.

No surprise, a quick look at Table 7 also reveals that after *Thelma and Louise* fictionally committed suicide by driving off the Grand Canyon-like rim, the same ball started rolling in reality on the South Rim.

1993, a year after *Thelma and Louise* came out in home rental video, became a bonanza year for emulators of *Thelma and Louise.* On January 15, 1993, Patricia Locke Astolfo, age 37, recently divorced and now too broke even to pay the Park entrance fee, tried to drive her Chevy Suburban across the snow and off the South Rim at the Abyss. Despite the cynical saying in some Grand Canyon Village circles, "You just can't miss at the Abyss" (if success in suicide is one's aim), Astolfo did.

Her Suburban high-centered on a rock outcropping on the edge of the roadway a few yards before the rim and lurched to a halt. This was not like *Thelma and Louise* at all. Astolfo, an investigation found later, had obsessively watched this video multiple times. She now exited her Suburban and walked to the rim. Then she jumped off. But again she had chosen a poor route. She fell about thirty feet before landing very seriously injured on a ledge. Leaving a puddle of blood, Astolfo got up, and, stumbling but determined, she crawled along the rocky bench. Then, making her third and final suicide attempt, she cartwheeled off a 100-foot precipice to her death.

Four months later, on May 8, Daniel McCourt drove an Enterprise rental car off Pima Point to his death. While any role of *Thelma and Louise* may remain hypothetical, McCourt did seem to possess a possible reason to drive off the edge. He was reportedly HIV positive.

Later that same year, on November 19, Michael Balboa Swinger, age 19, sped his car around the parking lot at the South Kaibab Trailhead then aimed it directly off the edge. This motor plunge into thin air proved fatal. And it was the third copycat suicide drive-off plunge from the South Rim in 1993.

Only three days later, backpackers reported a collapsed hiker at the base of a 30-foot cliff below the west edge of the Grandview Trail and Horseshoe Mesa atop Cottonwood drainage.

Although no one would learn of this for a while, the man they had found, Michael S. Walchle, had used his knife inside Crystal Forest Cave to slice his left antecubital fossa with three long slashes (at the inner side of the elbow) in a suicide attempt. He failed to sever his artery, but he had cut his brachial vein and had begun bleeding heavily. Contented, he fell asleep in the cave. He awoke to daylight streaming into the entrance. Staring at the crust of blood painting his arm, he now felt stupid for still being alive. He also now experienced second thoughts and decided to hike back out of the Canyon for help. He tossed his "kinda dull" knife off the cliff. He had earlier thrown away his driver's license so that his body could not be identified.

Although for eight years in the 1980s he had driven tours and worked a front desk at the South Rim, he was now living in Las Vegas. He'd had a break-up argument with his girlfriend. She had thrown hot coffee on him. This proved the last straw. Depression and a feeling of worthlessness had driven him to reenter the Canyon one last and final time. But now, not far up from his reconsideration point, Michael felt dizzy and weak. He collapsed and slid down 30 steep feet of cliff.

This is where one of those backpackers witnessed him tumble. They helped him to Horseshoe Mesa. He explained that he had cut his arm in a fall. The backpackers handed off Michael to four other campers they met, all physicians. These new caretakers warmed up Michael, dressed his wound, and treated him for dehydration and hypothermia. Meanwhile two of them trekked up through a storm to fetch help.

NPS rangers hiked in that night and found the 30-year-old patient. When the rangers radioed Dispatch, the dispatcher on duty, Barb Brutvan, was suspicious of Michael's story of having cut himself during a fall. She prompted the rescuers to question Michael more closely.

A quick search revealed the sleeve of his jacket had sustained no tear during the alleged injury. This prompted a confession: Yes, he admitted, he had tried to commit suicide.

Why?

Because of that row with his ex-girlfriend. And also because he was a diagnosed bipolar with obsessive compulsive order and was suffering from post-traumatic stress disorder. And he had quit taking his antidepression medications. His risk factors were even more considerable than these would imply. He had been raised in a series of foster homes. Indeed, his sister and five other family members had committed suicide. It seemed to run in his genes.

But his genes proved not to be his destiny. Fourteen years later Michael is not only still alive, but successfully married and is the father of a young daughter. To fight his demons he assiduously sees his therapist and psychiatrist and takes his antidepressant meds.

His regret? "I wish I could have been a Park Ranger or someone who helps others instead of being a burden on others."

Suicides Spurred By Canyon Experiences

In a few cases, the Canyon was not the opportunity for suicide, it was instead the precipitating factor.

An early example comes from a chapter "Lost Mines & Hidden Treasures" in George H. Billingsley, Earle E. Spamer, and Dove Menkes' book *Quest for the Pillar of Gold: The Mines & Miners of the Grand Canyon.* The story begins more than a century ago, when "Long Tom" Watson, a lone prospector who had combed Northern Arizona for gold, spent the winter in Flagstaff. He used old papers to start his fires. Among them he found a batch of letters, one envelope of which had an illegible address and had never been opened. Inside it Watson found a piece of brown wrapping paper with a note scrawled on one side and a map on the other. It had been written by a prospector to his brother.

The letter said he had found gold in Grand Canyon but he was also being followed by two men whom he suspected would rob him. He had filled a sack with his nuggets and hid it in a small cave behind a waterfall. The next morning the two men entered the prospector's camp. All three men had yanked their guns and fired at one another. The prospector had been hit and seriously wounded. Despite his wound(s), he managed to reach the Rim. Someone had found him there and had hauled him to Williams (60+ miles south) to see a doctor. It was here the wounded and possibly dying man had drawn his map and written his letter.

"Long Tom" Watson waited until spring before trying to follow the map. Then he combed tributary canyons from Havasu to Tanner, eventually guessing that the waterfall the prospector had used must have been an ephemeral one that flowed only in the spring or during run-offs. On the Tanner Trail he heard water and found a small fall nearby. Plunging through the water he found a rotting sack full of gold nuggets. Watson transferred many of these to his own sacks and pockets, then plunged back out through the falls. But in doing this, he lost his footing, so the story goes, fell, broke his leg, hit his head, and lost consciousness.

The next day he managed to climb atop his burro and escape up the Tanner. Yet another Good Samaritan found Watson—more or less as one had found the original discoverer of the gold. This rescuer hauled him to a hospital in Flagstaff.

Four months later, Watson shared the secret of the gold behind the waterfall with "Doc" Scanlon. Scanlon was interested. The two men entered the Canyon and combed the Tanner, now dry. Watson, however, could not relocate the region of the now-vanished waterfall no matter how hard they searched. "Watson, bitterly disappointed," write Billingsley, Spamer, and Menkes, "took his own life with his rifle near the Canyon rim." No one knows what happened to the nuggets or even to Doc Scanlon.

The above story may be apocryphal. It has all of the standard elements of the "lost gold" tales that emerge in any mining region. On the other hand....

Although nearly every suicide is a tragedy, and all are depressing, a few are truly astounding. The following episode transcends even the astounding. This story begins in the mid 1980s, when Carolyn (now Carolyn Castleman) was floating the Colorado on a private trip a few miles downstream of Lava Falls. Their group decided to hike up the Whitmore Trail at River Mile 188.

An hour or so later, she was surprised to see a solitary hiker atop the trail about to ride off on his mountain bike while wearing a life jacket. For a hiker in such a remote part of the Canyon, she thought, this guy was not carrying much of anything he really needed—and why the life jacket way up here? But he was drinking a Coke and he did offer them a cold one. The hiker was tall and lean, with long hair but a receding hairline. Allegedly, he was old enough to be have been a draft-dodger (an episode that he alluded to later) during America's Vietnam conflict. Curious, Carolyn and her husband talked to him and heard his story.

"I'm riding over to Toroweap to swim Lava Falls," he explained.

He had done all of this before, he assured them. This time he had driven out to the head of Whitmore Wash in his International Scout, and was now about to pedal from Whitmore to Toroweap Overlook, and then would hike down the trail to the Colorado River at Lava Falls (River Mile 179.5). After his swim he was planning on hiking back to the Whitmore Trail where he would then hike up and out to his Scout. From here he would drive to Toroweap to pick up his bike. This intrepid hiker identified himself as Lesley (a.k.a. Ed) Marr, from California. Marr was in his mid-thirties, of average build, and somewhat unkempt, Carolyn thought, but he seemed friendly enough. So friendly, in fact, that she and her fellow river runners offered Marr a ride downriver to Diamond Creek instead of continuing his plan to bike, hike down, swim, hike back up to his vehicle, then drive home.

He gladly accepted.

Becoming better acquainted over the next few days to Diamond, Carolyn and her husband asked Marr if he wanted to come along on another float trip on the Green River. He came along, had a good time, but showed some peculiar behavior. At times, for example, Marr chained his ammo box to himself to prevent its loss or theft. But what the heck? He seemed harmless enough.

They also found out that Marr had a girlfriend, and they invited Marr and this girlfriend onto the lower section of their next Canyon trip planned for the following year. Marr accepted yet again. They told Marr they would meet him and his girlfriend at the Phantom Ranch boat beach on a specific day in mid-June.

When that day came, Carolyn remembers floating toward the boat beach near Phantom Ranch. But only one person, a woman, waited on the beach. Lesley Marr was nowhere in sight. The woman was very upset.

She introduced herself as Marr's girlfriend and then told them what had gone wrong. She and Marr had hiked down the trail the night before and slept on the boat beach. Early that morning a ranger had approached them and told them that they had camped illegally by being outside of the campground. When the ranger next learned that the two campers had no permit at all for overnight camping, he said he was required to cite them for their violation of NPS backcountry rules.

Marr told the ranger that they were meeting a river trip. The ranger explained that that was irrelevant. As this ranger wrote the citation, Marr became extremely irate and belligerent. The ranger warned Marr that he was treading on thin ice and could be arrested.

At this, Marr acted even more belligerently. Finally, the ranger did arrest him. Next the ranger discovered that Marr's I.D. cards showed two different identifications. The ranger handcuffed Marr and had him flown to the South Rim. Marr's girlfriend seemed somehow immune to all of this and was simply left behind on the boat beach. So she waited there for the river trip.

After explaining her story, the boaters still offered her a ride downstream with them as planned.

"No," she explained with genuine worry, "Ed would kill me if I went downstream with you."

Carolyn, however, took this statement not at face value but as hyperbole, and told her, "Well, the only other way out of here is by hiking back up."

Marr's girlfriend grimaced and said something to the effect of, "No way am I going to do *that*...."

Carolyn then told her, "If you're not going to come downstream with us, and you're not going to hike out, then the *only* other way out of here is by a medical evacuation."

The river trip continued downstream. Marr's girlfriend ended up exiting the Canyon neither by river nor by foot but instead from Phantom Ranger Station via a medical evacuation helicopter. She had somehow "hurt her ankle" after talking with Carolyn.

Up on the Rim, NPS rangers released Marr from custody but issued a date for him to appear in Court before the magistrate at Grand Canyon in early July.

The date came. Marr never appeared. A warrant went out for his arrest. At about this same time, Grand Canyon National Park Headquarters received a bomb threat targeting Superintendent Dick Marks and the head of Law Enforcement, Dave Swickard.

Hundreds of miles away at this same time (July 5, 1987) during early morning in downtown Twentynine Palms, California, two highway patrolmen tried to stop a driver for a traffic violation. When the driver of the

International Scout failed to yield to them, the officers pursued him. During their pursuit, the officers observed the driver lighting a traffic flare inside the vehicle as he drove into Joshua Tree National Park.

When this fleeing subject approached that park's headquarters, he accelerated his vehicle through the parking lot and aimed it directly at the building's entrance.

The Scout crashed through a three-foot high retaining wall and lurched to a crunching stop.

The CHP officers stopped, took cover, and drew their weapons. They ordered the man in the Scout to place his hands on his head. Instead, the Scout's driver, still inside it, ignited yet another flare. The two CHP officers next heard the metallic clicks of a pump shotgun or rifle being loaded. Then they heard several shots.

Within seconds the interior of the Scout burst into flames.

Horrified, the CHP officers also saw the driver's head suddenly engulfed in flames. Even so, they again ordered him out of the car with his hands on his head. Soon the door of the Scout opened and the driver fell out of the Scout, collapsing onto the ground.

At significant risk (far higher risk than they knew at this moment), the two officers ran up and pulled the flaming driver away from the burning vehicle.

Seconds later, thousands of rounds of ammunition exploded inside it, along with several loaded guns, numerous bottles of compressed propane and acetylene, several cans of gasoline, and thousands of books of matches. The entire vehicle, they now realized in shock, had been loaded as a crudely designed carbomb.

The officers hospitalized the scorched driver of the exploded Scout. An investigation showed him to be Lesley Marr. Marr died from third degree burns over most of his body and from a self-inflicted .22 caliber gunshot wound to the head.

Yes, the bomb threat at Grand Canyon was confirmed to be linked to Marr. Marr's actions convinced law enforcement officials that he fully intended to kill several officials at the South Rim—along with himself as pilot of his carbomb. His Kamikaze trip to Grand Canyon National Park Headquarters to explode it and everyone inside it, however, had gone awry only because, en route, he had violated a routine traffic law.

So your mother was right: some hitchhikers can be real trouble.

What is the upshot on Canyon suicides? Several people apparently have traveled to Grand Canyon with the specific intent to commit suicide. More than three dozen of them have committed suicide in ways in which their bodies have ended up below the rims. Considering that nearly a century has passed during which this sort of thing was possible, and also considering that as many as fifty million people have deliberately visited Grand Canyon, this suicide rate off the rims is remarkably low.

On the other hand, in 1993, the year after the Hollywood video *Thelma and Louise* was released, three people suicided in three independent copycat drive-offs from the South Rim; and two more people failed in their suicide attempts by foot. One quarter of all 40 suiciders listed (ten of them) have done so by driving off the South Rim. These three in 1993 comprise a statistical anomaly. Throughout the entire eighty-year period during which this type of suicide was possible, only those ten people have driven off, in eight vehicles (many of them rental cars). Thus the statistical "anomaly" of more than a third of the cars having driven off in 1993 is very likely a nonrandom product of these victims copycatting a Hollywood glorification of an internal-combustion-powered death-plunge suicide presented in technicolor as a desirable means of exploring infinity.

Beyond copycatism, and as we have seen thus far in this book, men far more than women become victims of fatal mishaps in the Canyon. Does this also hold true for deliberate suicides? Yet again, yes. Of those 40 suiciders, only 9 (22.5 percent) were women. The ages of both genders, however, were more or less similar. The range for women was 18 to 49 years old, for men it was 17 to 54 years old (or perhaps 72, if Ambrose Bierce truly died in the Canyon—see Table 7). The average age of all suiciders was 32+ years old.

Suicide, however, shows an inverse seasonality to that of visitation—and also to that of all other types of fatal mishaps. Unlike accidental falls from the rims, 26 of those 40 suicides (nearly two-thirds of the total) occurred during the six "off" months (October through March) of very low visitation to the Canyon. In contrast, with accidental falls from the rims the opposite pattern holds: 35 of those 50 victims (70 percent) fell during the six "summer" months of high visitation. During the six "off" months, only 15 people (30 percent) fatally fell by accident. June was the peak month for accidental fatal falls, with 7 victims, versus October being the peak month for suicides, with 8 jumpers.

In summary, while the suicide season in the Canyon occurs during times of low visitation, the actual number of people who commit suicide in ways that deposit their bodies within Grand Canyon is far lower than most people would expect or imagine. For perspective on this, for each and every person who committed suicide listed in Table 7, *nine times more* were killed accidentally and tragically due only to air crashes in and around the Canyon. For additional perspective, note that well over 400 people have committed suicide by leaping off Niagara Falls. Of course the human population living close to Niagara Falls is much larger than that near Grand Canyon. Perhaps also the prospect of landing on water is more appealing—even for a suicidal visitor. Or perhaps the vista of Grand Canyon from either rim is so ethereal and is such a powerful reminder of how precious the gift of being alive on this planet is, that this spectacle discourages suicides among its five million visitors per year instead of facilitating them.

Table 7. SUICIDAL DEATHS BELOW GRAND CANYON'S RIMS.

Name, age	**Date**	**Location**	*Circumstances*

? Ambrose Gwinnet Bierce, 72 — 1914 — below the South Rim ?
The mysterious disappearance of former Civil War purple-heart veteran and noted journalist Bierce is under research by writer Scott Thybony. He has assembled a convincing case based on circumstantial evidence that Bierce detoured from a putative journey into Pancho Villa's Mexico and instead committed suicide within the Canyon at a years-long, pre-decided location, possibly by shooting himself with a new German pistol he admired.

Unidentified male, adult — 1931 ? — Shoshone Point, below the rim
The male victim's decomposing body was found on June 3, 1933, with a "cheap" .32 caliber revolver and a bullet hole in his cranium just above and behind the right ear. His pocketbook contained 40 cents and nothing else, no identification.

Ida M. Rusk, 40 — June 3, 1933 — Hermit Rapid (River Mile 95)
Rusk departed home in Maywood, California, leaving a note that she intended to commit suicide. She hiked down the Hermit Trail, left a suicide note at Santa Maria Springs and leaped into the river above Hermit Rapid. Rusk drowned. Her body was found near Hoover Dam six days later.

Charles Cuma, 48 — June 30, 1949 — Kaibab Suspension Bridge (River Mile 87.5)
Cuma had told people he planned to hike down to the Colorado and jump off the bridge. He was seen hiking down the Bright Angel Trail. Cuma subsequently vanished.

Mildred Violet Allen, 40+ — October 5, 1951 — Maricopa Point
Allen was sitting on the rim holding onto the bottom rung of a railing, when she suddenly shoved her body out and away from the ledge and let go. She fell 400 feet. She left a suicide note.

Tony Plachke, 40 — June 22, 1957 — near Lookout Studio
Plachke was a salesman from Phoenix and a former Fred Harvey Company butcher. He was last seen walking alone along edge of rim. He wrote a suicide note and left it in a Bright Angel Lodge cabin he had rented. Plachke jumped off and fell 150 feet below the rim.

George Lewis Kinsey, 33 — December 7, 1962 — "Duck-on-a-Rock," East Rim Drive
Kinsey's body was found on a ledge and with a bullet hole to the heart. A French-made 32-caliber automatic and a copy of the German poet Goethe's "Faust" ("On one's own initiative") were found next to him.

Marion Leroy Bates, 46

June 1965   a ledge below Hermit's Rest
A hiker found Bates in 1969 in a small crevasse under a ledge below rim, a .38 caliber revolver gripped in his skeletal hand. Death was due to gunshot wound.

Osan Kang, 54

March 28, 1967   Lipan Point
Kang drove a Hertz rental car off an ideal "launch ramp" on the rim, plunging a clean 1,000 feet. Kang had been a very dignified and courteous small-time con man who had recently been down on his luck. (see text)

Dorothy Dowdy, 49

October 1971   Mather Point
Dowdy was found huddled under a ledge below the rim with a paper sack over her head and a pistol shot into her head. Dowdy had recently been released from a mental institution and was disturbing the other guests at the Bright Angel Lodge. Ranger Vic Vieira checked with her doctor, who assured Vieira that Dowdy was not a threat to herself, or anyone else, nor was she welcome back at the institution.

Robin Ruth Myers, 18

November 3, 1972   Maricopa Point
Myers was found with a suicide note in her pocket. Hers was an unwitnessed apparent jump. She was a former mental patient with prior suicide attempts.

Stephen S. Steiner, 24
Peggy J. Horner, 31

February 2, 1974   Yaki Point
Couple drove to the Canyon on their prized motorcycle, rented a Hertz car, and, in apparent suicide pact, drove it off the rim at high speed, plunging 1,500 feet. (see text)

Gregory F. Bansberg, 32

October 13, 1978   behind Yavapai Museum
Bansberg, a troubled Vietnam vet, was seen taking a few "giant" steps along the rim and then into the Canyon.

Edward E. Walters, 36

June 15, 1980   Navajo Bridge/Marble Canyon
Walters wrote two long suicide notes, weighted himself with rocks, and leaped off Navajo Bridge. (see text)

Myung Sun Kim, 28

December 26, 1980   First Trailview Overlook
Kim stepped past the guard rail and ignored pleas of her family to step back from the rim. Seconds later, when her family looked away, she "fell" 300 feet. She was depressed over personal issues.

Unidentified white male,
  25–30

December 30, 1980   Pima Point
The body of a young adult white male dead from having fallen was found well below the rim wearing a black leather jacket, blue Levis, and hiking boots. No I.D.

William Joseph O'Brien, 38

August 12–22, 1984   Mather Point
O'Brien had terminal cancer. He had informed his former wife and friend of his intent to jump, and then he did, falling 300 feet.

Eric B. Lopez, 19

March 15, 1985   The Abyss
Lopez drove a car off West Rim Drive near The Abyss. He was the fourth suicide victim to die by driving off the rim (in the third vehicle driven off).

Laura Lynn Allen, 30
Richard Lee McMillan, 50

June 29, 1986   East Rim Drive past Yaki Point
Double suicide. Allen was despondent over her disability, and also was about to be arrested for child molestation of her own children. She apparently formed a suicide pact with Richard McMillan, also about to be arrested for molestation of Allen's children. Witnesses saw the couple as McMillan drove his International Scout at high speed off the rim to plunge 1,000 feet. (see text)

Peter K. Schrieber, 23

July 20, 1986   Toroweap Overlook
Schrieber wrote a note to his parents then jumped off 400 feet.

Alan Heaton, 41

September 9, 1987   Point Imperial
Died of gunshot to head (details unclear).

Michael Hope-Ross, 31

December 15, 1987   Yavapai Point
Hope-Ross, an unemployed airline pilot, left a journal indicating suicidal thoughts. NPS concluded he jumped off, falling 500 feet. His family, however, notes that Ross had $30,000 in the bank and a girlfriend whom he was thinking of marrying.

"R.K.",
  unidentifiable male

Winter 1987–88   ½ mile east of Hopi House
The victim jumped 300 feet with note and item with "R.K." initials. A tape player was found with acid rock tape. The body of this white male, 5 feet, 6 inches tall, was found years after his suicide, except for his skull, which was crushed into fragments. These had been dragged away by small animals, hence the identification problem.

John F. Zitko, 21

October 24, 1989   Yaki Point
Zitko left home on a "self-seeking" journey. He told his family, "You'll hear from me when I find myself." He jumped off.

Scott Mark Clements, 33

October 26, 1990   The Abyss
Clements wrote a detailed note then posted it, taped, to the guard rail. This note included an arrow pointing downward and instructions for whomever found the note to contact NPS rangers. Clements also tied a rope to his rifle and tethered it to the railing. When Clements shot himself, he fell off the rim. But his leg caught in the rifle tether he had rigged, and he fell less than ten feet, instead of hundreds. Clements had left several instructions that, among other things, his expensive assault-type rifle should be returned to his relatives.

Scott Beug, 17

September 14, 1991   Mather Point
Beug was in trouble at school. He took the family car and firearms from his South Dakota home. He jumped off 250 feet.

Bruce Ciniello, 21

October 15, 1992   unnamed Point
Ciniello jumped off, falling 500 feet.

Patricia Locke Astolfo, 37

January 15, 1993   The Abyss
Astolfo had obsessively viewed her THELMA & LOUISE *video 50 times. She tried to drive her Chevy Suburban across the snow and off the rim but it high-centered before it could drop off. Astolfo opened the door, walked to the rim, and jumped 20 feet onto the rocks below. Injured seriously but still alive, she crawled to a precipice and dropped off its edge 100 feet. (see text)*

Daniel McCourt, 31

May 8, 1993   Pima Point
McCourt drove a 1993 Nissan (Enterprise Rental car) over the South Rim. He was reportedly HIV positive. (see text)

Michael Balboa Swinger, 19

November 19, 1993   South Kaibab Trailhead
After racing his car across the parking lot, Swinger then drove it over the edge at high speed. He hit 700–800 feet below. (see text)

Joseph Seitz, 34

May 1, 1994   ⅓ mile west of Hopi Point
Seitz jumped off, falling 500 feet.

Christopher White, 25

December 30, 1994   Powell Memorial
White wrote a suicide note, then smashed his watch on the rim (as if to symbolically end his time). He next drew an arrow pointing toward the Canyon, then he jumped off, falling 540 feet.

Michael S. Gardner, 27

January 18, 1996   Mather Point
Gardner had stolen some money and gambled it. He arrived at the NPS entry station with too little to pay the entrance fee. So he parked—leaving his keys in his car—outside the park, then walked several miles to Mather Point. He jumped off, falling 250 feet. He had been reported as despondent prior to his jump.

Roberta Kay Beard, 21

March 1, 1997   Worship Site, Rim Trail
Beard, a Fred Harvey employee, reportedly had been depressed. She walked off her job that night and jumped off the rim.

Matthew J. Garcy, 20

October 24, 1997   Cape Royal
In a bizarre act of extreme emotional disturbance, Garcy asked a bystander to take his photo and to mail a letter on the front seat of Garcy's car. The bystander asked "Why can't you mail it yourself?" Garcy said, "I'll show you why," then he handed his glasses to the bystander, took a few steps, and jumped off the North Rim, falling 400 feet. He left a 6-page suicide note.

? Steven Vincent Mylan, 20

Sept. 1997– Feb.1998 (?)   Little Colorado River Gorge (?)
Mylan left his home in Ontario, Canada, and visited Rainbow Bridge in Glen Canyon. A Navajo found Mylan's car parked with keys in the ignition at the jewelry stands at the Little Colorado Gorge Overlook and drove it for a few months until it broke down. In early 1998, Mylan's car was found stripped off State Route 64. Interviews led to an unsuccessful search for his body in the Little Colorado Gorge. Mylan, who did not seem a good candidate for suicide, may have become a victim of foul play.

Andrew Gradzik, 42   April 23 (?), 1998   E of Yavapai Point
On September 26, 2001, NPS SAR rangers recovering suicider Richard W. Gibbs discovered a nearby skeleton scattered over 200 sq. feet, 400+ feet below the rim. Dental records identified it as Gradzik, from Toronto, with a previous suicide attempt. He went missing from El Tovar on April 26, 1998. On April 23, Gradzik had sent a postcard saying that he had met a man who offered to take him on "private hikes." A 14-day SAR in 1998 failed to locate him.

Murray M. Marshall, 51   November 11, 1998   Maricopa Point
Marshall pawned some personal belongings, then drove to the rim, and jumped off 480 feet.

Kahlil Williams, 28   February 2000   The Abyss
A routine overflight on March 29 noticed a "new" vehicle about 1,000 feet below the rim. The pilot recommend an investigation. Searchers found Williams' body (he was from Phoenix) well above the car and 450 feet below the rim. Williams was the tenth drive-off suicider, using the eighth vehicle to be driven off.

Robert William van Rooden, 27   February 20, 2000   ½ mile east of El Tovar Hotel
van Rooden's personal effects were found abandoned in his hotel room on February 20, but searchers below the rim found no body. An NPS overflight on March 31 spotted the body 250 feet below the rim as suspected, but unproven suicide.

Brady Matthew Forrester, 20   October 18, 2000   First Trailview Overlook
Forrester, reportedly "appeared to be bungee jumping" as he "swan-dived" off the rim, falling 300 feet. Identification took over one month. Victim had pending warrant for his arrest.

The following entries are not included in text, statistics, or the index.

Richard W. Gibbs, 52   September 26, 2001   E of Yavapai Point
Gibbs took a tour bus from Las Vegas to Grand Canyon Village. He was seen sitting on the edge of the rim. Witnesses saw Gibbs arch his back then jump off purposefully. He fell 400-450 feet.

Saifuddin Taibjee, 35   November 9, 2002   Mather Point
Plagued by "mental problems," Taibjee stripped off his clothes and scattered them beyond the guard rail. His naked body was found 400 ft. below the rim by Ranger Greg Moore using a spotting scope.

James Allen Jorgensen, ?   February 15 or 16, 2003   Quartermaster Canyon
Jorgensen apparently drove off the rim, plunging 600 feet.

Timothy Clam, 25   June 10, 2004   over White Butte into Travertine Canyon
Clam had tried in Tusayan to book a front "shotgun" seat on a Papillon Airways tour helicopter but had been turned away. The next day he was sold that seat, separate from other passengers. 2 miles into the canyon, passing over Dripping Springs, Clam unclipped his seat harness, pulled open the door and forced his way out into a free-fall of 3,700 feet. Pilot Maria Langer tried to stop Clem but could not manage while still controlling the airship.

Michael Alvarado, ?	September 13, 2005　Yavapai Observation Point *Jumped. (Freedom of Information Act request pending)*
Donald Hansen, Jr., 56	December 23, 2005　Yavapai Observation Station *Witnesses watched Hansen, who had made previous suicide attempts, leap 500 feet off the rim.*
Garret Barry, 24	May 15, 2006　　　Maricopa Point *Jumped 600 feet. (Freedom of Information Act request pending)*
Cynthia Ann Fairham, 40	August 22, 2006　　Angel's Window, Cape Royal *An NPS employee found Fairham's car parked with the door swung open and the radio playing. Footprints led to the edge. Rangers found her body 350 feet below an apparent suicide jump.*
French male, 60	October 31, 2006　　Mojave Point, The Abyss *A routine helicopter flight spotted an Alamo red Pontiac Crossfire convertible 600 feet below the rim on the Coconino, then a body 150-feet higher. The car contained cash. Identification of the driver is pending. Likely suicide.*
Eric Reddish, 24	April 2, 2007　　　Mather Point *At 4:15 a.m., mule wranglers on the S. Kaibab trail reported seeing a steady light below the rim. Rangers rappelled 300 feet and found Reddish, deemed suicidal via other evidence.*

If you are contemplating suicide, please do not come to Grand Canyon to commit it. Instead, seek help, call 911.

Chapter Eight

Murder

"I know Powell did some bad things," Wallace Stegner was quoted as saying during the pre-publication reviewing of his highly regarded book, *Beyond the Hundredth Meridian: John Wesley Powell and the Second Opening of the West*, "but he's not going to do them in my book."

Well, Powell *is* going to do them in this book....

Nearly every book of the hundreds written so far on Grand Canyon has described—often in chapter length or longer—the heroic first river exploration of the Canyon by Major John Wesley Powell and his crew of eight men. Most of these treatments canonize Powell. Indeed the most famous and highly praised book on Powell, his explorations, and his largely ignored legacy of intelligent land use of the West thus far is Stegner's *Beyond the Hundredth Meridian*. And, as Stegner's opening quote hints, Powell emerges in this book not just as a genius, but also as a saint. Stegner did eliminate questionable facets of Powell's life. Yet Stegner's amusing, "but he's not going to do them in *my* book" quote hints at just how hunky dory Powell's 1869 expedition of exploration down the Colorado River in Grand Canyon might have been.

In truth, Powell *was* visionary in the extreme. His realistic appraisal of the limits of potential water development in the West and his warnings of the tragic and destructive consequences of exceeding these limits via over-optimistic and excessive federal, instead of local, water projects would prove prophetic. Even so, this should not be misread to say that Powell was the original Colorado River conservationist. He was not. As historian and Powell biographer Donald Worster notes, Powell was in no way a conservationist in the modern, or even the old, sense: "I cannot find in Powell anywhere," notes Worster, "not even in his commonwealth idea, any room for this awareness....[that the West] holds treasures of natural beauty and biological diversity that should be preserved against all threats of development or use." In short, John Wesley Powell was neither John Muir nor Henry David Thoreau nor Aldo Leopold. Powell stood firmly in the "man over nature" camp—but only if that ascendancy was done right (i.e., locally, Powell's way).

Powell's legacy remains complicated. He was personally responsible for several enlightened advances in his time and ahead of his time. For example, in Washington, D.C., Powell originated the Smithsonian's Bureau of Ethnography, recording the customs and languages of many North American tribes before they were lost. At the same time, however, he advocated concentrating Western tribes on restricted reservations away from important natural resources, such as forests, which, he said, they would otherwise wastefully burn. Powell also directed the U.S. Geological Survey for years and fought unsuccessfully against rapacious water development. Powell often tried in other ways to inject his brand of "science" into the exploration of the West.

Important to our investigation of murder in Grand Canyon, however, is to look beyond Powell's science and politics to his ability to lead men when the chips were down. John Wesley Powell, it would prove, did not possess the skills of a Captain Meriwether Lewis or a Captain William Clark, who commanded and orchestrated the most famous exploration of unknown wilderness on North America—over a period of two years—without losing a single man to accident or to violence. Instead, in just over three months the self-absorbed J. W. Powell lost three men. To murder.

In 1869, John Wesley Powell recruited nine men. One of them, John Colton Sumner, claimed to have been a co-founder of Powell's 1868 idea to explore the Green and Colorado rivers flowing along unknown courses through unknown canyons of the West and Southwest. In 1868, nearly a thousand miles of these rivers remained unexplored as the "last great unknown"—and thus the last great exploration opportunity—in the continental United States. Powell's chosen crew included Sumner as head boatman. It also included Powell's younger brother Walter (whom the rest of the crew considered demented as a result of his feverish confinement in a Confederate prisoner-of-war camp), plus Oramel G. Howland and his younger brother Seneca. The crew further included William H. Dunn, William Rhodes Hawkins, and Sergeant George Young Bradley. At virtually the last minute, Powell also recruited Andrew Hall and Frank Goodman, an Englishman wandering the West in search of adventure, at the start of the trip at Green River Station, Wyoming.

The ten men set off from Green River on May 24, 1869, in four boats. One of these was Powell's 16-foot pine scoutboat, the *Emma Dean*. The other three were 21-foot Whitehall haulers of oak that Powell had paid for with money from Illinois Industrial University and from the Chicago Academy of Science ($500 from each source) and from private pledges and possibly from his own funds as well. He had instructed the boatbuilder, Bagley of Chicago, to modify them with double ribbing and also with sealable 5-foot-long compartments fore and aft for buoyancy and storage. Named by their crews *Maid of the Cañon*, *Kitty Clyde's Sister*, and the *No Name*, these were not bad boats. But, loaded heavily, they were extremely difficult to steer. They also had the flaw of taking on tons of water in the open 11-foot-long bilge while running rapids. This latter flaw would prove indirectly lethal. Note that all published etchings and photos of Powell's boats are not of the above mentioned boats of 1869 but instead of the boats from his 1871–72 trip. Powell's original boats had neither a steering oar nor sweep mounted off the stern. With only nine able-bodied men (Powell could neither row nor steer) to row eight pairs of oars, there remained only one man who might have used a steering oar, yet four boats to steer. This man was Oramel G. Howland who, instead of rowing (or steering), drew maps and made notes all day from the boat's deck. Even after the wreck of the *No Name* (see below), there remained, below the Uinta confluence, only eight able-bodied men to row six pairs of oars; again, one of these was O. G. Howland, who stayed at his cartographic duties. Hence there would, even then, have been only one man to steer three boats via a sweep oar. Nor did Powell's 1869 boats possess a compartment amidships or a chair mounted there for Powell himself. All of these additions Powell made in 1871.

And while Powell religiously wore an inflatable rubber, "horse-collar" life jacket in 1869 to compensate for the loss of his right arm during the Battle of Shiloh, this was the only life jacket on the trip. Robert Brewster Stanton researched this issue and concluded that Powell never admitted, publicly or otherwise, to having possessed this life jacket even to the day he died. His crew of 1871–72, for instance, was certain that he had *not* possessed any life jacket in 1869. At any rate, for everyone on this 1869 expedition, this was a dangerous trip.

Sixteen days downstream from Green River, in the Canyon of Lodore, the Howland brothers and Goodman missed pulling into shore and instead rode one of the 21-footers, the *No Name*, swamped and out of control into Disaster Falls. The *No Name* smashed into midstream boulders and disintegrated in successive collisions. The men aboard her barely escaped to a midstream island alive.

After a daring rescue by John Sumner, who rowed the *Emma Dean* across to the midstream island to scoop up the three men stranded there, the expedition re-united. The Howland brothers and Goodman were alive, but otherwise everything aboard the *No Name* except a couple of barometers and a small keg of whiskey were lost. Vanished to the bottom of the Green were one third of the expedition's ten-month supply of food and equipment. With it went the three men's rifles, revolvers, clothes, and other personal gear.

Understandably, Major Powell was upset about this huge loss. Goodman quit the trip after this at his first opportunity, two weeks later, at the Uinta.

Seventy-four days later (August 5) and seven hundred miles out of Green

River, Wyoming, Powell and his eight remaining stalwarts rowed their three beat-up boats past the future site of Lees Ferry. Here they entered Grand Canyon. Powell named these first 61.5 miles of Grand Canyon "Marble Canyon." Five days of rowing carried Powell's crew to the foot of Marble Canyon at the Little Colorado. By now the men were reduced to starvation rations of flour balls, dried and moldy apples, a few beans, and a lot of black coffee. Deer and bighorn sheep seemed to have long since vanished from the Inner Canyon. Even the fish refused to bite for Bradley, a consummate fisherman. Worse, the monsoons had begun, and the men were reduced to one blanket for every two of them.

The explorers camped for three days at the Little Colorado River (River Mile 61.5) while the Powell brothers geologized and geographied. This "lothesome [sic] little stream, so filthy and muddy that it fairly stinks" (as Bradley wrote) frothed with mud from the Painted Desert. Sumner called it "as disgusting a stream as there is on the continent....Half its volume and 2/3 of its weight is mud and silt." Discontent too seethed here beneath the surface of most of the men's attitudes about lingering on less than half rations among dust and hordes of insects next to this cesspool of a stream. "The men are uneasy and discontented," Bradley confided to his journal here on August 11, "and anxious to move on. If Major does not do something soon I fear the consequences, but he is contented and seems to think that biscuit made of sour & musty flour and a few dried apples is ample to sustain a laboring man."

Eventually the expedition shoved off downstream into what Powell would later refer to as the "Great Unknown." Strangely, posterity knows only a little about how this expedition proceeded from here.

In Powell's very brief journal he wrote little to nothing about this part of the journey in the Canyon. What he did write about at length (now using his left hand because he had lost his right years earlier) was only geology. Only months to years later, back East, would Powell compose what would be published as his "journal" of running the river itself. Meanwhile the only other surviving journals—the official one of Sumner and the secret journal that Bradley wrote in nearly microscopic script—do express undisguised disgust and impatience at their predicament with Powell in the Canyon. Interviews of John Sumner and of Billy Hawkins conducted later by Robert Brewster Stanton revealed even worse dynamics.

It seems that a conflict of wills and attitudes had begun at Disaster Falls between Powell and Oramel G. Howland, the older of the two brothers. Powell had held him particularly responsible for the wreck of the *No Name*. This conflict festered for the rest of the trip. Howland, in turn, found fault in Powell's decision-making regarding food resupplies in tit-for-tat spats. A bit later yet another, parallel, bad relationship allegedly began between Major Powell and William Dunn, a colorful, buckskin-clad, long-haired mountain man. It too grew worse in Grand Canyon.

This deterioration occurred in part because Powell allegedly gave Dunn, the best swimmer of the crew, the more risky posts perched on boulders in the river as the crew lined the boats along the edges of rapids. (Powell's crew lined roughly one hundred of the biggest rapids on the trip; the men did not row the boats through anything that Powell considered too dangerous.) During one of these episodes, a swinging rope knocked Dunn off his rock and into the Colorado. Still in Dunn's pocket from some previous chore was one of Powell's watches—the last one that worked. Powell's watch was ruined.

At dinner Sumner remarked that Dunn had come close to drowning. Walter Powell said that would have been but little loss. Then (both Sumner and Hawkins agree) Major Powell was so angry that he actually ordered Dunn to pay for the ruined watch then and there or else leave the trip and exit Grand Canyon. Dunn's exit would have demanded that he climb 4,600 feet up cliffs to the middle of a waterless nowhere. The closest escape would have been to the south on the uninhabited and unexplored Coconino Plateau. Dunn responded, "Not even a bird could get out here." But Powell seemed serious. For as long as Dunn were to delay his departure from the trip, Powell allegedly demanded, he must pay a boarding fee: $30 or $50 per month (Sumner and Hawkins disagree over Powell's stipulated fee). Later Powell decided that Dunn could pay $30 for the ruined watch after the trip.

Powell's tantrum may seem merely high-handed and morale-busting, but things apparently spiraled farther downward. For example, not much farther downstream, Hawkins noted in a far more serious allegation, Powell "saw his chance to drown Dunn" while he was perched on a boulder out in a rapid, again lining one of the boats. Although Powell normally had not assisted in this sort of work, Hawkins said, he now yanked on a rope in just the right way to catch Dunn's legs and dump him into the swift, deep water of the rapid. Dunn, struggling, swam to shore successfully. But he was upset with Powell.

Dunn allegedly told the Major that but for his swimming ability, he and maybe the boat too would have been lost. Powell answered, as Walter had, that losing Dunn "would be but little loss" and then called Dunn some sort of "bad name."

Dunn answered that if Powell were not a cripple he would not survive calling Dunn such a bad name. (Sumner admitted, "I think that only the fact that the Major had but one arm saved him from a broken head, if nothing worse.")

Walter Powell, the biggest man on the trip, then announced that *he* was not a cripple. (Sumner also said of Walter: "Captain Walter Powell was about as worthless a piece of furniture as could be found in a day's journey. O. G. Howland was far his superior physically and morally and, God knows, away above him mentally.") Walter now started toward Dunn swearing an oath to kill him.

As Walter Powell passed him, Billy Hawkins grabbed him by the hair and yanked him over backwards into the river. Then he held him under, face down, afraid to let him get a gasp of air too soon.

"For God's sake, Bill," Dunn said, "you will drown him."

Finally Hawkins did let Walter out of the river. He got up sputtering and calling Hawkins every name in the book, including a "Missouri puke." Walter then hurried to his boat to grab his rifle, saying that he would kill both Hawkins and Dunn. But as he was reaching for his gun, Andrew Hall punched him in the side of the head. When Walter turned around, he was facing the muzzle of Hall's revolver.

Major Powell, distressed, asked Hawkins how he could go back on him as he was doing. Hawkins told Powell that he had gone back on himself with his treatment of Dunn, adding to Powell that he "had better help the Captain get the sand out of his eyes and that if he monkeyed with me any more, I would keep him down next time."

The expedition at this juncture had stretched its thin thread of solidarity to the breaking point. As Hawkins tells it:

> Sumner and I had all we could do to keep down mutiny. There was bad feeling from that time on for a few days. We began not to recognize any authority from the Major. We began to run races with the boats, as the loads were almost gone. It was fun for the first two days but then the water began to get rough. Hall, [Seneca] Howland, and myself were in my boat. I had become an expert in bad rapids. We ran several that the other two boats were let over with ropes.

Sumner adds: "Major Powell did not run the outfit in the same overbearing manner after that. At a portage or a bad let-down he took his geological hammer and kept out of the way."

These statements disparaging Major Powell's leadership and accusing Walter Powell of attempted murder were made during Stanton's lengthy 1907 interviews of Sumner and Hawkins—and also during a 1919 interview of Hawkins by William Wallace Bass. Some historians and biographers who would like to preserve Powell's image unblemished have discounted both Sumner's and Hawkins' testimonies as nothing more than bitter grapes.

But what "bitter grapes?"

A hand-written copy of Powell's original contract for this trip hired only three of the nine men present for $75 each for the duration of the expedition (anticipated to last up to a year). The men were also to be allowed time on their own to trap and prospect. All three of these men were to run the boats and work in all general capacities on the expedition from June 1, 1869, until, if needed, May 31, 1870. Dunn was also supposed to take twice-daily barometric readings and also determine elevations of cliffs. Sumner was to take readings with the sextant. Oramel G. Howland was contracted as the expedition cartographer to draw maps of the entire 1,000+ miles of river canyons that the expedition explored as it traversed them. As mentioned earlier, Howland did this, sitting day after day on the deck of the boat (and often on a sack of flour). Using a compass, pencil, rule, et cetera, he drew these maps.

No other known written record or contract survives regarding what anyone else on the 1869 trip was to expect as payment—if anything. Hawkins, however, was the expedition's hunter and chief cook. He prepared every meal. He even washed Major Powell's one hand for him prior to meals and then served him his meals. Few Powell scholars believe that Hawkins did this gratis. Hawkins says that, several months before the 1869 trip, Powell promised him a daily wage of $1.50 to cook for the expedition and also promised transportation expenses after the expedition to return to Colorado. Hawkins said he also sold to Powell for an agreed upon price of $960, a stock of provisions, trade goods, and two horses. Powell did not pay him, Hawkins said, he instead issued him a receipt for moneys due and said that he expected to be able to pay Hawkins after Congress issued him several thousand dollars for his explorations. Hawkins does mention, however, that at Separation Canyon (see below), where Powell had (temporarily, at least) allegedly resolved to quit the expedition with the Howlands, that Hawkins told Powell he would accept the *Kitty Clyde's Sister* as partial payment on moneys owed him by Powell. Were Powell to make that hike, Hawkins adds, Powell would have wanted to cache the *Sister* for his own use should he later return by land to complete the exploration downriver. Hawkins wanted the *Sister* then and there so he could continue down the river .

Sumner's account mirrors Hawkins'. Sumner says that he too was out more than $1,000 on equipment and supplies lost or used on the 1869 expedition for which Powell said he would reimburse Sumner after the expedition and after Congress issued him the money.

Hawkins also notes that, beyond these reimbursements, Major Powell allegedly promised him and Sumner each $1,000 in salary *if* Powell received a grant of $12,000 that he was expecting from Congress. Of this, Hawkins added, Powell said he intended to keep $2,000 for himself. Powell did receive $10,000 from Congress after 1869, but he never reimbursed his 1869 crew one penny for lost equipment or supplies or promised wages. At the Rio Virgin, Powell did pay Sumner his $75 as originally contracted. Powell also paid Hawkins $60 and Andy Hall $60 (again, for a 99-day trip). Hawkins thought that Powell had also paid Bradley, but Hawkins did not know what amount. Here too at the Rio Virgin, Hawkins added, Powell promised again to send him and Sumner "a government voucher for the rest" of the money owed to them. Again, Powell never did. Both Sumner and Hawkins felt to their dying days that Powell had deliberately welshed on his debts to them. So maybe "bitter grapes" is one way of expressing Hawkins' and Sumner's disappointment in Major Powell's capacity for keeping promises.

Critics of Sumner's and Hawkins' accounts also point out that Sumner's journal mentioned no such attempted expulsion of Dunn, nor did it mention fights. But Sumner was writing his journal at Powell's behest to supplement Powell's own very weak one. Under such conditions Sumner could not have been expected to spell out in it any mistreatment by Powell of his crew. Sergeant George Y. Bradley's secret journal (microscopically penned while fishing), however, also reveals no specifics about Powell vs. Dunn. Bradley does say, as we've seen, that Powell was oblivious to the true feelings of his crew toward him, and these feelings were often anything but favorable.

Hawkins' and Sumner's interviews late in life were conducted independently hundreds of miles apart, months apart, years apart, and by different interviewers. Stanton's interviews included not only a stenographer to take every word down exactly, but also a notary public to swear that the words written were indeed those that each man had spoken. Sumner's and Hawkins' accounts—despite being independent—agreed on Powell's mistreatment of Dunn, et cetera. In short, if these two separated men—both brave, capable, and loyal to Powell during the 1869 expedition—were indulging in fictions to vent their spleen, they were doing so with a phenomenal coincidence of specific detail—and also doing so out of character.

The upshot? By the time Powell's first trip entered the Great Unknown, it was disintegrating. Again, somewhere in mid-Canyon Hawkins and Hall began running their boat, *Kitty Clyde's Sister*, independently of Powell's decisions. Until River Mile 239.5. At this point even Hawkins knew that he should wait for Powell to catch up in the *Emma Dean*.

The rapid here not only looked horrendous, cliffs on both sides precluded a portage. River Mile 239.5 is now called Separation Rapid because, after hours of scouting it and finding no clean route, Oramel G. Howland and William Dunn decided here to hike away from the trip. They planned to exit the north side canyon and seek the Mormon settlements many miles farther north. Seneca Howland, out of loyalty to his brother, decided to accompany them. Powell would later write for publication in his book, *The Exploration of the Colorado River and its Canyons* (a.k.a. Powell's "journal"), that he paced all night trying to decide what to do. He knew, he wrote, that the end of their journey, the Rio Virgin, could not lay more than seventy miles downstream (this was an accurate distance, but Powell only wrote these words long *after* having run those 70 miles). Even so, neither Powell nor the men who decided to continue downriver—Hawkins, Hall, Sumner, Bradley, and Walter Powell—could change the minds of the Howlands or Dunn.

On the morning of August 28, 1869, the trip split their guns, cash, food, and copies of some notes and journals (in haste, some parts of these accounts may have been split unequally, with duplicate copies of some sections going by land while no copies went by water) between the three hikers and the six boaters. It is unclear whether or not Powell paid O. G. Howland and William Dunn their $75 each in wages, but it seems that he may have. Powell did ask the hikers to tote a $650 barometer (or chronometer). The three also carried a batch of personal letters to be mailed, and Sumner's watch—to go to his sister in the event that he drowned. Here too Major Powell abandoned his 16-foot *Emma Dean*.

That morning the three hikers helped the other six men line and portage the two oak boats partway down the rapid. Farewells were accompanied by tears from some of the men, each of whom thought he was taking the safer of the paths. The six rowed those two surviving oak boats, *Kitty Clyde's Sister* and *Maid of the Cañon*, into the forbidding rapid. Bradley notes (again in his secret journal, which Powell would never learn existed) what happened next:

> We rowed with all of our might until the billows became too large to do anything but hold on to the boats and by good fortune both boats came out at the bottom of the rappid [sic], well soaked with water of course but right side up and not even an oar was lost. The three boys stood on the cliff looking at us and having waved them adieu we dashed through the next rappid where we stopped to catch our breath and bail out the water from our now nearly sunken boats. We had never run such a rappid before....

Sumner explained to Robert Brewster Stanton what happened below Separation Rapid:

> We waited about two hours, fired guns, and motioned for the men to come on, as they could have done by climbing along the cliffs. The last thing we saw of them they were standing on the reef, motioning us to go on, which we finally did.

Hawkins also told Stanton that the Howland Brothers and Dunn refused to rejoin them: "We all landed and hallooed to the other boys we had left on the rock to come. But they would not."

Clearly, while it may have been fear of the river at this point that drove the Howlands and Dunn to hike out and to emphatically refuse to rejoin the other six below Separation Rapid, but it was no longer fear of this rapid itself (Andrew Hall was certain that Dunn and O. G. Howland were indeed afraid of Separation Rapid) they now could have hiked around.

Interestingly, Powell would later write somewhat differently of the aftermath of running Separation Rapid:

> We land at the first practicable point below, and fire our guns, as a signal to the men above that we have come over in safety. Here we

remain for a couple of hours, hoping that they will take the smaller boat and follow us. **We are behind a curve in the canyon and cannot see up to where we left them, and so we wait until their coming seems hopeless, and then push on.** [Bold ours]

In reality, the river corridor immediately downstream of Separation Rapid runs phenomenally straight for more than two miles. Bradley's and Sumner's and Hawkins' accounts of the men's final separation seems more accurate (and less self-serving) than Powell's report. Powell's actual *entire* journal entry for that fateful day reads: "Boys left us. Ran rapids. Bradley boat broke. Camp on left bank. Camp 44."

After running Separation Rapid, Powell handed his prized life jacket to Hawkins in appreciation for Hawkins (and Hall's) rowing expertise through its daunting dangers. Hawkins still possessed this jacket during the twentieth century and showed it to Stanton. The six in the boats ran six more miles of fast river, then, mostly out of control, they survived a truly hair-raising, willy-nilly run down the worst rapid of the entire trip, Lava Cliff. Ironically, the next day, Powell and his surviving five men rowed past the Grand Wash Cliffs, thus exiting Grand Canyon and escaping the last whitewater dangers. Yet another day later, 99 days and a thousand miles out of Green River, they rowed into the mouth of the Rio Virgin.

Here the Powell brothers decided to go north overland and catch a train back East. The other four men would row downriver for the hell of it. Before they separated, Major Powell asked the small Mormon community up the Rio Virgin to pass the word to help the Howland brothers and Dunn were they discovered.

On September 8, twelve days after the morning of the Separation incident, The *Deseret News* reported that the Howlands and Dunn had been helped by friendly Indians "almost five days ago," who "put them on a trail leading to Washington, in Southern Utah. On their journey they saw a squaw gathering seeds and shot her; whereupon they were followed by three [Shivwits] and killed."

Soon thereafter, Powell received a telegraph message back East from Utah informing him that the Howlands and Dunn had been killed by Indians. No evidence exists to indicate that Major Powell attempted to conduct anything resembling an earnest effort to investigate these murders. Some historians consider this to be one of Powell's worst mistakes in his life.

A year later, however, Powell did finally return for more exploring. He visited the Uinkaret Indians, neighbors to the Shivwits Indians whose territory straddles the route the Howlands and Dunn would have taken. The Uinkarets requested for Powell an interview with the Shivwits. Jacob Hamblin, Mormon scout and proselytizer assigned by Brigham Young to guide Powell, interpreted for him the Shivwits' explanation of the fate of his three men. As Powell would later write, the Shivwits, Hamblin said, had met the three as they were trying to exit the Canyon. The Shivwits had helped them with food and directions. But after the three continued on, Indians from the south (or "east") side of the Colorado arrived and told the Shivwits that they were chasing some drunken miners who had abused and murdered a squaw. At this information, Hamblin explained, a few of the Shivwits pursued, then ambushed the Howlands and Dunn, murdering them in retribution and in sympathy with these other Indians.

Hamblin himself gave a sightly different account. The Shivwits, he said, had told him that:

> —some of their friends from the other side of the river crossed on a raft and told them that miners on their side of the river abused their women. They advised them to kill the three white men who had gone back from the river, for if any mines were found in their country, it would bring great evil among them. The three men were then followed, and killed when asleep.

This same basic story of how and why Powell's three men who hiked out were killed by the Shivwits exists in every book that discusses Powell's full journey. But even on cursory examination, it makes little sense. The full story itself—of miners killing a squaw and Powell's three men being misidentified as these miners—did not seem to surface until nearly a year after the Howlands and Dunn had been killed. This late breaking of this story is itself strange in light of the Mormons having reported for a year that the Shivwits had killed the Howlands and Dunn over a murdered woman. If the Mormons knew that these Indians had killed these three whites, why had they never during a year of opportunity asked all the details of *exactly* why? This lack was not because relations between the Shivwits and Mormons were too weak. The Mormons had baptized the entire tribe en masse into the LDS church seven years earlier, in 1862.

Indeed, this "We-killed-them-by-mistake-because-other-Indians-who-had-rafted-the-Canyon-came-and-told-us-that-they-were-bad-miners-who-shot-a-squaw" story is improbable on most levels. The Howlands and Dunn were well-armed and well experienced with Indians, while their adversaries were few and had only bows and arrows. On top of this, the two Indians who "confessed" were never arrested by the Mormons. Nor were Powell's chronometer, the barometer, or the expedition's records ever mentioned as having been recovered from this tribe by the Mormons. Besides, who *were* those bad miners who had allegedly perpetrated the rape-murder? Where did they come from and where did they go? This is even weaker. There exist virtually no written records of mining or prospecting activity for this region of Western Grand Canyon—which indeed was terra incognita for whites, including Jacob Hamblin himself—in 1869. Claim records found by George Billingsley, E. E. Spamer, and D. Menkes in their exhaustive history of Canyon mining *Quest for the Pillar of Gold: The Mines & Miners of the Grand Canyon* postdate Powell's 1869 trip. Indeed, it was *this* trip that gave the green light to pursuing riches *in* Grand Canyon. Moreover, during the years 1867 to 1869, the Hualapai Indians living in the Western Grand Canyon south of the Colorado were locked in a brutal war against the U.S. Cavalry. Lengthy scorched-earth campaigns by the army against the Hualapais finally fizzled out during 1869–1870. In short, 1869 was not a likely year for miners to have been prospecting in this region. As local historian Michael Belshaw—who followed on foot the Howlands' and Dunn's hike out Separation—notes:

> *That a small group of Indians or a solitary Indian from the South would be motivated to cross the river and carry the news to unrelated tribes is on the thin edge of probability. The story is less plausible because no mining had been carried out within a hundred miles of Shivwit territory* [until 1872 in Kanab Canyon and in Grand Gulch] *and should have been of little interest to them. Frederick S. Dellenbaugh reports that the Indians were incited by members of their own band, who reported outrages to the north....It is also most unlikely that the* [Powell's] *three men wantonly killed an Indian woman as reported in the Deseret News.*

Is it impossible that there could have been any miners in this region at the end of August in 1869? No, but there have been few worse years in known history for a miner to survive—let alone prospect—in Western Grand Canyon. Even so, according to anthropologists Henry F. Dobyns and Robert C. Euler, mining *had* been taking place since 1864, but 60 air miles south-southwest of the edge of Shivwits territory (about 100 miles by an overland route), and hence may not have been unknown in concept to the Shivwits. More to the point, Dobyns and Euler add, some Shivwits had moved south of the river to Pine Spring near camps of their southern trading partners, the Hualapai, and thus *could* have been the "friends" who crossed the river to the north as Jacob Hamblin reported. On top of all this, because the Hualapais had been very badly treated by the U.S. Cavalry, the Shivwits too may have looked upon any white men—including the Howlands and Dunn—as enemies.

Yet upon full analysis, Hamblin's story of *bad* miners abusing Indian women, as translated from the Shivwits, seems a concoction made up post hoc by the Indians to justify their killing and robbing innocent men—or else made up instead by someone else to cover their own unjustified murder of the Howlands and Dunn.

The initial story of Indians having killed the Howlands and Dunn even seemed flimsy in 1869. Jack Sumner doubted from the beginning that the Indians could have killed his three comrades. Sumner told Stanton that, even while Powell's six were still inside Grand Canyon on their final day (and afterward):

> *The boys discussed the conduct and the fate of the three men left ashore. They all seemed to think the red bellies would surely get them. But I could not believe that the reds would get them, as I had trained Dunn for two years in how to avoid a surprise, and I did not think the red devils would make an open attack on three armed men. But I did have some misgiving that they would not escape the double-eyed white devils that infested that part of the country. Grapevine reports convinced me later that that was their fate....*
>
> *I heard about two months afterwards, while at Fort Yuma, California, that they [Mormon searchers] brought in the report that the Howland brothers and Dunn came to an Indian camp, shot an Indian, and ravished and shot three squaws, and that the Indians then collected a force and killed all three of the men. But I am positive I saw some years afterward the silver watch that I had given Howland [to pass on to Sumner's sister]. I was with some men in a carousal. One of them had a watch and boasted how he came by it. I tried to get hold of it so as to identify it by a certain screw that I had made and put in myself, but it was spirited away, and I was never afterwards able to get sight of it. Such evidence is not conclusive, but all of it was enough to convince me that the Indians were not at the head of the murder, if they had anything to do with it.*

Not only was Sumner "positive" about the watch being his, way back on August 30, 1869, when he, Hawkins, Hall, Bradley, and the Powell brothers arrived at the Rio Virgin, he was also suspicious about motives of at least one of the local whites they met there. This being only two days after the Howland brothers and Dunn had started their hike up Separation Canyon, Powell and the others explained to these friendly Mormons the three men's predicament and location, asking that help be sent if possible. During this request, as Sumner later complained in disgust:

> *But when Major Powell made the foolish break of telling them the amount of valuables the boys had, I noticed a complete change in the actions of a certain one of the men present. From one with a listless demeanor he instantly changed to a wide-awake, intensely interested listener, and his eyes snapped and burned like a rattlesnake's, particularly when Major Powell told him of an especially*

valuable chronometer for which he had paid six hundred and fifty dollars.

Aside from this insight into which of Powell's priorities might be served by asking these Mormons to render assistance to Dunn and the Howlands, Sumner's observation also clarifies how a significant monetary motive could quickly have developed for a robbery-murder of the missing three men. It also offers a possible explanation for why almost nothing at all that was carried by the Howlands and Dunn was ever visibly recovered from the Mormons' friends, the baptized Shivwits, who had little use for barometers, chronometers, or notes of river expeditions.

In 1919, Billy Hawkins, then an old man, mentioned to William Wallace Bass, also old, that "some years afterwards [after 1869] I, with a party of some others, buried their bones [the Howlands' and Dunn's] on the Shewits [sic] Mountains, below Kanab Wash." No more has been said on this burial. Nor has anyone found its location or that of the murders. Nor, again, have the items the Howlands or Dunn carried been found—other than that watch Sumner was positive was his.

Could the Howlands and Dunn have been murdered by Mormons for a simple robbery? Or was it something more?

That something more would likely be the same set of conditions that prompted the September 7, 1857, Mountain Meadows Massacre perpetrated by Indians and Mormons in southern Utah. Indeed, without understanding this massacre, the murders of the Howlands and Dunn make little sense.

In late summer of 1857, a wagon train of about 140 people from Arkansas crossed Utah from northeast to southwest. This train was led by one of the three Baker brothers (Captain John T., George W., and Abel) but has been identified historically as the "Fancher party" after Alexander Fancher, the outspoken member of the group. Fancher, for example, had named his oxen after prominent Mormons, such as Brigham Young and Heber C. Kimball. And he boasted of how he loved to beat them. The train not only insulted, but even threatened, Mormons. It also tried to buy food from them, but unsuccessfully. Members of the Fancher train allegedly trampled Mormon crops, shot a Kanosh Indian, stole Indian cattle, and may have poisoned a water hole that killed more cattle and more Indians. Next, before leaving Utah, the Bakers and Fancher made the foolish decision to camp at Mountain Meadows in southwestern Utah to fatten their oxen and other livestock before crossing the bleak Nevada deserts.

As is told in detail by Juanita Brooks in her *Mountain Meadows Massacre*, the Paiutes, roughly 300–600 strong, gave an ultimatum to the Mormons of southern Utah, whom they outnumbered by nearly 4:1. The Paiutes' threat? "Either you help us attack this wagon train or else we will fight *with* the U.S. Army, now en route to Utah, *against* you when they arrive." These Indians had attacked the Fancher party earlier in retaliation for some of its members having shot some Paiutes. But the Paiutes had failed to overrun the train. A few Indians had been killed and several wounded. And all for naught. The Fancher party had continued to withstand the Indians' siege for a week.

The Indians thus enlisted/extorted Mormon help to break this stalemate. John Doyle Lee, a prominent Mormon and the local Indian Agent, acted as intermediary. Lee first tried to save everyone's lives by telling the Indians to simply take all the train's livestock and go home. But they refused. Making things even more impossible, Lee was subordinate to Major John M. Higbee of the Mormon militia, who had orders from Isaac C. Haight to kill "all the immigrants who could talk."

So Lee convinced the train to surrender their weapons.

If this seems to make no sense, remember that only ten years earlier the infamous Donner Party had suffered a hideous disaster tainted by cannibalism due to having reached the east slope of the Sierra Nevada too late to cross it, but then having tried anyway by pioneering a new route that left them bogged down in unseasonably deep snow. Perhaps the Fancher party worried that they too might not reach the southern Sierra in time for a safe crossing unless they left Utah soon. At any rate, the Fancher party agreed to Lee's conditions.

The Mormons convinced the fifty men of the train to separate from the wagons by a few hundred yards and then formally surrender their arms. Then, as soon as each man handed his gun over, his Mormon counterpart shot him dead (some Mormons of this militia refused to commit murder, but others nearby did it for them). Meanwhile the Paiutes spent the next half hour murdering all the women and most of the children with knives and hatchets. They spared the 18 youngest for adoption into Mormon families. After killing 120 people, the Paiutes and Mormons alike stole everything the victims had owned. Most important, everyone involved swore a "Covenant of Silence." The entire wagon train and the Fancher party simply ceased to exist.

Despite several federal investigations over the years, by 1869 no one had been arrested, tried, or punished for this mass murder. But the U.S. government still wanted to know who had done it.

Knowing this, the question immediately arises: Was Jacob Hamblin's explanation of the Shivwits having killed Powell's three men a cover-up to hoodwink Powell? Was Hamblin reliable? John D. Lee, who worked with and around Hamblin, referred to him as "Dirty-Fingered Jake" and called him an habitual liar. But what might Hamblin have been covering up with his Shivwits story?

And what *really* happened to the Howland brothers and Dunn?

One might guess that if we did not know by now, we never will. But this could be wrong. "New" information surfaced recently via a fluke discovery made by Wesley P. Larson, professor emeritus and former dean of the College of Science at Southern Utah University. In the 1980s, Larson purchased the old historic house built by John Steele in Toquerville. Steele, born in Ireland in 1821, was an unpublished but accomplished explorer of the plateaus of southern Utah and northern Arizona. At one time, for example, he rode around the entire Grand Canyon. Steele was also a Parowan judge, a Mayor, and a county recorder. Larson, also a Mormon, had sifted through a trunk of old documents and letters that John Steele's great grandson, Gary Callister, had turned up. Larsen found among them a letter, verified as authentic, written to John Steele in 1883 by William Leany, apparently in response to a letter that Steele—by then an old man—had written to him suggesting that it was time for them both to confess to and repent their sins.

William Leany, born in 1815, was a Parowan City Council Member and Harrisburg Water Master. He had fallen from the Church's graces, however, in 1857 when he gave food to William Aiden, one of the members of the doomed Fancher party soon to be massacred at Mountain Meadows. Leany had given William Aiden food because he was the son of Dr. S. R. Aiden, who had saved Leany's life earlier in Tennessee from an anti-Mormon mob while Leany was on a church mission. For this minor repayment for saving his life—by giving food to an "enemy," as Fancher's wagon train was dubbed—local Mormons ambushed Leany at night on his own front porch. They broke a club over Leany's head, fractured his skull, and left him for dead. Leany failed to die, though years passed before he recovered.

Leany's 1883 letter back to Steele was anything but repentant. He had nothing to repent, he said, adding that his accusers were "drunken, adulterous, murderous wretches." Leany continued, as Larson interprets, to "spill his guts" to his old friend Steele:

> —*God shall bear me witness that I am clean of all of which they* [President Erastus Snow and others] *accuse me & they guilty of all that I accuse them & much more.... And I cannot see that for me to confess to a lie would make me more worthy or they less guilty & here let me say that my object is & has been to stay the overwhelming tide of thieving whoredom murder and Suicide & like abominations that threaten to desolate the land & you are far from ignorant of those deeds of blood from the day the picket was broken on my head* **to the day those three were murdered in our ward & the murderer killed to stop the shedding of more blood**....*As the old Prophets said of the blood & violence in the city & blood tondreth blood if that was not fulfilled in* **the killing of the three in one room of our ward** *please say what it was & for all this & much more unrighteous dominion shall we be cast out of the land....Be assured that I will, God being my helper, clear my skirts of the mobbing, raking, stealing, whoredom, murder, suicide,*

lying, slander & all wickedness & abominations even in high places. [Bold ours]

Larson admitted that this letter led him to suspect that Powell's three men had succeeded in their hike through Shivwits country. The three must have been seen, Larson concluded, and then brought to Toquerville, the county seat and local center of Church authority. Only weeks earlier in 1869—Larson also found out—Brigham Young had ridden circuit through southern Utah to warn faithful Mormons that there would soon come yet another attempt by Gentiles to invade Utah. The coming "war," Young warned passionately, would be so hellacious that blood would flow as deep as the bridles of their horses. To avoid being attacked by surprise in this war, the Latter-day Saints posted sentries at passes leading into southern Utah.

Hence, the Howland Brothers and Dunn *were* likely spotted as they hiked north. And, once spotted, they would have been brought to Toquerville.

Leany's letter mentioned to Steele, "*our ward.*" Larson looked into this and found that the only time that Leany and Steele had shared a ward was in 1869. On top of this, Leany mentioned "*in one room of our ward.*" The only ward of that time, Larson found, which contained more than one room was that in Toquerville.

Larson next wondered if all of this could refer to some other three people murdered or killed somehow. So he searched the records of 1869 for the local region of southern Utah. Only one trio had been killed in that year, the Howland Brothers and Dunn.

But why would they have been murdered?

1869 was another year of prejudice against Mormons, of federal investigation concerning the as-yet-unsolved Mountain Meadows Massacre, of Mormon paranoia about being punished, and of Mormon vigilance against federal spies. Into this climate of paranoia and fear wandered three very beat-up river runners from a river that not only had never been run before, but whose name was synonymous with impossibility—almost with death itself. In this climate, when most strangers were suspected to be federal spies, the Howlands and Dunn would have been doubly suspect given their improbable story about having boated down the impossible Colorado in Grand Canyon. In short, to some inquisitors, they would have been unbelievable. Hence, they were lying. Hence they must have been covering something up. Something like being federal spies. The three, Larson suspected, might have been killed outright once they were brought from somewhere along the trail from Separation Canyon to Mount Trumbull and then past the Hurricane Cliffs to Toquerville—even without sanction from higher church authorities.

If this did happen, then a day or so later word of their execution would have reached Salt Lake City—some message to the effect that "we just executed three federal spies whose cover story was that they had just boated Grand

Canyon." Such a message would have arrived at virtually the same time as word from John Wesley Powell at the Rio Virgin reached Salt Lake saying that his expedition had been successful, but three of his men had hiked north from Western Grand Canyon and would need assistance. Together these two messages would have caused instant turmoil—if not panic.

Larson suspects that church authorities quickly sent word back to Toquerville commanding that the executioner himself must be executed and the entire crime itself be covered up completely to avoid further bloodshed. Leany's passage in his 1883 letter, "*& the murderer killed to stop the shedding of more blood*," suggests too that this is what happened. Larson suspects further that the blame for the three killings was officially placed on the Mormons' Indian allies (who also took the blame for the Mountain Meadows Massacre and for uncounted other deeds committed by Mormon militias who dressed up as Indians to rustle Gentiles' cattle or to assassinate enemies).

Indeed, the discovery that the Indians had killed the Howlands and Dunn was announced by Mormons only about ten days after the killings actually happened. After this coverup, Larson suspects, everyone involved was sworn to a blood oath "covenant of silence" similar to that sworn after the Mountain Meadows Massacre.

In Hurricane, Utah, Wes Larson told Flagstaff author Scott Thybony that, while this scenario was the only one that added up to account for all the facts, he wanted to corroborate his hypothesis with more evidence. Larson had a friend who submitted for him a request to examine documents of that era in the Mormon Archives. Larson arrived there, hoping to find any messages which had passed back and forth from Toquerville.

After being kept waiting for an hour, he was confronted by the chief archivist who demanded to know on whose authority Larson could view such documents. Larson said, "Well, I'm a Mormon."

The archivist denied Larson access and told him to leave.

"I guess you have to be a *good* Mormon," Larson said wryly to Thybony—the irony being that earlier during the heat of that day, Larson had steadfastly refused a cold beer because of his religion.

Thybony asked Larson if he was worried about repercussions from the church if he published what he had put together. "Hell yes, I'm worried."

But Larson did not give up. One of the most important missing pieces to this puzzle was who, specifically, had murdered the Howlands and Dunn and then was executed himself. As Larson dug deeper, it seemed clear to him that the murderer was Eli N. Pace. Pace was a son-in-law of John D. Lee and had killed all three, Larson reckoned, to protect Lee from the three armed federal men coming out of "nowhere." Pace died on January 29, 1870 (five months after the Howlands and Dunn) under mysterious—and suspicious—circumstances, shot with a Remington revolver positioned to suggest that he had done it by his own hand. Not long after this, Brigham Young would send John

D. Lee himself to the confluence of the Paria and Colorado rivers to build and run a ferry—Lees Ferry. Not only was the ferry necessary to colonize northern Arizona, its desolate location would keep Lee isolated from federal marshals.

Just before Larson and Thybony parted company, Larson answered Thybony's question of why he had gone to all the trouble he had to investigate the killings of the Howland Brothers and Dunn. "If these were Mormons who did it," Larson answered, "and the Paiutes got the damn blame for everything, it's...it's...." He stopped. Later he admitted, "I only wish I'd felt this way fifty years ago."

Between 1863 and 1864, U.S. Brigadier General James H. Carlton master-minded and commanded a politically-motivated and apparently illegal scorched-earth war against the Navajo Tribe. This led to the fruition of his scheme to relocate all of the 5,000 Navajos he estimated to be alive (those not already being held in slavery) via the "Long Walk" to a "reservation" at Fort Sumner (a.k.a. Bosque Redondo) on the Pecos River in east-central New Mexico. Each of the more than 300-mile Long Walks by captured or surrendered Navajos from Arizona to Fort Sumner in early 1864 resembled the Japanese-mastered Bataan Death March of American and Philippine troops during 1942. Each Navajo Long Walk was brutal. Along the way, unscrupulous New Mexicans stole Navajo livestock and captured straggling Navajos as slaves. Yet these Indians may have been some of the lucky ones, as historian Ruth Roessel explains:

> There were a few wagons to haul some personal belongings, but the trip was made on foot. People were shot down on the spot if they complained about being tired or sick, or if they stopped to help someone. If a woman became in labor with a baby, she was killed. There was absolutely no mercy.

Even though one out of ten Navajos on the Long Walks died en route, by 1865 their numbers at Fort Sumner had swelled to 9,022. Many of these starved or died of disease. So, during the next three years (during which General Carlton was relieved of duty) before the Navajos were allowed to return to *Dinetah* (Navajoland), many Navajos escaped to flee into the most recondite alcoves of the canyonlands of the Colorado Plateau, to the foot of Navajo Mountain, or even into Apache territory—as many Navajos had done even earlier to escape persistent slave raiders operating out of New Mexico. A best estimate is 2,000–4,000 Navajos had also escaped capture and/or surrender to the Long Walks themselves during the 1863–1864 war. A few of these early refugees from Navajoland and later ones from Fort Sumner were desperate enough to flee into *Tsechiikolh* ("Red Cliff Canyon," a.k.a. Grand Canyon).

One young family—a man, his pregnant wife, and their young child—seeking this vast sanctuary had almost reached its zone of safety. They were nearing the area of the South Rim from which, twenty years hence, Captain John T. Hance would build a trail down to River Mile 77 to facilitate his mining of asbestos. Now, in the 1860s, however, no trail had been built. Even so, the route Hance's trail would follow had already seen the passing of countless hundreds of Native Americans, from at least as far back as the *Anasazi* Puebloans a thousand years ago. It was still a good path. This young Navajo family fleeing the U.S. Cavalry knew that the Inner Canyon would offer them refuge, at least for a few months. There would be bighorn sheep to hunt and several wild foods—honey mesquite, agave, prickly pear, and many other plants—to gather. It would not be an easy life. But it would at least be one distant from enemies and capture and possible death. Besides, everyone knew that no *bilagaana* (white man) could find their way into the huge, forbidding fastness of Red Cliff Canyon. Yes, down there life would at least be safe.

But to enter this refuge without being tracked, the young Navajo man knew that he had to be thorough now. So he lagged behind his wife and child as they rode their horse ahead. He brushed away their footprints and removed other signs of their passing. Later, he caught up with them at a part of the South Rim that whites would someday name Grandview. To his surprise and alarm, he found his wife, instead of riding their horse, sitting on the ground in tears and hugging their child to her pregnant belly, swollen almost to term.

Alert now, he scanned for the cause of his wife's despair. Ahead, in a place just north of the future site of Hall's cabin, he saw some strange Navajos squatting over their murdered horse and butchering it for meat. Nearby stood a few more Navajos of a type the young man knew instantly to be bad men.

Without hesitation, the young husband raised his rifle, took careful aim, and fired at the man sitting atop a rock ledge and sharpening his knife. The other rogues spun in shock as their comrade crumpled to the ground mortally wounded. With barely a glimpse of the angry young husband, the brigands scattered and fled into the forest of pinyon pines and junipers.

The slain man, it turned out, was, among Navajos at least, public enemy number one by the name of Aah'yi'd digish. He was a murderous renegade Navajo robber who led a small gang of robbers and killers who preyed on members of their own people. He was infamous among the tribe as a very bad man. When eventually other Navajos—many of whom were also fleeing from Carlton's relentless U.S. Cavalry—learned of the death of this notorious robber and killer, they rejoiced. Now at least the tiny hidden enclaves of wilderness sanctuary remaining to them might be safe.

Having just killed public enemy number one and also having earned the gratitude of thousands of his people, however, did not free the young husband from a harsh reality: the disagreeable task of now butchering his family's slain horse. In such desperate times as these, nothing could be left to waste.

He also examined Aah'yi'd digish's body. He removed the dead man's medicine bundle. Later, as he and his family continued their hegira down into Red Cliff Canyon via the route with would ultimately become the Hance Trail, he stopped at a cave and hid his slain enemy's medicine bundle.

On nearly the last night of the last trip of 1971, a 20-day run operated by Grand Canyon Expeditions, trip leader Rick Petrillo regaled his passengers around the campfire with the unsolved mysterious disappearance of Glen and Bessie Hyde (see Chapter 4). As usual, Petrillo's small audience was captivated and intrigued by the Hydes' reckless bid for stardom and then their mysterious fate. Later, as the boatmen on this trip, George Billingsley, O. C. Dale, and Regan Dale, sat around the fire the tables turned.

A little old lady on the trip, Liz Cutler, announced that she had a confession to make. Billingsley had already been impressed by this woman. She frequently seemed to know more about the Canyon than she should have for a first timer. This time she dropped a bomb shell. She said she knew some of what had happened during the Hydes' fateful journey because she had known them. When pressed about how this could be, she confessed that she knew them because *she* was Bessie Hyde.

O. C., who considered Liz a good-humored trickster, asked something like, "Well, if you're Bessie, where's Glen?"

Liz became serious. Glen, she said, had changed when he got on the river. He was no longer the man she had fallen in love with. He had become abusive, she explained. "He was a son of a bitch who beat me all the time." Liz (a.k.a. Bessie) explained that she had wanted to quit the river at Hermit, but Glen had forced her into the boat. She knew, she said, from Emery Kolb that the worst rapids—232-Mile, Separation Rapid (River Mile 239.6), and Lava Cliff Rapid (River Mile 246)—were downstream of Diamond Creek. So Diamond represented her last chance to escape. That night above Diamond, their 42nd night on the trip, they had camped on the south side of the river. Fearing now for her life, she had waited until Glen fell asleep. Then she took a knife and stabbed him to death. She then pushed his body into the river. Next she reloaded the boat and shoved it into the river too. At dawn she hiked a few miles down to Diamond Creek and then hiked the 23 miles out to Route 66 where she caught a bus to a new life.

Pausing for a moment, Liz regathered herself. She reached into her pocket and retrieved a small pocket knife. "And this, " she said, displaying it, "was what I did him in with."

The Dale cousins never took Liz seriously. But Billingsley, with his scientist's take on the world around him, thought to himself, "You never know..."

How possible was Liz's story?

Emery and Ellsworth Kolb, Jim Brooks, Rollin C. Hyde, and Deputy Sheriff John Nelson visited Diamond Creek on Christmas Eve of 1928 to search for

Glen and Bessie. Weeks later, the elder Hyde and Nelson had hiked upriver. More than a dozen miles upstream of Diamond lay an abandoned camp site. Because the river level was dropping into winter, nothing had washed away. The beach held foot prints, an empty jar of lima beans, an empty can and that jar from southern Idaho. *Someone* suspiciously like the Hydes had camped there recently, and the route from there to Diamond, while not easy, *was* walkable.

So if Liz was Bessie, why did she come back and why would she confess to murder? When asked why she came back, Liz answered, "Because I loved him so much." When asked why she confessed, she said, "I've lived my life. And no one is going to believe my story anyway." Was this because it was so outlandish? Or because it was in fact untrue and Liz knew no one would take it seriously?

Strangely, no one followed up on this for years. But in the meantime the plot thickened. On December 11, 1976, Emery Kolb finally died. We say "finally" because he had been living on the South Rim since 1902, and had shown up there as an adult. He died at age 95. Indeed Emery still holds the record for length of residence at the South Rim's Grand Canyon Village, nearly 74 years. He also holds an even more interesting record. In 1911–1912 he and his brother Ellsworth had each built a boat and had rowed them during an epic trip from Green River, Wyoming, to beyond the foot of Grand Canyon. During parts of this trip they had taken moving pictures. The two spliced together a movie. Emery showed it daily and narrated it live, and later via audiotape, at the South Rim Kolb Studio from 1912 to 1976. It was, and still is, the longest running movie of all time. At any rate, when Emery Kolb died, his studio was jammed with the impedimenta of ages.

As the workmen cleared it out they found a canoe-type boat (given to Kolb by David Rust) hiked up to the rafters. They lowered it. Inside the boat were canvas bundles. One contained a set of old clothes. The other held the skeleton of a man. The skull, stored inside a coffee can, had a bullet hole in the temple. Inside the skull a bullet was lodged against the opposite side. Someone said, "Hey, that looks like it could be Glen Hyde."

At this time Bruce Babbitt was Governor of Arizona. The skull was clearly of a person who had been murdered—or committed suicide—hence it became state's evidence in an unsolved crime. Governor Babbitt was a Canyon-phile of the first order. Nothing Canyonesque was beneath his interest. And the skeleton of a murder victim in Emery Kolb's Studio was a kind of Canyon Cleopatra's Needle. Who knew what mysteries from the past it might translate? Babbitt ordered a special forensic investigation of the skeleton and the clothes.

Norm Tessman, Curator of the Sharlot Hall Museum in Prescott, examined the clothes. Yes, they were 1920s vintage, or maybe 1930s. But the belt buckle included with them did not match the one worn by Glen Hyde in Emery Kolb's photos of the honeymooners.

Forensic anthropologist Walter H. Birkby in Tucson examined the bones and the skull for architecture and degree of suture closure (for age). The skeleton seemed to have lain exposed to the elements for a year or more before being gathered into a more protective environment. Yes, the hole was a bullet hole. And the slug inside the cranium was from an H & R .32 caliber revolver. The trajectory of the bullet strongly suggested homicide, not suicide. The cranial sutures suggested that the skull was a 23-year-old man's. Moreover, Birkby's anthropomorphic measurements revealed the eye orbits to be angled wrong for what Glen Hyde looked like in life. The cheek bones were too wide. The chin too square. The whole skeleton was too stocky. "These bones that were submitted for analysis," Birkby reported, "are not the bones of Glen Hyde. Period."

On top of these anthropometrics was credibility. Birkby scoffed, finding the notion "preposterous that he [Emery Kolb] would off somebody and then keep the damn body around."

But why would anyone suspect Kolb to have Glen Hyde's skeleton to begin with? The chain is weak but seductive enough to raise an eyebrow. First, Western historian Michael Harrison was a young NPS ranger in 1928 in Grand Canyon. He explained to one of us (Ghiglieri) that Emery Kolb almost completely sequestered Glen and Bessie Hyde after they reached the South Rim Village. Second, Emery Kolb had badgered Glen to take his own life jackets. When Glen refused them, Kolb suggested that Glen at least take something else to provide floatation, such as inner tubes from the Fred Harvey Stable. Third, Emery's daughter, Edith, was a young woman of twenty, much like Bessie only more Western and outdoorsy. Edith, in fact, was the first woman ever (at age 15) to run a Grand Canyon rapid, Hance Rapid, with a whopping drop of 30 feet, in her dad's boat when he was the head boatman of the 1923 U.S. Geological Survey Expedition in Grand Canyon. In Bessie, Emery may have seen his daughter Edith in but two more years, entwined with some idiot egotist in a stubbornly dangerous stunt to achieve stardom regardless of the risk to the woman he bullied along while refusing life jackets. Rescuing Bessie was, in a golden-rule sort of way, rescuing Edith.

The plot really thickens when the next rumor is added. Around the end of November, 1928, at the time when Glen and Bessie were to pass Diamond Creek and finally make their quick run to Needles, Emery is rumored to have disappeared from the South Rim. Supposedly, the rumor goes, he went to Peach Springs and then down to Diamond Creek to try one last time to save Bessie (and Glen's) life with his life jackets.

At Diamond Creek the two men found one another so irritating that they got physical and somehow Glen came out the loser.

In which case Bessie would have not knifed Glen, she instead would have been the beneficiary of Emery's rescue. And her confession in 1971 would have been a cover for Kolb, her rescuer, who still lived at the South Rim.

From Diamond, Bessie and Emery Kolb could have gone out to Route 66, her to a new life and him back to the rim....(with Glen Hyde's body?)

No, the skeleton really does not make much sense, does it? And indeed Emery's old friend, Art Gallenson, finally explained where it had come from. Kolb had found it at an old mining site, he said, in the Canyon below Yavapai Point. He had collected it and donated the bones to the local, tiny, Grand Canyon School. Edith Kolb, born in 1908, was the first non-Native child to grow up at the South Rim; she attended this school. Finally, when the school acquired one of those articulated skeletons, they returned the disconnected bundle of bones to Kolb.

Even so, when one of us (Ghiglieri) asked Bruce Babbitt in late 1988 what, exactly, that forensic investigation had actually found, he paused, looked puzzled, and answered, "What ever *did* happen with that, anyway."

When Emery Kolb stashed the skeleton in Rust's boat, he joked to Art Gallenson, "when I die and somebody finds that skeleton, it's gonna cause a lot of commotion....Take it to the school in Kanab, would you?" But Gallenson never did.

What about Liz? Did she have a life before 1928? Two river sleuths dogged her early trail. In the 1980s, writer and river runner Scott Thybony finally called Liz Cutler (a.k.a. Bessie) to interview her. Yes, she remembered the trip very well. She described details the boatmen themselves had forgotten: bad runs in Horn Creek Rapid, a girl who broke her arm and had to be evacuated, and the broken lower unit on O. C.'s motor. But when Thybony asked Liz what she knew about the Glen and Bessie Hyde story, "She drew a complete blank." She even denied having told the story. "I'm not Bessie. [she said on the phone] I don't even know the name, 'Hyde.'"

Not long after this, river sleuth and Dock Marston protegé Martin J. Anderson became intrigued by this same enigma. He researched both Bessie and Liz back to each one's birth certificates. Bessie was born Bessie Haley in Washington, D.C. on December 29, 1905, and lived later in Parkersburg, West Virginia. She attended college with Earl Helmick, whom she secretly married on June 4, 1926, and she majored in art at Marshall College in Huntington, West Virginia. Liz Cutler was born on December 2, 1909, in Pomeroy, Ohio, (maybe 40 miles from Parkersburg) as Elizabeth Arnold. After Bessie abandoned Earl and was attending the California School of Fine Arts in San Francisco, Liz was attending the fourth annual Arnold family reunion at Rock Springs Fairground. What, then, are the chances that Bessie escaped the Canyon, assumed Liz Cutler's identity, and then grew four inches taller?

Infinitesimal.

What are the chances that Liz herself as a late teenager had read in the local newspapers about the romantic and mysterious Grand Canyon disappearance of local girl Bessie Haley/Hyde in 1928?

Pretty good.

Was Liz an impostor? Not really. Girls just want to have fun.

But being charged with murder in Arizona isn't much fun.

Marty Anderson also contacted Earl Helmick. In the past, Helmick had refused to talk to people about Bessie. And to Anderson, he was only slightly more open. When he asked Helmick what he thought about the stories going around that Bessie was alive ("Unsolved Mysteries" at this time was airing a television pseudo-documentary on Bessie and Glen), he simply said: "No, she is dead."

When the Kolb brothers and Brooks found the Hydes' scow, Bessie's purse was still aboard it. Inside her purse were a couple of dollars. Had Bessie killed Glen and decided to hike out, would she have left her money behind?

Maybe.

As we went to press with this book, new and very strange information surfaced. It surfaced—and was published in a one-page article—because of the generosity and enthusiasm of yet another river sleuth, Brad Dimock. Dimock, who, while working on a book-length biography of Bessie and Glen Hyde, recently interviewed Bill George, an owner of Western River Expeditions, which had bought Georgie White's Grand Canyon Royal River Rats company from her while she lay on her death bed in 1992. A big shocker to George came from Georgie's nurse/employee of more than a decade, Lee McCurry (now also deceased), who tried to sort out Georgie's papers just before her funeral. McCurry told him, "Bill, we don't know who we are burying today," and then showed him "Georgie's" birth certificate. It read "Bessie DeRoss," DeRoss being Georgie's maiden name. Bessie had lived in Denver, McCurry explained, not Chicago as Georgie's biographies tell it. (As subsequent biographers have found, notes Brad Dimock, Georgie's "autobiographical notes are often pure fiction.") "Georgie" also had a marriage certificate stashed in her lingerie drawer (along with a pistol), certified and stamped by a notary. Who got married on this certificate? Bessie Haley and Glen R. Hyde.

Bill George tried to add up this very bizarre two plus two. Georgie, during all of the time he had known her, would never remain for even one second in the same room with Emery Kolb, no matter how important the overall meeting might be that was taking place in that room. Why she refused to, George never learned. He only knew, "She *hated* [Emery]. With a *passion.*" Remember, Kolb had been the most important known player in warning Glen and Bessie about how bad the river would be in Lower Granite Gorge. On top of all this, both McCurry and her brother Marty Hunsaker (who drowned in Crystal Rapid as trip leader for Georgie on June 14, 1989) both suspected that Georgie *was* Bessie Hyde (the photo match between Bessie at her high school graduation and of Georgie in middle age are eerily similar, as are the years of their birth). Georgie, McCurry and Hunsaker also noticed, evinced a "black widow" predatory fantasy of murdering her own mate.

Where does this leave us with regard to Bessie Hyde's fate? Well, despite Georgie being several inches taller than Bessie, and despite the Hydes' marriage license being a *copy*, it leaves us anxiously seeking Brad Dimock's book: *Sunk Without a Sound*.

No one who knows the Canyon's history doubts that there exist untold—and maybe untellable—tales of murder that unfolded in real life below its rims. The inaccessibility of so many parts of this gigantic labyrinth lends itself to converting a run of the mill homicide into the "perfect" murder. "Perfect" in that the location of the victim and the details of what happened to him or her may remain hidden for eternity. The Canyon is the dry rock version of the middle of the ocean.

Despite this seeming convenience to the potential murderer, as with suicide within the Canyon, murder within it almost does not happen. Considering that more than half a million people have run the Colorado in Grand Canyon, and at least a million more people have hiked or camped within it, the very low number of known suicides and murders in the Canyon is impressive. As we saw in the previous chapter, suicides successfully initiated below the rims can be counted on one's fingers. The same is true of murder in the Canyon. Yet on the rims and plateaus, homicides, both successful and attempted, have been far more frequent (see Table 8).

In mid-June of 1927, for example, Bert Lauzon, custodian of the Bright Angel Trail and constable at Grand Canyon, received a strange warning from the sheriff's office of Okmulgee, Oklahoma. Five men, the sheriff warned, were reportedly traveling in a Buick, Packard, and a Studebaker to Grand Canyon around June 20. Their intent was to rob the Grand Canyon payroll. The sheriff's warning included names and descriptions and even photos of the five would-be robbers. Instantly NPS rangers were on the alert.

Late in the morning on June 23, a Buick sedan drove into Grand Canyon National Park. Leo Smith, the registry officer, recognized its driver as Matthew Kimes, one of the "bad five" from Okmulgee. Kimes was truly a hard case. At age 21, he had already been convicted of bank robbery and murder in Oklahoma.

Smith passed word ahead that Kimes—driving the Buick with its owners George Keady and his wife—was approaching the Village. At 2:30 p.m., Coconino County Sheriff John Parsons spotted Kimes near a Bright Angel cottage. Parsons told Kimes to come with him to the administration building. Both men climbed into the Buick. But as Kimes drove down the hill by El Tovar, he said, "The brakes won't hold!"

As he shot past the building he reached down and yanked the emergency brake. When his hand came back up, however, his fingers were wrapped around the butt of a Colt .45. Parsons grabbed Kimes' hand and the gun. For an amazing 15 minutes the two men fought all over the interior of that Buick. They piled into one seat, wrestled their way to the next seat, then slid onto the floor.

During this epic car-shaking frenzy, Curley Ennis, the garage foreman for

Fred Harvey Co., happened along. He reckoned the two men were drunks locked into an impressive argument. But when Ennis looked into the car, the muzzle of the .45 swung into his face. "Get away," someone commanded. Ennis then recognized Parsons' face under the steering wheel.

At this same moment George Cravey, the trail foreman, joined Ennis and also peered into the jiggling Buick. The .45 now swung into his face.

Bizarrely, neither Ennis nor Cravey could manage to get into a position to haul Kimes off of Parsons. So the two desperate men in the car—one trying to kill, the other fighting for his life—continued to weave and wrestle and grunt around the inside of the Buick. Finally Ennis ran to the garage for his gun. En route he heard three shots, then five more.

Kimes had broken out of Parsons' grip, exited the Buick, and run. Now Parsons had a chance to grab his own gun. He fired twice at Kimes. Ordinarily Parsons was a dead shot. But his hands had been torn by the hammer of Kimes' gun while wrestling over it and were now bleeding and unsteady. Both of Parsons' shots missed Kimes. Kimes turned around and fired several times back at Parsons. His shots also missed.

Kimes ran to the rim and dropped over the edge onto a sloping descent. Within ten minutes, at least thirty Grand Canyon residents carrying rifles or pistols deployed themselves along the Rim Trail in a semi-circle reaching from El Tovar to Yavapai Point. Ennis and Cravey tracked Kimes through a myriad of other tracks. They too dropped off the rim. They saw where Kimes had dug his heels into the steep slope, loosening some gravel.

Three hundred feet down they hit the rim of a cliff falling off several hundred feet. At this same instant they spotted Kimes, about twenty feet away.

"I give up," Kimes said. "I know when I've had enough."

This sounded good. But maybe too good. Ennis and Cravey could only see Kimes' left hand. Both pursuers ducked behind bushes. Then Ennis saw that Kimes' right hand was also up. Ennis kept his rifle aimed at Kimes while Cravey went up and took Kimes' Colt. Every chamber of the revolver had been reloaded.

Kimes and the Keadys were placed under arrest. Kimes was later executed by the state of Oklahoma.

Forty-five years later, Fred Bustillos trudged up to the Kaibab National Forest observation station on Red Butte, south of the national park entrance. It was still cold. It seemed a bit early to be using this place. But already, in the beginning of March, 1972, the forest was dry and would soon become vulnerable to fire. Bustillos had just driven several miles east of Highway 64 onto Red Butte to make this routine, pre-season inspection of the high lookout station. As a relief fire dispatcher for the U.S. Forest Service, his job didn't pay much. But the view was excellent.

Bustillos' senses suddenly shifted into close focus. Someone had broken into the observation station. The place had been trashed, but not by malicious vandals. Something far more sinister and violent had been unleashed in this cabin. Spatters of dark red blood speckled the floor. Shocked, Bustillos backed up out of the station and turned around to call the Tusayan Ranger Station.

More Forest Service rangers arrived. They soon concluded that someone had used the place for a few days before trashing it. Oddly, the only thing missing from the USFS supplies was a tarp. Left in trade were a bloody ice pick and a .22 pistol.

Even more ominous, outside the station the rangers saw a large drag trail leading to a nearby cliff. About fifty feet below the cliff the rangers spotted the tarp. Something big now lay wrapped up in it.

Unwrapping the tarp was no picnic for the Coconino County Sheriff's Department deputies called to the scene. The body of the middle-aged woman inside it was naked from the waist down, badly bruised and beaten with a pipe wrench, stabbed forty-two times with an ice pick, and then gunshot multiple times. Then, about four or five days before Bustillos had arrived, it had been dragged to this cliff and dumped off.

The Sheriff's Department quickly matched a missing person's report with this corpse. Authorities became convinced that the dead woman was Addie Lee Venturini, age 46, who lived in Jackson, Mississippi. A mother of five, she had abruptly left her children and prominent husband about two weeks earlier. Before vanishing, she had run up a considerable bill buying legal stimulants and depressants from local drugstores.

Venturini, it was known, had been traveling with Thomas J. Smith, age 48, who was driving a two-tone, beige-over-brown 1966 Buick with white Mississippi license plates lettered 25D13083 in green. Smith, a former chef and restaurant manager, had most recently been unemployed. Smith and Venturini had been traveling west in his car but on her credit cards. Why they had come all the way to Grand Canyon was a mystery.

Law enforcement agencies were now alerted to be on the lookout for Thomas J. Smith, considered armed and very dangerous. Smith and his Buick, however, seemed to have vanished.

Five weeks after the grisly find near the Red Butte lookout station, a Kaibab National Forest fire observer was driving home from it. His eye caught a glint of sunlight on metal about two miles from the station. He stopped. Yes, it was a car. He drove closer, then walked over to investigate. The 1966 Buick had white Mississippi license plates with green lettering 25D13083. The car was hidden under a thick stand of trees, but not hidden well enough. With a sinking feeling, the USFS observer re-entered his own vehicle and drove back to Highway 64 to alert the Coconino County Sheriff's Department.

The department arrived with about thirty-five Search and Rescue Unit members. They immediately found a note on the car that said something to the effect of: "The occupants of this car have gone camping, please do not disturb anything."

The SAR team spread out in a wide search pattern. A few hours later and two miles from the Buick, an SAR member spotted a body in a rough gorge. It lay face down. A .22 caliber bullet had entered its right temple. The revolver lay rusting on the carpet of cedar needles beside the body. I.D.s found on the body were those of Thomas J. Smith. Identifying tatoos and other marks on it were also an exact match for Smith's.

Again, what bizarre sort of relationship had led Venturini to flee her family and her home in Jackson and to jump into an old Buick with an unemployed chef and a sack full of drugs and then drive on credit to Grand Canyon only to be murdered by him in one of the most grisly and hate-filled ways possible is anyone's guess.

Murder and low life seem to go together. And while most of us expect the Inner Canyon to be free of the former if not the latter, such expectations may not be completely realistic. On July 7, 1979, trail guide Brad Jones reported to NPS rangers that he had been panhandled then assaulted by a man living in a cave on Horseshoe Mesa (roughly halfway between Grand Canyon Village and Desert View and three miles down inside the Canyon).

Rangers identified the assailant as Lee Devereaux, also known as "Patent Leather" (an unexplained nickname). NPS officers had already reprimanded Devereaux several times on the rim for aggressive panhandling. Realizing that they had a "hard case" on their hands that could get harder, NPS rangers decided to try to nip Devereaux in the bud.

So, on the following day, July 8, NPS law enforcement officers Dave Swickard, Steve Schneider, David Bunch, and Fred Hemphill donned civilian clothes to impersonate vulnerable tourists. They hiked down to Horseshoe Mesa to "investigate" and to, well, appear vulnerable.

Only one quarter of the way down, the undercover boys spotted someone ahead matching Lee Devereaux's description. The foursome decided to walk past him and to act as bait. Afterward they stopped to sit in the shade. Here they tried to be both inconspicuous and, you guessed it, vulnerable.

Devereaux followed them. Two minutes later, the undercover rangers heard a voice booming down the trail saying, "It's hot! And I'm hungry."

Seconds later, Devereaux came into view. He pulled a .22 revolver from an athletic bag he was carrying and announced, "All right, guys, this is a robbery."

Swickard and Bunch sat on the right. Hemphill and Schneider were to the left. They all faced Devereaux.

"Don't move," Devereaux commanded. "Take off your packs and put them on the ground."

In the foursome's endeavor to appear vulnerable, each ranger had stashed his gun in his pack. This decision now loomed as a flaw in their planning. Now they *were* vulnerable.

Devereaux repeatedly pointed his revolver at each ranger as he gave commands. He held it at waist level. Eight of the ten eyes present studied that revolver.

The four men removed their backpacks and placed them between Devereaux and themselves. Devereaux next said, "I want your money. Put it all on the ground too."

Ranger Hemphill took a twenty from his wallet and placed a rock over it as per Devereaux's instructions. Devereaux next told Ranger Bunch who said he had no money, to give him his folding belt knife and wrist watch. Bunch did so. But when Swickard told Devereaux that he too had no money and showed Devereaux his empty wallet to prove it, Devereaux said, "Then give me your canteen."

Swickard threw his canteen at Devereaux's feet. Schneider next explained that he did not even have a wallet.

"Then," Devereaux demanded, "give me your shirt and sunglasses."

Schneider took off his shirt and glasses and laid them on the backpack on the ground.

"You think this thing is loaded?" Devereaux asked the four men as he brandished his gun pointedly. The question was rhetorical. Devereaux cocked the revolver and added, "I'll use it if I have to."

Devereaux then waved his gun up the trail and said, "Take off."

The four rangers started up the trail, disgusted at the course that events had taken. But before they got more than a few steps, Devereaux noticed Bunch's hiking boots. "Stop," he told Bunch. "Take those boots off."

When Bunch got his first boot off, Devereaux noticed Bunch's socks. "Gimme the socks too."

As Bunch started pulling off his second boot and sock, Swickard asked, "You're going to make him hike out barefoot?"

Devereaux looked toward Swickard. As he did so, Bunch leaped up and tackled Devereaux and grabbed the revolver. The other three jumped in to help and to prevent the gun going off. As they struggled to restrain Devereaux and handcuff him, he yelled, "I'll kill you! I'll kill you! I'll kill you!"

Devereaux's gun was in fact loaded. Devereaux was convicted on several counts of assault and other felonies and sentenced to seven years in prison.

A dozen years later, in the summer of 1992, hundreds of law enforcement personnel stormed Grand Canyon during the largest manhunt in the history of the state of Arizona. The fuse for this explosion of manpower at Grand Canyon was lit as an almost unrecognized fizzle on June 26.

The sun had just set. NPS Patrol Ranger Donny Miller sat in his patrol car and wondered why a frantic boy was running across the parking lot of Babbitt's General Store and waving to flag him down. Nothing all evening had seemed unusual. Until now. Well, no rest for the wicked.

Obviously panicked, the boy now had trouble getting his words out. Miller tried to be patient. He reassured the boy that he should calm down and just speak clearly. He had to understand him to be of any help.

The boy pointed across the parking lot and blurted, "You've got to stop him, he's taking my Dad! He's kidnaping my family!"

Shocked, Miller turned and saw that the boy was pointing to a car parked next to an R.V. fifty yards away. Several people stood nearby. It seemed as if they were merely talking. As Miller started to drive over to investigate, the boy yelled, "He's got a gun!".

As Miller approached the R.V. he had not the foggiest idea that here, in Babbitt's parking lot, he was about to play a long game of touch tag with public enemy number one. Miller was about to become Wile E. Coyote. The Roadrunner was waiting just a few yards away.

Six weeks earlier, on May 12, convicted Winslow bank robber and child molester Danny Ray Horning, age 35, had been about to stand trial—with his brother—for their parts in the mutilation-dismemberment murder of catfish farmer and alleged marijuana dealer Sam McCullough, age 40, near Stockton, California, in 1990. But Horning had sneaked out of his cell in Florence State Prison in southern Arizona and into the infirmary. There he donned a white medical coat. He pinned onto it a forged photo identification card. Then he hefted a medical bag. Successfully posing as an orderly, Danny Ray Horning walked out of the prison unchallenged—leaving behind four consecutive life sentences unserved.

He fled Florence on foot into the desert.

To re-arm, he burglarized a nearby ranch, exiting it with a Ruger Blackhawk .44 magnum revolver. Then he returned to Florence. Two days later he hitched a ride to Tucson. There he planned, then carried out, an armed robbery of the Valley National Bank. Now well-funded as well as armed, Horning hitched a ride toward Flagstaff. The law enforcement bureaucracy had issued a "Be On The Lookout" bulletin for Horning. Despite the massive manhunt organized in southern and central Arizona (even the U.S. Border Patrol was on the lookout for him), for the next three weeks Horning not only remained at large, he left no trace at all of his whereabouts.

Finally, on June 3, a USFS Fire Prevention Officer recognized Horning near Blue Ridge Reservoir, 75 miles south of Flagstaff. Horning vanished before law officers arrived, beginning a trend that would embarrass Arizona law officers again and again in the next several weeks.

Two days later, Horning was spotted south of Mormon Lake. Arizona Department of Corrections set a dog team on his trail. Horning eluded them too and vanished again.

On June 10, Governor Fife Symington declared a state of emergency in Arizona to help release state funds for counties participating in the search for Horning.

Two days later Horning burglarized several homes and stole a pickup truck in Pine, Arizona, 90 miles southeast of Flagstaff. In some victims' homes Horning left notes of apology for his thefts. He also left a note for police telling them to send his backpack to his parents and to stop following him! Richard Lynd (away from home on vacation) lost from his Pine cabin his favorite pick-up truck, a .22-caliber rifle and ammunition, a chainsaw, a 13-inch color television, food, sleeping bags, a tool box, dress clothes, and even Lynd's electric razor. "It's kind of weird," Lynd reported, "the stuff he took."

Lynd's son-in-law was first to the cabin. The break in was immaculately done with a neatly slitted window screen, "I'll say one thing for him," the son-in-law said, "he's probably about the neatest burglar I've ever seen." Then he added that, even so, "We're down to our last truck. I hope he doesn't come back."

From Pine, Horning drove to Socorro, New Mexico. It seemed he would now flee the Southwest. What was Danny Ray Horning's ultimate goal? Was he planning to flee the U.S. and head to Mexico, Canada, or the Caribbean?

More than a month after his escape, on June 21, a citizen in Payson, Arizona, reported seeing Horning driving Lynd's stolen pickup. But before law officers arrived in Payson, Horning was already driving over Chavez Pass to Meteor Crater and onto Interstate 40. In Flagstaff, a police officer spotted Horning on Lake Mary Road. The officer pursued him onto a remote USFS dirt road south of Mormon Mountain. Horning abandoned the stolen truck and fled on foot into the forest, successfully vanishing yet again.

Several days later, Horning made his way to Flagstaff. There he stalked the Little America Truck Stop in search of potential hostages. Not finding the "right" ones, he went deeper into town. A local police officer stared Horning in the face, scrutinizing him. Horning nonchalantly walked past him, then ducked into a nearby hotel.

Capitalizing on a Hollywood-style coincidence, Horning spotted a fire down the street and reported it to the desk clerk in the hope that the emergency call would divert that suspicious officer outside. Having successfully eluded the officer with this ruse, Horning waited outside a veterinary clinic on Route 66 to scout for victims. He did not have to wait long. He soon kidnaped a man and woman, both Flagstaff residents, outside the clinic.

Now, on June 25, six weeks after his escape, he forced his two hostages to drive him on a circuitous 330-mile route to the South Rim of Grand Canyon. En route, in between bragging about the big .44 magnum in his belt and about his "lifestyle" of crime, Horning told his hostages that he would kill any policeman who tried to pull them over. He also informed them that his goal was to kidnap an affluent family with a motor home and hold them hostage. Even more amazingly, after driving 150 miles to Kingman, then backtracking 180 miles to Grand Canyon through Williams (where the hostages withdrew $1500 from their bank account for him), all without arousing suspicion, Horning and both hostages spent the night unchallenged at El Tovar Hotel!

Here at the South Rim Village was where Horning planned to hijack that expensive motor home and kidnap its affluent owners for that fat ransom.

Being organized, he had prepared in advance a tape recording of his ransom demands. His tape revealed, among other things about Horning's character, that he intended to kidnap and hold six hostages for a $1 million ransom plus his freedom and that of his older brother (serving time in Florence for sexual misconduct with a minor and also awaiting that trial for murder). On June 26, Horning pulled into the parking lot at Babbitt's General Store....

As Ranger Miller slowly drove his cruiser toward the R.V., he expected a domestic violence situation. He radioed his imminent investigation of the boy's report of a felonious man with a gun. Miller had never received the APB about Horning, but he did know of the situation. He had even cut Horning's photo from the local newspaper and was keeping it in his back pocket. Still, not in his wildest dreams had he imagined what was about to happen next.

Near the R.V., Miller saw three people standing close together. He guessed they were the boy's family. Next to a nearby car stood a man wearing a baseball cap pulled low over his strawberry blond (no longer dark brown) hair. The uplifted collar of his windbreaker concealed his face, now clean shaven. This man stared at Miller, but he neither moved nor showed any expression. A man and a woman in their mid-thirties (who had been kidnapped in front of that Flagstaff veterinary clinic) sat rigid and staring straight ahead in the back seat of the man's car.

Miller stopped his NPS cruiser by the car.

About a mile away, off-duty NPS Rangers John Piastuck, Keith Lober, and Chris Fors were all enjoying a party for a co-worker at a friend's house when they heard Miller's call about a man with a gun at Babbitt's. Piastuck and Fors ran to Piastuck's car and jumped in. Lober ran to his vehicle. Both cars accelerated toward Babbitt's.

Miller stepped halfway out of his patrol car and told the man with the baseball cap to step to Miller's side of the vehicle. At the same time Miller tried to ready his shotgun. Horning raised his right hand over the roof of the car and aimed the .44 Ruger at Miller.

Miller ducked back into his car and tried to shift it into reverse. But the boy had just run up behind him. So, instead, Miller chambered a shell in his shotgun and radioed that the man *did* have a gun. Next Miller asked for backup. He drew his own handgun but did not fire it because the parking lot was crawling with people.

A bullet from Horning's .44 would have penetrated Miller's cruiser like a hot knife through butter. But Horning, too, did not fire.

Escape, not a gun duel, was his priority. Horning jumped back into the car containing his two hostages and accelerated it across the parking lot. He raced past Yavapai Lodge and drove into the parking lot by the Shrine of the Ages and the Visitor Center. Miller pursued at high speed. This parking lot too was crowded. An evening ranger interpretive program had just ended. Horning streaked between tourists ambling back to their cars, then abruptly thought that the parking lot looked like a cul de sac. Horning tried to turn back on the main road. His right front tire dropped into a ditch. The hubcap flew off and rolled onward in an escape of its own.

Rangers Piastuck and Fors raced past all this on the main road. Horning saw them. He fired one shot at their vehicle. It missed. Lober, right behind Piastuck and Fors, saw Horning's gun arm and the muzzle blast. He swerved his vehicle toward Horning's to block his exit onto the main road.

Horning swerved around Lober and accelerated down the main road toward El Tovar Hotel. Miller spun around in pursuit.

Horning blurred past El Tovar and the Bright Angel Lodge on Village Loop at seventy miles per hour. Normally thirty is pushing it. Seconds later Horning missed the hairpin turn. He lost control and crashed into the West Rim Drive traffic gate. The driver's window exploded. Shattered glass flew everywhere, striking tourists lined up at the gate. The car skidded to a stop. About fifteen yards behind it, Miller too screeched to a halt.

Miller stepped out with his shotgun and yelled at Horning to step out of his car. Bystanders stared open-mouthed.

Horning slammed his gear selector to reverse, jockeyed the car, and maneuvered through the barricade. Then he accelerated up the hill past Bright Angel Trailhead on West Rim Drive. He aimed his Ruger out his shattered window and fired two rounds back at Miller. Tourists hit the dirt en masse.

Miller tore after him through the broken barricade.

Horning spun around and, just as his woman hostage ducked, fired two more rounds out the back window at Miller, blowing the glass into flying shards. Miller saw the muzzle flash and for an instant thought that it was the dome light and that one of the hostages was trying to escape out the back door. Miller backed off so as not to run over this escaping hostage.

No one jumped out. But as Miller passed Hopi Point and then rounded a blind corner in delayed pursuit, he saw Horning standing on the road about 45 yards away, outside the car stopped in the middle of the road. As Horning frantically yanked at a backpack to get it out of the car, Miller slammed on his brakes and skidded sideways to a stop.

Miller and Horning stared at one another for a split second. Then Horning raised his gun and fired at Miller.

Miller ducked down in his car and grabbed his shotgun. As he emerged with it, Horning's shadowy figure vanished into the woods.

Rangers Piastuck, Fors, and Lober caught up. They exited their vehicles, took cover, and surrounded Horning's car with the two Flagstaff hostages still in it. To no avail. Horning had apparently crawled back around them to the rim and then followed the Rim Trail eastward, either back toward the Village or into the Canyon itself via the Bright Angel Trail. NPS personnel and other law enforcement officers suspected that Danny Ray Horning had indeed dropped into the Canyon, possibly in search of more hostages.

The day after Horning vanished into the dark, June 27, Grand Canyon National Park set up a dozen roadblocks manned by law enforcement officers. Over the next several days, hundreds of law enforcement personnel—NPS rangers, State Police, Sheriff's Deputies, and FBI—swarmed into and over the park in an intensifying manhunt for Danny Ray Horning.

This same day hikers told police that they saw a man who matched Horning's description in the newspaper walking down the Bright Angel Trail into the Canyon.

At this same time one of us (Ghiglieri) was running a commercial rowing trip. We had just camped at Cremation Creek (River Mile 87) preparatory to sending most of our clients up and out of the Canyon the next morning via the Bright Angel Trail beginning at River Mile 89. NPS rangers at Phantom gave us (Michael Fabry, Rob Pitagora, Liz Hymens, Chris Dippold, and me) the lowdown. This lowdown was a big question mark surrounded by a lot of embroidery consisting of the many possible tactics that Danny Ray Horning might or might not be about to adopt in his next hostage-taking location. Roads and trails, including the Bright Angel, were being patrolled. But people could still leave. *If* they could avoid Horning.

We in the OARS' crew argued over what to tell our people who were hiking on their own up the Bright Angel Trail. Was ignorance bliss? Or was it better to inform our people to stay in one group for security? Luckily, two of our trainees running the baggage boat on this trip were Flagstaff Police sergeants Ray Martinez and Chuck Martin. Their advice was prudence is better than bliss.

Our passengers hiked out as planned. Luckily their experience added nothing new to the Horning saga.

But he was still out there somewhere, either in the Canyon with us or on the rim. Again, roadblocks blocked every road. Search dogs and SWAT teams roamed the Village and the pine woods around it. Residents had been warned to lock their doors and windows and to stay inside. Many of them also kept loaded weapons at hand. Trails into the Canyon were closed to entry while armed searchers scoured below the rim.

Three days after Horning's wild escape from Ranger Miller, Horning reappeared on the South Rim and struck again. Two tourists from Oregon, Jana Cerny, age 21, and Zdenek Kel, age 29, had pulled their overheated station wagon into the Grandview parking lot at about 7:00 p.m. As Cerny peered under the hood of the 1978 Chevy Caprice, Horning approached him unseen and said, "Get into the car. You have to help me."

Kel told Horning, "The car is broken; it won't run."

"I'll fix it for you," Horning said as he pulled his Ruger .44 magnum out from behind his back.

"I'm not going anywhere with you," Kel said. "If you want to shoot me, shoot me right now."

Horning hesitated. Kel yelled at Cerny, "Run!" Then he started to run himself.

Horning pointed his gun at Kel. Kel froze in his tracks. Then Horning aimed it at Cerny. She also stopped. "I thought he would shoot me," she said "But he didn't. Then I started to run."

Then Kel ran as well. Both ran down the road.

Horning jumped in the station wagon and drove it after them, chasing them down the road. He pulled up even with Cerny and looked her in the eyes. Horning commanded her, "Get in the car."

"I was really scared," Cerny admitted. She slowed her running and glanced behind her. She saw Horning looking in the rearview mirror. Maybe he was spooked by a another car, she surmised. "He stepped on the accelerator and took off as fast as he could."

As he accelerated away, Kel and Cerny hid in the woods. They emerged later to flag down a Ford Bronco driving by.

The next day park rangers found the couple's car smashed into a tree. Cerny was upset, mostly about not being warned: "When we entered the park, nobody told us to watch out for a fugitive."

Horning continued to elude everyone. Having learned evasion lessons during his eleven-month stint in U.S. Army reconnaissance in the late 1970s, he now used every trick he could remember. He walked in circles to confuse the hounds tracking him. He traveled during the day when he could be careful enough in choosing his path as to leave no tracks. Even so, to escape the Coconino Plateau, Horning needed a vehicle—he also wanted those affluent hostages as his ticket to paradise.

Despite these hundreds of law officers from ten law enforcement agencies and their helicopters, hounds, and high-tech impedimenta, Horning continued to elude capture. Now, in fact, he could watch his 385 pursuers, the platoons of Coyotes, and listen to the statements they made on TV—at least he would have been able to were he still dragging around that 13-inch TV he had stolen in Pine.

Even more weird, due to his outrageous Roadrunner-like success in escaping these government Coyotes, Horning was fast becoming a sort of folk hero, a real-life Rambo. A survivalist who could—and did—survive for yet another week despite seemingly impossible odds. The land and the elements were his allies. His outwitting hundreds of cops eager to nail him seemed miraculously easy.

On July 4, Horning struck yet again twenty miles east at Desert View, still inside the park. Unnoticed amidst a small crowd of visitors at Desert View Lookout, Horning squatted down between cars. There he pulled his gun on and abducted two British medical students. He forced Sally Edwards and Caroline Young, both age 27, to sit up front in their rented Nissan Sentra and chauffeur him. Horning "back-seat" drove them toward the Village, then south on U.S. 64. Horning chose the Fourth of July, he explained to his captives, precisely because it was the busiest time he could imagine for park rangers to deal with.

Horning faced three roadblocks. The first one, the terrified hostages later said, was easy for him. But at the second roadblock south of the Park in Valle (a.k.a. Flintstone Village), an Arizona Department of Public Safety Officer asked Horning to step out of the car.

Danny Ray Horning stepped out.

"Please remove your straw hat."

Horning did so. And while the officer compared a photo of Horning to the real thing, his two hostages in the front seat sat rigid. They were not only so paralyzed with fear that they could not bring themselves to tip off any of the officers manning the roadblock, they were so scared that they would not even talk to each other.

"Please open your trunk," the officer asked.

Horning popped it open. The trunk's interior did not look suspicious. "Is there anything wrong, officer?" Horning asked innocently.

The officer shook his head and thanked Horning then let him and his hostages drive on. Horning, it seems, by having changed his clothes, shaved, and bleached his hair, did not resemble Horning.

Ten miles north of Williams, near Red Lake, Horning pulled off the highway. About ten minutes from the road he tied both of his hostages to a tree.

"Please don't shoot us," the women begged.

Horning told Edwards and Young that he did not want to hurt them but that he did need at least 30 minutes to get away. Horning left both women tied to that tree. He headed east on I-40 back toward Flagstaff and Walnut Canyon National Monument. He still hoped to steal an R.V. and to kidnap some new and richer hostages.

While passing through Flagstaff, he was spotted by a state patrolman who gave chase. This patrolman lost Horning, but another officer, an explosives technician, picked him up.

Horning fired at the officer. One bullet penetrated the officer's trunk and a bag full of detonation equipment. Luckily, none of it exploded.

Horning lost control during his high-speed escape and crashed south of Flagstaff on I-17. Again like the Roadrunner, he ran into the woods. And despite his carrying a large case, he vanished yet again.

The next day, July 5, a woman residing near Sedona spotted Horning as he borrowed a garden hose to get a drink of water. The woman grabbed her gun and her phone, then dialed 9-1-1.

Yavapai County Deputies and Border Patrol officers using a bloodhound zeroed in on a deck perched on a nearby hill. They stealthily advanced on it.

Curled up in exhaustion under the deck, stolen .44 magnum in hand, lay Danny Ray Horning, the Roadrunner, asleep.

A Border Patrol Agent pointed a gun at Horning's head and said, "If you move, you're dead."

Danny Ray Horning found himself back in Florence. This time there would be no visit to the dispensary. The woman with a gun near Sedona who'd had her eye on her garden hose had just ended, after 54 days, the largest single manhunt in the history of Arizona. This massive and protracted manhunt sought a blue-collar felon whose admitted goal was simply to extort a few innocent but rich people at gunpoint, and, by threatening to murder them, gain the leverage to free his brother from prison and to steal the money he needed to live the good life. After his capture, Radio Station KFYI interviewed Horning, who spelled out his simple plan:

> *After I would have gotten a million dollars and my brother, I would have gone out of the country, most likely to Mexico, and I'd have hired about ten different families, men, wives, and kids. I would have set them up for life and lived in a nice little ranch and whenever I would have wanted something I would have given them the money and they could go get it for me.*

In yet another interview, with KTAR Radio, Horning admitted to robbing the bank in Tucson and to kidnaping all of his hostages, but he denied murdering Sam McCullough.

Two years later, however, Horning failed to convince a California jury of this. In 1994, Danny Ray Horning stood trial in San Joaquin County Superior Court for shooting Sam McCullough in the head in 1990. McCullough had apparently caught Horning burglarizing his home. Allegedly, Horning (being a "neat" burglar) methodically sawed off McCullough's head and limbs and stuffed them all into plastic bags, which he later dumped into a gully called Burns Cut. After hearing all testimony, on July 15, the jury convicted Danny Ray Horning of first degree murder. Judge William R. Giffen was so impressed with the "dastardly" cold-blooded execution style of the murder that he sentenced Danny Ray Horning to the death penalty.

"It's been four years of hell," admitted McCullough's wife, Carol, and the mother of his two sons. "The only peace that I find is that Danny Ray Horning can't do this to someone else."

Smirking, Horning walked out of the courtroom saying, "*Que sera*'" (What will be...).

A month later, while waiting on San Quentin Prison's lengthy death row in a segregated cell where "he's not allowed to be around anybody," Danny Ray Horning was stabbed three times by an unknown assailant. He survived but was in critical condition. Horning's brother, Mark Anthony Horning, also said, "He wasn't there long enough to make enemies. He wasn't there long enough to get into any trouble. I think it was a contract hit."

If so, someone had to return their fee. Five years later, in 2000, Danny Ray Horning still sat on death row. And, as hundreds of other murderers sentenced to death in California are doing, Horning too awaited developments on his lengthy appeal process.

Brain cancer *and* lung cancer. Sometimes nature is too cruel, reflected Robert Merlin Spangler, age 67, as he lay in his bed during early fall of 2000 in the Grand Junction home of himself and his fourth wife, Judith. Learning that your cancer has metastasized and that you have only months to live is shocking, to put it mildly.

A lot of things were about to end. One of them, his sojourns into Grand Canyon. Among other things, Spangler was something of a Canyon addict. His second wife, Sharon Spangler, had ignited his passion for the vast majesty of Grand Canyon. She was so entranced with the Canyon that she wrote the popular 1986 book *On Foot in the Grand Canyon: Hiking the Trails of the South Rim*. In this book, Sharon acknowledged: "My husband, Bob Spangler, took photographs, helped me to remember things, encouraged me through the rough times, and, being an accomplished writer, offered suggestions to make the text read better."

Cancer or not, you could not buy memories and accomplishments like these.

Robert Spangler had met Sharon (then Sharon Arst Cooper) in 1976 when she applied for a job with the company he worked for. He had been impressed by her. At the time, however, Spangler was married to someone else. Indeed he'd been married to Nancy Spangler since 1955, more than twenty years. Robert and Nancy had moved from Iowa to Arapaho County, Colorado, where, by 1976, Spangler had landed a good job as a public relations manager for American Waterworks. Robert's and Nancy's two children, David and Susan, were now 15 and 13 years old.

Two years later, however, a horrifying disaster shattered Robert Spangler's picture perfect suburban life. On December 30, while Spangler was at work, a neighbor and friend of young Susan Spangler stumbled upon a grisly tableau writ in incomprehensible gore in the Spanglers' Colorado home. Spangler's son David, now age 17, lay dead in his bed with a .38 caliber bullet in his chest. Susan, only 15, lay slain in her bed with a bullet wound to her back. Downstairs, sprawled their mother, Nancy, age 45, shot in the head with the same revolver. Close at hand investigators found a typed suicide note signed with Nancy's initial.

Investigators ultimately concluded that this tragedy had been a double homicide-suicide by the distraught mother.

Less than a year following this hideous tragedy, in 1979, Robert married Sharon. Although Sharon was not fond of children, she did love landscapes. Sharon had gone on two river trips in the 1970s and fallen in love with Grand Canyon—and now with Robert. She combined these two loves during their honeymoon wrap-up by beginning an avocation of hiking off the South Rim. She tackled the Hermit Trail with her new husband, who, as she confessed admiringly, was "a natural athlete" on a trail that left her stumbling. In the 1970s era of free-love-and-love-nature-too, Bob and Sharon Spangler's hand-in-hand sojourns into the Seventh Natural Wonder of the World seemed to prove that love indeed conquers all.

For years, at odd intervals and locations of Sharon's choosing, the two hikers became an ever more entrenched part of the Canyon landscape. We can imagine it: Robert, trim and bald-headed and with a thick white beard, striding along confidently, and Sharon, with her hiking diary, becoming ever more adept on the treacherous terrain.

Surprisingly, however, in 1988, Sharon and Robert Spangler divorced after a bitterly fought contest over their financial assets. Sharon had been on medication for years to control severe anxiety attacks, suicidally inclined, that had manifested themselves during her relationship with Spangler.

A year later, in 1989, Donna Sundling, a mother of five grown children and a well liked bookkeeper for Warrior Oil Company, decided to shoot for greater happiness by taking a risk. She answered a personal ad. The ad had been placed by Robert Merlin Spangler. Almost immediately, Spangler swept Donna off her feet.

On August 18, 1990, Robert Spangler married yet again, this third time to Donna Sundling. They moved to Durango where Spangler became a country music disc jockey for KRSJ-FM and developed a following. Spangler was a paragon, it seems: trim, healthy, cheerful, and a giver. He officiated at soccer and basketball games. Spangler, however, had quit visiting Grand Canyon during his first two years with Donna. Then, abruptly, his passion for Grand Canyon fired originally by his now ex-wife, Sharon, resurged even as his relationship with Donna seriously deteriorated due to a lack of mutual interests.

One fly in this ointment, however, was that Donna was afraid of heights. Robert chipped away at Donna's fear by convincing her that the Canyon was truly so important to him that he could not bear her not sharing it with him.

On Easter Sunday, April 11, 1993, Donna and Robert Spangler finally hiked the Grandview Trail and beyond. The views were stupendous. But, suddenly, disaster struck. Spangler explained later to NPS rangers that while he had his back turned to adjust his tripod for a photo of Donna standing on the rim of a Redwall cliff along the Page Springs Trail, she somehow had fallen off. Maybe, he speculated, a freak gust of wind had stolen her balance. He'd heard nothing, he added, possibly because his hearing aid had been turned off. As Robert Spangler explained during an interview:

> *We were only maybe a hundred yards up that trail* [Page Springs] *when, on one of these switchbacks, came this beautiful sunrise morning—Easter sunrise, as a matter of fact. We decided to stop*

and take one last picture back down the Canyon and at the area that we had been….I turned around and she was gone. She wasn't there. And I can only surmise that she, you know, adjusted her pack, or got it out of balance, or she moved slightly and stepped on a rock that rolled under her feet, something. At any rate, she just went over the edge, and about 200 feet down….The Canyon didn't take her life. God didn't take her life; it just happened. Those things occur. When you are in a place that does have precipitous terrain, the possibility is always there.

Despite Spangler's reasonable explanation, some of Donna Sundling's friends kept the case of Robert Merlin Spangler and his vanishing wives on a back burner. Although no actual evidence implicated Spangler, to Donna's friends the history of violent death among those closest to him reeked.

Next, despite Sharon's divorce from Spangler, after Donna's tragic accident in Grand Canyon, Sharon moved back into his attractive Durango home, reportedly in a now platonic relationship. Disaster soon struck again. In October of 1994, Sharon Spangler, age 52, also died tragically, of a drug and alcohol overdose. Although initially suspicious of foul play, investigators concluded that, based on "strong evidence," Robert Spangler had "nothing" to do with Sharon's death.

Indeed, quite the opposite, it seems that Spangler still thought of his Grand Canyon Sharon in the most positive of lights. Spangler's March, 1998, tribute to Sharon reveals almost nothing but respect for her:

But I think the main reason she was here was to discover the remarkable nature of the Grand Canyon and to translate her experiences in such an interesting, informative and persuasive manner that thousands of others, with similar surprise, would find themselves drawn there, too.

The book was her crowning achievement and I am so proud of her, so glad to have participated in its creation. Sharon had in mind to do a second book, one that would dig into the delights of hiking on the North Rim. But it never came to pass. She was the victim of an insidious disease that didn't show much, but was consuming her through the years. We were together in Durango, Colorado, when she died October 2, 1994.

I have continued to hike the Canyon, delighting especially in communicating with other aficionados and helping newcomers get started. I love guiding first-timers and experiencing their thrills and joy as Sharon and I first experienced it all those years ago.

I miss her very much, but like so many of you, I have her book to remind me not only of her, but how much she helped popularize this place we love so much. What a wonderful, talented, creative woman was Sharon Spangler, one the Grand Canyon's most eloquent friends.

In 1994, Arapaho County Sheriff's investigator Paul Goodman heard about Donna Spangler's 1993 fatal fall in the Canyon and felt queasy about it. To Goodman, as to others, something just did not add up. But, if a crime had been committed, it had apparently been a perfect one. Goodman could not put his finger on any piece of evidence that implicated Robert Spangler. Only…Only the reports of the rangers who had interviewed Spangler after Donna had fallen to her death continued to haunt him. Spangler had, they agreed, seemed less distraught than what one might expect for a man losing his wife in such a hideous way. On the other hand, Spangler seemed to some rangers an honest man who seemed to tell his story of loss forthrightly.

Even so, another NPS ranger working at Grand Canyon, Beverly Perry, also felt queasy about writing off Donna Spangler's death to accidental causes. Something was wrong here. Perry felt certain. Only how would she ever get proof?

Goodman next heard about Sharon Spangler's suspicious death by overdose.

Goodman recalled too the grisly 1978 case in which Robert Spangler's two teenaged children were brutally murdered and his wife allegedly suicided. This horror had occurred during Goodman's rookie year with the Sheriff's Department.

Goodman saw so much smoke in all this that his mind refused the believe the nonexistence of a fire. But, again, no real evidence existed to reveal that fire.

In August of 1998, Spangler renewed an acquaintance with Judith Hilty in Grand Junction, Colorado. They wed, Spangler's fourth trip to the altar, two years later, at nearly the same time that the news and symptoms of his cancer metastasizing surfaced. Judith didn't care that their months together might be few, she cared only that they be together. But the invading growth inside Spangler changed almost everything in his view of life.

Almost everything.

With the Grim Reaper now breathing down Spangler's neck, he began telling his friends and neighbors that he had only months to live. As they brought him cakes and pies in sympathy, he told his friends bravely that he expected that death "will treat me about as quickly and gently as one could hope."

By 1998, under a push by Assistant U.S. Attorney Camille Bibles, an Arizonan who had long suspected that Donna Spangler's demise had resulted from murder, an inter-departmental team was assembled to monitor Spangler. This team included National Park Service Criminal Investigations Special Agent Beverly Perry, Flagstaff FBI Agent Leonard Johns, and Arapaho County's Officer Paul Goodman. The team had full FBI resources at its disposal. When routine FBI monitoring of Spangler caught his medical tests indicating cancer, the team knew they had to act immediately.

"We just knocked on his door," Goodman explained. "He didn't seem surprised…"

Under two days of very sophisticated interviewing of Robert Merlin Spangler masterminded by Agent Johns, Spangler soon matter-of-factly confessed to an astonishing list of heinous misdeeds—then he signed his confession.

"It was his [Spangler's] opinion," reported Arapaho County Undersheriff Grayson Robinson, that "he was a model citizen and a good human being except during two days of his life when he did something terrible."

When Spangler entered court in Grand Junction at the end of September, 2000, he walked in jauntily and winked at his wife Judith, who, at this point, still refused to believe that his confession was real. On October 7, 2000, the FBI transferred Spangler to a federal holding facility in Florence, Arizona, to stand trial for the first degree murder of Donna Spangler committed in Grand Canyon.

What about those "two days of his life when he did something terrible?"

On one of them, in 1978, having decided that his suburban life with Nancy and their two children was no longer the life he wanted now that he had met Sharon, Robert Spangler engineered his exit. On the pretext, he admitted, of saying that he wanted to write a Christmas note, he convinced Nancy to initial a blank piece of paper. Then he typed her bogus suicide note on it. Later he told Nancy that he had a surprise for her downstairs in the basement, but that she first had to sit in a chair and cover her eyes. Once she complied with his conditions, he shot her in the forehead with a .38 handgun. Then he left the note.

He next gunned down his 15-year-old daughter Susan by shooting her in the back as she slept in bed, killing her instantly. Finally he entered his 17-year-old son's, David's, room and shot him in the chest as he tried to rise, alarmed at having heard the shot that had killed his sister. Spangler's quick shot failed to kill his son. So he rushed forward and smothered the critically wounded teenager with a pillow until he too was dead.

Then he left the house, following his usual routine.

As the years afterward had passed, Sharon Spangler, whose relationship with Robert Spangler had begun prior to the murders of his first family, had begun to suspect that her new husband had played a role in them. Then, at some point, according to at least one of Sharon's close friends at Grand Canyon, she knew. And this hideous knowledge likely metamorphosed into, as Robert Spangler himself put it, that "insidious disease that was consuming her through the years."

As time passed, that event on Robert Spangler's *other* day of doing "something terrible"—Easter Sunday of 1993, when that "gust of wind" on the Page Spring Trail below the Grandview Trail "maybe" pushed Donna Spangler to her death, may have also nudged Sharon Spangler over her own edge. With Robert Spangler still in the house and with her, Spangler's ghastly misdeeds likely nudged Sharon so hard that she swallowed a fatal overdose of alcohol and drugs.

What about that gust of wind in Grand Canyon that blew Donna Spangler, who was deathly afraid of heights, from atop a cliff to plunge almost two-hundred feet to her death?

Robert Merlin Spangler confessed to Johns and Goodman and Perry a new and different explanation. It was not wind after all. It was instead Spangler again adjusting his life circumstances ("as quickly and gently as one could hope") with a big shove over the edge. He and Donna's relationship had stopped being rewarding to him many months earlier. So, here in Grand Canyon, Spangler saw the opportunity for yet another perfect crime—and perfect solution to his lack of contentment.

He waited until he and Donna had reached the upper section of the Page Springs Trail in the Redwall Limestone where it offers a guaranteed lethal exposure. He knew, from his hikes with his second wife, Sharon, that no perfect vertical exposures remained above this trail. It was here that it had to happen, or not at all.

Upon reaching this perfect spot, Robert Merlin Spangler walked up to his wife and, facing her face to face, simply shoved her off the cliff to plummet 160 feet to her death. What terrified and dismal thoughts passed through her shocked mind during her long plunge toward the jagged rock below no one will ever know.

Afterwards Spangler hiked out. Then he stood in the back of the line at the NPS Backcountry Office to patiently wait his turn. When it finally came, he told the ranger that his wife had accidentally fallen to her death off the Page Springs Trail.

"It was easier," Spangler later explained his murderous decision to Johns in the summer of 2000, "than getting a divorce."

On December 27, 2000, Robert Merlin Spangler entered a plea of guilty to the premeditated murder of Donna Sundling Spangler. He now faces a life sentence in prison as well as a terminal cancer he expects will "treat" him "quickly and gently." At times, as we have seen, Mother Nature can seem cruel and uncompromising. Yet at other times, even at her worst, she may seem not half cruel enough. As it would turn out, Spangler would die slowly.

Table 8. MURDERS WITHIN GRAND CANYON OR ON ITS RIMS.

Name, age	Date	Location	*Circumstances*
"Tanner Man," 34-40	1000–1200 A.D.	Tanner Trail 1¼ mile below trailhead	

The partial skeleton of a robust male Puebloan about 5'4" was found under a Supai boulder exposed by natural erosion and overlayed with recent trash from hikers. The investigation in February, 1997, found stone arrowheads of the "Virgin Anasazi" or Fremont culture style of post-1000 A.D.—one, over an inch long, was found by Yavapai Co. Sheriff Captain Scott Mascher situated in the area of the chest cavity. Nearby lay a yellow travertine finger ring. The site lay off the Tanner Trail above a Basketmaker III/Pueblo I midden of pot sherds, a mano, etc., all near the 75-Mile Canyon saddle. The Park decided this was likely a prehistoric burial site not a forensic scene. But was it a post-homicide burial?

Aah'yi'd digish, adult Navajo male	1864–68	north of the site of the future Hall'smale cabin at Grandview

The husband of a Navajo refugee family from the Long Walk found the infamous outlaw/brigand Navajo, Aah'yi'd digish, in the act of butchering the horse that the husband's pregnant wife had just been riding. The husband shot and killed the man who had stolen, slain, and butchered this horse. (see text)

William H. Dunn, under 30 Oramel G. Howland, 36 Seneca B. Howland, 26	August 30– September 3, 1869	uncertain location either between Mount Dellenbaugh and Parashant Wash or Toquerville, Utah

Dunn and the Howland Brothers separated from J. W. Powell's first exploration down the Grand Canyon Colorado on August 28, 1869, and hiked north. The three were murdered. (see text)

Archimedes McClurg, adult	Fall 1894	Navajo Spring (5 miles S. of Lees Ferry)

McClurg, a self proclaimed Mormon missionary intending to "preach the gospel of salvation to the sinners" of Flagstaff, passed through Lees Ferry in fall, 1894. In mid October of 1894, Seth Tanner and some Navajos found McClurg's body—with a bullet hole through the chest and pockets turned inside out—partially buried by rocks and sand. McClurg was buried at Lees Ferry.

Unidentified male, 23 ? (a.k.a. "Kolb Skeleton")	1916–1919	"mining site" below Yavapai Point

As explained by Art Gallenson, a long-time friend of Emery Kolb, Emery found this skeleton of a six-foot-tall young man at an abandoned mining site and "collected" it. After being used at Grand Canyon School, the skeleton was returned to Kolb, who stowed it away in Rust's canvas boat. Upon doing so, Kolb joked to Gallenson, "When I die and somebody finds that skeleton, it's gonna cause a lot of commotion....Take it to the school in Kanab, would you?" (Gallenson never took it.) Years later, forensic anthropologist Walter Birkby examined the skull and concluded: 1) It could not be that of Glen Hyde, and 2) the trajectory of the .32 caliber bullet in it suggested homicide as a cause of death, not suicide. Identity of dead man may never be known. (see text)

? Milo "Sonny" Craig Jaycox, 2	July 28, 1927	near home in Grand Canyon Village

Ten minutes after Milo's mother saw him playing, he vanished. A troubled local youth, Raymond Sandoval, age 12, confessed to killing Milo but told twelve different versions of disposing the body, none of which were true. After Sandoval's father talked to him, he denied all wrong doing. Several weeks later, Milo's body was found in the woods nearby with no cause of death determined. Sandoval was sentenced to the state reformatory until age 21.

? Glen R. Hyde, 29

December 1, 1928   Uncertain location between Diamond
                    Creek and Mile 237
Homicide is one hypothetical explanation of Hyde's otherwise unsolved mysterious disappearance. (see text)

George Wilson, 65

June 26, 1935   Marble Canyon gas station
Wilson was shot by one of three armed robbers—Albert White, age 19, Carl White, age 17, and Carl Cox, age 29—on June 23. He died three days later. Albert White was convicted of 1st degree murder, but escaped jail. He was shot and killed near Bitter Springs during his escape attempt.

Mary Hunsaker, adult
Norman Bennett, adult
Ray Goodman, 44

December 28, 1950   Grand Canyon Village at Norman
                    Bennett's home
Ray Goodman, a 44-year-old dishwasher at Bright Angel Lodge, shot Norman Bennett in the head with a .22 revolver after Mary Hunsaker refused to go out on a date with Goodman, then he emptied his revolver into Hunsaker's chest. He reloaded but told Norman Bennett's wife that he would spare her if she stayed still. Goodman then walked into the woods and shot himself in the head.

Bert Brown, adult

July 15, 1951   outside El Tovar Hotel
Bert Brown, John Paul Harris, and Charles Read entered El Tovar at 10:30 p.m. and robbed the desk clerk at gun point of $12,000, then fled. A law officer shot Brown fatally in the chest in front of El Tovar Hotel. Read and Harris were apprehended 30 miles north of Flagstaff.

?Connie Smith, 10–15

Summer, 1957?   Skinner Ridge (near Tusayan)
Connie Smith disappeared at age ten in July 1952, from Camp Sloane in Salisbury, Connecticut. A man, later determined to be a "mental case," made a bogus confession to the police that he had picked up Connie Smith while she was hitch-hiking to Lakeside, CT, but he then drove her to Arizona where his partner killed her. Later, a third man, William Redmond, confessed to murdering her and passed a lie detector test but was not believed. A girl's body found near the Canyon in October 1958 was identified via dental records to possibly be that of Smith.

Addie Lee Venturini, 46
Thomas J. Smith, 48

February 27, 1972   Red Butte (6 miles S of National Park)
After a Relief Fire Dispatcher entered the fire observers cabin and found it in disarray and spattered with blood, searchers found the body of Addie Lee Venturini (mother of five and from Jackson, Mississippi). She had been dragged to a nearby cliff then tossed fifty feet to the bottom. An autopsy revealed that she had been stabbed 42 times with an ice pick, beaten with a wrench, and shot several times with a .22 pistol. She had been traveling with Thomas J. Smith, age 48. On April 11, Smith's 1966 Buick was found not far off. Smith was lying nearby, face down with a .22 bullet wound to his right temple. (see text)

Michael A. Sherman, 28
Charolotte H. Sherman, 28

January 22, 1977   Powell Memorial, parking lot
A Canyon visitor found both Shermans shot in the head by a small caliber gun about an hour earlier. The apparent motive for this double homicide was minor robbery (the Shermans were moving from the East to Norton A.F.B. in California with their possessions, which the killer left intact). Neither a murder weapon nor a suspect was ever found. This senseless murder devastated Dr. Sherman's parents and siblings for the rest of their lives.

Robert Leeds Layne, Jr., 35

June 8, 1984   El Tovar Hotel
A Fred Harvey Company mule wrangler, Robert Hinckle, age 36, was arguing with his girlfriend in the piano bar when an uninvolved tourist, Layne, tried to intercede by saying something like, "Hey, leave the woman alone." The wrangler pulled a .357 magnum revolver and shot the Good Samaritan tourist fatally.

Robert E. Diggs, 23

August 7, 1986   Victor Hall/Fred Harvey employee housing
Diggs was slain by a gunshot wound to the throat inflicted by a fellow Fred Harvey employee.

Donna K. Spangler, 59

April 11, 1993   Page Springs Trail in the Redwall below Horseshoe Mesa
Based on the confession of her husband, Robert Merlin Spangler, then age 61, he shoved Donna Spangler into the abyss to avoid the inconvenience of a divorce. She fell 160 feet. After signing his confession to four murders, Robert Spangler requested an NPS permit to have his ashes spread over Grand Canyon. U.S. District Judge Paul G. Rosenblatt ordered the NPS to deny this permit. During a strong wind in the Canyon, you will not have to worry about sipping the ashes of a serial killer in your tea. (see text)

Antonio Castillo, Jr., 31

December 13, 1996   Tusayan
Castillo was an invited guest at a Christmas party at a local motel when Harry Manchee, age 58, heavily intoxicated, stabbed him in the chest. Manchee had mistaken Castillo for someone who had admonished Manchee earlier to stop harassing some of the women present. Castillo died less than a half hour later at Grand Canyon Clinic due to a severed internal thoracic artery. Manchee was convicted of second-degree murder.

Sandra Marie Elizondo, 18

February 20, 2001   Rim Trail near Grandeur Point
Elizondo, from Ontario, California, was seen by two couples on the Rim Trail as they hiked. When the couples returned, Elizondo's personal items were still present on and below the rim, but she had vanished. Her journal entry for that day indicated no discontent with life. SAR Rangers found Elizondo's body 360 feet below the rim.

Kim Suzette Quanimptewa, 30 June 12, 2001   Trailer Village, Grand Canyon Village
Quanimptewa, a native of the Hopi village, Hotevilla, was found hidden under a bed and stabbed to death. Motive unknown. (not in text or text statistics or index)

The following entries are not included in text, statistics, or the index.

Tomomi Hanamure, 34   May 8, 2006   upstream of Navajo Falls, Havasu Canyon
Hanamure of Yokohama, Japan vanished hiking from Havasupai village en route to Havasu Falls. She was found 5 days later in a shallow eddy below a waterfall. She had been stabbed 29 times— both while facing toward and also away from her attacker. Her hands, arms, and wrists showed cuts and bruises consistent with self defense. Forensics suggests she was raped. A teenaged Havasupai suspect, Randy Redtail Wescogame, awaits trial.

Epilogue

What Can We Learn From All This?

The mass phenomenon of people seeking adventure for its own sake is a fairly recent one. Why do we do it? Adventure writer Sebastian Junger says it's because modern society has been "designed to eliminate as many unforeseen events as possible, [but] as inviting as that seems, it leaves us hopelessly underutilized." This lack of purpose is where the idea of "adventure"—being any situation in which the outcome is not entirely within our control—comes in. "Threats to our safety and comfort have been so completely wiped out," Junger concludes, "that we have to go out of our way to create them."

Indeed, in our preoccupation with safety, "adventure" has become such a highly desired commodity in the last half of the twentieth century that it has become profitably marketable in almost every form. Lethal trips up Everest titillate us so much that some of us even shell out $65,000 to go there and get frostbite, breathe from an oxygen tank, and generally experience insane misery—just so our lives suddenly will have some meaning, some definition, some adventure. Some of these people are not just seeking a self-defining adventure, of course, they are seeking special status, the ability to boast, however subtly, "Oh yeah, I've done the toughest thing there is." Others of us are stimulated enough just by reading about it or by watching the IMAX film. We then set our own sights on adventure of a more survivable—and affordable—caliber.

But for American society in general it can be well argued that, in our generations-long quest for security, we have domesticated ourselves. We train and hire specialists to do nearly everything for us so that we don't have to take the risk of doing it ourselves. We hire police to protect us from sociopaths, contractors to build our houses, farmers to grow or raise our food, programmers to battle Y2K, Ralph Nader to make our cars and skies safe, guidebooks to keep us on the safe routes, and Hollywood to flash vicarious yet extremely danger-ous adventures in our faces so that we don't risk experiencing anything like the real thing in order to jack up our adrenaline levels. If Hollywood pales, we still have organized sports, with lots of rules for safety and referees to enforce them. We've laced our social lives into a network wherein rights and wrongs are defined by hundreds of thousands of laws. And we have airbags and para-chutes and orthopaedic surgeons and seat belts and life vests and helmets to protect us when something does go wrong. If all of these fail, we call one of those lawyers we see on daytime TV and sue somebody. In short, we are what would be referred to in biology as a domesticated species. We are no longer wild *Homo sapiens*. Instead, psychologically, many of us are sheep.

Baaa....

As sheep—or, if you prefer, domesticated *Homo sapiens* (*Homo sapiens domesticus* or *Homo sapiens touristicus*)—many of us now make the habitual and unquestioned assumption that somebody else is supposed to be watching out for our best interests for us. We blindly follow the rest of the flock and assume that the sheepherder, wherever he is, is keeping his eye peeled for the wolves.

This sort of lack of self-responsibility by so many of the visitors to U.S. national parks is all too obvious. And, as we've seen, it all too often proves lethal.

As Lee H. Whittlesey reports in *Death in Yellowstone*, between the time Yellowstone became a National park in 1872 until 1995, over 300 people died in it traumatically, mostly due to their own errors. As with the nearly twice as many traumatic fatalities in Grand Canyon too, these casualties teach us vital lessons in survival. Perhaps the first of these lessons, Whittlesey notes, is: "Nature demands of us that we pay attention." More often than not, however, this lesson goes unheeded. Every day, Whittlesey says, someone enters a wilderness area unprepared.

Certainly this is true in Grand Canyon. But what should we do to fix this situation? Law students do exist who firmly believe that every possible loca-tion in the American West where someone might die accidentally should be labeled with warning signs. *Every* location. But even after posting several mil-lion signs, these places would still be dangerous to people who failed to think—or even to read the signs. Should we then pave, sanitize, declaw, and defang American wilderness so that those of us who have no respect for its reality will not be able to hurt ourselves in our blissful ignorance and arro-gance? In our current era at the end of the twentieth century, a time during which money-chasing lawyers and irresponsible jurors have nearly abolished the legitimacy of the concept of self-responsibility for the consequences of one's own personal actions, this question is a complicated one. Making feder-al wilderness so "safe" that mentally and/or physically unprepared people are guaranteed to survive in it unscathed is a tort lawyer's dream come true. This is because making the world safe cannot be done; lethal human foolishness is unlimited, while wilderness itself offers an infinite number of opportunities for someone to carelessly hurt him or herself. Hence, if a mandate did exist to force an attempt to make wilderness safe, America's one million lawyers (70 percent of all lawyers on Earth) would be assured of litigation income forever. Thus the logical answer seems to be to bar all human entry by land, water, or air into U.S. wilderness.

Crazy? Maybe. But the question of the degree to which federal or state governments should be required to *change* anything in wilderness involves several complicated issues of legality, morality, value, and practicality. The 1916 U.S. National Park Organic Act dictates that the NPS must leave national parks in their natural state, unchanged and unencumbered to the future enjoyment of posterity. So, no one is legally allowed to "fix" national park wilderness to make it safe. Instead, the NPS and state park systems are legally required only not to be *negligent* in safeguarding visitors. Mainly this safeguarding consists of forewarning people of common dangers in a systematic, easily understandable way through warning pamphlets, signs, radio broadcasts, and so on. Unfortunately, warnings that 999,999 people out of a million agree are quite clear and useful, number 1,000,000 does not bother to read or understand or heed and, in his ignorance, kills himself. Here, again, is the lawyer's bread and butter.

Each "frivolous" suit forces the government agencies to install more warning signs, erect more railings, pave more trails, forbid any step off the trail, continually lower and restrict visitor access, and in general treat most people as something less intelligent than a blind cow. Many of us find this increasing trend to be a very negative one when it comes to *enjoying* a visit to a national park or other natural area. And because protecting the ignorant or foolish from their own mistakes is an endlessly spiraling arms race between NPS administrators and human stupidity, NPS restrictions will only increase in this endless war to protect people who are too lazy or naive to protect themselves.

Nor can the NPS bring more resources to bear on this war. In other words, as mentioned above, making federal wilderness safe is both illegal and impractical (to put it mildly) even if funds were unlimited, which they are not. Between 1978 and 1998, the National Park Service budget decreased 40 percent in constant dollars while recreational usage increased 48 percent. The backlog in maintenance, resource management, construction, and land acquisitions for the national parks alone is estimated at $6 billion to $8 billion. Hence, the NPS has no choice but to employ the cheapest possible weapons in this war. Unfortunately, the cheapest possible weapon is simply *restricting* the places that a visitor can visit.

Beyond the questions of legality and practicality are the perhaps even more important questions of morality and value. As has become increasingly clear in the past fifty years, the human population on this planet and in this country is exploding. Humanity is not an endangered species (yet). Meanwhile wilderness—and merely pleasant and quiet natural scenery—is shrinking as people co-opt every scrap of unprotected landscape for economic use. Our shriveling wilderness not only contains, and is vital to the survival of, uncounted endangered species, wilderness itself *is* an endangered environment. Many of us insist that not only do we have a moral obligation to preserve such species, such habitats, and such ecosystems, we also are guilty of committing murder if we do not. Therefore, sanitizing and "human-proofing" the wilderness is not only illegal, impractical, and ultimately impossible, morally it is unconscionable ecocide.

So where does that leave us? Morality and practicality both dictate that when it comes to the question of man versus protected wilderness, the onus is on humankind to take on the personal responsibility to prepare its members for *all* of the environmental challenges that wilderness poses to the visitor. If a prospective visitor is unwilling to show the wilderness and his fellow humans this respect, he should stay out of the wilderness. Instead, he should rent the video.

Most of the five million people each year who drive or fly out of their way to visit Grand Canyon—a World Heritage Site and one of the most impressive of the World's Seven Natural Wonders—do not do so because they have been assured that it has been made as safe as (or safer than) their local neighborhood park. Instead they come to experience a truly inspirational chunk of *wilderness*. Few of them want to see it "improved" or "safety-proofed." Again, it is our job to safeguard ourselves by respecting the natural world, and most of us know it.

This respect is at the root of our love for wilderness. We know that wilderness is not only something bigger than all of us, it is also the source of all of us. It molded much of our own nature. Our ancestors survived in wilderness for millennia only by respecting its impersonal dangers. Our psyches were molded by these dangers and also by the rewards the wilderness offers to those who pay attention. In essence, we are surviving great-great-grandchildren of the wilderness. Our five senses were fine-tuned by its demands. To see its vastness, hear its thunder, smell its springtimes, and to feel the bite of its winds, the heat of its sun, and the chill of its rains brings us back to our childhood, to our very roots.

Most of us know, however, that the wilderness in turn cares not a whit for us. It reciprocates neither our fascination nor our love for it. If we fail to respect its dangers, we realize, not only might those dangers hurt us, they may kill us—or an innocent child who's depending on us.

Most of us would have this relationship be no other way.

The take-home lesson here—one obvious in the first six chapters of this book—is that the people who die traumatically in Grand Canyon die main-ly—almost universally—due to their own, or their guide's, poor judgement. It is impossible for the rest of us to protect them fully from these personal fail-ings. We can only hope to do our best to inform people of the real dangers the Canyon wilderness poses and always will pose.

Forewarned, it is then up to the personal responsibility of each of us to avoid killing ourselves—and thereby also avoid tacitly accusing the wilderness of being our murderer. We hope this book does just that, forewarn each of us of the dangers the Canyon poses. Forewarned enough, perhaps we *and* our vanishing wilderness will both survive.

Continuing Research

As we explained at the onset of this book, finding all of the information and then determining whether or not this information is accurate regarding fatal episodes in Grand Canyon is an unending task. If you possess personal knowledge of any episode at odds with what we have written, or instead know of an episode that we have missed, we would appreciate your information. One of our top priorities here is that this book be accurate. High accuracy makes its lessons that much more reliable. If you wish to share any information you possess, please contact us by letter via Puma Press, P.O. Box 30998, Flagstaff, AZ 86003 USA.

Authors' Profiles

MICHAEL P. GHIGLIERI earned his Ph.D. in Biological Ecology from the University of California at Davis for his pioneering research project on wild chimpanzees in Kibale Forest, Uganda. In addition to teaching university level courses in primate behavior and ecology and in human evolution and also directing several different university semesters in sustainable resource management overseas, he has worked as a wilderness river guide since 1974, running more than 600 commercial whitewater trips plus treks and educational programs in Australia, Canada, Ethiopia, Java, Kenya, Papau New Guinea, Palau, Peru, Rwanda, Sumatra, Tanzania, Turkey, the Turks & Caicos Islands, Uganda, and the U.S.A.. His expeditions include well over 100 two-week trips in Grand Canyon as a rowing or paddling guide/trip leader plus a few as an NPS river ranger. Ghiglieri has spent more than 1,500 days inside the Canyon, hiked roughly 2,500 miles in it, and has rendered assistance as an EMT during many accidents. A Flagstaff resident, married with three children, Ghiglieri is the author of six other books, three of which deal with wild chimpanzees and the violent natural history of men, and of the documentary screenplays "River of Stone" and "Artists of the West." His previous book on Grand Canyon, *CANYON*, was hailed by the *Library Journal* as "**the single best introduction to a myriad of aspects of this 'most impressive place' this reviewer has seen. Recommended for all—**"

THOMAS M. MYERS earned his M.D. from the University of Arizona and worked as a physician at Grand Canyon for nearly a decade, living at the South Rim with his family. Myers began exploring Grand Canyon at age ten and never stopped. He has hiked the Canyon backcountry extensively and rowed the Colorado River several times. Myers has seen, responded to, treated, and tried to understand the ontogeny of thousands of injuries and of all too many traumatic fatalities occurring in the Canyon. Myers, with co-authors Chris Becker and Larry Stevens, made the first-ever detailed statistical analysis of river-running accidents in their book *Fateful Journey: Injury and Death on Colorado River Trips in Grand Canyon*, dispelling many previously held myths about the risks of running the Colorado. Tom Myers also holds a degree in history from Northern Arizona University, is married with three children, and now lives back in his hometown of Flagstaff, Arizona.

TO ORDER COPIES of PUMA PRESS BOOKS:

Photocopy this page and fill out your order. Please print legibly.

Please send _____ copies of *OVER THE EDGE: DEATH IN GRAND CANYON*, $22.95 softcover (if being shipped to an Arizona address, please add $1.68 sales tax per copy) subtotal = _____

Please send _____ copies of *OFF THE WALL: DEATH IN YOSEMITE*, $24.95 softcover (if being shipped to an Arizona address, please add $2.03 sales tax per copy) subtotal = _____

Please send _____ copies of *FIRST THROUGH GRAND CANYON: The Secret Journals and Letters of the 1869 Crew Who Explored the Green and Colorado Rivers*, $19.95 softcover (if being shipped to an Arizona address, please add $1.62 sales tax per copy) subtotal = _____

Please send _____ copies of *GRAND OBSESSION: Harvey Butchart and the Exploration of Grand Canyon*, $19.95 softcover (if being shipped to an Arizona address, please add $1.62 sales tax per copy) subtotal = _____

Shipping & Handling: please add $3.00 for the first book, $1.00 for each additional book. shipping subtotal = _____

TOTAL = $ _____

Order via our website: **pumapress.org** or

Enclose your **check or money order** for the total above **payable to: Puma Press P.O. Box 30998, Flagstaff, AZ 86003 USA**
Thank you for your order. Please allow 3 weeks for delivery.

_____

ADDRESS TO WHICH YOU WISH YOUR ORDER TO BE SHIPPED
(*please print*)

NAME _____

ADDRESS _____

CITY _____

STATE _____ ZIP CODE _____

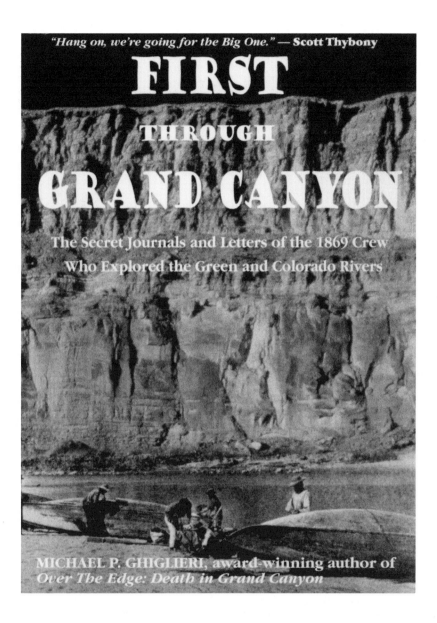

"Hang on, we're going for the Big One." — **Scott Thybony**

FIRST

THROUGH

GRAND CANYON

The Secret Journals and Letters of the 1869 Crew
Who Explored the Green and Colorado Rivers

MICHAEL P. GHIGLIERI, award-winning author of
Over The Edge: Death in Grand Canyon

References

Notes for Introduction: *WHY A BOOK ON DEATH?*

Udall, S. L. 1998. Foreword. in Farabee, C.R. "B.", Jr. (ed.) 1998. *Death Daring and Disaster: Search and Rescue in the National Parks.* Boulder, Colorado: Roberts Rinehart.

Whitman, D. 2000. Don't get **foolish** in the great outdoors; the bison do butt. *U.S. News &World Report* July 3, 129(1):48–49.

Farabee, C.R. "B.", Jr. 1998. *Death Daring and Disaster: Search and Rescue in the National Parks.* Boulder, Colorado: Roberts Rinehart.

Notes for Chapter 1. *"SAY, HOW MANY PEOPLE FALL HERE?"*

Falls From The Rims

Bowen, W. date? Grand Canyon National Park—South Rim—7/15/46 to 10/15/47 Unpublished NPS ranger's report.

staff. 1946. Fall in Canyon nearly fatal to dress designer. *Arizona Daily Sun* September 20.

McAuliffe, K. and M. Nash. 1997. Fatal Fall: Lana Virginia Smith. *U.S. Department of the Interior Grand Canyon National Park Service Case Incident Record, Incident # GRCA9700001689.* May 11.

Ken Phillips. 2000. Personal interview by T. Myers, February.

staff. 1908. Brush saves his life: Survives greatest dive ever made into the great gorge—lands on thick brush on narrow ledge. *Coconino Sun* Friday, August 14. p. 1.

staff. 1925. Doubt that death at Grand Canyon suicide. *Coconino Sun* Friday, April 3. p. 12.

staff. 1925. Aged man, alone, killed when car slid off into Canyon near Lee's Ferry. *Coconino Sun* Friday, November 6. p. 1.

staff. 1927. Killed in fall from Rim of Canyon. *Coconino Sun* Friday, November 4. p. 1

staff. 1928. Steel worker fell to death in the Colorado River from new bridge. *Coconino Sun* Friday, June 15. p. 1.

staff. 1929. Memorandum for the Director. January 6. U.S. Department of the Interior, NPS, Grand Canyon National Park. Superintendent's Monthly Report, Dec. 1929, #54734. p. 1.

Sun's own Bureau. 1947. Bus boy tumbles to death from rim as horrified visitors watch. *Arizona Daily Sun* Friday, July 18. p. 2.

staff. 1949. 500-foot fall fatal to woman at Canyon. *Arizona Daily Sun* Thursday, September 15. p. 1.

staff. 1957. Body of missing salesman found: Man killed in Canyon fall. *Arizona Daily Sun* Saturday, June 29. p. 1.

Fred Harvey Fatality File 1963, NAU Cline Library Special Collections, Fred Harvey Collections, ms #280.

Hodge, C. 1958. Gorge swallows 2 boys: Climbers recover bodies(Unknown publication)

staff. 1958. Car rolls into Grand Canyon: Parents watch helplessly as sons plunge to deaths. (Unknown publication) June 9.

Northern Arizona Bureau. 1965. Fall victim at Canyon identified. *The Arizona Republic* April 8.

Northern Arizona Bureau. 1966. Boy survives 120-foot Grand Canyon plunge. *The Arizona Republic* June 1.

Rushlo, M. 1999. Kneivel clears Canyon. *Arizona Daily Sun* Friday, May 21. p. 1.

staff. 1963. Youth falls 75 feet from Canyon wall. *Arizona Daily Sun* October 10. p. 8.

staff. 1971. Canyon fall kills coed. *Arizona Daily Sun* April 13.

staff. 1972. Supai Canyon crash claim man's Life. *Arizona Daily Sun* August 21.

staff. 1974. Ex-LDS leader's son dies in fall. *Arizona Daily Sun* August 24.

staff. 1975. Another Canyon tragedy. *Arizona Daily Sun* October 7.

staff. 1976. Grand Canyon fall kills Phoenix man. *Arizona Daily Sun* June 19.

staff. 1978. Canyon fall victim ID'd by deputies. *Arizona Daily Sun* June 18.

staff. 1978. Canyon fall claims life. *The Arizona Republic* July 12.

staff. 1979. Canyon plunge kills California picture-taker. *The Arizona Republic* April 10.

staff. 1979. Fall victim's body pulled from Canyon. *The Arizona Republic* December 29.

staff. 1981. Sheriff's deputies hope to identify mystery body. *Williams News* January 8.

staff. 1981. Skeleton identified. *Williams News* January 29.

staff. 1981. Body of British tourist recovered after plunge into Grand Canyon. *The Arizona Republic* Wednesday, April 29.

staff. 1981. Girl reportedly killed in Canyon fall. *Arizona Daily Sun* October 9.

staff. 1982. California tourist dies in Grand Canyon fall. *The Arizona Republic* September 2.

staff. 1982. Fall at Canyon fatal. *Williams News* September 2.

staff. 1985. California tourist slips, falls to death in Grand Canyon. *Arizona Daily Sun* January 11.

staff. 1993. Grand Canyon demands high price for carelessness. *Fort Donelson National Battlefield* November 30. p. 1.

staff. 1989. West German tourist falls to death. *Grand Canyon News* March 14.

staff. 1989. Life claimed in fall. *Grand Canyon News* March 23.

staff. 1994. Falls into Canyon not new: official. *Arizona Daily Sun* Saturday, May 26. p. 3.

Trausch, S. 1993. The canyon is real. *Boston Globe* Friday, December 3. p. 2.

Associated Press. 1993. Canyon deaths traced to carelessness. *The Arizona Republic* Saturday, November 27. p. B13.

staff. 1999. Visitor falls to his death at Grand Canyon. *Arizona Daily Sun* Saturday, August 21. p. 3.

Falls Within The Canyon

Ghiglieri, M. P. 1992. *Canyon.* Tucson, Arizona: The University of Arizona Press.

Castaneda, Pedro, de. et al. 1596 (edited by George Parker Winship in 1933 [1990]. *The Journey of Coronado.* New York: Dover Publications. pp. 22–23.

Billingsley, G. H., E. E. Spamer and D. Menkes. 1998. *Quest for the Pillar of Gold: The Mines & Miners of the Grand Canyon.* Grand Canyon: Grand Canyon Association. pp. 9 & 37.

staff & William Wallace Bass. 1929. Recalling tragic death of Mooney at Grand Canyon. *Coconino Sun* Friday, March 29, section 2.

Editor & Doheny, E. I. 1929. How the Mooney Falls in Cataract Cany'n got name. *Coconino Sun* August 23.

Reilly, P. T. 1966. The sites at Vasey's Paradise. *The Masterykey* (October– December) 40(4):126–139.

staff. 1950. Mystery bones found in Canyon skeleton minus skull found on bar south of Marble Canyon. *Arizona Daily Sun* Friday, July 21. pp 1 & 8.

Billingsley, G. H., E. E. Spamer and D. Menkes. *Ibid.* p. 35.

Billingsley, G. H., E. E. Spamer and D. Menkes. *Ibid.* p. 45.

Farabee, C. R. "B.", Jr. 1998. in Farabee, C. R. "B." Jr. (ed.) *Death Daring and Disaster: Search and Rescue in the National Parks.* Boulder, CO: Roberts Rinehart. pp. 207–208.

staff. 1940. Glendale girl dies from fall at Grand Canyon. *Coconino Sun* Friday, August 9. p. 7.

staff. 1951. *Supplement to Superintendent's Annual Report, Grand Canyon National Park.* Grand Canyon National Park.

staff. 1959. Search in Canyon for missing pair: Boy found dead in Inner Gorge. *Arizona Daily Sun* Monday, July 27. p. 1.

staff. 1959. Padre found dead; still seek youth. *Arizona Daily Sun* Tuesday, July 28. p. 1.

Sweitzer, P. 1959. Last diary entry reveals goal of ill-fated hikers.*Arizona Daily Sun* Tuesday, July 28.

staff. 1959. Searchers use bloodhounds to trace boy's Canyon trail. *Arizona Daily Sun* Wednesday, July 29. p. 1.

staff. 1959. Canyon searchers lose hope: "Just looking for body now." *Arizona Daily Sun* Thursday, July 30. p. 1.

Miller, R. 1959. Youth tells full story of ordeal. *Arizona Daily Sun* Saturday, August 1. pp. 1 & 2.

Madsen, R. 1959. Youth tells story of Canyon ordeal. Credits faith, instinct for survival. *Deseret News* August 1.

Owens, J. M., III. 1959. Youth's own story: No scout training, just used instinct. *Deseret News* August 1.

Davis, D. 1959. Ranger tells rescue story. *Deseret News* August 1.

staff. 1959. Boy's own story of ordeal in Grand Canyon: Father flies to him in hospital.*New York Herald Tribune* August 2. p. 5.

staff. 1959. 'Hog-hungry' boy at Canyon gains ten pounds in one day. *Arizona Daily Sun* Monday, August 3. p. 1.

Davis, D. 1959. Letter to Harvey Butchart, August 5.

Harvey Butchart. 2000. Personal interviews by T. Myers, on February 4 & 29.

Northern Arizona Bureau. 1968. Woman, 25, dies in fall. *The Arizona Republic* August 24.

staff. 1968. Plunge from high ledge kills Grand Canyon hiker. *Arizona Daily Sun* August 24.

staff. 1972. Canyon death ruled accident. *Arizona Daily Sun* July 6.

staff. 1972. Youth's body found in Grand Canyon. *The Arizona Republic* September 30.

staff. 1973. Foul play ruled out in death of hiker. *Arizona Daily Sun* May 11.

staff. 1973. Climber is killed in 1,200-foot fall. *The Arizona Republic* July 20.

staff. 1974. Service slated for Las Vegan found dead in Grand Canyon. *Las Vegas Republic Journal* January 27. p. 24.

staff. 1974. Hiker dies in plunge from Grand Canyon ledge. *Arizona Daily Sun* June 26.

staff. 1974. Students missing on Canyon hike. *Arizona Daily Sun* September 9.

Northern Arizona Bureau. 1974. Canyon hikers' plea for aid found. *The Arizona Republic* September 9.

staff. 1974. Hikers' bodies found in Canyon. *Arizona Daily Sun* September 10.

Northern Arizona Bureau. 1974. Bodies of ASU students found below Grand Canyon North Rim. *The Arizona Republic* September 10.

staff. 1974. 2 ASU students: Inquest planned in Canyon deaths. *The Arizona Republic* Saturday, September 14.

Phillips, B. 1977. Death, Charles Walter Rienecke: *U.S. Department of the Interior Grand Canyon National Park Service Case Incident Record, #4783.* August 2.

staff. 1977. Combined search efforts locate hiker's body. *Williams News* Thursday, August 4.

Stiles, E. 1978. Grand Canyon's vastness concealing missing hiker? *Tucson Daily Citizen* Thursday, June 15.

Northern Arizona Bureau. 1978. North Rim hiker killed in night fall. *The Arizona Republic* October 2.

staff. 1979. Grand Canyon victim identified. *Arizona Daily Sun* August 13.

staff. 1979. Body of Grand Canyon hiker found. *Williams News* August 16.

Leoben, K. 1979. Grand Canyon fall kills California man. *Arizona Daily Sun* May 6.

Jensen, M. O. 1979. Fatal fall, Gordon Stanley Grace. *U.S. Department of the Interior Grand Canyon National Park Service Case Incident Record.* Incident No. 2554. May 31.

Olson, D. 1979. Coconino County Sheriff's Department Witness Statement, D.R. #4-0579-1371. May 31.

Weiss, P. 1979. Coconino County Sheriff's Department Witness Statement, D.R. #4-0579-1371. May 31 (anomalously signed by Weiss giving date, "May 31, 1975.")

Anderson, P. R. 1980. Fatal fall, Joseph Anthony Dean. *U.S. Department of the Interior Grand Canyon National Park Service Case Incident Record.* Incident No. 4192. November 5.

staff. 1982. Body recovered in Canyon. *The Arizona Republic* December 4.

Burak, G. 1998. Lost! *The Ol' Pioneer* Spring 1998. pp. 11–14.

staff. 1984. Hiker's body recovered in Canyon. *Arizona Daily Sun* May 8.

staff. 1984. Canyon fall kills serviceman. *The Arizona Republic* June 11.

staff. 1985. Deputies probe Canyon mishap. *Arizona Daily Sun* March 7.

staff. 1985. Hiker falls to death at Grand Canyon. *Arizona Daily Sun* March 8.

staff. 1985. Body recovered from Canyon. *Arizona Daily Sun* August 21.

staff. 1985. Hiker died from fall. *Arizona Daily Sun* August 23.

Kuncl, Ernie W. 1986. Fatal Fall: Connie Wernette. *U.S. Department of the Interior Grand Canyon National Park Service Case Incident Record.* Incident No. 862791. August 21.

Phillips, K. 1989. Fatal fall: Ronald D. Hight. *U.S. Department of the Interior Grand Canyon National Park Service Case Incident Record.* Incident No. 89-3534. August.

Hutton, J. and Farias, J., Jr. 1990. Death, Michael Jacobs. *U.S. Department of the Interior Grand Canyon National Park Service Case Incident Record.* Incident No. 903811. September 23.

Short, V. 1990. Michael Jacobs. *boatman's quarterly review* 3(4):1.

Phillips. K. 1994. Fatal fall, Richard Flowers. *U.S. Department of the Interior Grand Canyon National Park Service Case Incident Record.* Incident No. 94-2448. July.

staff. 1995. Tourist slips off Canyon's rim in dark, falls 500 feet to his death. *The Arizona Republic* Wednesday, May 10. p. B2.

staff. 1996. Youth alive due to efforts of 30 rescuers. *Williams/Grand Canyon News* April 24.

Regan Dale. 2000. Personal communication to M. P. Ghiglieri. March and April.

Phillips, K. 1994. Fall, Julie Chaibineou. *U.S. Department of the Interior Grand Canyon National Park Service Case Incident Record.* Incident #944508 October 13.

Bryan Wisher. 1999 & 2000. Multiple personal interviews by T. Myers (on rescue of Jared King), April 28, 1999 & February, 2000.

staff. 1998. California woman falls to death in Grand Canyon. *The Arizona Republic* Sunday, May 10. p. B2.

Notes for Chapter 2. *THE DESERT CRUCIBLE: ENVIRONMENTAL DEATHS WITHIN THE "INVERTED MOUNTAIN"*

Harris, Thompson, & Kirschner, M. 1990. Interview of Karen Stryker. C.I. #90-1953/SAR 90-0199. Coconino County Sheriff's Department. June.

Audretsch, B. 1998. The Death of Casimar Pultorak: A Narrative History. Unpublished 3-page ms.

Fred Harvey Fatality File 1963, NAU Cline Library Special Collections. Fred Harvey Collection, ms #280.

staff. 1939. Detroit tourist found frozen in Grand Canyon. *Coconino Sun* February 10.

Hamilton, W. F. 1939. Death, Casimar Pultorak. Accident Report, Grand Canyon National Park Service. February 28.

1903. *Coconino Sun* August 15.

Anderson, M. F. 1998. *Living at the Edge: Explorers, Exploiters and Settlers of the Grand Canyon Region.* Grand Canyon: Grand Canyon Association.

staff. 1928. Hero threw villain into Colorado, drowning him—but it's only picture. *Coconino Sun* Friday, January 13. P. 3.

Eddy, C. 1929. *Down the World's Most Dangerous River.* New York: Frederick A. Stokes. p. 279.

staff. 1906. A Canyon mystery. *Coconino Sun* April 7. p.5.

Beer, B. 1994. Willie Taylor revisited. *boatman's quarterly review* 7(4):8.

Farabee, C. R. "B.", Jr. 1998. Rescue came, well, sort of. in Farabee, C. R. "B.", Jr. (ed.) 1998. *Death Daring and Disaster Search and Rescue in the National Parks*, pp. 193–194. Boulder, Colorado: Roberts Rinehart.

staff. 1960. Navajo's body found in Canyon. *The Arizona Republic* Sunday, June 26. p. 1.

staff. 1960. Old Navajo medicine man third Tanner Trail victim. *Arizona Daily Sun* Monday, June 27. p. 1.

James Peshlakai. 2000. Personal communication to M. P. Ghiglieri, August 3.

Northern Arizona Bureau. 1966. Skeleton identified as Missourian's. *The Arizona Republic* Wednesday, June 1.

Northern Arizona Bureau. 1966. Youth from Iowa dies on Grand Canyon trail. *The Arizona Republic* June 11.

staff. 1967. *Arizona Daily Sun* June 6.

staff. 1968. Canyon trail takes second life in 10 days. *The Arizona Republic* June 7.

staff. 1969. Sierra club hiker dies in G. Canyon. *Arizona Daily Sun* June 2.

staff. 1969. Autopsy slated in hiker's death. *Arizona Daily Sun* June 3.

staff. 1974. Body of 1967 storm victim found. *Williams News* October 31.

West, S. 1981. Death, Ed L. Agnew. *U.S. Department of the Interior Grand Canyon National Park Service Case Incident Record.* Incident No. 002192. July 30.

Kolb, E. L. 1914. *Through the Grand Canyon from Wyoming to Mexico.* New York: Macmillan. pp. 224–225.

Oltrogge, D. 1989. Death, Carolyn Guerra. *U.S. Department of the Interior Grand Canyon National Park Service Case Incident Record.* Incident No. 894800. October 12.

Almond, E. 1995. "Summer danger in the Grand Canyon: Hikers risk heatstroke and death." *Los Angeles Times* July 23.

Nichols, C. L. 1975. Death, Brad Riner. *U.S. Department of the Interior Grand Canyon National Park Service Case Incident Record.* Incident No. 006727. November 4.

Gottlieb, R. 1977. Good Morning. *Boulder City News* July 21.

staff. 1980. Canyon hiker dies. *Arizona Daily Sun* August 10.

staff. 1975. Young man survives ordeal in Grand Canyon. *Arizona Daily Sun* July 15.

staff. 1975. Searchers find woman lost 20 days in Canyon. *The Arizona Republic* August 21.

staff. 1975. Hiker's terror in Canyon. *San Francisco Chronicle* Friday, August 22. p. 3.

staff. 1976. Lost 19 days in 1975: Nurse keeps word, returns to Canyon. *Arizona Daily Sun* August 28.

Steller, T. 1992. Killer heat waterless Boy Scouts lacked Canyon permit. *Arizona Daily Sun* Friday, June 7. p. 1.

Palaski, K., Sgt. 1996. Death, accidental, David B. Phillips. Coconino County Sheriff Offense Report case number 960600063. December 15.

staff. 1996. LAW & ORDER Teen boy dies, was with 7 others illegally hiking trail in Canyon. *The Arizona Republic* Friday, June 7. p. B–2.

Maffly, B. 1996. Boy dies in Grand Canyon, heat, no water lead to tragedy. *The Salt Lake Tribune Utah* Saturday, June 8. p. B–2

Walsh, D. 1996. Does Boy Scouts Organization live up to its motto? *The Salt Lake Tribune Utah* Wednesday, June 12. p. B3.

staff. 1996. More scouts evacuated from Grand Canyon. *Las Vegas Sun* June 13.

staff. 1996. Boy dies in canyon; cause unknown. *Arizona Daily Sun* Wednesday, July 24. p. 3.

staff. 1996. Body of hiker is recovered from Canyon. *The Arizona Republic* Tuesday, September 10. P. B3.

staff. 2000. Prescott man dies after Grand Canyon hike. *Arizona Daily Sun* Monday, February 7. p. 2.

Ann Anderson. 2000. Personal communication to M. P. Ghiglieri, June 3.

Fuqua, B. 2000. Belgian tourist dies on Tonto Trail hike. *Williams Grand Canyon News* Wednesday, June 7.

Notes for Chapter 3. *"FLASH FLOOD!"*

staff. 1963. 2.02 inches of rain hit Bisbee; 2nd Canyon victim's body sought. *The Arizona Republic* August 4.

Garrett, W. E. 1978. Grand Canyon: Are we loving it to death? *National Geographic* 154(1):2–51.

Nixon, B. 1963. Hunt for boy in fifth day at Canyon. *The Arizona Republic* August 6.

staff. 1963. Boy's body recovered. *The Arizona Republic* August 7.

Clubb, M. D. 1963. Letter to H. C. and Mrs. Bryant. Unpublished letter, December 21.

Ramsdell, B. 1997. Eleven hikers feared drowned flash flood sweeps Page canyon. *Arizona Daily Sun* Wednesday, August 13. pp. 1 & 5.

Miller, E. 1997. Deadly wall of water `Never saw water like that.' *Arizona Republic* August 14.

Associated Press. 1997. Ninth flood victim found amid debris limits of warning systems debated. *Arizona Daily Sun* Monday, August 18. p. 1.

Mims, B. 1997. Hikers beware: Seek expert guides. *Arizona Daily Sun* Monday, August 18.

Ramsdell, B. 1997. Cleared: Antelope Canyon guide won't face prosecution for role in drownings. *Arizona Daily Sun* Monday, September 29. p. 1.

Glasenapp, T. 1998. A flood of memories two bodies still missing on anniversary of deluge. *Arizona Daily Sun* Wednesday, August 12. pp. 1 & 6.

Associated press. 1997. Flash flood forces Supai evacuation. *Arizona Daily Sun* Monday, August 11. p. 1.

Tolan, M. 1997. Hikers missing in Canyon in flash flood. *Arizona Daily Sun* Friday, September 12. pp. 1 & 10.

Associated Press. 1997. Body found in Grand Canyon. *The Arizona Republic* Friday, October 3. p. B2.

Associated Press. 1997. Body in river identified. *The Arizona Republic* Sunday, October 5. p. B2.

Janecek, T. 1997. Parked in the no-parking zone. *boatman's quarterly review* 10(4):19–21.

anonymous. 1988. Havasu day. *boatman's quarterly review* 1(2):3–4.

Jeffe Aronson. 1992. Personal communication to M. P. Ghiglieri, Grand Canyon.

Lober, K. and D. Davis. 1992. Deaths: Walter A. Jaskowiak and Miriam L. Epstein. *U.S. Department of the Interior Grand Canyon National Park Service Case Incident Record.* Incident No. 923020. Major SAR 8226-2029-178, SAR 92- 332 (Entire SAR file). August 30.

Cornish, I.D. Officer Dep. B., #45. 1992. *Coconino County Sheriff Offense Report.* Report # WC2J 460. September 2.

The Associated Press. 1992. 2 Canyon deaths tied to flood. *The Arizona Republic* Friday, August 28. p. B7.

McGibben, S. E. 1992. Forensic Entomology Report. AFOSI communication, file #921815D6-S719048. September 14, AFOSI District 18/RFC, Norton AFB, CA 92409.

Sidoti, F. 1997. Moran Fatalities, Case #97-4142. Investigative Report-Supplemental, National Park Service, Grand Canyon National Park. September 10.

Anderson, M. F. 1998. *Living at the Edge: Explorers, Exploiters and Settlers of the Grand Canyon Region*. Grand Canyon: Grand Canyon Association. pp. 94–95.

Bryan Wisher. 1999 & 2000. Multiple personal interviews by T. Myers, October–February.

Cue, E. 1999. An extreme sports report. *U.S. News & World Report* 127(6):33.

Notes for Chapter 4. *THE KILLER COLORADO*

Sumner, J. C. 1947. J. C. Sumner's Journal, July 6-August 31, 1869. *Utah Historical Quarterly* 15:113–124. p. 123.

Watkins, T. H. 1969. Chapter III: The Profitless Locality. in T. H. Watkins (ed.) *The Grand Colorado The Story of a River and Its Canyons*, pp. 61–87. Palo Alto, California: American West Publishing Company.

Lethal Errors While Running The River

Stanton, R. B. 1932 [1982]. *Colorado River Controversies*. Boulder City, Nevada: Westwater. pp. 3–93.

Stanton, R. B. 1965. *Down the Colorado, Edited and with an Introduction by Dwight L. Smith*. Norman, Oklahoma: University of Oklahoma Press.

Billingsley, G. H., E. E. Spamer and D. Menkes. 1998. *Quest for the Pillar of Gold: The Mines & Miners of the Grand Canyon*. Grand Canyon: Grand Canyon Association. p. 3.

staff. 1950. River expedition finds grave of drowned explorer. *Arizona Daily Sun* Friday, June 16. p. 4.

staff. 1896. A dangerous trip. *Coconino Sun* Thursday, January 8. p. 1.

Ghiglieri, M. P. 1992. *Canyon*. Tucson, Arizona: The University of Arizona Press.

O. Connor Dale. 1992. Personal communication to M. P. Ghiglieri.

Michael Harrison. 1992. Personal communication to M. P. Ghiglieri.

staff. 1928. Through Canyon on a flat boat. *Coconino Sun* November 16. p. 1.

Dimock, B. 2000. Bessie Haley's Bohemian friend. *boatman's quarterly review* Spring 13(2):25.

Anderson, M. J. undated. A perfect place to Hyde. Unpublished manuscript sent to M. P. Ghiglieri by author. Also in Cline Library Special Collections, Martin J. Anderson Collection, ms #77.

Thybony, S. 1985. Parting Shot: Mystery: What Happened to Bessie Hyde? *Outside* October, p. 108.

Tessman, N. 1986. "I wonder if I shall ever wear pretty shoes again": The disappearance of Glen and Bessie Hyde. *Sharlott Hall Gazette* (Prescott, Arizona) 13(1):1–6.

Farabee, C. R. "B.," Jr. 1998. The mystery of Glen and Bessie Hyde—70 years later. in Farabee, C. R. "B.," Jr. (ed.) 1998. *Death Daring and Disaster: Search and Rescue in the National Parks*, pp. 87–90. Boulder, Colorado: Roberts Rinehart.

Dimock, B. 2000. Glen Hyde's pop. *boatman's quarterly review* 13(1):10.

Dimock, B. 2000. "Glen & Bessie Hyde" A talk given for Mountain Air Community Radio, March 31, 9:00 p.m., Beaver Street Brewery, Flagstaff, AZ.

Dimock, B. 2001. *Sunk Without a Sound: The Tragic Colorado River Honeymoon of Glen and Bessie Hyde*. Flagstaff: Fretwater Press.

Nelson, J. 1931. re: Ervin and Payne (Talmadge) Experiences of June 1931 (Report sent September 3, 1948).

Stevens, J. E. 1988. *Hoover Dam: An American Adventure*. Norman: University of Oklahoma Press.

Ervin, J. R. 1966. Experience in Grand Canyon. Ms. prepared in 1966, Corrections of the record inserted by Dock Marston 10 XII 1966.

Garrison, L. 1948. Part of letter of Lon Garrison, Acting Superintendent, Grand Canyon National Park, October 20. Written from "Excerpt from files—Grand Canyon National Park, Oct. 31, 1938."

Holmstrom, H. 1938. Letter written to Julius F. Stone. Oct. 23. NAU Cline Library Special Collections, Haldane Holmstrom Collection, ms #311.

Watkins, W. 1948. Letter to Mr. Otis Marston from P.O. Box 107, Banning, California. (no date)

Bryant, Superintendent Harold. 1946. *Superintendent's Monthly Reports*, October, 1946, Grand Canyon National Park: National Park Service. #54706 (364).

Anonymous. 1947. *Memo to Director*. June 10, 1947, p. 2 Grand Canyon National Park: National Park Service. (#54706)

staff. 1946. Man travels river on raft. *The Arizona Republic* October 25. p. 1.

staff. 1946. Man riding raft down Colorado seen at Canyon. *Arizona Daily Sun* Friday, October 25. p. 4.

staff. 1949. Boatman drowns on Colorado River. Bert Loper dies as boat sinks in rapids. *Arizona Daily Sun* Monday, July 11. p. 1.

Marston, O. ("Dock") 1961. List of fatalities among those who have attempted a water traverse of the Grand Canyon prepared July 19, 1961, by Otis "Dock" Marston, for *LIFE*. (unpublished list from Marston Collection, Huntington Library).

Ives, R. L. 1976. *Journal of Arizona History* (Spring 1976) 17(1):49–54. p 51.

Westwood, R. E. 1992. *Rough-Water Man: Elwyn Blake's Colorado River Expeditions*. Reno, Nevada: The University of Nevada Press.

Beer, B. 1988. *We Swam the Grand Canyon: The True Story of a Cheap Vacation that Got a Little Out of Hand*. Seattle: The Mountaineers.

Myers, T. 1997. River runners and the numbers game. *boatman's quarterly review* 10(1):22–23.

Myers, T. M., C. C. Becker and L. E. Stevens. 1999. *Fateful Journey: Injury and Death on Colorado River Trips in Grand Canyon*. Flagstaff, Arizona: Red Lake Books.

staff. 1955. Kin identifies Jensen body. *Arizona Daily Sun* Wednesday, July 13. p. 1.

staff. 1965. Ranger dies in accident on Colorado. *The Arizona Republic* February 22.

staff. 1965. Spilled from canoe Sunday: Autopsy set here in death of ranger at Lee's Ferry. *Arizona Daily Sun* Monday, February 22. p. 1.

staff. 1967. River trip chief drowns. *The Arizona Republic* June 19.

Holland, A. 1998. Shorty's back. *boatman's quarterly review* 11(3):14–23.

staff. 1970. Colo. River victim sought. *The Arizona Republic* April 24.

Harrigan, J. J. 1971. Northern Views: Grand Canyon Hazards. *The Arizona Republic* Tuesday, August 24. p. 10.

staff. 1972. Two Canyon drownings are revealed. *Arizona Daily Sun* July 29.

Clark, G. White and D. Newcomb. no date. *Georgie Clark: Thirty years of River Running*. San Francisco: Chronicle Books. pp. 13, 15, 46, 52, 103, 104, 114-115.

staff. 1973. Student drowns in Canyon area. *Arizona Daily Sun* April 30.

staff. 1973. Boating accident claims a victim. *The Arizona Republic* May 22.

staff. 1973. Body recovered from Colorado River. *Williams News* August 30.

staff. 1974. Youth's body found near lake Mead. *The Arizona Republic* August 28.

Thomas, J. R.. M. O. Jensen and G. J. Kuipz. 1977. Drowning, Andalea Buzzard. *U.S. Department of the Interior Grand Canyon National Park Service Case Incident Record*. Incident No. 6184.

Drifter Smith. 1998. Personal communication to M. P. Ghiglieri, December 16.

Sauer, C. L. and T. Powers. 1981. Drowning, Terry Evans. *U.S. Department of the Interior Grand Canyon National Park Service Case Incident Record*. Incident No. 3636. December 2-12.

anonymous. 1981. Tribute to Terry D. Evans, January 6, 1955-December 2, 1981. in *Aquatic Resources Management of the Colorado River Ecosystem: Proceedings of the 1981 Symposium on the Aquatic Resources Management of the Colorado River Ecosystem, November 16–18, 1981, Las Vegas, Nevada*. p. 69.

Baker, P. and C. L. Sauer. 1983. Drowning: William Russell Wert. *U.S. Department of the Interior Grand Canyon National Park Service Case Incident Record.* Incident No. 831592. June 25–27.

Evans, J. 1983. Drownings: Dick B. Roach and David Sheperski. *U.S. Department of the Interior Grand Canyon National Park Service Case Incident Record.* Incident No. 833887. (plus entire SAR #83-0250 file). November 18.

Sauer, C. 1984. Drownings: Dick B. Roach and David Sheperski. *U.S. Department of the Interior Grand Canyon National Park Service Case Incident Record.* Incident No. 840703. March 24.

Sauer, C. 1984. Drownings: Dick B. Roach and David Sheperski. *U.S. Department of the Interior Grand Canyon National Park Service Case Incident Record.* Incident No. 843063. September 11.

Clayton, M. 1983. Drowning: Richard Bruce Sheperski. Coconino County Sheriff Offense Report case number 5-1183-2620. November 16.

staff. 1984. Officials identify skull. *Arizona Daily Sun* September 12.

Ron Stark. 2000. Personal communication to M. P. Ghiglieri.

Blomquist, B. and C. L. Sauer. 1984. Drowning, Tom Pillsbury. *U.S. Department of the Interior Grand Canyon National Park Service Case Incident Record.* Incident No. 841327. June 7.

Castleman, C. 2000. e-mail from Carolyn Castleman to T. M. Myers, March 14, Subj: Grand Canyon Story (regarding Tom Pillsbury's drowning below Crystal Rapid).

Castleman, C. 2000. e-mail from Carolyn Castleman to T. M. Myers, March 29, Subj: More on Tom).

Marley, Robert R. 1999. e-mail from Bob Marley to Grand Canyon Boaters, RE: '84 Death at Crystal (Bob&Sue@kwagunt.net) Thursday, July 1. 3:15 p.m.

Marley. R. R. 2000, multiple email letters to T. M. Myers and M. P. Ghiglieri, October 14–18.

Sauer, C. 1984. Drowning: Norine Abrams. *U.S. Department of the Interior Grand Canyon National Park Service Case Incident Record.* Incident No. 842832. August 26 & October 16.

John Davenport. 1999. Personal communication to M. P. Ghiglieri, July 3.

Clark, G. White and D. Newcomb. no date. *Georgie Clark: Thirty years of River Running.* San Francisco: Chronicle Books. pp. 46, 58–59, 60, 103.

Westwood, R. E. 1997. *Woman of the River: Georgie White Clark White-Water Pioneer.* Logan, Utah: Utah State University. p. 106.

Kim Crumbo. 1984. Personal communication to M. P. Ghiglieri, August 27.

Law, M. E. 1986. Drowning, William B. Blair. *U.S. Department of the Interior Grand Canyon National Park Service Case Incident Record.* Incident No. 863237. September 21.

Law, M. E. 1989. Drowning, Martin Hunsaker. *U.S. Department of the Interior Grand Canyon National Park Service Case Incident Record.* Incident No. 892092. June 19.

Curtis "Whale" Hanson. 1989. Personal communication to M. P. Ghiglieri, June 21.

Law, M. E. 1990. Drowning, Gene Elliot Stott. *U.S. Department of the Interior Grand Canyon National Park Service Case Incident Record.* Incident No. 901018. April 29.

staff. 1991. Stranded boater tells emotional Canyon tale. *The Arizona Republic* November 30.

Whittlesey, D. 1994. Personal letter to T. Myers, August 19.

Ken Phillips. 2000. Personal communication to T. M. Myers. March.

Chris McIntosh. 2001. Personal communication to M.P. Ghiglieri, February 26.

Darla Ekbom. 2000. Personal communication to M. P. Ghiglieri, December 8.

Sidoti, F. 1995. Death, Emilio Solares *U.S. Department of the Interior Grand Canyon National Park Service Case Incident Record.* Incident No. 945066. January 5.

Dave Desrosiers. 1999. Personal communication by M. P. Ghiglieri, July 16.

Joan Nevills Staveley. 1998 & 2000. Personal Interview by T. Myers. December 12, 1998 and February 15, 2000.

River Crossers Who Didn't
Schieffelin, E. 1996. Chapter 7. The grandest of all canyons, in *Destination Tombstone Adventures of a Prospector.* pp. 51–61. Mesa, Arizona: Royal Spectrum Publishing.

Reilly, P. T. 1969. How Deadly is Big Red? *Utah Historical Quarterly* 37(2):244–260.

McKee, T. H. 1922. Brighty, free citizen: How the sagacious hermit donkey of the Grand Cañon maintained his liberty for thirty years. *Sunset Magazine*, August, pp. 42 & 70 (and from original manuscript annotated by McKee's granddaughter, Martha Krueger).

McKee, T. H. no date. "The Passing of Bright Angel: A Saga of the Grand Canyon." (unpublished manuscript).

staff. 1911. Man and team drowned at Lee's Ferry. *Coconino Sun* Friday, March 17. p. 1.

staff. 1928. Three lost from Lee's Ferry boat. *Coconino Sun* Friday, June 8. p. 1.

staff. 1928. High wind primary cause recent triple Lee's Ferry drowning. *Coconino Sun* Friday, June 22. p. 8.

staff. 1928. Carried dead man up Canyon wall from Colorado River to new grave. *Coconino Sun* November. p. 1 & ?.

Reilly, P. T. 1999. *Lee's Ferry from Mormon Crossing to National Park*. Logan, Utah: Utah State University Press. pp. 326–330.

von Wiegand, K. H. 1900. Lost in the Grand Canyon of the Colorado. *The Wide World Magazine* 5(28):431–437.

staff. 1903. Lost in the Colorado. *Coconino Sun* August 8.

staff. 1903. Give up the search. *Coconino Sun* August 15, 22, & 29.

Coder, C. 1994. "Historical Archaeology," in Fairley, H. et al. (eds.) *The Grand Canyon River Corridor Survey Project: Archaeological Survey along the Colorado River between Glen Canyon Dam and Separation Canyon,* p. 127.

Sykes, G. G. 1967. Scraps from the Past, Unpublished ms., the Sykes Collection, Arizona Historical Society, Tucson.

Sturdevant, T. R. and M. Harrison. 1998. 1929 Grand Canyon Tragedy Revisited nearly 70 years later. *Ranger: The Journal of the Association of National Park Rangers* Summer 1998:14–16.

Tillotson, M. R. 1929. Our Sorrow. *Grand Canyon Nature Notes* February, 1929.

Farabee, C. R. "B.", Jr. 1998. Two rangers drown. in Farabee, C. R. "B.", Jr. (ed.) 1998. *Death Daring and Disaster: Search and Rescue in the National Parks*, pp. 90–91. Boulder, Colorado: Roberts Rinehart.

Cox, N. 1994. The story of Iven Bundy. *boatmen's quarterly review* 7(2):9–11. (excerpted from *Footprints on the Arizona Strip.*)

Garth Bundy. 1999. Personal interview by M. P. Ghiglieri, September 8.

Harvey Butchart. 1994. Personal interview by T. Myers, June.

Swimmers Who Drowned Between Phantom Or Pipe Creek
staff. 1935. Boy lost in Colorado at Grand Canyon. *Coconino Sun* Friday, July 26. p. 1.

Brooks, Chief Ranger Jas. P. 1935. Report of Accident, July 23.

staff. 1937. Officers seek Indian's body. *The Arizona Republic* Sunday, August 8. p. 2.

staff. 1966. Search ends for body in river. *Arizona Daily Sun* November 8.

Northern Arizona Bureau. 1966. Weather delays search for youth in Canyon. *The Arizona Republic* November 9.

Nixon, B. 1968. Mystery skeleton a woman's. *The Arizona Republic* April 24.

staff. 1968. Skeleton identity pending. *Arizona Daily Sun* April 26.

staff. 1970. Grand Canyon river victim identified. *Arizona Daily Sun* June 30.

staff. 1971. Body found in Grand Canyon. *Arizona Daily Sun* Friday, May 7. p. 1.

staff. 1973. Boy hunted at bottom of Grand Canyon. *The Arizona Republic* June 12.

staff. 1973. Youth's body found in Canyon river. *Arizona Daily Sun* June 27.

Jensen, M. O. 1977. Drowning: Gil Aparicio. *U.S. Department of the Interior Grand Canyon National Park Service Case Incident Record*. Incident No. 001106. April 8.

Phillips, K. 1995. Drowning: Louis John Stano, III. *U.S. Department of the Interior Grand Canyon National Park Service Case Incident Record*. Incident No. 951747. August 4.

Phillips, K. 1995. Drowning: Troy M. Fortney. *U.S. Department of the Interior Grand Canyon National Park Service Case Incident Record*. Incident No. 954005. December 6.

Herrmann, J. J. 1995. One swimmer missing; 2nd one is rescued. *Grand Canyon News* November 29.

Swimmers Who Drowned Elsewhere In The Colorado

Sauer, C. 1983. Drowning: Jeffrey Kaplan. *U.S. Department of the Interior Grand Canyon National Park Service Case Incident Record*. Incident No. 832449. August 7.

Law, M. E. 1990. Drowning: Matthew Cranny. *U.S. Department of the Interior Grand Canyon National Park Service Case Incident Record*. Incident No. 900610. March 23.

Law, M. E. 1990. Drowning: E. Meredith Akers. *U.S. Department of the Interior Grand Canyon National Park Service Case Incident Record*. Incident No. 901955. June 22.

McGinnis, M. J. and R. P. Thompson. 1990. Drowning: Bert Francisco. *U.S. Departmentof the Interior Grand Canyon National Park Service Case Incident Record*. Incident No. 902669. July 27.

Law, M. E. 1992. Drowning: Christopher Guetschow. *U.S. Department of the Interior Grand Canyon National Park Service Case Incident Record*. Incident No. 923169. September 4.

Ken Phillips. 1999. Personal communication to T. M. Myers, November.

Michael Wynn. 1999. Personal communication with M. P. Ghiglieri, March 13.

Accidental Swimmers Who Fell In From Shore

staff. 1919. Eastern tourist is killed in Colorado River. *Coconino Sun* May 23.

Anderson, M. F. 1998. *Living at the Edge: Explorers, Exploiters and Settlers of the Grand Canyon Region*. Grand Canyon: Grand Canyon Association.

Sinclair, M. A. and L. C. Van Slyke. 1983. Drowning: Josephine 'Jody' Mack. *U.S. Department of the Interior Grand Canyon National Park Service Case Incident Record*. Incident No. 830795. May 5.

anonymous. 1998. Unlikely angel. *boatman's quarterly review* 11(1):31.

Law, M. E. 1989. Drowning: Sebastian Karl Jacobi. *U.S. Department of the Interior Grand Canyon National Park Service Case Incident Record*. Incident No. 892093. June 19.

Arlan Lazere. 1999. Personal communication to M. P. Ghiglieri, May.

staff. 1999. Canyon death. *Arizona Daily Sun* Tuesday, June 1. p. 1.

staff. 2000. Man dies in river. *Arizona Daily Sun* Monday, January 31. p. 3.

Mysterious Disappearances Who Drowned From Camp

Judd, J. E. 1973. Disappearance: Marcos (Mark) Ortega. Officer's Report, the Coconino County Sheriff's Department, Case # 0673-2441-4, June 27.

staff. 1980. Missing man's body found. *Arizona Daily Sun* August 21.

staff. 1980. Search still under way for missing man. *Arizona Daily Sun* Tuesday, August 5.

Northern Arizona Bureau. 1980. Kansan apparently drowns while rafting on the Colorado. *The Arizona Republic* Wednesday, August 6. p. B9.

Sauer, C. L., J. R. Thomas and D. J. Daniel. 1981. Drowning: Charles Robert Hunter. *U.S. Department of the Interior Grand Canyon National Park Service Case Incident Record*. Incident No. 1947. July 10.

Willis, S. and M. D. Vandzura. 1997. Drowning: John Anthony Frye. *U.S. Department of he Interior Grand Canyon National Park Service Case Incident Record*. Incident No. GCCA9700004193. September 14.

Myers, T. M., C. C. Becker and L. E. Stevens. 1999. *Fateful Journey: Injury and Death on Colorado River Trips in Grand Canyon*. Flagstaff, Arizona: Red Lake Books.

Lessons of Safety and Survival from the Grand Canyon Colorado
Myers, T. M., C. C. Becker and L. E. Stevens. 1999. *Fateful Journey: Injury and Death on Colorado River Trips in Grand Canyon.* Flagstaff, Arizona: Red Lake Books.
staff. 1999. *Foundation Findings #31: Alcohol and Boating—January 1999.* Alexandria, VA: The BOAT/U.S. Foundation for Boating Safety.

Notes for Chapter 5. *IF LOOKS COULD KILL: DEATH FROM THE AIR*

staff. 1944. Rescuers contact three fliers marooned on isolated promontory in Grand Canyon and entire party now on way to Rim. *Coconino Sun* Friday, June 30. pp. 1 & 5.
Farabee, C. R. "B." Jr. 1998. "Greetings, you are in Grand Canyon." in Farabee, C. R. "B." Jr. (ed.) *Death Daring and Disaster: Search and Rescue in the National Parks.* Boulder, CO: Roberts Rinehart. pp. 162–165.
Cadwalader, M. H. 1957. Air mystery is solved: A step-by-step reconstruction of the Grand Canyon crash suggests ways to prevent the rare but nightmarish cases of airplane collision. *LIFE* April 29. pp. 151–164.
Sweitzer, P. 1971. June 30, 1956: the day two giants collided. *Arizona Daily Sun* June 30. pp. 1 & 8.
L.M.H. 1976. Airline Collision over Grand Canyon—1956. 6/9/1976.
Sweitzer, P. 1986. On collision's 30th anniversary: Grave is mute reminder of Grand Canyon air crash. *Arizona Daily Sun* June 29.
Sweitzer, P. 1996. 40 years later, mystery lingers: Today marks anniversary of Grand Canyon crash. *Arizona Daily Sun* June 30. pp. 1 & 4.
Farabee, C. R. "B.", Jr. 1998. 128 die. in Farabee, C. R. "B.", Jr. (ed.) 1998. *Ibid.* pp. 214–217.
staff. 1966. Pilot dies, three injured: Copter crashes in Canyon. *Arizona Daily Sun* April 12.
Northern Arizona Bureau. 1966. Crash in Grand Canyon kills helicopter pilot. *The Arizona Republic* Wednesday, April 13.
staff. 1967. Canyon Crash kills 5. *Arizona Daily Sun* Thursday, November 2. p. 1.
Northern Arizona Bureau. 1967. 6 sightseers, pilot killed in Canyon crash. *The Arizona Republic* July 28.
staff. 1969. Air search begins today for 4 canyon sightseers. *The Arizona Republic* May 7.
staff. 1969. Plane crashes: California couple dies in flaming wreckage. *The Arizona Republic* July 6.
staff. 1969. Plane crash at Grand Canyon brings suit. *Arizona Daily Sun* August 1.
staff. 1971. Plane crash kills ten near Canyon. *Arizona Daily Sun* Monday, October 18. p. 1.
Northern Arizona Bureau. 1980. 4 unhurt after plane lands on Canyon floor. *The Arizona Republic* July 8.
staff. 1969. Victims still unidentified. *The Arizona Republic* August 1.
staff. 1969. Dead tourists identified. *The Arizona Republic* August 2.
staff. 1969. Fourth this year: 'Copter pilot dies in Canyon Crash. *Arizona Daily Sun* December 16.
staff. 1969. Helicopter crash victim identified. *The Arizona Republic* December 17.
staff. 1969. Crash kills copter pilot. *The Arizona Republic* December 16.
staff. 1970. 'Copter suit filed. *Arizona Daily Sun* August 6.
staff. 1970. Weather blamed for crash. *The Arizona Republic* June 15.
staff. 1970. Plane wreck on Arizona Strip is identified; six bodies found. *The Arizona Republic* August 1.
Twenter, C. 1971. Officials disagree over cause of fatal plane crash. *The Arizona Republic* October 19.
Lamb, B. 1974. 2 died in plane crash. *Arizona Daily Sun* Friday, July 12. p. 1.
Northern Arizona Bureau. 1975. Bodies of 4 from Italy taken from North Rim plane crash. *The Arizona Republic* January 14.
staff. 1978. Canyon plane crash kills 3. *Arizona Daily Sun* Thursday, June 29. p. 1.

staff. 1980. Canyon crash kills 4 persons from Montana. *Arizona Daily Sun* Thursday, February 28. p. 2.

staff. 1980. 7 Killed in Canyon air crash. *Arizona Daily Sun* Tuesday, July 22. p. 1.

staff. 1981. Bodies of plane victims recovered. *Arizona Daily Sun* January 15.

staff. 1981. Canyon plane crash kills 2. *Arizona Daily Sun* Tuesday, March 3. p. 3.

staff. 1981. Survivors of honeymoon crash are victims this time. *Tucson Daily Citizen* March 6.

staff. 1981. 1 dead in Grand Canyon air crash. *Arizona Daily Sun* May 25.

staff and wire services. 1982. 3 bodies of TV film crew recovered after copter crash in Colorado River. *The Arizona Republic* April 19.

Schroeder, J. 1983. All 10 aboard tourist plane feared dead: Crash wreckage found on cliff just below Canyon's South Rim. *The Arizona Republic* August 19.

staff. 1983. Bodies removed from crash site. *Arizona Daily Sun* August 22.

Daniels, S. 1984. Copter may have struck tree before fatal crash. *The Arizona Republic* August 2.

Calhoun, C. A. 1995. *Operation of Glen Canyon Dam Final Environmental Impact Summary*. Salt Lake City: Bureau of Reclamation, U.S. Department of the Interior. March.

Farabee, C. R. "B.," Jr. 1998. Helicopter crashes upside down into the Colorado River. in Farabee, C. R. "B.," Jr. (ed.) 1998. *Death Daring and Disaster: Search and Rescue in the National Parks*, p. 369. Boulder, Colorado: Roberts Rinehart.

staff. 1985. 1 killed in crash of copter. *The Arizona Republic* July 13.

staff. 1985. Italian actor killed in crash. *Arizona Daily Sun* Sunday, July 14. p. 1.

Associated Press. 1985. Plane wreckage located in Canyon; 2 feared dead. *The Arizona Republic* October 1.

staff. 1985. Climbers recover bodies of victims. *Arizona Daily Sun* October 3.

Ed Wagner. 2000. Personal communication to Tim Ellis, February 4. (personal communication to M. P. Ghiglieri by Ellis, February 4, 2000)

Farabee, C. R. "B.," Jr. 1998. 25 killed in midair collision. in Farabee, C. R. "B.," Jr. (ed.) 1998. *Death Daring and Disaster: Search and Rescue in the National Parks*, pp. 386–387. Boulder, Colorado: Roberts Rinehart.

staff and wire reports. 1987. Suit filed in Grand Canyon crash case. *Arizona Daily Sun* July 22.

Hatch, C. 1986. Helicopter's mast hit plane's landing gear in Canyon crash. *The Arizona Republic* June 28. pp. B1 & B4.

Brinkley-Rogers, P. 1986. Skies over Canyon silent: Fliers, friends and families gather to mourn lost pilots. *Arizona Daily Sun* June 21.

staff. 1986. 25 killed aboard 2 aircraft. *San Francisco Chronicle* June 19.

Thybony, S. 1997. *Burntwater*. Tucson: University of Arizona Press. p. 110.

staff. 1986. Plane occupants dead in crash. *Arizona Daily Sun* Wednesday, January 15. p. 1.

staff. 1988. *Private Pilot Manual*. 2nd ed. Jeppesen Sanderson: Englewood, Colorado.

Accident Prevention Staff. no date. accident prevention program, Density Altitude. U.S. Department of Transportation, Federal Aviation Administration FAA-P- 8740-2/ AFS-800-0478: Washington, D.C.

Richardson, J. E. 1981. accident prevention program Wind Shear. U.S. Department of Transportation, Federal Aviation Administration FAA-P- 8740-40/ AFO-800-0582: Washington, D.C.

Bartimus, T. 1986. Officials call off search for plane in Grand Canyon. *Arizona Daily Sun* August 25.

staff. 1986. Crashed Page plane found in river. *Arizona Daily Sun* November 11.

staff. 1986. Officials confirm ID of body. *Arizona Daily Sun* November 21.

Associated Press. 1987. California tourists die in Canyon air accident. *Arizona Daily Sun* Sunday/Monday, November 16, 1987. p. 1.

staff. 1988. Officials search for cause of plane crash. *Arizona Daily Sun* Thursday, May 19. p. 2.

Shaffer, M. 1988. Tourist at Canyon sees 4 new friends die in plane crash. *The Arizona Republic*. September 5.

Smith, F. 1989. Survivor of Canyon crash won't forget tiny details. *The Arizona Republic* Friday, September 29. pp. A1 & A12

Sandy Chris Cancro. 2000. Personal interviews by M. P. Ghiglieri, January 24 & February 1.

Jean Louise Custer. 2000. Personal interviews by M. P. Ghiglieri, February 3 & 4.

staff. 1991. Canyon Crash kills 7, pilot was Chandler Resident. *Arizona Daily Sun* Tuesday, May 14. pp. 1 & 3.

staff. 1991. No survivors. *Williams-Grand Canyon News.* Thursday, December 19.

staff. 1992. Plane crash kills 10. *Arizona Daily Sun* Saturday, June 20. p. 3.

staff. 1992. Third crash in six months raises air safety questions. *Arizona Daily Sun* Sunday, June 21. p. 3.

staff. 1992. Canyon crash pilot taught accident-prevention classes. *Arizona Daily Sun* Monday, June 22.

Fritze, D. and K. Pearce. 1995. Family left decimated by Canyon crash: Survivor's identity a bit of a mystery. *The Arizona Republic* Wednesday, February 15.

Herrmann, J. J. 1995. Tusayan businessman, passenger, killed in plane crash. *Grand Canyon News* November 29.

staff & Associated Press. 1996. Crash kills 1. *Arizona Daily Sun* Saturday, August 3. pp. 1 & 3.

Associated Press. 1996. Canyon crash victim identified. *The Arizona Republic.* Sunday, August 4. p. B7.

Associated Press. 1996. Grand Canyon crash victims from Belgium. *Las Vegas Sun* October 7.

Associated Press. 1996. Belgian tourists crash victims. *Arizona Daily Sun* October 7. p. 2.

staff. 1997. Missing plane found, two believed dead. *Williams Grand Canyon News* Wednesday, April 9.

Whittlesey, L. H. 1995. *Death in Yellowstone: Accidents and Foolhardiness in the First National Park.* Boulder, Colorado: Roberts Rinehart. pp. 187-193.

Morris, J. and C. Ragavan. 1999. A wing, a prayer, a puzzler. *U.S. News & World Report* November 29. 127(21):30–32.

Lopez, B. 1978. *Crossing Open Ground.* reprinted in "Gone back to the Earth," in S. O'Reilly, J. O'Reilly and L. Habegger. (eds.) 1999. *Grand Canyon True Stories of Life Below the Rim,* pp. 14–24. San Francisco: Travellers' Tales. p. 20.

Abbey, E. 1981. Foreword to *A River Runner's Guide to the History of the Grand Canyon* by K. Crumbo. Boulder: Johnson Books.

Glasser, J. and C. Ragavan. 1999. Drive or fly? Gauging aircraft safety. *U.S. News & World Report* November 29, 127(22):33.

Editorial. 1999. Bring Grand Canyon sightseeing flights down to earth. *Arizona Daily Sun* Sunday, July 18. p. 6.

Ghioto, G. 2000. Tour operators blast Canyon air rules. *Arizona Daily Sun* Wednesday, March 29. pp. 1 & 9

Maureen Oltrogge. 2000. Personal communication to M. P. Ghiglieri, April 3,

Pittenger, T. 2000. The sky above, the Earth below. *Nature Notes: A Publication from Grand Canyon National Park* (Summer 2000) 16(1):1-3.

Notes for Chapter 6. *LIGHTNING NEVER STRIKES TWICE: FREAK ERRORS AND ACCIDENTS*

Farabee, C. R. "B.," Jr. 1998. "Last piece of Nature's handiwork he should ever behold." in Farabee, C. R. "B.," Jr. (ed.) 1998. *Death Daring and Disaster: Search and Rescue in the National Parks,* p. 19. Boulder, Colorado: Roberts Rinehart.

staff. 1993. Lightning strike kills Canyon hiker. *Williams-Grand Canyon News* Thursday, May 20.

Tolan, M. 1997. Hikers missing in Canyon in flash flood. *Arizona Daily Sun* Friday, September 12. pp. 1 & 10.

Rock Falls
Billingsley, G. H., E. E. Spamer and D. Menkes. 1998. *Ibid.* p. 67.
Smith, D. M. 1930. *I Married a Ranger.* Stanford, Calif.: Stanford University Press. pp. 61–66.
staff. 1968. Freak Canyon accident kills visitor from Japan. *Arizona Daily Sun* October 21.
staff. 1968. Rolling boulder kills Canyon hiker. *Arizona Daily Sun* October 22.
West, J. D. (Sam) and C. L. Sauer. 1982. Death: Ralph R. Voss. *U.S. Department of the Interior Grand Canyon National Park Service Case Incident Record.* Incident No. 2540. August 6–18.
Packer, J. 1990. Falling rock kills camper in tent. *The Arizona Republic* Monday, July 23
staff. 1992. Rock slide kills hiker. *Williams-Grand Canyon News* Thursday, May 28.
Patterson, C. J. 1996. Death, Randy Thompson. *U.S. Department of the Interior Grand Canyon National Park Service Case Incident Record.* Incident No. GCCA9600000818. February 26.
Keith, J. L. 1996. Park safety faulted in crew death. *Arizona Daily Sun* Wednesday, June 12. pp. 1 & 7.

Venomous Creatures
staff. 1999. *Desert Medicine Course sponsored by the Wilderness Medical Society*, September 28–October 2. Tucson, Arizona: Wilderness Medical Society.
Auerbach, P. 2001. *Wilderness Medicine: Management of Wilderness and Environmental Emergencies.* 4th ed. Mosby.

Freak Errors and Accidents
staff. 1912. Funeral of Charles Bell. *Coconino Sun* August 16.
staff. 1965. Californian drowns in Havasupai Falls. *The Arizona Republic* June 28.
staff. 1970 Camper in Grand Canyon killed by wind-blown tree. *The Arizona Republic* August 29.
staff. 1970 Park Service identifies victim. *The Arizona Republic* August 31.
staff. 1921. Three pack horses plunge over wall on canyon trail. *The Coconino Sun* Friday, January 28. p. 9.
Sloan, S. 1991. Unpublished report. March 26.
Harrigan, J. J. 1971. Northern views: Grand Canyon hazards. *The Arizona Republic* Tuesday, August 24. p. 10.
staff. 1972. Two Canyon drownings are revealed. *Arizona Daily Sun* July 29.
staff. 1977. Supai Man's death attributed to toxic weed. *Williams News* September 19.
staff. 1983. Boxing champion jumps to death. *Williams News* July 14.
Phillips, K. 1998. SAR: Sylvia Ann Leimkuehler: Grand Canyon National Park - Emergency Medical Services, July 26. Grand Canyon National Park. Case # 98-2446/SAR # 98-193
Tiffany George. 2001. Personal email communication to T. M. Myers, February 25.
Sylvia Ann Leimkuehler. 2001. Personal email communication to Tiffany George, emailed to T. M. Myers, March 1.
staff. 1993. Parachutist killed, other hurt in jump at Grand Canyon. *The Arizona Republic* Tuesday, May 11. p. B2.
staff. 2000. Boating fatality. *Arizona Daily Sun* Monday, July 24. p. 2.

Notes for Chapter 7. *SUICIDE*

Ghiglieri, M. P. 1999. *The Dark Side of Man: Tracing the Origins Male of Violence.* Reading, MA: Helix/Perseus. Chapter 5. Murder.
Holden, C. 1992. A new discipline probes suicide's multiple causes. *Science* 256:1761-1762.
Workman, T. and S. Martin. 1980. Death, Edward Enzor Walters. *U.S. Department of the Interior Grand Canyon National Park Service Case Incident Record.* Incident No. 1884. June 25.

Walters, E. E. 1980. Suicide notes: "To My Family" and "To the Police" (filed with GCNPS Incident Report # 1884, 1980.)

Thybony, B. 2000. "Ambrose Bierce and the Grand Canyon" A talk given for Mountain Air Community Radio, March 31, 8:30 p.m., Beaver Street Brewery, Flagstaff, AZ.

staff. 1933. Decomposed body of unknown man found, had shot himself. *Coconino Sun* Friday, June 9. p. 1.

staff. 1933. California woman drowned in Colorado River Saturday eve. *Coconino Sun* Friday, June 9. p. 1.

staff. 1949. Lost NMU prof may be suicide: Search continues at Grand Canyon for man who left home on June 26. *Arizona Daily Sun* Wednesday, July 6. pp. 1 & 8.

staff. 1951. Woman killed in Canyon leap. *Arizona Daily Sun*. Sunday/Monday, October 8. pp. 1 & 2.

Hoyt, W. 1962. "Mr. X" body tentatively identified. *Arizona Daily Sun* Friday, December 14. p.1.

staff. 1962. Man identified! FBI says "Mr. X" is Indiana man. *Arizona Daily Sun* Monday, December 17.

Northern Arizona Bureau. 1965. Skeleton found at Grand Canyon apparently that of army man. *The Arizona Republic* August 27.

staff. 1965. Graveside services held for man dead at Canyon. *Arizona Daily Sun* December 31.

Dedera, D. 1967. End of road for Mr. Kang. *The Arizona Republic* April 9.

staff. 1969. Hiker finds skeleton in Canyon area. *Arizona Daily Sun* April 7.

staff. 1969. Skeleton is identified as Illinois man. *Arizona Daily Sun* April 21.

staff. 1972. 'Canyon victim' identified as Tucson resident. *Arizona Daily Sun* April 13.

Northern Arizona Bureau. 1974. Couple's Canyon death stumps jury. *The Arizona Republic* Saturday, December 21.

Sweitzer, P. 1975. Skeletal remains identified. *Arizona Daily Sun* October 27.

staff. 1978. Suicide/fatality. *Williams News* October 19.

staff. 1980. Californian ignored pleas before falling into Canyon. *Arizona Daily Sun* December 29.

staff. 1981. Body found in Canyon is identified. *The Arizona Republic* September 24.

staff. 1984. Body found at Canyon. *Arizona Daily Sun* September 24.

UPI Int/*Republic* staff. 1986. 2 believed to be dead in Canyon: Truck plunges 1,000 feet; rescue team hiking to site. *The Arizona Republic* June 30.

Hatch, C. 1986. 2 victims of plunge 'wanted.' LA Police suspected pair in molestations. *The Arizona Republic* July 2. p. 2B.

staff. 1993. Man attempts suicide at Grand Canyon. *Arizona Daily Sun* November 25.

Billingsley, G. H., E. E. Spamer and D. Menkes. 1998. *Ibid.*

staff. 1996. Kansas man first suicide at Canyon in '96. *Williams Grand Canyon News* February 28.

Berkowitz, P. D. 1995. July 5, 1987, Joshua Tree National Monument, California, NPS Headquarters Bldg/CHP Officers, in *U.S. Rangers—The Law of the Land: The History of Law Enforcement in the Federal Land Management Agencies*. Redding, California: CT Publishing Company. p. 322.

Carolyn Castleman. 1999. Phone interview by T. Myers, September, and also e-mail communications February, 2000

Notes for Chapter 8. *MURDER*

Babbitt, Bruce. 1988. Personal communication to M. P. Ghiglieri on Colorado River, October 31.

Stegner, W. 1953, 1954 [1962]. *Beyond the Hundredth Meridian: John Wesley Powell and the Second Opening of the West*. Boston: Houghton Mifflin Co./ Cambridge: The Riverside Press.

Powell, J. W. 1879 [1983]. *Report on the Lands of the Arid Regions of the United States with a More Detailed Account of the Lands of Utah*. (Facsimile of the 1879 Edition). Harvard and Boston, MA: Harvard Common Press.

Worster, D. 1994. *An Unsettled Country: Changing Landscapes of the American West*. Albuquerque: University of New Mexico Press. p. 29.

Ambrose, S. E. 1996. *Undaunted Courage: Meriwether Lewis, Thomas Jefferson, and the Opening of the American West*. New York: Simon and Schuster.

Powell, J. W. 1895 [1961]. *The Exploration of the Colorado River and its Canyons*. New York: Dover.

Powell, J. W. 1947. Major Powell's Journal. *Utah Historical Quarterly* 15:125–131. Also copy of original in script.

Darrah, W. C. 1951. *Powell of the Colorado*. Princeton: Princeton University Press.

Stegner, W. 1953, 1954 [1962]. *Ibid*.

Powell, J. W. 1869. Copy of unpublished "agreement" between J. W. Powell, party of the 1st part and parties of the 2nd part: J. C. Sumner, William H. Dunn, and O. G. Howland. In Univ. of Arizona Dellenbaugh Collection, Box 5, folder 9.

Anderson, M. 1979. First through the Canyon: Powell's lucky voyage in 1869. *The Journal of Arizona History* 20(4):391–408.

Billingsley, G. H., E. E. Spamer and D. Menkes. 1998. *Ibid*.

George H. Billingsley. 2000. Personal interview by M. P. Ghiglieri, February 4.

Sumner, J. C. 1947. J. C. Sumner's Journal, July 6–August 31, 1869. *Utah Historical Quarterly* 15:113–124.

Bradley, G. Y. 1947. George Y. Bradley's Journal. *Utah Historical Quarterly* 15:31–72. Also copy of original journal in script.

Stanton, R. B. 1932 [1982]. *Colorado River Controversies*. Boulder City, Nevada: Westwater. pp. 95–232.

Hall, A. 1869 (1948-1949). Three letters by Andrew Hall. edited by W. C. Darrah *Utah Historical Quarterly* 16–17:505–508.

Lavender, D. 1985. *River Runners of the Grand Canyon*. Grand Canyon: Grand Canyon Natural History Association. p. 17.

McGuire, T. R. 1983. Walapai. in *Handbook of North American Indians Volume 10 Southwest*, pp. 25-37. Washington, D.C.: Smithsonian Institution.

Belshaw, M. 1979. The Dunn-Howland killings: A reconstruction. *The Journal of Arizona History* 20(4):409–423.

Dobyns, H. F. and R. C. Euler. 1980. The Dunn-Howland killings: additional insights. *The Journal of Arizona History* 21(1):87–95.

Powell, W. C. 1948–49. Journal of Walter Clement Powell: April 21, 1871—December 7, 1872 (edited by Charles Kelly) *Utah Historical Quarterly* 16–17:257–478. pp. 397–406, 410.

Little, James A. 1881. *Jacob Hamblin: A Narrative of His Personal Experience, as a Frontiersman, Missionary to the Indians and Explorer*. Salt Lake City: Juvenile Instructor Office. p. 97.

Dellenbaugh, F. S. 1902 [1962]. *The Romance of the Colorado*. Chicago: Rio Grande Press. pp. 227–230.

Brooks, J. 1950 [1991]. *The Mountain Meadows Massacre*. Norman: University of Oklahoma Press.

Larson, W. P. 1993. The "letter" Or were the Powell men really killed by Indians? *Canyon Legacy* #17, Spring, pp. 12–19.

Anderson, V. 199?. Did murders happen in Mormon Ward? 1883 letter may solve mystery of trio. *The Salt Lake Tribune*. date & page ?

Ghiglieri, M. P. 1992. *Canyon*. Tucson, Arizona: The University of Arizona Press.

Roessel, R. A., Jr. 1983. Navajo History, 1850–1923. in A. Ortiz (ed.) *Handbook of North American Indians, Vol. 10, Southwest*, pp. 506–523. Washington, D.C.: Smithsonian Institution.

Roessel, R. (ed.) 1973. *Navajo Stories of the Long Walk Period.* Tsaile, Arizona Navajo Community College Press. pp. 103–104.

James Peshlakai. 2000. Personal communication to M. P. Ghiglieri, August 3.

O' Connor Dale. 1992. Personal communication to M. P. Ghiglieri.

Michael Harrison. 1992. Personal communications (several) to M. P. Ghiglieri.

Anderson, M. J. undated. A Perfect Place to Hyde. Unpublished manuscript sent by author to M. P. Ghiglieri. NAU Cline Library Special Collections, Martin J. Anderson Special Collection, ms #77.

Martin J. Anderson. 1991 & 1992. Personal communications to M. P. Ghiglieri.

Thybony, S. 1985. Parting Shot: Mystery: What Happened to Bessie Hyde? *Outside* October, p. 108.

Thybony, S. 1985. A river mystery. in C. O'Conner, (ed.). *First Descents.* Birmingham, Alabama: Menscha Press.

Scott Thybony. 1990–2000. Personal communications to M. P. Ghiglieri.

Tessman, N. 1986. "I wonder if I shall ever wear pretty shoes again": The disappearance of Glen and Bessie Hyde. *Sharlott Hall Gazette* (Prescott, Arizona) 13(1):1–6.

Bruce Babbitt. 1988. Personal communication on Colorado River to M. P. Ghiglieri, October 31.

Ghiglieri, M. P. 1992. *Ibid.*

Dimock, B. 2000. Bessie, Woman of the River. *boatman's quarterly review* fall,13(3):42.

Dimock, B. 2001. *Sunk Without a Sound: The Tragic Colorado River Honeymoon of Glen and Bessie Hyde.* Flagstaff: Fretwater.

staff. 1927. Bank bandit and murderer caught in Grand Canyon yesterday after gunfight with sheriff Parsons. *Coconino Sun* Friday, June 24. p.1

Reilly, P. T. 1999. *Lee's Ferry from Mormon Crossing to National Park.* Logan, Utah: Utah State University Press. pp. 382–384.

Stone, J. 1972. Deputies probe death of woman near Canyon. *Arizona Daily Sun* Monday, March 6, pp. 1 & 2.

Stone, J. 1972. Man sought in Canyon slaying case. *Arizona Daily Sun* Tuesday, March 7, p. 1.

staff. 1972. Body, car found at Canyon. *Arizona Daily Sun* April 13. p. 1

Stone, J. 1972. Body is identified as slaying suspect. *Arizona Daily Sun* April 14, pp. 1 & 2.

staff. 1927. Little boy lost Grand Canyon Saturday; still missing; fear foul play.*Coconino Sun* Friday, July 29. p. 1.

staff. 1927. Disappearance Grand Canyon Baby baffles officers; few clues. *Coconino Sun* Friday, August 5. pp. 1 & 6.

staff. 1927. Suspect in Jaycox baby death to reformatory. *Coconino Sun* Friday, December 9. p. 1.

staff. 1950. *Coconino Sun* December 30.

Hoyt, W. 1962. 'Miss X' mystery near climax. *Arizona Daily Sun* Thursday, November 22. pp. 1 & 2.

staff. 1977. Detectives seek clues in Grand Canyon murders. *Arizona Daily Sun* Monday, January 24. p. 1.

Swickard, D. 1979. Lee Devereaux. Grand Canyon National Park Service Case Incident Report #3771. July 8.

Berkowitz, P. D. 1995. June 26, 1992: Grand Canyon National Park, Arizona NPS Rangers: *U.S. Rangers—The Law of the Land: The History of Law Enforcement in the Federal Land Management Agencies.* Redding, California: CT Publishing Company. pp. 398–400.

Faught, A. 1992. Horning left calling card; Escapee took Pine family's truck. *Arizona Daily Sun* Friday, June 26. p. 1.

Schill, K. 1992. Horning in Canyon: Escaped convict releases hostages, still eludes manhunt. *Arizona Daily Sun* Sunday, June 28. pp. 1 & 4.

O'Brien, C. 1992. Excitement filled run in with Horning: Fugitive came out of nowhere, stole couple's car, but failed to kidnap them. *Arizona Daily Sun* Wednesday, July 8. p. 5.

staff. 1992. Horning's goal: rich in Mexico. He admits to Tucson bank robbery, denies killing man in California. *Arizona Daily Sun* July 8. pp. 1 & 4.

Donny Miller. 1999. Personal interview by T. Myers, May 9.

White, H. 1994. Judge: Horning must die. *Stockton Record* September 8

Villa, J. 1994. Danny Ray Horning wounded critically in California prison. *The Arizona Republic* Sunday, October 9. p. B4.

Keller, K. 2000. Murder, Antonio Castillo, Jr. *U.S. Department of the Interior Grand Canyon National Park Service Case Incident Record.* Incident No. 96-6039,

Spangler S. 1986/1989. *On Foot in the Grand Canyon: Hiking the Trails of the South Rim.* (1st & 2nd editions) Boulder:Pruett.

Barnett, Z. 2000. Junction man killed 2 wives, kids, feds say. *Grand Junction Sentinel.* October 5.

Associated Press. 2000. Man admits to pushing wife off Grand Canyon cliff. *Arizona Daily Sun* Thursday, October 5. p A3

Drapaer, E., N. Lofholm and M. Robinson. 2000. For suspected killer, death part of his life. *Denver Post* Sunday, October 8.

United States District Court District of Arizona. 2000. United States of America (Plaintiff) V. Robert Merlin Spangler (Defendant), Plea Agreement CR-00-0968-PCT-PGR, December 27. Phoenix, Arizona: U. S. Courthouse.

Hendricks, L. 2001. Coroner: Canyon death was murder. *Arizona Daily Sun* Friday, March 1, pp. 1 & A7.

Notes for *EPILOGUE*

Junger, S. 1999. The Life: Colter's Way. *National Geographic Adventure.* Vol. 1 (1):73–79.

Whittlesey, L. H. 1995. *Death in Yellowstone: Accidents and Foolhardiness in the First National Park.* Boulder, Colorado: Roberts Rinehart. pp. 195-198.

Roosevelt, T., IV. 1998. Abusing the public trust. *Defenders of Wildlife Magazine* Summer, pp. 42–44.

Index